# NATURE'S WEB

*About the author*

Peter Marshall grew up by the sea in Sussex, England. After sailing around the world as a cadet in the Merchant Navy, he spent a year teaching English in Senegal, West Africa. He returned to England to pursue his studies, obtaining a BA in English, French and Spanish and an MA and D Phil in the History of Ideas. He has taught philosophy and literature at several British universities. In the late seventies, he was a founding member of a rural community in Buckinghamshire. Since 1980 he has been a full-time writer living in Snowdonia, North Wales. His circumnavigation of Africa in 1992 was made into a major TV series.

His previous books include:

*William Godwin (1984)*
*Journey through Tanzania (1984)*
*Into Cuba (1985)*
*Cuba Libre: Breaking the Chains? (1987)*
*William Blake: Visionary Anarchist (1988)*
*Journey through Maldives (1992)*
*Demanding the Impossible: A History of Anarchism (1992)*
*Around Africa: From the Pillars of Hercules to the Strait of
   Gibraltar (1994)*

# NATURE'S WEB

*Rethinking Our Place On Earth*

# PETER MARSHALL

CASSELL

Cassell
Wellington House
125 Strand
London WC2R 0BB

First published in Great Britain by Simon & Schuster Ltd 1992

First published by Cassell (with corrections) 1995

**British Library Cataloguing-in-Publication Data**
A catalogue record for this book is available from the British Library.

ISBN 0-304-33539-8

Cover illustration: 'Orpheus Charming the Animals' by Roelandt Jacobsz Savery
(1576–1639), private collection, U.S.A./The Bridgeman Art Library, London.

Printed and bound in Great Britain by Biddles Ltd, Guildford and Kings Lynn.

*For Cai, Jack and Lucy*

# THE BIRTHDAY

It was my daughter's eighth birthday.
There was a dark cloud girding Snowdon,
But then there are often dark clouds girding Snowdon
In this rain-drenched land.

Friends came from afar to our cwm,
Bringing quartz crystals, jays' feathers,
Coloured shells and a hot-air balloon.
We played in the sloping field
Enclosed by stone walls and twisted oak.
The cries of infant joy echoed across the ridge,
Scattering sheep and sending the fox to his den.

In mid-afternoon the dark cloud rolled over,
Casting its shadow across the hills.
Heavy drops of crystal rain fell silently
On the heads of babies and sheep,
Glistening like dew in their curly locks.
We quenched our thirst from the swelling stream
And laughed and splashed in its cool waters.

Only later we learned by chance
That the dark cloud girding Snowdon
Had blown across Europe,
Bringing birthday greetings from Chernobyl.

*Peter Marshall*

# CONTENTS

Part III *Green Visions*

Part IV *The Joining of the Ways*

# ACKNOWLEDGEMENTS

I would like to thank warmly my brother Michael and my neighbour Richard Feesey for commenting on different chapters of this book and for sharing their scientific and philosophical knowledge. Above all, I am grateful to Jenny Zobel for having deepened my vision, supported me throughout my work, and read the entire manuscript.

My children Dylan and Emily have brought me down to earth and helped me appreciate the essential things of life. Cai, Jack and Lucy in their different ways have enabled me to realize that human beings differ only in degree and not in kind from other animals. The conversations and experiences I have shared over the years with my friends Jeremy Gane, Graham Hancock, David Lea and John Schlapobersky have all greatly contributed to my understanding of our place within nature. Finally, I am indebted to the editorial director, Carol O'Brien, the editor, Sian Parkhouse, of Simon & Schuster and the copy editor, Ingrid von Essen, for their excellent advice.

Croesor, 28 January 1992

I read the proofs of this work off the Ogooué river, Gabon, during a voyage around Africa. It was on the same river that Albert Schweitzer realized that reverence for life should form the basis of morality. The ship I was sailing on was carrying hardwood from the Equatorial rainforests to South Africa. The principle remains; the problems continue.

at sea near the Cape of Good Hope, 16 May 1992

I am indebted to Philip Ball and John Clark for their detailed comments on the text. They have inspired some of the revisions in this second edition.

Peter Marshall, Borth-y-Gest, 24 March 1994

# PREFACE

I live in one of the most beautiful places on earth, in a small valley by the sea surrounded by mountains in Snowdonia National Park in North Wales. My dwelling is an isolated house called Garth-y-foel, which means in Welsh the 'enclosure on the hill'. It can only be reached by a rough track which winds up and down through several fields and copses and over a river which turns into a torrent after heavy rain.

At first sight, it would seem an ideal place to live for a writer, halfway between heaven and earth, part of society and yet separate from it. To the south, a reclaimed estuary stretches out towards the sea; on all other sides, rugged mountains reach to the overarching sky. The house is surrounded by small fields scratched out of the rocky ground, with clumps of twisted oak, tall beech and silver birch growing near their stone walls. From a rocky outcrop at the back of the house, Snowdon, the highest mountain in Wales and England, stands watch over the surrounding peaks. A few hikers sometimes wander by disturbing the sheep and crows, looking for a taste of the wild, free and natural.

They follow in the footsteps of earlier hikers who sought the sublime, like the Romantic poet Wordsworth. He gloried in the awesome grandeur of the mountain range, and found in Snowdon

> the perfect image of a mighty Mind
> Of one that feeds upon infinity,
> That is exalted by an underpresence,
> The sense of God, or whatsoe'ever is dim
> Or vast in its own being.

Not long ago, I climbed a local mountain after the first fall of snow on the peaks. Following an old drover's track over rough pasture, I eventually came across a new barbed-wire fence. It marked the outer boundary of land recently reclaimed from the ancient bogs and moors of the uplands. The contrast between the two sides of the fence could not have been starker.

On the one side were the dull browns and greens of a great variety of sedges, rushes, grasses, mosses and lichens in uneven terrain criss-crossed by little streams and brooks. On the other stretched a flat expanse of bright green grass on heavily limed and fertilized soil. The sheep rushed off in a great white mass at my approach. The barbed-wire fence marks the battle line between nature left to itself and man's steady and inexorable encroachment.

What place does barbed wire have in nature's web? Only industrialized man, who learned how to mine coal and iron from the earth and fuse them with fire, is able to create barbed wire. It was barbed wire that destroyed the American hinterland; it continues to unfurl throughout the world, transforming the earth into the preserve of our rapacious species. Nature has evolved for all beings to enjoy, but only human beings have tried to control it and make it their own. By trying to humanize nature, they have denaturalized themselves.

I continued on my walk further up the mountainside. There were signs of earlier human workings. The tumbled stones of an ancient hut circle could just be discerned, suggesting that the climate must have been warmer several thousands of years ago for humans to live comfortably at 800 feet in these parts. The Romans had come this far north, scratching for copper and silver in an otherwise barren land. I then came across a sweeping track which ended in a jagged heap of broken slabs of slate, clawed from the subterranean depths of the mountain – a stark reminder of the demand earlier this century to shelter the bursting population of Europe. Wordsworth's 'perfect image of a mighty Mind' lay for ever blasted and scarred. Medieval thinkers likened mining in the earth to the rape of Mother Nature; it is easy to see why, with the discarded workings of the violent boring into the mountain's womb.

As I reached a watershed, I saw at the bottom of a steep precipice a dark and gloomy reservoir, its sinister waters pumped up from the lake below by electricity from the nearby nuclear power station squatting in the ancient hills. The town of Blaenau Ffestiniog lay at my feet, surrounded by grey tips of broken slate. When the architect Clough Williams-Ellis drew up the map of Snowdonia National Park, he drew a ring around Blaenau Ffestiniog, so that it would stand as an oasis of industrial ugliness in an area of 'outstanding natural beauty'. Yet many who glorify the Industrial Revolution feel more at home in the grey, drab streets of Blaenau than on the windswept mountain peaks standing firm against the Atlantic westerlies. Tourists, disgorged by the veteran steam trains, rush headlong into the disused mines rather that turn their gaze to the heavens.

Turning my back on modern agriculture on one side and modern industry on the other, I climbed past the snowline for the ascent of Moelwyn Mawr. The first snow of the year, which lay deep and crisp, covered the tracks of summer hikers and the fissures of frost-broken rock. The place seemed utterly pure and pristine. The air was sharp and bracing. Swirls of mist passed over me, hiding the winter sun, cutting me off from all except the rolling expanse of white snow around. As I placed one foot after the other in the crisp snow, my head emptied of the chatter of the valley and the petty daily worries. I felt one with the white mountain which stood like an old man who had taken many knocks but still maintained his integrity.

But as I neared the summit, I suddenly felt strangely melancholy. However much I tried, I could not prevent the stark truth invading my mind. The snow around me was not pure and pristine; it was made from acid rain and was contaminated with radioactivity. The air was not clean; it contained an artificial axcess of hydrocarbons. A man-made layer of carbon dioxide lay between me and the sun, inexorably heating up the globe. In a hundred years, there might not be any more snow falling on this mountain. Nature, in the sense of the world independent of man, has come to an end. The human species, which has sought to climb the highest mountains and to dive into the deepest seas, has so dominated nature that it has begun to transform it irredeemably.

At the top of the mountain, a few crows had left their mark in the snow. As if to confirm my gloomiest thoughts, a red fighter aeroplane roared low up the valley below, practising no doubt with dummy nuclear weapons.

Beneath its surface beauty, nature has become scarred and poisoned. Humans have triumphed and only the faintest glimpse of Wordsworth's 'mighty Mind' can be discerned in the roar of the mountain torrents and the whistling wind of the peaks.

# INTRODUCTION

Drive my dead thoughts over the universe
Like withered leaves to quicken a new birth!
Percy Bysshe Shelley

This green and blue planet spinning in space is under severe stress. Like the human body the earth can take only so much damage before its health is seriously impaired. If we continue to defile the planet at the present rate, prevailing conditions of life will be threatened. *Hubris*, human pride before a fall, will be followed by *nemesis*, nature's revenge. Whatever happens, evolution will continue in some form or other but it is hardly reassuring to think that we may be recycled like the dinosaurs.

Not all is lost, however, for a new awareness of what humans are doing to the planet is burgeoning. The green movement has helped transform the way we think and act in the world. There has been a tidal wave of 'green' books telling people how to save the planet and themselves.

The term 'green', the colour of plant life, is appropriate for the word may be applied to describe anything that is life-enhancing in the broadest sense. A 'green' person is thus someone who wishes to live harmoniously with nature; he or she is life-centred and shows respect for nature and all its forms.

Everyone understands the meaning of the sentence 'Man should respect life and nature'. But the exact meaning of man, nature and life is not always clear. Western thinkers have often opposed man to nature. Even the term 'man' is misleading as a collective noun, for humanity is made up of men and women of different social groups. Many writers on ecological matters use the term 'man' or 'we' loosely, when they should strictly speaking specify whether they mean all men or women, or some particular men or women. I realize that I too sometimes use the term 'man' as a convenient alternative to humanity or human beings, but it is not intended to have any sexist overtones.

Again many refer to man and animals as if they were metaphysically different. While I might appear to fall into this habit on occasion, I consider man to be an animal and only differing in degree and not in kind from other animals. Although I discuss in conventional terms human rights and animals rights as if they were separate, strictly speaking human rights should be considered a branch of animal rights.

The word nature is one of the most complex words in the language, but it has developed three main areas of meaning. These are the essential quality and character of something (as in human nature, or the nature of wood); the inherent force which influences the world (as in Mother Nature); or the entire world itself. The last can be taken to include or to exclude human beings, as the phrase man and the natural world implies.

I consider humans to be an integral part of nature, although they are also the beings most capable of interfering with its processes. A central drive of Western 'man' has been to conquer 'nature', as if it were an object separate from him. Hence it has become common to distinguish between what is natural (existing without man's interference) and artificial (man-made). In this way, nature is opposed to nurture, civilization to the natural state. For many urban dwellers living permanently amongst concrete and glass, nature itself has come to mean little more than the countryside.

Nature and life are sometimes seen as the same thing, yet life is only one aspect of nature. Life in its broadest sense may be defined as a process which increases the complexity of forms by converting energy. It swims against the current of universal entropy, opposing the flow of energy to a more disordered state. But when an organism dies, it can no longer grow or maintain itself. Some obscure vital factor has left it; its body will rot. Modern science calls this vital force energy: energy is released from a dead body and will be transformed into other forms.

I consider this mysterious quality of life to be valuable in itself. Anything which strives to maintain itself, whether a bear, a tree, a lake or the earth itself, has inherent value. Even a stone, which on its own cannot be said to be alive in actively striving to maintain itself, nevertheless forms part of a system which makes up a living whole.

## Ecological thinking

This book explores the nature of ecological thinking. It is concerned with the meaning of the earth and our rightful place within it. This means developing a philosophy of nature and a morality to guide our actions. It attempts to provide the wider green movement with a comprehensive vision which will enable it to lay the foundations of an organic and sustainable society.

The words 'green' and 'ecological' are often used synonymously, and the term 'ecology' has come to mean little more than the intermingling of all aspects of life in an organic whole. As a scientific term *oekologie* was first used by the German biologist Ernest Haeckel in 1866 as the study of animals and plant systems in relation to their environment. It was not until 1930 that the science assumed professional status with its particular emphasis on the interdependence of different life-forms.

Derived from the Greek words *oikos*, meaning 'house', and *logos*, meaning 'knowledge', ecology is now employed to describe all aspects of our dwelling in the Earth House Hold. By extension, the politics of ecology concerns itself with the interaction between our species and our environment. Other key words in the subject are 'ecosystem', an interdependent group of items forming a unified whole, the 'biosphere', the earth's ecosystem functioning together on a global scale, and the 'ecosphere', the part of the universe, especially the earth, where life can exist.

Ecology as a science has gone some way in providing a framework for the green movement. It has undoubtedly inspired a new understanding of humanity as one element in an intricate web of nature. It endorses the values of unity in diversity, organic growth and interdependence. It suggests that all organisms have intrinsic value in a non-hierarchical world: humans and animals are different but they are worthy of equal consideration. It presents biotic communities and the whole of nature as self-regulating organisms. Applied to society, ecological principles point in the direction of participatory democracy, cooperation and mutual aid in decentralized and self-managing communities.

Although the green movement is like a river with many tributaries and springs rising in different soils, its members share certain common assumptions and beliefs. They nearly all agree that there is little ground in the natural world for human notions of hierarchy and domination; they consider it impossible to sustain the present rate of consumption and economic growth; and they believe in the essential harmony and beneficence of nature. Above all, they are all aware that we are an integral part of nature and that if we harm any part of it, we harm ourselves.

Green sympathizers are not necessarily religious but they often betray pantheistic or animistic feelings which express themselves in a reverence for life. They tend to adopt an aesthetic attitude to nature, appreciating its beauty and spontaneous order. They are often critical of traditional science but believe in the reality of the external world and the possibility of objective truth. They celebrate the fact that modern science seems to confirm the ancient beliefs about the cosmic dance of energy.

In their morality, members of the green movement tend to be 'ecocentric' rather than 'anthropocentric', concerned not only with human welfare but with the well-being of the earth as a whole. Involved with furthering animal rights, they would like to extend the moral community to include non-human beings and even things. They do not wish to work against the course of nature but with it, as companions rather than as lords and conquerors. They believe in the responsibility of each individual for his or her actions. Taking on board the insights of ecology, they would like society to develop in an organic direction.

Ecological thinking is unique in that it draws on science as well as philosophy and religion for inspiration. In their search for ancestors, ecological thinkers have delved into Taoism and Zen Buddhism, invoked the Greek Goddess Gaia, and looked to the old ways of American Indians for a model of a harmonious relationship with Mother Earth. Within Christianity, they emphasize the idea of human stewardship of rather than dominion over nature and find inspiration in figures like St Francis of Assisi and St Benedict. They have turned to a minority tradition in Western metaphysics, represented by such thinkers as Spinoza, Whitehead and Heidegger, who stress the organic unity of nature. But not all these varied traditions and thinkers have been fully understood or integrated into a larger philosophical whole.

## Changing views of the world

Ecological thinking is rising in human minds like sap in spring. What is taking place is not merely a concern with cleaning up our environment but a fundamental shift in consciousness – as momentous as the Renaissance. In order to solve existing environmental problems, it is simply not good enough to close ageing nuclear reactors or to put filters in coal-fired stations. It is beginning to dawn on people that what is wrong is not merely our present industrial practices but industrialism itself. Consumers who have switched to environment-friendly goods are now beginning to question the nature of consumption itself. What is wrong is nothing less than the way we see and act in the world.

The assumptions behind the traditional Western world-view are that we are makers of our own destiny; that our history has been a history of progress; that whatever problems we encounter in the future, we will be able to solve them. At the same time, it assumes that humans are fundamentally different from other creatures on earth, unique in the possession of reason, speech, moral conscience and soul. Nature is considered mainly as a collection of resources to be used at will, an unlimited opportunity to exploit.

This world-view has been supported by the mainstream Judaeo-Christian tradition which depicts God as giving man dominion over nature in order to subdue it to his own ends. The rationalist tradition from Plato onwards also separated the mind from the body, the observer from the observed, and humanity from nature. The cleavage between humanity and nature was deepened by the mechanical thinking of the Scientific Revolution in the seventeenth century which tried to put nature on the rack in order to force her to reveal her secrets. The instrumental rationality and the arrogant humanism of the Enlightenment further led to the disenchantment of nature. The rise of capitalism and industrialization fundamentally altered our relationship with the natural world and encouraged the dream of achieving the ultimate conquest over nature.

This dominant world-view which fires our industrial, technocratic and man-centred civilization is however beginning to unravel. A new vision of the world is emerging which recognizes the interrelatedness of all things and beings and which presents humanity as an integral part of the organic whole. It not only develops the insights of ancient religions and philosophies but is confirmed by modern physics and the science of ecology. It recognizes that our own welfare depends on the well-being of nature as a whole.

If we are to live in a habitable world these insights must be translated into action and form part of a democratic and sustainable society which is in harmony with nature. Such a prospect involves not only changing our ways of production, but reconsidering the whole range of our present needs and wants. It requires nothing less than a major shift in human consciousness and a new direction for Western civilization.

Although the old world-view is undoubtedly fading, a coherent ecological philosophy has not yet replaced it. The 'metaphysical reconstruction' which green activists like E. F. Schumacher and Jonathon Porritt have called for has only just begun. Few involved in the green movement are aware of the deep-rooted tradition which underpins their beliefs. While a handful of historians and philosophers have begun to sketch the outlines of a green cultural and intellectual tradition, as yet no comprehensive overview has appeared. Moreover there is a need for a philosophy of nature in which to ground our moral values and social action. Such a rigorous and radical philosophy can be the only real foundation for sound environmental ethics and effective green politics.

The aim of Nature's Web is to fulfil this need and to strengthen and deepen ecological thinking. It traces the emergence of the dominant world-view of Western civilization and the origins and evolution of the ideas and values which have led to the present ecological crisis. At the same time, it uncovers an alternative cultural tradition in different religions and philosophies and describes the growth of an ecological mind and sensibility. Once part of a counterculture, this now seems set on replacing the dominant one.

Nature's Web tries to be an inspiration as well as a comprehensive study. It not only offers a contribution to a new philosophy of nature, but also sketches the outlines of a sustainable and democratic society. It sets out to reaffirm the continuity between human beings and other animals and the rest of nature: we do not stand separate from or above nature, but form just another strand of its living web. The book should appeal to all those who treasure the beauty of our common dwelling in the Earth House Hold and who care about its long-term well-being.

*Part I*

# ANCIENT ROOTS

# 1

## TAOISM

### *The Way of Nature*

Horses live on dry land, eat grass and drink water.
When pleased, they rub their necks together. When angry,
they turn round and kick up their heels at each other.
Thus far only do their natural dispositions carry them.
But bridled and bitted, with a plate of metal on their
foreheads, they learn to cast vicious looks, to turn the
head to bite, to resist, to get the bit out of the mouth or
the bridle into it. And thus their natures become depraved.

Chuang Tzu

The first clear expression of ecological thinking appears in ancient
China from about the sixth century BC. Chinese society at the time
was passing through a feudal and bureaucratic phase and the empire
was divided into warring states. Law was becoming codified and the
followers of Confucius were calling for a rigid hierarchy in which
every citizen knew his or her place. The Taoists, on the other hand,
resented their meddling and believed all could live in spontaneous
harmony with nature. They offered the most profound and eloquent
philosophy of nature ever elaborated and the first stirrings of an
ecological sensibility.

Both Taoists and Confucians believe that human nature is fundamentally good: human beings have an innate predisposition to
goodness which is revealed in the instinctive reaction of anyone
who sees a child fall into a well. Both claim to defend the Tao, or
the Way, of the ancients. But whereas the Taoists are principally
interested in nature, the Confucians are more worldly-minded and
concerned with society. The Confucians celebrate traditionally 'male'
virtues like duty, discipline and obedience, while the Taoists promote
the 'female' values of receptivity and passivity. The former wish to
dominate and regulate nature; the latter to follow and harmonize
with it. The struggle between the two world-views, one authoritarian
and the other libertarian, is still with us.

The only reliable source of the teachings of Confucius (551–479 BC) is the *Lun-yü* (*Analects*), a collection of brief dialogues and sayings recorded by his disciples, mostly young gentlemen preparing for government office. Confucius' *Tao* is the proper way of life for humanity. It presupposes that the hierarchical structure of the old society corresponds to a natural world order. Each person has a moral obligation by virtue of his position, whether father or son, ruler or ruled. The cardinal virtue is *jen*, usually translated as 'benevolence', although in Chinese it is a homophone for 'humanity'. It embraces the moral qualities of loyalty, reciprocity and dutifulness and celebrates the ideal of the *chün-tzu* (gentleman) who is sincere, polite, righteous and generous. Confucianism has often been called a system of morality without religion, and the master formulated the golden rule: 'What you do not wish to be done to yourself, do not do to others.'

In social terms, Confucius was a utilitarian. He wanted to promote the general good, which he thought would be best achieved by a paternalistic government. He therefore urged rulers to bring about social justice by becoming moral themselves. A virtuous ruler would encourage the virtue of the ruled. Confucius felt that he failed in his aim to influence rulers but his disciple Mencius (371–289 BC), whose conversations were recorded in *Meng-tzu*, carried his message to the rulers of the warring states with some degree of success.

Although Buddhism held sway in Chinese society from the fifth century, there was a deliberate effort to revive Confucianism in the Sung period from the eleventh century onwards and it became a kind of state cult, the orthodoxy of a feudal and bureaucratic order. Its influence can still be seen at work in the hierarchical and authoritarian nature of the Chinese Communist Party.

Taoism, by contrast, never became an official cult, although it has helped shape Chinese thought as much as Buddhism and Confucianism. It had its roots in popular culture far back in Chinese history, possibly in an earlier matriarchal society, although it emerged as a remarkable combination of philosophy, religion, proto-science and magic at the beginning of the sixth century BC.

Its first principal exponent, Lao Tzu ('Old Philosopher'), is shrouded in mystery. Tradition has it that he was born *c.* 604 BC of a noble family in Ch'u (in modern Honan, or Henan, province). He rejected his hereditary position as a noble and became a curator of the imperial archives at Loh.

All his life he followed the path of silence – 'The Tao that can be told is not the eternal Tao,' he taught. But according to legend, when he was riding off into the desert to die in the west, he was persuaded by a gatekeeper in northwestern China to write down his teaching for posterity.

The exact date of the work attributed to Lao Tzu, *Tao Te Ching* (The Way and its Virtue), remains in dispute. Before the Second World War, scholars dated it about the fourth or even the third century BC, although since then there has been a tendency to revert to tradition and place it in the sixth century BC.[1] The *Tao Te Ching* remains the sole record of Lao Tzu's teaching and it stands as an unrivalled literary and philosophical masterpiece. The Chinese scholar Joseph Needham, the author of the monumental *Science and Civilization in China*, has called it 'without exception the most profound and beautiful work in the Chinese language'.[2] The text consists of eighty-one short chapters (5,250 words in Chinese). It is a combination of poetry and philosophical reflection. While it is sometimes obscure and paradoxical, a haunting beauty resonates throughout.

The other great Taoist text is written by Chuang Tzu (399–295 BC) and goes by the same name. More mystical than Lao Tzu, Chuang Tzu relates nevertheless many entertaining anecdotes and parables. The work still follows the light of reason and has a sensuous naturalism, but it develops more clearly the concept of *te* as Tao individualized in the nature of things. The idea of self-transformation is more central, as is the the need to adapt closely to the environment.

The influence of Taoism on Buddhism was great, especially in the development of Zen. It has also greatly inspired Chinese poetry and landscape painting. In the West, the Taoist view of reality as dynamic and ever-changing and the principle of unity in diversity find echoes in the philosophies of Heraclitus and Hegel. Taoism offers a path to mystical experience and philosophical enlightenment as well as a guide to right living. It provides the most fertile soil for the growth of a genuinely ecological sensibility.

## Philosophy of nature

The Taoist conception of nature is based on the ancient Chinese principles of *yin* and *yang*, two opposite but complementary forces in the cosmos. Together they constitute *ch'i* (matter-energy) of which all beings and phenomena are formed. *Yin* is the supreme feminine power, characterized by darkness, coldness and passivity and associated with the moon. *Yang* is the masculine counterpart of brightness, warmth and activity, identified with the sun. Both forces are at work within men and women as in all things, responsible for diversity within the overall unity.

> Know the strength of man,
> But keep a woman's care![3]

In the famous Taoist symbol of a circled S, the objective (white) emanates from the subjective (black); equally the subjective results from the objective. Both are for ever interrelated and flow into each other: black contains white and vice versa. The contraries of subject and object, good and bad, beauty and ugliness, dark and light, spring from subjective individuality; from the perspective of the whole, all distinctions merge. *Yin* and *yang* originally referred to the sunless and sunny sides of a mountain.

The Tao itself cannot be defined; it is nameless and formless. Lao Tzu likens it to an empty vessel, a river flowing home to the sea, or an uncarved block. The Tao follows what is natural. It is the way in which the universe works, the order of nature which gives all things their being and sustains them:

> The great Tao flows everywhere, both to the left and the right.
> The ten thousand things depend on it; it holds nothing back.
> It fulfills its purpose silently and makes no claim.
>
> It nourishes the ten thousand things,
> And yet is not their lord.[4]

The Tao is in all beings and things, yet it is not identical with them, neither differentiated nor limited. All proceeds from it and is under its influence.

Needham describes the Tao as a 'kind of natural curvature in time and space'. In one sense, there can be no wrong attitude to the Tao since there is no point outside it to take such an attitude.[5] The Tao, however, is not fixed; it is a flowing and creative process. The universe in a state of flux; everything changes, nothing is constant. Energy flows continually between the negative pole of *yin* and the positive pole of *yang*. Both being and nonbeing are aspects of Tao: 'The ten thousand things are born of being. / Being is born of not being.'[6] To be at one with the Tao is not therefore a static condition, a motionless identification. It is a process of creative self-realization, a process of becoming in which both being and nonbeing are two enduring presences.[7]

Taoists take a holistic view of the universe, recognizing the ecological principle of unity in diversity. The whole is greater than the sum of its parts, in nature as well as in society: 'A mountain is high because of its individual particles. A river is large because of its individual drops. And he is a just man who regards all parts from the point of view of the whole.'[8]

The Taoists speak of creation as the 'ten thousand things' merely as a way of expressing a large number since the outward shape of the universe is vast. The Tao folds them all into its embrace. Unity underlies all particular manifestations. The fulfilment of a part can only take place within the larger whole. 'All things spring from germs. Under many diverse forms these things are ever being reproduced. Round and round, like a wheel, no part of which is more the starting-point than any other. This is called the equilibrium of God.'[9] The Tao is thus an interrelated process which results in natural order. Taoists refer back to a golden age which preceded hierarchy and domination, state and patriarchy, when all formed an integrated community. But they also look forward to a restored organic society.

The Chinese phrase usually translated as 'nature' is *tzu-jan*, which means literally 'of itself so'. The concept stresses the creative spontaneity of nature; indeed, *tzu-jan* may best be translated as spontaneity.[10] Nature is self-sufficient and uncreated; there is no need to postulate a creator. All parts of the single organism regulate themselves spontaneously.

But the universe is not random, for its has its own organic pattern (*li*). *Li*, a concept also found in Buddhism, may best be translated as 'principle'. But *li*, the principle of principles, cannot be stated in terms of law (*tse*). The difference is beautifully expressed in the root meanings of the words; *li* referred to the markings in jade, the grain in wood or the fibre in muscle; *tse*, to the writing of the imperial laws upon sacrificial cauldrons. The laws cannot be changed; they are fixed and static. But the markings in jade are 'formless' in the sense that they create a flowing, complex pattern. Thus Huai Nan Tzu (died 122 BC) declares: 'The Tao of Heaven operates mysteriously and secretly; it has no fixed shape; it follows no definite laws [*tse*]; it is great that you can never fathom it.'[11]

## Being in the world

The artist creates beauty by understanding the nature of his material, the grain in wood or stone, the notes of a musical instrument, the colours of the palette. The nature of the material is *li*, which is discovered not by logical analysis but by *kuan*, a kind of quiet contemplation, an open awareness without conscious concentration. The Taoist will contemplate in silence, without words. Language does not structure the world, as Wittgenstein argued; nature is prior to language which only classifies – often misleadingly – the world into beings, things and events.

The hexagram *kuan* in the *I Ching*, or *The Book of Changes*, stands for contemplation, combining 'wind, gentle, wood, penetration' with 'the earth, female, passive, receptive'.[12] The Chinese character for *kuan* shows the radical sign for 'seeing' beside a bird. It may have something to do with the ancient Chinese practice of watching the flight of birds for omens. It may also evoke the still alertness of a heron as it stands by a pool without apparently focussing on anything in particular.

The *I Ching*, written about 770 BC after the collapse of the Chou state, was an oracle used for divination which inspired both Taoism and Confucianism. The *I Ching* is much more determinist than Taoism, since it believes that the future develops in accordance with fixed laws, according to calculable numbers: if these numbers can be discovered it is possible to predict future events.

*Kuan* does not imply an empty mind, but rather a mind empty of its habitual thoughts and goals. It does not struggle to understand; it is simply like a mirror, which never refuses to show anything but retains nothing afterwards. It resonates to natural things without prejudice or foresight. It does not even make an effort not to make an effort, realizing the folly of struggling to sleep or forcing an orgasm. Since this involves abandoning focus, it may well explain the love of Chinese and Japanese painters for clouds and mountains, seen as if through half-closed eyes, or for water and sky where the one flows into the other.

Modern scientists could well benefit from *kuan*, contemplating without strained attention, using 'no-knowledge' (no preconceptions) to attain knowledge. This is all the more relevant since modern physics describes the world as a dance of energy in a way which is remarkably similar to the Taoists'.[13]

The approach to nature recommended by the Taoists is one of receptivity and passivity. Where the Confucian wants to conquer and exploit nature, the Taoist tries to contemplate and understand it. One of the favourite symbols of Taoism is water, which yields but nevertheless erodes the hardest rock.

> The highest good is like water.
> Water gives life to the ten thousand things and does not strive.
> It flows in places men reject and so is like the Tao.

Therefore, 'Be the stream of the universe!'[14] Flowing like water, finding the point of least resistance, the individual will eventually wear away the hard and unyielding. By not blocking itself, the self will reach a state of *wu-hsin* or 'egolessness'.

Taoism celebrates the low and soft, not the grand and rigid:

> The valley spirit never dies;
> It is the woman, primal mother.
> Her gateway is the root of heaven and earth.[15]

Yet this attitude does not lead to an unthinking acceptance but actually encourages a scientific outlook among Taoists. By not imposing their own preconceptions, they are able to observe and understand nature and therefore flow with its energy beneficially. If the wise abandon prejudices and study nature they will be able to increase general wellbeing. The Taoist philosophy of nature restores the original sense of its seamless unity without loss of individual consciousness. It implies an approach to the universe and the immediate environment which does not interfere deeply with the natural course of things.

Taoist art, especially poetry and landscape painting, is not considered 'artificial' but spontaneous, created without strain or conscious intention. Naturalness is a kind of self-determining spontaneity. 'Communing with nature' is not therefore a form of escapism, but direct contact with reality, a state in which the observer and observed are no longer felt as separate.

The Taoists are primarily interested in nature but their conception of the universe has important corollaries for society. The individual is a microcosm of the universe, in that if left alone both spontaneously follow the Tao. As such the individual is a matrix of relationships; one can only realize oneself in relation to the whole. Realizing one's own Tao involves participating in the universal Tao and realizing the Tao of others. One should not therefore flee from oneself into the arms of others in spurious neighbourly love: 'Annihilation of the Tao in order to practice charity and duty to one's neighbour, – this is the error of the Sage.'[16] If each person keeps to him- or herself, the world would escape confusion. Unlike Christians, Taoists believe that the best way to help one's neighbour is to perfect one's own life. If one improves oneself, everyone will benefit.

The Taoists hold that only when society begins to deviate from nature, morality arises:

> Therefore when Tao is lost, there is goodness.
> When goodness is lost, there is kindness.
> When kindness is lost, there is justice.
> When justice is lost, there is ritual.[17]

A person of Tao will be good spontaneously without any judgment, without any utilitarian calculation of intentions or consequences of his actions. He will be sincere, simple, spontaneous, generous and detached. He will not force others to do things, but let them organize themselves. His virtue will be passive rather than active. The importance of inaction (*wu-wei*) is stressed time and time again in Taoist writings. It is not a form of idleness but rather a mental attitude of equilibrium and tranquil stillness which nothing can disturb:

> A truly good man does nothing,
> Yet leaves nothing undone.

It is a demanding ideal:

> Are you able to do nothing?
> Giving birth and nourishing,
> Bearing yet not possessing,
> Working yet not taking credit,

Leading yet not dominating,
This is the Primal Virtue.[18]

The person of Tao avoids competition and trying to win. Joy, anger, sorrow, happiness find no place in his heart. He uses his mind like a mirror: 'It grasps nothing: it refuses nothing. It receives but does not keep.'[19]

He who would follow the Tao never loses sight of the natural conditions of his existence. The more humans try to control the world, to check the natural flow, the more chaotic it will become. Coercion always hinders. Spontaneity and order are not opposites, but identical. The sage will therefore move with the natural flow of things, like an old sailor who does not tighten his muscles on a pitching boat.

But what is natural? The answer is simple: 'Horses and oxen,' answered the Spirit of the Ocean, 'have four feet. That is the natural. Put a halter on a horse's head, a string through a bullock's nose, – that is the artificial.'[20] The wise person will not interfere with nature, but let it be. He is not aggressive or assertive. He disregards externals; success and profit will have no value for him. He travels like a bird, leaving no trace behind. Above all, he is as spontaneous as a newborn child who can cry all day without becoming hoarse, who acts without knowing what it does. He acts without distinguishing between right and wrong.

Although Taoism is loath to elaborate a strict moral code, it does have certain values, notably compassion, frugality and nonassertion – 'daring not to be ahead of others'.[21] Compassion is not merely for fellow humans, but for all creatures; it is antihumanist in the sense that it has no favourites. The universe is not human-hearted: 'Heaven and earth are ruthless.' It follows that if a person wishes to be in harmony with the universe, he or she will also not be human-hearted: 'The wise are ruthless.'[22]

Man is not therefore the measure of all things: 'He who delights in man, is himself not a perfect man. His affection is not true charity,' Chuang Tzu claims.[23] Charity is the universal love of all creation, not of a particular manifestation. Taoists thus advocate a kind of ecocentric impartiality which results with identifying with the whole and which respects all beings as intrinsically valuable.[24]

The Taoist ideal is not the nonattached and passionless one of the Buddhists or the Hindus. Nor is it quietist and defeatist. Taoists advocate repose, but they offer a practical guide for right conduct. They teach peace and strongly oppose domination and oppression. They advocate not withdrawal from the world, but involvement in it. By following the Tao, a person's nature is not annihilated but fulfilled.

The Taoist natural philosopher is receptive and observant, not imposing his conceptual grid on nature, but aware that he is part of what he is observing. Because of their successful experimentation, the Taoists gave a considerable impetus to the development of science and medicine in ancient China.

At the same time, Taoists recognize that not all new technology is beneficial. They are fully aware that some technological innovations can be used to dominate and degrade humanity and nature. 'Destruction of the natural integrity of things, in order to produce articles of various kinds, – this is the fault of the artisan,' declared Chuang Tzu.[25] He related the story of an old gardener who prefers to water his patch with a pitcher from a well rather than use a well-sweep. It involves great labour with very little result. When questioned about this time-consuming practice, the gardener replies: 'Those who have cunning implements are cunning in their dealings, and those who are cunning in their dealings have cunning in their hearts . . . and those who are restless in spirit are not fit vehicles for TAO.'[26]

Lao Tzu makes a similar point: 'A small country has fewer people. Though there are machines that can work ten to a hundred times faster than man, they are not needed.'[27] Taoists recognize that technological developments are not value-free, and that while they may be apparently time-saving and efficient they can create artificial desires and prevent self-realization. They are moreover unnecessary to transcend natural scarcity – a notion which developed with the building of cities dependent on the surrounding land. Nature left to itself is fecund, abundant and overflowing. Unlike humans, it takes from those who have too much and gives to those who do not have enough. It continually tries to regulate itself and reach an equilibrium.

'There is no greater sin than desire,' Lao Tzu writes.[28] What he condemns is the inordinate desire for wealth, power and reputation which inevitably leads to unhappiness, not the desire for truth and sex. Far from condemning sexual desire, the Taoists felt that sexuality mirrored the cosmic flow of energy between the creative forces of *yin* and *yang* and that *ch'i* or energy was increased by sexual stimulus.

Life is thus nourished and not undermined by sexuality. As in Tantric yoga, the Taoists believed that sexual love could be transformed into a spiritual exercise in which the participants become embodiments of the universe and symbolize its union.

The gentle peacefulness recommended by Taoists is not a form of defeatist submission. Certainly good results are not achieved through violence for 'force is followed by loss of strength' and 'a violent man will die a violent death'.[29] Giving way is often the best means to overcome:

> Under heaven nothing is more soft and yielding than water.
> Yet for attacking the solid and strong, nothing is better;
> It has no equal. The weak can overcome the strong;
> The supple can overcome the stiff.[30]

When the Taoists advocate non-action (*wu-wei*), it is not inactivity but rather work without effort and complication. *Wu-wei* can be translated as 'non-striving' and 'non-making'. Real work should therefore go with and not against the grain of things, the flow of nature. Natural forms are not made but grow; artefacts, like houses and machines, should be shaped like sculpture. If work were approached from this perspective, it would lose its coercive aspect. Rather than being avoided as something which alienates and prevents self-realization, it would be transformed into spontaneous and meaningful play. It is useless trying to be useful; better to work for the intrinsic value of the activity itself, not for its possible consequences.

The deepest roots of the Taoist view of *wu-wei* probably lies in the nature of peasant life. Peasants by long experience refrain from activity contrary to nature and realize that in order to grow plants they must understand and cooperate with the natural processes. And just as plants grow best when allowed to follow their natures, so human beings thrive when least interfered with. The world is ruled by letting things take their course. If people followed this advice, the Taoists suggest, they would live a long life and achieve physical and mental health. Indeed, earthly longevity became one of their central goals. 'Whatever is contrary to Tao will not last long,' they teach, while he who is filled with virtue is like a newborn child.[31] In order to prolong their lives, some Taoists resorted to yoga-like techniques and even alchemy.

## *Ecological society*

The Taoists stress repeatedly that the causes of social conflict
and natural disasters are to be found in human domination and
hierarchy:

> that the the conditions of life are violated, that the will of God
> does not triumph, that the beasts of the field are disorganized,
> that the birds of the air cry at night, that blight reaches the trees
> and the herbs, that destruction spreads among creeping things,
> – this, alas! is the fault of *government*.[32]

To try and govern people by laws and regulations is the ultimate folly:
'To attempt to govern mankind thus, – as well try to wade through
the sea, to hew a passage through a river, or make a mosquito fly
away with a mountain!'[33] People should not therefore be coerced
into obeying artificial laws, but be left alone to regulate themselves.
The wise person knows that forceful actions will accomplish nothing,
and therefore does nothing.

The social ideal of the Taoists was a form of agrarian collectivism
which sought to recapture the primordial unity with nature which
human beings had lost in developing an artificial civilization. They
were extremely critical of the bureaucratic, warlike and commercial
nature of the feudal order of their own day which the Confucians
defended and enhanced. Lao Tzu specifically saw the excessive wealth
of a few as causing misery:

> When the court is arrayed in splendour,
> The fields are full of weeds,
> And the granaries are bare.

By claiming wealth and titles, the ruling elite created disaster in the
land. Lao Tzu more than any other ancient thinker realized that the
coercive apparatus of government was the cause and not the remedy
of social disorder. It is only when 'the country is confused and in
chaos, that loyal ministers appear'.[34] It follows that:

> The more laws and restrictions there are,
> The poorer people become.
> The sharper men's weapons,

The more trouble in the land.
The more ingenious and clever men are,
The more strange things happen.
The more rules and regulations,
The more thieves and robbers.

Therefore the sage says:

I take no action and people are reformed.
I enjoy peace and people become honest.
I do nothing and the people become rich.
I have no desires and people return to the good and simple life.[35]

The Taoists' social background tended to be the small middle class situated between the feudal lords and the mass of peasant farmers. The *Tao Te Ching* is addressed to rulers as well as would-be sages, but it is not a Machiavellian handbook of statecraft. Lao Tzu suggests that a ruler should act with the people, not above them. The best ruler, however, dissolves his own rule: he leaves the people alone to follow their own peaceful and productive activities. He trusts their good faith and lets them get on with things. The country will then reside in peace and contentment.

Unlike the meddling and authoritarian Confucians, the Taoists had the social ideal of an anarchist society without government and state, in which people live simple and sincere lives in harmony with nature. It is a decentralized society in which goods are produced and shared with the help of appropriate technology. The inhabitants in such an ecologically sound community would be strong but with no need to show their strength; wise, but with no pretence of learning.

A small country has fewer people.
Though there are machines that can work ten to a hundred
    times faster than man, they are not needed.
The people take death seriously and do not travel far.
Though they have boats and carriages, no one uses them.
Though they have armour and weapons, no one displays them.
Men return to the knotting of rope in place of writing.
Their food is plain and good, their clothes fine but simple,
    their homes secure;
They are happy in their ways.

Though they live within sight of their neighbours,
And crowing cocks and barking dogs are heard across the
  way,
Yet they leave each other in peace while they grow old
and die.[36]

Chuang Tzu makes a similar point:

They were contented with what food and raiment they could
get. They lived simple and peaceful lives. Neighbouring districts
were within sight, and the cocks and dogs of one could be heard
in the other, yet the people grew old and died without ever
interchanging visits.[37]

He also states the fundamental proposition of libertarian thought
which has reverberated through history ever since:

There has been such a thing as letting mankind alone; there has
never been such a thing as governing mankind.
    Letting alone springs from fear lest men's natural dispositions
be perverted and their virtue left aside. But if their natural
dispositions be not perverted nor their virtue laid aside, what
room is there left for government?[38]

But while pursuing their own interests, people would not forget the
interests of others. It is not a sullen selfishness that is recommended.
The pursuit of personal good involves a concern for the general
wellbeing: the more one gives to others, the greater one's abundance.
Human being are individuals but they are also social beings, part of
society, and society in turn is part of the wider environment of beings
and things.
    Anticipating the findings of scientific ecology, the Taoists also
believed that the more individuality and diversity there is, the greater
the overall harmony. The spontaneous order of society does not
exclude conflict, but there is an ultimate identity of opposites and
reconciliation of contradictions at the cosmic level. Thus society is
described as 'an agreement of a certain number of families and
individuals to abide by certain customs. Discordant elements unite
to form a harmonious whole. Take away this unity and each has a
separate individuality.'[39]
    The philosophy of nature and society of Taoism offers the first

and most impressive expression of libertarian ecology. Although containing elements of mysticism, the Taoists' receptive approach to nature encouraged an experimental method and a democratic attitude. They recognize the unity in the diversity of nature and the universality of change and transformation. In their ethics, they espouse self-reliance, self-realization and spontaneous behaviour, but always within the context of a larger whole of society and nature. They not only urge rulers to leave their subjects alone and oppose the bureaucratic and legalistic teaching of the Confucians, but ultimately propose as an ideal a free and cooperative society without government, which is in harmony with nature.

In its later forms Taoism degenerated into a quest for immortality and even hardened into a religious sect. But in its purest form, it has remained remarkably subtle and relevant. While some more aggressive thinkers may find in Taoism a philosophy of failure or quietude, a way of getting by in troubled times by keeping one's head down, it presents in reality the profound wisdom of those who have experienced power and wealth and know their inherent destructiveness. It provides the philosophical foundations for a genuinely ecological society and a way to resolve the ancient antagonism between humanity and nature which continues to bedevil the world.

# 2

# HINDUISM

## The Way of Understanding

Man is made by his belief. As he believes, so he is.
*Bhagavad-Gita*

Hinduism admirably illustrates the ecological principle of unity in diversity. It has always been tolerant of and hospitable to different beliefs and practices. More like a tree than a building, Hinduism is unique among the world's major religions in having no organization or formal institutionalized controls.

There are an infinite number of paths to the Absolute. Depending on their cultural traditions, different peoples have become attached to particular figures in Hindu mythology, the gods as well as their several incarnations (avatars). But they are all manifestations from the same source. The many currents of worship in Hinduism all flow towards the wide ocean of the Absolute. Some people require images to help them fix their mind on the object of their prayers. But they recognize that ultimately there is only one God and individual deities are only particular manifestations of the Absolute. Images are ladders to be thrown away as one begins to grasp the all-pervading nature of being.

There are many schools of Hinduism but from the very beginning there was a feeling of awe and wonder at the inexhaustible mystery of life. The *Upanishads*, written some eight hundred years before Christ, reveal the doctrine of the all-pervading nature of being. They were followed by the *Bhagavad-Gita*, with its ideal of selfless work for the good of the whole and its doctrine of *ahimsa* (non-injury or non-violence). The compassionate message of Hinduism was further developed by its offshoots Jainism and Buddhism.

Unlike the mainstream Christian tradition, many aspects of Hinduism are deeply ecological. It has never been man-centred and recognizes that the knower, known and knowledge are one. It is a religious tradition without a founder or prophet, and may be considered more of a culture than a creed. Although it accepts a spiritual hierarchy in the chain of being and a social hierarchy in the form of a caste system, its doctrine of reincarnation does not place an unbridgeable gulf between humans and other animals. Depending on their conduct, or *karma*, men and animals can go up or down the chain of being in the cycle of rebirth (*samsara*) until they achieve release (*moksha*) when the wheel of existence comes to an end.

Far from separating human beings from the rest of creation, Hinduism sees them as integral parts of an organic whole. All beings and things are the creation of the Supreme and therefore united and connected. The Sanskrit phrase *Tat twam asi* is known by all Hindus: 'Thou art that.' It was therefore possible for the smiling Indian yogi to tell the British soldier who bayoneted him in the stomach: 'I am thou.'

The whole of nature is seen as vibrating with life: trees, rocks and waterfalls become shrines; mountains and forests symbolize the power of nature. While spiritually advanced yogis seek desolate regions or wildernesses in order to discover ultimate reality, the broad masses travel to rivers, which are seen as the source and support of spiritual life – the symbol of life without end. The respect for animals expresses itself in the universal reverence for the cow, which is allowed to wander through town and country as it pleases. Even the small minority who still sacrifice animals do so because they consider them sacred and they offer them to the gods as a great gift.

Like the Greeks, modern Hindus, Buddhists and Jains speak of a golden age in the past – an 'age of truth' when humans knew neither illness nor want and lived peaceful, simple and virtuous lives. Then human greed developed and people began to accumulate private property. This was the original downfall of humanity, for it led to the introduction of disease, poverty and hunger into the world. Things have since grown progressively worse until the present dark (*kali*) age which will end in a universal deluge. The scenario fits in well with the more pessimistic ecological forecasts.

But that is not the end of it. After the total destruction of all life by the flood, the earth will emerge afresh and a new golden age begin. The ecological analogy breaks down here for Hindus think in cyclical rather than linear terms – the cycle of rise and fall will continue for ever. There is of course no historical evidence of an earlier golden age, and the stages of the myth are remarkably similar to the seasonal life of an Indian village, which ends and begins with monsoon floods.[1]

## The creation of the Vedas

The earliest known civilization in India is the Indus Valley Civilization, an urban culture based on a matriarchal society which was already quite advanced by 2500 BC. Excavations in the early twentieth century unearthed many figurines that suggest that these early people worshipped a mother goddess, symbol of creativity and the flow of life. Each village seems to have had its own goddess. There are also figures of a male god, shown in the position of a yogi in a state of contemplation. He is often surrounded by animals and may possibly be the original form of the later Hindu god of creation, Shiva, 'Lord of the Animals'. *Lingam* and *yoni* symbols, representing male and female sexual organs, have also been found, and show the central importance given to fertility. There are traces of tree, serpent and other animal worship.

It was probably from this matriarchal society that the worship of the mother goddess (Devi) as well as the mother image of spiritual power (Sakti) emerged.[2] The universal reverence for the cow in Hindu culture was also probably an offshoot of the ancient cult of the mother goddess. The cow remains in India the living symbol of Mother Earth and of the abundance she bestows on humanity. Feeding the cow is an act of worship; even its urine is seen as sacred and used in purification rituals.

The Indus Valley Civilization declined in the middle of the second millennium, possibly owing to the invasion of people known as Aryans, who spoke a language from which Sanskrit is derived. Their religion, presented in the *Vedas*, appears polytheistic like those of the Greeks and Celts, and their pantheon recalls the gods of the *Odyssey*. They worshipped in the open air. Where pre-Aryan worshippers gathered principally around water, the Aryans performed ceremonies around fire.

The *Vedas* and the religion they represent form the bedrock of Hinduism and Hindu civilization. They are collections of prayers and hymns meant for incantation in an ancient form of Sanskrit. They were written some time between 2500 BC and 1500 BC. Their main heroes are the gods, most of whom represent forces of nature, such as the sun, the moon, sky, storm, wind, rain, dawn, fire and water.

Worshippers would try to influence them by putting grain, butter, spices, goats and even horses into the flames of a sacrificial fire.

The most popular Vedic god seems to have been Indra, god of rain and thunder (and later of heaven), a warrior who overcomes powers of evil and brings the world into being. Agni, the personification of sacrificial fire, is also prominent. As in all early religions, the spiritual and physical realms are not separated. The marriage of the divine parents, Heaven and Earth, symbolizes the indissoluble links between the two. 'May Heaven and Earth protect us from fearful evil' goes the refrain in a hymn to them both.

Deeply spiritual, the *Vedas* are also life-affirming and have an earthy naturalism. There is a sense of awesome mystery in the universe which escapes human understanding. The account of genesis given in the 'Hymn to Creation' relates that in the beginning there was the 'One' which 'breathed windless' in dark, undiscriminated chaos. Thereafter rose Desire, the 'earliest seed' produced by thought. But since the gods were born after the creation of the world, 'Then who can know from whence it has arisen?'[3] This scepticism later led not only to doubt about the possibility of knowing the ultimate source of things, but to agnostic ridicule of the gods.

At the same time, the *Rigveda* ('Songs of Knowledge') reveal an intimate bond between the believer and his or her environment, a sense of kinship with the spirit that dwells in all things. As the hymns to the night, forest and dawn demonstrate, a profound spiritual meaning was combined with a great sensitivity to and appreciation of the beauties of the natural world. This is particularly true in the beautiful hymn to Earth:

> You bear truly, Earth,
> The burden of the mountains' weight;
> With might, O One of many streams,
> You awaken the potent one, the soil.
>
> With flowers of speech our songs of praise
> Resound to you, far-spreading one,
> Who send forth the swelling cloud,
> O bright one, like propelling speed;
>
> Who, steadfast, hold with thy might,
> The forest-trees upon the ground,
> When, from the lightnings of thy cloud,
> The rain-floods of the sky pour down.[4]

Although the hymns show a sense of awe in face of the mysterious universe, there is little trace of the fear found in Celtic and Christian tales. Humans live in a world which is portrayed as essentially friendly if its ways are respected.

This sense of wonder and awe at life on our planet comes through in the 'Hymn to Goddess Earth' in the *Atharvaveda*, a collection of magical formulae which form part of the *Vedas* written more than three thousand years ago:

> Thy snowy mountain heights, and thy forests, O earth, shall be kind to us! The brown, the black, the red, the multi-coloured, the firm earth, that is protected by Indra, I have settled upon, not suppressed, slain, not wounded . . .
>
> Rock, stone, dust is this earth; this earth is supported, held together. To this golden-breasted earth I have rendered reverence.
>
> The earth, upon whom the forest-sprung trees ever stand firm, the all-nourishing, compact earth, do we invoke.[5]

While the import of the hymn is to implore the earth, 'mistress of that which was and shall be', to prepare a 'broad domain' for humanity, the attitude is one of reverence, completely at odds with the conquering spirit of Genesis in the Old Testament. The moral principles which emerge from the *Vedas* are predominantly ascetic, and love and kindness to all, both the human and the nonhuman, is the prevailing tone.

Despite the overall sense of unity in the world of the *Vedas*, there are some distinctions. One of its least attractive legacies is the caste system. In an anthropomorphic symbol, the concrete universe was created out of Purusha, the 'primal man', and from his body arose the different castes: his mouth gave rise to the priestly caste of Brahmins, the Aryan elite, his two arms the *kshatriyas*, the warriors, his thighs the *vaisya*, the traders and peasants, and at his feet are the *shudras*, the workers and serfs, doubtless made up of the darker-skinned indigenous people conquered by the Aryans. Moving from society to nature, the moon is said to have been born from his spirit, the sun from his eye, the middle sky from his navel, the heavens from his head, and the earth from his feet.[6] The analogy however emphasizes the link between man and the universe, the microcosm and the macrocosm.

On occasion, the *Vedas* appear dualistic or atomistic, but this is misleading. Throughout the *Vedas* there is a strong sense that one supreme being is being worshipped in different aspects. Indeed, the idea of a single being is made explicit: 'He is one, [though] wise men call Him by many names.'[7] This unity in diversity also comes through in the central notion of *rita*; that is, of a spontaneous order that is reflected in each part of the creation and pervades the whole. It represents the unity or rightness which underlies the ordered universe. Virtue is thus in conformity with the cosmic order, and enjoins an orderly and consistent life.

In the sixth century BC the movements of Jainism and Buddhism reacted against Hindu civilization's priestly ritual and sacrifices. Both rejected the caste system and taught a new way of release and salvation. They also placed the doctrine of *ahimsa* (non-injury) at the centre of their ethics and preached reverence for all life. Although the Jain and Buddhist movements had a great influence on Hinduism, turning the majority of Hindus into vegetarians, their beliefs were considered unorthodox by many later Hindu teachers.

## The forest wisdom of the Upanishads

Orthodox Hindu teaching draws on writings that emerged in the sixth century BC, the *Upanishads*. Their name comes from the Sanskrit words for 'near' and 'sit', evoking the position of learners gathered around their teachers, or gurus. Unlike the *Vedas*, with their songs to particular forces of nature, the *Upanishads* focus on the ground of being which is prior to all existence. Like modern ecology, they teach the apparent paradox of a transcendent yet immanent unity underlying the diversity of the world:

> By the Lord [Isa] enveloped must this all be –
> Whatever moving thing there is in the moving world.
> With this renounced, thou mayest enjoy.
> Covet not the wealth of anyone at all . . .
> Now, he who on all beings
> Looks as just in the Self
> And on the Self as in all beings –
> He does not shrink away from Him.[8]

The *Upanishads* do not separate man from the creation or its creatures. We find the same analogy between man and the universe, the microcosm and the macrocosm, as in the *Vedas*. In the *Upanishad* known as the 'Great-Forest Book', it is written that 'in the beginning this world was Self [atman] alone in the form of a Person [*Purusha*].'⁹ But the primal man finds no pleasure in being alone, so he divides himself into male and female and the two halves copulate. Wondering how 'he' can embrace her after producing her from himself, 'she' decides to hide. In the process, she transforms herself into various kinds of animal and the couple then procreate the different species. The creation myth vividly shows the presence of the male and female principles throughout the universe, and the continuity between humanity and the rest of the creation. By stressing the close correspondence between the human body and the universe, humanity is portrayed as an integral part of a gigantic organism.

Central to the *Upanishads* are the notions of atman, the self, and Brahman, the all-pervading Absolute or Universal Self. The two are one and the same; the Absolute manifests itself in every individual self.

The exact meaning of Brahman is obscure and opaque; it is described in the *Upanishads* as:

> Hidden in all beings, all-pervading, the self within all beings,
> watching over all works, dwelling in all beings, the witness, the
> perceiver, the only one, free from all qualities. He is the one ruler
> of many who do not act; he makes the one seed manifold.¹⁰

Brahman manifests itself in every being. Through the cycle of rebirths man approaches his final end, identity of his self (atman, the ground of his self, not his individual personality) with the Universal Self (Brahman). The realization of the Brahman pervading all being frees us from the chains of illusion and enables us to recognize reality as the dwelling of pure being (*sat*), pure consciousness (*cit*), and pure delight (*ananda*). The latter is joyful release from the sufferings imposed by our ego through ignorance. Once unity with Brahman has been realized, all rituals become superfluous, death loses its sting, and the mind becomes calm, contented and free. It is incompatible with hatred, greed and injury. This belief is at the core of mainstream Hindu thought.

Where as Vedic India studied knowledge of the natural world, the forest civilization of the *Upanishads* sought to discover the principles which give unity to the world. They asked not only the question

'Who am I?' but 'Who is the knower?' They attempted to find the answer by meditation, a process of pure concentration which trains the mind to focus without wandering until it is absorbed in the object of contemplation. It does not create dullness or emptiness but a state of inner wakefulness.

While Brahman and atman are one, the world is not pure illusion. External objects are not just forms of personal consciousness. The world may be a manifestation of Brahman, but it still exists in a fashion. The Hindu philosopher Samkara uses the analogy of a rope and a snake to explain this apparent paradox. The rope may appear to be a snake until it is properly examined. The world may be likened to the snake and Brahman to the rope. The precise relationship between the world and Brahman is called *maya*. The relationship between Brahman and the world is not reversible. There would be no world without Brahman, but Brahman can exist without the world.[11]

There is a marvellous anecdote about a Greek philosopher who came across some '*brahmanes*' lying naked on a rock in the midday sun of the Deccan. Knowing their reputation as wise men, he approached them and enquired whether they would discuss the nature of the universe with him. 'Of course,' they said, 'as soon as you get your clothes off and get down on this rock.'[12] The anecdote expresses a profound truth. Like modern physicists, the sages of the *Upanishads* recognize that it is impossible to know anything objectively; no entity really exists objectively as a separate item. The only way to know something is to identify with it.

The Hindu tradition has highlighted three key utterances in the *Upanishads*: 'The Self is Brahman', 'Consciousness is Brahman', and 'I am Brahman'. They form the ground of the Hindu belief that all is one. What links all phenomena together is energy, or *prana*. It is similar to the Chinese concept of *ch'i*. It supports life, sustains evolution and reveals itself in the mind as thoughts and desires. The *Upanishads* build around the notion of *prana* a seamless theory of life which covers everything from morality to health:

> The Self [within the body] asked himself, 'What is that makes
> Me go if it goes and stay if it stays?'
> So he created *prana*, and from it
> Desire; and from desire he made space, air,
> Fire, water, the earth, the senses, the mind

> And food; from food came strength, austerity,
> The scriptures, sacrifice, and all the worlds;
> And everything was given name and form.[13]

*Prana* links up the subjective to the objective, the animate to the inanimate. In its external form it is the sun, radiant energy; in its internal form it is consciousness. *Prana* supports both the external and the inner world.

The central insight of modern ecology – unity in diversity – is also central to the *Upanishads*. The unknown authors revel in the sheer diversity of life on earth:

> He is this boy, he is that girl, he is
> This man, he is that woman, and he is
> This old man, too, tottering on his staff.
> His face is seen everywhere.
>
> He is the blue bird, he is the green bird
> With red eyes; he is the thundercloud,
> And he is the seasons and the seas.
> He has no beginning, he has no end
> He is the source from which the worlds evolve.[14]

This forest vision of life is tempered by a profound awareness of the unity at the heart of being. The creation of the manifold world comes from the unitary self; the many come from the one. This is made clear in the cosmic-egg theory of creation given in *Chandogya Upanishad*:

> In the beginning this world was merely non-being. It was existent. It developed. It turned into an egg. It lay for the period of a year. It was split asunder. One of the two eggshell-parts became silver, one gold.
>
> That which was of silver is this earth. That which was of gold is the sky. What was the outer membrane is the mountains. What was the inner membrane is cloud and mist. What were the veins are rivers. What was the fluid within is the ocean.[15]

There is an overall unity not only in space but in time. This is expressed in the mystic symbolism of the syllable *Om* which is pronounced during meditation:

> *Om!* – This syllable is this whole world.
> Its further explanation is: –
> The past, the present, the future – everything is just the
> word *Om*.[16]

*Om* is also heard by the one who meditates as the voice of
the world.

Once a person realizes that he or she is not separate from the rest
of the creation, there is no longer any ground to feel threatened or
alien in the world:

> Those who see all creatures in themselves
> And themselves in all creatures know no fear.
> Those who see all creatures in themselves
> And themselves in all creatures know no grief.
> How can the multiplicity of life
> Delude the one who sees its unity?[17]

Explicit in the Upanishadic teaching of unity is the notion of *ahimsa*
or non-injury. To harm other things or beings is to harm oneself.
The central ethics of Hinduism is therefore *ahimsa paramo dharma*:
'There is no higher conduct than non-violence.'[18]

To realize the self-in-the-Self, to unite atman and Brahman, to
become enlightened, does not involve deprivation. Renouncing the
material ways of the world, particularly wealth, power and fame,
brings freedom and joy. Indeed, the *Upanishads* claim that the
knower of Brahman has a shining face, feels healthy and even smells
good. The inner personal freedom of *swaraj* involves channelling
passions, not negating them; directing thoughts, not suppressing
them. 'Only those who find out Who they are and what they want
find freedom, here and in all the worlds.'[19]

For many Hindus the natural world has importance only as the
manifestation of the Absolute. The whole sensuous drama of life on
earth is like a theatrical performance; once its message is understood,
it becomes superfluous. 'As a dancer stops dancing after displaying
herself on stage, so Nature stops, after having shown herself to
Mind.'[20]

### Bhagavad-Gita *and the good of the whole*

The great epic of *Bhagavad-Gita* (composed around 500 BC)
focuses on how humans should act in the world. The three principal ways of reaching God also become clearer, through *inana*
(knowledge or meditation), *karma* (action) and *bhakti* (devotion).

The *Bhagavad-Gita* takes the form of a conversation between
Arjuna, a great warrior, and his charioteer, Krishna, just as they
are about to enter battle. To many it appears as a spirited defence
of detachment, the caste system, and the warrior ethic. But the
whole narrative is symbolic, with Krishna as the incarnation of
Brahman, and the approaching battle representing spiritual and
moral struggle. Its central themes of Love, Light and Life emerge
from an ecological vision of God in all things and all things in
God: 'God dwells in the heart of all beings.'[21]

Right conduct, or *dharma*, is more important than belief to Hindu
culture. The *Bhagavad-Gita* proclaims the ideals of selfless work,
detachment, honesty and love: 'Let the wise man work unselfishly
for the good of all the world.'[22] The moral community is not as
in the Judaeo-Christian tradition restricted to human beings; in the
words of Krishna, the virtuous man is 'the man who has a good will
for all [born beings], who is friendly and has compassion; who has
no thoughts of a "I" or "Mine", whose peace is the same in pleasures
and sorrows, and who is forgiving'.[23]

### *Hindu sects*

While the *Upanishads* and the *Bhagavad-Gita* form the foundation
of Hindu metaphysics and ethics, there are many sects in the Indian
sub-continent reflecting a great combination of different religious
influences and communities. In later Hindu mythology, the most
common gods are the triad Brahma, Vishnu and Shiva. They represent
three aspects of the Absolute – the creator, preserver and destroyer,
the last being necessary for further creation. Traces of earlier beliefs
remain. Some Hindus worship a river, a mountain or particular trees
and animals. Others take a particular deity as the object of their
worship, like Ganesh ('Lord of the Folk'), who is half human and
half elephant. The cult of Kali, the folk goddess, is still widespread.
It probably derives from the mother goddess found in the Indus Valley

Civilization, for she emerges as a mother-force of the universe. She can be merciful and all-suffering, but also ruthless and devouring. It is under the latter aspect that the notorious thuggee worship her.

Various non-Vedic cults have developed over the centuries within Hinduism, with varying degrees of awareness of the self-in-atman and of respect for nonhuman life. The Natha cult, for example, worships Shiva as the lord of the animals. Like the yogis, the Natha followers claim to find all the religious mysteries in the human body. They see the solar and lunar currents within the nervous system, and claim that by uniting them it is possible to open the psychic centres of the body known as *chakras*. They acknowledge the equilibrium of Shiva and Sakti, the male and female deities, as two different aspects of the divine force.

An offshoot of these beliefs is Tantrism, according to which sexual energy is part of cosmic energy, and sexual activity expresses spiritual forces at work in the universe. Making love is not making love to an individual but uniting male and female principles operating throughout the universe. A woman should not love a particular man, but the Absolute made manifest in him and vice versa. The path of Tantra involves the gradual uncoiling of the *kundalini*, or the spiritual current in humanity. As it uncoils and rises upwards, it frees a series of *chakras* in the body culminating in *sahasrara* – a thousand-petalled lotus in the mind or the crown of the head. Like the Buddhists and the Jains, the Tantric practitioners reject the caste system and rigid social hierarchy, and, as might be expected, women play an important role in the sect.

One of the most intriguing sects to have emerged in recent times are the Bauls of Bengal, a movement which grew out of the ruins of Buddhism and Tantrism in the region. *Baul* means madcap and probably comes from the Sanskrit word *vayu* for wind. Certainly they consider themselves as free as the wind and wish to leave no trace behind them. As Narahari Baul puts it in a song:

> That is why, brother, I became a madcap Baul.
> No master I obey, nor injunctions, canons, or custom.
> Man-made distinctions have no hold on me now.
> I rejoice in the gladness of the love that wells out of my
>     own being.

In love is no separation, but a meeting of hearts forever.
So I rejoice in song and I dance with each and all.
That is why, brother, I became a madcap Baul.[24]

The song expresses some of the central beliefs of the Bauls. They are uncompromising free spirits, seeking freedom from all outward constraints. They accept no divisions of society, such as class or caste. They will have nothing to do with special deities or temples. 'What need we of other temples,' they ask, 'when one body is the temple where our Spirit has its abode?' They refuse to wear the traditional ochre-coloured clothes of Indian hermits and monks. They do not go on pilgrimage and consider every moment sacred. They are not celibate and claim that earthly love helps them to feel divine love. Not surprisingly, this has earned them a notorious reputation in more orthodox quarters.

They place great stress on independent thinking and prefer the spoken to the written word. All the scriptures they need are written within the heart for all to read. Like William Blake, they will not accept another person's system but create for themselves: 'Brave men rejoice in their own creation. Only cowards are content with glorifying their forefathers because they do no know how to create for themselves.' They tend to express themselves in direct and moving songs.

Although they learn from teachers or gurus, they only have them as stepping stones to their personal development. Indeed, they sometimes deny in their poetry that human gurus exist and use the term metaphorically to refer to whatever makes them think and understand: 'Every wrench at your heartstrings that makes the tears flow is your *guru*.' In order to remind themselves that they can learn from everything around them, they even call their guru *sunya*, literally meaning 'nothing' or 'emptiness'.[25]

They disregard the history of their sect but this does not mean they are not interested in the passing of time. On the contrary, they seek harmony between past, present and future in order to appreciate the continuity of life. They also try to achieve harmony between material and spiritual needs. Like all Hindu religious sects, however, the Baul have as their ultimate aim the realization of the self as part of the universal whole. To be completely free is to die to the life of the world, even when one is in it.

The movement draws support from the lowest social strata of the

Hindu and Muslim communities but embraces householders as well as wanderers and vagrants. Their ideal is to be *sahaj* (simple or natural); they follow the *sahaj* way and leave no trace behind them: 'Do the boats that sail over the flooded river leave any mark? It is only the boatmen of the muddy track, urged on by their petty needs, that leave a long furrow behind.'[26]

## Vedanta and the self-in-the-self

While many different sects form part of religious practice, Hindu religious thought has also developed into half a dozen systems of philosophy. As in Western philosophy, a variety of cosmologies stand side by side, ranging from monism and dualism to pantheism. The most influential and holistic school of thought is the Vedanta, which derives from the *Upanishads* and focuses on the concept of Brahman. Its most celebrated exponent was Samkara, who lived in south India in the eighteenth century AD and who elaborated the theory of *maya*. The word comes from the Sanskrit root *ma- (matr-)*, meaning to measure. *Maya* thus means the world-as-measured, divided up into things and events. As such, it is an illusion.

While one school in Vedanta tolerates a degree of dualism, Samkara and his school were strictly non-dualistic, preaching the doctrine of *advaita* (literally, 'not two'). The basis of their teaching is the ontological identity of the self and the Absolute: all entities are identical with each other through their common origin in Brahman, the substratum of all phenomena.

In terms of Western philosophy, the Vedantists make no distinction between the mental and the physical, rejecting the dualism of mind and matter as unreal: 'All sense-objects, including our body, exist solely as notions, in other words, that they exist only when thought of.'[27]

The greatest exponent of *advaita vedanta* (non-duality) in the twentieth century has been the Indian sage Ramana Maharshi. He taught that 'the One Self, the Sole Reality, alone exists eternally' and that the 'world owes its appearance to the mind alone'.[28] The supreme method of attainment is to destroy the ego and be as the Self. This can only be achieved through a long process of self-knowledge; to know anything else is simply a form of ignorance. Using a modern analogy, he declared: 'Brahman or the Self is like a cinema screen and the world like the pictures on it. You can see the picture only so long as there is a screen. But when the observer himself becomes the screen only the Self remains.'[29]

## The Jains: they would not hurt a fly

At the time that the *Upanishads* were being written, around 800 BC, there were several other currents developing in India which were reacting against the earlier Vedic religion. The Vedic ideal of a pleasant life in heaven was challenged by movements who believed in renunciation and selfless work here on earth. Chief among these were the Jains and the Buddhists. Both opposed the caste system, and sought to escape the cycle of rebirth (*samsara*) through right faith, right knowledge and right conduct.

The leading exponent of Jainism was Vardhamma, known to his followers as Mahavira (the Great Hero). He lived in the sixth century BC. Like his younger contemporary, the historical Buddha, he came from a wealthy family but left it to wander in search of salvation. He achieved this at forty-two, becoming a conqueror (*jina*) of his passions and emotions. As a result, his soul was released from the consequences of its actions (*karma*) and its imprisonment in matter.

Jainism is an austere sect that aims at passionless detachment, which is to be obtained solely by self-effort and without the help of any god. Its adherents believe that *karma* consists of fine particles of matter: bad deeds hold down the soul while good ones lighten it. Full salvation is possible if a devotee decides to starve himself to death – a view which appealed to the German philosopher Schopenhauer.

Unlike the monistic teaching of the *Upanishads* which affirms the One as ultimate reality, Jains believe in the plurality of beings: each soul is an entity in its own right. There is an infinite number of animate and inanimate substances which exist independent of our perception. The world continually goes through cycles of growth and decline without beginning and without end; at present, we are in descent. Jainism is fundamentally atheistic, rejecting the notion of a creator or of providence operating in the world. It is also pessimistic in believing that human beings can only rely on themselves to achieve salvation.

The Jains believe in a ladder of Being which they grade according to the five senses: at the lowest level of touch, there are the four elements and vegetables; at the second level of the two senses of touch and taste, there are creatures like worms and shells; at the third level of touch, taste and smell there are ants, bugs and moths; at the fourth level of touch, taste, smell and sight, there are wasps, locusts and butterflies; and finally, at the fifth and highest level of the five senses, there are animals, humans and infernal and heavenly beings. There is no gap, as in Judaeo-Christian and Greek-Stoic traditions, between humans and other animals.

Jainism is predominantly an ethical system and its ecological importance lies in the area of environmental ethics. The Jain code of conduct includes five virtues or vows: nonviolence, truth, honesty, continence and renunciation of pleasure in external objects. Jains therefore lead ascetic lives and are strict vegetarians. The first of the five virtues – nonviolence (*ahimsa*) – is the most important and it was interpreted to mean respect for all living beings. It was adopted by Buddhism and Gandhi went on to claim that it was the fundamental element in Hinduism.

Although their ascetic attitude means that Jains tend to devalue the physical world, their rigid interpretation of *ahimsa* has meant they are the most caring of all the Hindu sects. To injure living beings, even by mistake, is considered bad *karma*. Since the world is pulsating with life, Jains have to take extreme precautions and go to extraordinary lengths to avoid doing harm. As a result, a Jain layman should be a strict vegetarian and only eat leftovers. He must not be a farmer, for when ploughing the soil he might injure animals and plants, as well as the soil itself. He must not practise certain crafts, for the metal on the blacksmith's anvil and the wood under the carpenter's chisel suffer excruciating pain when worked. He should not become embroiled in earthly pursuits which might lead to the destruction of life: he should not engage in hunting or touch a weapon. He should stay in his region and not travel far.

To avoid the accidental killing of insects, Jain monks wear face masks and sweep the ground before them when walking. They pull out their hair rather than cut it. They extend the Hindu respect for cows to all animals. They not only provide schools and hospitals for humans, but have set up many animal hospitals and refuges where they take care of injured and aged animals. While helping to heal animals, they refuse to put them out of their misery if infirm or wounded. Nature must be allowed to take its course.

But as in most strict sects, the application of their principles has led to some strange anomalies. Since Jains are not allowed to engage directly in any activity which involves killing, they have traditionally taken to finance and in the process some have become very rich. Blood, they believe, does not stick to gold. Jainism began as a simple movement free from the rule of priests, but later became priest-ridden. Many simple believers have adopted Hindu deities to worship and entreat. Although extremely ascetic in its practices, Jainism has given rise to magnificent temple architecture, with wonderful fretted ceilings and ornamental pillars, perhaps the finest in the world.

Jainism has wielded an influence out of all proportion to its size. Jains are still numerous in Rajputana, Gujarat and some parts of southern India. Their concern with animal welfare and commitment to non-injury has also inspired many involved in the animal-liberation movement in the West.

Hinduism and its offshoots like Jainism thus has much to offer for the growth of an ecological sensibility. While its other-worldliness may devalue life on earth and its ultimate aim is salvation and detachment from the natural world, its belief in Absolute Being, its doctrine of unity in diversity, and its stress on the mutual interdependence of all aspects of reality provide a challenge to Western mechanism and atomism. Its moral principle of *ahimsa* and its respect for all living things, including trees and stones, offer a framework for a genuine environmental ethics. All would do well to breathe the cosmic energy of *prana* and to meditate on its source.

# 3

# BUDDHISM

## *The Way of Compassion*

'What is the ultimate teaching of Buddhism?'
'You won't understand it until you have it.'

*Sih-t'ou*

In the sacred Sri Lankan city of Anuradhapura, founded about 400 BC, there stands an old tree supported by props surrounded by thick walls intended to keep out elephants. The tree is allegedly a sapling taken from the bo tree under which Buddha obtained enlightenment, and was brought to Sri Lanka in 230 BC by the daughter of the Indian emperor Asoka.

The man who realized himself in its shade was born around 568 BC as Prince Siddhartha Gautama, the son of the ruler of a small kingdom at the foot of the Himalayas. His father educated him to become an enlightened ruler but insisted that he must not see any signs of suffering. When Siddhartha was nearly thirty, he ventured out of the palace grounds and for the first time saw an old man, an ill man and a corpse. After talking to a monk about the spiritual life, he decided to renounce the material world. He left his sleeping wife and child one morning and withdrew into the forest. At first he lived the life of an extreme ascetic, but after six years he chose the trackless path of meditation and eventually obtained enlightenment (Buddha means the 'enlightened one'). He realized that all earthly things are a hindrance and release from them is necessary before one can leave the wheel of life.

Existence in this world is, the Buddha taught, inevitably miserable. The cause is to be found in ignorance. Striving for one's own interest and craving, whether for possessions, wealth, power or status, invariably leads to suffering. As long as a person remains ignorant and attached to such material things, he or she will be chained to a cycle of reincarnation.

This teaching was summed up in the Four Noble Truths of Buddha:

the omnipotence of suffering; its cause, wrongly directed desire; its cure, the removal of the cause; the eight-fold path (right views, right intention, right speech, right action, right livelihood, right effort, right mindfulness, right concentration) which leads to the end of suffering.[1]

The only way to escape from the cycle of rebirth (*samsara*) is thus to overcome one's ego and dissolve all desire. One must recognize that the world of appearances, of permanence and diversity, is *maya*, an illusion. At the same time, one should recognize that one is part of the universal whole. If this is achieved, then individual consciousness will pass into the state of *nirvana*, nothingness or nonexistence.

What can such a seemingly otherworldly belief offer to the growth of an ecological sensibility? How is it possible to reconcile the teachings of the Buddha with the triumphant Sinhala state in Sri Lanka, whose nationalism is supported most vehemently by the Buddhist clergy? Buddhists in the capital Colombo trap rats and take them down to the beach each evening and release them (they run back to their neighbours' houses) and yet Buddhists and Tamils hack each other to death.

In the beginning Buddhism was principally restricted to moral action and meditation. It separated from Hinduism by rejecting the scriptures, rituals and priestly organization. The Buddha spoke against the caste system and felt that all people are equally capable of enlightenment. The 'Buddha-mind' was from the beginning associated with 'a great compassionate heart' which desires the liberation of all sentient beings.

Buddhism provides fertile soil for the germination of the ecological self. It presents reality in such a dynamic and interrelated way that categorical subject–object, man–nature, God–world distinctions dissolve. Buddhism is also ecological because it goes beyond anthropocentric religions and moralities to stress compassion for all as the central guide to right action. Although deeply felt, the personal self is an ephemeral and illusory construct of the senses. As we proceed on the path to enlightenment, in which we realize we are an inseparable part of the whole, we become a Bodhisattva, an 'awakening being'. An awareness of the suffering in the world leads to *mahakaruna*, the great compassion which manifests itself as a 'boundless heart' in active identification with all beings. It does not rest with the human species, but identifies with all living beings, and ultimately experiences an all-embracing love for the universe as a whole.

The Bodhisattva who is no longer concerned with his own salvation is committed to the good of all beings. On obtaining enlightenment, he does not leave the world behind him, but devotes his compassionate skill to the aid of others. 'For with the help of the boat of the thought of all-knowledge, I must rescue all these beings from the stream of Samsara, which is so difficult to cross . . . I must ferry them across.' Such a person will be happy, for if a person acts or speaks with a pure thought, 'happiness follows him, like a shadow that never leaves him'.[2]

The teaching of the Buddha spread steadily throughout India and was dominant three hundreds years before Jesus. It split into two separate branches, one becoming more rationalistic, formalized and scholastic (Theravada, or Hinayana, the 'Lower Vehicle') and the other, more mystical (Mahayana, the 'Higher Vehicle'). The former pays attention to historical fact, while the latter aspires to the universal. In the third century it was dominant throughout India from the Himalayas to Cape Comorin. It began to decline and by 1200 it had practically disappeared in India to be replaced by Hinduism and Islam, but it has remained well established in Sri Lanka, Tibet and Thailand.

When Buddhism first developed in China in the fifth century, it took a highly idealistic form and became known as the 'Consciousness-Only School'. The most philosophical of Buddhist schools, it was originally called *Yogacara* (the way of yoga) and was founded by Asanga (c. 410 – c. 500) for the purpose of mystical enlightenment through metaphysical reflection. The central doctrine of the school is that we reap what we sow. Each person must therefore become his or her own spiritual gardener in order to reach enlightenment.

It was not long before different schools developed in China. The Consciousness-Only School was followed in the sixth century by the T'ien-tai Philosophy of Perfect Harmony which asserted that the *dharmas* (elements of existence rather than right action as in Hinduism) have no nature of their own and 'the three thousand worlds [are] immanent in an instance of thought'.[3] This in turn gave way in the seventh century to the 'One-and-All Philosophy' of the Hua-yen school, with its belief in the harmonious combination and spontaneity of the sea of being.

The Hua-yen philosophy was fully developed by Fa-tsang (596–664). It represents the highest development of Chinese Buddhist thought. It came to be known as the 'One-and-All Philosophy' because of its stress on the unceasing process of transformation of the *dharmas* which interact and interpenetrate each other to form a perfect harmony. The *dharmas* on their own have no substance, but through their interaction the one is in all and all is in one. In the treatise on the golden lion, it is written:

> In each of the lion's eyes, ears, limbs, joints, and in each and every hair, there is the golden lion. All the lions embraced by all the single hairs simultaneously and instantaneously enter a single hair. Thus in each and every hair there are an infinite number of lions, and in addition all the single hairs, together with their infinite number of lions, in turn enter into a single hair.[4]

The geometric progression is infinite. It is likened to the jewelled net of Indra (the Hindu king of Heaven). The net is decorated with a bright jewel on each knot of the mesh, with each jewel reflecting all the other jewels and the reflections in them, and so on to infinity. There could be no more beautiful metaphor of nature's web, with each part containing the whole.

### Zen Buddhism

Ch'an or Zen Buddhism in the meantime emerged to become the most ecological of all the schools of Buddhism. Although at first it was mainly an Indian transplant in Chinese soil, by the seventh century Ch'an Buddhism, with its close affinity with Taoism, began to overshadow the Consciousness-Only movement. Strictly speaking, the name of the school should be Meditation, since this is the meaning of the Sanskrit word *dhyana*, which is pronounced in Chinese *ch'an* and in Japanese *zen*. At first, meditation involved the Taoist sense of preserving nature, conserving vital energy and breathing properly, but eventually it went beyond sitting in meditation and mental concentration, and aimed the direct enlightenment of the mind.

Zen Buddhism has rightly been called the 'apotheosis of Buddhism'.[5] It is uniquely iconoclastic, attempting to reach truth and enlightenment directly without the use of concepts, scriptures or ritual. Where Theravada Buddhism became neatly arranged and systematized, with a 'twelvefold chain of causation', Zen adepts see in the Buddha the first rebel. 'The Buddha was not the mere discoverer of the Twelvefold Chain of Causation,' the Japanese writer D. T. Suzuki informs us; 'he took the chain in his hands and broke it into pieces, so that it would never again bind him to slavery'.[6] The familiar props of religion are thrown away. The four central statements of Zen are:

A special transmission outside the Scriptures;
No dependence upon words or letters;
Direct pointing to the soul of man;
Seeing into one's nature and the attainment of Buddhahood.[7]

The purpose of Zen is not anti-intellectual; it aims to achieve knowledge which is beyond the intellect. The last act of reason is to realize its inadequacy; it should voluntarily give way to an intuitive awareness in which subjectivity and objectivity, the perceiver and the perceived, merge into one. The Zen way of direct enlightenment can be achieved immediately by everyone. It is based on learning by direct and immediate experience.

According to tradition, the philosopher Bodhidharma (c. 460–534) began the Ch'an school in China, arriving from India in AD 520. He became the first of twenty-eight teachers over the next five hundred years, traditionally known as patriarchs. Bodhidharma handed down the *Lankavatara Sutra* (Scripture about [the Buddha] Entering Lanka), which emphasized ultimate reality or the true nature of the *dharmas*. It taught that 'pure in its own nature and free from the category of finite and infinite, Universal Mind is the undefiled Buddha-womb, which is wrongly apprehended by sentient being'.[8]

But with Hung-jen (601–674) Ch'an took a radical turn; he taught the *Diamond Sutra*, which declared: 'What is known as the teaching of the Buddha is not the teaching of the Buddha'. He made the mind the central focus of Chinese Ch'an. Divergent tendencies further emerged in the north with Shen-hsiu, who stressed gradual enlightenment, and in the south with Hui-neng, who advocated sudden enlightenment.

Both schools accepted the Buddhist principles of idealism and universal salvation; nirvana is identical with the original substance of the Buddha-mind (also called Buddha-nature) and all humans can become Buddhas. The Buddha is in all things:

One Nature, perfect and pervading, circulates in all natures,

One Reality, all comprehensive, contains within itself all real-
ities.
The one Moon reflects itself wherever there is a sheet of
water,
And all the moons in the waters are embraced within the one
Moon.[9]

But whereas the northern school taught that the pure mind can only
arise after eliminating false thoughts and disturbances, the southern
school claimed that the mind cannot be divided into two parts and
all its processes are part of ultimate reality.

It is the latter school that is the most ecological and that became
most influential. The Buddha-mind is considered to be everywhere
and its realization can occur at any moment in any place: 'See
one's nature and become a Buddha' was the deep insight. The Third
Patriarch of Ch'an taught that the Way knows no difficulties except
that it refuses to make preferences and cherish opinions:

Pursue not the outer entanglements,
Dwell not in the inner void;
Be serene in the oneness of things,
And dualism vanishes of itself.

When the ten thousand things are viewed in their oneness, we return
to the origin and remain where we have always been. Once you
comprehend 'One in all, and all in One', there is no more worry
about being perfect.[10]

The Ch'an masters did not follow the Buddha but aspired to be his
friends and to place themselves in the same responsive relationship
with the universe. Unlike the Indian Buddhists, who saw the body
as an obstacle to spiritual freedom, Chinese Ch'an adepts believed
that it is possible to become 'a Buddha in this very body'. The body
is not like a refuge, but more like an inn. At the same time, they
argued that the Three Worlds (of desires, matter and pure spirit) are
nothing but the mind and all *dharmas* are consciousness only.

From the ninth to the eleventh centuries, new and unusual techniques were developed: one master taught how to empty the mind
of thoughts and characters, another to forget our feelings, and yet
another to let the mind take its own course. This is not a cult
of unconsciousness but rather having 'no mind one's own'; that
is, no mental attachment which would enslave the mind. Some

recommended staying at home and living a life of absolute calmness; others advocated travel, which would broaden and enrich the mind to such an extent that the song of a bird or the fall of a leaf could suddenly trigger off enlightenment.

Chinese meditation often works with the aid of external influences in the world. Since reality is everywhere, enlightenment can be achieved anywhere. The master I-Hsuan told his congregation:

> Seekers of the Way. In Buddhism no effort is necessary. All one has to do is to do nothing, except to move his bowels, urinate, put on his clothing, eat his meals, and lie down if he is tired. The stupid will laugh at him, but the wise one will understand. An ancient person said, 'One who makes effort externally is surely a fool.'[11]

But the most novel and famous method was the *kung-an* (*kōan* in Japanese). It was most commonly a question, to which the answer was often illogical, paradoxical and enigmatic. Ch'an masters also turned any story or situation to shock their listeners. Even shouting and beating were resorted to. The aim is to make the alert mind aware that conceptualization alone cannot reveal Buddha-nature and that words too can be misleading.

The practice of the koan was therefore intended to help the Zen aspirant to jump out of his or her self-centred and anthropomorphic thought processes and to have sudden insight into the ground of being. One of the most famous koans was uttered by I-Hsuan, who declared to a bewildered monk with characteristically earthy naturalism: 'What dried human excrement-removing stick is the pure man who does not belong to any class of Buddhas or sentient beings!'[12] It is intended to imply that the Buddha, like the Tao, is every where.

The basic teachings of Ch'an are recorded in the *Liu-tsu t'an-ching* (Platform Scripture of the Sixth Patriarch). It records the teaching of Hui-neng (also known as Wei-Lang) of the southern Chinese school. He is the most holistic of Zen teachers: both wisdom and calmness are the foundation of his method since they are one substance and not two. Equally, in his method there is no distinction between gradual and sudden enlightenment. Of the word *zazen*, which became central to Buddhist practice, he said: 'Outwardly to be in the world of good and evil yet with no thought arising in the heart, this is Sitting (*Za*):

inwardly to see one's own nature and not move from it, this is Meditation (*Zen*)'[13] In addition, to become enlightened not only transforms the individual but also the world. Since each individual is part of the whole, if one becomes enlightened all appear enlightened: 'With enlightenment, even in a single instant of thought, all living beings become the same as a Buddha. Hence we know that all dharmas are immanent in one's mind and person.'[14]

Despite his name, the Sixth Patriarch, Hui-neng, was totally demo-cratic and egalitarian. 'Perfect wisdom is inherent in all people,' he insisted.[15] Human nature is originally pure. It is only because people are deluded in their minds that they cannot attain enlightenment by themselves and need the help of 'good and learned friends' to show them the way to see their own nature.

This of course is not always necessary, and indeed the search for a master can check one's development. Self-reliance is a keynote of Buddhism. When Daiju visited the master Baso in China,

> Baso asked: 'What do you seek?'
> 'Enlightenment', replied Daiju.
> 'You have your own treasure house. Why do you search outside?' Baso asked.
> Daiju inquired: 'Where is my treasure house?'
> Baso answered: 'What you are asking is your treasure house.'
> Daiju was enlightened! Ever after he urged his friends:
> 'Open your own treasure house and use those treasures.'[16]

The Buddha's last words – 'Work out your own salvation with dili-gence' – are a constant refrain. No one can escape the consequences of his or her acts, and no one can enlighten another. Enlightenment can only be achieved by oneself, not through another's power. Buddhism knows no authority for truth save the intuition of the individual. There are therefore no set rules or regulations in Ch'an. At all times the end dominates the choice of means; indeed, the means are ends in the making. As the greatest exponent in China, Hui-neng, declared: 'If I tell you that I have a system of Law to transmit to others I am cheating you. What I do to my disciples is to liberate them from their own bondage with such devices as the case may need.'[17]

Ch'an Buddhism is profoundly libertarian as well as ecological. Its goal is self-disciplined freedom. Our 'mind-forged manacles' are not the true condition of existence but put on by ignorance. These chains of illusion are wrought by the meddling intellect and sensuous infatuation. Thus all the treatment of the Ch'an teachers is to bring the enquiring soul back to the original state of freedom. When asked to define mental liberation, the Fifth Patriarch, Po-Chang Huai-Hai, replied in negative terms:

> Don't seek Buddha or understanding; exhaust feelings of pure and impure. Also don't hold on to this non-seeking as right. Don't dwell where you exhaust feelings, either. Don't dread the chains of Hell and don't love the pleasures of Paradise. Don't cling to any dharma [truth or principle] whatsoever. Then you may begin to be called liberated without hindrance; then body and mind *all* may be called liberated.[18]

We are thus free to seek our own salvation. Ch'an Buddhism finds no contradiction between free will and determinism. It accepts that there is universal determinism, and that all effects have causes. A person's character is the sum total of her or his previous thoughts and acts. Our lives and all existence are ruled by the endless chain of cause and effect, of action and reaction. But while the present is always determined by the past, the future remains free. Every action we make unavoidably depends on what we have come to be at the time of making it, but what we are coming to be at any time depends on the will. Every person is free within the limitations of his self-created *karma*. By right thought and action, I can therefore change myself and shape my destiny.

### Japanese Zen: boiling oil over a blazing fire

Chinese Cha'an Buddhism reached Japan in the twelfth century. Here two main sects developed; Rinzai, which carried on the 'sudden' technique; and Soto, the larger and more gentle way. Both continue to develop the ecological and libertarian tendencies within Buddhism.

Although traditionally Zen aspirants learn from a 'master' who helps them break their everyday perceptions and intellectual habits, they are not slavish disciples. Buddhist masters are teachers and exemplars, not intermediaries between the individual and God or reality. They may exact strict discipline on their students but the intention is to free them from their everyday perceptions. 'To the question, "What is Zen?" a master gave this answer, "Boiling oil over a blazing fire." The student has to go through this scorching experience before Zen smiles on him or her and says, "Here is your home."[19] As the poet Gary Snyder has observed, the dialectic of Rinzai Zen practice is that you live a totally ruled life, but when you go into the *zazen* room, you have 'absolute freedom'.[20] The ritual is simply a ladder which is finally to be discarded. To enter enlightenment is a gateless gate. The adept Zen student eventually learns to control the senses and transforms his or her everyday life.

Although there are no set rules in Zen, two principal devices have been developed in Japan over the centuries, especially in the Rinzai school, in the sudden path to *satori*, or enlightenment. One is the mondo, a form of rapid question and answer between teacher and student which aims to take the thought process to its limits. The other is the koan. Perhaps the most famous koan is Hakuin's development of the Chinese proverb 'A single hand does not make a clap' into the question 'What is the sound of one hand?' Such a question is as absurd as to ask whether it is possible to obtain knowledge of one's own real nature from someone else.

The effects of *satori* may better be observed than expressed. One sees directly into one's own nature and realizes that it is not separate from nature but part of an organic whole. Opposites are transcended. One laughs. One feels clear, calm and whole. One is uncircumscribed and free. One is beyond conventional definitions of good and evil, man-made morals and laws. If you have Zen, you have no fear, doubt or craving. You live a simple and disciplined life, entirely self-sufficient:

> Imperturbable and serene the ideal man practises no virtue;
> Self-possessed and dispassionate he commits no sin;
> Calm and silent he gives up seeing and hearing;
> Even and upright his mind abides nowhere.[21]

### When mountains are mountains

While ultimately concerned with enlightenment which transcends the duality of this world, Buddhism offers a persuasive view of man's place within nature, and some guidelines for ecological living. It may not offer a strict code of morality, wishing to avoid preferences and notions of right and wrong, but a number of moral values emerge. Overriding all is the Buddhist sense of compassion for all beings ('the law of all laws') since life is one and indivisible. Whoever breaks the eternal harmony of life will suffer accordingly, since they are part of the whole. By hurting others, they will only delay their own development. Even when trying to separate himself from nature, man is still part of nature; his being is rooted in nature. There should not therefore be any hostility between the two.

Human beings may experience themselves as separate from nature, but this is an illusion. One Zen master recounts: 'When I began to study Zen, mountains were mountains; when I thought I understood Zen, mountains were not mountains; but when I came to full knowledge of Zen, mountains were again mountains.'[22]

Naturalness and spontaneity are central to Zen, and can be seen in its various art forms such as poetry, archery, flower arrangement (ikebana) and the tea ceremony. To create spontaneous beauty, the mind must become a harmonious whole, without one side interfering with another. It results in the calm wisdom of letting things take their course:

> Sitting quietly, doing nothing,
> Spring comes, and the grass grows by itself.[23]

Humans are thus simply beings among other beings in the natural world.

Within Zen Buddhism, there are no grounds for hierarchy or domination: human beings are born free and equal. This equality is spiritual in that all people are equally capable of achieving enlightenment, of realizing their Buddha-nature. In their monasteries, Zen monks live communally and are expected to contribute to the running of the place. Both master and pupil have equal obligations; as the Chinese Zen master Hyakujo taught: 'no work, no food'. They also should receive equal treatment; if necessary 'sour miso' for all.[24] Zen Buddhism is absolutely no respecter of persons. One story has it that when the governor of Kyoto visited a master, his visiting card was returned. He was only received when he sent it in again with his title crossed out.

While Buddhism seeks personal enlightenment, it does not turn its back on this world. Like the Taoists, Mumon commented:

> Do not fight with another's bow and arrow.
> Do not ride another's horse.

Do not discuss another's faults.
Do not interfere with another's work.[25]

Although only the individual can work out his own salvation, he or
she should not neglect others. When some Japanese soldiers came
to the temple of the Zen master Gasan demanding special treatment
because they defended the country, he insisted on giving them the
same fare the other monks received. He reminded them sternly: 'Who
do you think we are? We are soldiers of humanity, aiming to save
all sentient beings.' On another occasion, he went further and told
his pupils:

> Those who speak against killing and who desire to spare the
> lives of all conscious beings are right. It is good to protect even
> animals and insects. But what about those persons who kill time,
> what about those who are destroying wealth, and those who
> destroy political economy? We should not overlook them.[26]

Zen Buddhism goes beyond conventional definitions of good and
evil, and has no commandments enforced by threat of punishment.
Indeed, evil itself is not part of nature but man-made: demons are
human creations. The source of suffering in the world is craving
– craving for possessions, reputation and power. This insight has
important social implications. The desire for wealth is just one more
chain preventing spiritual development and ultimate enlightenment.

Many Zen stories illustrate this theme. When a thief came to
Shichiri Kojun, he first told the thief not to disturb him and to
take the money in a drawer. A little later, he asked him to leave
some money to pay taxes with. As the thief gathered up most of the
money and started to leave, Shichiri added: 'Thank a person when
you receive a gift.' When the intruder was eventually arrested and
confessed, Shichiri declared: 'This man is no thief, at least as far as
I am concerned. I gave him the money and he thanked me for it.'[27]
After serving his sentence, the man became his disciple.

By contrast, Zen Buddhists reiterate that natural beauty is the most
valuable thing which no one can take. When a thief visited the Zen
master Ryokan, who lived the simplest kind of life in a hut with a
leaking roof in a forest, he found that there was nothing to steal.
On seeing the thief, Ryokan declared: 'You may have come a long
way to visit me and you should not return empty-handed. Please

take my clothes as a gift.' Naked, watching the moon, he mused: 'Poor fellow. I wish I could give him this beautiful moon.'[28] Ryokan (1758–1831) was a kind of Japanese St Francis who thought of the lice on his chest as insects in the grass. When there was no money, he was not perturbed for

> The wind brings
> Fallen leaves enough
> To make a fire.[29]

The Buddhist idea that the giver should be thankful for having the opportunity to give, which is found among many tribal peoples, not only fuses the bonds of the community but refuses to exploit its members. It is the opposite of the mercantile mentality which has developed in the West and many parts of the East and sees profit as the supreme motive. Buddhism places compassion and good will at the heart of economics, a view recognized by E. F. Schumacher, author of *Small is Beautiful*, who recommended a form of 'Buddhist economics' which encouraged fulfilling and creative work adapted to local conditions.

In the Buddhist scale of values, it is not power, rank or wealth that is true prosperity, but life itself. When a rich man asked the Zen master Sengai to write something for the continued prosperity of his family, he wrote a large sheet of paper: 'Father dies, son dies, grandson dies.' 'Why do you make such a joke as this?' the rich man demanded. 'No joke intended,' Sengai explained.

> If before you yourself die your son should die, this would grieve you greatly. If your grandson should pass away before your son, both of you would be broken-hearted. If your family, generation after generation, passes away in the order I have named, it will be the natural course of life. I call this real prosperity.[30]

# 4

## ANCIENT EGYPT

### Waters on High

I am One that transforms into Two
I am Two that transforms into Four
I am Four that transforms into Eight
After this I am One.
                    *Coffin of Petamon, Cairo Museum*

Ancient Egyptian civilization remains one of the greatest mysteries and one of the most outstanding achievements of humanity. Little is known of the people who lived before its first flowering in 3100 BC, except that they were hunters and used animal tusks as pendants, no doubt to bring them luck. About 3400 BC a great change took place, with Egypt passing rapidly from a Neolithic culture with a simple tribal character to two well-organized monarchies, one centred on the delta and the other in the Nile Valley. Following the incursion into the Nile of a new people, of whom little is known except that they were devotees of the god Horus, a sophisticated and even luxurious civilization appeared within a hundred years or so. The art of writing, a highly developed and monumental architecture, and refined arts and crafts emerged rapidly. This great civilization lasted for nearly three millennia until the Romans conquered the land in 30 BC.

The sudden appearance of Egyptian civilization has continued to baffle archaeologists and historians. No known civilization, either before or after, seems to have developed so quickly. There may well be a connection with the civilization which developed about the same time on the Euphrates in Mesopotamia, but it does not seem to have been one of cause and effect. The common features and fundamental differences between Mesopotamia and Egypt suggest that they may both have originated from a third lost civilization.[1]

One intriguing piece of evidence for this bold hypothesis is the nature of Egyptian papyrus boats. Although used by the Egyptians only on the gentle waters of the Nile, they are designed to be extremely seaworthy. Their original form may well have been handed down from an earlier seafaring people. The pharaohs were buried with boat kits next to their pyramids in the middle of the desert. The practice may have partly been prompted by the fear of a kind of flood in the ancient world, recorded in the Old Testament, and partly by the hope of sailing in them with Osiris, the god of the underworld, in the next life.

Egypt's entire civilization was based on religion. For ancient Egyptians, the world was alive as a whole and infused with divine spirit and consciousness. All activities, whether ploughing, sowing, reaping, brewing or building, were considered earthly symbols of divine activities. Although the popular view is that the Egyptians worshipped many gods, their religion was strictly speaking monotheistic. They considered the universe to be the result of a conscious act of creation by one great and supreme God. Their 'gods' (*neterw*) may best be regarded as divine principles responsible for the order and maintenance of the universe.[2] All the 'gods' were merely personifications of the names of Ra.

Many Egyptian beliefs may appear strange to the modern reader, and Egyptian theology undoubtedly challenges rational logic. But the Egyptian mind is remarkably dialectical, rejecting linear notions of cause and effect and mechanical ways of seeing. In this it reflects the findings of modern ecology and physics. In the first place, it assumes that every notion has its inverse indissolubly connected with it – in Hegelian terms, every affirmation has a negation. Secondly, it has a strong sense of the crossing of disparate elements, of the warp and weft of truth. Thirdly, it appreciates simultaneity: many of its myths present several themes at one time rather than in a logical sequence. Finally, its calendar, parts of which still remain mysterious, does not follow a linear pattern.[3]

The exact meaning of Egyptian religion is obscured in mystery. No ancient Egyptian sacred book exists and no contemporary study of Egyptian theology was written. The Egyptians had many myths depicting relationships between men and gods, but very few survive. Scattered references have to be pieced together in order to get an overall picture.

What does seem clear is that they all believed in an afterlife, in the sense of both personal resurrection and immortality. Man might be born mortal, but he contains within himself the spark or seed of the divine. The purpose of life is to nurture that seed, and the reward is eternal life. The inevitable fact of resurrection is apparent in two principal metaphors, symbolizing death and rebirth: the daily path of the sun and the yearly cycles of the seasons.

At the same time, the Egyptians believed that a certain vital part of each individual continues to exist in the neighbourhood of his body; it therefore became important for the body to be preserved in a tomb designed as a house – hence the pyramids for the pharaohs. Individuals would be resurrected in a similar body to their earthly ones, and judged for their deeds by the gods after their death.

The Egyptians saw the universe as infused with consciousness and naturally harmonious. A central notion which colours all the myths, the morality and the life of the ancient Egyptians is 'Maât'. It is the Egyptian word for consciousness, which pervades all levels of being from the the individual to the cosmos. Humans as well as divine beings live 'by Maât, in Maât and for Maât'. The name expresses all notions of equilibrium and poise and is a symbol of justice, truth, authenticity and integrity. It is usually represented as a kneeling bird-woman with outstretched wings. In the New Kingdom era of ancient Egypt – after 1567 BC – harps were often decorated with a figurine of Maât. This conscious principle of harmony is a cosmic law. Like the Taoists, the Egyptians believed in a natural order:

> Whatever be the disorder that man or fortuitous natural accident may provoke, Nature, left to herself, will put everything in order again through affinities (the Consciousness in all things). Harmony is the *a priori* Law written in all of Nature; it imposes itself on our intelligence, yet it is in itself incomprehensible.[4]

According to the Egyptians, the awakening of consciousness (Maât) provokes the first breath (Shu) issuing from the nostrils of the Creator. It is Shu who sustains life; in one myth, he brings forth the initial egg of the origin of time. The god Hathor is also identified with Maât as a principle of order, equilibrium and harmony in the universe.

Water was central to the Egyptians' way of life and as a result many of their creation myths suggest that the universe emerged from water. Life was impossible without the Nile: if its flood came when expected, it turned the surrounding plains into a lush oasis; if it failed to rise, then all would become desolate with famine.

But the Nile was not only an earthly but also a heavenly source. Its flood transformed Egypt into a vast sea. In the beginning, Egyptians believed that there was a primordial ocean, the Nun, and their divine beings sailed on the 'waters on high'. No doubt inspired by the annual rising and falling of the Nile waters, they imagined the universe as originally filled with water from which a hill arose on which life began. The Nile therefore re-enacts the mystery of the creation: as the flood waters recede, the rich dark soil recalls the 'first earth'.

The Nun, the infinite source of the universe, is sometimes envisaged as a swampy mire, seething with life.[5] It is the dwelling place of the lotus, with its roots in mud, its stem in water and its leaves and flowers opening out in the air, symbolizing the four elements.

The child that comes forth from the primordial lotus is Ra, variously known as the king of the gods, father of humanity, protector of kings, and the sun god. He was later identified with Amun. But Ra is not so much the sun as the principle of light itself. Ra is all: 'I am he who made heaven and earth, formed the mountains and created what is above. I am he who made the water and created the celestial waves.'[6] The sun and the moon are the right and left eyes of Ra. He is 'a self-created being, who made the heavens and earth, and the winds [which give] life, and the fire, and the gods, and men, and beasts, and cattle, and reptiles, and the fowl of the air and the fish of the sea'.[7]

A female counterpart of Ra is Hathor, the sky goddess, who later became a cow goddess, goddess of love and dance, lady of the underworld and mistress of the stars. Under multiple names, Hathor represents a synthesis of all notions concerning cosmogenesis (identified narrowly with Aphrodite by the Greeks). She takes the role of the creator; her son is the falcon Horus, the sky god of Lower Egypt, who rises up out of the Nun. In a hymn to Hathor, she is hailed as 'Mysterious one who gives birth to the divine entities, forms the animals, models them as she pleases, fashions men ... O Mother!' She often appears in the form of a cow. But it would be wrong to consider her exclusively as a female principle. Under the name of Neith she is addressed as 'Lady of Sais, that is to say Tanen, two thirds masculine and one third feminine'.[8] The gods and goddesses of Egypt possess male and female sides, both anima and animus.

### Father Earth, Mother Sky

Like the Chinese Taoists, the Egyptians associated different aspects of the universe with male and female principles: Shu was the male 'void'; Tefnat, the female counterpart of moisture. But they did not consider the earth to be a mother goddess.

The earth is represented by Geb, the personification of material fecundity. He is often depicted as a man, painted green, fallen to the earth, with penis erect. He has one arm raised and one knee bent, symbolizing the mountains and the seas. The Greeks equated Geb with Kronos, the father of the gods. He might also be associated with the Green Man which proliferated throughout medieval Christian Europe in churches as a symbol of wild nature.

While the earth was male for Egyptians, the sky was female. Nut is the sky, the great mother of the universe and the cosmic source of nourishment. She is often depicted as a naked woman standing on her legs and arms arching over earth, her breasts hanging down offering sustenance to the male earth. She may well represent space as an all-embracing womb in which the universe is brought to birth.

The aptness of the symbol undermines the culturally specific argument of some Western feminists that the hatred of women and the hatred of nature are intimately connected and mutually reinforcing. For the Egyptians, the natural environment was not a passive female presence, but an active male one.

The fact that the earth in ancient Egypt is not presented as a female waiting to be exploited or abused may well have something to do with the status of women in Egyptian society. Compared to ancient Greece and Rome and medieval Europe, they were comparatively well off. Generally a woman could not hold public office, but queens like Hatshepsut came to power. The legal rights of women were better than in virtually all other ancient societies. Daughters could inherit their father's wealth, and were usually well provided for. When a woman married, her property still remained her own and she could leave it to whomever she wished. Divorce was easy. Many of these privileges were not recognized in parts of the West well into this century.

The periodic rise and fall of the Nile is also associated with the myth of Osiris, divine principle of perpetual return, death and rebirth, as symbolized by the annual cycle of vegetation. Osiris is the god of vegetation and fertility, and later became the supreme god of Egypt. The Pyramid Texts, as first recorded by the Greek historian Plutarch, tell us that Osiris, the son of Nut, the sky, and Geb, the earth, inherited his father's throne, but was slain by his brother Seth. He was launched in a coffin into the Nile and washed out to sea, but was recovered by his sister Isis (queen of the gods and mother goddess). When Seth discovered the body, he cut it up and scattered the pieces, but Isis buried each part where it came to rest.[9] The myth further reflects the close relationship in ancient Egypt between men and gods, sky and earth, water and life.

Women in Egypt played an important role not only on earth but also in heaven: the one related to the other. Isis became more and more revered and, according to one legend, she made a bold attempt to wrest the power of Ra from him and to make herself mistress of the universe.[10] Isis became the principal goddess of ancient Egypt, forming with her husband-brother Osiris and their son, Horus, the major triad of deities. She was represented as a queen, with a double crown of horns and a solar disc. As the patron saint of mariners in Alexandria, she was identified with the moon: the cow was sacred to her, with its horns representing the crescent moon.

Although the Egyptians did not identify her with nature, she became identified as such in the West, a process which reflected the increasing domination of man over woman and man over nature and the changing of its gender from male to female. It was the Greeks and Romans who first represented Isis as the goddess of nature. By the second century AD, Apuleius in the *Golden Ass* described her as the 'universal mother nature'. Depictions of her suckling her son Horus may well have been the prototype of the Madonna and Child. 'To lift the veil of Isis' came to mean to penetrate the heart of a great mystery, in particular the mystery of nature, a penetration which increasingly took the form of rape.

### Animal worship

Placing humanity firmly within nature, the Egyptians were careful observers of nature and delighted in the presence of nonhuman creatures. Their extraordinarily close observation of the natural world is visible in the hippopotamus hunt in swamplands depicted

on the tomb of Meruka, Saqqara, in the sixth dynasty, c. 2300 BC.
The fish, birds and other animals are outlined with such accuracy that
naturalists can easily identify the different species. Hippos were
hunted not for meat but because they descended in herds on farmers'
fields and devastated their crops. In myth the male hippopotamus was
associated with Seth, enemy of light, who causes the monthly waning
of the moon and the eclipses. On the other hand, Taweret, the goddess
of childbirth, was usually shown as a pregnant hippopotamus, friend
to mothers and children.

The gods of ancient Egypt as represent in temples and tombs
present a bewildering complexity of strange forms, half-animal
and half-human. Many of the gods represent strong forces in
the natural world. Since the country's prosperity depended on the
daily reappearance of the sun and the annual flooding of the river,
these and other natural forces were encouraged by worship. They
were often portrayed as animals. The Egyptians saw animals as
embodying certain divine principles and functions, not as separate
gods themselves. Each animal was chosen as a symbol of a particular
aspect of divinity. The hawk, which flies high in the sky, represented
the sun; the cobra, which was often found basking on the hot
threshing floors, stood for the harvest goddess; the ibis-headed god,
Thoth, was thought of as the god of scribes and writing; Khnum, the
ram-headed deity, was presented as the creator of men on his potter's
wheel. The cat was sometimes the incarnation of Ra or Bastet. Each
part of its body was identified with parts of the bodies of gods.

How animals were actually treated in ancient Egypt varied according to time and place. In some cases, all animals of one species were
considered sacred: baboons, crocodiles, ibises, cats and dogs were at
different times mummified in large numbers. On the other hand, one
individual animal was often singled out as the incarnation of a god.
At several places a particular bull was chosen and taken into the
temple, pampered throughout its life, and mummified and interred
ceremoniously after its death. Since it had been the dwelling of a god,
it was treated in the same way as a human body so that it could enjoy
immortality. Although the Eyptians who built the great pyramids and
temples worshipped the animals only as symbols of the gods, some
of the populace came in time to worship them for themselves.

The feeling of closeness with other creatures comes through in the
Egyptians' depiction of the afterlife. One of the greatest delights a
mortal could look forward to was the power to assume the form of

any animal, bird, plant or living thing, as he or she saw fit. Twelve chapters of the Egyptian *Book of the Dead* – a guide to the deceased on their journey in the afterlife – are devoted to the words of power which would enable the deceased to transform themselves into a hawk, a lotus, a heron, a swallow, a serpent or a crocodile. In the form of a bennu bird (a kind of phoenix) an Egyptian could become part of the 'soul of Ra'.[11]

But while Egyptians undoubtedly delighted in the bird and plant life around them, treated animals as sacred, and looked forward to taking their shape and sharing their pleasures in the afterlife, they were still interested in mastery of the natural world. They had, after all, with their irrigation skills, controlled to a large extent the annual flow of the Nile. In the form of a lotus, for instance, the deceased human would have mastery over the plants of the field, just as in the form of the god Ptah, he would become more powerful than the lord of time and be given mastery 'over millions of years'.[12]

Egyptian 'animal worship' provoked the merriment of the cultured Greeks, while the Roman and early Christian writers picked it out for their abuse and ridicule. This is not surprising, given their humanist arrogance and contempt for nonrational creatures. But Hebrews, Greeks and Romans simply failed to understand the logical conception underlying the Egyptian reverence for certain animals. Just as the souls of the departed could assume the form of any living creature or plant, so could the gods. Egyptians paid honour to certain animals because they thought they possessed certain characteristics of the gods. The bull, for instance, symbolized strength and procreative power and became the god of reproduction in nature, with the cow the female counterpart.

From the earliest to the latest period of Egyptian civilization, a respectful attitude to animals remained an integral part of the Egyptian's religion. They were far more advanced than subsequent Greek, Roman and Christian thinkers in believing that the gap between men and other animals is one only of degree and not of kind. Although Plato recognized in his *Timaeus* that the Greeks gained much of their knowledge from the Eygptians, their ecological wisdom was largely lost to subsequent Western civilization.

# 5

# EARLY GREECE

## *Gaia*

All things come out of the one, and the one out of all things.

Heraclitus

The legacy of ancient Greece to the West is a mixed blessing. Much of early Greek religion and philosophy was organic: the Greeks saw nature as a living being. But in many ways Western civilization went wrong after Plato, who separated the mind and the body, the world of reason and the world of the senses. Dominant Western metaphysics came to reject its holistic and organic origins and saw the world as a collection of discrete entities, substances or atoms. It saw properties as distinct from substances, so that even if properties changed the substance would remain the same. This implied that it was quite possible to alter the qualities of the earth without fundamentally changing its nature, a view which has had disastrous ecological consequences. There are, however, other trends in Greek civilization, and it was never as rationalist and mechanical as its critics suggest. Many different and often opposing traditions may be traced to early Greece.

The ancient history of Greece covers some 6,000 years, from the first permanent settlement based upon grain agriculture (barley and wheat). Only about one tenth of the rugged land area was cultivable, and the greatest effect the agriculturalists had on the landscape was the progressive removal of woodland. The impact of this Neolithic agriculture resulted in a sudden growth in population: where hunting and gathering were practised, one person could live to every square mile; under farming conditions, one square mile could support from ten to a hundred people. Given the limited amount of space, the population growth in ancient Greece led to migrations as well as the practice of infanticide through the exposure of the newborn. But it took a technological revolution – metalworking, especially copper and tin – to provide the economic base for the emerging Mycenaean and Minoan civilizations.

The Mycenaean civilization ended in destructive violence around 1100 BC, with a sudden decline in population. The subsequent shift from bronze to iron only encouraged more bloodshed and war among the emerging city-states (*polis*). But even at its height, Hellenic civilization from the sixth century BC was not widespread. The democratic running of Athens did not involve more than one fifth of the population; the rest of society consisted of slaves, resident aliens, women and children, who had few rights or privileges. Non-Greeks – Egyptians, Libyans, Scythians and Persians – were collectively considered 'barbarians' – that is, incapable of Greek language and 'civilized' Greek thought.

The early Greeks were much closer to primal society and primitive religion than is traditionally assumed. Although portrayed in Homer in human terms, the gods were considered immortal. Greeks considered that fate determined all, and the anger of the gods, like the anger of men towards one another, must work out its destined course. The gods therefore filled men with awe, dread, fear and shame. In response, the Greeks felt impelled to pray, entreat, praise and offer sacrifices to the gods to win their favour and avoid their wrath.

But not all Greeks were impressed by the gods. After the Persian wars in the fifth century, a group of writers called the Sophists, led by Thucydides, presented men as capable of creating great disasters, with the Olympian gods remaining remote and unexemplary. Aristophanes went on further to ridicule the gods in his plays.

The Greeks, like the Taoists and the Hebrews, believed in a golden age in the past when men were not aggressive and destructive and all nature flourished. The philosopher Empedocles wrote that in such an age of love, trees bore fruit all the year round and 'all things were tame and kindly to man'. It was a time when 'no altar was wet with the shameful slaughter of bulls'.[1] Man's primal sin was not in eating of the tree of knowledge, as the Hebrews suggested, or in working against the ways of nature, as the Taoists implied, but in killing animals, initially for sacrificial purposes and then for meat.

The poet Hesiod recorded in the eighth century BC that there was once a golden race of men, subjects of Cronus,

> who lived without cares or labour, eating only acorns, wild
> fruit, and honey that dripped from the trees, drinking the milk

of sheep and goats, never growing old, dancing, and laughing much; death to them, was no more terrible than sleep. They are all gone now, but their spirits survive as genii of happy rustic retreats, givers of good fortune, and upholders of justice.[2]

The next race was the silver race, eaters of bread and completely subject to their mothers (presumably in a matriarchy). Because they were ignorant and antagonistic, Zeus destroyed them. Then came a brazen race, who ate flesh as well as bread and delighted in war. Black Death took them. The fourth race was also bold but more generous, fathered by gods on mortal mothers. They became heroes and dwell in the Elysian Fields. The last race is the race of iron, ignoble descendants of the previous one; they are cruel, unjust, untrustworthy and degenerate. They would seem still to be living today, an age in which iron men fight and squabble and destroy the earth.

As Hesiod implies, very early Greek society may well have been matriarchal. In the earliest creation myth of pre-Hellenic Greece, woman is the dominant sex and man her anxious victim. In the beginning Euronyme, the 'Goddess of All Things', rose naked from chaos and, finding nothing for her feet to rest on, divided the sea from the sky and danced lonely upon its waves. Dancing south she created a wind, and rubbing this north wind in her hands she created the great serpent Orphion (Boreas), with whom she coupled. She then took on the form of a dove and laid the Universal Egg. When it hatched, out came all that exists: sun, moon, planets and the earth with its mountains and rivers, its plants and living creatures. Orphion and Euronyme lived on Mount Olympus, but when he annoyed her by claiming that he was author of the universe, she kicked him down to the dark caves below earth.[3] Perhaps a more appropriate name for the earth in our age would be Euronyme, meaning Wide Wandering, rather than Gaia. Whereas Gaia is somewhat passive, trying to heal the wounds inflicted by man on her, Euronyme might well take her revenge.

The English poet and scholar Robert Graves has argued persuasively that Greek society, like most of ancient Europe, originally had a great white goddess whom men feared and loved.[4] She was the head of a matriarchal society. The goddess became identified with seasonal changes in animal and plant life and thus with Mother Earth. As the moon goddess, she passed through three phases of maturity: maiden, nymph and crone. In Greek mythology, this triad was conceived as

Selene, the maid of the upper air; Aphrodite, the nymph of the earth; and Hecate, the crone of the underworld. They all came together in the Greek goddess Hera.

The tribal queen probably chose an annual lover for sacrifice at midwinter when the year ended, making him a symbol of fertility. His blood served to fructify trees, crops and flocks and his flesh, it seems, was eaten raw by the queen's fellow nymphs. Sacred kingship began even though the king remained under the queen's control. But once the male role in conception was discovered, men gradually acquired more power. When the Hellenes overran Greece in the early part of the second millennium BC, they destroyed the goddess's chief shrine – Medusa – and seized her sacred horses. A male military aristocracy became reconciled to female theocracy. Animals were substituted for young men on the sacrificial altar and the king refused death at the end of his reign. The Dorians at the end of the second millennium finally put paid to matrilineal tradition and established patriarchal royalty. The familiar Olympian system of gods and goddesses was then agreed upon as a compromise between Hellenic and pre-Hellenic views.[5]

## Mother Earth, Father Time

Early Greek religion was much closer to the primal mind and stressed the organic interconnectedness of things. Gaia, popularized recently by James Lovelock, was the Greek word for the earth goddess. It is from the name Gaia or Ge that we derive the root 'geo' as used in words like 'geography'. But though Gaia today has come to be considered in the West as a nurturing and loving earth goddess, the Greek view of her was very different. In the Olympian creation myth, Mother Earth or Gaia emerged in the beginning from chaos and bore a son called Uranus as she slept. 'Gazing down fondly at her from the mountains, he showered fertile rain upon her secret clefts, and she bore grass, flowers, and trees, with the beasts and the birds proper to each. This same rain made the rivers flow and filled the hollow places with water, so that lakes and seas came into being.'[6]

It was this patriarchal myth of Uranus that gained official acceptance under the Olympian religious system. The name of Uranus came to mean 'the sky', thereby inverting the sex of the Egyptian god and goddess of the earth and sky. It was only after the Hellenic invasions of ancient Greece that the prevailing matriarchy gave way to patriarchal principles.

According to Hesiod, Uranus fathered the Titans upon Mother Earth after throwing his rebellious sons, the Cyclopes, to the Underworld. The vengeful Gaia persuaded the Titans to attack their father. 'Ah, my children,' she exclaimed, 'and children, too, of a nefarious father – will you not hear me and punish your father for this wicked ill-doing? He was the first who ever devised a shameful deed!'[7] Led by Cronus, they surprised the sleeping Uranus and Cronus castrated him with a sickle given to him by his mother. The Titans then released the Cyclopes and gave the sovereignty of the earth to Cronus – whom later Greeks read as Chronos, Father Time with his relentless sickle. In a modern development of this myth, the sons of Uranus have not only emasculated their father but have used their machines to attack their mother.

Although the Hellenes introduced patriarchy, they still believed that the earth was a living organism, able to reward humanity with her bounty for kind treatment or to revenge abuse. Xenophon, the historian and military commander who came under the influence of Socrates, wrote in his *Economics* four centuries before Christ: 'Earth is a goddess, and she teaches justice to those who can learn: for the better she is served, the more good things she gives in return.' The advice is couched in terms of rational self-interest.

Xenophon was a mercenary, fighting for and against the Persians. He became a friend of the king of Sparta, who gave him an estate. He wrote guides on commanding cavalry and on hunting. But while he killed humans and other animals without regret, he was remarkably enlightened when it came to horse training, convinced that what a horse does under compulsion it does badly. 'Anything forced and misunderstood can never be beautiful,' he wrote, quoting the earlier Simon of Athens. 'If a dancer were forced to dance by whip and spikes,' he asserted, 'he would be no more beautiful than a horse trained under similar circumstances.'[8]

## The Greek mysteries

The irrational and primal aspect of the Greek mind revealed itself in the 'mysteries' first mentioned by Herodotus, which were probably practised at least as early as the eighth century BC. The main mysteries of Eleusis, near Athens, were centred on the goddess Demeter and her daughter and associated with cereal grains during the ploughing season. It involved initiation ceremonies and rituals, promising happiness, sometimes in a glorious vision of the god. They seemed to have absorbed many Eastern myths. The cult reflected the crucial importance of agriculture to Greek civilization; without its surplus, the cities would have been unable to flourish.

The central symbols were corn, pomegranates and poppies, referring to the unseen forces affecting mankind through the vegetable world, building the body and informing the mind. The complex and wonderful nature of this relationship was illuminated in the climax of the mystery, which was the display of an ear of wheat.[9]

Another cult was that of Dionysus. It started in the autumn with the grape picking and lasted into the spring when the new wine was tasted, accompanied by cycles of plays and comedies. The cult of Dionysus, associated with wine and drunkenness, gave rise to a profound mysticism. The ritual produced an ecstatic delirium in which the worshipper felt one with the god. The worship of Dionysus remained fundamentally animist but Orpheus and his disciples substituted mental for spiritual intoxication, hoping to achieve eternal bliss in the transmigration of souls by becoming 'pure' in this life.

Those living in the country tended to worship Hermes and Pan, and had a multitude of fertility cults. In Athens in the fifth century BC, Pan, whose original name was probably Paon, meaning feeder or shepherd, came to be interpreted and worshipped as the god of all. From this god was derived the word 'pantheism', the identification of god with nature.

Many of the Greek mystery cults involved animal sacrifice. In the temple cult of Asclepios, the god of healing, there were several stages of initiation. These involved ritual bathing before entering the inner sanctum of the temple where small animals were offered on a sacred hearth. At a much later stage, in the second century AD, the apse of the temple was reconstructed into a *taurobolium* so that a bull or goat could be slaughtered with its blood drenching the priest or initiate below a grate. This may have been the source of the later Roman Mithras cult.

### Early Greek philosophy

The pre-Socratic philosophers were holistic thinkers, looking for a common substance to the universe. They were at the fountainhead of the mainstream in Western metaphysics, reinforced by Aristotle,

which depicted nature as a substance with distinct properties, each
of which can be separately changed without modifying anything else.

The philosopher Thales (flourished 580 BC), the first of the Ionian
school, claimed everything was made of water. All things derive from
and resolve into water. His journeys as a merchant took him to the
Middle East, to Babylon and Egypt, where he acquired astronomical
techniques. He is said to have invented geometry by refining them
through deductive reasoning.

Thales' successor Anaximenes, on the other hand, claimed that all
things come from air. Air is the primal substance, infinite and
eternal. It 'encompasses all the worlds', for our world is only one of
many. A kind of necessity or natural law holds the different elements
in balance and prevents one from conquering the others. 'Into that
from which things take their rise they pass away once more, as is
ordained, for they make reparation and satisfaction to one another
for their injustice according to the order of time.'[10] This reflects the
Greek sense of justice as the golden mean, as not overstepping the
bounds.

While some philosophers looked for a common substance, others
tried to define the ultimate nature of things. Heraclitus (flourished
500 BC) anticipated modern evolutionary theory by arguing that
everything is in constant flux, and ecology by describing nature
as a complex system of interacting processes which vary in their
stability. You cannot therefore do one thing at a time. Each system
which form parts of the whole can survive – like a flame – only if it
continues to interact with surrounding systems in certain ways,
giving and taking from them. Human beings are only one system
among others, not lords of creation or devils of destruction, and
their apparent uniqueness lies merely in their special relationships
with other systems.

Heraclitus stands at the source of the Western metaphysical
tradition which stresses process and flux in nature. He regarded fire
as the fundamental substance; everything, like a flame in a fire,
is born by the death of something else. He pictured the world as 'an
everliving fire, kindling in measures and going in measures'.[11] It is
'reason' or 'destiny' that keeps everything in order and ensures the
orderly succession of events.

Heraclitus' most famous doctrine is that everything is constantly
changing: 'You cannot step twice in the same river; for fresh waters
are ever flowing in upon you.' Change occurs through the dynamic

interplay of opposites: 'cold things warm themselves, warm cools'. But since all opposites are polar, they must be united: 'the way up and the way down is one and the same'.

The unity in the world is a unity formed by the combinations of opposites: 'All things come out of the one, and the one out of all things.' Here are the beginnings of the dialectic which grew to fruition in Hegel's philosophy. But while there is unity in diversity, Heraclitus often implies that unity is paramount; 'good and ill are one'. Like Anaximenes, he believed in a kind of cosmic justice which prevented one element from gaining the upper hand in the strife of opposites: 'The sun will not overstep its measures.'

Heraclitus had a very low view of humanity and was nicknamed the 'weeping philosopher'. He argued that only force will compel people to act for their own good: 'Every beast is driven to the pasture with blows.' But he also recognized natural appetite: 'Asses would rather have straw than gold.'[12] He thought that war is common to all things and strife is justice. His ethics is a kind of proud asceticism. He is at one with the more misanthropic ecologists who see humanity as the cause of evil in the universe.

While the pre-Socratic philosophers developed an organic and holistic approach, the seeds of the downfall of Western civilization were sown in the rich soil of Greek thought. Pythagoras, who lived in the sixth century BC, was a mathematician and a mystic, combining both theology and science. Born in Samos, he gained knowledge of the Ionian school of philosophers and, through his travels, the beliefs of the Egyptian priests. He founded around 530 BC a communal religious order which was ascetic, regulated and antidemocratic. This involved abstaining not only from flesh-eating, because it was cruel, but also from beans, which might excite the passions. The strict rules included not plucking garlands to avoid wanton waste.

Pythagoras believed in the transmigration of souls and reincarnation. It is claimed that he taught:

> first, that the soul is an immortal thing, and that it is transformed into other kinds of living things; further, that whatever comes into existence is born again in the revolutions of a certain cycle, nothing being absolutely new; and that all things that are born with life in them ought to be treated as kindred.[13]

Like St Francis, he is said to have preached to animals. He was certainly one of the first in the Western tradition to argue against cruelty to animals:

> For as long as Man continues to be the ruthless destroyer of the lower living beings, he will never know health or peace. For as long as men massacre animals, they will kill each other. Indeed, he who sows the seeds of murder and pain cannot reap joy and love.[14]

Pythagoras thought that the only way to escape the 'wheel of life' was to become a philosopher who devotes himself to the disinterested pursuit of science. This involved the study of the relations of numbers. Mathematics, in the sense of demonstrative deductive argument, begins with Pythagoras. By asserting that 'all things are numbers', Pythagoras anticipated the abstract approach to science developed by Galileo and other scientists in the seventeenth century which transformed nature into a machine to be exploited at will.

Democritus and the Atomists further destroyed the holistic world-view of the early Greek philosophers. They were led to atomism in an attempt to mediate between monism, the theory that all phenomena make up one substance, and pluralism, the theory that they form many different substances. These two positions were represented by Parmenides and Empedocles respectively. Parmenides argued in opposition to Heraclitus that nothing changes and everything forms part of permanent being. Empedocles, on the other hand, assumed that there are four primitive independent elements, air, water, fire and earth, and two moving powers, love and hate or affinity and antipathy.

Democritus is remembered for continually laughing at the folly of humanity. He travelled widely in the East and collected the works of other philosophers. His own system assumes an infinite number of atoms which from their combinations form the vast aggregate called nature. He recognized in it law but not design. This view, developed by Epicurus and Lucretius, came to prevail in Western science until the twentieth century.

The Atomists believed that the atoms are physically indivisible and indestructible, always in motion and infinite in number. Between the atoms is empty space. As strict determinists, they believed everything happens in accordance with natural laws. Unlike Plato and Aristotle, they sought to explain the world without the notion of purpose or final cause. When John Dalton put forward his famous atomic theory at the end of the eighteenth century, which made chemistry into a science, he was standing in an ancient philosophical tradition.

## Plato and Gaia

Socrates and Plato continued the process in Western philosophy of separating humanity from the world of nature by their stress on the unique rationality of man and by their separation of the soul from the body.

Despite his overriding rationalism, Plato (c. 427–327 BC) was still sufficiently close to the primal roots of Greek civilization to consider the world to be a living creature. In his account of the creation, he wrote in *Timaeus* that the creator created 'a single visible living being, containing within itself all living beings of the same natural order'.[15] In a remarkable passage which celebrates unity in diversity and anticipates the modern Gaia hypothesis, Plato records how the creator made

> this world a single complete whole, consisting of parts that are wholes, and subject neither to age nor disease. The shape he gave it was suitable to its nature. A suitable shape for a living being that was to contain within itself all living beings would be a figure that contains all possible figures within itself. Therefore he turned it into a rounded spherical shape ... And he put soul in the centre and diffused it through the whole and enclosed the body in it. So he established a single spherical universe in circular motion, alone but because of its excellence needing no company other than itself, and satisfied to be its own acquaintance and friend. His creation, then, for all these reasons, was a blessed god.[16]

Plato further insists that there is a close correspondence between the microcosm and the macrocosm, between the structure and behaviour of the world in general and of human beings in particular, between the planet and the person.

At the same time, Plato often interprets the physical world in an anthropocentric way, in terms of purpose and function as in psychology and biology. It marks a departure from earlier and more ecological Greek speculation about the origin of the world, which saw it largely in terms of sexual reproduction and growth: the Orphic world-egg was laid and hatched. The more philosophically oriented, like Democritus, also presented the creation in evolutionary terms, describing it as developing from material origins by some inherent but undesigned power.

In *Timaeus*, however, Plato introduces the notion of a creator-god, variously described as father, maker or craftsman, who fashioned the world out of chaos; that is, an indeterminate substance which resembles space in confused motion. Although the creator is never equated with Zeus, Plato further develops the Greek belief in a hierarchy of divine beings and extends it to the human and animal world. Indeed, in his doctrine of the transmigration of souls, he suggests that men came first, then women and finally animals. At once sexist and speciesist, Plato maintains that men who lived cowardly or immoral lives in the first generation were reborn in the second generation as women; empty-headed sensuous men interested in the heavens became birds; men who had no use for philosophy and followed their feelings became land animals. As for the most unintelligent and ignorant, these poor souls were turned into creatures of the sea.

The notion of hierarchy based on rationality dominated Plato's thinking. He is the fountainhead of the great authoritarian river which has swamped Western thought. In his ideal *Republic*, he depicts a rigidly hierarchical society ruled by an elite of guardians and soldiers. Religion is chosen on utilitarian grounds and poets are banished. Women are second-class citizens and slave labour enables the philosophers to speculate and rule.

Like many authoritarian and hierarchical thinkers, Plato was something of a conservationist. He liked to imagine a brave new world, but he also lamented the degradation of the environment in his day. He observed that the wood in some Greek temples could no longer be obtained because of the wanton destruction of ancient forests. Indeed, he blamed deforestation for causing erosion, climate changes and crop failure in the vulnerable Mediterranean environment. In Attica, he records, sacred memorials stood in an arid landscape once criss-crossed by streams and rivers:

> There are remaining only the bones of the wasted body, as they may be called . . . all the richer and softer parts of the soil have fallen away, and the mere skeleton of the land being left. But in

the primitive state of the country, its mountains were high hills covered with soil, and the plains . . . were full of rich earth, and there was abundance of wood in the mountains.[17]

Accounts of natural catastrophes and ecological disasters are not only confined to Judaic tradition. Plato developed the myth of Atlantis, an island to the West of the pillars of Heracles (Straits of Gibraltar) which was swallowed up by the sea. Atlantis disappeared as a result of some ecological disaster. It is a reminder of the truth that there is 'at long intervals a variation in the course of heavenly bodies and a consequent widespread destruction by fire of things on the earth' and that 'the gods purge the earth periodically with a deluge'.[18]

Yet, despite Plato's view of the world as a living, interrelated organism, and his concern with ecological damage in the past, he helped elaborate the basic beliefs that underlie the separation of Western civilization from nature. Dividing what is into two orders of Becoming (Heraclitus) and Being (Parmenides), he argued that only the real world, the world of Being, contains forms and ideas which are objects of rational understanding and the operations of logic and mathematics. The world of Becoming contains objects of our senses and provides no firm knowledge. Only in logic and mathematics can truth be discovered; physical science, based on empirical knowledge, could at best be only probable. We are habitually enclosed in a cave of ignorance, taking shadows cast on the walls to be real. It is the task of the philosopher to lead us from the cave of our five senses out into the noonday light of truth and reason.

Plato developed the dualistic view of the world, celebrating the superiority of the mind over the body, reason over emotion, the 'real' world of ideas and forms over the 'illusory' world of the senses. In *Phaedrus*, he compared the psyche (soul or mind) to a charioteer controlling two horses, one representing the appetite and the other emotion. In *Timaeus*, he located three parts of the psyche in different parts of the body: the powers of reason and decision in the head; the emotions and feelings in the heart; and the physical appetites in the belly. Only in the head resides the divine and immortal part of the soul which, like the world-soul, has its eternal circles of 'Same' and 'Different'.

On the positive side, Plato stressed the close connection between mental and physical disease, thereby reinterpreting the old Socratic paradox 'no man does wrong willingly' to mean that wrongdoing is often a result not of deliberate choice but of a failure to coordinate mind and body. Vice is merely a form of ignorance. But with Plato ends the earthy naturalism of the early Greek thinkers; abstract ideas of the rational man become more important than the sights and sounds of the sensuous man.

Although most of Plato's works were lost to the West for centuries, his *Timaeus* survived in the Middle Ages in Latin translation and provided a starting point for the first gropings towards a scientific cosmology. His account of the creation of the universe could be assimilated to that of Genesis. Above all, it reinforced the contempt for the visible universe in Christian doctrine and influenced the philosophers of the Renaissance by its combination of rational, spiritual and aesthetic contemplation of the universe.

### Aristotle and the end of nature

Aristotle, Plato's great pupil, took a much more empirical approach to knowledge. Not merely concerned with abstract speculation, he tried to test his hypotheses through observation and experience, and collect data and evidence for his theories. Although a great formal logician, Aristotle approached ethics and psychology with the inductive method of biology rather than the deductive method of mathematics. In his school, called the Lyceum, he spent much time talking to his students in a garden called the *Peripatos*, or 'Walk' – so that his teaching was called the 'Peripatetic Philosophy'.

While he carefully observed natural processes, Aristotle held that the earth was a solid stationary ball at the centre of the universe and that the sun and moon revolved around it – a view later elaborated by Ptolemy but exploded by Copernicus. But his view of the universe was distinctly ecological in the sense that he saw it as a vast complex of organisms with each one striving to attain the end assigned to it by nature. For this reason Aristotle's philosophy is called teleological, *telos* in Greek meaning 'end'.

Aristotle was chiefly preoccupied with the notion of development; he was the first to explain the nature of an organism in terms of its potential. He also introduced the method of classification by genus and species. Like Plato, he believed that the soul consists of reason, sensation and appetite, with reason the supreme controlling power. It is human reason that cuts us off from the rest of the creation, for only man is capable of considered action. 'The life of the lower animals is defined by the capacity of sensation, of man as the capacity for sensation *plus* thought.'[19]

Aristotle defines man as a social and rational 'animal'. Moreover, 'the brutes do not share with man the power of deliberate choice, but like him they feel desire and passion'.[20] Although he recommended the dissection of animals, and reprimanded a 'childish distaste' against examining them, he insisted: 'We should approach the inquiry about each animal without aversion, knowing that in all of them there is something natural and beautiful.'[21] Like men, animals pursue pleasure and shun pain and have feelings: the feeling between parents and their offspring seems to have been 'implanted by nature' in birds and most mammals as well as men. There is even such a thing as 'natural' virtue – the good qualities which men share with the lower animals. Every animal has a pleasure, as it has a function, of its own, and its pleasure is derived from the exercising of that function.[22]

But although man shares a common nature with other animals, Aristotle insists that this does not qualify the latter for equal consideration. Only creatures with the same degree of rationality can be considered equal. A slave, who has inferior reasoning power, is merely a 'living instrument'; though remaining a human being, he or she is also 'an article of property'. There can be justice only where there can be friendship, and friendship only where there is shared understanding. This is simply not possible between men and animals, masters and slaves.

Aristotle was aware that there were many possible ways of classifying the natural world, but he was mainly responsible for arranging all living beings into a single graded *scala naturae* according to their degree of 'perfection'. In *De Anima*, he proposed a hierarchy based on the 'powers of the soul' possessed by each being. Each order possesses all the powers of the order below it and peculiar to it, from the nutritive (plants) to the rational (man).[23] Those with less reason in the hierarchy are intended to serve those with more:

> Plants exist for the sake of animals, and brute beasts for the sake of man – domestic animals for his use and food, wild ones (or at any rate most of them) for food and other accessories of life, such as clothing and various tools.
>
> Since nature makes nothing purposeless or in vain, it is undeniably true that she has made all animals for the sake of man.[24]

It is this rationalist and anthropocentric view, not Pythagoras' more mystical biocentric one, that became a central part of the Western tradition. In the Middle Ages, this zoological and psychological hierarchy came to be known as the 'Great Chain of Being' composed of a countless number of links. It dominated the European conception of nature and its creatures until the end of the eighteenth century.[25]

### Canine wisdom

Among the several schools of philosophy which flourished in ancient Greece after the death of Socrates, the Cynics are the most ecologically minded. They sought peace and guidance in a period of social turmoil, celebrating the authority of nature instead of that of the state. They looked to a world of universals in nature beyond civil society. Where the theories of Plato and Aristotle were for a few, they extended their teaching to all people.

The Cynics of the third century BC reinterpreted the fundamental Greek concepts *physis* ('nature') and *nomos* ('custom') in a radical new way. Where Aristotle tried to reconcile the two by imposing law on the natural occurrence of things, the Cynics rejected *nomos* in favour of *physis*. They wished to live solely 'according to nature', and rejected the artificial encumbrances of civilization; their name comes from the Greek word *kunikos*, 'canine', because they were said to live like dogs. They flouted conventional standards of decency and wandered with a knapsack and staff, living like beggars. They wished to travel lightly and live a simple life in harmony with nature.

Diogenes is the most famous Cynic. He was born in Sinope in Pontus but went to Athens, where he lived for a time the life of a rake and spendthrift. Coming under the influence of Socrates' friend Antisthenes, the founder of the Cynic school, he suddenly became an ascetic, wearing coarse clothing, eating the plainest food, and sleeping on the bare ground. He eventually took up residence in a 'tub' (probably a large earthenware pot). He condemned slavery, having been made a slave temporarily when seized by pirates on a voyage. Practical good was the chief aim of his philosophy.

Diogenes professed brotherhood with all beings, including animals. He abstained from flesh-eating, declaring: 'We might as well eat the flesh of men as the flesh of other animals.'

Alexander the Great visited him in Corinth and tried to corrupt him by offering him anything he liked; Diogenes merely replied: 'You can stand out of the sunlight!' It is reported that the greatest man in the known world said, as he left: 'If I were not Alexander, I would be Diogenes.' It would have been better for the world if he had been.

The Stoics developed some of the doctrines of the Cynics but did not reject all the benefits of civilization. They found in the law of nature a guide prior and superior to human customs and laws. By looking to the world of universals in nature, they developed the ideals of individualism, equality and cosmopolitanism. Not surprisingly, they found adherents in the outlying parts of the Greek world, especially in Asia Minor, where Greeks and Orientals intermingled.

The founder of Stoicism, Zeno of Citium, identified God with nature, which is the most excellent of all things. He taught like the Taoists that the wise person will see how natural processes occur and confirm his will accordingly. To live in agreement with nature is also to live according to reason:

> The end may be defined as life in accordance with nature, or, in other words, in accordance with our own human nature as well as that of the universe, a life in which we refrain from every action forbidden by the law common to all things, that is to say, the right reason which pervades all things, and is identical with Zeus, lord and ruler of all that is.[26]

Zeno recommended that people should live as a single herd or tribe without family and property, without distinctions of rank or race, and without money or courts of law. Above all, there is no need for coercion, for left to themselves people will spontaneously fulfil their natures. Their stateless society could spread across the whole globe.

But the Stoics believed that what exists does so only for the rational; man, the rational being *par excellence*, should therefore have dominion over nature. It was a view later developed by the Roman Stoics and taken up by early Christians.

### The living fountain of universal benevolence

Not all Greeks adopted the Stoical attitude to animals and considered nature to be shaped solely for human ends. Plutarch, the great historian, biographer and philosopher of the first century AD, was one of the first to consider the moral interests of animals, separate from any belief in the transmigration of souls. He is best known for his *Lives*, but his good humour, warm sympathy and compassionate

concern come through in his collection of short treatises known as
*Morals.*

Plutarch accepts that there are certain things that we must do in
order to live, but they do not include killing or torturing animals,
although he thought torturing a living creature (in an experiment or
for sport) was no worse than slaughtering outright. To extend justice
to animals does not corrupt humanity. On the contrary, if we maltreat
animals it is very easy to maltreat men; if we kill animals, it is a short
step to murder. Plutarch seems to have been the first to call for the
kind treatment of animals on the grounds of universal benevolence:

> The obligations of law and equity reach only to mankind, but
> kindness and benevolence should be extended to the creatures
> of every species, and these will flow from the breast of the true
> man, as streams that issue from the living fountain.[27]

He further condemned the hunting of animals, arguing that 'sport
should be joyful and between playmates who are merry on both
sides'.[28]

The natural corollary of Plutarch's doctrine of universal benevolence applied to all beings was abstention from flesh-eating. He
considered it an unfeeling, irrational and immoral practice:

> I, for my part, wonder of what sort of feeling, mind or reason
> that man was possessed who was first to pollute his mouth with
> gore, and allow his lips to touch the flesh of a murdered being;
> who spread his table with the mangled form of dead bodies,
> and claimed as daily food and dainty dishes what but now
> were beings endowed with movement, with perception and with
> voice.[29]

## Western hubris

The Greeks did not make great advances in technology. This was
partly because they saw science and philosophy as inextricably
linked and as philosophers they were primarily concerned with
understanding nature rather than changing or controlling it. They
were prepared to observe, but not to dominate.

Nevertheless, it was the Greeks rather than the Hebrews who were
mainly responsible for the notion of man as the rightful master of
nature, which came to be a central tenet of Western Christianity.

Traditional Greek religion taught that to seek mastery of the world would amount to *hubris*: by attempting to vie with the gods, man would in the end be punished for his arrogance. *Hubris*, pride before a fall, was inevitably followed by *nemesis*, revenge. Since nature is in some way divine, too much power over nature would be disrespectful and court disaster.

Aeschylus understood this. In *The Persians*, he suggests that Xerxes, who led the Persians against the Greeks in 480 BC, came to grief because of his arrogant imperialism against nature as well as Athens. By building a bridge across the Hellespont, he not only tried to enslave his fellow men but also the sea.

The Greek Enlightenment from Plato onwards tended to reject the notion of *hubris* and forgot about *nemesis*. Thereafter it became increasingly common for philosophers to maintain that the world was intended for humanity and that the rest of creation, including all its beings, existed for their sake. The dominant Western tradition became wedded to a view of man as a rational and perfectible being, whose history can be seen in terms of linear progress. Despite the myth of Prometheus, who stole fire from the gods only to be condemned to eternal punishment for going beyond his proper place, Western man has come to believe that he can conquer nature and interfere with its processes with impunity.

# 6

## THE ROMANS

### *Second Nature*

Each being contains in itself the whole intelligible
world. Therefore All is everywhere. Each is there All,
and All is each.

Plotinus


The ancient history of Rome begins in the eighth century BC and
extends to the fifth century AD. Never before or since has Europe
known such an empire. The Romans built straight roads and
magnificent buildings, but their cultural legacy is not so clear-cut.
Since the Roman empire was based on conquest and force, military
virtues were celebrated and sympathy for the weak despised. They
may have had a high regard for public duty, but there were limits to
their moral feelings. They did not include in their moral community
criminals, captives, foreigners or nonhumans.

The attitude of many Romans to other peoples as well as to animals
reflects little reverence for life. The killing and torturing of humans
and animals in the Roman 'games' helped harden the imperialist
and bellicose tendencies of Roman citizens as well as providing an
emotional outlet for potential troublemakers. The Roman games not
only pitched men against each other, but men against animals, and
animals against animals. Four hundred bears in a single day were
killed under Caligula, and under Nero four hundred tigers fought
with bulls and elephants. A leader during Rome's decline would be
more unpopular if he neglected the games than if he neglected the
distribution of corn: circuses became more important than bread,
such was the craving for blood. But not all Romans condoned the
mass slaughter of animals for sport or even food: Ovid, Virgil and
Seneca all advocated a non-flesh diet. Ovid in particular argued in
his *Metamorphoses* that all beings have a right to live.

## Roman gods and cults

Religion is a Latin concept – the Greeks had no word for or clear idea of it. Cicero defined religion (*religio*) as 'the worship of the gods'. The Roman like the Greek world was peopled by spirits and gods. But for the bureaucratically minded Romans the gods were considered to have specific functions and were assigned precise offices. Thus there were gods for all the basic processes of agriculture, from Vervactor for the first ploughing to Insitor for sowing. They adopted some foreign gods and in particular modified the Greek deities into their state cult. Zeus, the supreme god of the Greeks, became Jupiter. Roman religion has been called a religion of field, city and hearth. At the cosmic level, the primeval trinity consisted of heaven (Uranus), earth (Gaea) and their son the sea (Oceanus). At the same time, different family cults flourished, and nearly every house had a private shrine.

Fertility was essential to life, and there were many statues associated with fruitfulness and reproduction of such gods as Silvanus, Flora, Faunus and Priapus. Wreaths of vegetation, horns of fruit and phalluses were common. In one of the temples at Sentinum from the third century, there is a mosaic of Tellus (earth) surrounded by the seasons – a symbol of the peace and harmony which the Pax Augusta had brought to the world. A male figure turns the circle of the Zodiac, and the whole gives the impression of Earth and Heaven forming a single happy family. In the late Roman Empire several classes of intermediate deities like the muses, sirens, graces and seasons populated the world. Although during the Roman republic, there was a growing sense that superstition was improper, nature for the Romans was always animate and infused with spirits.

It was normal for Romans to sacrifice animals during the festivals for their gods. The Greeks had sacrificed bulls in their temples, but in the second century AD, a Mithras cult of the bull developed throughout the Roman Empire, with temples as far north as Hadrian's Wall in northern England and as far south as Alexandria in Egypt. It has been called the 'Freemasonry of the Roman world'.[1] The cult was particularly popular among the military, and, not surprisingly in the male-dominated Roman world, women were excluded.

Mithras was said to have been incarnated on 25 December to redeem mankind who was suffering on earth under Ahriman, the Zoroastrian god of darkness and chaos. In this, there are obvious parallels with the coming of Christ. He is sometimes identified with the sun; sometimes opposing it.

The main theme of the cult is Mithras slaying a bull. The god is generally depicted with his left knee on the bull's back, pulling back his head with his left hand and stabbing the bull with his right hand in its shoulder. A dog and a snake are sometimes seen leaping towards the blood from the wound, while a scorpion grasps the bull's genitals. The animals may well have astrological significance, but nothing in Roman times represents so well man's destructive mastery of the animal world. The warrior who was part of the cult had to make his life a continuous re-enactment of the sacrifice, mortifying the body symbolized by the bull, to release the spirit.[2]

For the ritual sacrifice of the bull, the cult developed the *taurobolium* in which an initiate stands in a pit and is drenched from the warm blood of a bull killed on a platform above. The vital forces of the bull were meant to enter the devotee, who was eternally 'reborn'. Ironically, Mithraic celebration of the birthday of a new sun on 25 December was later taken over by the Christians.

The mother goddess appears in the Roman world in the form of Juno, the wife of Jupiter, but in the masculine republican world of imperial Rome she was considerably downrated. The Roman state religion was dominated by warrior gods and national heroes. However, for five hundred years Cybele was worshipped in a temple on the Palatine Hill as if to redress the balance.

Where as the mother goddess often appears as loving and nurturing, as in the Egyptian Isis and the Greek Hera, Cybele takes on the devouring and destroying aspect of the Greek Hecate or the Indian Kali. On seeing her son fall in love with a nymph, in a fit of jealousy she makes him mad; he castrates himself and dies. He is then reborn and reunited with his mother.

The devotees of Cybele therefore worshipped a jealous goddess and her mutilated son. The central ritual, as in Mithraism, was the sacrifice of a bull, drenching initiates in blood. The shedding of bull's blood may well have been a substitute for human sacrifice. Some of Cybele's most devout followers castrated themselves like her son and became wandering beggars.

The Egyptian goddess Isis was also worshipped in Rome for four centuries as universal Mother Nature, from the first unformed matter of the universe down to the birds and plants. But she always appeared in a kind and nourishing form. The cult never involved the taking of animal life: milk, honey or herbs were the usual offerings.

The Dionysus cult of ancient Greece also reached Rome. Although the Greek Dionysus changed his name to the Roman Bacchus, he did not change his nature. He has been called the 'Archetypal Image of Indestructible Life'; he certainly represents dynamic energy and orgiastic inspiration.[3] Wine, opium, ivy and toadstools all seem to have contributed to the collective frenzy of his worshippers, and they may well have been used as springboards for mystical trances.

The first Dionysus was born of Zeus and Persephone, but killed as a child by the Titans. He was then reborn after Zeus mated with the mortal Semele, who was annihilated in the act. As a son of Zeus, Dionysus was a creative deity but very much part of the earth. The purpose of Bacchic initiation ceremonies, however, was to awaken individual consciousness to an awareness of the universal mind of which it is a part. But whatever the higher symbolism, the Bacchantes practised phallic and sacrificial rites which included eating raw flesh. For all his vitality, it would be difficult to include Bacchus in a pantheon of environmentally sound gods.

## The nature of things

Just as Roman religion tended to be state-oriented, martial and sacrificial, so the mainstream of Roman philosophy was anthropocentric and humanist. The main schools – Stoics, Cynics and Epicureans – all agreed that matter is the sole reality and the senses are the sole source of knowledge. Ultimate happiness was to achieve a calm and untroubled mind. They developed the Aristotelian view that justice was only possible among those who shared the same values: foreigners and nonhumans were beyond the pale.

The Stoic view was that the world was made for man. The Stoics considered the world ruled by a divine rationality (*logos*), manifested as fate, and closely related to human reason. In his *De Natura Deorum* (*On the Nature of the Gods*, 45 BC), Marcus Tullius Cicero makes the Stoic Balbus declare: 'The produce of the earth was designed for those only who make use of it; and though some beasts may rob us of a small part, it does not follow that the earth produced it also for them.'[4] Like Aristotle, Cicero argued that plants are made for animals and animals are made for humans. It is self-evident to Cicero that the necks of oxen were naturally made for the yoke and their shoulders for the plough. Since everything on earth is for man's use, it follows that he can alter it as he sees fit: 'We alone have the power of controlling the most violent of nature's offspring, the sea and the winds . . . Likewise the entire command of the commodities on land is vested in mankind . . . by means of our hands we try to create as it were a second Nature within the world of Nature.'[5]

The Epicureans are popularly remembered for taking pleasure as the supreme value, but they portrayed man's place within nature in a very different light to the Stoics. In his great work *De Natura Rerum*, Lucretius (died 55 BC) popularized the philosophies of Democritus and Epicurus and felt it was silly to imagine that this world – 'so foolish the design, contrived so ill' – should have been created by a god solely for human use. Anticipating Darwin, Lucretius developed a theory of natural selection, in which men at first competed with other species for survival and multiplied only with difficulty. Like modern ecologists, he saw human beings as not only using, but also being used by other living beings around them. It is only this evolutionary view that can bring a calm and tranquil mind.

Seneca was another Roman philosopher and poet who developed Stoic philosophy with important Epicurean modifications in the first century. Seneca's principle was: 'The blessing is not in living, but in living well.' But this did not include living off other beings, or aping the ways of the crowd. In particular, it implied voluntary abstinence from flesh, even if it involved swimming against the tide of society. 'If true,' he wrote,

> the Pythagorean principles as to abstaining from flesh, foster innocence; if ill-founded they at least teach us frugality, and what loss have you in losing your cruelty? It merely deprives you of the food of lions and vultures. We shall recover our sound reason only if we separate ourselves from the herd . . . the very fact of the approbation of the multitude is a proof of the unsoundness of the opinion or practice; let us ask what is best – not what is customary. Let us love temperance – let us be just – let us refrain from bloodshed.[6]

## Neoplatonism

Neoplatonism, originating in Alexandria in the third century AD, was strongly eclectic, based to some extent on Pythagoras and Plato, with additions from Aristotle and the Stoics. The philosophy of

Neoplatonisn was one of divine unfolding. From the fullness of the divine unity emerged *nous* or pure intelligence, and from *nous* emerged the world-soul. The human soul is of divine origin but imprisoned in material clothing, and as a result is tainted, gross and dark. It is the individual's duty to cleanse the soul of its bodily form, so that it might return to God. The Neoplatonists advocated extreme ascetism, fasting and chastity in order to purge the soul of its material impurities.

The legacy of Neoplatonism was mixed. Its Gnostic separation of mind and body, spirit and matter, encouraged the dualism at the heart of Christianity. At the same time, its sense of the overall unity of an animated world continued as an important undercurrent in Western thought, emerging during the Renaissance and Romanticism to counter the dominant mechanical and atomistic philosophy.

Plotinus, the principal founder of Neoplatonism, was probably born in Egypt in AD 205 and settled in Rome in 244. He declared that 'he blushed that he had a body'. He taught that the Ultimate One is the ground of existence and the source of all values. In his trinity, the One or God is at the top; spirit, which is the intellectual principle, second; and finally the soul, which is the author of all living things. World-mind and world-soul suffuse all nature. The purpose of human nature is through will and understanding to achieve a kind of ecstatic union with the One.

Like the Hindus and Buddhists, Plotinus insists that all is one and one is all. The apparent diversity of life forms an overall unity. 'Each being contains in itself the whole intelligible world. Therefore All is everywhere. Each is there All, and All is each. Man as he now is has ceased to be the All. But when he ceases to be an individual, he raises himself again and penetrates the whole world.'[7] Plotinus inferred the necessary existence of this world, with all its imperfections, from his notion of the self-sufficient One. In his view, whenever anything reaches its own perfection, it cannot endure to remain in itself and therefore produces some other thing: 'The One is perfect because it seeks for nothing, and possesses nothing, and has need for nothing; and being perfect, it overflows, and thus its superabundance produces an Other.'[8] From the One was begotten the Many, and every possible variety of being must be produced in a descending series – for ever onwards until the confines of the possible are reached.

The first stage in the descending process is the intelligible world, which is outside time and space; then comes the universal soul, which is the parent of nature; then reason, peculiar to man; and finally the 'sentient and vegetative natures' (animals and plants). In this 'Scale of Being', an earlier version of the medieval Chain of Being, 'the world is a sort of Life stretched out to an immense span, in which each of the parts has it own place in the series, all of them different and yet the whole continuous, and that which precedes never wholly absorbed in that which comes after'.[9]

Anticipating Leibniz, Plotinus argued that this is the best possible world because it is full – 'the whole earth is full of a diversity of living beings, mortal and immortal, and replete with them up to the very heavens'. The best world must also contain all possible evil; in his terms, all the possible gradations of deprivation of good. The difference of kind is equivalent to a diversity of rank in a hierarchy, but all are necessary parts of the whole. As a modern ecologist might argue, to harm one is to harm the whole: 'Those who would eliminate the worse from the universe would eliminate Providence itself.' To eliminate the 'lowly' beings would be to spoil the beauty of the whole for it is by means of all beings, both high and low, that the world becomes complete and perfect. 'We are like men,' Plotinus sagely suggests, 'who, knowing little of painting, blame the artist because the colours in his picture are not all beautiful – not seeing that he has given to each part what was appropriate to it.'[10]

Diversity is therefore necessary for moral, aesthetic and metaphysical reasons. Such an optimistic view which maintains partial evil is universal good can of course be used as an excuse to condone suffering. Plotinus argues that the perpetual war among animals and among men is necessary for the good of the whole, since the good of the whole consists mainly in the variety of parts; the lion and the deer are both necessary for the abundance of life. Indeed, Plotinus maintains that conflict is a special case of diversity: 'Difference carried to its maximum *is* opposition.' This did not prevent Plotinus from abstaining from eating flesh, since there was no need for rational man to increase the suffering of the nonrational and sinless animals.

In the third century AD, Porphyry became the principal expositor of Neoplatonism. He studied at Athens under Longinus and at Rome around AD 263 under Plotinus. Influenced by Plotinus and Pythagoras, whose lives he wrote, he saw the end of his philosophy as the salvation of the soul though strict asceticism and knowledge of God.

Porphyry showed great concern for animals and considered that the voluntary abstinence from flesh symbolized the triumph of the spirit over the body. He proved to be one of the earliest and most eloquent defenders of animal rights and vegetarianism. In his influential essay *On Abstinence from Animal Food*, he even recommended eating fruits that plants do not need for reproduction.

Porphyry also came out against animal sacrifice, which was the most common form of magic practised in the ancient world: the life force of the victim was offered to a god or spirits to be placated out of fear or entreated for a favour. Porphyry argued that none of the three main ends of sacrifice – homage, necessity and gratitude – is disinterested and therefore they cannot be considered moral. Animal sacrifice, moreover, could not possibly influence the gods, and always had a negative effect on the sacrificer.

Although the arguments of Porphyry were lost for nearly a millennium and a half of Christianity, he became the favourite author of Montaigne, who was one of the first in Christendom to condemn cruelty to animals not for the moral effect on humans but for the sake of the animals' welfare.

### Philo of Alexandria

One of the last great synthesizers of the philosophical and religious traditions of the ancient world was Philo of Alexandria in the first century. His own life and philosophy show the close relationship between Egypt, Greece and Rome at the time, with its wider contacts with the Middle East. Born in Alexandria in Egypt, of a wealthy Jewish family, he was brought up in Greek culture but remained faithful to his Jewish religion. He went to Rome when over fifty years old to plead for certain Alexandrians who had refused to worship Caligula. Most of his writings have been lost but three were recorded in the Pentateuch which emphasize the unity of nature. They show that he fused Neoplatonism, Pythagoreanism and Stoicism with the Jewish scriptures in a way that later inspired both Christians and Jews.

Philo was exposed to the Hellenistic mystery religion which flourished among the Jews of the Diaspora between 200 BC and 100 AD. He transformed the anthropocentric and personal God of the Old Testament into Absolute Mind which pervades all the universe. The highest good is to achieve immediate contact with this supreme being. But it is not to be realized through suppressing the passions. 'The rout and destruction of the passions, while a good, is not the ultimate good; the discovery of Wisdom is the surpassing good. When this is found, all the people will sing.'[11] Since nature is infused with the divine, human beings should not turn their backs on it but try to imitate its beneficent ways. Philo's approach is the opposite of the Gnostic and Christian view of a corrupt and fallen nature: 'Even though a man be incapable of making himself worthy of the creator of the cosmos, yet he ought to try to make himself worthy of the cosmos. He ought to transform himself from being a man into the nature of the cosmos and become, if one may say so, a little cosmos.'[12]

The Roman empire collapsed of course from over extending itself, from the pressure of the Celtic and Teutonic tribes, and from its growing corruption of manners exemplified in its games. Christianity too had a considerable influence in its downfall, introducing to the Roman world the idea of the uniqueness of man which it developed from Judaism. The Christians were opposed to the gladiatorial fights – they had after all been thrown themselves to the lions – but they only confirmed the anthropocentric legacy of the Graeco-Roman world which was to cast long shadows over Western civilization.

# 7

## CELTIC MYSTERIES

### Neither This nor That

I am Roar of Sea ...
I am Fairest of Flowers ...
I am a Word of Skill.
                *The Book of the Taking of Ireland*

Where I live in Wales, the local inhabitants proudly boast of their Celtic origin. They still speak *Cymraeg* in this remote mountainous region, a version of the Brythonic language which was once in use throughout Europe before the Roman conquest. They are resentful of intruders, and I will always remain in their eyes (despite some Celtic ancestry) a *Seis* – Saxon – from the lowlands of England. The dragon on their national flag swishes his tail and snorts fire; he is not dead yet.

The lost culture of the nomadic Celts was predominantly oral and the principal records of their beliefs and customs made by the invading Romans share the inevitable bias of all conquerors. To justify the imposition of their own civilization, the Romans dwelled on the primitive savagery of the Celts. The literature and arts of the early Celts which have survived, however, show that they had a rich and subtle relationship with the world around them. They were inextricably interwoven with nature like their common knotted and interlaced designs.

Where the Celts came from is still a mystery, but they share many affinities with Indo-European warrior groups who overran the Indus Valley Civilization about 2000 BC. They emerged from the Rhinelands of central Europe as a distinctive group of clans or tribes between 1000 and 500 BC. The earliest remnants of Celtic culture in central Europe are usually dated between 800 and 450 BC. The later Celtic phase, known as La Tène culture, continued until Roman times. While many of their beliefs can only be surmised, they believed in the afterlife – as grave goods testify – and Julius Caesar implied that they believed in the transmigration of souls.

There is some evidence to suggest that at some stage they had ties with Vedic India.

The key to Celtic mysteries is to be found in the intertwining of the spiritual, physical and imaginative realms in their world-view. Although their gods and heroes were often mingled around a specific site, they had no strict pantheon of gods like the Greeks and Romans but were at one with the elements and the Great Spirit. They believed that magical agencies pervaded every aspect of their lives and surroundings and tried to direct them through ritual, sacrifice and the recitation of myths.

Central to their belief was the Earth Mother, who was invoked under many different aspects and names. As in many Indo-European myths, the Celtic Earth Mother is a symbol of creation and destruction; she is ruthless and bountiful; she must be propitiated as well as entreated.

The devouring aspect of the Earth Mother recurs in Celtic symbolism: grotesque images of her, for instance, known as sheela-na-gigs, are common in Irish castles and churches. Their stylized and enlarged vaginas are the counterpart of the Celtic phallic symbolism of standing stones, reflecting male fear-fantasies of the all-absorbing mother. The Earth Mother may well be the forerunner of the vigorous female figures in Irish stories who often appear in groups of three. On a more practical level, the double aspect of the Earth Mother also reflects the perilous character of the Celts' existence and their fragile dependence on the whims of nature.

The Celts were a warrior people; blood-letting was common in war and peace. They changed the methods of warfare of the first millennium BC through their innovations, which included the wielding of large iron hacking swords, the throwing of spears from fast two-horsed chariots, and the use of screaming naked riders to create terror and confusion among their enemies. With their great hilltop forts and fierce reputation, Celtic tribes controlled trade routes between the west, the Mediterranean and the Middle East for almost a thousand years.

It is not surprising that to their enemies they should appear bloodthirsty, cruel and savage. The Greek geographer Strabo called the whole nation 'war-mad, and both high-spirited and quick for battle although otherwise simple and not uncouth'.[1] They were great head-hunters and the severed head is the most widespread feature of all Celtic imagery. They used human skulls as decorations in their buildings and to protect them from evil spirits. Human sacrifice as well as the sacrifice of animals was common. In Bouches-du-Rhône, France, there is a stone statue known as the Monster of Noves, with a half-eaten leg protuding from its mouth, huge claws clamped on twin severed heads, and an erect phallus, a gruesome reminder of the close connection for the Celts between killing and fertility, death and rebirth. Their economy was based on cattle-rearing and slaughter was natural to them. Blood sustained the Celtic warrior.

But these bloody rituals were not merely a base expression of cruelty or indifference to suffering. The Celts believed that the decapitated heads had great spiritual power. In the story 'The Entertaining of the Noble Head' in the thirteenth-century collection of stories known as the *Mabinogion*, the companions of Bendigeid Vran experienced eighty gloriously happy years after severing his head and keeping it.

The need for sacrifice and the identification with animals carried on into the Middles Ages, despite the overlay of Christianity. In his *Description of Ireland* (1185), the Welsh historian Giraldus Cambrensis recorded his disgust with the 'barbarous and abominable rite of enthronement' of the leader of an Ulster clan in northern Ireland which involved the sacrifice of a mare. He who is to be inaugurated comes before the people:

> on all fours, confessing himself a beast with no less impudence than imprudence. The mare being immediately killed and cut into pieces and boiled, a bath is prepared for him from the broth. Sitting in this he eats of the flesh which is brought to him, the people standing around and partaking of it also. He is then required to drink of the broth in which he bathes, not drinking it in any vessel nor even in his hand but lapping it with his mouth. These unrighteous rites duly accomplished, his royal authority and dominion are ratified.[2]

Blood sacrifice was considered necessary by the Celts to propitiate the Earth Mother to prevent her wrath and ensure her fertility. Their individual lives and the continuance of their tribes depended upon it. They lived in a world where the living and the dead intermingled, where spirits were as real as the creatures moving around them.

This no doubt explains the Celtic fascination with in-between times and places: dawn and twilight, sea shore and river ford, sea mists and mountain clouds, even the act of dying. Objects which are 'neither this nor that' have a mysterious value. They defy classification, like spring dew, which is neither rain nor sea, river nor well water; it appears at dawn when it is neither day nor night, on a May morning when it is neither winter nor summer. Mistletoe is another example, neither a tree nor a shrub, with roots yet not growing in the soil.

The whole of nature was a living organism for the Celts, and they identified with its elements. The Celtic veneration of 'sacred oak groves', mistletoe rites and other rituals in forests or on hilltops were part of widespread animistic belief that trees and stones were embodiments of the spirits of dead ancestors. They undertook their rites in special places where they felt that the energies of the earth were located – places whose mysterious atmosphere can still be dimly felt today.

Water sources, especially wells and springs, also had special significance to the Celts. Water of course is essential to the fertility of the soil and the support of life. They dedicated the main river sources of Western Europe as sanctuaries to Mother Earth, the fertility goddess, as is shown by the large number of votive offerings – figures, skulls, precious metals, weapons and domestic objects – found in their vicinity. Any river or stream was seen as a living expression of Mother Earth. Each sacred spot had its own guardian spirit who could materialize as a cat, bird, fish or in whatever form was most pleasing to the goddess. Just as burial sites were considered womb places of the Mother Earth, so the sources of streams were regarded as womb openings.

Nature could be harsh but she could also give pleasure, especially in the spring and summer. As late as the fourteenth century, the Celtic bard Dafydd ap Gwylym expressed this pagan sense of erotic ease in nature. He sends birds and animals as messengers to his lovers and invites them to trysts in houses of leaves. Addressing a nun, his voice is that of the pre-Christian wild man:

> Is it true, the girl that I love,
> That you do not desire birch, the strong growth of summer?
> Be not a nun in spring,
> Asceticism is not as good as a bush.
> As for the warrant of ring and habit,

A green dress would ordain better.
Come to the spreading birch,
To the religion of the trees and the cuckoo.[3]

The maypole, a symbol of male fertility, was traditionally a birch tree.

The strong ecological sensibility of the Celts and their identification with nature come across in the *Lebor Gabála Érenn*, 'The Book of the Taking of Ireland', which combines parts of Hebrew mythology and Celtic legends. It tells of the journey of 'the Sons of Míl' from Egypt to Ireland. The Celtic substratum of the story comes through in the poem of the judge Amairgen when he lands in Ireland. Like Krishna in the *Bhagavad Gita*, he embodies the primal unity of all things on the sea of nonbeing:

> I am Wind on Sea,
> I am Ocean-wave,
> I am Roar of Sea,
> I am Bull of Seven Fights,
> I am Vulture on Cliff,
> I am Dewdrop,
> I am Fairest of Flowers,
> I am Boar of Boldness,
> I am Salmon in Pool,
> I am Lake on Plain,
> I am a Word of Skill . . .[4]

The Celts were inveterate hunters, but they had great respect for their quarry. In a strange process of identification, hunter and hunted, predator and prey, became one. It is almost possible to talk of a kind of biocentric egalitarianism at work, for men and animals were both considered members of the same community in life and death. The spirits of dead animals and ancestors were remembered and respected. Even the fact that humans were sacrificed as well as animals means that they were placed on the same spiritual footing in the rites to the Earth Mother.

The Celtic hunter particularly identified with the stag, and made it the ancestral symbol of his clan. They portrayed this god as a man with antlers and made offerings to him in order to propitiate his spirit. There is a statue of the stag god in Rheims inscribed with the name Cernunnos, probably meaning the 'Horned One' or the 'Lord of All

Stags'. As a god of prosperity and good fortune, in Gallo-Roman art he became identified with Pan. While he clearly was a god of fertility, with his consort Mother Earth, he was sometimes associated by the Romans with their warrior god Mars. In British folklore he was known as Herne the Hunter, mentioned by Shakespeare as associated with an oak in Windsor Forest.

The widespread figure of the Green Man, who emerges in obscure corners in many Gothic churches with foliage sprouting from his mouth like grass bursting through heavy paving stones, is probably a descendant of the Celtic horned god.[5] For the early Christians he represented sexual sin, but for the Gothic artists he became a symbol of renewal and resurrection. Animals, birds and monsters inhabit the carved forest surrounding him. One of the most outstanding examples is in Exeter Cathedral in England.

The Green Man, or Jack-in-the-Green, as he is sometimes called, also seems to have been linked with the Celtic head cult, for he usually lacks a body. Related to Wodwo, or the wild man, he was popular throughout western Europe in the Middle Ages. The closest in British literature of the time is the fourteenth-century story of the Green Knight who arrives in Arthur's court in winter and challenges Sir Gawain to return to his dwelling after a beheading game. He is clothed entirely in green, riding a green horse with a holly bough in one hand, 'ande al grayped in grene pis gome & his wedes' on 'a grene hors gret & pikke'.[6] He leaves the court carrying his own severed head in his hand.

The figure undoubtedly draws on ancient Celtic fertility myths and rites of prophecy and sacrifice. It represents the archetype of the ancient European mind emerging through layers of Christian civilization, evoking the male spirit in nature. At the same time, the Green Man, brought into Gothic churches like holly at Christmas into the drawing room, symbolizes a new stage in the taming and humanization of nature.[7]

The Celts did not separate themselves off from the creation and its creatures as the later Christians did. A common feature of their tales is 'shape-shifting' in which humans realize their animal natures, whether as bull, stag, horse, boar, cat, bird or fish. Indeed, the art and literature of the Celts contain a rich bestiary which shows the great power animals had for them. The most favoured animals were the stag, the bull, the boar and the horse, all associated with strength and fertility. In their rituals, it seems that animals were identified with the

ancestral spirit who presided over the fortunes of the tribe. The horse
was the animal of power of the early nomadic Celts; the bull became
important to the pastoral Irish. The sacred nature of these animals
comes through in the many stories of magic hunts and shape-shifting
in Gaelic tales.

Originally nomads, the Celts kept the wandering spirit alive in
their culture. There are many Celtic legends surrounding the Isles
of the Blessed as well as stories about wonderful lands that have
disappeared in the sea. In the sea voyages of early Irish literature,
crystal boats on a sea of glass carry many a hero to the 'land of
Promise'. The journey was symbolic of the life of the soul and the
cycle of experience it must encounter. Not only do humans turn
into animals in these epics, but the elements themselves undergo
a metamorphosis. The stories of Mael Dúin's epic voyage suggests
that they may be the remnants of an ancient oral tradition that
charts the worlds beyond death; they may even be comparable to
the Tibetan and Egyptians books of the dead. A visitor from another
realm reminisces about a loch:

> It was yellow. It was blossoming. It was green. It was hilly. It
> was a place of drinking. It had silver in it and chariots. I went
> through it when I was a deer. When I was a salmon. When I
> was a wild dog. When I was a man I bathed in it. I carried a
> yellow sail and a green sail . . . I know not father nor mother.
> I speak with the living and the dead.[8]

Few passages describe so vividly the intimate interlacing of the Celtic
world between humanity and nature, this world and the next. This
interlacing is beautifully demonstrated in the first three letters of the
ancient Irish alphabet of the trees, Beth-Luis-Nion, which correspond
to the birch, rowan and ash.

The spiritual leaders of the Celts were the Druids, who performed
the roles of shaman, priest, poet, physician, judge and prophet.
Strabo called them 'students of moral philosophy'. As shamans,
the Druids extended their range of consciousness through strictly
observed rituals in special places such as groves or hilltops which
inspired their visions. In their quests, they entered dream states where
past and present, psychic and physical planes merged. They achieved
this often with the use of riddles and wordplay, reminders of the
origin of all sacred mysteries – breath.

Being so close to the forest which covered northern Europe, the Druids foretold the future from bird calls, the paths of animals, and the casting of yew sticks. Strabo records that the Druids read omens by killing a human victim with a sword stroke in the back and noting the way he fell, the nature of the convulsions, and the flow of blood. Julius Caesar also describes the Druids of the Gauls as concerned with divine worship, performance of sacrifices, and interpretation of ritual questions. According to his account, they worshipped Mercury (the Roman god of travellers and thieves) above all gods, while keeping appropriate worship for Apollo, Mars, Jupiter and Minerva. Caesar also mentions that human victims were burned in wickerwork colossi to propitiate their gods.[9]

The Celts had fairly egalitarian relationships among themselves – women had the same rights as men in making marriage and divorce and each family was related through matrilineal descent and took the clan name of the mother. But the power of the Druids was absolute. This was achieved not by force but through spiritual ascendancy over the tribe: the hardest penalty that could be imposed on a member was exclusion from the rites.

The classical writers had little respect for the 'natural religion' of the barbarians in their great forests of northern Europe. The invading Romans in the first century desecrated native shrines and sanctuaries not only because of the savage beliefs they represented but for their gold and silver objects. Nevertheless, the conquerors absorbed some of their beliefs: inscriptions in Britain and France show Romanized expression of the older Celtic religion.

The English followed the Romans in Wales and tried to impose their customs on the population, but for centuries the Celtic spirit lived on in the Welsh language, legends and stories, standing stones and sacred springs. But it has now virtually evaporated. The great forests have gone and the spiritual link with the earth has been broken. Hunters go after the fox at night with high-velocity rifles and powerful torches which blind their prey. Animal sacrifices take place only in slaughterhouses with blaring radios and there is no wish to propitiate the spirit of the dead. The travelling urge of the Celts, which made the telling of their journeys as much of a religion as the ceremonies themselves, has been extinguished. The neat, plain chapels of Nonconformity have replaced the sacred groves and hilltop shrines. Roman law and English commerce have triumphed. The wonder voyages are over.

# 8

# THE JUDAEO-CHRISTIAN TRADITION

## Man's Dominion over Nature

And God said, Let us make man in our image, after our likeness: and let them have dominion over the fish of the sea, and over the fowl of the air, and over the cattle, and over all the earth, and over every creeping thing that creepeth upon the earth.

So God created man in his *own* image, in the image of God created he him; male and female created he them.

And God blessed them, and God said unto them, Be fruitful, and multiply, and replenish the earth, and subdue it: and have dominion over the fish of the sea, and over the fowl of the air, and over every living things that moveth upon the earth.

Genesis 1:26–8

In this account of the creation in Genesis, man is depicted at the apex of the creation and given dominion over the rest of nature. The account could not be more anthropocentric. As John Calvin wrote in his commentary on Genesis, 'the end for which all things were created [was] that none of the convenience and necessities of life might be wanting to men'.[1]

In a meditation on the human condition, similar sentiments are expressed in Psalm 8:5–8 in the Bible:

For thou hast made him a little lower than the angels, and hast crowned him with glory and honour.

Thou madest him to have dominion over the works of thy hands; thou hast put all *things* under his feet:

All sheep and oxen, yea, and the beasts of the field;

The fowl of the air, and the fish of the sea, *and whatsoever* passeth through the paths of the seas

Thou hast given him.

If Genesis had been written by a dog and not a man, we would undoubtedly have had a different story. It seems as if the God of the Old Testament was invented by man merely to sanctify the rule they had already usurped for themselves over the cattle of the field, the fowl of the air and the fish of the sea.

It has been argued that the force of the anthropocentric and arrogant message of the first chapter of Genesis is assuaged somewhat in the second, which offers an image of companionship and stewardship in Adam's relationship with nature. According to Chapter Two, which was allegedly written first, God placed man into the Garden of Eden and instructed him 'to dress it and to keep it' (2:15). But even this is the old image of man as the improver of nature. Moreover, the account goes on to say that God brought every 'beast of the field, and every fowl of the air' to Adam for him to name them. By naming them, he made them his own. Like the arch-imperialist Robinson Crusoe and his man Friday, Adam did not enquire what the animals thought about the situation or what they called themselves.

Semantics support the negative interpretation of the relationship between man and nature given in Genesis. Hebrew scholars confirm that the operative words in Genesis 1:28 – *kabash*, translated as 'subdue', and *radah*, given as 'have dominion over' or 'rule' – are used throughout the Old Testament to mean a violent assault or crushing. Both words are used to describe the act of enslavement; they evoke the image of a conqueror placing his foot on the neck of a defeated enemy in total domination.[2] It comes as no surprise, therefore, that Christians should have traditionally interpreted the divine command of Genesis to mean that man should conquer, enslave and exploit nature for his own ends.

### The Fall of man and the corruption of nature

Having created the Garden of Eden and introduced Adam and Eve into it, God for some mysterious reason became dissatisfied with his originally good creation. He next introduces evil in the guise of the serpent in order to beguil Eve into tempting Adam with fruit from the tree of knowledge of good and evil. God, being the omnipotent creator, sets the whole scene up but when the serpent succeeds in the task set for him, 'Lord God' curses the serpent 'above every beast of the field' and condemns it to eat dust all the days of its life. As for the luckless pair, after they have eaten the forbidden fruit and fallen into sin, the Lord says that Adam will '*rule*' over Eve and that he will eat in sorrow for the rest of his days. Above all, nature itself becomes corrupt because of man's wickedness – 'cursed *is* the ground for thy sake' (3:17). So much for cosmic justice in the Judaeo-Christian tradition: man's domination of woman is reflected by man's domination of nature.

The consequences are disastrous: after Adam and Eve are banished from Eden, humanity is condemned to painful childbirth, hard work and finite existence. It leads to the domestication of plants (Cain), the domestication of animals (Abel) and to murder between members of the same species (Cain versus Abel).

Before the Fall of man and the subsequent corruption of nature, Adam and Eve seem to have been fruitarian gatherers in the Garden of Eden. After the Fall they are condemned to live by the sweat of their brow, engaged in farming. They also become flesh-eaters. God not only accepts animal sacrifice but moreover expresses an inexplicable preference for those who raise and slaughter animals. When Cain makes an offering of the 'fruit of the ground' and Abel offers up the 'firstlings of his flock and of the fat thereof', God spurns Cain's vegetarian offering in favour of Abel's meat.

The ensuing conflict between the two brothers begins the rivalry between pastoralists and agriculturalists which has reverberated down the centuries. When Cain kills his brother Abel, the Lord does not offer forgiveness for an act he provoked but declares that Cain is 'cursed from the earth' and that when he tills the ground it shall not yield its strength to him (4:11–12).

This account has profound social implications. Anthropologists have argued that the management of herds and domestic animals first gave rise to an interventionist and manipulative conception of nature and political life. A pastoralist dominates his animals and orders them here and there. In order to herd them, he must impose his will on them. The domestication of animals therefore tends to generate an authoritarian attitude and to become a model of social subjugation.

On the other hand, those societies, as in Polynesia, who lived by vegetable gardening, which requires very little intervention, seem to have despised rulers and ruling. They cannot impose their will on plants and have to cooperate with the rhythms of nature to encourage them to grow. Soil, not blood, is on their hands. The result is that such societies assume that human beings can organize their affairs without regulation and believe nature should be left to take its course.[3]

It would seem, however, that Western civilization develops from the farmer Cain. Civilization tries to counteract the destructive forces of nature, hold it at bay and prevent man from becoming its victim. The word 'civilization' comes from the Latin word for city. The leisure and communal organization of the first cities enabled arts and sciences to develop. And cities can only grow when farmers in the country produce a surplus to maintain its citizens.

According to Genesis, Cain, the inventor of agriculture, which demands a settled existence and fixed dwellings, built the first city. His offspring – the sons of Lamech – invent both 'artifices in brass and iron' and musical instruments; that is, technology and art. Since then, killing among humans has not ceased and the connection between murder and invention, which derives from agriculture and civilization, has not yet been broken.[4]

### Cursed is the ground for thy sake

It is the Christian doctrine of the Fall that is the most difficult to accept from an ecological point of view. Before God introduced man into the world he saw everything that he had made and it was 'very good'. It implies that to begin with nature had intrinsic value, as deep ecologists would put it. But the original blessing gave way to original sin. Because Adam listened to Eve and ate of the tree of knowledge, God declared 'cursed *is* the ground for thy sake' (Genesis 3:17). God's vengeance on the innocent and good creation did not stop there. When he saw the wickedness of man, the Lord said:

> I will destroy man whom I have created from the face of the earth; both man, and beast, and the creeping thing, and the fowls of the air; for it repenteth me that I have made them . . . The earth also was corrupt before God, and the earth was filled with violence. And God looked upon the earth and, behold, it was corrupt; for all flesh had corrupted his way upon the earth [Genesis 6:7, 11–12].

As a result, the primal harmony is destroyed and man moves from vegetarian gatherers to carnivorous agriculturalists and pastoralists.

Not only did God make all the creatures on earth man's subjects, he deliberately allowed the innocent spectators of man's wickedness to perish during the flood. Because of human wickedness, the Lord repents having made the creatures of the earth in the first place. This unjust act of revenge is further compounded by God's discrimination towards nonhuman creatures. He classifies the animal world into 'clean' and 'unclean beasts', and discriminates against the unclean, only allowing two 'unclean beasts' to every seven 'clean' ones to take refuge in the ark.

After the flood, in which God nearly wipes out the whole of creation, including animals and plants, in order to punish man for his wickedness, the Bible states:

> And God blessed Noah and his sons, and said unto them, Be fruitful, and multiply, and replenish the earth.
>
> And the fear of you and the dread of you shall be upon every beast of the earth, and upon every fowl of the air, upon all that moveth *upon* the earth, and upon all the fishes of the sea; into your hands are they delivered.
>
> Every moving thing that liveth shall be meat for you; even as the green herb have I given you all things [Genesis 9:1–3].

Thus God gave the final seal to man's dominion of the earth; no wonder most animals veer away from man in fear. It is the basic position of the ancient Hebrew writings towards nature and its creatures.

Because of man's primal disobedience, the whole of nature loses its sacred character and becomes corrupt and evil. There has been an attempt to give the doctrine of the Fall an ecological slant by saying that it shows how closely entwined man and nature were, so that when man transgresses, nature suffers.[5] But there can be little justice in this.

During the Christian centuries in Europe, nature became consigned to the 'Satanic order', and the Satanic forces working within nature became almost as real as the divine.[6] Moreover, the comparatively late development of science in Europe may well have been partly due to the fact that nature was considered to be a realm of evil.[7] As John Calvin declared, Adam's sin 'perverted the whole order of nature in heaven and on earth'.[8] The corruption of nature after the Fall and man's supreme position within nature became the central pillars of Christian doctrine.

More eloquently than anyone else, the French philosopher and mathematician Blaise Pascal in the seventeenth century summed up this arrogant and anthropocentric attitude. The Christian faith, according to Pascal, consists almost wholly in establishing 'the corruption of nature and the redemption of Christ'.[9] As a result, human beings should have little to do with the animal world. Unlike man, animals are slaves of their instincts: 'The parrot wipes its beak although it is clean.' The wise therefore conclude 'let us not delight in creatures'; indeed, Pascal insists that 'everything which drives us to become attached to creatures is bad, since it prevents us from serving God'.[10] Pascal reflects the ingrained dualism of the Judeao-Christian tradition when he asserts that man is composed of 'two opposing natures of different kinds, soul and body'; he is the battlefield of a 'civil war' between reason and passions.[11] And although, faced with the infinite universe, man appears as nothing, Pascal goes on to celebrate his greatness because he alone is conscious: 'Man is only a reed, the weakest in nature, but he is a thinking reed . . . even if the universe were to crush him, man would be nobler than his slayer, because he knows that he is dying and the advantage the universe has over him. The universe knows nothing of this.'[12]

## Judaism

The teaching of the Old Testament forms the bedrock of Judaism and Christianity. Although they developed in different directions, both religions are anthropocentric and sanction man's dominion over nature. The Jews considered mastery over nature to be acquired by knowledge of the Ineffable Name.[13] Man moreover has a duty to improve on nature. In order to justify circumcision, rabbis argue that nature does not produce anything quite ready for man's use, and expects man to improve upon its creations. This is true of the human body, as well as external nature.[14]

The Jews believe that the world was made for man, even though he was a latecomer among its creatures. It was God's design for man to find all things ready for him. At the same time, they hold that the body of man is a microcosm of the whole world, and the world in turn is an image of man: 'The hair upon his head corresponds to the woods of the earth, his tears to a river, his mouth to the ocean . . .' But man is more than a mere image of the world. He unites both heavenly and earthly qualities. He resembles the angels in four qualities: his power of speech, his discriminating intellect, his upright walk and the glance of his eye. But in four others he resembles animals: he eats and drinks, excretes and urinates, reproduces and dies – 'like the beast in the field'.[15]

Part of the Western contempt for animals may be traced to the

Jews. Animals were considered to have few good inclinations; if a man follows evil, he is likened to an animal; if he follows good, he is 'higher than an angel'.[16] The view is at the root of the concept of the Great Chain of Being which developed in the West: halfway between the beasts and angels, man must repress the animal within him in order to realize his celestial potential.

While the Hebrew world-view is thoroughly man-centred, it is in some ways more holistic than the Christians'. There is no word in ancient Hebrew corresponding to the word 'nature', which implies that the Israelites did not distinguish between the world of man and the rest of the world. Again, in Hebrew thought, in the category of living beings – nefesh hayya – humans are included with beasts, birds, fishes and insects. It has also been argued that the original dominion did not include the right to kill animals for food since Adam and Eve are portrayed as vegetarians before the Fall.[17] In reality, Jews never discounted nature as wholly bad and corrupt. They believed that morals could be derived from nature, and that the monogamy of the dove, for instance, could be a model for humanity.

Everything in nature was thought to have a mission to perform, so that even the bad might be applied as a means to attain the good. The conception that animals and all created things chant praise to God – expressed in Psalms 65:14 – is genuinely Jewish and occurs frequently in the Talmud and Midrash. In Isaiah 55:12 it is written: 'For ye shall go out with joy, and be led forth with peace: the mountains and the hills shall break forth before you into singing, and all the trees of the field shall clap their hands.' Moreover, the Jews believe that there is nothing inanimate in nature and 'all things in creation are endowed with sensation'.[18] The Jewish mystical tradition known as Kabbalah developed this ecological tendency within Judaism.

### Kabbalah: the way of the Jewish mystic

Although mainstream Judaism, informed by the Old Testament, has been generally anthropocentric, Kabbalah has been much more ready to embrace a holistic and biocentric view of the universe. Kabbalah ranges from the contemplation of the Bible's secret meanings to ecstatic prayer and techniques of meditating on the Hebrew alphabet. The tradition was initially passed down orally, but in thirteen-century Spain much of it came to light in a book called the Zohar ('Book of Splendour'). Although Kabbalah is first and foremost a mystical practice, much of its inspiration comes from the Jewish book of instruction called the Torah (the Pentateuch or five books of Moses) and the Laws.

Kabbalah teaches a 'panentheistic' philosophy rather than pantheism. Instead of seeing, like the pantheist, God in everything, its disciples assert that 'God's place is the world, but the world is not God's place'.[19] At the same time, there is nothing else apart from God since all is God. Everything in the universe is one; as the great sixteenth-century Kabbalist Moses Cordovero put it: 'The Creator is Himself, at one and the same time, knowledge, the knower, and the known ... There exists nothing which is not united to Him and which He does not find in His own essence. He is the type of all being, and all things exist in Him under their most pure and most perfect form.'[20]

Jewish mystical practice literally assumes that the part may indeed be taken for the whole. Made from the same basic substance as the stars, a man could become one with the most distant star; vibrating with the same energy as the birds, he could learn their language.

Although the universe is one, there are different levels of reality which correspond to the physical, psychological, spiritual and divine worlds. They are, however, all interconnected and the physical is not despised or downrated since it is the dwelling of God. In the eleventh century, for instance, Bahya ben Joseph ibn Paquda, a judge in the rabbinical court at Saragossa, Spain, encouraged students in *The Book of Direction to the Duties of the Heart* to begin with a study of nature before moving to a more abstract plane. Of the ten gates it is necessary to pass through in the practice of 'self-reckoning', the first is to realize the unity of God in the plurality of the creation. This can be done by studying the active workings of the divine in nature. Indeed, the intensive study of the organic world will enable a person to understand the prevailing philosophical, social and artistic systems on earth. Bahya therefore advised his disciple to investigate minutely every aspect of nature, just as a modern ecologist would. 'The relationship between seed, soil and the growth of fully developed plants; the changing colours of light at dawn and dusk, the seasons, even the insect crawling across the wall in front of him may elevate a man to the level of Awe.'[21] A disciple eventually leaves the realm of Awe for the more deeply personal realm of Love. The study of nature enables a person to unify the physical and the spiritual, but the final goal is his loving encounter with God.

One of the earliest forms of ecstatic contemplation was to explore the 'cosmic body'. Since man is made in God's image, Abot de Rabbi Nathan wrote in the second century, 'one man is equivalent to all Creation. One man is a World in miniature,'[22] Although this might appear anthropomorphic, it linked the person to the planet. Kabbalists imagined journeying along the body until they reached the nine paths within the beard of the formless Absolute.

A mystic brotherhood tried to put into practice Bahya's teachings in the northern Galilee town of Safed in the sixteenth century. In a system modelled on the Essene commune, all members participated in the work of their own homes and the community. Under the influence of Solomon Alkabez, a group calling themselves the *Chaverin* ('comrades') tried to turn their hearts into the 'abode of the *Shekhinah*' (immanent presence and female aspect of God) and to purify their minds and bodies by refraining from cruelty to animals as well as hypocrisy and anger. Further inspired by Moses Cordovero, they attempted among other 'divine attributes' to achieve forbearance in the face of insult, patience in enduring evil, pardon to the point of erasing the evil suffered, total identification with their neighbour, and compassion for the suffering without judging them.[23]

As concrete images are more easily reinforced than abstract terms, Cordovero taught his disciples to picture their own body as an analogue of the great cosmic tree of life. The image of the tree of life is central to Kabbalah. 'What is this Tree that you speak of?' asked the twelfth century *Book of Bahir* in Provence. 'All the Divine Powers are arranged in a series of layers like a Tree, and as a tree brings forth fruit when watered so do the Divine Powers when charged with the water of God.'[24]

The crown of the cosmic tree is humility – the key to all. It stands above the branches of understanding and wisdom, which in turn stand above judgement and loving kindness and so on. In all there are ten Sefirot, that is, divine attributes or manifestations of the Absolute, which make up the tree. At the bottom of the tree is the most accessible part of the divine body – the very presence of the living God in the world, known as *Shekhinah* or *Matrona*, the mother of the universe. The Kabbalist or *chaver* learned to unify his 'male' and 'female' selves in marriage and work until he was ready for total ascetic isolation. He would eventually leave behind his ego and find his personal life cycle indistinguishable from that of the universe.

Perhaps the greatest Kabbalist was Isaac Luria, known as Ari, born in Jerusalem in 1534. After travelling and studying the *Zohar* for eight years, he eventually moved to Safed and became its leading teacher after the death of Cordovero. Ari taught that one should love all creatures without preference. Like the Jains in India, he carefully avoided harming even insects and worms, insisting that they too could evolve through the transmigration of souls. Everything was sacred and alive. Even inanimate things could be communicated with through the language of the spirit. In order to achieve 'mindfulness', Ari encouraged his disciples to follow strict rituals and meditative techniques.

Although concerned with the ultimate meeting with God, Kabbalists were not otherworldly. Meditating on something in this world – a tree, a body or a letter of the alphabet – was tantamount to meditating on the entire creation. In fact, there are very close parallels between practices of the *Zohar* and Taoist meditation. Both try to achieve enlightenment through gradual nonattachment. Both compare the human body to the macrocosm, the Kabbalists' cosmic man and tree of spheres being very close to the Taoists' 'diagram of the ultimateless'. Finally, both see all things interdependent and unity in diversity, culminating in the Universal One.[25]

While much of Kabbalah is esoteric and opaque, the movement known as Hasidism for the first time tried to make Jewish mysticism accessible to the masses through simple prayers. It was Baal Shem Tov who took the cosmology and practice of Lurianic Kabbalah and made it into a popular system. Like the teachers of the 'crazy wisdom' of Zen Buddhism, Hasidic enthusiasts used antics to awaken their followers. For them ecstasy did not occur as a result of arduous contemplation of the worlds within worlds, but as 'a spontaneous overflow of energy in response to *this* world and to the God that lives in its every stone, crawling insect, and child'.[26] Rejecting the legalistic 'small way' of the fastidious observance of commandments and rituals, they advocated the 'great way' of uniting with God suddenly and overwhelmingly, breaking through 'all skies in one act'. For Baal Shem Tov, a person's prayer completes God, for man is a divine spark: 'Every single letter contains universes, souls and godliness, and as they ascend one is bound to the other and they become unified.'[27]

This holistic way of perceiving the world comes through even stronger in the work of his disciple Dov Baer in the eighteenth century. This itinerant preacher, known as the Maggid of Mezerich, told his followers: 'Think of your soul as part of the Divine Presence as the raindrop in the sea.'[28] Even though some Hasidic disciples wished to subdue the 'animal self' through prayer, rituals and the Torah as a means of releasing the divine spark within humanity, it did not imply a dualistic separation between spirit and body. Such prayer continually spiritualized the entire physical world, including animal, vegetable and mineral life.

The most important ecological message of Kabbalah is that the universe forms not only an integrated whole but all within it is interrelated. The *Zohar* declares:

> When the Holy One who created the Universe wished to reveal its hidden aspect, the light within the darkness, He showed how things were intermingled. Thus out of darkness comes light and from the concealed comes the revealed. In the same manner does good emerge from evil and Mercy from Justice since they are intertwined.[29]

In the cosmic tree of the divine attributes, there is a universal process of balanced interaction between upper and lower, active and passive principles. Like a tree on a mountainside, for Kabbalists, the deeper one penetrates the earth, the higher one reaches into the heavens. And God is everywhere, all in one and one in all.

# 9

# CHRISTIANITY

## *The Good Shepherd*

Praise be, my Lord, for our sister, Mother Earth.
St Francis of Assissi

Many of the ecological ills of modern civilization may be traced to the Judaeo-Christian tradition. The anthropocentric trend in Judaism was reinforced in Christianity by the Greek Stoic view of man's superiority over the rest of nature and the Gnostic stress on the corrupt nature of the physical world. Christianity not only stands accused of deep-seated patriarchy (woman after all is presented as man's 'spare rib' and Adam 'rules' over Eve), but it has also been called 'the most anthropocentric religion the world has seen'.[1]

By giving man 'dominion' over the earth, God would seem to have endorsed the wholesale exploitation of the earth and its creatures. By encouraging man to multiply and subdue nature, God apparently took no heed of the pressure of human population on limited resources and other species. Man moreover is portrayed as being metaphysically unique in having a 'living soul' whereas the 'beasts' are lost in sensuality. In order to release the soul, the Church taught that it was necessary to crush the 'beast' within the body. Finally, the doctrine of eternal punishment and the torture of the damned hardly encouraged the kind treatment of other creatures.

By denying that nature is sacred, traditional Christianity implies that man has no moral obligations towards it.[2] In 1930 John Dickie, professor of systematic theology at Aberdeen University and moderator of the General Assembly of the Church of Scotland, summed up Christian teaching on nature as follows: 'The world exists for our sakes and not for its own. That follows from the truth that it is only personal beings capable of responding to Love that be objects of Love in the true meaning of the term. God wills the world therefore as a means, but only as a means.'[3]

The teaching of the Gospels only confirms the Old Testament's depiction of man as the lord of creation. They are lacking in any injunction against cruelty to animals or any recommendation to consider their interests. Christ may have been with the 'wild beasts' (Mark 1:13) during his temptation in the wilderness, but the key events in his life and death – his crucifixion and resurrection – take place in man-made gardens. His main encounter with the natural elements was to show his mastery, as when he stilled the wind and walked on water (Mark 4:35–41). God may know every sparrow who falls to the the ground (Matthew 10:29) but Jesus appears to have been indifferent to the sufferings of animals and the wellbeing of plants. Referring to the incident where Jesus induced two thousand swine to hurl themselves into the sea, and to the episode in which Jesus cursed a fig tree, St Augustine wrote:

> Christ himself shows that to refrain from the killing of animals and the destroying of plants is the height of superstition, for judging that there are no common rights between us and the beasts and trees, he sent the devils into a herd of swine and with a curse withered the tree on which he found no fruit ... Surely the swine had not sinned, nor had the tree.[4]

Jesus, according to this interpretation, was not punishing or blaming the swine and tree; he merely demonstrated that animals and plants are not part of our moral community and we can do with them as we like.

This has generally been the dominant Christian view of nonhuman creatures. St Thomas Aquinas in his vast *Summa Theologica* summed up the attitude to the natural world which prevailed in Christendom until the Reformation and continues in Roman Catholicism. Aquinas tried to reconcile theology with philosophy, especially that of Aristotle. In the outcome, he adopted the Greek philosopher's teleology and his dualism between man and nature:

> There is no sin in using a thing for the purpose for which it is. Now the order of things is such that the imperfect are for the perfect ... things, like plants which merely have life, are all alike for animals, and all animals are for man. Wherefore it is not unlawful if men use plants for the good of animals, and animals for the good of man, as the Philosopher [Aristotle] states [*Politics*, I, 3].[5]

Aquinas goes on to refer to Genesis 1:29, 30 and 9:3 to support his
view that it was God's commandment for man to kill animals for his
own use. Moreover, he nowhere says that cruelty to animals is wrong;
indeed, there is no category for sins against them. If this is not plain
enough, Aquinas insists that charity does not extend to irrational
creatures since they are 'not competent, properly speaking, to possess
good' and cannot attain the fellowship of everlasting happiness.[6]

Aware of the Old Testament injunction 'The just regardeth the life
of his beast' (Proverbs 12: 10), Aquinas recognizes that it is possible to
feel pity for animals which are sensible to pain. But it is recommended
purely because it will make a person more disposed to take pity on his
fellow men. From a rational point of view – which is paramount – 'it
matters not how man behaves to animals, because God has subjected
all things to man's power . . . and it is in this sense that the Apostle
says that God has no care for oxen, because God does not ask of
man what he does with oxen or other animals'.[7]

Since Aquinas' views became part of the canon of the Roman
Catholic Church, it comes as no surprise to learn that as late as
the middle of the nineteenth century, Pope Pius IX refused to allow
a society for the Prevention of Cruelty to Animals to be established
in Rome on the grounds that to do so would imply that human beings
have duties towards animals.


## Sacred groves and wells

Traditional Christianity, like Judaism, is monotheistic, and the first
commandment was to worship only Yahweh, and not gods, spirits
or idols. God is presented as a transcendent deity, separated from
the world, partly in order to distance it from earlier pantheistic
cults. But the process had dire consequences for nature. By banish-
ing pagan animism, it became much easier to exploit nature for it
was no longer considered sacred and protected by guardian spirits.
Early Christians cut down the sacred groves of northern Europe
where pagans worshipped their deities. (Indeed, the practice may
well be behind the ritual of felling Christmas trees.) Christians
became indifferent to the supposed feelings and interests of natural
objects. People no longer felt obliged to placate a guardian spirit
before cutting down a tree, mining a mountain or blocking a river.

Since, with the Fall of man, nature became corrupt, it became a
symbol of the absence of God's grace. The earth, too, in its wild

state, untransformed by man, was considered particularly dangerous, a permanent threat to Christian civilization. Adam and Eve were blissful in the Garden of Eden before they were expelled, and Jesus spent much of his time in gardens. The image of the Promised Land in the Bible is a well-tended garden where man has perfected nature. The traditional Christian view of wilderness is that of a cursed land, 'the antipode of paradise'.[8] So powerful was this theme in the Old and New Testaments that nature was considered worthless until 'humanized'. The Christian approach to wilderness in the New World, in both North and South America, was one of subjugation and conquest and continues to be so. Not only was a good Indian a dead one, but a good prairie was a fenced prairie.

Even this century, many Christians continue to argue that man has dominion over corrupt nature and its creatures. The Catholic archbishop Robert Dwyer attacked in Los Angeles in 1973 the 'worship of the Environment' and the 'new cult of Nature Unspoiled' as 'anti-human'. Wilderness was a constant threat to civilization and the country could easily invade the cities. Instead of adopting an ecological perspective, it was better to consider 'Nature as Enemy, the alien force, to be conquered and broken to man's will'.[9]

## Gnosticism and the beast within

The separation of man from nature, spirit from matter and soul from body became a central feature of Christianity. In the Great Chain of Being, man's place was given as halfway between the 'angels' and the 'beasts'; his task was to suppress the latter within him in order to emulate the former. Only by denying his 'natural' instincts could he achieve eternal bliss. In order to realize his 'divine' nature, man must crush the 'beast within' and release himself from ties to the external world. Christianity is therefore fundamentally otherworldly – the goal of every Christian is to save his soul and enter heaven. His temporary passage on earth is the testing ground for the future; in itself, the earth has no value.

This dualistic view deep within Christianity was strongly influenced by the Gnostics, a cult which first developed in Palestine in the first century BC. They in turn were probably influenced by Zoroastrianism, developed by the Persian poet Zoroaster about 1500 BC, which taught that the world was the battleground of two separate good and evil forces. The Manichees further developed the concept

of the universe in the grip of two opposing forces in Persia during
the second century AD. Manicheism portrayed God as the ruler of
light, Satan as the ruler of darkness. Satan has imprisoned Adam in
a material body, but God has sent Christ, a being created from his
own substance, to offer the means by which humanity can claim
their divine inheritance. Since nature is fallen and the body steeped
in sin, the Manichees laid great stress on self-control and asceticism,
condemning the eating of animal food not because it was cruel but
because all flesh was unclean.

This disenchanted attitude to the body and the material world
comes through in Gnosticism, which stressed salvation through
secret 'knowledge of the true nature of things' (gnosis). Although
the Gnostics were considered heretics by the Church Fathers of
the second century, their sharp dualism between spirit and matter
profoundly influenced traditional Christianity. Their system opposed
a transcendent and hidden God to an ignorant demiurge, or creator.
The cosmos is evil, and governed by a malicious and tyrannical
deity. All matter is part of the satanic darkness that emerged from
chaos.[10]

Not only the cosmos but also humanity are fundamental errors.
Fashioning a world in error, the demiurge created an abortive race
of humans. Indeed, the doctrine that man is steeped in original sin
is the cornerstone of Gnostic theology; man is Satan's creature and
can do no good works. His body is a fabric of pollution. The creation
of woman is an even greater source of evil, for procreation is the
multiplication of souls in bondage to the powers of darkness.

But there is a way out of this darkness and chaos on earth. Man
has a soul which is not made by the demiurge and alone possesses
divine light. Nevertheless, only a few 'spiritual' humans are destined
for salvation, awakened by Christ, in the form of gnosis. Only they
are able to leave the prison of their body and cross the planetary
spheres of hostile demons to be reunited with God. Alone man is
literally hopeless, but with Christ there is hope. Through knowledge
(gnosis) of Christ one can love the transcendent God.

By identifying nature with evil as the Gnostics did, Christianity
encouraged the dualistic separation between matter and spirit, body
and soul. The Christian rejection of metempsychosis, or transmigration of souls, further separated nature from man. After death the
soul of the Christian was destined to either heaven or hell, not to
be reincarnated in an animal or a tree. After all, you might think

twice about eating flesh if you thought that the chicken you were about to eat was once your grandmother.

The early Christian Church in Rome further institutionalized dualism. It brought into the Roman world the idea of the uniqueness of man, insisting even more than the Greeks on the importance of man's immortal soul. By taking the creator out of the creation, traditional Christianity dissolved the holy in the world. By investing all spiritual power in its clergy, the Church tried to suppress traditional forms of spirituality as pagan and to strip nature of its primeval magic and mystery. The Church then claimed to be the sole interpreter of divine truth, using biblical verses like 'God fixed the earth upon its foundation, not to be moved forever' to check any opposition to its anthropocentric and hierarchical creed.

From this perspective, Western science and technology simply reflect traditional Christian arrogance towards nature. Since man was capable of receiving God's grace and Christ had come to redeem man on the cross, many Christians came to believe that humanity could create a new Garden of Eden by transforming nature. The results of this ultimate arrogance are now being felt throughout the world.

## Green saints and heretics

Although Christianity may be the most anthropocentric religion in the world, there has been an ecological undercurrent in the Christian tradition which has tried to bridge the gap between humanity and the creation and to stress man's responsible stewardship.

But while there have been a few ecologically aware Christians in the past, they remained a minority current and their teachings were often fraught with contradictions. The sixth-century St Benedict of Nursia was the first to call for a new attitude to nature. He founded the abbey of Monte Cassino in Italy and his followers spread his monastic system throughout Europe. Not only was he a pioneer of a theology of the earth but he has been called the 'patron saint of those who believe that true conservation means not only protecting nature against human misbehaviour but also developing human activities which favour a creative, harmonious relationship between man and nature'.[11]

St Benedict was the first to encourage monks to employ themselves in manual labour as well as religious exercises. He implied in his writings that labour is a kind of prayer which creates paradise out of chaotic wilderness. The Benedictine monks drained swamps, cleared forests, improved fields and tended gardens. In their sheltered life, they worked as farmers and builders, establishing close contact with the natural world in their daily and seasonal rituals.

Benedict stands in the green pantheon for stewardship and husbandry. But is keeping herb gardens and stealing honey from bees central to ecological awareness? Are the monastic rules of chastity, obedience and poverty guides for ecological living? Is improving God's creation or giving it a more 'human' expression truly ecological? The kind of improvement of nature undertaken by followers of St Benedict is precisely the kind of development that defenders of the wilderness today are trying to stop. Mankind, Benedict believed, was in charge of the world and ought to manipulate nature to his own best interests, even if nature was ultimately God's property and not his own. His self-interest might be enlightened but it is self-interest none the less.

Another saint to adopt a green mantle was St Bernard of Clairvaux in the twelfth century. He was the founder of the Cistercian order, an ascetic and eloquent man. A strong ecological sensibility comes through his writings and he underplays the division between man and nature and the mind and the body.

He was not afraid of the wilderness, and learned of God in the book of nature rather in the works of man. He wrote: 'What I know of the divine sciences and Holy Scripture, I learnt in woods and fields. I have had no other masters than the beeches and the oaks.' In another letter, he says: 'Listen to a man of experience: thou wilt learn more in the woods than in books. Trees and stones will teach thee more than thou canst acquire from the mouth of magister.'

He maintained that as spiritual creatures we have a need of a body in order to obtain knowledge of those things that make us blessed. He also held that God 'in his simple substance, is all everywhere equal', although he can only be comprehended by rational creatures.[12] Yet at the same time, Bernard was a fighting father of the Catholic Church. He drew up the statutes of the Knights Templar in 1128 and helped kindle the enthusiasm in France of the second crusade against Islam.

The saint who had the greatest green vision was the thirteenth-century St Francis of Assisi. Certainly St Francis was an outstanding exception in the Christian tradition in his treatment of nonhumans.

The son of a merchant, he spent a youth pursuing pleasure until he decided to live a life of poverty. He founded in 1209 the Order of Friars Minor, who were distinguished by their joyous worship of Christ and their voluntary poverty. In 1224, he is supposed to have received stigmata on Mount Alvernia. He was canonized two years after his death. He is usually depicted in a drab green or brown cassock with a winged crucifix before him, preaching to the birds or kneeling before a crib.

Unlike St Benedict, St Francis considered all life forms and even inanimate things to be part of the fellowship of God. He considered all creatures equal and interrelated. For him there is no hierarchy, no chain of being or dualism but a seamless web of life.

Unlike Christ, he showed kindness towards nonhuman creatures on many occasions. He often removed, like a Jain monk, worms from paths to prevent them from being injured. He wanted to pray to the emperor to issue an edict prohibiting anyone from catching or imprisoning 'my sisters the larks, and ordering that all who have oxen or asses should at Christmas feed them particularly well'. He extended the moral community to embrace wild and dangerous animals. It is said that he gave sermons to birds and pacified a man-eating wolf in the village of Gubbio by reminding him of his membership in the Christian community.

There are many stories of his kindness to mammals, birds and fishes. Unlike Jesus, who worked miracles with dead fish, when St Francis was offered a large fish, he addressed it as brother in his usual way and put it back into the water. The fish, his disciple and biographer St Bonaventura records, 'played about in the water in front of the man of God; and as if it were attracted by his love, it would not go away from the ship until it received from him permission with a blessing'.[13]

If not in a mystical trance St Francis seems to have spent much of his time in a state of heightened consciousness. His contemporaries described him as taking 'inward and outward delight' in almost every creature. This delight was also inspired by water, rocks, flowers and trees. And it was not only creatures that he called sisters; he addressed a canticle to 'Brother Sun, Sister Moon':

> Praise be, my Lord, for our sister,
> Mother Earth,
> Who sustains and governs us

And brings forth diverse fruits with
many-hued flowers and grass.

Nevertheless, St Francis's ecstatic love for all creatures did not affect his anthropocentric view of the universe which was in keeping with medieval Christian theology. The sun itself, he thought, shone for man and he affirmed: 'Every creature proclaims: "God madde me for your sake, O man!"' And while he called all creatures his brothers and sisters and felt compassion for them, he still apparently continued to eat them. In his rules for his order of friars, he suggested only that they should abstain from meat on certain fast days.[14]

One story goes that when a brother fell ill and told his fellow disciples that he had a longing for pig's trotters, the latter in 'great fervour of spirit' cut the trotters off a living pig. St Francis upbraided them, not however for the callousness of the act but rather for having damaged someone's property. He urged him to apologize to the owner of the pig, not to the pig itself.[15]

St Francis's attitude to nature seems to have been very close to that of the Psalms, where nature is seen as worshipping God. As his disciple St Bonaventura makes clear in the opening of *The Soul's Journey to God*, the natural world is not valuable in its own right but as part of God's creation: 'Whoever is not enlightened by such splendour of created things is blind for every creature is by its nature a kind of effigy and likeness of the eternal wisdom.'

Although the Franciscan order flourished, St Francis's view of animals and birds had little influence in the Catholic Church. Franciscan theologians continued to accept the mainstream Aristotelian-Stoic separation between man and animals. While Protestant biographers tend to stress St Francis's fellowship with nature, Catholic ones emphasize his orthodoxy. In the past, he has been remembered more for his voluntary poverty than for his ecological sensibility. Nevertheless, St Francis stands out in the Christian tradition for his spiritual egalitarianism and his readiness to see birds, wolves and rocks as members of a spiritual family. As part of God's creation, the nonhuman world had an intrinsic value separate from man.

Although condemned as a heretic, the German Johannes Eckhart deserves rehabilitation as a green saint. He joined the Dominican order and was appointed vicar-general of Bohemia in 1307. He taught a mystical version of pantheism, of God in nature. When arraigned in 1325 for heresy by the archbishop of Cologne, he abjured any possible religious errors which he might have made.

Eckhart's starting point and end is that God forms the divine ground of all things: 'The more God is in all things, the more He is outside them. The more He is within, the more without.' God is immanent and transcendent, one in all and all in one. The divine is within us as it is within nature; indeed, 'any flea as it is in God is nobler than the highest of the angels in himself'. Again, 'every creature is a word about God and is a book of God'.

Like Eastern mystics, Eckhart thought that people should think less about what they ought to do and more about what they ought to be. Spiritual growth involves going beyond a sense of this or that, of mine and yours; it involves identifying with the whole of the universe. Man's final end is to love, know and be united with the universal divine spirit.

Two years after his death in 1327, Eckhart's writings were condemned by Pope John XXII, and they are still considered by orthodox theologians to be too pantheistic. This, however, has not prevented them from influencing philosophy and providing fertile soil for an ecological sensibility.

One of the most influential Catholic theologians to reconsider our place in nature was Pierre Teilhard de Chardin (1881–1955). A French Jesuit priest, geologist and palaentologist, he was in his lifetime also forbidden by his superiors in the Catholic Church to publish his unorthodox views. Chardin saw no conflict between faith and science, and believed in a unitary concept, based on science, of the world and Christ. Christianity and evolution, for instance, are not two irreconcilable points of view, but 'two ways of looking at things that are designed to dovetail together, each completing the other'.[16] He argued that the course of evolution was towards increasing consciousness and complexity and the goal of history was to reach an 'Omega Point' in which man would become one with God. In his philosophy of 'creative union' of God and the world, he stressed the priority of the whole in the universe, seeing the myriads of life forms making up one immense unity. In our evolutionary phase of the cosmos, everything happens 'as though the One were formed by successive unifications of the Multiple'.[17]

He not only adopted process metaphysics, seeing everything developing and interrelated, but considered matter to be charged with spiritual power. Spirit and matter are not therefore opposed as two separate things, but two directions of evolution within the world. The

spirit of God not only insinuates everywhere but it sustains everything in the universe:

> From the ultimate vibration of the atom to the loftiest mystical
> contemplation; from the lightest breeze that ruffles the air to
> the broadest currents of life and thought, he [Christ] ceaselessly
> animates, without disturbing, all earth's processes. And in return
> Christ gains physically from every one of them. Everything that
> is good in the universe (that is, everything that goes towards
> unification through effort) is gathered up by the Incarnate
> Word as a nourishment that it assimilates, transforms and
> divinises.[18]

Teilhard de Chardin sought to teach how to see God everywhere, 'to
see him in all that is most hidden, most solid, and most ultimate in
the world'. There is a general 'drift' of matter towards spirit. Just
as every process of material growth in the universe is ultimately
directed towards spirit, so every process of spiritual growth is directed
towards Christ.

Teilhard de Chardin sees his ideas as a superior form of pantheism.
Tradional pantheism gives only 'fusion and unconsciousness';
Christianity on the other hand pushes to the furthest possible limit
the 'differentiation among creatures'. Ultimately the goal of human
history is to move beyond the earth to God. Whereas the pagan
pantheist loves the earth in order to enjoy it and confine himself
within it, the Christian does so in order 'to make it purer and draw
from it the strength to escape from it'.[19]

Teilhard de Chardin transcended the view of man as the geometric
and static centre of the universe by presenting him as an evolving
creature riding the cosmic wave towards spirit. Yet he embraced
the Enlightenment idea of progress through science, and the gradual ascent of technological man. 'Superhumanity', in his view, is
biologically inevitable. Homo sapiens is metaphysically unique, the
only species which in spreading over the globe has resisted division
into further species.

For all his organic awareness, Teilhard de Chardin was unable to go
beyond the traditional Christian concern with man's multiplication of
his species and his domination and control of the world. 'God's first
wish', he insists, 'is that his creatures should increase and multiply.
And to be true to him they must first develop themselves and conquer
the world.'[20]

Above all, Teilhard de Chardin's view of man's stewardship was not one of a partner in development, but rather the captain or overseer. He called on man in no uncertain terms 'to seize the tiller of creation'; the ship might be earth sailing in the ocean of space but the animals are the crew. Teilhard de Chardin's steward is the sublunary director of the universe.

## The greening of Christianity

Despite the devastating ecological legacy of mainstream Christianity, there has not only been an attempt to rehabilitate 'green saints' but also to argue that 'God is green'. But it requires more than merely 'stripping off a whole series of alien layers that have accumulated to reveal the original greenness of the Garden of Eden and the cross of Calvary'.[21] It is almost impossible to reconcile Christianity with those ecologists who make a religion of ecology and revere nature in a pantheistic or pagan way. Worship of the earth goddess has no place within Christianity.

The most substantial green revision of Christianity has been to interpret man's God-given dominion over nature not in terms of control but of stewardship. This interpretation can partially be supported by God's placing of Adam into the Garden of Eden in order 'to dress it and to keep it' (Genesis 2:15). The 'dominion' of Genesis from this point of view is interpreted as a form of trusteeship: man was thus directed to take care of the rest of God's creation, not to conquer and exploit it. He might be the most privileged creature on earth and unique in having an immortal soul, but his earthly task is to look after the wellbeing of the planet.

A better case for a progressive Christian notion of stewardship might be made from the 'covenant' God is said to have made with Noah after the flood: 'This *is* the token of the covenant which I make between me and you and every living creature that *is* with you, for perpetual generations' (Genesis 9: 12, Cf. 6: 17–20). Indeed, it has even been argued that the tale of Noah and his ark is an 'ecological parable' which tells of God's concern for his creatures and points to the role of humans as stewards and protectors of other species. From this perspective, Noah appears as a wildlife conservationist.[22]

But can this really be so? God first makes man the lord of creation. When man does wrong, God then wipes out virtually all the innocent creatures on earth. He then makes man a steward over the creation. In reality, man's 'stewardship' hardly appears an improvement over his lordship. It still involves domesticating animals, keeping wild ones at bay, and killing for meat.

Even those who try to argue that 'God is green' recognize that the Bible portrays humans as occupying a unique place in nature and fulfilling a key role in the working-out of God's plan for the whole of creation. The Bible presents nature as incomplete and assigns a special role to humans to improve and perfect it. This attitude was put most persuasively by the English judge Matthew Hale in the seventeenth century:

> The end of man's creation was that he should be the viceroy of the great God of heaven and earth in this inferior world; his steward, bailiff or farmer of this goodly farm of the lower world. Only for this reason was man invested with power, authority, right, dominion, trust and care, to correct and abridge the excesses and cruelties of the fiercer animals, to give protection and defence to the mansuete and useful, to preserve the species of divers vegetables, to improve them and others, to correct the redundance of unprofitable vegetables, to preserve the face of the earth in beauty, usefulness and fruitfulness.[23]

The whole tone of the passage displays an arrogant and interfering attitude to the rest of the creation. It is noteworthy that Hale describes man's stewardship in terms of an imperialistic viceroy, of a bailiff who carries out the wishes of his property-owning landlord, of an improving farmer and gardener. The saying that you are never nearer God than in a garden may well be right: in a garden, man is fulfilling his special role as improver of rude nature. But ownership itself is a form of theft if not slavery. It is difficult to extend the notion of stewardship to the sea or to wilderness areas outside human interference and control.

The notion of stewardship raises more questions that it solves. Why should humans be 'charged with the awesome responsibility of carrying the rest of creation up to God'?[24] Why do animals need us to find God, or the physical world need us to be lifted up to God? Indeed, why should man be responsible for the rest of the creation?

The type of stewardship presented in Genesis is far from inspiring. The covenant between God and Noah from which the notion of stewardship is derived comes *after* God 'delivered' all the creatures into the hands of Noah and his sons, suggested that the 'fear of you and the dread of you' will be upon all of them, and offered 'every moving thing that liveth'[9] as meat for them (Genesis 9:2–3). After the flood, Noah might have become a 'husbandman' and planted a vineyard, but he and his offspring continued to use nature for their own ends and exploit and kill animals to eat.

The most persuasive concept of stewardship asserts that nature belongs to God and not to human beings. It stresses that God originally liked the world he created, finding it 'very good' (Genesis 1:31). However much it violates the original Hebrew meaning, from this perspective 'dominion' means loving care. Nature is not to be valued merely as a useful object or instrument, but for itself; that is to say, nature has intrinsic value. But few Christians are ready to accept that man is an equal member with other species in a biotic community. One such theologian is the American Paul Santmire, who has adopted St Francis's idea of 'sister earth' to argue that God, humanity and nature form a system of interrelationships. In this context, nature and civilization are 'fellow citizens of the Kingdom of God', each with certain inalienable rights.[25] Nature has its own right to natural fulfilment.

The American philosopher John Cobb has also recently tried to develop a theology of ecology. Inspired by the belief that all matter is significant for the universe, he argued that it also has intrinsic value in the eyes of God. As such the nonhuman world has rights which humans should respect. Cobb extends the natural rights to liberty, life and happiness, enshrined in the American Constitution, to the nonhuman world.[26]

But despite his fine effort, Cobb's theology is embedded in his atomistic culture. The liberal theory of rights is applied to individuals, and he fails to make clear in his 'religion of life' how a subatomic particle can be said to have a right in the same way as an oak tree, an elephant or an ecosystem. What criteria will decide when a conflict of rights arises? In addition, rights are a quasilegalistic notion and require a coercive agency, usually in the form of government, to enforce them. Above all, in his scheme man is still at the top of the pile: 'The new Christianity must substitute a vision of a healthy biotic pyramid with man at its apex for the absoluteness of man.'[27]

The most fruitful development in modern theology, however, has been the gradual recognition amongst more radical Christians that nature is God's and not man's, thereby recognizing nature to have an intrinsic value and an independent claim to exist and flourish. It follows that it is morally wrong to harm nature and its creatures, even if it might appear to benefit humanity in the short term.

Another way of greening Christianity is to play down the difference between man and the rest of the creation. Although God made man in his image and breathed into him a 'living soul' – something not extended to the beasts of the field who preceded him – he is made from the 'dust of the ground'. Man therefore comes from the earth as much as he comes from the heavens.

In addition, the doctrine of the incarnation can be interpreted to show that God clothed himself in the form of a human body in Jesus. The physical body cannot therefore be wholly bad.

Rather than stressing the transcendence or the hidden nature of God, it is possible to make a case for God sustaining the whole of nature. This comes through in Psalm 104: 10–19.

> He sendeth the springs into the valleys, *which* run among the hills.
> They give drink to every beast of the field: the wild asses quench their thirst.
> By them shall the fowls of the heavens have their habitation, which sing among the branches.
> He watereth the hills from his chambers: the earth is satisfied with the fruits of thy works . . .
> The trees of the LORD are full *of sap*; the cedars of Lebanon, which he hath planted . . .
> He appointed the moon for seasons: the sun knoweth his going down.

But the stress in the Psalm is still on the mighty power of God and the advantage to man of his wonderful providence: 'He causeth the grass to grow for the cattle, and herb for the service of man: that he may bring forth food out of the earth' (Psalm 104:14).

The Old Testament seems less anthropocentric in the book of Job, where the prophet cries to God for an explanation of his suffering. The answer comes in a series of questions in which God reminds Job that much of what happens on earth has no relevance to man:

> Who hath divided a watercourse for the overflowing of waters, or a way for the lightning of thunder;

To cause it to rain on the earth, *where* no man *is*; *on* the wilderness, wherein *there is* no man;
To satisfy the desolate and waste *ground*; and to cause the bud of the tender herb to spring forth? [Job 38:25–7]

Who hath sent out the wild ass free? or who hath loosed the bands of the wild ass?
Whose house I have made the wilderness, and the barren land his dwellings. [39:5–6]

The wild ass might well be an exemplar of the modern ecologist who makes it his duty to defend the wild, natural and free. But the predominant attitude towards the wilderness in the Bible is one of fear. The Israelites, for instance, pass through wild deserts as a scourge searching for the Promised Land which is depicted as a country well-managed by man – a land overflowing with milk and honey, products stolen from animals and insects by man.

These passages from Job, it might be argued, present animals and birds, plants and rivers as having value in their own right, outside the control and interference of man. But the purpose behind the nature poetry is to humble Job and to convince him of God's mighty works and his own ignorance and imbecility. At the end of his rhetorical questioning, God refers to the Leviathan and asks Job: 'Canst thou fill his skin with barbed irons? or his head with fish spears?' (41:7)

The question seems singularly inapt nowadays. Man with his exploding harpoons and factory ships has hunted the descendants of Leviathan to near extinction. The whale might have helped Jonah in his salvation and repentance, sheltering him for three days and nights, but the sons of Jonah who take to their boats to hunt the sea's most intelligent mammal do not return the compliment.

God finally asks Job about Leviathan: 'Will he make a covenant with thee? Wilt thou take him for a servant for ever?' (41:4) The question clearly demonstrates the nature of the covenant God had in mind between Noah and the creatures of the earth. It is not an agreement made by equal parties in a commonwealth, but a contract between unequals, between master and servant. Thomes Hobbes did not miss the point when he called his apology for state dictatorship *Leviathan* (1651).

It is difficult not to conclude that the Bible rejects reverence of nature in favour of worship of a transcendent and wrathful God. However, Christianity evolves like any other religion, and has taken on board the ecological concern with the wellbeing of the earth as a whole and not merely the salvation of humanity. No longer satisfied with human history, it embraces the history of the cosmos and all within it.

Inspiration may be drawn from the Eastern Orthodox Church, which has always been less anthropocentric than Catholic and Protestant churches. Matter for the Orthodox is never inert but animated by latent energy. God is seen as both transcendent and immanent, especially through the incarnation of Christ. Moreover, Christ's redemption is extended to the whole of the universe, not just humanity, so that physical matter made profane and corrupt by the Fall is restored to its original sacred and blessed state. The Christ of the Eastern Orthodox Church is therefore worshipped in cosmic terms as the redeemer of all creation.

Apart from stressing the nature poetry found in Psalms and the Book of Job, the new ecological tendency within Christianity celebrates a dynamic and reciprocal relationship between God and nature in a dance of creation. The text to support this interpretation is in Isaiah, where inanimate objects take on life and rejoice in the presence of God: 'For ye shall go out with joy, and be led forth with peace; the mountains and the hills shall break forth before you into singing, and all the trees of the field shall clap *their* hands' (Isaiah 55:12).

While not accepting pagan animism, an immanent and pantheistic conception of God can be culled from St Paul when he declares that 'Christ *is* all, and in all' (Colossians 3:11). This view, which rejects the transcendent or hidden God, can be supported by the doctrine of the incarnation and the practice of the sacraments as a way of recognizing God's presence through Christ in the physical world. The English theologian Don Cupitt has recently argued: 'The Gospel says that man is not a blight on nature, but crowns her; that God is not the God of the past, but of the future, and that through the incarnation of God in man redemption avails for man himself, and through man's God-inspired work, for nature.'[28]

Then of course there is Christ's teaching that tomorrow should take care of tomorrow and that we should live like the lilies in the valley.

A greener Christianity will stress the variety and fullness of God's earth, and his care for its creatures from cedars and lilies of the valley to falling sparrows. It will point out that after making the earth, 'God saw every thing that he had made, and, behold, it *was* very good' (Genesis 1:31) – and still is, despite human wickedness, greed and cruelty. This is underlined by the fact that the whole creation, especially in Psalms, praises the Lord (see Psalms 96:11–13).

Archbishop William Temple in the early twentieth century tried to elaborate a philosophy of religion which did not separate God from the creation or place an unbridgeable gap between man and animals. He argued in *Nature, Man and God* for a universe of different levels, rising in value, and interpreted God as 'Supreme Value' and hence 'Ultimate Reality'. He was concerned not only with suffering humanity and the poor but with the whole creation:

> The treatment of the Earth by man the exploiter is not only imprudent, it is sacrilegious. We are unlikely to correct our hideous mistakes in this realm unless we recover the mystical sense of our oneness with nature. Many people think this is fantastic. I think it is fundamental to our Sanity.[29]

The New Theology is now taking on board the findings of ecology. The 'green bishop' Hugh Montefiore in particular, as chair of the Board of Social Responsibility, has tried to get the Anglican Church to accept *Our Responsibility for the Living Environment* (1986). He stresses the creative task of humans: 'Man acts not only as the co-creator with God in nature but also as co-redeemer in the sense that he assists the purposes of God in the natural world.'[30]

Even the Pope made St Francis the 'patron saint of ecology' in 1980. A decade later, he eventually admitted that the Church had wronged Galileo when he was condemned by the Inquisition in 1633 for backing the Copernican view that the sun and not the earth is the centre of the known universe. The biblical view that 'God fixed the earth upon its foundation, not to be moved forever' has now been adapted to take into account modern scientific findings.

Yet despite these welcome if belated developments, there is still a long way to go to overcome the devastating legacy of Christianity in its traditional teaching of humankind's relationship with nature. A revaluation of the Christian idea of stewardship is long overdue which sees man not as the guiding force in nature but as an equal member of the biotic community and a co-partner in evolution. The view of the Christian as a good shepherd should be extended to embrace the entire creation. Then perhaps the vision of the natural world as interwoven, bounteous and good can shine forth in all its glory.

# 10

## ISLAM

### *The Goodly Tree*

Every grain of barley given to a horse is entered in
Allah's book of good deeds.

*The Qur'an*

Islam grew out of Judaism and Christianity and began in Mecca about
AD 610 when Muhammad claimed to be the messenger of God. The
dominant religion of Arabia at the time was a form of the old Semitic
religion, with shrines to various gods and goddesses in many places,
although there was also a tendency to believe in a supreme God,
Allah. The gods mentioned in the Qur'an which Islam sought to
replace are all female ones: al-Lat, al-Uzza and Manat, which
represented the Sun, the planet Venus and Fortune, respectively.
At Mecca, they were considered the daughters of Allah. Al-Uzza was
the most important for the Meccans, and tradition says that in his
youth Muhammad sacrificed a white sheep to her. The cult of al-Lat
– meaning 'the goddess' – was mentioned by the Greek historian
Herodotus; she was the great mother goddess whose worship was
widespread in the ancient world. The religion was strongly animistic
and involved the worship of a god or spirit who was believed to dwell
in stones, rocks, trees and wells. Blood sacrifices were made on the
sacred stones, while trees were hung with scraps of clothing.[1]

Islam of course tried to eradicate these beliefs, and missions were
sent out by the prophet Muhammad to smash the pagan idols. He
taught a strictly monotheistic religion; 'There is no God but Allah' is
the fundamental credo of Islam. Allah in Arabic means 'the One'. He
is supreme and all-powerful – all-seeing, all-hearing, all-willing. It is
the duty of all Muslims to worship Allah and to practise Islam, which
literally means 'surrender to God'. Although men appear to have the
freedom to choose between good and evil, ultimately it is God who
decides and controls the course of events: 'Allah guides whom he will,
and lets whom he will go astray.' Each individual is an *abd* of God, a

term which carries the twin meanings of 'worshipper' and 'servant'. All life is thus lived under the command of God.

Muslims praise God as 'the Merciful', 'the Compassionate' and 'the Generous'; he can also be a stern and wrathful figure. In a final judgement, God decides who will go to heaven or hell depending on their earthly conduct. He can destroy nations if a people misbehave and condemn individuals to eternal punishment. It is in his power to reduce the world into barren dust if his word is not heeded. In the Qur'an, it is written: 'Hast thou not seen that Allah hath created the heavens and the earth with truth? If He will, He can remove you and bring (in) some new creation' (Surah 14:19).[2]

Unlike Jesus, Muhammad did not claim to be the son of God but simply a messenger of Allah. From about AD 610 he claimed to receive messages or revelations from God through the archangel Gabriel for the benefit of humanity; these were later collected in the form of the Qur'an. Although not divine, Muhammad is considered the best of men and the last and greatest prophet in a long line which stretches back to the biblical figures of Jesus, Solomon, David, Moses, Abraham, Noah and Adam.

The universe is depicted in Islam as the personal creation of God. Since his work is faultless, it is considered perfect. It was enough for God to say 'Be' and 'It was'. This encourages an attitude of wonder and awe, for all that is in heaven and earth is seen as the glory of God. The only purpose of prayer is to thank God for his creation. 'Praise be to Allah, Lord of the Worlds' is the beginning of 'The Opening', the Lord's Prayer of the Muslims.

Islam depicts the world as an organic whole, consisting of a complex unity of multifarious parts, both material and spiritual. Muslims do not separate the spiritual and the material; indeed, the world would not be complete if the material did not embrace the spiritual. The Qur'an sees body and spirit as inseparably combined in the wholeness of worship. Islam has no term for 'spirituality'; its devotion seeks to preserve a balance between 'outer' and 'inward' aspects of life. The world is full of angels, with Gabriel the chief of them, while Satan as a fallen angel works with assistants. As the book of *Thousand and One Nights* and countless other Arabic tales narrate, the earth is peopled by djinn, or spirits, who must be appeased or avoided.

One consequence of the entwining of the physical and the material in Islam was that it permitted the early development of science. It was possible for Muslims, as for Taoists, to integrate a science of nature with a spiritual vision of the universe. Islamic scholars, encouraged by the Qur'an, practised *taffakur*, the study of nature, and *taskheer*, the mastery of nature through technology. They studied and developed classics of Greek science and philosophy lost to the West. Muslim philosophers and naturalists laid down between the ninth and fourteenth centuries the foundations of science on which Western civilization is built. Without the Islamic contribution, it is unlikely that the scientific revolution would have taken place in the seventeenth century in Europe.

Although science was able to develop within Islam because it was not seen as a threat to the faith, a 'supernatural' incentive to study the natural world was still required. This was supplied by Mahmum, caliph of Baghdad from AD 813 to 818, who saw the ghost of Aristotle in a dream and was convinced by the Greek philosopher that there was no contradiction between religion and reason. Mahmum then ordered a 'house of wisdom' to be built, and began to collect all available books in the library. The works of Greek, Persian and Indian writers were translated into Arabic and their thinking examined and developed. The result was a great flowering of knowledge about the world. Through the Muslim philosophers such as Averroes (Ibd Rushd) and Avicenna (Ibn Sina), Aristotle was rediscovered in the West.

Like the Greeks, the Muslims assumed that behind the visible chaos of the world there is a fundamental order which follows general laws and is accessible to human reason. The aim of their science was therefore to discover the basic laws of the world. But unlike Western scientists, they did not make a rigid distinction between the observer and the observed. The only way to know something is to realize it. As one mystic declared: 'If [one] loves a stone, he becomes a stone; if he loves a man, he is a man; if he loves God – I dare not say more, for if I said that he would then be God, you might stone me.'[3]

Muslims made enormous strides in both theoretical and practical knowledge. In medicine, they developed the knowledge of ancient Persia, discovered the circulation of the blood and undertook operations with anaesthetics. Their body of knowledge, known as *Avicenna* (after the great philosopher and physician Ibn Sina), was an important source for the alchemists and remained a textbook in the universities of Europe until the seventeenth century. Developing Indian mathematics, Muslims adopted the decimal system and used the concept of

zero – *sifr* (the empty one). Algebra, which uses symbols to represent
unknown quantities, was also a Muslim invention.

The Arabs had long used the stars as guides in the desert and
at sea, and references to the stars abound in the Qur'an. Coming
across the work of Ptolemy in the eighth century, they began to
study the sky more closely, and gave many names to the stars as
well as coining such terms as 'zenith', 'nadir' and 'azimuth'. They
calculated the circumference and diameter of the earth. Al-Farghani,
a ninth-century astronomer, assumed that the Ptolemaic cycles fitted
so tightly between the planetary spheres that 'there is no void
between the heavens'.[4] As great travellers and geographers, they
further mapped the known world, and their atlases and travel guides
were used well into the Middle Ages. Without them it is unlikely that
the European age of discovery would have got underway.

Bringing science and religion neatly together, the Sufi poet Jalal-
uddin Rumi declared: 'The astrolabe of the mysteries of God is love.'[5]
But while the growth of science was not hindered by religion, the same
cannot be said of Islamic art. The Qur'an taught that the object and
its image are magically united. It was probably for this reason that
representational art became prohibited. The 'Islamic style' which
developed therefore revelled in the decorative, endeavouring to turn
the natural appearance of things into abstract designs and patterns.

The Islamic occupation of southern Europe gave an enormous
impetus to Western civilization. Sicily became a centre of Arabic
philosophy and science, but the greatest influence took place in
Spain. The architecture of Muslim towns such as Córdoba and
Granada from the tenth century was magnificent. Everything was
planned to make life pleasant and agreeable, from street lighting to
ornamental baths, from marzipan to perfumed oranges. The spread
of Islamic civilization reached its peak in the thirteenth century, but
after the sacking of Baghdad by Mongol invaders in 1258 it went
into gradual decline.

## The Ladder of Being

Islam is strongly hierarchical. According to the Qur'an, Allah sits
on a high throne in the seventh heaven, surrounded by angels who
serve him the way kings are served by ministers and attendants. The
Devil is an angel who fell through pride and now with his assistants
tries to obstruct the plans of Allah on earth and to tempt men to

go astray from the right path. But because men can choose between obedience and rebellion they are superior not only to other creatures but also to the angels: God ordered the angels to prostrate themselves before them.

The created world is thus ordered into a ladder or chain of being, with God at the top, followed by the angels, humanity, animals, plants and minerals. The poet Jalal-uddin Rumi describes the ascent of the ladder as a process of spiritual evolution towards ultimate union with God:

> I died a mineral and became a plant.
> I died a plant and rose an animal.
> I died an animal and I was a man.
> Why should I fear? When was I less by dying?
> Yet once more I shall die as man, to soar
> With the blessed angels; but even from angelhood
> I must pass on. All except God perishes.
> When I have sacrificed my angel soul,
> I shall become that which no mind ever conceived.
> O, let me not exist! for Non-Existence proclaims,
> 'To Him we shall return.'[6]

It was within this framework that Persian poets saw the love of a human being as a ladder towards the love of God. Jami expressed it in this way: 'Beholding in many souls the traits of Divine beauty, and separating in each soul that which it has contracted in the world, the lover ascends to the highest beauty, to the love and knowledge of the Divinity, by steps of this ladder of created souls.'[7]

Like Judaeo-Christianity, Islam is a strongly anthropocentric religion. Man is metaphysically unique and holds a privileged position in the creation. At the centre of Islam is the belief in a primordial covenant between God and humanity, a fact of meta-history, as understood from the Qur'an. Before creation, God called the future humanity out of the loins of the not yet created Adam and said 'Am I not your Lord?' and they replied: 'Yea, verily, we testify' (7:172).

God then created the world for humanity: 'He it is Who created for you all that is in the earth' (2:29). Man is the microcosm and is created for God's sake, who in turn created everything for man's sake. Adopting the story of Adam and Eve, the Qur'an says that God created man as his *khalifa* or deputy on earth – 'a viceroy in the earth' (2:30) – whose duty is to look after it and to be good. God created the animals and plants, the sun and the moon for man's benefit and they are all forced into his service:

> He it is Who sendeth down water from the sky, whence ye may drink, and whence are trees on which ye send your beasts to pasture.
> Therewith He causeth crops to grow for you and the olive and the date-palm and grapes and all kinds of fruit. Lo! herein is indeed a portent for people who reflect.
> And He constrained the night and day and the sun and the moon to be of service unto you, and the stars are made subservient by His Command. Lo! herein indeed are portents for people who reflect.
> And whatsoever He hath created for you in the earth of divers hues, lo!, therein is indeed a portent for people who take heed [16:10–13].

While Islam condemns usury in the human sphere, it has no problems with humanity exploiting the rest of the creation.

'Know ye that every Muslim is a brother to every other Muslim,' Muhammad declared. Alms-giving is one of the basic duties of every Muslim, the key pillar of social action. It is the duty of sharing one's wealth with all who are less fortunate yet equally members of the Muslim community. The intention is more important than the amount; according to the Qur'an, when alms are offered 'in search of God's pleasure and for the strengthening of their own souls, it is as the likeness of a garden on a hill; the rainstorm smites it and it brings forth its fruit twofold'.[8]

But this love and benevolence are not extended to other creatures. The Islamic attitude to animals is that they are made for man's use and sustenance. Some animals are despised: dogs and pigs are considered unclean because they eat carrion. Whereas Hinduism made the cow sacred, the Qur'an specifically rejects their teaching as idolatry and insists 'And of the cattle (He produceth) some for burdens, some for food' (6:143). Again, it states: 'And the cattle hath He created, whence ye have warm clothing and uses, and whereof ye eat' (18:5).

Animals are invariably slaughtered for the two main feasts in the Muslim calendar. The 'little feast' takes places after a month of fasting at the end of Ramadan. The 'great feast' is the sacrifice of Id al-Adha when pilgrims outside Mecca in the neighbouring village of Mina ritually offer up live animals. The event is intended to recall Abraham's readiness to sacrifice his son to God. The Qur'an tells how in joyful recollection of God's divine mercy the pilgrims should offer the sacrifice of sheep or camels: 'their flesh and blood reach not to God, but your devotion reaches him.'[9] Muslims throughout the world join with the pilgrims in Mina for the 'Feast of Slaughter'.

### Sufis and mystical Islam

The great mystics of Islam, the Sufis, are generally anti-worldly. Their coreligionists nicknamed them Sufis from their custom of wearing garments of undyed wool (suf, 'wool'). They chose to lead a life of voluntary poverty and asceticism. They were critical of Islamic philosophy influenced by Greek thought and were particularly contemptuous of the rationalism of Ibn Sina (Avicenna). Like the Taoists, they disliked superficial cleverness and prefer the path of silence. The Hadith, a collection of stories about Muhammad's deeds and sayings, which is sometimes translated as 'traditions', asserts: 'Knowledge is the greatest veil.' In place of rational thought, the Sufis believed in intuition and immediate experience; they 'strove to lift veils, not to collect books'.[10] Within two centuries after the death of the prophet, they had worked out a detailed method of attaining the gnosis, or knowledge of God, through various practices, which included the dance of the whirling dervishes.

The early ascetics considered the created world to be a detestable veil that distracted them from God. It had no intrinsic value and its worth depended on man's relation to it. The aim of the mystic is to return to the experience of the time when only God existed, before the creation. It involves the intellectual perception of the unity of being as well as union with God.

The Sufi ascetics believed that they should not only renounce the world but renounce the happy feeling of having renounced it. The world ought to be regarded as so insignificant that it should no longer be noticed. This world is a place of exile; as one Bektashi poet wrote:

> This universe is a tree – man became its fruit.
> That which was intended is the fruit – do not think it is
> the tree![11]

The Sufis thus longed for their true home in heaven in its primeval state. Man is imprisoned in 'six walls' of the created world and must go through six doors to reach God who lives in the seventh heaven. To achieve this, they organized themselves in tightly knit groups with novices giving blind obedience to their spiritual directors; members were known as *faqirs* or *darwishes*, poor men or beggars, and devoted their lives to meditation and various physical exercises.

The most negative aspect of this otherworldly mysticism is the depiction of the earth as a hag. Despite Muhammad's praise of women, and the veneration of Fatima in Shia circles, the attitude to women of Islam in general and of Sufism in particular is ambivalent to say the least. It is written in the Qur'an:

> Men are in charge of women, because Allah hath made one of them to excel the other, and because they spend of their property (for the support of women). So good women are the obedient, guarding in secret that which Allah hath guarded. As for those from whom you fear rebellion, admonish them and banish them to beds apart, and scourge them [4:83].

In classical Sufism the world is equated with an old harridan who tries to seduce men, a mean prostitute or a mother who devours her children.[12] The lower soul, or *nafs* – man's worst enemy – is also compared to a woman who tries to ensnare the pure spirit and bring him down into the trap of worldly life. The 'animal quality' prevails in woman. This misogyny is as lamentable as any found in medieval Christianity.

However, there is another strand in Islam which sees nature as the revelation of God and the hand of God in all things and beings. It emerges from the text: 'Wherever ye turn there is the face of God.'[13] God not only created but continues to sustain life. From this perspective, it is the duty of humanity to establish a harmony between heaven and earth through right conduct and speech. 'A goodly saying, as a goodly tree, its roots set firm, its branches reaching into heaven' (14:24).

From the beginning, there were Sufis who insisted that the created world had a spiritual meaning. Since the world is God's revelation, all beings recollect God. Not only was a red rose created from Muhammad's sweat during his ascension, but according to the *Hadith*, a red rose is part of God's glory. The Qur'an further asserts that everything created worships God, expressing praise in its own tongue. Dhu'n-Nun, an Egyptian mystic of the ninth century (died 874), wrote:

> O God, I never hearken to the voices of the beasts or the rustle
> of the trees, the splashing of the waters or the song of the
> birds, the whistling of the wind or the rumble of the thunder,
> but I sense in them a testimony to Thy Unity, and a proof
> of Thy incomparability, that Thou art the All-Prevailing, and
> All-Knowing, the All-True.[14]

Many Sufis stressed the mutual love between the creator and the creature, and sought to be absorbed in God like a drop of water in the ocean. Love for love's sake is a central theme of Sufism, although it is always love for the creator and not for his creation. For Jalal-uddin Rumi, dynamic love is at the centre of all: 'If this heaven were not in love, then its breast would have no purity, and if the sun were not in love, in his beauty would be no light, and if earth and mountain were not lovers, grass would not grow out of their breast.'[15] It is only for the sake of the lovers that the sky revolves and the spheres turn, Rumi claims, and not for the sake of the baker, blacksmith, magistrate and pharmacist. The poet and saint Kabir, who was claimed by Muslims and Hindus as a coreligionist, wrote that 'the devout seeker is he who mingles in his heart the double currents of love and detachment, like the mingling of the streams of the Ganges and Jumna'.[16]

As a distinctly monotheistic, hierarchical and anthropocentric religion, Islam, like Christianity, does not have a great deal to offer in creating an ecological sensibility. Its sense of the unity of being and of the divine nature of the world, especially in its Sufi mystical tradition, is suggestive, but the general perception of this world is that of a seedbed for the afterlife, a rotting and impermanent world full of temptations and snares. Only in the nature poetry of the Sufis emerges the idea that the world is a revelation of God, and that his beauty and wisdom are revealed in the creation.

Living traditionally in such harsh environments, constantly preoccupied with survival, Muslims not surprisingly see the wilderness, especially in the form of the desert or sea, as inimical to man. Rain clouds are signs of divine mercy. Their vision of heaven is nature transformed into a resplendent garden, with singing fountains and carefully cultivated pomegranate and date trees. They long for the rest of the oasis, not the harshness of the desert which they must pass through. The voyage of life for them has long been a risky business, and the gleaming surface of divine nature which manifests itself in this world can often appear like a mirage. Not all are bold enough to take the plunge into the ocean of being. The tenth-century Muslim saint Niffari, the Egyptian, put it in characteristically enigmatic terms:

> God made me behold the sea, and I saw the ships sinking and the planks floating; then the planks too were submerged. And God said to me, 'Those who voyage are not saved.' And He said to me, 'Those who, instead of voyaging, cast themselves into the sea, take a risk.' And He said to me, 'Those who voyage and take no risk shall perish.' And He said to me, 'The surface of the sea is a gleam that cannot be reached. And the bottom is a darkness impenetrable. And between the two are great fishes, which are to be feared.'[17]

# 11

# NATIVE AMERICANS

## *The Way of the Eagle*

One does not sell the earch upon which the people
walk.

Tashunka Witko (Crazy Horse)

Many North American Indians now live impoverished lives in
reservations of poor land or on the margins of white consumer
society. The tipi, symbol of independence and wholeness, has given
way to the rectangular corrugated shack. The chapel stands where
the medicine lodge once was. The Indians have lost their freedom
to roam the open prairies and they can no longer worship at their
sacred sites. Defeated, they live as extras for films extolling the might
and right of the American cavalry, or as tourist attractions.

Ever since Columbus landed in the New World 500 years ago, the
story of the contact between Europeans and the indigenous Indians
has been one of conquest and devastation. From the Spaniards the
Indians obtained the horse, which transformed their lives on the
plains, but they also learned the practice of torture and scalping.
Contact with Europeans gave them knowledge of the forked tongue
of white men and of their religion and their whisky. They could
not comprehend why the intruders from the east – the direction of
illumination in the Sioux medicine wheel – wanted to destroy all that
was beautiful and free.

As Heinmot Tooyalaket (Chief Joseph) of the Nez Percés told the
great white chiefs in Washington after being forced into a reservation:
'You might as well expect the rivers to run backward as that any man
who was born free should be contented when penned up and denied
liberty to go where he pleases.' The land the whites chased the Indians
from was part of their very being: the measure of the land and the
measure of their bodies was one and the same. It was not a question
of ownership – the concept was alien to Indians – but a question of
everyone being free to enjoy its fruits. The land was not man's for

him to do with as he chose; 'the one who has the right to dispose of it is the one who has created it'.[1]

Despite the rude intrusion of Europeans, the Indians still kept their circles complete, holding the earth together in their travels along its sacred ways. They lived in comparative harmony with the natural world, following the cycles of nature and developing a subtle and profound understanding of their surroundings. They were true conservationists, realizing that life depended on the wellbeing of the earth. The earth was considered a goddess and was worshipped for her fertility and abundance. Strongly animistic, they lived in close contact with other creatures and believed that all nature is an interconnected living organism: 'In the Circle of Life every being is no more, or less, than any other. We are all Sisters and Brothers. Life is shared with the bird, bear, insect, plants, mountains, clouds, stars, sun. To be in harmony with the natural world, one must live within the cycles of life'.[2] The art, music, stories and spirituality of these tribal peoples were intimately comlected with their environment.

Like many aboriginal peoples, American Indians were notable for their respect for the individual as well as having a strong sense of community which gave them personal security. The community guaranteed the basic minimum of food, shelter and clothing to their members irrespective of their contribution, and they recognized individual needs.[3] It was a way of life that did not fit in with encroaching Western civilization with its ethos of personal power and its desire to exploit nature to the hilt.

## The triumph of Western civilization

The pioneer spirit of the American West exemplifies the uncontrolled greed and conquest of nature at its worst. The 'wilderness' was a sacred dwelling for the indigenous people, their way of life carefully adapted to their environment and the buffalo which sustained them. There were no enclosures; everything drew free breath. Yet, within a matter of decades, a combination of the gun, the railway and barbed wire put an end to open plains teeming within between 30 and 50 million buffalos.

As the railways travelled across the continent in the 1860s, a great industry followed and grew fat on the hunting of the buffalo. Between 1872 and 1874 alone over 3 million were killed. By the turn of the century, fewer than a thousand remained. It was beyond comprehension. The very web of nature which sustained life was being destroyed. Having seen how the soldiers had cut down all the trees and killed the buffalo, Satanta, chief of the Kiowas, asked: 'Has the white man become a child that he should recklessly kill and not eat? When the red men slay game, they do so that they may live and not starve.'[4]

The Indians went down after the buffalo. Ecocide was followed by genocide. It fell to General William Tecumseh Sherman, named with dreadful irony after the Indian prophet, to lead the campaign of extermination in the Midwest and West of America. In the early 1860s he wrote to his brother: 'The more we can kill this year, the less will have to be killed the next war, for the more I see of these Indians the more convinced I am that all have to be killed or maintained as a species of pauper. Their attempts at civilization are simply ridiculous.'[5] Soon after congratulating General George Custer for having wiped out and scalped Black Kettle of the Cheyennes, Sherman declared in 1868: 'The only good Indians I ever saw were dead.' The judgement was honed down in time to the good old American saying: 'The only good Indian is a dead Indian.'[6]

The land of the buffalo and the antelope, which belonged to nobody but the wind, the rain and the sun, was then appropriated. A square grid was superimposed on it, regardless of the lie of the land or the flow of the water, and rectangular plots sold off. The sacred sites were also ignored. The Western spirit had triumphed.

But there was one last act of resistance. Among the Plains Indians, the Sioux spread the news of the ghost dance: 'The dead are to return. The buffalo are to return. The Dakota people will get back their own way of life. The white people will soon go away, and that will mean happier times for us once more!'[7] A prophet or messiah had told the people that if they danced the ghost dance, the Great Spirit would come. The Indians would go to the mountains and a great flood would come and drown all the whites on the plains. The dream was passed on. The earth would roll up like a carpet, with all the white man's works:

> the fences and the mining towns with their whorehouses, the
> factories and the farms with their stinking, unnatural animals,
> the railroads and the telegraph poles, the whole works. And
> underneath this rolled-up white man's world we would find

again the flowering prairie, unspoiled, with its herds of buffalo and antelope, its clouds of birds, belonging to everyone, enjoyed by all.[8]

The sweat lodges were set up and people were purified in great numbers for the dance. But the government agency in the area got the jitters and called out the military. In a preliminary free-for-all Sitting Bull was shot. A little later, over two hundred men, women and children were massacred in an encampment at Wounded Knee in 1890. Where the Sioux once roamed free with the buffalo and the antelope is now Custer State Park. Paradise was not to be regained. The long, painful journey of the American Indians to independence evaporated in the gunsmoke once and for all. But the ghost voices of the past live on.

### The Divamish: man did not weave the web of life

The Indians of the north Pacific coast are famous for their totem poles, which symbolize their clan. Salmon-fishing is an important part of their life. Above all, they are known for their practice of potlatch, which involves the lavish distribution of gifts. They were among the last tribes to be conquered. They were also among the most poetic.

In a myth of the Indians of the northwest coast, it is said that the Earth lived up in the sky at first, but because she complained of the Sun's ardour, the Old One put her down below. He told her:

> Henceforth you will be the earth and people will live on you and trample on your belly. You will be as their mother, for from you bodies will spring, and to you they will return. People will live as in your bosom and sleep in your lap. They will derive nourishment from you, for you are fat; and they will utilize every part of your body.[9]

The myth did not say that men from the east would come and rape and quarter and poison her.

One of the most eloquent messages from Indian culture to Western civilization comes in the alleged declaration by Chief Seattle to the great white chief in Washington in 1854, when the US government forcibly purchased the land of the Divamish Indians. Although written for a film script, the words capture the authentic voice of the Divamish:

If we do not own the freshness of the air and the sparkle of the water, how can you buy them?

Every part of this earth is sacred to my people. Every shining pine needle, every sandy shore, every mist in the dark woods, every clearing and humming insect is holy in the memory and experiences of my people. The sap which courses through the trees carries the memories of the red man . . .

We know that the white man does not understand our ways. One portion of land to him is the same as the next, for he is a stranger who comes in the night, and takes from the land whatever he needs. The earth is not his friend but his enemy, and when he has conquered it, he moves on . . .

He kidnaps the earth from his children, and he does not care ... His appetite will devour the earth and leave behind a desert . . .

What is man without the beasts? If all the beasts were gone, man would die from a great loneliness of spirit. For whatever happens to the beasts, soon happens to man. All things are connected . . .

Teach your children what we have taught our children, that the earth is our mother. Whatever befalls the earth, befalls the sons of the earth. If men spit upon the ground they spit upon themselves.

No one has described so well the intricate strands which go to make up nature's web and warned so persuasively against arrogant human interference with its delicate fabric:

This we know: the earth does not belong to man; man belongs to the earth. This we know. All things are connected, like the blood which unites one family. All things are connected.

Whatever befalls the earth befalls the sons of the earth. Man did not weave the web of life; he is merely a strand in it. Whatever he does to the web, he does to himself . . .

The whites too shall pass: perhaps sooner than all the other tribes. Contaminate your bed, and you will one night suffocate in your own waste.[10]

## The Haudenosaunee: coming to one mind

In the eastern woodlands lived the Haudenosaunee or Iroquois. There was the land of the longhouse, of Hiawatha, of ceremonial masks and the Peace Tree. The Haudenosaunee developed a confederacy of their five nations which stands as the greatest model of democracy in an organic society in the Western hemisphere. It offers a vision of a decentralized society of self-governing communities.

In the culture of the Haudenosaunee, the family is the centre of life. People develop a sense of morality not through an imposed ethical code but through sharing and thinking about their experiences. While they develop a collective understanding of reality, it results from each individual thinking about it for him- or herself. Kinship is by clan, and people can be adopted into clans. The clans extend across national groups. The Wolf clan of the Mohawks, easternmost nation of the Haudenosaunee, is considered as one with the Wolf clan of the Seneca, the westernmost nation.

The Haudenosaunee have a strong sense of spirituality, teaching that nature and the universe are both benign. Their story of creation recounts how the world — this physical world which humans experience — was created by twin spirits. But it is not a story of stark opposition between good and evil principles: 'One twin creates the world of ascending life, the green and flowering world of reproduction which delights mankind. The other creates another, perhaps less appealing aspect of life, which includes creatures like the insects and the vulture.' Yet they recognize that both aspects are necessary for life to continue in this world. Since nature is not considered an irrational and threatening 'wilderness', they have no desire to tame or conquer it.[11]

In their cosmology, the Haudenosaunee place themselves in a balanced familial relationship with the universe and the earth. Chief Segwalise has observed:

> In our language, the Earth is our Mother Earth, the sun our Eldest Brother, the moon our Grandmother and so on. It is the belief of our people that all elements of the Natural World were created for the benefit of all living things and that we, as humans, are one of the weakest of the whole Creation, since we are totally dependent on the whole Creation for our survival.

Recounting the history of his people, Segwalise asserts:

> Ours was a wealthy society. No one suffered from want. All had the right to food, clothing and shelter. All shared in the bounty

of the spiritual ceremonies and the Natural World. No one stood in any material relationship of power over anyone else. No one could deny any one access to the things they needed. All in all, before the colonists came, ours was a beautiful and rewarding Way of Life.

He goes on:

There was a time when our lands were torn by conflict and death. There were times when certain individuals attempted to establish themselves as the rulers of the people through exploitation and repression. We emerged from those times to establish a strong democratic and spiritual Way of Life. The [confederacy] of the Haudenosaunee became the embodiment of democratic principles which continue to guide our people. The Haudenosaunee became the first 'United Nations' established on a firm foundation of peace, harmony and respect.[12]

The Haudenosaunee chiefs were recallable, and sometimes elected by women as well as men. Matrilineal descent prevailed. The people worked voluntarily together in their fields. They made their decisions always in open councils, considering the counsel of the women as well as the needs of future generations.

The Grand Council assembles the leaders of the clans to raise issues and solve problems. Given the best possible information, they discuss it with great respect for each other's views and give each person their say until they 'come to one mind'.[13] There is therefore a tradition of consensus in making decisions, although the 'one mind' does not require complete agreement between all parties. It offers a model of participatory democracy. The federations of the Haudenosaunee are completely at odds with the hierarchical and despotic empire of the Incas. Their democratic and libertarian relations among themselves are reflected in their relations with other creatures and with nature as a whole.

### The Sioux: remembering the bear

Sioux were Plains Indians dependent on the buffalo. They were nomadic, following the buffalo, living in tipis. They got their horses from the Spaniards; they called it *sunka wakan*, 'holy dog'. Within decades they became expert horsemen.

Kinship was central to the life of the Sioux and was coextensive
with their domain. It was based on blood tie, with relatives established through marriage. Kinship held everything together and every
other consideration – property, personal ambition, glory, happiness,
life itself – was considered secondary. This was symbolized by their
camp circles in which the tipis faced the council tipi in the centre,
which was the focus of community life and thought. All the families
of the circle operated as a single unity in most activities, the women
putting up the tipis and the men going hunting.

The Sioux fulfil the classic image of the Indians in the West. They
wore war bonnets of eagle feathers and fringed buckskin garments.
They were fierce warriors and engaged in intertribal warfare for sport
and glory. And yet they lived in balance with their environment,
wasting nothing and treading lightly on the earth. They were deeply
religious, enfolded in symbols as in a blanket. According to them, the
universe is infused with a Great Spirit – something holy, mysterious
and moving – which they called Wakan Tanka. It made the flowers,
trees and rivers and takes care of them, 'the spirit splitting itself up
into stones, trees, tiny insects even, making them all *wakan* by his
ever-presence. And in turn all these myriad of things which make
up the universe flowing back to their source, united in the one
Grandfather Spirit.'[14]

The Sioux were careful not to disrespect the Great Spirit. They
saw gods in separate things but all are united in Wakan Tanka. They
did not worship individual rocks and trees: 'They are not themselves
Wakan, but the Wakan is in all things. When our people wished to
pray, they selected some common tree or rock, untouched by man,
and set it apart for its sacred use by painting it red. And then they
addressed it, for now it was Wakan.'[15]

The Sioux considered the buffalo, who provided them with everything they needed, to have power and wisdom. They considered it
their brother, and there are many Sioux legends of buffalo changing
into men. It was the Buffalo Woman who brought them the peace
pipe, which is at the centre of their religion. After she taught the
tribes how to worship with the pipe, she changed herself into a white
buffalo calf. The smoke of the sacred pipe is the breath of the Great
Spirit: 'Sitting together smoking the pipe, we form the circle without
end, which contains within it every living thing upon this earth.'[16]

The Sioux Medicine Wheel is also a circle that acts like a mirror
in which everything is reflected. 'The Universe is the Mirror of the

People,' the old teachers said, 'and each person is a Mirror to every other person.' Any idea, person or object can be a medicine wheel, a mirror, for man. The wheel is constructed with stones in a circle, with each stone representing one of the many things in the universe. All things are contained within the Medicine Wheel; it is the total universe. All things on the wheel have spirit and life, including the rivers, rocks, earth, sky, plants and animals. Man may be a determiner but 'our determining spirit can be made whole only through the learning of our harmony with all brothers and sisters, and with all the other spirits of the Universe'.[17] Each direction within the Medicine Wheel represents an aspect of life and thought: to the west, introspection (represented by the bear and the colour black); to the east, illumination (eagle, yellow); to the south, innocence (mouse, green) and to the north, wisdom (buffalo, white). People should travel around the Medicine Wheel and experience its manifestations; they would then walk in balance on the Earth Mother.[18]

The most famous and important ceremony of the Sioux each year was the annual sun dance, to ensure continued fertility of the tribe and the earth. Those men who had cried out in distress to Wakan during the year offered themselves in fulfilment of their pledges. When choosing a tree for a sacred pole, they performed a little rite called 'Apology to the Birds' for taking their dwelling. During the dance the men would carry out in detail the vows they had made to Wakan, cutting and piercing their flesh. Just before dawn on the second day, the holy man would wail, holding the pole on behalf of his people; the sun returned and the people retired quietly to their tipis.

'Lonely is the man with vision.' Apart from the sun dance, Sioux religious life was solitary, consisting mainly of individual vision quests. They believed that there was something within them, 'something like a second person almost'.[19] First the seeker must prepare himself in a sweat lodge (*inipi*), a cleansing lodge which represents the womb of the Earth Mother who sustains all life. Fasting for many days, he would be led by a relative to a place of his own choosing where he would be left alone until someone led him into the *wakan* realm in order to make him a better man. If a bird or animal approached, he might see it as the spirit to guide him in his vision. Afterwards he would hold the animal in great reverence and in order to obtain its help again, he would identify with it and act out the role of the animal in a characteristic way. The act of calling on the help of a spiritual brother was called 'remembering oneself as bear' or eagle, or whatever.[20] Nothing illustrates so clearly the close identification of the Indians with nature and its creatures.


## The Hopi: the further you go, the harder it gets

For thousands of years, the Hopi Indians lived in peace among the hills and mesas of the desert southwest of America, in northeastern Arizona. They led a highly spiritual life, evolving rituals and ceremonies to help them nurture the delicate natural balances that made life possible in their arid land. They built their villages into the sides of cliffs. Each one was a self-governing community; the very idea of central government was considered a violation of the patterns of nature.

The Hopi are fiercely independent. Although the Spaniards set up a Christian mission in the town of Oraibi in 1679, the Indians rebelled a year later and rejected Christianity as the 'slave church'. Towards the end of the nineteenth century, Senator Henry L. Dawes, concerned that in Indian society 'there is no selfishness, which is at the bottom of civilization', tried to introduce a General Allotment Act to turn their collective land into private plots.[21] The Hopi would have none of it.

All the basic tasks of Hopi society continue to be done cooperatively, from growing maize to preparing food. Children are involved from the beginning, and their sense of solidarity is so strong that they find it difficult to understand the competitive games of Europeans. Their profound feeling of unity between the individual and the community reflect their sense of oneness with nature.

In their cosmogony, they believe that humans live through a succession of worlds. As in the Greeks' golden age, all was well in the beginning. The creator Taiowa created his nephew Sótuknang, who in turn created the universe out of endless space and then Kókyangwúti, Spider Woman, to be his helper on earth. Following his instructions, the Spider Woman shaped the earth and created its life forms. The first people were happy and began to multiply.

But this primal harmony was progressively disturbed. As human achievements came to dominate in each world, the changes led to quarrelling, greed and disorder on a new level, so that only a few still remembered the creator and his plan. The rest were destroyed and saved for the next world. The present fourth world, Túwaqachi, which means 'World Complete', has 'height and depth, heat and cold, beauty and barrenness: it has everything for you to choose from'.[22]

It is such a mixture because the easier life was made for men, the more likely they were to fall into evil ways. The Hopi thus stress 'the further you go, the harder it gets'.[23]

As agriculturalists whose staple diet is maize or corn, the Hopi believe that the living organism of the earth reveals itself most specially in the form of the Corn-Mother. They regard corn as a living entity with a body similar to their own, and they build 'its flesh into their own'.[24]

All their ceremonies are intended to ensure the due processes of nature. They do not try to impose their will on nature, but cooperate with its rhythms. Nothing is insignificant in nature: plants, rocks, animals, humans, the living and the dead all have a share in the maintenance of the universal natural order. The entire being of the Hopi individual affects the balance of nature; and 'as each individual develops his inner potential, so he enhances his participation, so does the entire universe become invigorated.'[25]

The word *hopi* means 'peace' and the Hopi call themselves the People of Peace. They are dedicated, since their first emergence, to a universal plan of creation which seeks to maintain an unbroken harmony in the lives of every item – mineral, plant, animal and human. In our time they have made known a prophecy carved in stone by their ancestors outside the ancient village of Oraibi. In the 1600s the Hopi prophesied that the whites would come and destroy their land. But they also foretold a Time of Purification when red and white brothers would reunite, a time when corrupted people, who only think with their minds, would rediscover the natural way, the way of peace. This would follow a time of great restlessness and dislocation and the disruption of the seasons. They believe that this Fifth World has already begun, being made by humble people of little nations, tribes and racial minorities.[26]

In response to the atheistic and materialistic age of the West, many 'New Age' seekers, specially in North America, wish to live closer to the land and follow the 'old ways' of the Indians. It represents a revival of Romantic 'primitivism', of a belief that many aspects of existing civilization are evil and that people lived a better life in earlier, more 'primitive' times. American Indians therefore often appear as Romantic 'noble savages', despite their present degradation in an alien society. The American poet Gary Snyder in particular has called for a return to their tribal way of life. He is part of an ecological movement which seeks to rearrange American society into a new tribalism based on 'bioregions', living in areas not defined by political boundaries but by natural and cultural bonds.

But tribal culture is not necessarily an ideal to emulate. Many tribal societies are warlike and show little respect for the dignity of those who do not share the same blood. They are often conformist and intolerant. Women are not given equal voice and male elders generally rule. Shamans often become leaders as well as protectors of their groups, and together can form a ruling elite.[27] In times of war and mounting population pressures, tribal democracy breaks down and coercive rulers appear.

Nevertheless, the North American Indians like other organic societies can provide great inspiration by offering alternative ways of organizing society and relating to the earth. As the anthropologist Claude Lévi-Strauss has written:

> The study of these savages does not reveal a Utopian State in Nature; nor does it make us aware of a perfect society hidden deep in forests. It helps us construct a theoretical model of society which corresponds to none that can be observed in reality, but will help us to disentangle 'what in the present nature of Man is original, and what is artificial'.[28]

The ways of the American Indians should not be forgotten. Their interweaving of humanity and animals and their reverence for nature stand as a model of a harmonious way of relating to the earth. Their societies demonstrate the advantages of tribal groupings, based not on blood but on common interests, living in bioregions shaped according to the contours of the land rather than the maps of the centralized nation-state. Combined with a modern sense of individuality, their practice of cooperation and mutual aid points the way to a genuinely ecological society.

# Part II

# SEEDS BENEATH
# THE SNOW

# 12

# ALCHEMY

## Sacred Philosophy

Art is the imitation of nature in her mode of operation.
Alchemists' adage

It is usual to dismiss alchemy in scientific circles as a primitive forerunner of modern chemistry. In the popular mind, the alchemist was a mad fanatic, an early Dr Frankenstein, consulting strange hieroglyphics in a fuming subterranean laboratory in order to transform base metal into gold. As far as good Christians were concerned, if not actually practising black magic, the alchemists were doubtless disturbing evil spirits.

In reality, there was a great deal more to alchemy. Alchemists were natural philosophers trying to discover the Philosopher's Stone, also known as the elixir or tincture. The stone was believed to be not only a transmuting agent, having the power to turn inferior material into gold, but also the key to knowledge, which could be used responsibly only by a wise person. Its power was both physical and spiritual:

> The Philosopher's Stone is called the most ancient, secret or unknown, natural, incomprehensible, heavenly, blessed, sacred Stone of the Sages ... the cure for all unsound and imperfect metals – the everlasting light – the panacea for all diseases – the glorious Phoenix – the most precious of all treasures – the chief good of Nature.[1]

Alchemists always worked on both a physical and a symbolic level. The gold they sought was superior to the gold found in the earth. 'The gold engendered by this art,' wrote the English scientist Roger Bacon in the sixteenth century, 'excelleth all natural gold in all properties, both medicinal and other.'[2] It was nothing less than 'philosophical gold'.

In psychological and spiritual terms, the alchemists' attempt to turn

151

base material (*prima materia*) into gold may be seen as man's search
to perfect his own nature. In modern times, Freud borrowed the
alchemical term 'sublimation' to describe the process of transforming
forbidden desires into socially acceptable behaviour. His pupil Jung
further argued that the alchemists' quest for gold exemplified the
sublimation of the instincts into a psychic whole, a reconciliation
between the individual psyche and the collective unconscious.[3]

Although alchemists never actually managed to transmute gold,
their fruitless search helped to prepare the ground for the scientific
revolution of the seventeenth century. They followed a deliberate
method which was both profound and original and they recognized
the influence of the observer on the observed in a scientific experiment.[4] As an esoteric discipline drawing on the Hermetic tradition,
alchemy carried forward and developed many ideas from mystical
Christianity and the Kabbalah.

Alchemists did not separate man from nature as later scientists
did; on the contrary, they considered our species to be an integral
part of nature, with man as a microcosm reflecting the macrocosm
of the universe. In this sense, alchemy may be said to offer a science
of the cosmos as well as a science of the soul. It became a way of
life for their practitioners, who referred to it in terms of 'our sacred
philosophy' or 'the Great Work'.[5]

The origins of alchemy are shrouded in mystery, which makes it
all the more intriguing. It may well have existed since prehistoric
times; it certainly goes back at least to the first millennium before
Christ in Far East and Middle East civilizations. The ancient interest
in gold and silver was not simply because they were rare or had
special qualities; since recorded history they have always been valued
as earthly reflections of the sun and the moon.

European alchemists trace their roots back to the ancient Egyptians.
Certainly the working of gold in ancient Egypt was a priestly craft
centred on the temple of the god Ptah at Memphis. The oldest extant
alchemical drawings are to be found on Egyptian papyri. The word
*alchemia* derives from Arabic *al-kimiya*, which is said to derive from
the ancient Egyptian *kême* – a reference to the 'black earth' which
bordered the Nile and was the name for Egypt. This would define
alchemy as 'the Egyptian art' or 'the black art'. Another root may
be from the Greek *chyma* meaning 'smelting' or 'casting'.[6] From
Egyptian civilization, alchemy seems to have spread over Europe
and the Middle East, and perhaps even influenced Indian alchemy,

taking on widely different forms and practices as it adapted to local circumstances.

Where alchemy in the West focused on metals and minerals, the alchemy of the East was mainly concerned with longevity. The Taoists were particularly involved. Taoism presents life as a ceaseless flow of changes and transmutations, and its emphasis on experiment, close observation of nature and spiritual growth coincide with the early spirit of alchemy. *I Ching*, the Book of Changes, is a classic text showing how changes occur in nature as well as in society and humanity. It seems that Taoists used alchemy along with yogic practices as a way of bringing natural energies into harmony.

Around the Mediterranean, alchemy first developed in Alexandria, founded by the emperor Alexander in the fourth century BC on the north Egyptian shore. It was a marvellous cultural melting pot, and early alchemy brought together aspects of Egyptian, Persian, Syrian, Jewish and classical Greek thought. Many mystical teachings and myths, such as the worship of Isis and Osiris, Eleusian mysteries, Gnosticism, Manicheism and Neoplatonism, were transmuted into the alchemical tradition.

From Alexandria two principal currents emerged, one predominantly artisanal, concerned with transforming metals, and the other symbolic, using the metallurgical processes as analogies for spiritual growth. The Western school then shifted from Alexandria to the Arabic world, reaching Europe, especially through Sicily and Spain, towards the end of the 'Dark Ages'.

The founder of alchemy in the West is usually taken to be Hermes Trismegistus, the 'thrice-great Hermes', identified with the ancient Egyptian god Thoth who presided over all priestly arts and sciences. The *Corpus Hermeticum* comprises texts ascribed to Hermes and forms the foundation of the 'Hermetic tradition'. The texts are not, however, a summation of Egyptian wisdom; they are written in Greek and strongly influenced by Gnostic, Jewish and Neoplatonic teaching. Another important text called The *Emerald Tablet* (*Tabula Smaragdina*), probably dating from the early centuries of the Christian era, is also ascribed to Hermes Trismegistus. It is only known in Arabic and Latin translations. Much of the knowledge was passed down orally, so that it would not reach the uninitiated, hence alchemy's esoteric reputation. Its secrets are also couched in opaque language; for instance, in *The Book of Seven Chapters*, also attributed to Hermes Trismegistus, it is written: 'See, I have opened unto you what was hid: The [alchemical] work is with you and amongst you; in that it is to be found within you and is enduring; you will always have it present, wherever you are, on land or sea.'[7] By conveying their tenets and findings through mythological symbols, the alchemists escape precise definition.

The 'Hermetic art', as it came to be known, entered the world of Islam as the doctrine of 'oneness of existence' (*wahdat-al-wujûd*) which gave a new spiritual impetus to art. Alchemy made its entry into Christendom through Byzantium and later through Islamic Spain where Jâbir ibn Hayyan founded a school in the eighth century. The famous thirteenth-century Catalan or Italian, who resumed the whole of medieval alchemy in his *Summa Perfectionis*, assumed the Latinized name Geber probably in honour of his illustrious Muslim predecessor.

Since they were disapproved of by the Christian Church for adopting pre-Christian and heretical doctrines, the alchemists tended to drop out of mainstream medieval society. They formed a rich and elaborate subculture which often took a visionary and apocalyptic direction. Observing their dual role of trying to make gold and reveal a path to enlightenment, most of their contemporaries could not make up their minds whether they were pure sages or idolatrous charlatans.[8]

With the Renaissance a new wave of Byzantine alchemy reached the West, and in the sixteenth and seventeenth centuries many texts were printed; for the first time its doctrines came out into the open. But alchemy soon suffered the twin onslaught of the scientific revolution and new humanism, and fell into decline. It was discarded by mainstream science as a form of exploded error. It was left to a few isolated scientists and thinkers like the great German writer Goethe to maintain the Hermetic tradition until the revival of interest in the twentieth century, which took a mainly psychological and philosophical form. Alchemy however, like its cousin smelting, is still considered suspect by some.

In archaic and simple cultures, where the spiritual and the practical are interwoven and the unity between humanity and the cosmos remains intact, the preparation of ores has always been considered a sacred process. Many tribal people consider mining as a direct violation of Mother Earth. The process must therefore be sanctified and Mother Earth appeased. Moreover, since ores can be used for evil as well as good, their removal from the earth is fraught with dangerous possibilities. From the very beginning of the metallurgical age this two-edged aspect was recognized. 'We revealed iron,' the Qur'an asserts, 'wherein is evil power and many uses for mankind' (57:25).

The process of smelting – changing the nature of a substance by the application of fire – is considered by many tribal peoples as meddling with the laws of nature. The mixing of ore and fire might be useful but it can also corrupt the mixer. In many African tribes, the smelter or smith is considered to be an unauthorized intruder into the sacred order of nature, and suspected by many of practising black magic.[9] The artisan working gold in Guinea, for example, must first of all purify himself by washing himself from head to foot and by abstaining from sexual intercourse. Like the medieval alchemists, in order to make outward gold in the external world, he must first make inward gold in his soul. His art is a sacred art, invoking the spirit of the fire, the spirit of the wind and the spirit of the gold itself.[10]

## Cosmology of alchemy

Hermetic cosmology adopts one of the oldest images of earth as a disc covered by the starry vault of heaven. Heaven, bringing rain and sunshine, is the masculine pole of existence; the earth, giving life, is the feminine pole. This was combined with the picture of the world developed by the second-century AD Greek astronomer and geographer Ptolemy in which the globe of the earth is at the centre of the universe. The planets revolve around it in a variety of orbits and spheres and it is surrounded by the heaven of fixed stars. Outside this is the starless empyrean, representing the prime mover and the all-embracing universal intellect. According to the Arab philosopher Averroes, who lived in Spain and profoundly influenced Christian Scholasticism, the unbroken movement of the starless heaven is the mediator between time and eternity. It was thought that as the soul ascends through the spheres to reach the undivided whole, it leaves behind the world of multiplicity and change. The Ptolemaic system held sway throughout the Middle Ages until Copernicus in 1543 published his theory that the earth and the planets revolve around the sun.

The alchemists further developed a view of nature which combined elements of Greek philosophy and Christian theology. Their starting point was a belief in Aristotle's doctrine of 'prime matter' (*prima materia*) which forms the common base of the four elements of fire, air, earth and water. Although they believed in the immutable essence of each element, they managed to tally this with a belief in the transmutation of metals by arguing that the elements themselves are never present in bodies in their pure form.

The Seal of Solomon represents the synthesis of all the four elements and thus the union of all opposites:

fire  △  water  ▽  air  △̶  earth  ▽̶

As a whole, it symbolizes the four elements in unity, with the two joined triangles representing essence and substance, *materia* and *forma*, spirit and soul, sulphur and quicksilver, the volatile and the stable, and, finally, spiritual power and bodily existence:

The alchemists also followed Aristotle in their distinction between *materia* and *forma*, the latter being the material clothing of the former. Such a view stressed the unitary aspect of being, with the essence of God revealing itself through the qualities of an object.

In the book of the *Corpus Hermeticum* known as 'Poimandres', it is described how the universal intellect revealed itself to Hermes:

> With these words, He looked me long in the face, so that I trembled before his gaze. Then, as He raised His head again, I saw how in my own spirit (*nous*) the light which consists of a numberless number of possibilities, became an infinite All, while the fire, surrounded and so contained by an almighty power, had attained its immobile position: such is what I was able to grasp rationally of this vision.[11]

Hermes thus experiences the mystical vision of unity in diversity, of the multiplicity of things ascending to cosmic unity, which is part of the modern ecological concept of nature.

What is different is the Neoplatonic view that objects in the world are reflections of eternal prototypes or archetypes. Indeed, alchemists saw this world as a shadowy and imperfect reflection of an eternal and divine world. Base metal is on the mineral plane in the same condition as the lost soul. According to the great Muslim mystic and alchemist Muhyi'd-Dîn ibn 'Arabî, gold corresponds to the original condition of the soul which freely reflects the divine spirit in its essence, whereas lead corresponds to its 'sick' and distorted condition. But the true essence of lead is gold. Each base metal therefore represents a break in the equilibrium which gold alone exhibits.

As with the metals, so with the soul. In order to free the soul from its paralysis and 'coagulation', its *materia* and *forma* must be dissolved. After their 'divorce', they become 'married' again. The *materia* is dissolved and purified in order to be coagulated anew in the form of perfect crystal.

## Nature can overcome nature

The model for alchemical work is nature and nature comes to the aid of the practitioner who has mastered its mode of operation. The alchemist believed that he was merely speeding up processes that take place naturally on earth.

Western alchemy uses in general the language of Platonic metaphysics – *natura* or *physis* – to describe nature. The Neoplatonist Plotinus suggested that on being asked why she produces her works, Nature might reply, if indeed she deigned to answer at all, as follows:

> It would be more fitting not to ask, but to learn silently, even as I am silent . . . Thus the mathematicians write down figures as a result of their contemplation. I however write nothing down. I only watch, and the forms of the material world arise, as if they proceeded from out of me.[12]

In the Platonic universe of the alchemists, nature is situated between three realms. At the top is the 'universal spirit' (*nous*) which alone contemplates the ineffable One. Next comes the 'universal soul' (psyche), and then nature itself. Below nature is *materia prima*, the passive foundation of all being. From an alchemical point of view, one could call nature 'the maternal aspect of the *materia prima*, since it is she that "gives birth"'.[13]

According to Muhyi'd-Dîn ibn 'Arabî, universal nature is the feminine or maternal side of the creative act. She is the 'merciful "breathing-out" of God' which confers separate existence on the undifferentiated possibilities latent in nonbeing. The 'breathing out' is merciful but can also be confusing, for the multiciplity of things in this world is a deception and separation from the unity of God. Like shakti in the form of the Hindu goddess Kali, the universal mother can be both bountiful and devouring. In their 'outward work', nature for alchemists is the driving force behind all transmutations – the potential energy of things. In 'inward' alchemy, she appears as the maternal power which releases the soul from its sterile and earthbound existence. Always feminine, she can appear in the comely disguise of Dame Nature or in her terrible aspect as the Great Dragon which roams in all things.

The alchemists sought to 'master' the female energy of nature by understanding her rhythms. It is not a question of destroying the natural forces but rather of taming them, so that they can become vehicles of the spirit. The process is often described in terms of a rider mastering a mare in order to channel its energy in a positive direction.

This coaxing and yet dominating attitude to nature comes through in the anonymous alchemical work entitled *Purissima Revelation*. Borrowing on Greek mythology, nature is likened to

> a very thick wood into which many have penetrated in order to try and wrest its holy secrets from it. But they have been swallowed up, because they did not have the right weapons which alone could conquer the terrible dragon protecting the golden fleece. And those who were not killed, had to retrace their steps, gripped by terror and covered in shame and disgrace. Nature is also that measureless sea on which the Argonauts set out. Woe to sailors who do no know our art! For they may travel their whole life long without ever reaching harbour . . . Only the wise Argonauts, who strictly observe the laws of nature and are completely devoted to the will of the Almighty, can win the precious golden fleece.

The overall tone of this passage is one of ravishment, and nature appears in its two aspects of timorous virgin and devouring seductress. The golden fleece is ostensibly knowledge but is described in terms of stolen virginity.

> And woe to him who, like Jason, having conquered with the help of Medea, lets himself be seduced by his dangerous conquest and submits to nature the sorceress, instead of remaining constant and true to his divine bride, wisdom.[14]

The message seems to be that the alchemist should take care when violating nature. The violation itself is not questioned. Art may be the imitation of nature in her mode of operation, but another adage of alchemy is that 'nature can overcome nature'.

Alchemy sees the universe (macrocosm) and man (microcosm) as corresponding to each other as reflections in a mirror; whatever is in the one, must in some form be in the other. Although the relationship can be expressed in terms of the world, as object, and the human individual, as subject, they cannot be separated but exist in mutual relation. There is a correspondence between inside and out, so the whole of nature is a metaphor for the human mind. To study man was at the same time to study the universe and vice versa.

While recognizing the influence of the observer on the observed, natural magic followed an inductive method, formulating general laws from specific observations. Baptista della Porta, author of the leading manual of *Natural Magick* (1658) (a copy of which was in Newton's library), wrote:

> Magick is nothing else but the knowledge of the whole course of Nature. For, whilst we consider the Heavens, the Stars, the Elements, how they are moved, and how changed, by this means we find out the hidden secrecies of living creatures, of plants, of metals, and of their generation and corruption; so that this whole science seems merely to depend upon the view of Nature ... Wherefore, as many of you as come to behold Magick, must be perswaded that the works of Magick are nothing else but the works of Nature, whose dutiful hand-maid magick is.[15]

Alchemists talk in terms of the universal intellect whose object is not only the outward physical world but also the inner world of the human intellect and soul. The planets are also described in terms of the human family. As the *Emerald Tablet* (first mentioned in the eighth century) puts it:

> Whatever is below is like that which is above, and whatever is above is like that which is below, to accomplish the miracles of the one thing.
> Just as all things proceed from One alone by meditation on One alone, so also they are born from this one thing by adaptation.
> Its father is the sun and its mother is the moon. The wind has borne it in its body. Its nurse is the earth ...

Thus the little world is created according to the prototype of
the great world.[16]

It is noteworthy how the fifteenth-century alchemist Basilius Valen-
tinus interprets the alchemical keyword VITRIOL: *Visita interiore
terrae; rectifiando invenies occultum lapidem* (Visit the interior of the
earth; through purification thou wilt find the the hidden stone). The
interior of the earth is also the interior of the body; that is, the *materia
prima*. And *materia prima* is the mirror of the universal intellect.

In one sense to see the the universe as the macrocosm of man
is highly anthropomorphic, but in another it is deeply ecological
since it depicts the universe as a living organism, with humanity
as a cell of its body. The European alchemists, however, steeped
in Christianity, differ from the Chinese alchemists in conceiving
of man as metaphysically unique, unlike all other living creatures
on earth. While his body is mortal like that of other animals, he
alone has an immortal soul. Therefore his task is to develop his
powers, to become 'godlike' in order to apprehend God. This can
only be achieved by leaping clear of all that is corporeal. It is the old
Promethean dream: 'Think that for you too nothing is impossible;
deem that you too are immortal, and that you are able to grasp all
things in your thought, to know every craft and science; find your
home in the haunts of every living creature.'[17]

This vision became a vital ingredient of Rosicrucianism, which
came to prominence in 1614–15 when two texts – the *Fama
Fraternitatis* and the *Confessio Fraternitatis* – appeared, revealing
the existence of a secret society ready to meet the dawning of a
new age when the world would awake from its profound sleep. The
wisdom gathered by the Rosicrucian Order was to be 'a compendium
of the Universe', the 'perfection [of] all Arts', 'so that finally man
might thereby understand his own nobleness and worth, and why
he is called Microcosmus, and how far his knowledge extendeth to
Nature'.[18]

The medical practitioner Robert Fludd defended the Rosicrucian
Order and took spiritual alchemy as a central theme in his *History
of the Macrocosm and the Microcosm*. In describing how the divine
interacts with the human world, he presents nature 'not as a goddess,
but the proximate minister of God, at whose behest she governs the
sub-celestial worlds'. Alchemy in its physical aspect is nothing less
than the 'art of correcting Nature in the mineral realm'.[19]

The whole aim of alchemy is therefore to 'purify' and 'transmute' external and inner nature. Such an attitude assumes that nature is somehow inadequate and incomplete in its present form, and requires man to use his 'art' to improve it. Hermes Trismegistus wrote in *The Book of Seven Chapters*: 'In turning back on myself and meditating on the way in which nature produces metals in the interior of the earth, I perceived that true substance which nature has prepared for us, so as to enable us to perfect them *on* earth.'[20] Such a view clearly draws on the Neoplatonic and Gnostic notion of the baseness and impurity of matter and the body. In Christian terms, it presents much of nature in a state of corruption and imperfection as a result of the Fall of man and his expulsion from the Garden of Eden. Alchemists thus aimed to regain the original 'nobility' of human nature – Adamic virtue. Medieval Western alchemy may be considered a kind of Christian mysticism, although it is a mysticism without God. The inner 'soul' as much as outer 'nature' is a 'substance' which has to be purified, not by the miraculous intervention of God, but by man's own efforts.

Alchemy therefore intended to transform man and nature into a state of grace. The alchemist Nicolas Flamel in the fourteenth century wrote that the completion of the work

> makes man good by effacing from him the root of all sins, namely covetousness, so that he becomes generous, mild, pious, believing, and God-fearing, however bad he may have been previously; because from now on he is continually filled with the great grace and mercy which he has received from God, and with the depth of His wonderful works.[21]

In medieval Europe, alchemy became increasingly associated with Christianity. In *The Sophic Hydrolith* the life of Jesus is directly equated with the transformation of the Philosopher's Stone in the alchemical process. The German mystic Jacob Boehme specifically used the alchemical process to show how man might develop into a fully conscious being and unite with God. Beginning life as an untutored shoemaker, Boehme developed a highly complex and enigmatic style. As a dialectical thinker, he saw the warring elements in the alchemical vessel as an emblem of the activity of nature itself which cannot change without conflict:

> For the eternal nature has produced nothing in its desire, except a

likeness out of itself; and if there were not an everlasting mixing, there would be an eternal peace in nature, but so nature would not be revealed and made manifest, in the combat it becomes manifest . . .

This view impressed William Blake ('Without Contraries, there is no Progression') and has endeared itself to some modern deep ecologists. But Boehme is sufficiently steeped in Neoplatonic alchemy and Pauline Christianity to describe man as lost in sin, a corrupt being living within corrupt nature:

[Man] lies now shut up after his fall in a gross, deformed, bestial dead image; he is not like an angel, much less like unto paradise; he is the gross ore in Saturn, wherein the gold is couched and shut up; his paradisical image is in him as if it were not, and is also not manifest, the outward body is a stinking carcass, while it yet lives in the poison; he is a bad thorny bush, from whence notwithstanding fair rose-buds may bloom forth, and grow out of the thorns.[22]

Only if Christ is born and bruises the head of the serpent will a New Man arise in righteousness which puts forth its lustre 'as the hidden gold out of the earthly property'. It is a far cry from Blake's profound insight that 'everything that lives is holy' or the deep ecologist's insight that the thorns on a bush are as valuable as its buds.

## Alchemy and the Scientific Revolution

When Copernicus' theory of the universe was published in 1543 it marked the death knell of the old Ptolemaic system on which the cosmology of alchemy was based. Whereas medieval cosmology had seen space as a limited sphere encompassed by the empyrean, the new rationalist philosophy saw it as infinite. The Hermetic world-view which placed man at the centre of the universe saw him as part of the whole. Paradoxically, the new heliocentric view displaced the earth and man from the centre of the universe but in the process made man the measure of all things. The rationalist view of man which developed out of the scientific revolution and the Renaissance turned him into little more than a speck of dust, a thoughtless accident. But although he might have been a reed, he was a thinking reed, capable of analysing and mastering nature and its powers for his own ends.

Although the scientific revolution of the seventeenth century eventually displaced alchemy as a method of scientific enquiry, alchemy passed on several important discoveries, especially in distilling alcoholic spirits. The marvel of *aqua ardens* (brandy) demonstrated, for instance, the alchemical aspiration to combine the two elements of fire and water, for it was both liquid and inflammable.

But the legacy of alchemy was far more than its physical discoveries. The new science might have shown that elements cannot be transmuted, but it took up the fundamental drive of alchemy to reveal the secrets of nature and transform it – a desire which has become a central part of Western scientific tradition with tragic results for both humanity and nature.

In this context, it is not surprising that scientists like Robert Boyle and Isaac Newton should have had feet in both camps. Boyle was prepared to make his discoveries public and break the tradition of Hermetic secrecy. He went on in *The Skeptical Chymist* (1661) to attack the alchemical view that the four elements are the foundation of all matter, by demonstrating that earth, water, fire and air are not indivisible bodies but composed of various chemical constituents.

While Newton elaborated the system of mechanical and deterministic physics which long bedevilled the West, he was well versed in Hermetic teachings, the Kabbalah, and Neoplatonism. He had a well-stocked library of alchemical texts, and burned much midnight oil doing alchemical work in his own laboratory. His knowledge of alchemy was a direct trigger to his discoveries in physics. While he took up the current atomic theory of matter, he still believed that matter could be transmuted in another way. In his claim to have discovered 'philosophical mercury', he wrote:

> I have such a vessel in the fire with gold thus dissolved, where the gold was visibly not dissolved through a corrosive into atoms, but extrinsically and intrinsically into a mercury as living and mobile as any mercury found in the world. For it makes the gold begin to swell, to be swollen and to putrefy, and also to spring forth sprouts and branches, changing colours daily, the appearance of which fascinate me everyday.[23]

Chemistry took over from alchemy its accumulated knowledge, but where alchemy had been based on spiritual devotion, the new chemistry adopted the modern scientific method which insisted that only experiments that could be repeated and theories that obtained identical results under identical conditions could be considered proven. If a theory was not falsifiable, it could not be considered scientific. Chemistry shared alchemy's careful observation, but severed the link between the observer and the observed, matter and spirit, the microcosm and the macrocosm. The new scientific cult became one of passionless objectivity. Nature, once ridden sympathetically as a mare, was henceforth dismantled as a machine into its separate parts.

In the twentieth century, the Copernican system was once again challenged and a new paradigm emerged. The sun of our galaxy is no longer the centre of the universe but one of a stream of countless suns. Modern physics, influenced by relativity theory and quantum mechanics, has abandoned the notions of time and space as separate entities; time is described as 'curved' space flowing back into itself. Moreover, it is recognized that at a subatomic level the observer affects the observed in the act of observing. The basic oneness of the universe has been reasserted, and the more we penetrate matter, the more nature appears as 'a complicated web of relations with various parts of the whole'.[24]

But while modern physics has revived some of the insights of alchemy about the ultimate nature of the universe, the modern scientist proceeds in a different way from the medieval alchemist. Most modern scientists strain for objectivity and deny that their investigations have any moral or spiritual meaning. The nuclear scientist is the ultimate exemplar of this trend. By delving headlong into the heart of matter, by splitting the atom regardless of the consequences, he has released an energy which he cannot control and which threatens to consume him. He has no internal restraints, and is constantly tempted to use his acquired skill in a destructive way.

Although the modern scientist and the medieval alchemist are very different in their approach, they share a common desire to master nature. In their attempt to extract 'noble' metals from 'impure' ones, alchemists came up against what they considered the 'darksome and chaotic' forces of nature, just as the achievement of 'inward gold' demanded 'the conquest of all the dark and irrational impulses of the soul'.[25] In their Gnostic and Neoplatonic world, the alchemists saw within the crucible of nature the spirit suffocated by crude matter and evil forces locked in battle with the good.

Indeed, there are many aspects of alchemy that are anti-ecological. Its man-centred drive to transform nature and to create artificial gold reflects the ambition of Western science to conquer the world. It tries to bring nature to perfection by interfering with its course. Above all, it has a strongly hierarchical view of nature which reflects the hierarchical society in which the alchemists lived.

In their scheme of things, alchemists give different symbolic value to different metals, in both a social and a spiritual sense. In their natural hierarchy, lead represents the chaotic, heavy and sick condition of metal or of inward man. Gold on the other hand is a form of 'congealed light', an 'earthly sun' which expresses the perfection of both metallic and human existence. They not only have an aristocracy of metals, with 'noble' and 'base' elements, but call their work the *ars regia*, the 'royal art'.

Alchemists, ancient and modern, have always considered themselves as part of an intellectual elite, the carriers of hermetic and esoteric knowledge which the profane cannot understand. In their medieval underground, they formed a secret brotherhood not unlike Freemasonry today.

Not surprisingly, Plato in his deeply authoritarian and hierarchical dystopia *The Republic* associated the three classes of citizen with gold, silver, and iron and bronze. He makes the link in his notorious myth of the 'noble lie' which is used to ensure that people keep to their allotted place:

> You are, all of you in this community [*polis*], brothers. But when god fashioned you, he added gold in the composition of those of you who are qualified to be Rulers [which is why their prestige is greatest]; he put silver in the Auxiliaries [those who are responsible for government, the army and the police], and iron and bronze in the farmers and other workers.

The principal care of the Rulers, or Guardians, is to watch the mixture of metals in the characters of the children who must be promoted or degraded depending on whether traces of metals outside their class are found in their make-up. There is a prophecy, Plato pretends, that the state will be ruined when it has 'Guardians of silver or bronze'.[26]

Alchemy today is fashionable among new seekers and spiritual ecologists. It rightly sees that humanity is an integral part of nature and that humans should be aware of the dangers of interfering with its course. It accepts that the observer will affect the observed and that scientific endeavour is based on probability and not certainty. It recognizes the need for the scientist to make him- or herself authentic and responsible before attempting to reveal the secrets of nature. It teaches that a successful discovery in science is merely an external sign that the scientist has completed his work, just as a blindfolded Zen archer's arrow reaching its target demonstrates his inner concentration and wholeness.

But alchemy can hardly provide a paradigm for a new science. Paradoxically, it appeals to the 'base' instinct of self-interest in man by promising to 'ennoble' him. By holding out the prospect of eternal youth and boundless wealth, it encourages him to break the limits of nature. Rooted in the hierarchical world-view of the feudal order, it has strongly elitist and authoritarian connotations. Above all, it came to express in the West in the Middle Ages an arrogant and conquering spirit in its attempt to 'improve' and 'perfect' nature by artificial means.

Alchemists, like archaic man and the tribal blacksmith, instinctively recognized the dangers of mining and smelting, of clawing into the womb of Mother Earth and firing her entrails. They had to purify themselves so that the evil of what they were doing did not enter their own souls. But why undertake such a dangerous enterprise in the first place?

*The Book of Seven Chapters*, attributed to Hermes Trismegistus, is explicit about the physical, psychological and financial benefits of the 'royal art': 'With the help of Almighty God this [philosopher's] stone will free you and protect you against sadness and trouble, and especially against whatever may be harmful to body and soul. It will lead you from darkness to light, from the desert to home, and from indigence to riches.'[27] Alchemists were clearly as good as modern scientists in the justification of their work, and certainly more frank about its personal advantages. They did not need to appeal to progress and the general good.

But was personal advantage rather than a love of wisdom their principal motive? Alchemists may have been more morally responsible in trying to purify themselves than modern scientists, but they were no less prepared to interfere with the course of nature in order to 'improve' and 'perfect' it. They claimed to be searching for wisdom; how much of their search was motivated by greed? Why should gold be considered superior to lead, any more than a peacock to a chicken?

Light and darkness are both essential to life. Lead has it own intrinsic value, and without it, the shine of gold would not blind so many.

### An alchemical parable

The Kogi, who still live in the mountain fastness of Colombia, understand well the dangers of mining, fashioning gold and interfering with the course of nature. They believe that gold has a property that enables the world to protect itself. It is the remnants of the menstrual blood of Mother Earth. But man's rapacious search for gold and other materials is leading to the death of the world:

> If we plant an orange tree or any type of tree and then pull it up by the roots it will die. Digging out the earth's gold is the same thing. It could die . . . If I cut my foot off I cannot walk. When they dig into the earth and take its gold it is the same thing . . . Gold has its own thought and it can speak. It is a living being. They must stop stealing it. If they take all the gold the world will end.[28]

The Kogi know where the gold is in the mountains but they only make offerings to it. It is vital to the life of the Great Mother. They are right to think that it should be left alone, radiating out goodness from its hidden deposits, rather than firing the destructive greed of humanity.

The 'Elder Brothers', the Kogi, have recently decided to speak for the first time to the 'Younger Brothers' who are destroying the earth. They see before their eyes that the plants and creatures of the Andes are failing to breed. The world is sick at heart, and it shows among the lichens and heathers and streams of the mountains. The overweening ambition of modern science is killing the earth, and the Philosopher's Stone remains as elusive as ever.

# 13

# THE SCIENTIFIC REVOLUTION

## *Nature on the Rack*

> And it is said that nature can be understood only by
> reduction, that only by reducing her to numbers does she
> become clear. That without mathematics 'one wanders
> in vain through a dark labyrinth'. It is decided that
> which cannot be measured and reduced to numbers is
> not real.
>
> Galileo Galilei

The scientific revolution of the sixteenth and seventeenth centuries is
one of the chief sources of the dominant Western world-view. Where
as the Greeks saw nature as a vast living organism, science in the
seventeenth century discovered a world of dead matter in motion.
By depicting the world as a machine governed by universal laws
which must be weighed, measured and classified to be understood,
the philosophers and scientists of the day paved the way for modern
industrial and mechanical civilization.

It marked a fundamental shift in our relationship with the natural world, which was no longer considered a divine dwelling for
humanity but an object to be used. By insisting on a rigid split
between the observer and the observed, it further alienated man
from nature. No longer fearful of disturbing the vanished gods,
he could exploit the machine of nature to the hilt. Released from
earlier moral and religious curbs, he felt free to maximize his power
in the untrammelled pursuit of his own ends. In a double process,
it not only desanctified nature, but also gave man enormous power
over it.

There was also a shift from metaphysics to physics, from the
contemplation of being to the observation of becoming. Philosophy
abandoned its theological foundation and declared its independence
as a source of truth. The human mind no longer felt confined by
God, and turned from the contemplation of the absolute and eternal

168

to the knowledge of the particular and contingent. In the process, the mathematical science of the physical world and its phenomena took precedence over metaphysical accounts of the universe. It distinguished between an empirical 'fact' and a metaphysical 'truth'. Rather than contemplating Absolute Being or the Supreme Good, it looked towards what it could sense, control and direct – the motion of physical bodies on earth.

Whereas the medieval cosmology saw nature as an organism with certain inherent tendencies, the new science saw it as a clock governed by eternal laws. It broke down the distinction between celestial and terrestrial zones, maintaining that the laws observed on earth were true elsewhere in heaven. The earth was just another celestial body. Above all, it expanded man's power; if he could discover and understand natural laws, he could dream of absolute mastery over nature.

Just as Portuguese voyagers at the end of the fifteenth century opened up new worlds in the west and east for European colonization, so the scientists and the philosophers of the scientific revolution gave Europe power to control and direct natural forces. Both endeavours involved the use of telescopes and both led to the exploitation of 'virgin' territory. On the title page of Francis Bacon's *Great Instauration* (1620) a ship sails symbolically between two Neo-Classical pillars out into the wide ocean and the new worlds beyond. The slogan declares: 'Many shall pass through and knowledge will increase.'

## The indignity of animals

The attitude of the new science to nature perhaps comes across best in its treatment of animals. The more the powers of man were elevated, the more animals became degraded. They were considered beings created by God entirely for human use, and of no intrinsic value. Indeed, their feelings and welfare were completely disregarded. The Flemish anatomist Andreas Vesalius (1514–64) has been remembered for greatly advancing the science of biology by his anatomical work *De Humani Corporis Fabrica* (1543) with its description of the bones and the nervous system. He was the first to challenge the Aristotelian doctrine that the heart was the physical correlative of the personality, in favour of the brain and the nervous system. Above all, he was a master vivisectionist on live animals without anaesthetics.

Considering medicine to be 'by far the most beneficial, necessary, abstruse, and laborious' of the arts discovered by man, Vesalius trained himself without guidance in the dissection of what he calls 'brute creatures'. He recommended that after training on dead animals, students should proceed to living animals in order to investigate the action and use of the parts. It was his custom to explain the precise point to be observed to his audience before a public dissection of a living animal so that the students could concentrate on the cries of the animal. He particularly recommended performing a vivisection on a pregnant sow or bitch: 'It is better to choose a sow on account of the voice. For a dog, after being bound for some time, no matter what you do to it, finally neither barks nor howls, and so you are sometimes unable to observe the loss or weakening of the voice.'

The first thing to do is to fasten the animal to the operating table as firmly 'as your patience and your resources allow' in such a way that it lies upon its back and presents the front of its neck and the trunk of its body. Special attention must be given to the upper jaw, so that it may be firmly fastened to a plank: 'Do this with a chain or a strong cord fixed in front of the canine teeth . . . so that the neck may be extended and the head motionless, and the animal at the same time free to breathe and cry.'

The next thing to do is to make a long incision in the throat with a sharp razor, cutting through the skin and the muscles under it right down to the trachea. The enthusiastic Vesalius continues:

> Then I grasp the trachea in my hand, and freeing it merely with the aid of my fingers from the muscles that lie upon it . . . Then I also examine the recurrent nerves attached to the side of the trachea, and sometimes I ligature them, sometimes sever them . . . You can quickly examine without much loss of blood, and very nicely hear, what a powerful outward blast the animal produces.
>
> Then I pass to the abdomen . . . by these two incisions, we shall expose the intestines and uterus distended with the fetuses. But we must take particular care that one of the audience put his thumb on the vessels which descend below the breastbone and make for the abdomen. For these are the only vessels up to now from which much blood flows.[1]

Vesalius was sentenced to death by the Inquisition for 'body snatching' and for dissecting dead human bodies; there was no problem with the Church about dissecting live animals since they were not considered to have immortal souls. His death sentence was commuted to a pilgrimage to Jerusalem; he died on the return journey, confident that he had served humanity, but without any remorse for the untold suffering he had caused other animals. What Vesalius did to animals, the new breed of scientist were to do to nature as a whole. And the cries of Mother Earth would be ignored.

### The Copernican revolution

Although natural magic and alchemy prepared the way, the scientific revolution may be said to have begun with the publication of Polish scientist Copernicus' *On the Revolutions of the Heavenly Orbs*. Nicolas Copernicus (1475–1543) completed the work which made him the founder of modern astronomy in 1530 but it was not until 1543 that he touched the first printed copy with his dying hand. It destroyed at a stroke the Ptolemaic and medieval view of the geocentric universe, by asserting that the sun was the centre. The Copernican revolution in the history of Western thought was as important as Darwin's and Einstein's, and marked a new shift in human consciousness and the transformation of the scientific paradigm of the world.

Johann Kepler (1571–1630), a German astronomer, continued Copernicus' search for universal laws to explain the movements of the planets. Rejecting Aristotelian teleology, he held that every body tends to remain stationary. But to explain movement he argued that when one object approaches another there is a 'mutual affection', a kind of magnetic pull. Thus a stone falls to the earth because it attracts it just as the tides move because of the attraction of the moon. In our universe the sun and the planets work like magnets, and in rotating the sun acts as a cause, pushing the planets around with it. Kepler was explicit about the analogy between nature and and a machine:

> I am much occupied with the investigation of the physical causes. My aim in this is to show that the celestial machine is to be likened not to a divine organism but rather to a clockwork ... insofar as nearly all the manifold movements are carried out by means of a single, quite simple magnetic force, as in the case of a clockwork all motions [are caused] by a simple

weight. Moreover I show how this physical conception is to be presented through calculation and geometry.

Kepler was so intoxicated with geometry and its explicatory power that he exclaimed: 'Why waste words? Geometry existed before the Creation, is co-eternal with the mind of God, *is God himself.*'[2] Geometry thus provided God with a model for the creation, and was implanted in man as innate knowledge for him to uncover.

This view of God as the creator of a machine, the maker of a clocklike world, had obvious deterministic implications. It also exploded the ancient and medieval view of the world as *anima mundi*, an animated being.

With the Italian Galileo Galilei (1564–1642) the new science reached its maturity. Developing Kepler's views, he believed that the book of nature was written in the language of mathematics and could only be understood by a mathematician:

> Philosophy is written in that vast book which stands ever open before our eyes, I mean the universe; but it cannot be read until we have learnt the language and become familiar with the characters in which it is written. It is written in mathematical language, and the letters are triangles, circles and other geometrical figures, without which means it is humanly impossible to comprehend a single word.[3]

While formulating the basic principles of gravitation and planetary motion, Galileo further developed Pythagoras' view that 'all things are numbers'. Only those aspects of the universe that could be described by using mathematics had any real basis: mass, motion, shape, number and force are real; the complex messages of the senses are illusory. Reality thus is a complex of *quantities* in time and space and not *qualities*. He was not concerned with framing theories consistent with a body of doctrine, but with measuring the movement of physical bodies. He preferred the finding of his optic glass, as it surveyed mountains in the moon and planets in the sky, to the authority of the *Summa Theologica* of St Aquinas. Measurable quantities are objective and certain, while qualities are subjective and unreliable:

> I think that tastes, odours, colours, and so on are no more than mere names so far as the object in which we place them

is concerned, and that they reside only in consciousness. Hence
if the living creatures were removed, all these qualities would
be wiped away and annihilated.[4]

This had two important corollaries. Firstly, only the measurable is
scientific knowledge and what cannot be measured cannot be said to
exist. Secondly, only objective knowledge is 'true' whereas subjective
knowledge is not. The philosophical foundations of the new science
had been laid down.

The Church of course was not pleased with Galileo's view that
the earth was no longer at the centre of the universe and preferred
the authority of Scripture to that of the new science. The Inquisition
imprisoned him as a heretic but his view began to prevail in the
scientific community.

Galileo introduced the new principle of inertia in physics; the
God of Aristotle and Aquinas was no longer necessary to sustain
movement since motion, like immobility, will continue until affected
by some force. He admitted that he knew nothing of the ultimate
nature of the forces he was measuring, and remained silent about
the origin of the universe or the nature of gravity. But the effect
of his dethronement of man from the centre of the universe had
enormous repercussions. It soon become apparent that humanity had
far greater power over nature than he had ever imagined. Galileo and
his fellow scientists showed that science through careful observation
and mathematical analysis could transform the world and alter the
course of nature.

## Newton's light

The scientific revolution culminated in the work of Isaac Newton (1642–1727) a hundred and fifty years after the death of
Copernicus. Newton combined the astronomical revolution carried
out by Copernicus and Kepler with the new theories of motion
proposed by Galileo and Descartes. He acknowledged his debt in
the famous phrase 'If I have seen further it is by standing on the
shoulders of Giants'. Newton left them behind, however, to develop
his own distinctive style, creating in his *magnum opus, Philosophiae
Naturalis Principia Mathematica* (1687), a whole new mathematical
method and language to investigate natural philosophy.

Although he brought the scientific revolution to its fruition,

Newton appears as a transitory figure between the medieval and modern worlds. He was one of the last great Renaissance magicians. Not only was he an assiduous student of alchemy, but he left a stream of manuscripts on the Bible, especially the prophecies of Daniel and the Apocalypse.[5]

It is of course as a mathematician and scientist that Newton is primarily remembered, and the mechanical thinking of the scientific revolution came to dominate his thoughts. The immediate context of his work was Descartes' *Principia Philosophiae* (1644) in which the French philosopher had elaborated a mechanistic alternative to the Aristotelian natural philosophy with its fundamental distinction between terrestrial and celestial physics. For Descartes, as for Galileo, matter was the same in heaven as on earth, and the properties of matter strictly limited to their mathematical aspects; qualitative properties like inherent forces or those perceived by the five senses had no place. His philosophy was unswervingly mechanical, and he even explained magnetic attraction and repulsion in terms of streams of particles emitted by the magnet. His overweening confidence led him to assert at the end of his treatise on the principles of philosophy:

> And thus by simple enumeration, it is concluded that no phenomena of nature have been omitted by me in this treatise. For nothing is to be numbered among the phenomena of nature, except what is perceived by the sense ... thus ... there is nothing visible or perceptible in this world which I have not explained.[6]

Newton worked largely in reaction to Descartes. Descartes disapproved of atomism; Newton became a convinced atomist. Where Descartes depicted motion algebraically, Newton developed a dynamics written in geometry and founded a new branch of mathematics, calculus, to do so.

In his celebrated *Mathematical Principles of Natural Philosophy* (1687), Newton took off further from the mechanical philosophy of Kepler and Descartes, undertaking an investigation of forces and motions, of bodies on the earth and in the heavens. He was principally concerned with the properties of natural bodies in terms of quantity of matter or mass, quantity of motion or *momentum*, passive force or inertia, and three kinds of active *force*. He asserted the existence of immovable absolute space and absolute time, distinguishing them carefully from the relative space and relative time of the senses. In so doing, he described the world as a kind of machine and depicted the scientist as a mechanic trying to understand its workings.

The work was particularly influential in laying down a model of scientific method which proceeded by testing hypotheses against experience and observation. In his preface, Newton wrote:

> I offer this work as the mathematical principles of philosophy, for the whole burden of philosophy seems to consist in this: from the phenomena of motions to investigate the forces of nature, and then from these forces to demonstrate the other phenomena ... I wish we could derive the rest of the phenomena of Nature by the same kind of reasoning from mechanical principles, for I am induced by many reasons to suspect that they may all depend upon certain forces by which the particles of bodies, by some causes hitherto unknown, are either mutually impelled toward one another and cohere in regular figures, or are repelled and recede from one another.[7]

In his *Optics* (1704), Newton further determined the composition of white light, dividing the spectrum into the musical division of seven colour bands. He proposed the mechanical hypothesis that light consists of 'multitudes of unimaginable small and swift corpuscles of various sizes, springing from shining bodies at great distances one after another'.[8]

But although Newton depicted the universe as a machine composed of particles of matter governed by the law of gravity, the gravitational forces which work as powers of attraction remained a mystery. He rejected the notion of innate gravity: "'Tis unconceivable that inanimate brute matter should (without the mediation of something else which is not material) operate upon and affect other matter without mutual contact.'[9] But how gravitional forces operated continued to worry him. In his 1706 *Queries to the Optick*, he confessed the limits of his knowledge: '[W]hat I call Attraction may be performed by impulse, or by some other means unknown to me. I use that Word here to signify only in general any Force by which Bodies tend towards one another, whatsoever the Cause.'[10] Rejecting Descartes' first law of nature in his *Principles of Philosophy* that 'each thing, as far as it is in its power, always remains in the same state', he even was prepared to admit that 'particles have not only a *vis inertiae*, accompanied with such passive Laws of Motion as naturally result from that Force, but also they are moved by certain Active Principles'.[11] To many, this sounded suspiciously liked the 'occult qualities' of Aristotelian and medieval cosmology. The German mathematician Leibniz declared that 'gravity must be a scholastic occult quality or the effect of a miracle'. Voltaire suggested after a visit to London in 1730 that Newton's description of gravity with its animist and occult overtones proved the principal stumbling block to the acceptance of his theory in Paris.[12]

The mystery of gravity was only resolved when Einstein suggested that the gravitional field is not *in* space and time, but *contains* space and time. It underlies both material bodies and the space between them. The moon goes round the earth, not because it is pulled towards it by gravitational force, but because the space-time in which it moves is curved. Ironically, after three centuries of Newtonian science, gravity is now seen to act like a formative cause in a similar way to the *anima mundi* of the medieval cosmologists.

For Newton, the only way to explain gravitional force without reference to an innate property of matter was to fall back on the idea of God as a cause: 'There exists an infinite and omnipresent spirit in which matter is moved according to mathematical laws.'[13] Indeed, he saw the *Principia* as a contribution to theology as well as natural philosophy, and included a prose hymn to God the creator.

In his *Optics*, Newton wrote:

> The main business of natural philosophy is to argue from phenomena without feigning hypotheses and to deduce causes from effects, till we come to the very first cause, which certainly is not mechanical; and not only to unfold the mechanism of the world, but chiefly to resolve these and such like questions.

But how is it that nature does nothing in vain? From where does all the order and beauty we see in the world arise? Newton replied that every design must have a designer: 'Does it not appear from phenomena that there is a Being, incorporeal, living, intelligent, omnipresent ...?'[14] For Newton, the new physics demonstrated an old argument for the existence of God which became the focal point of deistic thought in the eighteenth century.

Towards the end of his active life, Newton further argued that the order of the cosmos was incompatible with mere mechanical necessity. Using the same argument of design employed in natural theology, he wrote at the conclusion of the *Principia*: 'This most beautiful system of the sun, planets, and comets, could only proceed from the counsel and dominion of an intelligent and powerful Being ... This Being governs all things, not as the soul of the world, but as the Lord over all.'

Although his God is a creator deity, Newton stood firmly within the Christian tradition by defining God as eternal, infinite, perfect and omnipotent. God intervenes in nature and is able to vary the laws of nature, creating particles of matter. Above all, He is not a remote first cause but a 'Lord God' and 'Universal Ruler' whom Newton believed we should treat as such: 'We reverence and adore him on account of his dominion: for we adore him as his servants; and a god without dominion, providence, and final causes, is nothing else but Fate and Nature.'[15]

The rigorous mathematician also believed in millenarian prophecies. Poring over the prophetic books of the Bible for textual evidence, he surmised that the second coming would bring Christ's judgement over all the earth and his reign would not last a thousand years but for ever. Newton may have been the principal architect of the mechanical philosophy which would hold sway until Einstein, but he was also a religious seeker who tried to recover the lost wisdom of the ancients, and elaborate golden prophecies for the future. As he contemplated the starry heavens, dissected rays of light or pondered over gravity, he never ceased to hear the distant 'music of the spheres' or the 'pipes of Pan' to which the whole of nature danced.[16]

Newton's contribution to science was enormous. He created an account of gravitation that encompassed both terrestrial and celestial phenomena which could be quantified in mathematics, thereby providing a physical basis for the Copernican universe. It had a lasting impact on the Western mind, and although Newtonian dynamics is now seen as part of Einstein's broader canvas, most people still think in Newtonian terms. Newton's laws work well enough to build bridges and to guide spacecraft to the moon.

Newton in fact was never satisfied with the mechanical philosophy which he did so much to promote. Although intellectually he accepted that particles in motion constitute physical reality, he could not help feeling that such a view was too confining. Partly for this reason he turned to alchemy, with its doctrine of *anima mundi*, which opened up new vistas for him.

None the less, his published ideas were to lead to the triumph of the mechanical philosophy which depicted the world as so much 'inanimate brute matter' in motion governed by mathematical laws. He helped develop scientific method as an impartial tool, stressing the independent autonomy of man separate from the rest of nature. In the long term, his way of thinking contributed enormously to the mechanistic and atomistic view of the world which came to prevail in the West. Coupled with the rise of capitalism and the Industrial Revolution, it enabled nature to be mastered and exploited without restraint. By joining the Royal Mint, Newton united symbolically in his own career the making of money with mechanical science, a union still graphically depicted by his portrait on the back of the one-pound note of British currency.

In his own lifetime, Newton was virtually deified. Voltaire, who did so much to publicize Newton's views of light, calculus and cosmology into France, wrote in 1736 that his compass measuring the universe had lifted the veil hiding the soul of nature.[17] The Augustan poet Alexander Pope wrote the epitaph:

> Nature, and Nature's Laws lay hid in Night.
> God said, *Let Newton be*! and All was Light.[18]

Newton became a national hero of England. He was appointed president of the Royal Society and became the first scientist ever to be knighted. But as a man, he was far from pleasant. He had little aesthetic sense: he dismissed great works of sculpture as 'stone dolls' and viewed poetry as 'a kind of ingenious nonsense'.[19] As a scientist, he was profoundly jealous of his reputation: he tried to steal the work of the Astronomer Royal, John Flamsteed, and in a dispute with Leibniz over who first developed calculus he found great satisfaction in 'breaking Leibniz's heart'. And as Warden of the Royal Mint, he sent several men to the gallows for counterfeiting.[20]

The popular image of Newton discovering the laws of gravity while sitting under an apple tree in a sheltered garden implies that he is at one with nature. But the scientific revolution of the sixteenth and seventeenth centuries marked the beginning not only of the Promethean voyage of Western science but also of the violation of Gaia, the earth goddess. Henceforth nature came to be seen as inanimate matter governed by external forces operating according to mathematical laws. In the words of the philosopher A.

N. Whitehead, nature became 'a dull affair, soundless, scentless, colourless; merely the hurrying of material, endlessly, meaninglessly'.[21] It was nature reduced to *naturata naturans*, merely what exists, not *natura naturata*, what might be generated. In the bright light of mechanical and instrumental rationality, the world soul, *anima mundi*, fled in terror. Although exploded by Einstein in the twentieth century, the mental framework lingers in the popular mind like smoke in the barrel of a gun.

# 14

## PHILOSOPHERS OF THE
## BRAVE NEW WORLD

Knowledge itself is power.
Francis Bacon

The Renaissance which occurred in Europe from the mid-fourteenth century to the end of the sixteenth marked a major shift in human consciousness. It proved to be a great cultural movement: a renewed interest in antiquity coincided with the flowering of the arts and sciences as well as the expansion of the philosophical horizon.

Classical works of art introduced into Italy by refugees and visiting scholars from the Byzantine world soon spread throughout Europe. The new humanists who revered the ancient writers of Greece and Rome wished to reinterpret their message for modern Christians in order to perfect human life on earth. Only later did humanism became primarily a secular philosophy devoted to the propagation of human values alone. Nevertheless, the stress on human potential not only led to the growth of individualism in private and public life, but also resulted in the elevation of humanity to the detriment of the 'lower' animals.

The principal message of the moral and theological writings of the sixteenth century was to define the unique status of man and his ascendancy over the rest of the creation.[1] Whatever the Bible might say, man's role was now definitely considered one of dominion, not of stewardship. Man might be in a fallen state on earth but Sir Matthew Hale spoke for his contemporaries when he declared that he was the 'Viceregent and Deputy of Almighty God'. He insisted that 'all the creatures were made for man, subjected to his government and appointed for his use'. And there was no room for sentiment in dealing with the rest of the creation; the Irish scientist Robert Boyle correctly realized that a 'veneration' of nature is 'a discouraging impediment to the empire of man over the inferior creatures'. After all, the whole purpose of studying nature was that 'being known, it

180

may be master'd, managed and used in the services of human life'.[2]

From Aristotle, the medieval Scholastics developed the view that the soul consists of three elements – the nutritive soul, shared by man with vegetables; the sensitive soul, shared by animals, and the intellectual and rational soul, peculiar to man. Man was thus elevated to special status, placed halfway between beasts and the angels in the Great Chain of Being. The notion was a source of much back-slapping and self-congratulation in the fifteenth and sixteenth centuries.

The fifteenth-century Italian thinker Giovanni Pico della Mirandola celebrated more than anyone else the divine attributes of man. The last of the medieval schoolmen with a mystical bent, he was sufficiently a humanist to suffer persecution from the Church of Rome. Drawing on Neoplatonism and Christianity, he set out to underline the unique dignity of man. Man for Pico is an 'incredible and wonderful thing', placed in the middle of the 'universal chain' of being:

> Man is the intermediary between creatures, the intimate of higher beings and the king of lower beings, the interpreter of nature by the sharpness of his senses, by the questing curiosity of his reason, and by the light of his intelligence, the interval between enduring eternity and the flow of time.

He believed that the 'Great Artisan' had set man in the centre of the world, confined by no limits and able to determine his own nature, in accordance with his own free will. He had endowed him with all kinds of seeds of every way of life, and whatever seeds each man cultivates will grow and bear fruit in him:

> If these seeds are vegetative, he will be like a plant; if they are sensitive, he will become like the beasts; if they are rational, he will become like a heavenly creature; if intellectual, he will be an angel and a son of God. And if, content with the lot of no created being, he withdraws into the centre of his own oneness, his spirit, made one with God in the solitary darkness of his spirit, which is above all things, will surpass all things.[3]

The Italian Platonist Marsilio Ficino (1433–99) concurred. President of an academy for the diffusion of Platonic doctrines, Ficino also became a canon of the cathedral of Florence. Developing a *Platonic Theology*, he called on the alchemists' mentor Hermes Trismegistus for confirmation that man is a 'great miracle, a living creature worthy of reverence and adoration'. If man uses the 'Platonic wings' of intellect and will, he will become godlike and fly towards God. At the same time, he is the immortal vicar of God, since he inhabits and cultivates all elements and is present on earth without being absent from the ether. Above all, as lord of the creation, he rules the whole world and makes use of all things:

> not only the elements, but also all the animals which belong to the elements, the animals of the earth, of the water, and of the air, for food, convenience, and pleasure, and the higher, celestial beings for knowledge and the miracle of magic. Not only does he make use of the animals, he also rules them. It is true, with the weapons received from nature some animals may at times attack man or escape his control. But with the weapons he has invented himself man avoids the attacks of wild animals, puts them to flight, and tames them ... Certainly he is the god of the animals, for he makes use of them all, rules them all, and instructs many of them.[4]

This view came to dominate in the West in the subsequent centuries, justifying the unrestrained domination and exploitation of nature and animals.

### Francis Bacon and the advancement of learning

It was the ambition of the English thinker and politician Francis Bacon (1561–1626) to sweep away the medieval cobwebs and the Christian attitude to science which Marlowe had so brilliantly and recently portrayed in his play *Doctor Faustus* (*c.* 1588). The medieval legend of a man who sold his soul to the Devil had became identified with a Dr Faustus, a sixteenth-century necromancer. In Marlowe's play, Faustus, weary of his work, calls up Mephistopheles, who offers the magician a pact to surrender his soul to the Devil in return for twenty-four years of life during which all his desires will be fulfilled.

The Faustus legend shows the fascinated dread in which the Middle Ages held natural science. Under Pauline and Augustinian theology, nature (including man) had been represented as depraved and corrupt because of the Fall. The divine order, the order of grace, was felt to be wholly separate from, and directly opposed to 'Nature'. In this context, natural science was considered a form of forbidden knowledge, and the attempt to unlock its secrets was seen as meddling dangerously with the Satan-ridden earth. Astrology and alchemy were aligned with black magic and the four elements were considered the abodes of evil spirits.

Bacon was chiefly instrumental in overthrowing this attitude; it was his task to prove that science was not Mephistophelean but Promethean, an activity not harmful but beneficial to man.[5] His work proved the culmination of a process from the late fifteenth and sixteenth centuries which led to the rebirth of confidence in 'Nature'. By reclaiming the physical world from the grip of Satan, Bacon successfully showed that science did not necessarily involve a Faustian pact with the Devil, but could be reconciled with religion. Indeed, he paved the way to a form of scientific deism, with God the Artificer revealing himself in his created world as much as in his scriptures.

But while sweeping away the medieval cobwebs, Bacon also laid down the disastrous Western scientific project to conquer and control nature. Having separated science from religion, it was only a short step for man to see himself as the measure of all things. The new scientist of the Renaissance became, like Marlowe's Dr Faustus, a man striving for infinite power, consumed by the ambition to become the 'great Emperor of the world'.

Bacon has long been venerated as the great champion of intellectual liberty, as the man who drew the attention of philosophers from abstract speculation to the direct observation of nature. It was his method 'continually to dwell among things soberly'. He insisted that those who 'determine not to conjecture and guess, but to find out and know; not to invent fables and romances of worlds, but to look into, and dissect the nature of this real world, must consult only things themselves'.[6] To achieve this end, Bacon wished to keep science separate from religion, constantly reminding his readers how the progress of science had been hindered by the conservative prejudice of Scholastic theologians. 'It is therefore most wise,' he wrote, 'soberly to render unto faith the things that are faith's.'[7]

What Bacon overlooked or did not care about was that to dissect is to murder. In his enthusiastic celebration of science shorn of sacred philosophy he inadvertently summed up the new conquering attitude towards nature in the brave new world of Renaissance science.

'Knowledge itself is power,' Bacon declared in 1597.[8] Rejecting the deductive reasoning of the Scholastic philosophers of his day, he proposed in Of the Advancement of Learning (1605) his own inductive method of interpreting nature by which the results of experience are studied in order to reach a general conclusion.

Science, he argued, would restore man's dominion over the animals which he had lost after the Fall. Having been expelled from the Garden of Eden through eating of the tree of knowledge, man's only way forward was to eat further of the tree and create his own garden in this vale of tears. It would be hard and painful work, but the goal was comfort and ease on earth. In this way Bacon reconciled traditional Christianity with the new technological optimism.

Bacon considered that man has a spirit or reasoning power which makes him like God and a bodily appetite which makes him like the animals. The virtuous man should therefore seek 'victory over his nature' and to 'alter and subdue nature' within himself as well as outside himself. The value of studies was precisely because they 'perfect nature' since natural abilities are 'like natural plants, that need pruning by study'.9

Bacon's considered nature incomplete and corrupt; it was the duty of man to transform and improve it. He is not only the lord of creation but its principle of order:

> Man, if we look to final causes, may be regarded as the centre of the world; insomuch that if man were taken away from the world, the rest would seem to be all astray, without aim or purpose . . . and leading to nothing. For the whole world works together in the service of man; and there is nothing from which he does not derive use and fruit . . . insomuch that all things seem to be going about man's business and not their own.10

Bacon was no proto-Romantic and castigated his contemporaries for taking an aesthetic interest in nature; 'we respect, contemplate and reverence Nature,' he insisted, 'more than is fit'. It is not something of value or beauty in itself since it 'took beginning from the Word of God by means of confused matter, and the entrance of prevarication and corruption'.11 It is therefore man's task to improve and perfect fallen nature through his science and art. And the way to achieve this is to try to understand it in order to control it. His belief that it was necessary to put nature on the rack and force her to reveal her secrets was akin to the rape of Mother Earth. It is a process not of seduction but of ravishment.

Bacon's attitude to nature comes across most clearly in his view of gardening. He felt making a garden, in which man imposes his will on nature, to be the purest of human pleasures. His ideal allows for the presence of the wild, but it is carefully controlled and circumscribed. In his blueprint there would be 'a green in the entrance, a heath, or desert, in the going forth, and the main garden in the midst, besides alleys on both sides'. The garden itself would best be square, encompassed on all sides with a 'stately arched hedge'.[12] It is the model of a bowling green, with the wilderness beyond the hedges intended to emphasize the security and comfort within.

As Bacon makes clear in his utopia *New Atlantis*, the avowed aim of his philosophy and the end of the foundation of his ideal society is 'the knowledge of cause, and secret motions of things; and the enlarging of the bounds of human empire, to the effecting of all things possible'.[13] But Bacon is not content to observe nature and direct it; he wishes to transform it. A central institution on the island of Bensalem is a centre for scientific study called Solomon's House. Its spokesman anticipates modern genetic engineering for plants and animals. He boasts that they experiment with grafting and inoculating, making by artificial means trees and flowers come on earlier or later than their seasons, and to reach fruition more speedily than by their natural course. They also make their fruit greater and sweeter, and of a differing taste, smell, colour and figure from their natural ones.

The most chilling and prophetic passage comes when he waxes lyrically about the trials they make upon beasts, birds and fishes:

> We have also parks and enclosures of all sorts of beasts and birds, which we use not only for view or rareness, but likewise for dissection and trials, that thereby we may take light what may be wrought upon the body of man. Wherein we find many strange effects, as continuing life in them, though divers parts, which you account vital, be perished and taken forth; resuscitating of some that seem dead in appearance, and the like. We try, also, all poisons, and other medicines upon them as well as chirurgery as physic. By art, likewise, we make them greater or taller than their kind is, and, contrariwise, dwarf them, and stay their growth; we make them more fruitful and bearing than their kind is, and, contrariwise, barren and not generative; also we make them different in colour, shape, activity — many ways. We find means to make conmixtures of divers kinds, which have

produced many new kinds, and them not barren, as the general opinion is.[14]

Bacon is the arch-imperialist of nature, wishing to extend human control to its furthest corners. The Royal Society was partly inspired by Solomon's House and, on its inauguration, was proud to invoke Bacon's name.

It comes as no surprise to learn that Bacon was a powerful statesman as well as a philosopher. Having served as Solicitor General, he eventually became Lord Chancellor. In the essay 'Of a King', it was his considered opinion that 'a king is a mortal god on earth, unto whom the living God hath lent his own name as a great honour' – a view which no doubt facilitated his own placement at the court. The Romantic poet and visionary William Blake was astonished by how much 'Contemptible Knavery & Folly' Bacon's *Essays* contained.[15] It was only in our century that the full nightmare of the Lord Chancellor's vision has been realized. Blake declared 'Bacon's philosophy has Ruin'd England'; two hundred years later one might add that it has ruined the earth itself.

## Descartes and the mastery of nature

The Frenchman René Descartes (1596–1650), who is considered the 'father of modern philosophy', also founded analytic geometry. Physics for him was nothing but mechanics, that is, applied geometry. All physical objects are matter in motion. It was therefore natural for him to liken the entire universe, including the human body, to a machine. Everything in his scheme of things consists of matter governed by mechanistic principles. God had set the universe in motion according to fixed mathematical laws, no different from the laws through which a king rules his subjects. In his *Discourse on Method* (1637), Descartes argued that the goal of science is to discover these laws in order to understand the elements in nature in sufficient detail so that 'we might put them in the same way to all the uses for which they are appropriate, and thereby make ourselves, as it were, masters and possessors of nature'.[16] Human freedom may have been the central goal for Descartes, but he could only see it in terms of mastery.[17]

Descartes proceeded by a method of systematic doubt, in which he subjected all inherited opinions to the test of reason. Turning over existing ideas and values was like looking through a barrel of apples, keeping the sound and throwing away the rotten before they infect the others. The process, however, was entirely that of a disembodied intellect. It is significant that Descartes should have tried to make a *tabula rasa* of all existing philosophy during the lull in a military campaign in Germany. It was winter and he lived, as he put it, without cares or passions to disturb him, spending the whole day 'shut up in a room heated by an enclosed stove'. In this state, cut off from the natural world outside, hovering over a man-made source of heat, he began to reject as absolutely false anything which gave rise to the slightest doubt in his mind. It was in this process that he realized that in the very act of thinking everything to be false, he could not doubt that he was thinking. He inferred: '*I think, therefore I am*' (*cogito ergo sum*). He made this certainty the first principle of his philosophy. He concluded: 'I was a substance, of which the whole essence or nature consists in thinking, and which, in order to exist, needs not place and depends on no material thing; so that this "I", that is to say, the mind, by which I am what I am, is entirely distinct from the body.'[18] He described himself as lodged in his body like a pilot in a ship.

The realization proved a watershed in human history, and one from which the world is still recoiling. By his own admission, Descartes was indifferent to external nature and only concerned with clear and distinct ideas: 'As for the notions I had of several other things outside myself, such as the sky, the earth, light, heat and a thousand others, I had not the same concern to know their source, because, seeing nothing in them which seemed to make them superior to myself.'[19]

Descartes was a Christian and adopted the traditional Christian view that man is metaphysically unique and has been given dominion over nature. He tried to escape the heretical view that man is a machine by identifying consciousness with the immortal soul – 'that part distinct from the body' whose 'nature is only to think'. Only humans combine matter with intellect and have separate souls. Man is a 'thinking thing' and the 'knowledge of the understanding must always precede the determination of the will'.[20] Only men, moreover, use language to convey their thoughts.

Animals, on the other hand, are 'thoughtless beasts', mere machines devoid of reason, unconscious automata: 'They do not have a mind, and . . . it is nature which acts in them according to the disposition of their organs, as one sees that a clock, which is made up of only wheels and springs, can count the hours and measure time more exactly than we can with all our art.'[21]

What makes animals move are the 'animal spirits', which are like a very subtle wind or a pure and lively flame. They are governed by the same principles as a clock; if their actions seem more complicated than those of a man-made clock, it is simply because they are made by God. Man is thus the master and proprietor; an animal is a *machina anima* which he may use as he wishes. This view not only separated man entirely from the rest of the creation, but provided an excuse to maltreat and torture animals in the pursuit of science and pleasure.

It seems that Descartes may have modified his doctrine in later years by acknowledging that animals may be capable of sensation. In a letter to the Cambridge Platonist Henry More, who claimed that the idea of 'beast-machine' was a 'murderous' doctrine, he wrote: 'I am speaking of thought, not of life and sensation. I do not deny life to animals, since I regard it as consisting simply in the heat of the heart; and I do not deny sensation, in so far as it depends on a bodily organ.'[22] Sensation in this sense is merely saying that they have sensory organs that can be stimulated by external stimuli; it does not imply consciousness. Descartes remained adamant that animals do not think. Since they exhibit no behaviour which cannot be accounted for in terms of natural impulse or external stimulation, it cannot be said that they have souls.

Descartes' supporters went even further. If animals squeal when cut with a knife, this does not mean that they feel pain. When a wagon wheel grates, it cannot be said to be in pain; it merely needs oiling. The cry of a beaten dog is therefore no different from the sound of an organ when the levers of its stops are moved. To nail a dog to a table like Vesalius and dissect it alive to study the circulation of the blood is therefore no different from dismantling a clock, and it is misguided sentiment to commiserate with the victim. Animals do not belong to our moral community and are not worthy of moral consideration.

The Cartesian view of animals spawned a vast literature and the attempt to define the differences between men and animals became the central preoccupation of European intellectuals for a century and half. Not all were impressed. In Britain, not only Henry More felt that the doctrine was monstrous but the philosophers John Locke and John Ray thought that it went against all evidence of sense and reason.

Most people would now agree with them. It is difficult to deny that a puppy with a broken paw is in pain, and we habitually give conscious motives to animals when we describe them as grieving at their owner's absence or happy at his return. Anyone who has seen the communication between a skilled shepherd and his dog when rounding up sheep would find it difficult to describe the animal as a *machina anima*. But then philosophy tries to go beyond our common-sense view of the world and its inhabitants. Descartes as a rationalist philosopher insisted that 'we perceive bodies only by the understanding, which is within us, and not by the imagination, or the senses'.[23]

To answer Descartes it is not enough merely to appeal to common sense to show that animals have awareness. It is necessary to show that human beings are not merely similar to animals but are animals and that both have a mental life. In the first place, if Descartes is right about animals, he fails to demonstrate that humans have consciousness simply because they have immortal souls. Secondly, Descartes' language test is faulty because it has now been shown that primates, including gorillas and chimpanzees, can use sign language. Thirdly, as a dualist he does not offer a satisfactory explanation of how mind and matter interact. To overcome the difficulty, Cartesians compounded the absurdity by the doctrine of 'occasionalism': when I put my finger in a fire, it is the occasion for God to cause my sensation of pain. Another absurdity is to say that God has wound up the clocks of the mind and body in unison, so that when one strikes the other does at the same time.

In pushing the European stress on the gulf between man and animals to its logical conclusion, Descartes justified the prevailing treatment of animals. By denying that animals felt pain, he assuaged the guilt of those who made them suffer. Theorists were then able to justify the common practices of domestication, hunting, meat-eating and vivisection.

The strategy of human domination, confirmed by Descartes, was a double-edged sword. Not only did it remove animals from the sphere of moral consideration; it also legitimized the ill-treatment of humans considered to be living in an animal condition. The domestication of animals therefore became a model for social subjugation. It was a simple step to argue that the dominion God gave Adam over animals could be extended to include the dominion of members of the human species. As a mental preliminary for persecution it became possible for the rich and powerful to dehumanize their human victims by reclassifying them as animals. Greed and lust (and unduly long hair) were considered particularly bestial whereas civility meant acting differently from animals. To describe a man as a beast became an excuse to treat him as such.[24] The psychological trick was not of course new; the Greeks called all non-Greeks 'barbarians' and proceeded to enslave them without a qualm. But Descartes gave new impetus to the process. Edward Gibbon, who delighted in tracing the rise and fall of the Roman Empire, asserted that 'our toil is lessened and our wealth increased by our dominions over the useful animals'. He then added: 'The human brute, without arts or laws . . . is poorly distinguished from the rest of the animal creation.'[25]

Discourses on Negroes stressing their beastlike sexuality and brutish natures (an eighteenth-century London goldsmith advertised 'silver padlocks for blacks or dogs') were used to justify slavery. American Indians, who crept on all fours like bears, could be shot like them. The training of children was likened to the 'breaking in' of a horse. The mad were put into cages like birds. Indeed, many men considered half of their own species in Europe – women – to be closer to the animal state, and a few even claimed that they had no reason or souls. Women then – and now – were showered with animal insults like bitch, vixen and shrew.

The poor might have resented being considered animals by their superiors, but that did not prevent them from tyrannizing in turn over animals. The popular protests in the seventeenth and eighteenth centuries against the game laws were not against hunting as such; the poor merely wanted to trap and shoot wild animals and take fish, which they considered everyone's property. And if kicked by their masters, they could kick their wives; after their wives, there was always the dog or the pig. It was a quick and easy way of exacting revenge for ill-treatment received from their superiors.

### Thomas Hobbes, fear and the mechanical state

Thomas Hobbes (1588–1679) best summed up the political implications of the new mechanical philosophy at the end of the sixteenth century. He was born in the year of the Spanish Armada, and later observed, 'my mother bore twins, myself and fear'. His whole philosophy was an attempt to overcome his sense of dread and insecurity in troubled times.

Hobbes was directly exposed to the teachings of the scientific revolution. After rejecting the Aristotelian philosophy taught at Oxford, he came under the influence of Galileo, whom he met in Florence. For a time he worked as Francis Bacon's amanuensis and adopted his master's scientific outlook and view of knowledge as power. Hobbes went on to write works concerning the body, man, laws and the citizen, but the book which brought him lasting fame was *Leviathan*. Published in 1651 in Paris, where Hobbes was a political refugee from the English Revolution, it was 'occasioned by the disorders of the present time'. Its atheistic implications made him notorious and the work was almost condemned by Parliament.

Hobbes's central concern was with security. Although he attempted to create a science of political philosophy, to reduce politics to the rules of reason, it is clear that he was primarily motivated by fear. His real intention was to show how civil peace and commodious living could be achieved.

Hobbes shared with Galileo the view that everything, including human sensation, is caused by motion and that motion is the natural state of things. Since all men wish to keep going, self-preservation is the fundamental law of nature. Impressed by Euclid, he further adopted the deductive method of geometry in his exposition, moving from simple self-evident propositions to more complex ones. Finally, he applied Galileo's scientific method to politics, resolving the machine of society into the motion of its parts.

In his depiction of humanity, Hobbes reduces the motion of a human being to the effect of the mechanical apparatus of sense organs, muscles, reason etc. Men are moved by appetites and aversions which determine their voluntary actions; willing is merely the last appetite or aversion. As a result, men desire 'felicity', which Hobbes describes as 'a continuall progresse of the desire, from one object to another'.[26]

In order to achieve satisfaction men must have power over others and over nature. The competitive struggle for power is therefore universal and unlimited. 'I put for a generall inclination of all mankind,' Hobbes writes, 'a perpetuall and restless desire after power, that ceaseth onely in Death.'[27] The universal war which results from men's drive for power can only be avoided if they make contracts with each other to obey an all-powerful sovereign. Only the fear of death can bring men to make such a contract.

At this stage in his argument, Hobbes introduces the famous concepts which came to dominate Western political thought – the state of nature, the right of nature and the social contract. In his view, in a state of nature without the law to restrain individuals, every man would be prey to violent invasion of his life and property by his fellows. There would be

> no place for Industry; because the fruit thereof is uncertain: and Culture of the Earth; no Navigation, nor use of the commodities that may be imported by Sea; no commodious Building; no Instruments of moving, and removing such things as require much force; no Knowledge of the face of the Earth; no account of Time; no Arts; no Letters; no Society; and which is worst of all, continuall feare, and danger of violent death; And the life of man, solitary, poore, nasty, brutish, and short.[28]

For Hobbes this is not merely hypothetical, for he claims that the 'savage people in many places in America' lived in such a brutish manner, in a condition of 'warre, as is of every man, against every man'. The vision has continued to haunt the Western mind and finds expression in William Golding's *Lord of the Flies*. But it is profoundly unhistorical and unanthropological, a flight of dark imagination and pathological dread.

The right of nature, Hobbes continues, is the liberty of each man to use his power to preserve his own life. The corollary is the law of nature 'a Precept, or generall Rule, found out by Reason, by which man is forbidden to do, that, which is destructive of his life'. But Hobbes deduces a second law of nature for reasonable men – to lay down their right to all things and limit their freedom if all do the same for the sake of peace. They would, however, have to form a contract and transfer their rights to a person or body who would make their agreement stick, since for the cynical Hobbes 'Covenants, without the Sword, are but Words'.[29] Obligation to the laws of the state would last only as long as the sovereign had sufficient coercive power to protect its citizens. Hobbes's sovereign is a self-perpetuating and absolute ruler who can only be changed by rebellion. As for man's obligations to animals, they do not exist, because to make covenants with 'brute beasts' is impossible.

Hobbes offers a brilliant analysis of Western man in a market economy striving for more power to obtain wealth and status. Indeed, he insists that 'the *Value*, or WORTH of a man, is as of all other things, his Price; that is to say, so much as would be given for the use of his Power'.[30] At the time Hobbes's account of equal obligation and natural right was an advance on the doctrine of the divine right of kings. He also recognizes the equal ability, equal right and equal obligation of all citizens. But he has a highly atomistic view of society as composed of calculating individuals.

The title page of *Leviathan* symbolically shows a crowned sovereign whose body is made up of a multitude of individuals. Wielding a sword in one hand and a mace in the other, he overlooks the ordered works of man in transforming nature: a cultivated landscape and walled city. He is flanked by a castle and a church which represent civil and ecclesiastical authority. It is significant that Hobbes should call his absolute state the Leviathan, the sea monster in the Bible, synonymous with a huge and powerful thing. He called his historical account of the Civil War the Behemoth, another gigantic animal, probably inspired by a hippopotamus. He wished to frighten his contemporaries with the power of these mythical creatures which could wreak havoc on frail humanity.

In the final analysis, Hobbes stands as the very antithesis of an ecological sensibility with his mechanical view of nature and man, his nightmarish depiction of the state of nature, his celebration of power, and his artificial and absolute state. Hobbes applies Galileo's and Bacon's mechanical philosophy to psychology and politics with disastrous results. His system fails to resolve the paradox that if human beings are as Hobbes describes them, then how can they rationally decide to make a contract to form a government or even hold together as a community? As his contemporary Sir William Temple observed; 'Nor do I know, if men are like Sheep, why they need any government: Or if they are like wolves, how can they suffer it.'[31]

# 15

## THE PHILOSOPHICAL
## COUNTER-REVOLUTION

It is a generally received opinion that all this visible
world was created for Man; that Man is the end of the
Creation, as if there were no other end of any creature
but some way or other to be serviceable to man . . . But
though this be vulgarly received, yet wise men nowadays
think otherwise.

John Ray

From the beginning of the Renaissance, there was a philosophical
counter-revolution which opposed the new mechanical thinking and
continued to see nature in organic and holistic terms. It refused to
separate radically the mind from the body and humanity from nature.
Although often contradictory and inconsistent, the current of thought
has continued to flow in our own era, when it is now beginning to
challenge the dominant culture.

### Giordano Bruno and the divine mother

The Italian Giordano Bruno (1548–1600) is a transitional figure
with one foot in the Middle Ages and another in the Renaissance.
A Dominican monk influenced by Copernican astronomy, he was
converted from Christianity to an extreme form of naturalistic and
mystical pantheism. He was steeped in the Hermetic tradition and
Neoplatonism (Plotinus was for him the 'prince of philosophers'),
and fused many of their insights in his organic philosophy.[1] But
it was not without personal cost. Obliged to leave Italy under the
accusation of heresy before he was thirty, he was eventually seized
by the Inquisition in Venice, tried in Rome for seven years, and then
burned at the stake.

Inspired by the medieval doctrine of the necessary plenitude of
divine nature, he became the principal exponent at the time of the

doctrine of the Great Chain of Being, of a 'decentralized, infinite and infinitely populous universe'.[2] Bruno argued that there must be an infinite world to afford room for all the possible permutations in its full scale: 'Because of the countless grades of perfection in which the incorporeal divine Excellence must needs manifest itself in a corporeal manner, there must be countless individuals such as those great living beings of which our divine mother, the Earth, is one.'[3]

It was self-evident for Bruno that innumerable individuals manifest 'divine Excellence' more than a finite number. Like modern ecologists, he saw that the greater the diversity in the world, the greater the overall unity and harmony. Moreover, he did not see the Chain of Being in terms of a rigid hierarchy, since every being was a valuable part of the whole; 'For whatever is small, trivial or mean serves to complete the splendour of the whole' and there can be no 'grade of being which, in its own place in the series, is not good in relation to the whole body.'[4] In the presence of the infinite, he felt that man is no more than an ant.

In his philosophical interpretation of the new astronomy, Bruno argued that all moves according to the same laws, not in a linear fashion – he rejected Aristotle's unmoved first mover – but with an inherent circular motion. The material world is thus infinite space with plastic and changing matter and inherent movement.

This view led to a pantheistic cosmology reminiscent of the one developed later by Spinoza. Bruno rejected the qualitative difference between terrestrial and celestial zones; God is the unifying substance from which all things in the universe are derived. At the same time, he believed that the universe could offer no genuine knowledge of the divine: 'Nature is nothing but a force implanted in things and the law by which all entities proceed along their proper paths.'

For Bruno, God and the universe are two names for one and the same reality. Reality itself may be considered the creative essence of all things, and the manifold of realized possibilities in which that essence manifests itself. He described an infinite universe of vast interrelationships, throughout time and space, which includes all phenomena, material and spiritual. Each part of infinitely numerous worlds moves on its own course, impelled by its twofold nature as an individual and as part of the whole in relation to other worlds. The main hindrance to natural knowledge is the failure to perceive in things the harmony between substances, motions and qualities. The philosophical mind should thus search for the one in the many, simplicity in variety, the eternal in the temporal.

Bruno's cosmology is entirely organic and pantheistic. The whole does not transcend this or that part; indeed, it is not the sum of the parts since the whole is immanent in all parts. Absolute being is immanent in all things, but it remains one and the same.

### Montaigne and the state of nature

The French writer Michel de Montaigne (1533–92) is best remembered for his *Essays* (1588). In them he appears as a man of considerable intellectual curiosity, condemning pedantry and espousing a tolerant morality and a sceptical philosophy. Attempting to answer the question 'What do I know?', he recognized the fallibility of human reason and the relativity of human science. A kind and easy-going man, he could not tolerate injustice or cruelty, whether to humans or animals. A close friend of Etienne de La Boetie, author of a *Discourse on Voluntary Servitude*, he was well aware of man's propensity for enslaving himself and others.

Montaigne did much to overcome the Christian culture of the Middle Ages which associated nature with the satanic order. Whatever the Bible or the theologians might say, life on his small estate convinced him that nature was good. He anticipated the naturalism of the late eighteenth century by exalting nature over conventions, codes and systems: 'Whoever contemplates our mother Nature in her full majesty and lustre is alone able to value things in their true estimate.' Despite his love of wisdom, he felt life was of supreme importance: 'If, by being overstudious, we impair our health and spoil our good-humour, the best pieces we have, let us give it over.'[5]

The age of the scientific revolution was also an age of discovery. The European explorers brought back wondrous accounts of their travels which inspired a series of imaginary utopias. Pigafetta, who had accompanied the Portuguese navigator Ferdinand Magellan on his voyage around the world, described how the Brazilian Indians followed nature, wore no clothes, were free of civilized vices and lived to one hundred and forty. In a similar vein, Montaigne declared that what he had seen of the manners of three 'savages' in the court of Charles IX surpassed 'all the pictures with which licentious Poesie hath proudly imbellished the golden age'.

But Montaigne does not leave it simply at that. In his essay 'Of Cannibals', which Shakespeare drew on in Gonzalo's utopian speech in *The Tempest*, he presents the natural society of the New World, in which there are no artificial restraints, governments, laws, contracts, private property or poverty, as superior to European civilization.

Whereas nearly all the early voyagers described the 'natives' of their 'discovered' lands as lesser breeds without the law, Montaigne turns the tables and asks who are the true 'savages':

> They [the Indians] are even savage, as we call those fruits wilde, which nature of her selfe, and of her ordinarie progresse hath produced: whereas indeed, they are those which our selves have altered by our artificiall devices, and diverted from their common order, we should rather terme savage. In those are the true and most profitable vertues, and naturall properties most lively and vigorous, which in these we have bastardized, applying them to the pleasures of our corrupted taste.[6]

His imagery raises the whole question of whether the gardener's art – and by extension the farmer's science – corrupts and bespoils nature or improves the stock. Unlike Bacon who wanted art to improve on nature, Montaigne concludes:

> There is no reason, art should gaine the point of honour of our great and puissant mother Nature. We have so much by our inventions surcharged the beauties and riches of her workes, that we have altogether overchoaked her: yet where ever puritie shineth, she makes our vaine and frivolous enterprises wonderfully ashamed ... All our endevour or wit, cannot so much as reach to represent the nest of the least birdlet, its contexture, beautie, profit and use, no nor the web of the seely spider.

While condemning the 'barbarous horror' of cannibalism, Montaigne cannot help thinking that there is more barbarism in 'eating' men alive under the pretence of religion (as was the practice in Europe) than to feed upon them after they are dead: 'to mangle by tortures and torments a body full of lively sense, to roast them in peeces, to make dogges and swine to gnaw and teare him in mammockes ...'[7] But Montaigne was not concerned only with human cruelty. His was one of the first voices to speak up for the 'brute creation'. Throwing a bridge across the medieval gulf between man and animals, Montaigne observed: 'We understand them no more than they us. By the same reason may they as well esteem us beasts as we them.'[8]

To raise this question demanded a great act of imagination at the time. Montaigne condemned the new arrogant humanism of the Renaissance as much as the Judaeo-Christian tradition which tried to separate man from the rest of nature: 'Presumption is our natural and original disease,' he wrote, ''Tis by the same vanity of imagination that [man] equals himself to God, attributes to himself divine qualities, and withdraws and separates himself from the crowd of other creatures.'[9] He roundly condemned man's 'imaginary sovereignty' over other creatures. In his view, there was 'a kind of respect and a general duty of humanity which tieth us . . . unto brute beasts that have life and sense . . . Unto men we owe justice, and to all creatures that are capable of it, grace and benignity.'[10] He even went so far as to urge that trees and plants should be treated with 'humanity'.

Montaigne's denunciation of cruelty to animals was based on his belief that they were God's creatures worthy of respect and that they possessed similar attributes to humans. But the ultimate source of his concern was his own sensibility: 'If I see but a chicken's neck pulled off or a pig sticked, I cannot choose but to grieve; and I cannot well endure a silly dew-dabbled hare to groan when she is seized upon by the hounds.'[11] He was one of the first since Roman times to argue that cruelty to animals is wrong in itself and not merely because it encourages cruelty in humans. Indeed, by breaking with the prevailing anthropocentric tradition, he helped start the great revolution in Western thought which has challenged the Scholastic dogma that the world exists for man alone.

Another Frenchman in the sixteenth century who shared Montaigne's love of the Earth was the potter Bernard Palissy (c. 1509–89). After many trials, he eventually discovered how to make enamels, but he delighted above all in nature and its creatures, as his coloured ware bearing plants and animals in high relief testifies. He was not only a potter; during 1575–84, he lectured on physics, natural history and agriculture, stressing the importance of experience and observation as a guide. In a dialogue on agriculture and philosophy, he wrote one of the first ecological tracts in praise of dung and good husbandry. 'It is necessary,' he repeatedly stressed, 'to carry the dunghills, muddy and filthy, and even the excrement and ordure of men as well as of beasts, if it were possible, in order to put back in place the very substance which has been removed.' Yet he was no mere practical man and insisted on the need for a philosophical understanding of nature:

> I tell you that there is no art in the world which requires more philosophy than agriculture, and I say that if agriculture is carried on without philosophy it amounts to a daily violation of the earth and the things it produces; and I marvel that the earth and its products do not cry for vengeance on certain murderers, ignorant and ungrateful, who every day do nothing but waste and ruin the trees and plants, without any consideration.[12]

## Spinoza, the lens of nature

A philosopher with more influence on the ecological movement has been the rationalist Baruch Spinoza (1632–77). Many green thinkers have looked to his philosophy as a unique Western basis for deep ecology, especially in his notion of God as Nature. Arne Naess, the Norwegian philosopher who coined the phrase 'deep ecology', sees him representing 'Middle Eastern wisdom *par excellence* . . . no great philosopher has so much to offer in the way of clarification and articulation of basic ecological attitudes as Baruch Spinoza'.[13] Other thinkers have also been impressed. 'To be a philosopher, one must be a Spinozist,' Hegel wrote, while Einstein avowed: 'I believe in the God of Spinoza.'

Spinoza was the son of a Portuguese Jewish family in Amsterdam who changed his name from the Hebrew Baruch to the Latinized Benedict. Although he tried to live a quiet and independent life making lenses, he was excommunicated from the Jewish community for heresy and his controversial views on the Bible were attacked by Christian theologians. In his lifetime, he earned the reputation of an impious atheist and materialist. His principal work, *Ethics*, was not published until his death.

Spinoza's philosophy is notoriously difficult. Written in Latin, it is expressed in a strictly logical sequence. Like Galileo, he felt that all genuine explanation is deductive; he therefore adopted an *a priori* geometrical method of reasoning which proceeds carefully with definitions, propositions and postulates. He felt it was possible to deduct from a few basic propositions or axioms a system of sound knowledge about man and the universe.

Philosophy for Spinoza was a search for salvation through reason.

He was the most ambitious of modern philosophers and wanted to understand the universe as an intelligible whole solely through the power of logical reasoning. Despite his personal modesty, he was convinced that he had discovered the only true philosophy.

Although principally interested in ethics, Spinoza felt that ethics without metaphysics is meaningless; before we know how to act, we must know our place in nature. It is therefore necessary to begin with the ground of being, what he called, in Aristotelian terms, 'substance'.

Unlike Aristotle, Spinoza argued that it is not possible to separate substance from its attributes. He also disagreed with his contemporary Leibniz who conceived of nature as a system of self-determining substances called 'monads'. If there were a plurality of substances, Spinoza argued, it would be impossible for them to interact, for one to be the cause of the other. He therefore concluded that there can only be one substance which is *causa sui*. This single substance is identified with the universe as a whole which he calls *Deus sive Natura* (God or Nature).

God or Nature is the eternal cause of all things and of itself; only it is free as self-causing and self-creating. At the same time, nature manifests itself in two different ways; as *natura naturans*, nature actively creating itself; and in a passive sense as what is created, *natura natura*. Both are aspects of the same substance. God or Nature is therefore eternal, has infinite attributes, and is free in the sense that it acts merely according to the laws of its own nature. In Scholastic terms, 'God is not only the effecting cause of the existence of things, but also of their essence'.[14] The world could not have been other than it is.

Individual items, whether mountains, sheep or plants, are temporary and finite modifications or 'modes' of the all-embracing, infinite substance. Physical bodies as well as the ultimate units of physics are not discrete atoms, but 'modes' of matter in extension. They are in a state of 'motion-and-rest' (a notion perhaps best translated as energy), constantly interacting with each other and with their environment.[15] Similarly, ideas are 'modes' of thought. Both modes are connected, as ideas coincide with their objects; in this sense, the real is the rational. There can be no idea without something extended of which it is the idea.

While this world picture as its stands overcomes Descartes' embarrassing dualism of mind and matter, it still remains static. Spinoza then introduces the notion of striving into his universe. Each particular thing, interacting with others within the natural order, has a drive to preserve its identity; it possesses a 'striving [conatus], so far as it lies in itself to do so, to persist in its own being'.[16] Every finite item, including a human being, tries to preserve itself and to increase its power of self-maintenance. This power, which takes on the form of vitality, may be described in mental terms as pleasure and pain. The degree of power of the item depends on whether it is causally active, whether change is the effect of changes within itself or of external causes.

The doctrine of *conatus*, the tendency to cohesion and self-maintenance of all particular things in the common order of nature, introduces a dynamic element into Spinoza's universe which is absent in Descartes' and Newton's and other mechanical and atomistic cosmologies. In human terms, as a natural drive for self-preservation and the extension of power and energy, *conatus* may be compared to Freud's notion of libido.

### Mind and body

The limited human intellect can conceive nature as a system of extended bodies, that is, an infinite spatial system, or as a system of thought. For Descartes, the two systems are self-contained and independent. In describing the human personality, such a dualistic position is awkward. Either the interaction between the mind and the body must remain a mystery or God must intervene to ensure that if one does not cause the other, one might at least be the 'occasion' of the other. By interpreting thought and extension as two aspects of a single reality, Spinoza's position is clearly an advance on both views. As he makes clear in a crucial note:

> The mind and the body are one and the same thing, which conceived now under the attribute of thought, now under the attribute of extension. From which it comes about that the order of concatenation of things is a single order, whether Nature be conceived under one or the other attributes; it follows therefore that the order of the actions and passions of our body is simultaneous in nature with the order of the actions and passions of the mind.[17]

In this way, Spinoza overcomes the dichotomy between mind and

body, subject and object, the individual and the world. It also breaks
down the gulf between man and animals in Descartes' philosophy:
all items, human beings, animals and stones are interconnected and
to different degrees animate, all part of Nature or God.

Given his metaphysical thesis of the unity of nature as a causal
system, Spinoza is a strict determinist in the sense that everything
that exists could not have been otherwise. Notions of free will
and deliberate choice have no place in his scheme. To be free is a
recognition of necessity, to understand that everything must exist
or happen as it does: 'Everything is determined by the necessity
of the divine nature.'[18] Since no one could have acted otherwise,
moral terms like good and bad, approval and disapproval, praise
and blame are not appropriate to humans any more than to stones.
It it meaningless to call a human or animal 'vicious'. Every human
action is one necessary link in the infinite chain of causes. If we are
to improve human beings we must therefore study the natural laws
of their behaviour in the same way we would study those of animals.
The exhortations of moralists are simply misguided vapourings and
wasted energy.

While rejecting the claims of traditional ethics, Spinoza still has
a notion of the 'good life'. He sees 'natural passions' or 'appetite'
as external and hostile to the developed personality. In our normal
condition, we are irrational weathercocks, 'agitated by contrary
winds like waves of the sea, waver and are unconscious of our issue
and our fate'.[19] The free and contented person is one who overcomes
the passions and follows the life of reason. I am free to the degree
I am unaffected by external causes. To be free is to understand the
true causes of our desires. Only the intelligent person can logically
be free.

The free individual, however, has active emotions and adequate
ideas springing from his whole personality, not, like the passions,
from just a part. He has an adequate knowledge of natural causes,
understands his place in nature, and is uninfluenced by fear and hope.
He aims 'to act well and to rejoice' (*bene agere ac laetari*). Such a
life of wisdom and self-disciplined freedom brings vitality and joy;
'there cannot be too much joy: it is always good: but melancholy
is always bad'.[20] A free person who lives according to the dictate
of reason alone does not fear death. On the contrary, 'a free man
thinks of nothing less than of death, and his wisdom is a meditation
not of death but of life'.[21]

The end of Spinoza's philosophy was to save and cure the irrational man. It was intended to make him more self-conscious, no longer attached to particular things and persons of his immediate environment, but to become part of the infinite whole. His real happiness comes from the contemplation and understanding of the whole spectacle and system of nature. Ultimately, the good life centres on 'the Intellectual love of God'.

The meaning of this phrase is not clear, but Spinoza used love in the sense of wanting to unite with the object loved; to love God or Nature is to unite or identify with it. If I achieve this, then I lose my individuality as a particular finite mode and live in eternity, *sub specie aeternitatis*, not in the sense of partaking in everlasting life but in the sense of my mind becoming part of the infinite idea of God. Such a state cannot be described but only experienced; glimpses of it are possible in moments of heightened consciousness when time stops still and the universe appears as a seamless whole.

Arne Naess has likened Spinoza's philosophy to Mahayana Buddhism, in which the sage identifies with all beings. Certainly it is possible to see Spinoza as a pantheist who interprets every natural phenomenon as a revelation of an immanent God. But although the Romantic poets Coleridge, Goethe and Shelley were impressed by this aspect of Spinoza's thinking, it is misleading to see him as a mystic or a Buddhist.

Spinoza wished to develop a unified science of all knowledge. The highest level of knowledge is a direct intuitive knowledge of particular things (modes), that is to say, grasping God as manifest in individual beings. To understand God we must understand nature, and, since God is nature, 'The more we understand individual things, the more we understand God'.[22] It is a form of understanding in which the subject/object distinction disappears and the knower experiences the union that the mind has with the whole of nature. All lower forms of knowing are based on the imagination which conceives things as mental images which are projections of sense-experience and therefore erroneous and misleading.

Despite these mystical overtones, Spinoza was above all a rationalist. He believed that man's identity with Nature or God could be achieved not by contemplation or meditation but by an act of philosophical understanding, an act which could result only from a rigorous process of cogitation. It cannot be helped by the imagination (Coleridge's key faculty), which is the prime source of confusion and error. Only by disciplined clear thinking can nature be made intelligible, a process which involves the healing and purifying of the intellect. The free person's intellectual love of God is thus the enjoyment of the union of himself with nature through reason.

In his own day, Spinoza was called an atheist, which he was in the sense of denying the existence of a personal God or a creator outside the creation. Today, ecologists are turning to him for his belief that all things are part of the whole, that there is unity in diversity, and that the physical and mental are two attributes of a single substance. Like modern ecologists, Spinoza believed that everything is ultimately explicable in a intelligible and self-sustaining universe. In order to understand and explain why particular things or beings are the way they are, it is necessary to see them as part of the total scheme of nature.

Spinoza would also seem to anticipate the notion of earth as Gaia, as a self-regulating organism. By describing the physical world in terms of 'motion-and-rest', he conceives it as an all-inclusive, self-generating and self-maintaining system of interactions in which the total amount of energy is constant. This dynamic concept of the universe as a configuration of energy is a considerable advance on Newton's and Descartes' mechanical one and fits in well with the findings of modern physics and ecology.

For all the ecological insights of Spinoza's organic philosophy, there still remain some thorny points for ecologists. In the first place, his principal concern is with the human species. 'I wish,' he wrote, 'to direct all sciences in one direction or to one end, namely, to attain the greatest possible human perfection.'[23] The whole structure of his philosophy culminates in his doctrine of human freedom and happiness.

Although Spinoza believed that all things are animated, he had a strongly hierarchical view of nature, believing that the more conscious a being is, the more reality it has. There is a hierarchy of ideas which coincides with a hierarchy of things; there are degrees of rationality and degrees of reality. The human body is therefore more excellent and contains more reality than animal or vegetable bodies. And since the philosopher is the most rational being on earth, he is the most real. Spinoza sees that the difference between human beings and animals is one of degree and not of kind, a degree of complexity in their organization and behaviour. He is even prepared to admit that there are many things observed in 'brutes' which far surpass human sagacity.[24] But the relatively elaborate patterns of animal behaviour can be explained solely in physical terms without any appeal to the faculty of judgement. Animals do not have an immortal mind. Only of human bodies can one say that the idea of them is a mind; that is, 'a created thinking substance' (*substantia cogitans creata*) which is immortal, 'part of the infinite intellect of God'.[25] Humans and other animals may all be part of nature, but the latter are more subordinate than the former.

All this hardly ties in with the notion of biocentric egalitarianism put forward by deep ecologists. As the English philosopher Stuart Hampshire has observed: 'Spinoza, like Descartes, showed an unsentimental and un-English disregard of the soulfulness of animals; they both held that we are entirely justified in exploiting them for our own purposes.'[26] It is not surprising that both philosophers tend to call animals 'brutes'. Spinoza's metaphysics may be admirably holistic and organic, but his thought is imbued with anthropocentrism. Within the hierarchy of nature, animals are inferior to men and may be treated as mere things for their own use. In some notes to his *Ethics*, Spinoza makes his position crystal clear:

> Besides man, we know of no particular thing in nature in whose mind we may rejoice, and whom we can associate with ourselves in friendship or any sort of fellowship: therefore, whatsoever there be in nature besides man, a regard for our own advantage does not call on us to preserve, but to preserve or destroy according to its various capabilities, and to adapt to our use as best we may.[27]

Spinoza's utilitarian attitude comes through most clearly in his politics. He respected Machiavelli, with his philosophy of might is right, and was indebted to Hobbes and considered his roaring Leviathan of a centralized state as the only alternative to chaos and tumult.

Spinoza tried to base his politics on what he considered a purely logical and scientific study of human society. He maintained that ethics has nothing to do with politics, which is solely concerned with the distribution of power within the state. All politics is necessarily power politics. There are therefore no such things as moral rights or duties; obedience to the state is only justified on the utilitarian grounds of rational self-interest.

The central criterion for any state in Spinoza's view is whether it establishes security and peace among warring individuals. As finite modes of nature, all men pursue their own pleasure, preservation and the indefinite extension of their power. The ensuing war of all against all can only be avoided by vesting superior power in a sovereign person or group of persons. Society is therefore 'always a balance between forces of self-assertion'.[28]

Despite his dynamic view of nature, there is no sense of organic community in Spinoza's view of society. Each individual consents to the state only if it brings him security, and obeys the law as long as it is expedient and the state can enforce it. In practice, Spinoza advocated a restricted 'democracy' with the opportunity of political power limited by property qualification. His contemporary ideal was the mercantile community of Amsterdam, which provided asylum to people of many creeds and denominations. He was principally concerned with achieving security for the quiet life of the intellectual and to this end he was ready to compromise with the prevailing system of law and punishment. As an ostracized thinker in his own community, he naturally espoused the liberal notions of freedom of thought and religious tolerance. 'The real disturbers of the peace,' he wrote, 'are those who, in a free state, seek to curtail the liberty of judgement which they are unable to tyrannize over.'[29] Spinoza's caution led him to avoid publication of his *Ethics* in his lifetime.

The authoritarian elements in Spinoza's social philosophy cannot merely be put down to the pressures of the time he was living in. His near contemporaries Etienne de La Boétie and the satirist Rabelais both entertained the idea of a free society of self-governing individuals. Spinoza may have called for a degree of freedom of opinion and religious toleration, but he felt that the state was right to proscribe views which might undermine its authority. For all his organic metaphysics, in his social views he starts and ends with the calculating individual who is the sole judge of his advantage. He will cooperate with others only as long as it is in his interest and it is natural that he will try to expand his power unless stopped by the greater coercive power of others.

Spinoza fails to realize that more often than not the state is the cause and not the remedy of social disorder. He does not apply his insight about self-regulation in nature to human society as modern social ecologists do. Instead, he falls back on the misanthropic views of seventeenth-century theorists like Machiavelli and Hobbes. Spinoza singularly lacked historical imagination despite the boldness of his logical reasoning. Deeply conservative, he believed that no political progress was possible: 'It is hardly credible that we should be able to conceive of anything serviceable to a general society, that occasion or chance has not offered.'[30]

Spinoza's naturalism certainly goes against the ancient Taoist and modern ecological view that human beings are self-organizing and self-regulating organisms. The Taoists believed in natural order; Spinoza in natural disorder. He held that left to themselves human beings would engage in a war of all against all; the wiser Taoists recognized that they flourish best when least interfered with. Nevertheless, for all his loss of insight when it came to human society and the relationship between humans and other animals, Spinoza's organic and holistic philosophy resoundingly challenged the prevailing mechanical and atomistic mentality.

## The Cambridge Platonists: the plastic power of nature

The so-called Cambridge Platonists, notably Henry More (1614–87) and Ralph Cudworth (1617–88), put forward a rational theology which inspired Coleridge and other Romantics to develop a spiritual and organic view of nature. They wished to follow the natural light of reason, which meant thinking philosophically. God was Reason deified. But they also recognized (like a Hindu adept) that it was necessary to purify the heart and discipline the will – to become godlike – in order to apprehend God. They found in the metaphysics of Plato and the Neoplatonists a defence against the mechanical materialism of Hobbes.

In his *True Intellectual System of the Universe* (1678), Cudworth defined God as 'a Perfect conscious understanding being (or mind) existing of itself from eternity, and the cause of all other things'.[31] Sensation is not the mere passive reception of motions from external bodies, but involves an act of intellectual perception. But despite his attack on materialism, Cudworth is no proto-Romantic. He declared works of imagination to be 'gross dew upon the pure Glass of our Understandings'.

Cudworth's fellow Platonist at Cambridge, Henry More, had a much greater sense of the divine presence interpenetrating all things. At first he was impressed by Descartes, who seemed to salvage the soul and God from Hobbesian materialism and atheism. More wrote to Descartes in 1648 that 'all the great leaders of philosophy who have existed, or who may exist, are pygmies in comparison with your transcendent genius'.[32] But he soon came to reject Descartes' definition of the soul as a *res cogitans*, a thinking substance. Wanting to reunite matter with spirit, More argued that the soul occupies space; indeed, spirit may be deemed as real as matter. But where matter is penetrable, the spirit is impenetrable and infinite, an attribute of the Infinite Spirit. The infinite extension of space is thus the divine ground of the universe, a view shared by Locke.

More was no dry thinker, and wrote a series of divine dialogues and philosophical poems. Adopting the doctrine of the Great Chain of Being, he contended that 'millions of spiritual creatures walk the earth' or ascend through the air into heaven. He not only gave credence to demonology, but, like the medieval alchemists, interpreted the *anima mundi* as a 'Soul of the World, or Spirit of Nature' pervading the universe; it was a mysterious 'plastical power' holding everything together.

### John Ray and the candle of the Lord

John Ray (1627–1705) was influenced by the Cambridge Platonists and as the founder of modern botany and zoology has been called the Linnaeus of his age. His three-volume *Historia Generalis Plantarum* (1686–1704) earned him an international reputation. But he was not content to remain a natural philosopher and as a 'physico-theologian' he set out in *The Wisdom of God manifested in the Works of the Creation* (1691) to describe man's place within nature.

Nature for Ray is no longer corrupt and imperfect as it was for the medieval theologians. It is the unimprovable manifestation of God's wisdom and benevolence, an eternal source of awe and wonder. The mechanical thinking of Galileo and Newton, which reduced God to a first mover and left a world of dead matter in motion, went wrong by taking geometry as its inspiration. What it fails to take into account is the organization of living beings, of plants and animals who adapt to their environment. In a devastating stroke, Ray raises the banner of ecology at the dawn of the eighteenth century: 'These mechanick Philosophers being no way able to give an account thereof from the necessary Motion of Matter, unguided by Mind for Ends, prudently therefore break off their System there, when they should come to Animals.'[33]

In order to explain the 'vital motions' and the preservation of the species, Ray appeals to a kind of Platonic demiurge which he calls a 'vegetative soul' or a 'plastick Nature' at work throughout the universe. It acts like a life force with a certain degree of independence, thereby exonerating God from the botches of the creation. It is responsible for all the wonders of design and the marvels of instinct on earth, from the timely appearance of wasps as plums ripen, to the maintenance of steady populations among species. Ray stands in the long line of religious scientists who can see God at the end of their microscopes, who look to the book of nature for spiritual nourishment as much as to the Scriptures.

Ray's careful observations of nature led him, two centuries before Darwin, to consider the natural selection of the fittest in the struggle for survival. But since it implied for him spontaneous generation, and therefore a flaw in God's omnipotence and the perfectly designed creation, he finally dismissed the doctrine as the 'grand subterfuge of Atheists'. Adhering to the doctrine of the Great Chain of Being, he lamely justified the existence of the lower ranks as necessary for the manifestation of the 'Infinite Power and Wisdom'.

Ray was convinced that it was sheer arrogance to think that the world was created for man's sole use as the Christian and Cartesian legacy would have it. Animals and plants do not exist merely for man but to enjoy themselves and to glorify God. They have their own intrinsic value. But Ray is no primitivist and does not line up with modern souls in search for wilderness to replenish themselves. Augustan civilization is always preferable to unpolished barbarism:

> If a Country thus planted and adorned, thus polished and civilized, thus improved to the height ... be not preferred before a barbarous and inhospitable Scythia ... or a rude and unpolished America peopled with slothful and naked Indians ... then surely the brute Beast's Condition, and manner of Living ... is to be esteem'd better than Man's, and Wit and Reason was in vain bestowed on him.[34]

Ray implies, like his contemporary colonizers in the New World, that those living without 'civilization' are less than human and closer to 'brutes'. God has put man in a 'spacious and well-furnished world' and it is his privileged duty to exploit and perfect it as far as possible.

According to Ray, what distinguishes man from the animals is reason. The creation can praise God only through man, who, with his erect posture and reason, is the crown of all. And the jewel within the crown? The immortal soul. No earthy naturalist, Ray like the Cambridge Platonists sees the body as a mere physical envelope: 'the Body is but the dark Lanthorn, the Soul or Spirit is the Candle of the Lord that burns in it'.[35]

Thanks to his background in botany and zoology, Ray showed the limits of the mechanical and materialistic philosophy of the Renaissance, but despite the promptings of his own perceptive observations of nature he was unable to escape the cultural limits of his age.

## John Locke and the state of nature

John Locke (1632–1704) turned his back on Platonic rationalism and looked to common sense as a guide through the labyrinth of philosophy. In doing so, he rejected Descartes' and Hobbes's mechanical philosophy. Like an active gardener, he tried to cut away all the tangled bushes which had encroached on the central issues. Deeply rooted in English soil, he stressed that people were a product of their environment in their particular corner of the universe. But while he reacted against the excesses of the philosophers of the scientific revolution, he also helped justify the continued exploitation of the earth.

In Locke's view, the mind is a blank sheet at birth without innate ideas, and our knowledge derives from experience. He distinguishes in his theory of perception between the observer, the idea and the object that the idea represents. But while the secondary qualities, such as colour, taste and sound, depend on the mind of the observer, primary qualities, such as extension, impenetrability and number, belong to material bodies. Nevertheless, if ideas only represent objects and are never objects themselves, then man would seem to be imprisoned in a sort of diving bell, receiving some signals from without and within but never having any definite knowledge of the world around.[36] But this does not lead Locke to despair; on the contrary, he has little ambition:

> We have no reason to complain that we do not know the
> nature of the sun or the stars, that the consideration of light

itself leaves us in the dark and a thousand other speculations in
nature, since, if we knew them, they would be of no solid
advantage, nor help to make our lives the happier, they being
but the useless employment of idle or over-curious brains.[37]

Locke also rejected Descartes' view that animals are mere automata.
In *Some Thoughts concerning Education* (1693), he argued that
animals can suffer and that it is morally wrong to make them do
so. He lamented the fact that many children '*torment*, and treat
very roughly young Birds, Butterflies, and other such poor Animals,
which fall into their Hands'. Indeed, he claimed that not only socially
useful animals like cattle and horses should be well treated but also
squirrels, birds and insects, and 'any living Creature'. This was not
for the sake of the animals but for the moral effect on human beings.
The ill treatment of animals should be checked because it hardens
the mind against the suffering of human beings; people 'who delight
in the suffering and Destruction of Inferior Creatures, will not . . .
be very compassionate, or benign to those of their own kind'. He
therefore encouraged parents to make sure their children look after
pets to help them become responsible members of society.[38]

Unlike Hobbes's war of all against all, Locke's 'state of nature' is
relatively benign. Men are naturally in 'a state of perfect freedom to
order their actions, and dispose of their possessions and persons, as
they see fit, within the bounds of the law of nature'. Although it is a
state of liberty, it is not a state of licence, since men have sufficient
reason to follow the law of nature which teaches them that all being
naturally free, equal and independent, 'no one ought to harm another
in his life, health, liberty, or possession'. Unlike a state of war, where
force without right is placed upon a person, the state of nature is
where men live together 'according to reason without a common
superior on earth, with authority to judge between them'.[39]

Many modern libertarians have argued that Locke's 'state of
nature' is precisely what we should try to create out of existing violent
and unequal governmental society. However, in Locke's view there
are certain inconveniences in the state of nature, particularly for each
person trying to punish the trangressions of others. It is for this reason
that people should consent to set up a government with known and
settled laws in order to enjoy their natural rights to life, liberty and
property in peace and safety. Locke thus employs the classic liberal
defence of government.

Although much of his common-sense philosophy is admirable, Locke remained profoundly anthropocentric. He stood firmly in the Judeao-Christian tradition by asserting that 'God who hath given the world to men in common, hath also given them reason to make use of it to the best advantage of life and convenience. The earth and all that is therein is given to men for the support and comfort of their being.'[40]

Locke was also the chief architect of the Western notion of the natural right to property. He argued that the natural rights to life, liberty and property, later enshrined in the United States Constitution, could all be reduced to the notion of 'estate' since a man can be said to 'own' all three rights. By claiming that man had a 'natural right' to property, he justified the division of the earth – and the life upon it – into privately owned parcels of land. The key factor was labour: by mixing his labour with nature, man created his own property. For Locke the chief end of government is to protect the private ownership of land.

Locke further defended slavery by arguing that if a man forfeits another his life, then the master does him no injury to make him work for him; master and slave remain in a state of war between a 'lawful conqueror and a captive'. He equally justified the exploitation of humans and animals by arguing that man has a right to the product of the labour of any creature which happens to be in his power:

> Thus the grass my horse has bit, the turfs my servant has cut, and the ore I have digged in any place, where I have a right to them in common with others, become my property without the assignation or consent of anybody. The labour that was mine, removing them out of that common state they were in, hath fixed my property in them.[41]

The only limit to this right of property is perishability; Locke elevates the adage of 'waste not, want not' into a principle. Anyone may gather the fruits of the earth, anyone may 'engross as much as he will' before it spoils, but it is a law of nature that whatever is beyond this is more than his share, and belongs to others. Locke quotes the Bible – 'God has given us all things richly' (Timaeus 7:12) – to support his view of natural abundance, but argues that the voice of reason tells us that there is a limit to our enjoyment of the advantages of life. Although this supports those who would argue for the conservation of the earth's resources, the inventions of modern technology make Locke's 'perishability' principle somewhat redundant.

Locke is the great philosopher of liberalism and his version of possessive individualism came to inform the dominant Western attitude to government and property. His ethics of cool self-love, his ordinary common sense and his placid comfort-seeking all inspired the *philosophes* of the Enlightenment. However, Locke may be celebrated for his stress on the close link between a person and his or her environment, and for his call for more humane treatment of animals. Once he had asserted the 'natural rights' of humans, it was but a short step for later moralists to extend them to nonhumans. Above all, he presented a benign picture of the state of nature which counterbalanced the nightmarish visions of Hobbes and Spinoza.

# 16

# THE ENLIGHTENMENT

## *The Disenchantment of Nature*

'I perceive', said the Countess, 'Philosophy is now
become very Mechanical.' 'So mechanical', said I, 'that
I fear we shall quickly be asham'd of it; they will have
the World to be in great, what a watch is in little; which
is very regular, & depends only upon the just disposing
of the several parts of the movement. But pray tell me,
Madam, had you not formerly a more sublime idea of
the Universe?'

Bernard le Bovyer de Fontenelle

The Enlightenment marked a great turning point in Western cultural
history. It developed in Europe in the eighteenth century and believed
in the triumph of civilization over nature through the development
of reason and science. It launched the modern idea of inevitable
progress, developing the Promethean view of man as maker of
his own destiny. Its principal thinkers, known as the *philosophes*
in France, believed that man is potentially rational and largely a
product of his circumstances. Vice is ignorance; all that is needed
is to educate and enlighten human beings and they will become wise,
virtuous and free. It was an optimistic creed which had disastrous
results for the earth.

Although many of the philosophers quarrelled, they were all members of the same family. The Enlightenment was a form of modern
paganism, but a paganism without local gods and goddesses. Inspired
by antiquity, they sought to oppose the pagan to the Christian in order
to achieve their intellectual independence and autonomy. They were
adept at criticism – of society and culture – and were interested in
gaining power in order that their views should prevail.[1]

The most general feature of the Enlightenment was that the
philosophers were aware that a cultural revolution was taking
place. There was a new confidence in the abilities of humanity
to transform itself and nature. In his *Essai sur les éléments de*

214

*philosophie*, the mathematician and encyclopedist Jean le Rond d'Alembert traced the revolution back to the fall of Constantinople in the middle of the fifteenth century which brought about a renaissance in Western literature and philosophy. The Reformation of the sixteenth century was the next great leap forward. Finally the new philosophy of Descartes in the seventeenth century had given an additional stimulus so that in the eighteenth century the progress of philosophy could not be denied. 'Natural science acquires new riches daily; geometry, pushing back its boundaries, has illuminated the parts of natural philosophy nearest to it; the true nature of the world has been discovered, developed and perfected.' But it was not a peaceful process recognizing natural boundaries. The new method in philosophy had transformed the hitherto 'cold and untroubled' study of nature into a lively intellectual ferment which, 'active in every sense by its nature, has turned its attention with a sort of violence to everything that comes before it, like a river that has burst its banks'.[2]

The German philosopher Hegel also saw the Enlightenment as marking an important and necessary stage in human history. In the great unfurling of spirit, he saw that in the seventeenth and eighteenth centuries, thought had involved 'the Harmony of Being in its purest essence, challenging the external world to exhibit the same Reason which Subject [the Ego] possesses. Spirit perceives that Nature – the World – must also be an embodiment of Reason, for God created it on principles of Reason.' The new way of thinking challenged tradition and authority:

> These general conceptions, deduced from actual and present consciousness – the Laws of Nature and the substance of what is right and good – have received the name of *Reason*. The recognition of the validity of these laws was designated by the term *Eclaircissement* [*Aufklärung*]. From France it passed over into Germany, and created a new world of ideas. The absolute criterion – taking the place of all authority based on religious belief and positive laws of Right (especially political Right) – is the verdict passed by Spirit itself on the character of that which is to be believed or obeyed.[3]

The Enlightenment was therefore a necessary stage in the inevitable development of history, a progressive movement in the realization of Universal Spirit. Its aspiration, however, remained abstract, for it posed an ideal rational order against the real world rather than seeking rationality inherent in the historical process.

The intellectual roots of the Enlightenment were in the science of Galileo and Copernicus, the sensationalism of Locke, the empiricism of Bacon and Newton, and the rationalism of Descartes. D'Alembert in his Preliminary Discourse to the *Encyclopédie* (1750), which tried to accumulate all useful knowledge, called for the free enquiry into all subjects. While most of the *philosophes* of the Enlightenment rejected Descartes' belief in innate ideas, they valued above all his method of systematic doubt. 'Descartes at least dared to show advanced minds how to shake off the yoke of scholasticism, of opinion, of authority, in a word of prejudices and barbarism,' d'Alembert wrote. 'He can be regarded as a rebel leader who has had the courage to rise up first against a despotic and arbitrary power.'[4]

The philosophers of the Enlightenment considered themselves to be living in what the French called the '*Siècle des Lumières*' and the British the 'Age of Reason'. Systematic doubt and rational analysis were two prongs for their attack. They held up authority and tradition to the test of enquiry; they wished to banish the shadows of medieval superstition, bigotry and ignorance; they undertook a crusade for abstract truth as they saw it. They applied all inherited beliefs to the test of reason, believing that all could perceive rationally universal truths and act accordingly in the interest of general wellbeing. This analytical spirit pervaded all that they undertook and this method of philosophizing is their chief characteristic. Reason was seen as the supreme faculty, 'a kind of energy, a force which is fully comprehensible only in its agency and effects . . . its most important function consists in its power to bind and to dissolve'.[5]

While the Enlightenment in France had a distinctly rationalist direction, in Britain, philosophizing took a more empirical turn, following Newton rather than Descartes, and looking to observation and experience and not abstract reasoning as a source of knowledge. Locke had stressed the importance of circumstances in the growth of consciousness, and held that the mind is 'a white paper void of all characters, without any ideas'. But his was a limited vision; we must find satisfaction in 'a quiet and sure possession of truth that most concerned us' and not 'let loose our thoughts into the vast ocean of Being'.[6] Locke's forte was an inspired ordinariness; he did not want to look beyond human affairs and the busy marketplace. Voltaire popularized Newton's and Locke's ideas in France, and Etienne de

Condillac in his *Treaty on Sensations* developed the Lockean claim that all knowledge is acquired through the senses.

Like Locke, David Hume was an empiricist, claiming that 'the science of man is the only solid foundation for the other sciences, so, the only solid foundation we can give to this science itself must be laid on experience and observation'.[7] He was concerned in his *Treatise of Human Nature* (1739) with the 'nature of the ideas we employ, and of the operations we perform in reasonings'. His conclusions were extremely destructive, denying the existence of the self as a continuous identity rather than merely a sequence of sensations.

Despite their different emphases, what united both the French and the British philosophers during the Enlightenment was their primary concern with the human understanding, their preoccupation with epistemology and psychology. In an age of examination, their main interest was to know how one knows. Rather than looking at nature, the philosophers wanted to look at the process of looking. By focusing narrowly on the human mind, they bracketed it from the world and deepened the gulf between the subject and the object, the observer and the observed, humanity and nature.

The Enlightenment further saw the triumph of the idea of progress in the Western world. From one angle, history might appear as Voltaire observed, a record of human follies and crimes, but from another it demonstrated steady and gradual amelioration. Turgot, a leading physiocrat who developed laissez-faire theories and was *Contrôleur-Général* of finance for Louis XVI, declared in a discourse in 1750 that the human mind was becoming more enlightened, trade and politics were uniting the whole globe and 'the totality of humanity, fluctuating between calm and agitation, good times and bad, moves steadily though slowly towards a greater perfection'.[8]

The faith in progress was so great that when the mathematician Condorcet was imprisoned in 1789 by the Jacobins during the French Revolution, he completed the ninth division of his *Esquisse* for the *Tableau historique des progrès de l'esprit humain* (1793–94) while under threat of execution during the Terror. He considered the indefinite improvement of humanity to be a 'general law of nature'. Progress would be brought about primarily through education: Condorcet not only called for universal public education but shocked his contemporaries by suggesting that the female half of the species might benefit from it.

Condorcet had a broad vision of humanity's place in nature.

Civilization had confused the 'natural' man with the 'civilized'. The truly natural man would be the enlightened man of the future who had thrown off the yoke of priest and prince and the manacles of ignorance. He would live according to nature in harmony with his fellows. Man was not condemned to an isolated existence, but could be 'an active part of the great whole and co-worker in an eternal enterprise. During a momentary existence on a point in space, he can by his efforts identify himself with all the world, be linked with every century, and be active long after his memory has vanished from the earth.'[9]

The doctrine of human progress became known as the 'perfectibility of man'. If man were not actually capable of perfection, at least he could be perpetually improved. With the overthrow of the doctrine of original sin, man was considered to be naturally good but corrupted by society; if society could be changed, then so could his character. Vice was therefore ignorance, and education and enlightenment would bring about virtue. This progress could best be achieved through the spread of science and technology.

## The Great Chain of Being

Without the doctrine of the Fall to explain the existence of evil in the world, the eighteenth century turned to the old notion of the Great Chain of Being which reconciled the one with the many, and perfection with imperfection. To suggest that the existence of evil demonstrates an imperfect God is a partial view of the subject. A perfect world must be a 'full' world, it must contain the greatest number of possibilities, including superior and inferior creatures; in short, it demands a Great Chain of Being. Man, according to Alexander Pope, was 'plac'd on this isthmus of a middle state', between animals and angels. It held up the prospect of something to avoid and to emulate; above all, it gave him a privileged position on earth.

The phrase the 'Great Chain of Being' came in the eighteenth century to be the most common phrase after 'Nature' to describe the world in which humanity found themselves. The concept, with its underlying principles of plenitude, gradation and continuity, enjoyed its widest diffusion and acceptance. It served as a metaphysical framework for scientific hypotheses about nature as well as a popular guide to understanding man's place within nature. It took on something of a sacred air, like the words 'evolution' in the second part of the nineteenth century and 'ecology' in the latter part of the twentieth.

The doctrine of course had a long pedigree. It had probably originated in Asia with the notion of the transmigration of souls up the ladder of existence. It came to the foreground in Greek thought, intimated in Plato's dialogues and made explicit in Aristotle's single *scala naturae* where all animals are graded according to their degree of perfection. The Neoplatonists then elaborated the idea into a system.

Alexander Pope gave the fullest expression to the idea of the Great Chain of Being in the eighteenth century:

> Vast chain of being! which from God began,
> Nature's aethereal, human, angel, man,
> Beast, bird, fish, insect! what no eye can see,
> No glass can reach! from Infinite to thee,
> From thee to Nothing! – On superior pow'rs
> Were we to press, inferior might be ours;
> Or in the full creation leave a void,
> Where, one step broken, the great scale destroy'd;
> From Nature's chain whatever link you strike,
> Tenth, or ten thousandth, breaks the chain alike.[10]

Even if one link were destroyed, Pope suggests, the cosmic order would collapse; with its plenitude punctured, it would no longer be full or coherent. He was writing at a time before the death of the dodo, before man had secured mastery over nature. But his awareness of the interrelated nature of all life is profoundly ecological.

At the same time, the doctrine remained hierarchical in Pope's Tory hands. Order for him means gradation of rank, a requirement of divine reason as well as social necessity:

> ORDER is Heav'ns first law; and this confest,
> Some are, and must be, greater than the rest,
> More rich, more wise.[11]

The doctrine of the Great Chain of Being, like so-called 'laws of ecology' in this century, was used by many to justify social inequality and indifference to suffering. Pope inferred that it meant in the social sphere that each should do his duty in his allotted state in life; equality is 'contrary to nature' and to seek to change one's place is to invert the 'laws of Order'.

Pope believed that this was the best of all possible worlds – despite the obvious evidence to the contrary. If Nature is the design of an omnipotent and perfect God, then it must by definition be the best possible design. To consider the world evil or badly made was simply to take a one-sided, unenlightened view. The problem of theodicy – of reconciling the ways of man with God and the existence of evil in the world – was thus solved at a stroke. It followed for Pope that 'whatever IS, is RIGHT'. This attitude might be called 'cosmic Toryism', a deeply conservative philosophy which pervaded the eighteenth century and has reappeared in modern ecology.[12]

The English philosopher Soame Jenyns in his *Free Enquiry into the Nature and Origin of Evil* (1757) went even further to argue that apparent evils of imperfection are merely 'privations' essential to the whole system. He anticipated ecology by insisting that 'the beauty and happiness of the whole depend altogether on the just inferiority of the parts'.[13] The ant and the bee are equally essential to the plenitude of the Chain of Being; each has a claim to his own special happiness. So far so good. The slug or the mosquito, however unpleasant to man, have their place in the order of things and should be allowed to follow their natures.

But Jenyns then uses the idea of the Chain of Being to justify the existing social order; the evils we labour under are due to superior beings between us and God who 'have power to deceive, torment, or destroy us, for the ends of only their pleasure or utility' in the same way that we human beings lord it over inferior creatures:

> Man is one link of that vast chain, descending by insensible degrees, from infinite perfection to absolute nothing. As there are many thousands below him, so must there be many more above him. If we look downwards, we see innumerable species of inferior beings, whose happiness and lives are dependent on his will; we see him cloathed by their spoils, and fed by their miseries and destruction, inslaving some, tormenting others, and murdering millions for his luxury or diversion; is it not therefore analogous and highly probable, that the happiness and life of man should be equally dependent on the wills of his superiors?[14]

He concludes from this state of affairs that one should not try to lessen suffering in the human and animal world but accept it as part of God's perfect and beneficial design.

When Jenyns, like many modern ecologists, slides from the natural to the social sphere, his injunctions are no less benign. The hierarchy in society is as divinely ordained as the hierarchy in nature. Ignorance, he argues, is the 'opiate' of the poor, 'a cordial, administered by the gracious hand of providence'. With one masterly stroke, he is able to justify the status quo and absolve any guilt about educating the lower orders. Ignorance, pain, poverty and toil are the necessary consequences of human nature. No other order can be imagined; 'the sufferings of individuals are absolutely necessary to universal happiness'.[15] Like so many before and after him, Jenyns projects his own social order on to nature. Not surprisingly, he considers self-interest as 'the great principle which operates in the political world in the same manner that attraction does in the natural'. Although many political institutions are irrational, they are all the more appropriate to irrational man. The upshot is that whatever is, is right, and the would-be reformer is merely unwisely rocking the universal boat.

The doctrine of the Great Chain of Being was not a generalization derived from experience and often flew in the face of the facts of nature. How, for instance, could it be tallied with the fossil record, cross-breeds or 'sports' of nature? Its social teaching of indifference and hierarchy were also repugnant to some. Dr Johnson, offended by Soame Jenyns, argued that the principle of plenitude contradicted observable facts and seemed to contradict itself. If the Chain of Being were a genuine continuum, there would have to be an infinity of intermediate members between two members, however close they might be. Since this is impossible, 'the Scale of Existence from Infinity to Nothing cannot possibly have Being'. In short, the whole idea must be 'raised by presumptuous Imagination, to rest on Nothing at the Bottom, to lean on Nothing at the Top'.[16]

Voltaire, who brilliantly satirized Leibniz's optimistic philosophy in *Candide*, also argued that the continuous series is nonexistent in the organic world on the following grounds: some species which once existed have disappeared; we can conceive imaginary intermediate species between living ones which do not exist; and to be complete, the Great Chain of Being must include the absurd notion of a vast hierarchy of immaterial beings above man.

# 17

## TO FOLLOW NATURE

First follow NATURE, and your Judgement frame
By her just Standard, which is still the same:
Unerring Nature, still divinely bright,
One clear, unchang'd, and Universal Light,
Life, Force, and Beauty, must to all impart,
At once the source, and End, and Test of Art.

Alexander Pope

Apart from the Great Chain of Being, the key concept in the eighteenth century was 'Nature' and nearly all thinkers urged their readers that if only they were to 'follow Nature' all would be well. Nature became the touchstone of beliefs in religion and politics. Robert Boyle of the Royal Society enumerated at least eight senses of the word used in philosophy and natural science. Its unqualified use gave rise to great ambiguity and contradiction.

The word 'nature' is one of the most complex in the language; a history of its uses would encompass a large part of the history of human thought. Its complexity of meaning also reflects the complexity of the processes of the world.[1] Over the centuries, it has evolved three distinct areas of meaning: 1) the essential quality of something; 2) the inherent force which directs either the world or human beings or both; 3) the material world as whole. Precise meanings, especially in the latter areas, are often confused if not opposed.

Its oldest meaning is that of an essential quality of something, as in the Latin *natura rerum* (the nature of things) or in the thirteenth-century English usage of the word. In the following century, it came to mean an inherent force. In the sixteenth and seventeenth centuries, it could denote the world as a whole. The abstract use of the word 'nature' presupposed a single prime cause or force as in the second sense, and something common behind the multiplicity of things and creatures in the third. Nature also became personified, as a shaping force such as 'plastic nature' or as a universal directing power, 'Mother Nature'.

The changing meaning of 'nature' reflected the changing structure of society. In medieval theology, God is primary and Nature is his minister. But reflecting the hierarchical nature of medieval thinking, God is also depicted as an absolute monarch who governs the world, and who will punish man if he does not obey. From the seventeenth century, it became possible to observe and study nature as the work of God, in order to praise the maker. But by the eighteenth century, nature came to be seen more in terms of a constitutional monarch, governed by laws. Nature increasingly became synonymous for the material world and the scientist acted like a constitutional lawyer interpreting and codifying universal laws.

Underlying all the main uses of the word in the eighteenth century was the idea that nature provided the foundation on which man was to build. It had come to mean the opposite to all that man had made of himself. The 'natural' was thus opposed to the 'artificial', nature to civilization, natural man to urban man. The 'state of nature' as a state of innocence, goodness and health was increasingly contrasted with the existing corrupt, artificial and mechanical society. Only by following or returning to nature could humanity be cured or regenerated.

At the same time, nature was appealed to as a clear authority – the laws of nature were considered to be the laws of reason, the same everywhere. They had only to be revealed in order to be acknowledged. Nature became identified with reason; the object of observation with the organ of observation. Reason was thus the 'natural light' of humanity which would reveal all the truths of nature.

The new philosophy of nature was not at first anti-religious; indeed, it might be said that the scientific revolution had in some sense rescued nature from Satan and restored it to God.[2] The Great Machine of Nature presupposed a divine mechanic. This argument from design was the mainstay of the deists who rejected the 'barbarism' and 'superstition' of the Middle Ages, but felt unable to live in a world of accidental atoms. Both Francis Bacon and Newton were theists and saw God as central to their universe. God revealed himself as much in his handiwork as in the Bible; Locke asserted: 'The works of Nature everywhere sufficiently evidence a Deity.' Even the mechanical materialists needed a first cause to get things going.

Science thus helped to 'divinize' nature, demonstrating that instead of chaos all was order, design and law. God was a distant first cause or creator; he did not suspend the laws of nature to make miracles, but he could be discerned in all his works. This became the basis of what was called 'natural religion', 'natural theology', 'physico-theology' and 'natural morality'.

## Shaftesbury and glorious nature

The most eloquent exponent of natural religion in the early eighteenth century was Anthony, Earl of Shaftesbury. Where the rational philosophers as much as the theologians had banished spirits from grove and well, Shaftesbury reintroduced universal mind into nature and saw it in organic and plastic terms. Influenced by the Cambridge Platonists, he opposed the mechanical philosophy of the scientific revolution not only because it was hostile to religion but also because it rejected the creative imagination. Shaftesbury was a typical moralist of the Enlightenment but as founder of the 'moral sense' school, he looked to immediate feeling and not to analytical reason as the basis of ethics. He rejected both Hobbes's account of nature as war of all against all and the traditional Christian view that it was corrupt and fallen. Man was not depraved by nature but because his natural affections had been spoiled.

Arguing against those atheists who saw the world as a senseless chaos of atoms, and against orthodox Christians who perceived it as a valley of tears, Shaftesbury asserted that both human nature and nature as a whole are good. Man is naturally good and social; herding in clans and tribes is as natural as eating and drinking. Virtue brings its own reward.

It is in his divinization of nature, however, that Shaftesbury is most interesting from an ecological point of view. In his collected writings *Characteristicks of Men, Manners, Opinions and Times* (1711), he insists on the divine perfection of Nature in the sense of the whole of the creation. Nature is a vast organic system of interconnected parts moving according to unalterable laws. 'All things in this world are united,' he insists, 'For as the branch is united with the tree, so is the tree as immediately with the earth, air, and water which feed it.' Contemplating all the things and beings on earth, we must of necessity view 'all in one, as holding to one common stock'. Indeed, he took it as an article of faith that 'divine Nature' forms 'the great and general ONE of the world'.[3] What we call 'evil' is due to our ignorance and our failure to see it as part of the whole.

Shaftesbury shared with Plato the sense of nature as a work of art and the conviction that the beautiful, the harmonious, the true and the good are synonymous: 'What is beautiful is harmonious and proportionable; what is harmonious and proportionable is true; and what is at once both beautiful and true is, of consequence, agreeable and good.'⁴ But he went beyond the Platonists to recognize God in nature. Natural objects are divine analogues, symbols of God. The beauty of the river, the sea, the constellations in heaven all flow from a universal mind, the same eternal source.

Nature moreover was not static but 'plastic', possessing a shaping power which is part of divine activity. Whereas for the Cambridge Platonists 'plastic natures' acted as forces executing the details of the creation under the control of the divine Will, for Shaftesbury the whole of nature is one plastic force. There is a creative process at work throughout nature which is responsible for growth and change.

In the dialogue entitled *The Moralists: A Philosophical Rhapsody*, the character Theocles appears as an early Thoreau. 'Ye fields and woods,' he exclaims, 'my refuge from the toilsome world of business, receive me in your quiet sanctuaries, and favour my retreat and thoughtful solitude.' In nature far from man, one can contemplate the cause of things, divine wisdom and the harmonious order of the works of the 'divine Artificer'. In rhapsodic excess, he continues:

> O glorious nature! supremely fair, and sovereignly good! all-loving and all-lovely, all-divine! ... whose every single work affords an ampler scene, and is a nobler spectacle than all which ever art presented! O mighty Nature! wise substitute of Providence! impower'd creatress! O thou impowering Deity, supreme creator! Thee I invoke and thee alone I adore.⁵

Shaftesbury was one of the first to appreciate the sublime in nature which leads the observer towards the infinite mind. He also stressed the importance of the disinterested appreciation of nature for its own sake, and not as a means to our ends. When observing a beautiful ocean, one should not want to command it 'like some mighty admiral', but contemplate it like a 'poor shepherd' who forgets his flocks while admiring its beauty. Indeed, Shaftesbury was one of the first to celebrate nature in the raw, nature unspoiled by man: 'The wildness pleases. We seem to live alone with Nature. We view her in her inmost recesses, and contemplate her with more delight in these

original wilds than in the artificial labyrinths and feigned wildernesses
of the palace.'[6]

Inverting centuries of Christian teaching, Shaftesbury asserts that
man is not the 'lord of all'. If anything, the subordination is the other
way round; 'if Nature herself be not for man, but man for Nature;
then must man, by his good leave, submit to the elements of Nature,
and not the elements to him'.[7]

The German writer Herder hailed Shaftesbury as the 'beloved Plato
of Europe' and he profoundly influenced Coleridge, Kant and Schiller.
But while Shaftesbury anticipated the Romantic poets, his optimistic
philosophy that partial evil is universal good in the best of all possible
worlds was profoundly conservative from a social point of view. It
simply overlooked the suffering of humans and animals in an unequal
and unjust world. His naturalism, moreover, is more progressivist
than primitivist in that the noble earl considered existing society the
natural condition of man. In his moral arithmetic, self-love and social
justice are the same.

## Holbach's and La Mettrie's system of nature

In France, as the eighteenth century progressed, those who did not
wish to follow Church and state began, like the Stoics before them,
to raise the cry of 'follow nature'.

This becomes immediately apparent in the *Système de la nature* by
Baron d'Holbach (1723–89). A German living in France, he developed
Cartesian mechanism to offer a completely materialist and determinist
picture of nature. For him nature consists of matter eternally in
motion: 'By Nature we understand that which really is, a whole of
which various parts have various properties, behave in accordance
with these properties, and are in a state of perpetual interaction upon
each other.'[8] All things are trying to become themselves.

In the same way, man, who is part of nature, seeks happiness but
is acted upon by causes like everything else. Since the 'soul' is part of
the body, medicine is the key to morality. It makes no sense to punish
someone; it is better to heal them. If they are wicked, it is because of
their environment – especially in the form of government, education
and public opinion. 'Man is bad, not because he was born bad, but
because he is made so.'[9] Just as all things tend to preserve themselves,
so man is directed by self-love. Holbach considered the moral man to
be merely a physical being from a different point of view. Man is no

more free to think than to act independently of the causes operating on him. Holbach thus overcame Cartesian dualism by identifying the soul with the body, the mind with the brain, and God with nature. The Cartesian mind as a separate substance is nothing more than a figment of the imagination.

Holbach, who contributed articles on minerals to the *Encyclopédie*, developed the idea of nature in a radical direction; in his hands, nature became a touchstone against which the accretions of Church and state could be measured. He habitually made a distinction between the 'natural' and the 'artificial' and opposed an 'unspoiled' nature to an erring humanity. All our misfortunes are caused by our departure from or neglect of nature.

At the same time, nature in Holbach's writings is constantly opposed to the 'super-nature' of the spirit and God. He insists on the necessity of atheism: 'Failing to know nature, he [man] created Gods.' Religion is nothing more than 'the art of intoxicating men with enthusiasm, so as to divert their attention from the evils with which their rulers load them here on earth'.[10] As an atheist, Holbach was primarily concerned with the tyranny, cruelty and ignorance perpetuated by the Church. Opposing *le bon sens* to Christian doctrine, he saw suffering humanity crushed under the double yoke of spiritual and temporal powers: 'Man was a simple machine in the hands of his tyrants and his priests, who alone had the right to regulate his movements: treated as a slave, he has had almost at every time and in every place the vices and character of a slave.'[11] The only way out is to use reason and to follow nature.

But what does nature actually teach us? It bids 'man to be sociable, to love his fellows, to be just, peaceful, indulgent, beneficent, to make or leave his associates happy'.[12] It also bids men to be self-reliant and to conquer removable evils by mastering natural laws. Like most of the *philosophes* of the Enlightenment, Holbach believed that virtue naturally brings happiness and is its own reward.

Although Holbach calls for atheism in order to become free, he celebrates nature with an almost religious fervour. Nature is the true deity in his writings. He condemns 'Spinozistic' pantheism, but his own 'Matter' has marvellous attributes and potentialities. He ends his *Système de la nature* with a veritable hymn to nature:

> Oh Nature! sovereign of all beings! and you its adorable daughters, virtue, reason, truth! forever be our only Divinities;

it is to you that are due the incense and the homages of the
earth. Show us then, oh nature! what man must do to obtain
the happiness which you have made him desire . . .[13]

For all his determinist and materialist philosophy, Holbach was
undoubtedly an optimist. He was convinced that there were no
natural ills without corresponding natural remedies. Vice is not
endemic in nature but a form of ignorance. The surest answers to
all human ills therefore lay in education. But who is to educate the
educators? Holbach summed up the faith of the *philosophes* of the
Enlightenment by insisting:

> It is only by enlightening men, by showing them evidence, by
> proclaiming the truth to them that it can be promised that
> they will be made better and happier . . . Let us then consult
> reason, call experience to our aid, interrogate nature, and we
> shall discover what must be done in order to work effectively
> for the happiness of the human race. We shall see that error is
> the true source of the ills of our species; that is . . . by taking
> the axe to the root of superstition, that we shall be able quietly
> to search for the truth, and find in nature the torch which can
> guide us to felicity. Let us then study nature . . .[14]

Although Goethe, reacting in his youth against the 'gloomy' spirit of
eighteenth-century French materialism, 'shuddered' at the *Système
de la nature* 'as at a ghost', Shelley was deeply influenced by it,
particularly in his great revolutionary poem *Queen Mab*.

Like Holbach, Julien La Mettrie (1709–51) repudiated Descartes'
distinction between mind and matter, body and soul on which man's
alleged uniqueness and separation from nature was founded. At the
same time, however, he developed Descartes' mechanical philosophy
to conclude that not only are animals unconscious automata but so
is man; he moved from *la bête-machine* to its ultimate conclusion
in *L'Homme machine* (1748). Since man is a machine, the true
philosopher is an engineer.

Not only did he consider questions of the origin and destiny of
the universe beyond investigation, but also natural order, matter
and movement. The soul detached from the body, he argued, is
'like matter though without any form; it is inconceivable'.[15] As
for the mind, it 'is only an empty term of which one has no idea
at all, and of which a sensible person should not make a use except

to designate the part in us which thinks'.[16] La Mettrie reaches the nadir of mechanical materialism: all mental attributes are properties or functions of matter. The human will is merely determined by the body's response to pleasure and pain from its internal constitution or external environment. The mind is a box containing ideas which are the mental equivalent of Newtonian particles.

Unlike other *philosophes*, La Mettrie thought that men in general are born bad, and without education there would be few good people on earth. There was moreover no necessary connection between virtue and happiness. His, and not Holbach's, was the truly gloomy system.

## Smith, Burke, Bentham and natural society

Appeals to nature had a revolutionary dimension in the hands of the French *philosophes*, but in Britain they were used in a reformist direction. The 'state of nature', particularly after Locke, was used by the emerging middle classes to assert their 'natural rights' against the divine right of kings and the remnants of the feudal and ecclesiastical order. They also appealed to nature to justify their economic programme of laissez faire, secure that in a free market 'natural laws' of supply and demand would bring about general wellbeing. Adam Smith in his *Wealth of Nations* looked to the hidden hand of God to transform self-interest into the general good. The 'Law of Nature' thus became a sanction for laissez faire and unrestrained competition for the good things of the earth.

Although in his maturity Edmund Burke became the scourge of the French Revolution and is remembered as the 'father of Conservatism', as a young man he was a supporter of both economic reform and American independence. He also wrote a remarkable work called *A Vindication of Natural Society* (1756).

Burke echoes the Chinese Taoists by insisting that 'if left to itself [nature] were the best and surest Guide'. In their original state of nature, Burke suggests that people lived 'with their Brethren of the other Kinds in much equality' and were wholly vegetarian. There were no shadows stretching from the Fall and nature was wholesome and good. In such a 'natural' society, people followed their 'natural Appetites and Instincts, and not in any positive institution'.[17] Governed by reason, they had no need for external government or law.

Unfortunately, human beings left this paradise by inventing artificial rules to guide nature; they created a political society held together by laws which were a violation of nature and a constraint on the mind. The Church then came to support the artificial and unnecessary state and finally empires were cemented in blood. The remedy, Burke suggests, is that 'we should renounce their "Dreams of Society", together with their Visions of Religion, and vindicate ourselves into perfect liberty' – a liberty that we originally enjoyed in harmony with nature and other creatures.[18]

Although Burke later claimed that the work was tongue in cheek, it inspired William Godwin and other anarchists who took its celebration of nature and criticism of artificial government seriously. There can be no doubt that Burke's *Vindication of Natural Society* contained a devastating exposure of existing political institutions.

The British philosopher and reformer Jeremy Bentham also took nature as his guide to develop a powerful critique of existing society. 'NATURE,' he asserted in 1780, 'has placed mankind under the governance of two sovereign masters, *pain* and *pleasure*. It is for them alone to point out what we ought to do, as well as to determine what we shall do.' It is therefore the role of reason to calculate the degree of pleasure or pain one might feel in any action.

Bentham was a utilitarian in ethics and politics; that is to say, he thought that the individual should contribute all in his power to the general good. It was thus on the principle of utility that he sought 'to rear the fabric of felicity by the hands of reason and law'.[19] It is a principle that approves or disapproves of every action according to its tendency to promote or oppose human happiness.

Since Bentham defined happiness as pleasure, he went to absurd lengths in drawing up a 'felicific calculus' in order to establish the degrees of potential pleasure in different actions. It marked the ultimate calculation in an age of calculators, with the individual becoming the supreme judge of his or her interest. The community for Bentham does not exist; it is a 'fictitious body' and the interest of the community is no more than the sum of the interests of the members who compose it.

In applying his principle of utility, Bentham advocated moral equality, in the sense that equality is not an assertion of fact but a prescription of how we should treat each other. Everyone's interests should be given equal consideration. He therefore proposed the formula: 'Each to count for one and none for more than one.' He did not, like Locke, extend rights only to the 'rational', thereby excluding by his definition women, children, fools and animals. On the contrary, he insisted that there was no insuperable line between men and animals. The claim to equal consideration does not depend on the faculty of reason or the faculty of discourse but on the capacity for suffering and enjoyment: 'The question is not, Can they *reason?* nor Can they *talk?* but, *Can they suffer?*'[20]

Bentham was one of the first to denounce 'man's dominion' over nature as tyranny rather than legitimate government by comparing the position of animals with that of black slaves. He looked forward to the time 'when the rest of the animal creation may acquire those rights which never could have been withholden from them but by the hand of tyranny'.

Adapting Bentham's principle of sentience as a criterion for moral consideration, it is possible to make a persuasive case for animal liberation. If the limit of sentience is the only defensible boundary of concern for the interests of others, and the principle of equality requires that the suffering of one being be counted equally with the like suffering of any other being, then it could be argued that animals as well as humans have rights.[21]

Nevertheless, while Bentham offers a strong argument to extend rights to nonhumans, he did not advocate abstinence from flesh-eating. 'There is very good reason,' he claimed,

> why we should be suffered to eat such of them as we like to eat; we are the better for it, and they are never the worse. They have none of those long-protracted anticipations of future misery which we have. The death they suffer in our hands commonly is, and always may be, a speedier, and by that means a less painful one, than that which would await them in the inevitable course of nature.[22]

By the principle of utility, Bentham also created the horror of the Panopticon, a 'model' prison based on a rational plan which enabled perpetual vigilance of inmates by the guards. It might be a symbol of our own punitive and totalitarian society.

### Kant's Copernican revolution

The humanism of the Enlightenment culminates in the German philosopher Immanuel Kant (1724–1804), who followed Descartes in opposing his intellect against tradition and authority. Kant saw the ability to think for oneself as the central feature of the Enlightenment:

> Enlightenment is man's exodus from this self-incurred tutelage. Tutelage is the inability to use one's understanding without the guidance of another person. This tutelage is self-incurred if its cause lies not in any weakness of the understanding, but in indecision and lack of courage to use the mind without the guidance of another. 'Dare to know' (*sapere aude*)! Have the courage to use your own understanding; this is the motto of the Enlightenment.[23]

Kant had almost equal reverence for Newton as the first to set forth the principles of natural science, and for Rousseau, whom he considered the first to discover the principles of conduct. Kant further developed the rationalism of Descartes and the empiricism of Locke; he was awakened from his dogmatic slumbers by Hume and went on to create a Copernican revolution in philosophy.

Kant is generally considered the founder of German idealism. His great ambition was to analyse human reason and to discover what it can and cannot do. Just as Copernicus explained the movement of the stars by suggesting that their apparent movements are partly due to the movement of the observer on earth, so Kant suggested in his *Critique of Pure Reason* (1781) that instead of our knowledge conforming to objects, 'objects conform to the mind'.

The mind has a creative role in perception by applying a kind of conceptual apparatus to the external world. This apparatus consists of *a priori* principles independent of experience such as the categories of causality, substance and time. Mind thus plays an active role, organizing what we experience. Kant's revolutionary idea is that by supplying a conceptual structure of the world, we in part construct the world around us. 'The order and regularity in objects, which we entitle *nature*, we ourselves introduce. The understanding is the lawgiver of nature.' It is therefore impossible to separate the observer and the observed as the architects of the scientific revolution had hoped.

This position, which is sometimes called critical idealism, limits the boundaries of possible knowledge. Kant did not deny the existence of the external world or suggest that it is all in the mind. The mind, however, can never know the real nature of 'things-in-themselves' (noumena) independent of our conceptual and sensory framework.

All it can do is to perceive them as they appear (phenomena); we thus construct the external world out of appearances. All science can do is anticipate experience; it can never reveal the true nature of things.

While drawing the limits of knowledge, and recognizing the mutual relationship between the observer and the observed, Kant still vaunted the Western ambition to dominate nature:

> It is only the principles of reason which can give to concordant phenomena the validity of laws, and it is only when experiment is directed by these rational principles that it can have any real utility. Reason must approach nature with the view, indeed, of receiving information from it, not, however, in the character of a pupil, who listens to all that his master chooses to tell him, but in that of a judge, who compels the witnesses to reply to those questions which he himself thinks fair to propose.[24]

Nevertheless, in his ethics Kant laid the foundations of a libertarian morality by insisting on the moral autonomy of the individual. He named the autonomy of the will as the supreme principle of morality; it is 'the ground of the dignity of human nature and every rational creature'.[25] The love of freedom was central to his ethics: 'There can be nothing more dreadful than that the actions of a man should be subject to the will of another,' he declared. In Kant's view, we retain our moral autonomy if we follow moral rules or obey laws which we have made for ourselves. And 'I ought' implies 'I can': as a rational being I must be able to determine the motives of my actions.

Kant tried to formulate a universal moral law in what he called the 'categorical imperative'. It is not a rule of skill or counsel of prudence, but a moral command. It declares: '*Act only on that maxim through which you can at the same time will that it should become a universal law.*'[26] If I steal a book, for instance, I should be prepared for others to steal all books, including my own. The fundamental presuppositions of this morality are that the rational will must be subject to universal law; that it must exist as an end in itself; and that the rational will must be the maker as well as the subject of the universal law.

A central feature of the categorical imperative is that we should treat every person as an end-in-himself or herself and never as a means to our own ends. Each person has intrinsic and not merely instrumental value. But while we have a duty to treat other human beings as ends-in-themselves, so far as animals are concerned, Kant argued that we have no direct duties. The criterion for him is not Bentham's capacity to suffer but Descartes' ability to think. 'Animals are not self-conscious, and are there merely as a means to an end. That end is man.'[27] Nonrational beings have 'only a relative value as means and are consequently called *things*. Rational beings, on the other hand, are called *persons* because already their nature marks them out as ends in themselves.'[28]

Kant makes the moral life of central importance. He rejects the traditional arguments to prove the existence of God but suggests that the moral law is independent of religion and the highest good is not realizable unless God exists. The cornerstone of Kant's philosophy of religion is that only a good life has religious meaning: 'Everything that man, apart from a moral way of life, believes himself to be capable of doing to please God is mere religious delusion and spurious worship.'[29] One can therefore be truly religious without adhering to any organized religion or external worship.

Kant's ethics are uncompromisingly rationalistic. No reliable incentives can be found in moral feeling or intuition, and the instincts always mislead. Reason is the governor of the will, he asserted, and there will always be a conflict betweed duty and desire. One's duty will always be disagreeable; indeed, if one feels an inclination to perform an action, it cannot have moral worth. The austere moralist in Kant insists that 'the more cultivated reason concerns itself with the aim of enjoying life and happiness, the farther does man get away from true contentment'. Nevertheless, Kant does allow that the moral life brings its own 'peculiar kind of contentment'.[30]

If we extend Kant's criterion of rationality for entrance into the moral community to include Bentham's principle of sentience, it is possible to argue that animals as well as human beings have intrinsic value and should be considered as ends-in-themselves. The practical imperative would therefore be: never treat sentient beings simply as a means but always as an end. Kant can thus provide a moral base for animal liberation.

# 18

# PRIMITIVISM AND THE NOBLE SAVAGE

Iron and corn first civilized men, and ruined humanity.
Jean-Jacques Rousseau

During the Enlightenment there were some dissident voices who
questioned the rational and mechanical foundations of Western
'civilization'. There was a growing interest in the 'primitive' which
coincided with an interest in non-European societies. This primitivism
took a chronological form, which viewed the earliest period in history
as the best, and a cultural form, which considered the achievements of
civilization to be evil and corrupt. It also tended to stress the gentleness
as well as the simplicity of the primitive life. It led to the ecological
belief that the best life is one of voluntary simplicity, unencumbered
by the trappings of civilization.

Primivitism as a whole crystallized in the myth of the 'Noble
Savage'. Just as science opened up the vista of nature, so adventurers,
missionaries and merchants were opening up the rest of the world
to European trade and culture. The early travellers brought back
evidence to support natural religion and natural morality, depicting
pagan societies living close to the earth and following nature. Even
Jesuit missionaries in Brazil, Paraguay, Canada, China and other
distant parts praised the virtues of natural man. American Indians
and Tahitians seemed to live idyllic lives compared to harassed
and anxious Europeans. The tales of the travellers of unspoiled
societies without government and property, where gracious and
healthy humans lived as in the Garden of Eden, were used as foils
against the corrupt and tyrannical European regimes. Accounts of
imaginary voyages provide many fertile suggestions for creating an
ecological society in harmony with nature.

## Foigny's hermaphrodites

One of the first and certainly most instructive was the French writer Gabriel de Foigny's *Les Aventures de Jacques Sadeur dans la découverte de la Terre Australe* (1676), where hermaphrodite deists live in perfect freedom and equality. The battle between the sexes is resolved once and for all.

Foigny's Australians are born free, reasonable and good, and worship by meditation rather than prayer. They have no written laws, no rulers and no private property; they are educated in communal houses. In this ecotopia, the inhabitants spend the first part of each day at school, the second part gardening and the third part in public exercise. As fruitarians, they have no need for agriculture beyond gardening. Industry is minimal since they wear no clothes and have little furniture. Their needs are simple and simply satisfied. Each morning food is brought from their gardens to the common storehouse when they meet for their daily conference. Population is not a problem since they are all 'hermaphrodites'.

Foigny was the first social ecologist, advocating a society without government. An elder whom Jacques Sadeur encounters explains that the essence of man consists in liberty and to be free means to follow nature:

> It was the Nature of Man to be born free, and live free, and that therefore he could not be subjected without being despoiled of his nature . . . The subjection of one man in another was a subjection of human Nature, and making man a sort of slave of himself, which slavery implied such a contradiction and violence as was impossible to conceive.[1]

These freedom-loving people find words of command odious; they only do what their reason tells them to do. All important decisions affecting their lives are taken in local assemblies of each district or neighbourhood. The spontaneous order which prevails flows from the 'Natural Light' of their reason.

## Swift and equine wisdom

In the following century, Jonathan Swift (1667–1745) used the device of utopia in *Gulliver's Travels* to criticize the follies of his own civilization and to suggest an alternative way of living. The Tory Dean had a low view of humanity and his misanthropy has echoes in the writings of many modern deep ecologists. The bulk of the English nation, he declared, is 'the most pernicious race of little odious vermin that Nature ever suffered to crawl upon the Surface of the Earth'.[2]

In *Gulliver's Travels*, Swift offers in the flying island of Laputa a direct satire of the state of England and Ireland, and Lilliput reflects the rigid social divisions and absurd political pretensions of European society. In Brobdingnag, the inhabitants are by contrast hard-working and live a life of few wants and simple virtue. But the most interesting ecotopia comes in the voyage to the country of the Houyhnhnms in Book IV, where he mounts an attack on European states with their laws, government, commerce and war.

The hairy creatures in human form called Yahoos who disturb the peaceful ways of the Houyhnhnms are remarkably similar to modern Europeans. They are greedy, perverse, cunning and destructive. They fight over food and shining stones and move around in packs waging war on each other. By contrast the Houyhnhnms are dignified horses, rational creatures who maintain that 'Nature and Reason were sufficient Guides for a reasonable Animal, as we pretended to be, in shewing us what we ought to do, and what to avoid'.[3] They practise universal benevolence and perfect sincerity. Their wants are few, Swift adopting the maxim that nature can very easily be satisfied. As a result, in their stone-age economy they have no metal or wheels to cause their downfall. Population is controlled by moral restraint and abstinence. All receive the same education which fosters temperance, exercise and cleanliness. They organize their affairs by periodic councils where they try to reach unaninimity; they do not issue laws, but merely exhort others to act in agreed ways.

There are of course some negative aspects to Swift's utopia – the economy is based on Yahoo labour and the family is strongly patriarchal. To influence others solely through reason and love can be oppressive if practised in the wrong way. There is little room for dissidence or awkwardness. Nevertheless, Swift's depiction of the 'state of nature' as a form of spontaneous order is undoubtedly more accurate than Hobbes's nightmare of all against all. By making horses his heroes and humans the villains, Swift overthrows the prevailing anthropocentrism of his day and makes an indirect plea for kind treatment of animals. It becomes quite understandable why Gulliver, on his return to England, should prefer to live in a stable among horses rather than with his grasping and restive fellows.

### Diderot and paradise in the Pacific

Denis Diderot (1713–84) was a leading member of the Politburo of the Enlightenment party. As editor of the *Encyclopédie*, he shared the confidence of his fellow *philosophes* in the march of progress through the gradual diffusion of theoretical and practical knowledge.

He was, however, an ambivalent and subtle thinker, and could always see both sides to a question. In principle he was a materialist and determinist, but he found it difficult to renounce moral responsibility. In the dialogue *Jacques le fataliste*, first published in 1796, Jacques believes in fate but acts as if he were free. Again in *Le Neveu de Rameau*, written in 1762 and not published until 1823, Diderot observes: 'In nature all species devour one another; all conditions of men devour one another in society. We mete out justice to one another without the law being concerned in it.'[4] Yet this did not lead him to call for the curbing of nature. In an article on the 'Passions' for the *Encyclopédie*, he argued that our happiness and perfection consist in following our nature. People speak different languages, but if all could hear the voice of nature and act upon it they would be virtuous. Corruption is not therefore the fault of the passions, but of false judgement:

> The passions always inspire us rightly, since they inspire us only with the desire for happiness; it is the mind which leads us astray, and which makes us follow false paths to its achievements. Thus we are criminals only because we judge wrongly; and it is reason and not nature which deceives us.[5]

Diderot gave flesh and blood to these philosophical principles in his *Supplément au voyage de Bougainville* (1796), an addendum to the French navigator Louis Antoine de Bougainville's account of his visit to Tahiti. America had long been the great inspiration for primitivist utopias, but after its conquest and the American Revolution, Diderot turned to the South Seas to situate his 'primitive paradise'.

Diderot, like Foigny and Swift, uses his utopia to attack Western civilization with its repressive religion and warring states as well as to suggest a more healthy and natural alternative. His Tahitians are noble and generous; they condemn by contrast the hypocrisy and meanness of Christian civilization. They follow the 'pure instincts of nature', have no word for 'mine' and 'thine', and enjoy free love. But this does not lead to overpopulation; there is a strict taboo on intercourse before maturity to avoid unwanted babies.

Diderot depicts a magnificent ecotopia. The Tahitians reject the 'artificial needs', greed and bellicosity of the West and choose to live a simple life in harmony with nature. Preferring repose above all else, they have reduced their needs to a minimum. Their only moral rule is the 'general good' and 'particular utility'. In this anarchist society without government, civil law is merely the enunciation of the law of nature. The Tahitian who scrupulously holds to the law of nature, Diderot observes, is closer to good legislation than any 'civilized people'. The whole is a celebration of natural order as opposed to civilized disorder.

Europeans have of course all but destroyed the gentle society in the South Seas. Paul Gauguin and Robert Louis Stevenson in the nineteenth century were still bewitched by the vision of a paradise in the Pacific but found that white mischief had already worked its ways. The fantasy still lives on in travel brochures about palm-fringed tropical beaches and in accounts of voluntary castaways. The vision of escaping from artificial and industrial society to a tropical island of peace and plenty continues to be a central fantasy of the West.

## Rousseau and the return to nature

The cult of primitivism, which operated historically in terms of a lost golden age, or geographically in the sense of a country far away, reached its apogee in the work of the French writer Jean-Jacques Rousseau (1712–78). He was the most paradoxical thinker of the eighteenth century, a product of the Enlightenment and yet one of its principal critics. While using his own reason to great effect, he attacked the rationalism of his age. A great libertarian in his early writings, he came to advocate the corporate state and totalitarian democracy.

Nevertheless, he was one of the most eloquent critics of the scientific revolution, which depicted the world as a machine, and of the Enlightenment, which upheld analytical reason as the supreme faculty. Seeing the misuse of reason in curbing natural instincts, he declared that the 'the man who meditates is a depraved animal'.[6] This did not mean that natural man would be immoral, for conscience is a 'divine instinct' and sure guide. Above all, Rousseau was one of the greatest critics of Western civilization and of its corrupt and unjust institutions. As such he is one of the great forerunners of the green movement as well as of Romanticism.

Rousseau's attack on Western civilization began with *A Discourse on the Moral Effects of the Arts and Science* (1750), in which he argued that the arts and sciences are misused by those in power to corrupt morals and to mislead the people. He then developed his central theme of humanity's tragic departure from their essential nature in *A Discourse on the Origin of Inequality* (1754). His stated intention is 'to distinguish properly between what is original and what is artificial in the actual nature of man'.[7] He stresses that he is not offering historical facts but proceeding by hypothetical reasoning.

According to Rousseau, man in a state of nature lived an independent and self-sufficient life. He was by nature gentle and compassionate. Man has two drives prior to reason, one which leads to self-preservation, and the other which makes him feel repugnance at the sight of the suffering of another sensible being. It is the latter – his innate sense of compassion – which takes the place of laws, morals and virtues in a state of nature.

Unfortunately, as man emerged from the state of nature he became 'a tyrant over himself and over nature'. As he began to cooperate with others, the desire for self-preservation became transformed into *amour propre*, a 'fictitious feeling' which made him obsessed with the opinion of others and fostered pride, ambition and competition. Thinking only made matters worse, for it is reason that engenders *amour propre*, and reflection that confirms it.[8]

The principal cause of the downfall of humanity, the origin of inequality, was the institution of private property:

> The first man who, having enclosed a piece of ground, bethought himself of saying 'This is mine', and found people simple enough to believe him, was the real founder of civil society. From how many crimes, wars, and murders, from how many horrors and

misfortunes might not any one have saved mankind, by pulling up the stakes, or filling in the ditch, and crying to his fellows: 'Beware of listening to this impostor; you are undone if you once forget that the fruits of the earth belong to us all, and the earth itself to nobody.'[9]

Thereafter, as people grew more industrious, their needs multiplied. Agriculture and industry speeded up the downward spiral: 'It was iron and corn which first civilized men, and ruined humanity'.[10] This argument has echoes among modern ecologists who believe that the best stage of human history was when a small population of hunter-gatherers moved over the earth without sufficient tools and knowledge to make large-scale disturbances of natural cycles.

The development of civil society based on agriculture and industry led to the creation of authoritarian and hierarchical institutions. Wishing to enjoy their property in security, the rich and powerful duped the people into accepting the need for government and laws: 'All ran headlong to their chains, in hope of securing their liberty.'[11] Government ended up ensuring the law of the strongest, which it was originally designed to remedy. It is this insight that makes Rousseau a great libertarian and a precursor of anarchism.

Rousseau appears in his *Discourse on the Origin of Inequality* as a great lover of liberty and defender of oppressed creatures. Liberty, the noblest faculty, is a gift of nature, to be found in animals and humanity alike. Rousseau will have no truck with those apologists of slavery who maintain that creatures have a natural propensity to servitude:

> When I see free-born animals dash their brains out against the bars of their cage, from an innate impatience of captivity; when I behold numbers of naked savages, that despise European pleasures, braving hunger, fire, the sword, and death, to preserve nothing but their independence, I feel that it is not for slaves to argue about liberty.[12]

At the end of his discourse, Rousseau develops the contrast between vigorous and healthy 'savages' in the state of nature and modern man in the 'civilized' world. This anticipates some of the most stringent accounts of alienation in the technological and military states of the twentieth century, where real wants have become artificial needs, where personal integrity is lost in the scramble for power and reputation, where everything is reduced to appearances, where property and laws have destroyed equality, and where the privileged few gorge themselves with superfluities and luxuries while the starving multitude lack the bare necessities of life. Our society offers us only 'an assembly of artificial men and factitious passions'. Rousseau suggests that the 'savage' and the 'civilized' man differ so much that what constitutes the supreme happiness of the one would reduce the other to despair:

> The former breathes only peace and liberty; he desires only to live and to be free from labour . . . Civilized man, on the other hand, is always moving, sweating, toiling and racking his brains to find still more laborious occupations: he goes on in drudgery to the last moment, and even seeks death to put himself in a position to live, or renounces life to acquire immortality. He pays his court to men in power, whom he hates, and to the wealthy, whom he despises; he stops at nothing to have the honour of serving them; he is not ashamed to value himself on his own meanness and their protection; and, proud of his slavery, he speaks with disdain of those, who have not the honour of sharing it. What a sight would the perplexing and envied labours of a European minister of State present to the eyes of a Caribbean! How many cruel deaths would not this indolent savage prefer to the horrors of such a life, which is seldom even sweetened by the pleasure of doing good![13]

Rousseau based his contrast on idealized accounts of travellers from the East and West Indies, journeys made possible only by the technological advances brought about by the scientific revolution. His observations, he reminds his readers, are conjectures. But while they might not be anthropologically accurate, his bold attempt to distinguish between the artificial and the natural is at the heart of modern green thinking. Moreover, at a time when it became the policy of colonialists to emphasize the barbarism of non-European societies in order to justify their rule and to impose their own civilization, Rousseau spoke out on behalf of the subject peoples whose traditional ways were threatened. In the process, he brought out the failings of his own industrious and oppressive society.

Voltaire, the supreme example of eighteenth-century court society, declared contemptuously that reading Rousseau's discourse made him want to fall down on all fours and eat grass. Rousseau deliberately cut his links with Voltaire's polished world and the Establishment of the day by radically changing his lifestyle. He chose to dress in simple clothes, symbolically took off his wig (the artifice of fashion) and unbuckled his sword (the cruelty of war). The son of a watchmaker, he broke his watch, symbol of the time-conscious and mechanical culture he found himself in, and of God the Great artificer. By breaking with the Establishment in this way, Rousseau was a forerunner of the hippies and New Age travellers who turn their backs on straight society and try to survive in their own way on its fringes.

Alone and abused in his bold attempt to take on Western civilization, Rousseau eventually succumbed to the pressure. He ended his days in bouts of mental confusion and paranoia. His brilliant *Confessions*, which narrate his attempt to transform his culture and society, end up as an exercise in self-justification. But his persecution complex was founded in reality: those in power did not like his message and for good reason for it was profoundly subversive.

Rousseau has been associated with the 'return to nature' movement. He opened his treatise on education, *Emile* (1762) with the words: 'Everything is good as it comes from the hands of the author of nature, everything degenerates in the hands of man.' He made famous the doctrine that man is 'naturally good', depraved and corrupted only by private property, oppressive government and false reasoning. His lyrical writings about nature in *Reveries of a Solitary Walker* and his ecstatic feeling for God in nature helped heal some of the ravages of the scientific revolution and paved the way to Romanticism. Indeed, he has been called the father of French Romanticism because of his closeness to nature, his individualism, his rebellion against the established order, and his celebration of the imagination and feelings.

Rousseau declared: 'Man is born free; and everywhere he is in chains.'[14] This cry inspired the mob which stormed the Bastille and has reverberated in the minds of revolutionaries ever since.

But he did not simply call for a return to some primal state of nature. He believed the happiest and most stable epoch for humanity was in the youth of society when the expansion of the mind kept 'a just mean between the indolence of the primitive state and the petulant activity of our *amour propre*'.[15] Furthermore, in his late work, the *Social Contract* (1762), he did not look backwards but forwards, calling for a new agreement between subjects and their rulers and a democratic state based on popular sovereignty and expressing the 'general will'.

Rousseau is a paradoxical man and thinker. Just as he thinks woman should be educated to be the plaything of man, so his ideal state is totalitarian. Starting out with the isolated individual in a state of nature, he ends up submerging him in a coercive community. As a holistic thinker, he argues that the 'general will' is greater than the sum of individual wills, yet leaves it to the legislator to determine the exact nature of this hazy concept. He defends popular sovereignty, advocates a form of direct democracy, calls for small states and favours federalism. At the same time, he believes that it is possible to 'force' people to be 'free'. He even advocates state religion, rigid censorship and the death penalty. Although his onslaught against Western civilization anticipates much of the contemporary ecological critique, the later Rousseau is no social ecologist.

# 19

## CHANGING SENSIBILITIES

What right, I pray, has man to all the corn in the world?

Thomas Tryon

There has always been a close correspondence between man's attitude to nature and the degree of his mastery over it. In early history, he classified nature according to its potential use, especially in terms of the edible and the inedible, the tame and the wild, the useful and the useless. The desire to know and classify the biological environment in order to impose some pattern upon their surroundings seems universal to all peoples.[1] The most important aspects of their environment received the greatest discrimination: the Inuit have many words for snow, the pastoral Nuer of the Sudan have six terms for the shape of cattle's horns, and the Lapland herders some fifty names for the colours of their reindeer.

In the seventeenth and eighteenth centuries, the classification of the animal world in Europe resulted in their separation into pets and pests, wild and tame animals. The members of each category were not universal: in the East dogs were considered filthy scavengers, while in the West ladies shared their silk beds with their perfumed four-footed darlings. The attitude to animals of the same species was often contradictory, depending on the closeness of them to humans: the English squire who revelled in killing foxes lay in a drunken stupor with his hounds.

The traditional anthropomorphic tendency to project human values on to the natural world continued. The natural world became the mirror of political organization and communities of animals were seen in terms of human society: the 'queen' bee, the 'leader' of the pack and the 'king' of the jungle all were eminently human. The whole natural world was ordered in a hierarchical scale, with eagle, whale and lion in popular imagery as the monarchs at the top. The more democratic rooks who squawk and squabble had a 'parliament'. As in the ancient world, the fox continued to be cunning, the goat lustful and the ant provident.

Nature could provide a lesson; the wild dogs of Puerto Rico according to an English traveller were 'a notable instruction to man ... how easily he may grow wild, if once he begin to like better of licentious anarchy than of wholesome obedience'.[2] Bernard de Mandeville in *The Fable of Bees, or Private Vices, Public Benefits* (1714) tried to demonstrate the vileness of the human species by arguing that society like a hive of bees thrives on a system of mutual rapacity and exploitation. Whereas in his *Theory of Moral Sentiments* (1759) Adam Smith argued that these all arise from sympathy, which is the basis of the fabric of society, in his *Enquiry into the Nature and Causes of the Wealth of Nations* (1776), he saw in the 'economy of nature' the division of labour, an abhorrence of waste, and the operation of a providential Invisible Hand which transformed private interest into the general good.

## Tame animals and wild beasts

In Europe, some animals became privileged species. The growth of the cities and the resulting alienation of urban man from the natural world led to an increasing number of tame animals being taken into the house as pets. As individuals retreated from the community into the privacy of the nuclear family, pets became company for the lonely, relaxation for the weary, compensation for the childless. They were often treated as honorary humans and, in some cases, given precedence over servants. Isolated from their own species, such domestic animals were used to compensate for the impoverished emotional life of their owners. In the country, the farmer kept his working dogs filthy and cold and underfed in an outhouse, while allowing his children to pamper a useless dog in the warmth of the kitchen.

The instinctive response to strange wild creatures was to reach for a gun. When confronting penguins and other sea birds for the first time during the voyages of John Hawkins and other Elizabethan adventurers, the reaction of the English seaman was to slaughter them indiscriminately. In the eighteenth century, the first impulse of many naturalists when seeing a rare bird was to shoot it. This desire to kill and classify and control led to the enormous collections of stuffed birds and addled eggs which filled private and public museums in the nineteenth century and which has meant that sites of rare nesting birds have to be guarded in our own era.

At first the kind of protest lodged in Thomas Tryon's *The Complaints of Birds and Fowls of Heaven to their Creator for the Oppressions and Violences Most Nations on the Earth do Offer Them* (1683) was a lonely voice in the wilderness. But in the eighteenth century the growing concern for the wild as well as the domestic slowly changed attitudes. Thomas Jefferson may have kept slaves but he wanted his garden to be an asylum for every kind of wild animal. The killing of the albatross brings retribution to Coleridge's Ancient Mariner. Once he has blessed the watersnakes – 'O happy living things!' – the curse is lifted from him. But he decides to travel the world to teach, by his own example, love and reverence to all things that God has created:

> He prayeth well, who loveth well
> Both man and bird and beast.
>
> He prayeth best, who loveth best
> All things great and small;
> For the dear God who loveth us
> He made and loveth all.[3]

Although the transformation of domestic animals into pets deprived them of many of their instincts, their close observation by their owners had some beneficial results. It encouraged a belief in animal intelligence and individual personality – 'Look how he begs; he's almost human!' This awareness supported the view that the interests of some animals at least were entitled to moral consideration.

While the narrowing gap sometimes worked to the animals' advantage, dogs caught killing sheep could still be hanged like criminals. The propaganda was so strong during the Napeolonic Wars that some monkeys washed ashore at Gateshead were hanged by the local people who thought they were French sailors.

Philosophers who liked to observe their dogs dreaming by the fire while they wielded the quill at their desks found it difficult to see them as unconscious automata. David Hume conceded to animals the 'power of experimental reasoning' – a kind of instinct shared by children, women and the majority of mankind. Sir Matthew Hale went further, to declare that foxes, dogs, apes, horse and elephants display 'sagacity, providence, disciplinableness and a something like unto discursive ratiocination'.[4]

The traditional distinctions between man and animals began to be questioned. In Protestant countries, the Catholic doctrine that only men have souls was not universally accepted; many hoped to meet their favourite pets in heaven. Even speech was no longer considered uniquely human as the idea of evolution gained ground. The Scottish philosopher Lord Monboddo believed that man had evolved by degrees from a vegetable state and argued that speech was not universal among human beings: orang-utangs, for instance, were no doubt a race of men who had not yet learned to speak. Rousseau too suggested that language was not an innate human attribute but an invention of human society.

To support their hypotheses, eighteenth-century philosophers jumped on 'wild children' who were periodically found in woods, naked and inarticuate, as examples of the condition to which any human being could revert. Indeed, there were still many stories of wild men, half man and half animal, lurking in the dark European forests and in jungles in the new worlds. Not only in Cuba but also in Ireland there were said to be men with tails. The colonial conquests in the West and East Indies, the growing slave trade, the awareness of the wide diversity and possible evolution of the human species all fired the incipient racism of white Europeans. By the end of the eighteenth century, the Manchester surgeon Charles White was analysing 'the regular gradation from the white European down through the human species to the brute creation, from which it appears that in some particulars wherein mankind excels brutes, the European excels the African'.[5]

## Crops and weeds

In their classification of the natural world, Europeans in the seventeenth and eighteenth centuries expressed the same attitude to plants as they did to animals, with a rigid distinction between useful 'crops' and useless 'weeds'. To the progressive farmer, a weed was and still is, the vegetable equivalent of vermin, to be hacked down, uprooted, poisoned and burned. The hierarchy of plants paralleled human society, with the noble oak at the top and the lowly buttercup at the bottom. Weeds and nettles were like the common people, unwanted and springing up everywhere.

A more neutral attitude was adopted by the early scientists, who recognized that even weeds and wild plants might be useful. Apothecaries had always believed that many neglected wild plants were valuable medically. Early botanists and naturalists allowed nothing to be weeds in their attempt at 'objective' classification and located wild plants as well as domestic ones. From the seventeenth century scientists began to study nature in its own right. The attempt of Linnaeus (the Swedish botanist Carl von Linné) and others in botany to classify plants not in terms of moral status or usefulness but according to their intrinsic qualities and structures was quite new. Indeed, Linnaeus is said to have fallen on his knees to give thanks when he first saw gorse in England – a hated enemy of the agricultural improvers.

In zoology, the distinction between wild and tame was also abandoned. Some scientists even recognized that all systems of classification are man-made devices to order the world. While attempting to draw up a neutral taxonomy, they criticized the vulgar error that birds, beasts and plants could respond sympathetically to human beings.

In general, however, the attempt to adopt an objective attitude to the natural world was part of the legacy of the scientific revolution which sought to classify and analyse nature in order to gain greater mastery over it. Linnaeus and his fellow naturalists stand in an imperial tradition amongst the forerunners of ecology. In his widely influential essay 'The Oeconomy of Nature' (1749), Linnaeus sought to discover the hand of God in nature. In the process, he presented an extremely static portrait of its interactions, bound together by the chains of sustenance, in which the human species occupies a special place of honour: 'All these treasures of nature . . . seem intended by the Creator for the sake of man. Everything may be made subservient to his use.'[6] It was man's prerogative to improve nature's economy to enrich the human economy, by eliminating the undesirable and multiplying the useful.

Towards the end of the eighteenth century with the growth of a Romantic sensibility, a new attitude to plants developed which went beyond the neutral. Weeds and wild plants began to be appreciated for themselves and for their success in escaping man's rapacious hand. John Clare devoted many poems to the beauty of plants that farmers hated: ragwort, yarrow, rushes, thistles, poppies in the corn. The Romantics preferred the common wild flowers to cultivated blooms, the violet which grew and died by the brook unseen by man to the rose above the cottage door. While most people continued to see the natural world largely in terms of its potential use, the Romantic poets and travellers went to the opposite extreme of the scientists' objectivity, giving way to the 'pathetic fallacy' and seeing in nature a reflection of their own moods and feelings.

Gilbert White's much-loved *Natural History of Selborne* (1789) reflects this new benign attitude to nature, advocating a simple life in peaceful coexistence with other organisms. As a 'philosopher' this curate and naturalist was intent on recording 'the life and conversation of animals' in his parish but it proved one of the most important early contributions to field ecology. He was particularly struck by the way 'Nature is a great economist' for 'she converts the recreation of one animal to the support of another!' The smallest organism is important to the overall harmony in the economy of nature. 'Earthworms,' he observed, 'though in appearance a small and despicable link in the chain of nature, yet if lost would make a lamentable chasm.'[7] But White still believed that Nature required a helping hand to eradicate obnoxious insects from her economy and to improve her stock for human benefit.

## Animal welfare

Despite the biblical justification for man's dominion over nature in the Judaeo-Christian tradition, the good Christian could find passages which reminded him to be lenient in his rule. One should not only turn the other cheek, but help the ass of one's enemy when it lay under its burden (Exodus 23:5; Deuteronomy 25:4). Animals, like humans, should be allowed to rest on the Sabbath (Exodus 23:5). Above all, 'a righteous man regardeth the life of his beast' (Proverbs 12:10). But these isolated examples of putting down the rod did not challenge the overwhelming sense of dominion that Christians felt over the rest of nature. Cruelty was condemned not because the victims suffered but because it was felt that those who torture animals would end up torturing their fellows. 'If any passage in holy scriptures seems to forbid us to be cruel to brute animals,' Aquinas asserted confidently, 'that is either . . . lest through being cruel to animals one becomes cruel to human beings or because injury to an animal leads to the temporal hurt of man.'[8]

In the seventeenth century a few writers in the Christian tradition began to question man's alleged sovereignty over other creatures. The Cambridge Platonist Henry More thought that creatures were made 'to enjoy themselves', as did the naturalist John Ray. Sir Matthew Hale argued that cruelty to beasts was 'tyranny', 'breach of trust' and injustice. A strict interpretation of the Christian doctrine of stewardship made it difficult to condone killing animals for sport. Samuel Pepys for one thought animal sport provided 'a very rude and nasty pleasure'.[9] Even if animals had been created for man's sake, as Genesis taught, that did not provide grounds for ill-treating them.

Philosophy in this case came to the support of the feelings. The creation could not be considered solely for man's use since it was increasingly difficult to believe that nature had an end at all. Greek teleology was abandoned for a purposeless world. Francis Bacon and Descartes had rejected the notion of final causes in natural history, while for Spinoza all final causes were human inventions. David Hume in his *Dialogues concerning Natural Religion* (published in 1779) described 'a blind nature, impregnated with a great vivifying principle, and pouring forth from her lap, without discernment or parental care, her maimed and abortive children'. Even Kant in his *Critique of Teleological Judgment* (1790) was unable to find 'any being capable of laying claim to the distinction of being the final end of creation'.[10]

The shift in consciousness was so great in the eighteenth century that by 1769 the English naturalist Edward Bancroft considered that the 'arrogance of humanity' had created the delusion that the whole of animate nature had been created solely for its use.[11] By the end of the century, the new sensibility towards the creation became increasingly apparent. Animals were no longer brutes or beasts, or even fellow creatures, but companions and even brothers. In a burst of revolutionary fervour, Coleridge extended the notion of fraternity from the human sphere to the animal world, and to 'A Young Ass' – 'Poor little Foal of an oppressed race!' – exclaimed: 'I hail thee *Brother*.' Blake, for whom everything that lived was holy, found a fellow in the insects:

> Am not I
> A fly like thee?
> Or art not thou
> A man like me?[12]

Byron not only condemned capital punishment but attacked angling as that 'solitary vice'. He took to task the author of *The Compleat Angler* (which had, since its first publication in 1653, by 1800 gone into nearly four hundred editions or separate reissues):

Whatever Izaak Walton sings or says:
The quaint, old, cruel coxcomb, in his gullet
Should have a hook, and a small trout to pull it.[13]

Once the gap was bridged between man and the rest of the creation, there was no stopping the widening moral community from embracing plants as well as mammals, insects and fish. 'And 'tis my faith,' Wordsworth wrote, 'that every flower enjoys the air it breathes,' adding: 'I would not strike a flower as many a man would strike his horse.'[14]

As the threat from wild animals receded – bears and wolves continued to exist in the imagination but not at the back door – a few insistent voices asked whether it was right to eliminate those wild animals left which posed no threat. As animals began to be enjoyed as pets and companions, and their uncomplaining toil for man appreciated, there was a growing concern for their wellbeing. Some people even began to question whether we should breed or hunt mammals, fowl and fish in order to eat them. Once it was accepted that animals should be treated with kindness, it became increasingly repugnant to kill them for meat.

It had long been a Christian millenarian dream that one day man would live on peaceful terms with animals and the lamb would lie down with the lion. All theologians agreed that man had not originally been carnivorous. As Alexander Pope put it, in the Garden of Eden:

Man walk'd with beast, joint tenant of the shade;
The same his table, and the same his bed;
No murder cloth'd him, and no murder fed.[15]

The Fall had inaugurated the carnivorous era and the act of meat-eating symbolized man's fallen condition. But since Abel was a herdsman and approved of by God, it was concluded that to domesticate animals and eat their flesh was permissible. The liberty of eating meat was also said to be confirmed by God to Noah. St Thomas Aquinas had approved of the practice for Christians. Nevertheless, the Old Testament prohibition on eating blood (Genesis 9:4) – a prohibition repeated in Acts of the Apostles (15:20; 21:25) – lingered on among early Christians and survived in the Eastern Church. There was also the injunction: 'God said, Behold, I have given you every herb bearing seed, which *is* upon the face of all the earth, and every tree, in the which *is* the fruit of a tree yielding seed; to you it shall be for meat' (Genesis 1:29).

Despite the distinction between clean and unclean animals, by the time of the Reformation in Europe it was considered by the Church lawful to eat all animals. National tastes varied – unlike the French, the English choked on horses, frogs and snails – but the prevailing view was that meat-eating was justifiable for human survival.

Spinoza took the Hobbesian view that humans live in a state of war with the 'brutes' and whatever rights they had to kill us we had over them. According to this holistic philosopher, the objection to killing animals was 'based upon an empty superstition and womanish tenderness, rather than upon sound reason'.[16] The statement shows only too well the thrust of the scientific revolution and the Enlightenment towards the domination of woman, animals and nature as a whole through the use of manly reason. In Spinoza's view, civilization could not exist if humanity acted justly towards nature, and man could not survive without being a predator on other creatures.

But Spinoza and his ilk did not get it all their own way. During the religious upheavals of the 1640s and 1650s, the Ranter Jacob Bauthumley asserted that 'God is in all creatures, man and beast, fish and fowl, and every green thing.'[17] John Ray believed that a vegetable diet was preferable to the 'butchery and slaughter of animals'. Newton allegedly found 'a frightful contradiction' between accepting that animals could feel and making them suffer; as a result he yielded only with reluctance to 'our barbarous usage of feeding on the blood and flesh of beings like ourselves'.[18]

Thomas Tryon pushed the argument to its logical conclusion and became a vegetarian. He admitted in 1683 that it was true that man was 'viceroy of the creation', but this rule was

> not absolute or tyrannical but qualified so as it may most conduce, in the first place to the glory of God; secondly to the real use and benefit of man himself, and not to gratify his fierce and wrathful, or foolish and wanton humour; and thirdly as it best tends to the helping, aiding and assisting those beasts to the obtaining of all the advantages their natures are by the great, beautiful and always beneficent creator made capable of.[19]

Tryon gave up eating meat and fish in 1657 and refused to wear leather. He elaborated all the principal arguments in support of

vegetarianism. He rejected flesh-eating partly because it encouraged
the baser animal element in the body, and partly because it was
unhealthy, but mainly because he opposed 'killing and oppressing
his fellow creatures'. But he still stood within the Christian tradition:
animals bore the image of their creator and were entitled to be treated
according to the golden rule: 'Do unto all creatures as they would be
done unto.' He associated the adoption of meat-eating after the Fall
with the beginning of fighting among men, and by inference believed
vegetarianism was a way of curbing aggression and violence. Carrying
on the libertarian tradition of the English Revolution, he also attacked
Negro slavery, war games, the criminal code, the harsh treatment of
the insane, and the practice of making all persons behave as if they
were naturally right-handed. He even defended the right of wild birds
to feed themselves from the farmers' fields: 'What right, I pray, has
man to all the corn in the world?'[20] He was was not without influence,
and his converts included Aphra Behn and Benjamin Franklin.

The teaching of antiquity about flesh-eating also began to be
considered anew. Many Christians were inspired by the pagan
writers Seneca and Porphyry, for whom the voluntary abstinence
from flesh symbolized the triumph of the spirit over the body.
Pythagoras' moral objections to animal food, based on his belief in
the kinship of all animate nature, also gained wide currency through
successive translations of his speech in Ovid's *Metamorphoses*. In his
version of 1700, Dryden included the lines:

> Take not away the life you cannot give:
> For all things have an equal right to live.[21]

The minister Dr Humphrey Primatt raised the issue of animal rights
with *A Dissertation on the Duty of Mercy and the Sin of Cruelty to
Brute Animals* (1776), in which he argued that cruelty to any form
of life in God's creation was atheism and infidelity.

By the end of the eighteenth century, all the main arguments
supporting the modern case for vegetarianism were already in
place. Not only did the slaughter of animals have a brutalizing
influence upon the human personality but the consumption of
meat was full of evil effects. It was among other things bad
for health; it was physiologically unnatural; it made men cruel
and ferocious; and it inflicted much suffering on fellow creatures.
In addition, the economic as well as the moral argument was

advanced: stock-breeding was less efficient and more wasteful than arable farming.

At the time of the French Revolution, a growing number of radical intellectuals were prepared to extend the notions of rights from the human sphere to the animal one. Bentham made a huge philosophical leap by making the ability to suffer the criterion of moral consideration regarding animals. A liberal English farmer, John Lawrence, further extended the notion of rights from the human realm to the nonhuman one. An ardent opponent of slavery and supporter of women's rights, Lawrence in *A Philosophical Treatise on Horses and on the Moral Duties of Man towards the Brute Creation* (1796) rejected the Christian idea that animals were 'merely for the use and purposes of man' as well as the Cartesian view that they were automata. His close association with animals had taught him that they were conscious like humans and, since 'life, intelligence, and feeling necessarily imply rights', the essence of justice was not divisible and applied to both.[22] But a belief in animal rights did not lead him to vegetarianism; he was unable to join the people – 'a step beyond me' – who refused to eat meat.

One such was the Scot John Oswald, who helped organize the revolutionary armies in France during the Revolution. During his stay in India with the Highland regiment, Hindus had persuaded him to become a vegetarian and he brought back to Europe his newfound beliefs. In his tract *The Cry of Nature* (1791), he confidently claimed that as the 'barbarous governments' of Europe were 'giving way to a better system of things, the day is beginning to approach when the growing sentiment of peace and goodwill towards men will also embrace, in a wide circle of benevolence, the lower orders of life'.[23]

Both Thomas Paine and Mary Wollstonecraft embraced the cause of animal welfare as well as writing in defence of human rights. The reflections of the misanthrope Mandeville on animal slaughter in *The Fable of the Bees* also led the literary antiquarian Joseph Ritson to become a vegetarian and he went on to write *An Essay on Abstinence from Animal Food as a Moral Duty* (1802). Ritson's work and John Frank Newton's *The Return to Nature* (1811) provided much of the arguments for Shelley's celebrated *Vindication of a Natural Diet* (1813).

Although the moral case for vegetarianism was to undergo little subsequent development, the early vegetarians made few converts

among the masses, for whom meat was still a precious luxury and a
matter of status. To attack roast beef during the Napoleonic Wars was
to attack a national symbol: it represented the assertive and bellicose
character of the British empire. The 'Pythagoreans' for the most part
remained isolated intellectuals and were considered by wider society
as cranks and eccentrics.

This remained the case throughout the nineteenth century, although
there were some important developments. In 1824 the Society for the
Prevention of Cruelty to Animals (after 1840 given 'Royal' approval)
was founded by British liberals who included prominent opponents
of the slave trade like William Wilberforce. John Stuart Mill, whose
reading of Coleridge had tempered his utilitarianism, argued in 1848
that the laws making it a crime to abuse children should 'apply not
less strongly to the case of those unfortunate slaves and victims . . . the
lower animals'.[24] Vivisection became a heated topic, and the historian
Arthur Helps wanted to extend rights even to insects, 'whirling about
in a mazy dance, and, as far as we can judge enjoying themselves very
much, and doing us no harm'.[25]

It was Henry S. Salt, however, who put forward the soundest
case for animal rights towards the end of the century. Inspired by
Godwin, Shelley and Thoreau, Salt was a libertarian socialist and
ardent pacifist. In 1885 he abandoned his post as schoolmaster at
Eton, where he had been a 'cannibal' in 'cap and gown' (living off
animals and the toil of others), in order to live a life of voluntary
simplicity in Surrey. He cut up his academic gown to tie up his
vegetables and vines.

In his *Animals' Rights* (1892) Salt emphasized the need for a
'true sense of kinship' with animals, and wanted to widen the
human community to include them. He turned anthropocentrism
on its head by making animals honorary humans, even ironically
calling them 'lower races': 'If we are ever going to do justice to
the lower races, we must get rid of the antiquated notion of the
"great gulf" fixed between them and mankind, and must recognize
the common bond of humanity that unites all living beings in one
universal brotherhood.'[26] Salt was well aware that rights are human
conventions and that humans and nonhumans cannot enter into
reciprocal moral relationships. But he saw it as part of human ethical
development to respect the rights of nonhumans. Above all, he wished
to expand democracy to embrace all animals, human and nonhuman,
in one great republic: 'The emancipation of men from cruelty and

injustice will bring with it in due course the emancipation of animals also. The two reforms are inseparably connected, and neither can be fully realized alone.'[27]

It had to wait until the twentieth century before a radical non-anthropocentric case for animal rights could be made, a case which recognizes the intrinsic rights of animals regardless of their relationship with humans.

## Woods and gardens

The wild wood, with its tangled roots and interweaving branches, has always posed a threat to humanity since they first emerged from it. It obstructs man's vision and movement, it provides a sanctuary for his quarry, and it escapes his control. Early man preferred the open country because it was safer and he could see what was around him. Like the unconscious, the wild wood is a place of strange fears and forbidden desires which are beyond the reach of the noonday light of rationality. In the wild wood, outlaws, witches, elves and dwarves live. It is the dwelling of the hobgoblins of the imagination which awake with the sleep of reason.

Since Mesolithic times human progress has depended to a large degree on the cutting-down of trees in order to clear land for pasture or tillage. The invention of the axe speeded up the process, as did the invention of the chainsaw in our own day. Even before the arrival of the Romans, the bulk of the forests in England had been cleared. By the late thirteenth century the familiar pattern of the landscape had been established, with irregular fields and winding lanes. Paradoxically, the demand for charcoal for the iron industry in the late fourteenth and fifteenth centuries meant that the forests sprang back, because they were carefully managed and coppiced, but the growing population in the following centuries rapidly cut them down again.

To many, the cutting-down of the forests, like the cutting-down of weeds in a garden, symbolized the triumph of civilization. As the word 'savage' (from *silva*, 'a wood') implies, the forest was long synonymous with wildness and danger. For the Elizabethans 'wilderness' signified a dense wood; Shakespeare's Forest of Arden, for instance, was 'a desert inaccessible under the shade of melancholy boughs'. John Locke contrasted the 'civil and rational' inhabitants of the cities with the 'irrational and untaught' denizens of 'woods and forests'. In New England, the Plymouth Pilgrims founded their

colony in a 'hideous and desolate wilderness . . . full of wild beasts
and wild men . . . and the whole country full of woods and thickets'.[28]
Only by leaving the woods could men become civilized. At the same
time, the forests remained areas of comparative freedom where the
law of the king could not reach: Robin Hood and his merry men
were not the only ones to live in forests as outlaws and free-born
Englishmen.

While natural forests have always been considered dangerous and
hostile, man-made gardens and groves have been symbols of peace and
prosperity. Since Anglo-Saxon times, monks in Britain had planted
trees for the sake of their beauty. In the seventeenth century there was
a burst of fruit-tree planting as orchards were increasingly considered
places of delight. As early as 1661 John Evelyn conceived the idea
of a garden city. This was followed by a considerable amount of
tree planting on the big estates in the eighteenth century. With
increasing mastery over the environment, trees were no longer
considered symbols of barbarism or mere commodities but part
of the aesthetic landscape of aristocratic life. The love of woods,
wrote Addison in 1713, 'seems to be a passion implanted in our
natures'. Trees were not only domesticated but assumed an almost
petlike status. At the time of the French Revolution the practice took
a more democratic turn, with the symbolic planting of the 'liberty tree'
in the hope that freedom would take deep root in the fertile social soil.
With the new sensibility associated with Romanticism, the right to life
of trees as well as animals was respected: John Clare grieved 'to see the
woodman's cruel axe employ'd', while Wordsworth commemorated
a yew tree in Lorton Cale 'Of form and aspect too magnificient / To
be destroyed'.[29]

A similar change in attitude occurred with gardens. At first, they
were appreciated for their formal lines; they were the ultimate
example of man imposing his will on his environment and taming
wild nature for his own ends. By the mid-seventeenth century the
Tudor bowling green surrounded by trees had become one of the
most distinctive features of the English landscape. For Bacon, the
arrogant philosopher of the scientific revolution, 'nothing is more
pleasant to the eye than green grass kept finely shorn'. Throughout the
eighteenth century, the Neo-Classical formality held sway. When the
English social reformer William Cobbett went to the United States in
1817 he lamented that 'there were no gentleman's gardens, kept clean
as drawing-rooms, with grass as even as a carpet'.[30]

What these early gardeners most appreciated was the power it gave them over nature in a small compass. 'In a garden,' John Lawrence wrote in 1716, 'a man is lord of all, the sole despotic governor of every living thing.' It comes as no surprise to learn that Sir Isaac Newton, the great ruler of nature, was 'very curious in his garden, which was never out of order, in which he would at some seldom times take a short walk or two, not enduring to see a weed in it'.[31] What he did in his garden, he wanted to do in nature at large: shape, control and direct it.

Towards the end of the eighteenth century, there was a Romantic reaction against the formal garden in favour of a more natural and flowing creation – the celebrated 'English garden'. But the ideal of a well-ordered, rectangular area of cultivation remained. Working-class vegetable gardens and allotments followed the traditional pattern. They too allowed the exploited labourer to have some control in his life, even if only over the vegetable 'tribe'. Away from the tyranny of the clock and the boss, he could decide the life and death of his own plants. But the link with the small patch of land also gave him a sense of self-esteem and identity. A non-utilitarian element crept in with the cultivation of flowers among the vegetables, and in the delight of giving away surplus produce.

Nineteenth-century farmers in Hitcham, Surrey were right in fearing that 'the holding of an allotment will give the labourer a spirit of independence that will interfere with the services he owes his master'.[32] It offered a refuge in a alienated world. By providing the worker with a safety valve to express his pent-up frustrations – like walking the dog or keeping pigeons – gardening may well have contributed to the the lack of revolutionary fervour in the British proletariat. Instead of taking to the barricades, they preferred to grow leeks and sweet peas.

## In search of the wild

In an age of reason – an age which valued reason precisely because it was aware of the disturbing forces of passion and instinct – the wild was considered a dangerous threat like the unconscious, ever ready to break through the thin veneer of civilization. It had to be kept back and repressed, and was only acceptable when tranformed – sublimated – into a safe arena. Towards the end of the eighteenth century, with the rise of Romanticism, however, an increasing number

of people – especially poets and travellers – wanted to climb over
the garden fence or park wall and get back to the wild woods
and unspoiled nature. Deserts, mountains, seas, woods and marshes
began to be appreciated for what they represented – the primeval, the
nonhuman, the instinctual, the natural.

For the agricultural propagandists of the sixteenth and seventeenth
centuries, untilled heaths, mountains and fens represented a 'standing
reproach'.[33] For them the cultivation of all available soil was a
symbol of civilization. They therefore proposed to impose a grid
on nature, carefully fencing off the wilderness, within which they
could transform nature through human labour and make it their
own. In the process, neatness and symmetry became the human way
of distinguishing between civilization and nature. The Neoplatonist
Henry More believed that no one, save those 'as stupid as the basest of
beasts', would not agree that a cube, a tetrahedron or an icosahedron
had more beauty in them 'than any rude broken stone lying in the
field or highways'.[34] (His near namesake Henry Moore was clearly
such a beast.)

The principal appeal of rural scenery to the cultivated in the
eighteenth century was that it reminded them of pictures, especially
those of Poussin and Claude. It was visually pleasing – 'picturesque' –
because it looked like a picture. The landscape was admired because
it was like a 'landskip', originally a term in painting. Nature imitated
art, not art nature. The taste for nature was schooled by exposure
to paintings. The British artist William Gilpin observed in 1791 that
most people found wild country in its natural state totally unpleasing:
'there are few who do not prefer the busy scenes of cultivation to the
greatest of nature's rough productions'.

The taste of the cultivated changed dramatically however. In
place of the formal garden, the English style of landscape garden had developed, which was so informal as to resemble an
uncultivated field. Reacting against the regularity and uniformity
imposed by agriculture, sensitive souls sought the wild and rugged. The tables had turned. 'A gentleman's park is my aversion,'
John Constable wrote in 1822. 'It is not beauty because it is not
nature.'[35]

Wild, barren landscapes were no longer detested but considered
sources of spiritual renewal; they were morally healing as well as
aesthetically pleasing. They provided a refuge for the city dweller
from the bustle, alienation and rat race of modern life, a place for

solitude, reverie and self-examination. The wilder the scene, the greater the response. Mountains were no longer Nature's shameful 'pudenda', deserts no longer bleak and hostile. Wide open spaces became a symbol of human freedom: 'A wilderness is rich with liberty,' Wordsworth asserted.[36] The same feelings of awe, terror and exultation which previous generations had reserved for God were transposed to the planets and stars in the heavens or to the mountains, oceans, deserts and tropical forests on earth. 'The farthest I ascend from animated Nature, from men, and cattle, and the common birds of the woods, and fields,' Coleridge wrote in 1803 after climbing the Kirkstone Pass in a wild storm, 'the greater becomes in me the Intensity of the feeling of Life; Life seems to me then a universal spirit, that neither has, nor can have, an opposite. God is every where, I have exclaimed.'[37] Rather than lowing cattle seen in meadows by an artificial lake, grey rugged rock and mountain torrents became *de rigueur*.

This fundamental shift at the end of the eighteenth century which led well-to-do poets and travellers to derive pleasure from scenes of desolation was not shared by the poor or the labourer. Then, as now, the visitor to the Lake District, Snowdonia or the Alps may have felt a *frisson* of the sublime in contemplating the mountain folds, but not so the local shepherd trying to scratch a living from poor, marginal soils. When contemplating his land, he worries about his money instead of feeling the solemnity, majesty and sublimity of its curves. His sheep are valued for their market price, not for their decorous embellishment of the mountainside.

Wordsworth, like many sensitive souls, found no pleasure in the growth of agriculture and industry which had led to the the destruction of forests, the slaughter of predators and birds, the uprooting of weeds and wild flowers:

> I grieve, when on the darker side
> Of this great change I look; and there behold
> Such outrage done to nature as compels
> The indignant power to justify herself;
> Yea, to avenge her violated rights . . . [38]

In the eighteenth and nineteenth centuries, the need for wilderness was gradually recognized by a few intellectuals opposed to the headlong rush of capitalism and empire. John Bruckner in *A Philosophical Survey of the Animal Creation* (1768), impressed by the 'wonderful economy of nature' in which the dead fed the living, was worried about the effect of the transformation of the American wilderness on the 'web' of life and the plan of Providence.[39] In 1848 John Stuart Mill based his case for a stationary population on the importance of preserving some areas where men could still be themselves. Being alone, he believed, was indispensable for human fulfilment. The presence of natural beauty and grandeur is 'the cradle of thoughts and aspirations' which are not only good for the individual, but which society could ill do without. Fearful of the developments of industrial Europe, he observed prophetically:

> Nor is there much satisfaction in contemplating the world with nothing left to the spontaneous activity of nature; with every foot of land brought into cultivation, which is capable of growing food for human beings; every flowery waste or natural pasture ploughed up, all quadrupeds or birds which are not domesticated for man's use exterminated as his rivals for food, every hedgerow or superfluous tree rooted out, and scarcely a place left where a wild shrub or flower could grow without being eradicated as a weed in the name of improved agriculture.[40]

As the settlers were pushing West in North America, wiping out the buffalo, displacing the Indians and putting up fences, Henry David Thoreau (1817–62) came to the defence of the wild. He celebrated the wilderness as 'absolute freedom', an oasis in the desert of modern urban civilization. His social ecology was so radical that he went beyond politics. Most revolutions in society had little power to interest, still less to alarm him, 'but tell me that our rivers are drying up, or the genus pine is dying out in the country, and I might attend'. For the wilderness was important not merely for the animals and plants within it but as a spiritual source of renewal for humanity. Thoreau argued that 'in Wildness is the preservation of the World'. He considered the wildest to be the most alive: 'When I would recreate myself, I seek the darkest wood, the thickest and most interminable and to the citizen, most dismal, swamp. I enter as a sacred place, a *sanctum sanctorum*. There is the strength, the marrow, of Nature . . . In short, all good things are wild and free.'[41]

This spiritual dimension of wilderness was recognized by the American ecologist Charles Elton at the end of the nineteenth century. He observed that reservations of scenery had become 'the cathedrals of the modern world'.[42] Freud too recognized the psychological value of nature reserves for preserving the wild within safe limits:

> The creation of the mental realm of phantasy finds a perfect parallel in the establishment of 'reservations' or 'nature-reserves' in places where the requirements of agriculture, communications and industry threaten to bring about changes in the original face of the earth which will quickly make it unrecognizable. A nature reserve preserves its original state which everywhere else has to our regret been sacrificed to necessity. Everything, including what is useless and even what is noxious, can grow and proliferate there as it pleases.[43]

This probably explains the symbolic value of ecozones, national parks and wildernesses (by definition, an area where man is not) for many modern urban people. The Amazon forest may be the 'lung' of the earth, but it is also one of the few remaining unexplored areas. The Antarctic is not only pure and virginal – white with snow – but contains secrets. The value of its secrets is precisely that they are secrets – exciting because unknown.

By the nineteenth century, a growing number of people had thus come to find man's ascendancy over nature unacceptable from a moral and aesthetic point of view. The growth of towns had created a longing for countryside. The advance of agriculture led to an appreciation of wilderness. The security from wild creatures awakened a concern to protect and preserve those, especially birds and mammals, still remaining in their natural state. As a result, there was a growing demand that the intrinsic value of all parts of the creation should be recognized.

But the change in sensibility had its contradictions: an aesthetic delight in animals, especially pets, did not prevent their continued use. The tender-hearted mother, charmed by lambs gambolling in the fields, served their joints for her children to gnaw on a Sunday after church. Humans had increased their mastery over nature in an unimaginable way, but this was based – and still is – on the unprecedented exploitation of animals, plants and minerals. The conflict between the new sensibilities and the economic foundations of modern civilization were a long way from being resolved.

# Part III

# GREEN VISIONS

# 20

## THE ROMANTIC MIND
## AND IMAGINATION

And what if all of animated nature
Be but organic Harps diversely fram'd,
That tremble into thought, as o'er them sweeps
Plastic and vast, one intellectual breeze
At once the Soul of each, and God of all?

S. T. Coleridge

Towards the end of the eighteenth century, a shift of consciousness as fundamental as the Renaissance and the Enlightenment began to take place in Europe. A sense of historical change was quickened by the American and French revolutions. The static and ordered hierarchy of nature and society gave way to a new world-view characterized by change and progress. The idea of natural evolution increasingly caught on. The dominant image of the age was no longer a machine, fixed, dead and complete, but a plant, with life, growth and potential.

As the Industrial Revolution began to bite into the earth, factories spread across the fields of Europe. With the dream of mastery over nature almost realizable, nature was no longer considered a threat; indeed, it was itself being threatened. A few sensitive souls like the Romantic poets realized what the break with nature might mean and some far-seeing scientists raised the voice of alarm. As European civilization began to triumph among conquered peoples in the West and East, there was a sense of nostalgia for the lost innocence of the pre-industrial age and a concern with disappearing peoples and ways of life. Mechanical philosophy had simply failed to explain all phenomena and there was a renewed pagan sense of animism. A growing ecological sensibility emerged with the love of unspoiled nature and wild places. But in general the voices lamenting the degradation of nature were lost in the clamour of the factories and the tinkling of the tills as the age of revolution gave way to the age of capitalism and empire.

This great reorientation in cultural life came to be called 'Romanticism'. To define Romanticism is notoriously difficult and at best it can only remain an approximate label. It cannot be neatly enclosed in a concept or definition, for by its very nature it seeks to overstep all boundaries.

The word 'romantic' was originally used to describe medieval romance. By the eighteenth century, the word had general overtones of something fictitious, as in 'wild romantic tales'. For Dr Johnson, it meant the fantastic or imaginary. Towards the end of the century, it took on a more positive meaning, as something captivating the imagination and associated with originality, creation and spontaneity.

At the same time, a recognizable cultural movement emerged which might be called 'Romantic' with a capital R. It took different forms in different countries at different times, emerging in Germany in the 1770s, in England in the 1790s and in France in the 1800s. The variants were so distinctive that some have preferred to talk of a plurality of Romanticisms rather than a single coherent movement. It certainly appeared more as a mood, a manner of feeling, than as a clear set of beliefs and ideas, expressed in literary, artistic and philosophical works. But while the Romantics are all highly individual, they bear a recognizable family likeness. And behind the great diversity, there are some common themes, notably a new attitude to the imagination, to nature and to style. Romanticism not only offers a modern way of experiencing reality, but forms the basis of a truly ecological sensibility.

Although its roots lay in the rich soil of the Enlightenment, especially in the works of Rousseau, Romanticism put forth very different fruit. Where the *philosophes* of the Enlightenment celebrated reason and progress and looked for a common humanity and universal truth, the Romantics looked to the individual, the particular and the relative. The Romantic artists rejected the Neo-Classical ideal of perfect beauty in favour of personal expression; rather than copying nature, they wished to interpret it. 'A painter must not paint merely what he sees before him, but also what he sees within himself,' wrote Caspar David Friedrich. Whereas Greek art is 'simpler, cleaner, more like nature in the independent perfection of its separate works,' August Wilhelm Schlegel wrote, Romantic art, 'in spite of its fragmentary appearance, is nearer to the mystery of the universe'.[1]

Romanticism marked a great opening-up, a throwing-over of tired conventions and stuffy aesthetics. The picturesque was out, the sublime in. There was a tremendous sense of movement, as ancient regimes toppled and new social experiments got underway.

The people were not only claiming their rights to life, liberty and happiness, but the individual artist insisted on exploring all levels of consciousness. It marked a quest for experience and a readiness to grasp life in all its enormous variety. Breaking out of the Bastille of reason, the Romantics revelled in the unseen and the intangible. Among their most common symbols were the sea, associated with a yearning for innocence as well as death, and the wind, an invisible power known only by its effects.

Pope had advised his fellow writers and artists: 'Learn hence from all ancient rules a just esteem / To copy Nature is to copy them.' In the new aesthetics, key words were not 'rules' and 'imitation' but 'genius', 'originality' and 'creation'. The spontaneous and natural were sought after, not the polished and formal. In his *Conjectures on Original Composition* (1759), the English poet Edward Young drew a distinction between imitation and originality, learning and genius, rules and free creation, the ancients and the moderns, thereby anticipating Romantic poetic theory: 'An original may be said to be of a vegetable nature, it rises spontaneously from the vital root of genius; it grows, is not made; imitations are often a sort of manufacture wrought up by those mechanics, art and labour, out of pre-existent materials not their own.'[2]

Such imagery was to dominate the age of Romanticism, and the works of both nature and art were seen in organic and dynamic terms. In philosophy as well as in aesthetics, the perceiving mind was no longer considered a passive mirror of the external world, but a creative organ which illuminated all around like a lamp.[3] The Romantic mind saw in the world a living organism, not Newton's and Galileo's machine. Indeed, the most distinctive feature of Romanticism was a growing sense of the universe as an organic whole rather than as a mechanical structure, subject to an eternal principle of growth and change. This underlying shift was a watershed in the history of thought, and it manifested itself most clearly in Romantic poetry which showed that nature could not be divorced from moral and aesthetic values.

### Reason and imagination

As the eighteenth century wore on, there was an increasing dissatisfaction with the claims of analytical reason to be the prime faculty and the most reliable source of knowledge. Mechanical philosophy

had simply failed to account for all phenomena. David Hume had
raised the alarm by declaring that 'reason is, and ought only to be
the slave of the passions'. Rousseau, the great Romantic son of the
Enlightenment, observed that 'General and abstract ideas are the
source of men's biggest errors.' Voltaire's protégé, Vauvenargues,
further insisted that 'reason does not know the interests of the heart.
Reason misleads us more than nature.'[4] The Romantics went on to
replace the familiar objective portrayal of nature with the subjective
feeling for nature. The landscape reflected the state of the mind of the
observer, apparently in sympathy with his or her moods and feelings.

The writers and artists of Romanticism thus turned their back on
naked reason and sought new springs of inspiration and knowledge.
'Thinking,' the German poet Novalis wrote, 'is only a dream of
feeling, an extinct feeling, only grey, weakly living.'[5] Romanticism
marked the triumph of life over art and thought. The analytical
and deductive methods of the scientists and philosophers of the
scientific revolution and the Enlightenment had merely destroyed
what they sought to understand and control: 'To dissect is to murder,'
Wordsworth reminded his contemporaries. This rejection of analytical reason took the form of praising the 'natural' wisdom of the savage, the peasant and the child, who still trailed clouds of glory and had
not yet been imprisoned in the mental workhouse of modern civilization. Their visionary perception shone through the darkening gloom.

The Romantics were not therefore content merely to operate on the
level of reason but wished to explore all levels of consciousness, hence
their interest in drugs, extremes of experience, and the supernatural.
They wanted to go beyond the here and now, the restrictions of rules
and conventions. 'Classic art portrays the finite,' the German poet
Heinrich Heine observed, 'romantic art suggests the infinite.' Above
all, they were like the Celts at home in the world of betwixt and
between, of swirling mists of the mind and remote heaths of the
imagination. They possessed what Keats called 'negative capability';
that is, 'when man is capable in uncertainties, Mysteries, doubts,
without any irritable reaching after fact and reason.'[6]

For Dr Johnson 'all power of fancy over reason is a degree
of insanity'; for the Romantics, it was reason uninformed by the
imagination and feelings that led to the madness of rational man. 'I
am certain of nothing,' wrote Keats, 'but the holiness of the Heart's
affections, and the truth of the Imagination.'[7] Although there had
been a growing appreciation of the powers of the imagination during

the Enlightenment, with Romanticism it came to the fore; indeed, the value which Romanticism gave to the imagination is perhaps its most distinctive feature.

The creative imagination thus ousted reason as the supreme faculty and as the principal source of knowledge. But it was also viewed in a new light. No longer Aristotle's power of visualization, it was considered to be a creative power able to form concepts and images not present to the senses, to forge new wholes out of existing materials, and to penetrate with insight into ultimate reality. As a great unifying power, it was able to go beyond the mechanical perception of the world as a dead and spiritless pile of atoms, and to experience it as a vibrant whole, in which all things flow together, like rivers into the sea.

A constant refrain of the English Romantic poets is the wondrous power of the imagination. For Coleridge, it has a 'synthetic and magical power', nothing less than the 'living power and prime agent of all human perception'. Blake insists that 'Nature is Imagination itself'. In similar vein, Keats wrote to his brother: 'I describe what I imagine.' Shelley in his *Defence of Poetry* not only defined poetry as 'the expression of the imagination' but gave it the greatest moral and social importance by insisting that poets are 'the unacknowledged legislators of the world'.[8] Where the philosophers of the scientific revolution and the Enlightenment looked to analytical reason to understand and control the world, the Romantics, like modern ecologists, believed that knowledge of oneself and one's natural environment could be achieved through intuition, sensibility, feeling and, above all, imagination. But it would be misleading to see Romanticism in terms of George Sand's formula of 'emotion rather than reason; the heart opposed to the head'. The Romantics felt that naked reason alone was inadequate when not completed by the flash of intuition, the flame of feeling or the urging of instinct. They wished to combine the head and the heart; the mind, the body and the soul. Ultimately the crude opposition between reason and passion is a false dichotomy; the mind can move as well as the body for, in Blake's words, 'a Tear is an Intellectual Thing'.[9]

## In search of the sublime

With the collapse of revolutionary hopes at the end of the eighteenth century, as the French Revolution degenerated into the Reign of Terror and then the Napoleonic Wars, a growing band of sensitive

individuals turned to nature, especially in its wilder aspects, for solace
and consolation in a cold and indifferent human world. At the same
time, humanity had more or less transformed nature in Europe, and
there were few truly wild places left. With the triumph of the Industrial
Revolution, the gap between town and country deepened, but an
increasing number of people began to value what was still left in
a relatively unspoiled, natural state. 'Nature-lovers' sought out the
countryside, mainly coming from the towns and cities, to enjoy the
views, creatures, plants and fresh air.

The idea of the 'countryside' was of course largely the creation
of townsfolk. It derived from the Latin *contra* – against – and in
its first separate meaning denoted a tract of land spread out before
an observer. For the first time, man-made features which had been
made long ago, such as hedgerows and ditches, began to be valued as
organic parts of the landscape. In time, even man-made deserts were
appreciated for being wild and abandoned places.

With the Romantics the quest for 'nature' no longer meant
following long-established aesthetic rules, but rather a pursuit of
the simple, spontaneous and pristine – the authentic – as opposed
to the artificial, conventional, sophisticated and false. The Romantic
poets who experienced something 'deeply infused' in nature were
only reflecting a wider change in consciousness and taste in society.

Urban dwellers increasingly came to value nature for its own
sake. Leaving behind the urban sprawl, blackening factories and
utilitarian politics, they sought solace and freedom in its embrace.
Uncultivated 'wasteland' was no longer an affront to God and man.
Wild landscapes, formerly dismissed as gloomy and horrid, became
sources of great spiritual nourishment; wild woods, seen as a threat
to the forces of civilization, now offered the opportunity of solitude,
contemplation and oneness with nature. The experience of nature
became a spiritual act; nature was not only beautiful, but was
mentally uplifting and morally healing. In this respect, the Romantics
anticipated the modern wilderness movement.

People turned their backs on the picturesque, put on boots and
knapsacks, and went in search of the sublime. The soothing baa of
the sheep and the sight of the rolling Downs were replaced by the
sound of roaring torrents and the jagged peaks of Meirionnydd, long
reputed to be the rudest and most rugged county of Wales. In the
middle of the eighteenth century it was considered a dismal region,
with its snow-capped mountains and dark and sinister valleys. But

with the change in taste at the end of the century, the monstrous excrescences of an earlier generation became revered objects of great beauty. Edmund Burke found in the mountains of North Wales – the 'British Alps' – the perfect manifestation of the 'sublime'; from its vast, rugged, dark and gloomy mountains 'came ideas elevating, awful and of a magnificent kind'.[10] The peak called Cnicht became known as the 'Welsh Matterhorn'. Coleridge, Wordsworth and Shelley all made the pilgrimage to experience the grandeur of the area.

It was not just the experience of walking up high inclines that they were after. The 'northern imagination', Madame de Staël wrote,

> delights in the solitary shore, the soughing winds, the wild heath ... [and] carries onward into the future, into another world than this, a soul weary with its lot. The imagination of the northern peoples reaches out beyond the world to which they are confined; it reaches beyond the clouds which bound their horizon.[11]

The Romantic poets were no longer content to be separate from nature, but wished to live within nature, so that the observer and the observed, the subject and the object could once again be reunited. Where the Classical writers had sought to mirror external reality, the Romantics attempted a mythic interpretation of the world. In Wordsworth's case this meant that the imagination could give symbolic meaning to natural objects, as when crossing the Simplon Pass, he saw the 'characters of the Great Apocalypse,/The types and symbols of Eternity'. It also meant that natural objects could inspire profound understanding, so for Wordsworth 'the meanest flower that blows can give / Thoughts that do often lie too deep for tears'.[12] Many Romantic poets, like Shelley in his 'Ode to the West Wind', felt that nature was so sympathetic and alive that it responded to their own moods and feelings – a belief that came to be known as the 'pathetic fallacy'.

Those who sought oneness with nature were not exempt from sadness. In the embrace of nature, there was often a sense of exclusion, as in Wordsworth's and Coleridge's laments at loss of vision and joy. Keats' love of sensuous life on earth was tempered by his awareness of impending death. 'I have two luxuries to brood over in my walks, your loveliness and the hour of my death,' he wrote to Fanny Brawne. 'O that I could have possession of them both in the same minute.'[13]

## William Blake: nature is imagination

The writers who perhaps best reflected the new attitude to nature
were the English Romantic poets Blake, Wordsworth and Coleridge.
William Blake (1757–1827) is an ecological poet *par excellence*,
a vibrating source of earth wisdom. He not only challenged the
mechanistic and rational premises of Western civilization but posed
an alternative vision which looks back to the millenarian sects of the
Middle Ages and anticipates the modern green movement.

'May God keep us,' Blake exclaimed, 'From Single vision &
Newton's sleep!' He associated Newton in his mythology with
the authoritarian tyrant Urizen, 'your reason', who tries to draw
a 'horizon' around the infinite and curb natural desire. Rejecting
Descartes' dualism of mind and body and the philosophers of
the scientific revolution, Blake called for a new revolution of the
imagination:

> The Negation is the Spectre, the Reasoning Power in Man . . .
> To come in Self-annihilation & the grandeur of Inspiration,
> To cast off Rational Demonstration by Faith in the Saviour,
> To cast off the rotten rags of Memory by Inspiration,
> To cast off Bacon, Locke, & Newton from Albion's covering,
> To take off his filthy garments & clothe him with
>     Imagination.[14]

The human essence for Blake is the imagination. He made no
distinction between the perceiving mind and the perceived world.
'Some See Nature all Ridicule & Deformity . . .' he wrote, '& Some
Scarce see Nature at all. But to the Eyes of the Man of Imagination,
Nature is Imagination itself. As a man is, So he Sees.'[15] For Blake the
science which only sees nature as a machine is the 'Tree of Death'.
But if we recognize that 'Nature is Imagination itself', its study can
become a 'sweet Science'. Like the Taoists, Blake thought that all
things develop in a dialectical way through the clash of opposite
forces, for 'without Contraries is no progression'. Like modern
ecologists, he also adopted a holistic approach to nature, stressing its
interdependence, its unity in diversity and its organic growth. Above
all, if we go beyond our five senses, if the doors of perception are
cleansed, then we will see that 'every thing that lives is Holy'.[16]

Blake was of course horrified at the callous treatment of other species. In *Auguries of Innocence*, he makes one of the most eloquent pleas for animal liberation:

> A Robin Red breast in a Cage
> Puts all Heaven in a Rage . . .
> A dog starv'd at his Master's Gate
> Predicts the ruin of the State.[17]

Further along the web of being, Blake sees plants and objects as having a spiritual quality; in his poems, clods of mud and pebbles talk, flowers feel.

Blake's profound ecological sensibility comes through again in his letters, where he laments the fact that in this fallen world, dominated by the cash nexus, to the eyes of a miser 'a Guinea is more beautiful than the Sun, & a bag worn with the use of Money has more beautiful proportions than a Vine filled with Grapes. The tree which moves some to tears of joy is in the Eyes of others only a Green thing that stands in the way.'[18]

## William Wordsworth: the vernal wood

William Wordsworth (1770–1850) has become the best-loved nature poet among the Romantics. He learned more during his walks as a boy among the hills and woods of his youth than in schools and cities. 'Let Nature be your teacher,' he declared later.

> One impulse from the vernal wood
> Will tell you more of man,
> Of moral evil and of good,
> Than all the sages can.[19]

While Wordsworth fled modern civilization to be in touch again with the permanent forms of nature in the Lake District, he never lost his concern for the simple and the poor. He defended the independent yeoman peasant threatened by the Industrial Revolution, and valued those solitaries who were so close to nature that they had hardly emerged from it. In his poems, they appear as natural as outcrops of rock in the landscape. He feels for the 'Old Cumberland Beggar', the 'Idiot Boy', 'Simon Lee the Old Huntsman', the 'Leech Gatherer', the 'Solitary Reaper', and the shepherd Michael. In his magnificently simple verse and ordinary language, he celebrated the most elemental feelings.

Wordsworth's feeling for nature is more than an appreciation of the countryside or landscape. As a boy, he communed with all that he saw as something not apart but inherent in his own 'immaterial nature'; many times while going to school, he would grasp at a wall or a tree to recall himself from 'this abyss of idealism to the reality'. As an adult, he was still able to enjoy moments of heightened awareness when all nature appeared an organic living whole. He experienced a 'visionary power' when looking at a flower, a tree or some other object in the countryside. A kind of light flowed from his mind and bestowed a splendour upon the object, which then lost its identity and became a presence, an energy or a force. It is cosmic and all-pervasive − 'a motion and a spirit'. This visionary power resembles primitive animism felt by many children and preliterate peoples. It is also a kind of pantheism, feeling a divine presence in all things. The joyous apprehension of the whole brings a deep sense of unity, harmony, tranquillity and love.

As Wordsworth grew older, he lamented the loss of his visionary power in *The Prelude*, but he never forgot his youthful raptures or their philosophical meaning. He considered the supreme faculty to be imagination, which 'is but another name for absolute power / And the clearest insight, amplitude of mind; / And reason in her most exalted mood.'[20] The imagination not only enables man to create but reveals something deeply interfused in nature. Indeed, he felt there was a kind of mutual fitness between the creative mind and the external world of nature:

> . . . my voice proclaims
> How exquisitely the individual mind
> (And the progressive powers perhaps no less
> Of the whole species) to the external World
> Is fitted: − and how exquisitely too −
> Theme this but little heard of among men −
> The external world is fitted to the mind;
> And the creation (by no lower name
> Can it be called) which they with blended might
> Accomplish.[21]

Wordsworth's pantheism and mysticism rose from his intense feelings about nature. But his idea of nature is not simple, and he uses the term to describe human beings and external nature. He thought of it as a sure guide, an influence for good, and an instrument of God. He found in nature

> The anchor of my purest thoughts, the nurse,
> The guide, the guardian of my heart, and soul
> Of all my moral being.[22]

Wordsworth echoes the understanding of the Zen Buddhists for rivers and mountains, and anticipates the 'mountain men' among the deep ecologists who retreat to the wilderness in order to escape from the busyness of urban man. Like them, he wanted to preserve wild areas, and, while writing a guide to the Lake District, he opposed the coming of the railway to the Lake District since it would bring crowds of people who would disturb the balance of nature.

### Samuel Taylor Coleridge: the unifying power of the imagination

As a young man, Samuel Taylor Coleridge (1772–1834) had been deeply influenced by the associationist psychology of David Hartley (naming his son after the philosopher) and the radical politics and rationalism of William Godwin (who remained a lifelong friend). But as the French Revolution degenerated into the Terror, Coleridge followed Wordsworth in finding larger meanings in nature than in society and in developing a more organic philosophy. After a stay in Germany at the turn of the century, where he studied Kant and the German idealists, his views became clearer.

Although he has been accused of plagiarism, Coleridge claimed that his fundamental ideas had matured before reading a single page of German philosophy, and that he merely found in the German philosophers a 'genial coincidence with much that I had toiled out for myself, and powerful assistance in what I had yet to do'.[23] Whatever the degree of indebtedness, Coleridge came to prefer German idealism to British empiricism and utilitarianism, since the German philosophers saw the mind as fundamentally active and organic as opposed to mechanical and atomistic. 'The pith of my system,' he admitted in later life, 'is to make the senses out of the mind – not the mind out of the senses, as Locke did.'[24]

Despite his initial enthusiasm for the French Revolution, Coleridge became a bitter critic of the rationalist and mechanical philosophy

which he saw as having inspired it. He singled out 'the extreme
overrating of the knowledge and power given to the improvements
of the arts and sciences, especially those of astronomy, mechanics,
and wonder-working chemistry'.[25]

Coleridge was not anti-science; indeed, he counted the scientists
Humphry Davy and Thomas Beddoes among his friends. But he
did not feel that the scientific mind could penetrate to the essence
of things. Wordsworth once responded to Newton's statue with
his prism and silent face as 'The marble index of a mind for ever
/ Voyaging through strange seas of thought, alone'. But Coleridge
came to believe that 'the Souls of 500 Sir Isaac Newtons would go
to the making up of Shakespere or a Milton'.[26] One of Newton's
main contentions had been that God had formed matter in solid,
impenetrable and moveable particles. Although in his youth Coleridge
had been a disciple of Newton and Locke, he came to reject this
doctrine of atomism because it not only reduced the diverse form
of activity in nature to the motions and collisions of inert particles
but left no place in the universe for God and the creative imagination.
He believed that Newton was a 'mere materialist' since mind in his
system was always passive – 'a lazy Looker-on on an external World'
rather than inherently creative.[27] In his view, deep thinking was only
possible by a man of deep feeling. Coleridge eventually broke off
his relationship with Davy because he could not agree with Davy's
atomistic vision of the world.

Under the influence of German idealist philosophy and the organic
philosophers Boehme, Giardano Bruno and Spinoza, Coleridge came
to see the world as active, organic and whole, developing through the
interplay of opposite forces. Although he was a disorganized thinker,
he made a lasting contribution to philosophy and literature with his
reinterpretation of reason and imagination.

Coleridge was highly critical of the kind of discursive reasoning,
which predominated in the Enlightenment. It forms for itself general
notions and terms of classification for the purposes of comparing
and arranging phenomena. Its chief characteristic is clearness without
depth. It contemplates the unity of things in their limits only
and is consequently a knowledge of superficial qualities without
substance.

In making his distinction between 'reason' and 'understanding',
Coleridge deepened his analysis and distinguished admirably between
an ecological and a mechanical way of seeing the world. Whereas

reason is the 'organ of the supersensuous', the understanding is the faculty by which we generalize and arrange the phenomena of perception. Reason is the 'source and substance of truths above sense', whereas understanding judges according to sense. The one seeks ultimate ends, the other studies means.[28] With the contemplation of reason we have 'that intuition of things which arises when we possess ourselves as one with the whole', which gives rise to substantial knowledge. On the other hand, the science of mere understanding, makes us think of ourselves as separate beings and places 'nature in antithesis to the mind, as object to subject, thing to thought, death to life'.[29] Only if the understanding is 'impregnated' with the imagination will it become 'intuitive, a living power'. Rejecting abstract reason as the mere organ of science and *a priori* schemes, Coleridge celebrates an intuitive and vital kind of reason which is the 'integral spirit of regenerated man' and contains the understanding and the imagination within itself.[30]

Coleridge also describes the imagination in organic and dynamic terms which reflect his profound ecological sensibility. When in his *Dejection Ode*, he exclaimed. 'Ah! from the soul itself must issue forth / A light, a glory, a fair luminous cloud', he was referring to 'My shaping spirit of Imagination', the power which gives meaning to 'that inanimate cold world' of matter. For Coleridge, as for Kant, the mind is not a passive receiver of impression, but active and creative.

As with understanding and reason, Coleridge distinguished between fancy and imagination. The fancy merely arranges existing materials, whereas the imagination creates new wholes which are greater than the sum of their parts. Coleridge called the imagination an 'esemplastic' power, claiming to have construed the word from the Greek meaning 'to shape into one'. He was probably inspired by the German word for imagination, *Einbildungskraft*, which he thought had connotations of 'organic unity'.

Another distinction emphasized by Coleridge was that between the inorganic and the organic: in the inorganic 'the whole is nothing more than a collection of parts', while in the organic 'the whole is everything and the parts are nothing'. When he viewed the forms of nature, he felt the whole of which they were an integral part. Thus, gazing at a flowery meadow, he felt 'an awe, as if there were before my eyes the same power as that of reason – the same power in a lower dignity, and therefore a symbol established in the truth of things'. Flowers in a field were proof of God's existence far more than an open Bible.

Coleridge more than any other British thinker clears the ground for an ecological philosophy. He conjures up the emotional implications of the mechanical philosophy when he experiences the universe as 'an immense heap of *little* things', while his mind aches to behold and know something great, 'something *one and indivisible*'.[31] When in moments of heightened perception he is able to achieve such a vision of unity in multiplicity, he is struck with the 'deepest calm of Joy'. One such occasion is recorded in 'This Limetree Bower my Prison':

> On the wide Landscape gaze till all doth seem
> Less gross than bodily, a living Thing
> Which acts upon the mind, and with such Hues
> As cloath th'Almight Spirit, when he makes
> Spirits perceive his presence!

Coleridge went beyond this early pantheism to believe in a personal God as the ground of all being, but he retained a Kantian belief in the creative aspect of the mind in the presence of nature:

> . . . we receive but what we give,
> And in *our* life alone does Nature live . . .
> Ah! from the Soul itself must issue forth
> A light, a Glory, and a luminous Cloud
> Enveloping the Earth![32]

Nature will respond if the soul takes the initiative, otherwise it can appear an 'inanimate cold World' perceived by the 'poor loveless ever-anxious crowd'. It is not a question of the mind injecting meaning into nature; the imagination is able to create a union between two living beings. In the metaphor of 'The Eolian Harp' (1796), Coleridge implies that a spiritual breeze animates all nature.

# 21

# ROMANTIC COSMOLOGY

All theory is grey, dear friend,
Green is the golden tree of life,
Johann Wolfgang von Goethe

The most important single feature of the cultural revolution towards the end of the eighteenth century was the discovery of unlimited time. It smashed the foundations of earlier static world-views even more thoroughly than the discovery of unbounded space had done at the time of the scientific revolution.[1] Following the biblical account of creation, it had generally been held that the world was about 4,000 years old – a span which was certainly within the grasp of the imagination. The French naturalist Georges Buffon, drawing on the evidence of the geological record, launched a philosophical time bomb by suggesting in his *Histoire Naturelle* (1749–88) that the earth might be an unimaginable 75,000 years old. Suddenly, the familiar horizon vanished, and thinking people were subsequently presented with the prospect of an evolving universe in infinite time.

Immanuel Kant too in his *General History of Nature and Theory of the Heavens* (1755) interpreted the whole universe as a product of historical development and offered the first systematic evolutionary account of cosmic history. The gradual development of order out of chaos, he argued, had taken a vast period of time: 'The future succession of time, by which eternity is unexhausted, will entirely animate the whole range of Space to which God is present . . . The Creation is never finished or complete. It did indeed once have a beginning, but it will never cease.'[2] Despite his awareness of cosmic evolution, man for Kant was still the legislator of the creation who extracts answers from nature by vigorous cross-examination. Evolution may have occurred in the universe, but the idea of evolution of the species remained distasteful to him. He felt moreover unable to prove the reality of purpose in nature or its organic totality.

Kant had taken a step towards a more dynamic view of nature, but it was his pupil Johann Gottfried Herder (1744–1803) who had a greater ecological sense. Inspired by the recent developments in electricity by Benjamin Franklin and Albrecht von Haller, he conceived the basis of the universe as 'force', a concept remarkably similar to that of 'energy' in modern science. This force manifests itself in various degrees, as chemical affinity and electricity in matter, as sensitivity in plants, and as nervous activity and thought in man – all forms of the omnipresent spirit of God. What we call matter is imbued with life; even hair and nails when detached from the body enter another realm of living forces.

In his *Thoughts on History* (1784–91), Herder put forward his theory of the organic growth of cultures. History in his view has a plan which is discernible through the scrutiny of nature. First the galaxy came into existence, then the sun and the system of planets. Among the latter is the earth which, being neither too hot nor cold, provided the fittest environment for the emergence of living things. Through a process of gradual evolution, man eventually appeared:

> From stones to crystals, from crystals to metals, from these to plants, from plants to animals and from animals to man, we see the form of organization ascend; and with it the powers and propensities of the creatures become more variant, until finally they all, so far as possible, unite in the form of man.[3]

With Herder, the Great Chain of Being is thus temporalized: the passage from 'lower' to higher marks a succession from 'earlier' to 'later'. Herder sees man as only one thread in the complex web of life: 'The God I seek in history must be the God who is in nature; for man is only a small part of the whole, and his history, like that of the worms, is interwoven with the fabric he inhabits.'[4]

Although this would seem to anticipate Darwin, Herder in fact did not conclude that the later creatures on earth were descended from earlier ones. For all his ecological insight, Herder was still wedded to the Judaeo-Christian view of man's privileged position as lord of the creation. The earth did not make man, but rather the earth was made for man: 'Man, therefore, if he was to possess the earth and be the lord of creation, must find his kingdom and his dwelling-place made ready; necessarily, therefore, he must have appeared later and in smaller numbers than those over whom he was to rule.'[5] It was the role of the human race once established on earth to carry forwards the 'purposes of Mother Nature'. Because of his erect posture, man became lord over the animal creation (*der Gott der Tiere*). He then began to realize his potential in diverse societies which developed organically at different rates. Thus in Herder nature and society are unified in a single process of development and the static Chain of Being was transformed into a dynamic web of cultures which evolved over time.

Although the Great Chain of Being was strictly hierarchical, its legacy was not wholly bad from an ecological point of view. In the first place, the degrees of being which resulted from the overflowing plenitude of the One formed an interrelated and organic whole. Secondly, where the scientists and philosophers of the scientific revolution and the Enlightenment sought to discover the uniform and universal laws governing nature and society, the doctrine of the Chain of Being continued to see diversity as a form of excellence. By emphasizing that every link was necessary for the completeness of the chain, it encouraged a respect for different life forms. Thirdly, by placing man on a narrow isthmus between the animals and the angels it denied – on the principle of graded continuity – any great chasm between them. It thereby curbed man's arrogance and fostered humility towards the complex and infinitely varied creation. Finally, the doctrine of the Chain of Being was inherently animistic and a natural ally of pantheism, since it presented the world as the overflowing manifestation of the One.

At the end of the eighteenth century this positive legacy was further enhanced by the discovery of time, a process which transformed the once immutable Chain of Being into a web of endless becoming. The cosmic order came to be seen not as a static order of infinite diversity, but as a dynamic process of increasing diversification. This change was the most distinctive single feature of the Romantic revolution, the one common factor underlying its diverse tendencies and strands.

It also paved the way for an evolutionary and ecological appreciation of nature. Whereas Spinoza as a man of the Enlightenment thought that the purpose of nature is to make men uniform, the Romantics like modern ecologists revelled in the idea of diversity and difference. They believed that diversity itself is the essence of all excellence and sought the fullest possible realization of difference in nature and human nature. They rejected the classical ideal of single perfection for a multiplication of forms;

they looked for the individual and particular rather than the
universal and general.

## Romantic science

The scientists of the Renaissance and the philosophers of the Enlightenment had reduced nature to mathematics; its sensory aspects –
colour, taste, feel, sound – were considered secondary attributes. The
Romantics, on the other hand, came to see nature as having its own
integrity; indeed, in some cases a purpose and meaning. The French
naturalist Georges Buffon set the scene as early as 1749 when, in
revolt against Newtonian and Cartesian science, he declared: 'The
true mainspring of our existence lies not in those muscles, arteries
and nerves which have been described with so much minuteness; it
is to be found in the modern hidden forces which are not bound by
the gross mechanical laws which we would fain set over them.'[6]

With the Romantics, a dynamic and organic view of nature replaced
the old static and mechanical one. As the inspirational model for
science, biology, which looked at the relations between organisms,
replaced mathematics, which was concerned with abstract numbers.
Lamarck in France proposed a form of evolution which claimed that
acquired characteristics could be passed on, while Erasmus Darwin
in Britain entertained the idea of evolution through natural selection.
Growth was no longer considered a linear development but a result
of the dialectical clash of opposing forces.

The new developments in science in the second half of the eighteenth
century made the old Newtonian model of the universe as a machine
governed by universal laws seem increasingly implausible. In 1752
Benjamin Franklin made the identification between electricity and
lightning; five years later, the Swiss physiologist Haller stimulated
dead animal tissue in the recently invented 'Leyden jar' in a way
which resembled life. It was electricity, more than anything else,
that gave the lie to the world as a pile of dead particles moving
through collision; electricity revealed a mysterious and intangible
force animating nature. Further discoveries in light, electricity and
magnetism inspired the idea of a universal life force at work in all
phenomena.

A new attitude to science developed and thinkers tried to achieve
a synthesis between reason and feeling, science and art. Erasmus
Darwin wrote up his scientific findings in verse. He included Newton

in his pantheon of scientific heroes in *The Temple of Nature* (1803) but the frontispiece was designed by the Romantic artist Henry Fuseli, who depicted a multi-breasted goddess of nature. Darwin was keen to go beyond the 'ratiocination of philosophy' and 'to inlist the Imagination under the banner of Science'. Another scientist who wrote poetry was Humphry Davy, whose discovery of nitrous oxide (laughing gas) inspired some of the visions of his friend Coleridge.

Modern ecologists who lie on ice and imagine they are glaciers in order to understand their nature are in this Romantic tradition, a tradition which denies the objectivity of science and the split between the observer and the observed. They might also aim at what Coleridge found in Wordsworth's early poetry: 'the union of deep feeling with profound thought; the fine balance of truth in observing, with the imaginative faculty in modifying the objects observed'.[7]

Romanticism thus involved a revolt against the scientific revolution and tried to defend a qualitative science, in which man is not separate from nature, against a quantitative science, which alienates the creator of science from his own creation by the total objectification of nature. It was for this attitude that Wordsworth scorned the man of science as 'One that would peep and botanize / Upon his mother's grave.'[8] Romantic science like ecology substituted organism for mechanism as the model of order, and biology for physics as the heart of science. It was more interested in becoming than in being, and its ontology lay in metamorphosis rather than atomism.[9] As the philosopher A. N. Whitehead argued, one of the most important lessons for modern science was the Romantics' 'protest on behalf of the organic view of nature, and ... against the exclusion of value from matter of fact'.[10]

## Western man's pact with the devil

The work of Johann Wolfgang von Goethe (1749–1832) offers a fine example of the Romantic union of art and science, as well as the contradictions at the heart of Romanticism. Inspired by Greek culture, he helped develop the Romantic cult of sensibility only to reject it.

Goethe is principally remembered as a poet, playwright and novelist, but he also made an important contribution to science. Charles Darwin regarded highly his research in plant biology, resulting in *The Metamorphosis of Plants* (1790) which argued that the leaf represents the characteristic form of a plant of which all other parts are variations. Hegel was also impressed by his work *On the Theory of Colours* (1810) – preferring it to Newton's *Optics*.

In these studies, Goethe reacted against the analytical tradition of the scientific revolution and adopted a more holistic approach. In opposition to the prevailing categorizing and classifying method, he always tried to see the individual phenomenon as part of an organic, developing whole. T. H. Huxley was so impressed by his approach that in the first issue of the journal *Nature*, he included Goethe's ecstatic exhortation:

> Nature! We are surrounded and embraced by her; powerless to separate ourselves from her, and powerless to penetrate beyond her ... She has always thought and always thinks; though not as a man, but as Nature ... She has divided herself that she may be her own delight. She causes an endless succession of new capacities for enjoyment to spring up, that her insatiable sympathy may be assuaged ... The spectacle of Nature is always new, for she is always renewing the spectators. Life is her most exquisite invention; and death her expert contrivance to get plenty of life.[11]

Goethe's spiritual love of and scientific interest in the natural world come across clearly in his literary as well as his scientific works. His early work was part of the *Sturm und Drang* (storm and stress) movement which led to Romanticism in Germany. It stressed the creative energy of the indvidual as opposed to the rationalist ideal of the Enlightenment and the formalism of Neo-classicism. In his poem *Prometheus*, written around 1774, Goethe summed up its import by insisting that the individual should not believe in the gods but in himself alone.

At the same time, Goethe depicted in *The Sorrows of Werther* (1774) the longing of a sensitive and intelligent individual who loses himself in fantastic dreams; torn by hopeless passions, especially love for a girl who marries another man, he commits suicide. Werther is the antithesis of the cool philosopher and the prototype of the Romantic artist who cannot soar in this barren world. Nature, however, is no solace and remains a destructive threat: 'The source of man's happiness is that of his misery as well ... My heart is undermined by the consuming power that lies hid in all of nature, which has formed nothing that does not destroy its neighbour and itself.'[12]

Ironically, after a trip to Italy, Goethe grew increasingly attached to the Classical view of art. Looking back on his early work and hectic youth, he concluded that 'Romanticism is disease, Classicism is health'. The Classical, he felt, sought a perfect state of balanced harmony, the rational order of unity and completeness; the Romantic revelled in extremes of feeling, disregarding form and discipline. His earlier Romantic tendencies began to reassert themselves, however, especially in Part II of his most famous work, *Faust*.

The transformation of the Faust legend in Goethe's hands demonstrates the distance covered in the seventeenth and eighteenth centuries. It originally expressed the popular dread of and fascination with alchemy and occult knowledge in the Middle Ages. Goethe turned it into a moral play about a world-weary individual who seeks to obtain the whole range of experience and delight. Faust is prepared to promise his immortal soul to the destructive tempter Mephistopheles in order to achieve his ambition. The pact is made; Faust is rejuvenated and then seduces the young girl Gretchen, who drowns their daughter.

In the second part of the work, a purified Faust tries to serve humanity. He attempts to justify his existence by reclaiming land from the sea in order to found an ideal society, but the project fails. But Goethe does not intend to demonstrate the folly of interfering with nature in this way; Faust's soul is finally rescued by a choir of angels who declare the motto: 'He who exerts himself in constant striving, / Him we save!'[13] Despite his organic approach in science, Goethe remained to the end prisoner of the dream of transforming nature which has bedevilled Western civilization.

### Promethean man

Percy Bysshe Shelley (1792–1822) also transformed an old myth. He wished to unchain Prometheus, who had been bound to a rock on a mountainside for trying to steal fire from the gods. For his daring, Prometheus had to suffer the torment of having his liver torn out by an eagle by day only to be healed by night – for eternity. In his great work *Prometheus Unbound* (1820), Shelley saw his liberation as inaugurating a wonderful era in which humanity would be transformed and live in harmony with nature. Tyrants would cease and men would no longer rule over each other. In his great work he envisages a time when women will be 'frank, beautiful, and kind / As

the free heaven which rains fresh light and dew / On the wild earth'.
As for man he would become

> Equal, unclassed, tribeless, and nationless,
> Exempt from awe, worship, degree, the king
> Over himself; just, gentle, wise . . .

But he would not be exempt from the laws of nature,

> From chance, and death, and mutability
> The clogs of that which else might oversoar
> The loftiest star of unascended heaven,
> Pinnacled dim in the intense inane.[14]

He adds, however, that man would be 'ruling them like slaves'. Even
Shelley, the most humanitarian of men, who extended his compassion
to other creatures and became a vegetarian, was not exempt from the
ambition to direct nature.

For Shelley, Prometheus is a symbol of the rebel and the artist, the
man who is ready to withstand the wrath of heaven in order to create
it on earth. In his poetic drama, Prometheus also stands for humanity
who throws off Jupiter, the symbol of rulers, and takes for his wife
Asia, who represents love and nature.

Nearly two centuries on, scientists have stolen 'fire' from the gods
and locked it up – temporarily – in nuclear power stations and bombs.
Their *hubris* has not yet been followed by *nemesis*, but it may be flying
low over the distant mountains.

A more appropriate myth for our time was written by Mary Shelley
– *Frankenstein: or, The Modern Prometheus* (1818). Partly inspired
by the recent discovery of electricity, it is a parable of man's attempt
to use his scientific knowledge to penetrate the mysteries of nature,
to break down the barrier between inanimate and animate matter,
to create life out of dead flesh. Frankenstein realizes the dreams of
the medieval alchemists and modern genetic engineers by stumbling
on the *elixir vitae*, the secret of life. In the process, by vying with
the creator, he creates a monster whom he cannot love and who
eventually destroys him.

The monster, for his part, is at first full of virtuous and affectionate
feelings, but, spurned by humanity, his love turns into hatred; the
'fallen angel becomes a malignant devil'.[15] Evil is not autonomous

but a human invention. When he tries to destroy what he has created, Frankenstein becomes locked in a chase across the Arctic wastes in which it is no longer clear who is the hunter and who is the hunted. The message is clear: in his attempt to understand and control nature, man fails to control and understand himself. He develops his intellectual and rational self at the expense of his emotional and intuitive side. Frankenstein becomes the slave and victim of his own artificial creation by trying to go beyond the boundaries of nature.

## German idealism: Fichte, Schelling and Schleiermacher

The starting point of Romantic cosmology was Kant's philosophy, providing a halfway house between Cartesian rationalism, which saw reason as the source of knowledge, and Lockean empiricism, which derived knowledge from sensory experience. Philosophers who came after Kant took idealism in different and often contradictory directions. Johann Gottlieb Fichte (1762–1814) developed it into complete subjectivism. By turning all knowledge of the external world into self-knowledge, he cut man off from nature entirely. In his *Science of Knowledge* (1794) nothing remains but the knowing subject: 'The ground of explanation of all facts of empirical consciousness is this: before all positing, the Ego must be posited through itself.'[16] He went on to develop egoism to the verge of solipsistic madness.

Although this can offer little of value for an ecological cosmology, it had important implications for art. If the world depends entirely on our perception, then we can reshape it constantly in our imagination. Only art will then be able to approximate the transcendental realm revealed by the imagination. Novalis was quick to take up this 'magical idealism', which presents the artist as a transforming magician in creative freedom. Friedrich Schelling (1775–1854), who is generally regarded as the principal philosopher of Romanticism, undoubtedly provides the most important groundwork for an ecological cosmology. He went beyond both Kant and Fichte in his early work *Weltseele* (*World Soul*, 1797–99) and *Naturphilosophie* (*Nature Philosophy*, 1800) by presenting the whole of nature as an embodiment of a process by which Spirit tends to rise to consciousness of itself. For him nature is 'objective reason' or 'frozen intelligence'.[17] All its sensations and views are manifestations of the spirit. Human consciousness is an outgrowth of nature become history. Art, however, is central to his scheme – the mind can only become fully aware of itself in art, a condition to which all philosophical reflection should aspire. In his major work *The System of Transcendental Idealism* (1800), he increasingly drew inspiration from the organic philosophers Boehme and Spinoza.

Schelling's belief in a world-soul took on a more Christian form in the work of the theologian and philosopher Friedrich Schleiermacher (1768–1834). A translator of Plato and the author of a life of Jesus, he taught that religion, philosophy and science do not contradict one another. Indeed, he offered one of the most eloquent expressions of the Romantic sense of union with the cosmic One, of the intimate correspondence between the microcosm and the macrocosm:

> I am lying in the bosom of the infinite universe, I am at this moment its soul, because I feel all its force and its infinite life as my own. It is at this moment my own body, because I penetrate all its limbs as if they were my own, and its innermost nerves move like my own . . . Try out of love for the universe to give up your own life. Strive already here to destroy your own individuality and to live in the One and in the All . . . fused with the Universe.[18]

### Hegel's barrel organ

Although Wilhelm Hegel (1770–1831) was a professional philosopher, he reflects the enormous cultural sea change that was taking place at the beginning of the nineteenth century. Many have been lost in the labyrinth of his thought, but he now stands as a towering figure in the minor Western tradition of organic and process metaphysics.

The key to Hegel's philosophy lies in the importance it gives to history; history is a process following necessary laws. The whole world is in a state of flux, evolving from the simple to the complex, from the unconscious to the conscious, from enslavement to freedom: 'the history of the world is none other than the progress of the consciousness of freedom'.[19]

Hegel was a monist and an idealist in thinking that all nature is composed of one spirit or mind (*Geist*): '*What is rational is actual and what is actual is rational.*'[20] It is impossible to isolate one part of reality and understand it; all objects are sets of relationships and can only be understood as such.

Hegel argued that the aim of philosophy is 'the actual knowledge of what truly is'; it requires diving immediately into the stream of consciousness and moving from one form to the next. Absolute knowledge is reached when the mind realizes that what it seeks is to know itself. Reality is thus the mind's own creation: 'mind knowing itself in the shape of mind'.[21] There is only one reality because there is only one mind. Mind and nature are therefore not separate entities, but one and the same, forming a self-conscious developing whole.

Although his holistic approach seems distinctly pantheist, Hegel rejected the label. Certainly God is not outside the world – that is a view of the alienated soul. Hegel believed that everything in the universe is part of God, but God is more than the universe. God might be said to need the universe as a person needs a body.[22]

Hegel was a dialectical as well as an organic thinker. He did not make any wild claims for his dialectial method; he called it 'a simple rhythm' to dance to. Like the Taoists, he thought that the evolving whole changes through the clash and reconciliation of opposite forces. A further stage in the development brings together all that went before. In logical terms, a thesis produces its antithesis, which in turn is subsumed in a higher synthesis. In his *Science of Logic*, Hegel suggests that the first thesis is *being*, which turns into *nothing*, but which is then subsumed in *becoming*. All that went before is taken up.

This dialectical process occurs in nature and in history. In the preface to his *Phenomenology of Mind*, Hegel illustrates the dialectical advance towards self-identity by an organic analogy taken from the natural world:

> The bud disappears when the blossom breaks through, and we might say that the former is refuted by the latter; in the same way when the fruit comes, the blossom may be explained to be a false form of the plant's existence, for the fruit appears as its true nature in place of the blossom. These stages are not merely differentiated; they supplant one another as being incompatible with one another. But the ceaseless activity of their own inherent nature makes them at the same time moments of organic unity, where they do not merely contradict one another, but where one is as necessary as the other; and this equal necessity of all moments constitutes alone and thereby the life of the whole.[23]

In his *History of Philosophy*, Hegel presents one dialectical movement dominating world history, from the community of the Greeks to its antithesis in the cult of the individual conscience of the

Reformation. It culminates in the synthesis of German society, which is a rationally organized organic community preserving individual freedom.

In his *Philosophy of Nature*, Hegel makes a distinction between nature and spirit: 'Nature is Spirit estranged from itself; in Nature, Spirit lets itself go, a Bacchic god unrestrained and unmindful of itself.' But Hegel wants man to bring out the rational in nature. 'The study of Nature is thus the liberation of Spirit in her; implicitly she is Reason, but it is through Spirit that Reason as such first emerges from Nature into existence.'[24]

Unlike Descartes, Hegel did not see physics as a model for rational thinking. He rejected the idea that 'nature makes no leaps' and believed that quantity could be transformed into quality. As an organic thinker, he further denied John Dalton's recent atomic theory in chemistry and revived the older Aristotelian theory of the four elements.

Hegel brilliantly described the alienation in the dominant Western attitude to nature in his exploration of the master–slave relationship. Man's relationship with the world is initially based on conflict. Human 'self-consiousness' cannot exist in isolation but needs a contrast, an object from which to differentiate itself. The object outside itself (the Other) appears as something foreign and hostile and yet desirable. To desire is to want to possess and transform it. In order to realize themselves fully, self-conscious humans must therefore set about changing the external world and making it their own.

In personal terms, each person threatens the self-consciousness of the other by failing to acknowledge him or her as a person. In the ensuing power struggle, the stronger turns the weaker into a slave. But there is a contradiction. On the one hand, the master sees the slave as a mere thing, but, on the other, he needs him to work for him and acknowledge his existence. At the same time, through his labour, by externalizing himself in objects, the slave 'becomes aware, through this re-discovery of himself by himself, of having and being a "mind of his own"'.[25] With this awareness, he tries to throw off his chains.

Humanity and nature have clearly entered in the West into such a master–slave relationship; nature appears as a hostile force that oppresses man. It must be mastered and made his own. There seems little prospect of nature however becoming sufficiently 'self-conscious' to throw off the burden of its human master.

In his social philosophy, Hegel argued (like many ecologists) that the individual could only be free and fulfil him- or herself within an organic community, where there is harmony between private and public interests. He described the atomized relationship of Western civilization where community has degenerated into a plurality of egos. He analysed with insight the indefinite multiplications of wants and the collision between producers and consumers in industrialized society. He pointed out the dangers of trying to create a new society entirely on a rational plan, as the French revolutionaries had attempted.

While praising the community and organic change, Hegel still saw the need for a state to encourage the potentially rational within existing society to reach its full expression. In Hegel's view, a person is free when he or she chooses rationally; it was rational to choose to serve the objective form of the universal law, namely the state. The ideal state should have absolute power against everything individual and particular within its boundaries. It is this apparent state worship that has earned Hegel the reputation of being a proto-fascist. While this might be going too far, it cannot be denied that he confuses the state with society and finds no distinction between rulers and ruled.

For all his organic and holistic insight, Hegel, like Spinoza, departs from the libertarian ecological tradition in his politics. The individual becomes totally submerged in the community; indeed, the Danish existentialist philosopher Kierkegaard rightly said that the individual is lost in the great barrel organ of Hegel's philosophy.

Hegel also felt some peoples are superior to others. Each people has a spirit which at different times in history carries forward the process of enlightenment which will culminate in a 'World-Spirit'. By a happy coincidence, he thought that the Prussian state in his own day happened to be carrying the torch in humanity's glorious march of progress towards total consciousness.

Finally, Hegel's philosophy remains highly anthropomorphic in that he believes that the goal of history is for man to become like God, self-causing and all-conscious. He believes that ultimately our true home is not the natural world but the spiritual world, and to enter it humans must overcome natural instincts and natural existence. We are not free when we act from desire, but only when we act from reason. Freedom for Hegel is when mind is in total control of everything else. It involves transforming the objective world according to the universal principles of human reason. While offering in his dialectical scheme the possibility of a reconciliation between subject (man) and object (nature) it is in fact a false identity since it involves the human domination of nature.[26]

Hegel's importance as an ecological thinker lies in his stress on process in history and nature, on unity in diversity, and on the organic wholeness of reality. He brought out well the existing relationship between subject and object, knower and known, and humanity and nature, and called for their transcendence. Above all, he made a lasting contribution by reintroducing a dialectical way of thinking into the mainstream of Western philosophy.

## The legacy of the Enlightenment and Romanticism

The legacy of the two great cultural movements which have dominated Western thinking since the eighteenth century are ambiguous and their full repercussions are still being worked out. The rationally minded tend to dismiss Romanticism as a sickly form of self-indulgence, whereas the more emotional see the Enlightenment as a form of arrogant humanism which murders to dissect. There is an element of truth in both generalizations, but the real situation is more complex.

In many ways the message of the Enlightenment was a liberating one, for it freed men and women from superstition and ignorance and encouraged them to think for themselves. It challenged the teachings of authority and tradition and was understandably considered subversive by the Church and the state. The *philosophes* had the courage to use their reason to search for knowledge.

At the same time, the Enlightenment elevated humanity as never before. The growing mastery over nature through technology and science made man more arrogant than ever. The Christian faith gave way to a humanist faith, a belief in the perfectibility of man and the inevitable progress of society.

The first half of the century was deeply optimistic, with Leibniz insisting that this was the best of all possible worlds, and Pope that 'whatever is, is right'. The Lisbon earthquake of 1755 shook this cosmic optimism, but this act of God encouraged the humanist view that the eradication of evil on earth was a human affair which required the transformation of society. Rather than trying to enter the city of God through faith and works, it became imperative to build the heavenly city on earth through conscious actions.

While the Enlightenment anticipated the best of modern liberalism in its sense of free enquiry, tolerance and concern with the wellbeing of all, it also proved a sinister foreshadowing of the twentieth century. Its political messianism and belief in an exclusive truth in politics culminated in the Jacobin dictatorship of the French Revolution and laid the foundations of totalitarian democracy.[27] The revolutionaries rejected what had grown gradually and organically over the centuries and tried to create a new society from first principles in the sole light of reason. The prevailing belief in universal truth denied the merit of other value systems, and resulted in a drive to impose European standards on conquered peoples throughout the world regardless of local circumstances.

The French Revolution overthrew the *ancien régime* and the monarchy, and promulgated a resounding Declaration of Rights to life and liberty, but in practice it limited civil rights were extended only to European property-owning males. When the Haitian Toussaint-Louverture, a general in Napoleon's army, tried to extend rights to blacks in the West Indies, he was crushed by his erstwhile employers.

During the Jacobin dictatorship, Robespierre tried to install a religion of reason. But this celebration of abstract and instrumental reason, uninformed by feelings and the imagination, led not only to a disenchantment with nature but to the moral corruption of humanity. The greatest symbol of destructive and analytical reason was perhaps the guillotine, the most 'rational' state machine for murdering opponents so far invented. The ships which first took the copies of the Declaration of the Rights of Man to the New World in 1789 returned with the guillotine in their prows four years later.

The characteristic *a priori* analytical reasoning of the Enlightenment overlooked other types of thinking, devalued intuition, imagination and feeling, and created a lopsided human being in a lopsided world. The material gains of the scientific method based on experience and observation led to the increased exploitation and destruction of nature. In the long run, it proved a false enlightenment because it was too centred on human reason and human welfare. It posed the questions 'What can I know?' and 'What should I do?' from a humanist perspective, and not an ecological one.

Marxism was strongly influenced by the revolutionary materialism of the Enlightenment, but Engels observed that the 'kingdom of reason' of the Enlightenment was nothing more than 'the idealized

kingdom of the bourgeoisie'.[28] In fact, the reason of the Enlightenment was often more subtle than it critics make out. At its best, it
upheld a notion of reason which involves high ideals and universal
values. At worst, it could degenerate into a view of reason as a
'reasonable' mentality to advance an individual's personal interests,
a form of instrumental reason which is merely concerned with the
most efficient means of reaching ends.[29]

The *philosophes* of the Enlightenment were primarily concerned
with defending the first kind of universal reason, but it was the
second kind of instrumental reason that came to prevail. It sought
to curb instincts and master the world. 'Progress' thus came to be
seen as increasing control over internal and external nature. Western
civilization henceforth intensified the struggle of reason to transcend
and transform nature: 'The disease of reason is that reason was born
from man's urge to dominate nature.'[30]

Of all the writers at the end of the eighteenth century, Goethe
expresses most vividly the tension between the Enlightenment and
Romanticism. Having contributed so much to the growth of Romanticism in his youth, Goethe turned his back on the movement which
seemed to lead to melancholy and despair, and reaffirmed the
classical principles of clarity and form of the Enlightenment. His
*Faust* demonstrated the dangers of searching for experience wherever
it might lead you, including a pact with the Devil. It could all too
easily lead to the paralysis of the soul, to decay, nihilism, confusion
and disorder.

Certainly, Romanticism at its worst degenerated into windy
vapourings and self-indulgent whimperings. It encouraged a morbid
concern with decay, a sense, in Keats' words, of being 'half in love with
easeful death'. It fostered a deep discontentment with one's lot which
did not always translate itself into action, a mysterious melancholy, an
inexplicable longing for another shore. For some, it led to a desire to
annihilate the troublesome will to live, as for Schopenhauer; to seek
deliverance through art, as for Schelling; or to escape in intoxication
and exultation, as for Wagner.

Although Romanticism celebrated individualism and revolt, there
was also a deeply conservative strand in the movement which looked
back to the romance of the Catholic Middle Ages, with its courts
and pageantry and injustices. The new sense of history, which
started with year one of the French Revolution, degenerated into
nationalistic ideals; in Walter Scott's novels, for instance, the idea of

national unity embraces the king and peasants despite their different economic interests. At the same time, there was undoubtedly an elitist and aristocratic superiority in the Romantic pose, with some lesser writers and artists finding consolation in the thought that only a few sensitive souls could fully appreciate a tragic sense of life and its poles of suffering and ennui.

Some Romantics were also fascinated with power. Chateaubriand considered Napoleon great not only because he created a powerful government but because he owed everything to himself and made thirty-six million subjects obey him. In our era, Romanticism has been linked to fascism, with its mystical 'blood and soil' philosophy; from this point of view Hitler is a perverted Romantic. But this is going too far. The Nazis may have quoted Herder – as they did Nietszche – out of context, but the efficiency of the Panzer divisions and the gas ovens owes more to a perverted rationality than to Romanticism. For all their love of extremes, the true Romantics stress freedom and individualism, which are diametrically opposed to Nazi values.

At its best, Romanticism marked a great transforming surge of energy which brought with it flexibility in form, freedom to experiment, and new vistas and possibilities. The search for new forms and symbols resulted in a reinterpretation of myths important for our own age. It led to the rediscovery of the creative depths of the imagination and to the regeneration of new feelings and sensibilities. Above all, it replaced the dead mechanical view of nature proposed by the scientific revolution with a new organic and dynamic vision of the universe. This naturalistic outlook challenged the artificial conventions of civilization based on the exploitation of human beings and animals. It paved the way for a genuinely ecological sensibility which recognizes the one in the many, the interdependence of humanity and nature, and the reverberating harmony of the universe.

In the final analysis, the dichotomy between the health of the Enlightenment and the disease of Romanticism is a false one. The excessively rational always fear feeling because it might upset their well-ordered universe. On the other hand, those who are anti-intellectual and reject reason out of hand often do so because they are unable to or cannot bother to think for themselves.

There is certainly a need to go beyond the narrow analytical or instrumental version of reason in order to create a libertarian rationality, which embraces intuition and sensibility and yet still has objective standards of truth and consistency. In this way, reason can retain the highest ambition of the Enlightenment to become emancipatory and life-affirming.

Reason need not be merely a tool of analysis, killing what is dissects. It can go beyond arranging the phenomena of perception, or judging according to the senses, and discover important truths about the world. It can clarify issues, solve problems, and decide on ultimate ends. We need not remain slaves of passion or playthings of chance. The wind of feeling and appetite may fill our sails, but reason can help us steer on the ocean of life towards chosen destinations and new ways of being.

If humanity is to survive the present ecological crisis, it must forge an Enlightened Romanticism, a synthesis of reason and feeling, science and poetry, form and meaning, all within the shaping power of the creative imagination, the great organ of morality. It would mean a cultural movement that does not degenerate into sensationalism or self-indulgence, but seeks to re-unite the human species and nature to the benefit of both. The heart must be bold enough to reassert its influence and reason sensitive enough to recognize its rightful claim; both then might give way to universal love. This new Enlightened Romanticism would recognize the importance of the Classical, with its sense of harmonious equilibrium, and the Romantic, with its imaginative and spontaneous drive. It would unite Dionsynian energy and fire with Apollonian order and harmony in a higher synthesis of ecological sensibility. It would dance on the edge of the world to the music of the spheres.

# 22

# UTOPIAN SEERS

Once annihilate the quackery of government and the
most homebred understanding might be strong enough
to detect the artifices of the state juggler who would
mislead him.

William Godwin

Among the most important prophets and seers who have helped shape
the green vision of decentralized and self-governing communities in
harmony with nature are William Godwin, Robert Owen, Charles
Fourier, Pierre-Joseph Proudhon, Peter Kropotkin and William Morris. Karl Marx and Friedrich Engels dismissed most of these thinkers
as 'utopian'. Although there were very strong elements of utopianism
in their own communist vision, and they looked to the ultimate
reconciliation of humanity and nature, the Marxist legacy has been
far from ecological.

### William Godwin, the father of anarchism

At the fountainhead of the great libertarian tradition in the nineteenth
century stands William Godwin (1756–1836). His work contains the
seeds of all later anarchism and socialism. In his own day, according
to William Hazlitt, 'he blazed as a sun in the firmament of reputation;
no man was more talked of, more looked up to, more sought after,
and wherever liberty, truth, and justice was the theme, his name was
not far off'.[1] The young Wordsworth and Coleridge came under his
spell and planned to put his ideal society into effect on the banks of
the Susquehanna in the New World. Shelley not only eloped with
Godwin's daughter Mary, the author of *Frankenstein*, but he put his
philosophy to resounding verse. Godwin's world is to Shelley what
the Bible is to Milton.

Godwin was the father of philosophical anarchism. In his *Enquiry
concerning Political Justice* (1793), he argued that though government had been intended to end conflict and injustice, it had only

perpetuated and aggravated them. Both Thomas Paine and Godwin
thought society a blessing, but whereas Paine reluctantly admitted
that government was a necessary evil for the time being, Godwin
concluded that it was harmful and unnecessary.

As a son of the Enlightenment, he believed in the perfectibility of
man. We are all products of our circumstances, but because we have
reason we can choose the motives for our actions and in turn change
our circumstances. And since our voluntary actions originate in our
opinions, if we can change people's opinions through education and
enlightenment we can change their actions. Godwin put his case in
the form of five propositions:

> Sound reasoning and truth, when adequately communicated,
> must always be victorious over error: Sound reasoning and truth
> are capable of being so communicated: Truth is omnipotent:
> The vices and moral weaknesses of man are not invincible:
> Man is perfectible, or in other words susceptible of perpetual
> improvement.[2]

People are therefore potentially rational, and as they grow more reasonable, there will be less need for external authority and government.
Godwin looked forward confidently

> to the auspicious period, the dissolution of political government,
> of that brute engine which has been the only perennial cause
> of the vices of mankind, and which ... has mischiefs of
> various sorts incorporated with its substances, and not otherwise
> removable than by its utter annihilation![3]

Through the early English socialists, Godwin's vision of the ultimate
withering away of the state began to haunt the socialist imagination.
It has today become one of the principal goals of the social
ecologists.

Godwin based his social philosophy on a system of ethics. As
a utilitarian, he defined ethics as a 'system of conduct which is
determined by a consideration of the greatest general good'. But
while emphasizing the importance of the general good, Godwin was
loath to submerge the individual in its interests. He was an act rather
than a rule utilitarian, warning against too rigid an application of
general moral rules. He did not want to reduce the enormous variety
of human actions to a common standard. Indeed, he maintained

that the best maxim is that 'Every case is a rule to itself'.[4] It therefore behoves every person to consider all the circumstances of a particular case and judge accordingly. It was this insight that led Godwin to reject the Procrustes bed of man-made law and become an anarchist.

In his definition of good, Godwin was a hedonist. He saw the end of morals and politics as promoting general happiness and defined happiness in terms of pleasure. He felt that intelletual pleasures are superior to physical ones, and moral ones are supreme, but the most desirable state is to have access to all sources of pleasure.

Combined with the principle of impartiality, Godwin's criterion of utility led to some novel conclusions. All human beings are entitled to equal consideration, but it does not follow that they all should be treated the same. When it comes to distributing justice I should put myself in the place of an impartial spectator and discriminate in favour of the most worthy. Thus if I am faced with an inescapable choice of saving one of two people in a fire, I should choose the one most likely to contribute to the general good – even if the one left to burn happens to be my mother or father. 'What magic,' Godwin asked, 'is there in the pronoun "my" that should justify us in overturning the decisions of impartial truth?'[5] Although this shocked his contemporaries, Godwin made clear that he did not undervalue the importance of the 'domestic affections'; he insisted, however, that while charity might begin at home it should not end there.

Godwin's doctrine of utility has also important implications for rights. Although he recognized the right of private judgement which expects a degree of noninterference from others, and the right to assistance when in need, he saw these as claims based on utility rather than as positive entitlements. In certain circumstances, it might well be just to forfeit our right to property and even to life in order to promote the general good. But in all cases it is for the individual to decide for him- or herself: coercion is always a confession of imbecility and can only alienate the mind. Promises and contracts – including the marriage contract – suffer the same fate in Godwin's hands; they are unwise undertakings for they do not allow room for change and growth in awareness. Past folly should never shackle future wisdom.

On the grounds of universal benevolence, Godwin thus rejected the ties of family, race and nation. Although he was concerned primarily with human wellbeing, he depicted a dog in his Romantic novel *St Leon* like a noble savage and in a children's adaption of Phaedrus' tale 'The Wolf and the Dog', he gets the starving wolf to declare to the well-fed but chained mastiff: 'Hunger shall never make me so slavish and base, as to prefer chains and blows with a belly-full, to my liberty.'[6] Extended beyond the human species and coupled with the principle of impartiality, Godwin's doctrine of utility encourages an ethic concerned with the wellbeing of all regardless of individual attachments and preferences.

In place of centralized nation-states, Godwin looked to a federation of face-to-face communities. They would govern themselves through popular assemblies at the local level of the parish, and would create national assemblies whenever necessary to resolve differences and coordinate defence. They would form no permanent centre of authority and any officials would be unpaid and supported voluntarily.

Since the practice of voting produces an unnatural uniformity and involves the tyranny of the majority, decisions would be made where possible through consensus. Courts and the judiciary would be replaced by popular juries and the aim would be to re-establish social harmony rather than mete out punishment. Public opinion would take the place of law to reform wrongdoers, although it would not be harsh and would recognize each person's sphere of discretion. Since the ultimate aim of education is to develop the mind and the imagination, and liberty is the school of the understanding, children should no longer be schooled into conformity but be allowed to learn through desire.

In his economic proposals, Godwin believed that the good things of the earth were a common stock and humans should act as stewards to use wealth to the best advantage. He maintained that every person should enjoy the fruit of their labours, but any surplus after the satisfaction of their basic needs should be distributed to the most needy. The result would be a form of voluntary communism. But it would not be based on a 'clockwork uniformity' and Godwin saw no need for common labour, stores or meals in a free society. People would cooperate if they saw fit, but would never be obliged to: 'Every man ought to feel his independence, that he can assert the principles of justice and truth without being obliged treacherously to adapt them to the peculiarities of the situation and the errors of others.'[7]

Godwin considered the most important social good was leisure, since it would enable people to develop their full potential. He therefore recommended the appropriate use of technology to alleviate unpleasant toil and reduce necessary labour-time if possible to half an hour a day. Like yogis and practitioners of holistic medicine, he felt that if the mind was left to expand it might one day become 'omnipotent' over matter so that a developed person would feel no pain. At the same time, he was not devoted to stoical simplicity for its own sake and felt that a free and equal society was not incompatible with 'considerable accommodation and even in some sense with splendour'.[8]

Godwin celebrated autonomy and individuality and condemned forced cooperation as evil. Nevertheless, he did not advocate a selfish individualism. In a free society, he thought that direct democracy would encourage a feeling of solidarity: 'Each man would be united to his neighbour, in love and mutual kindness, a thousand times more than now: but each man would think and judge for himself.'[9] More than any other thinker, Godwin tries to give meaning to the ideal of communal individuality.

Godwin sums up the optimistic message of the Enlightenment in his philosophy but he helped, partly under the influence of his companion Mary Wollstonecraft, to foster the Romantic cult of sensibility. He came to recognize the 'culture of the heart', the importance of the 'domestic affections', and insisted that reason is 'merely a comparison and balancing of different feelings',[10] His ideal was a small family circle living in harmony with nature. He also knew at first hand the alienating atmosphere of the new factories of the Industrial Revolution and condemned them for reducing men to machines.

Godwin's optimism inspired the Reverend Thomas Malthus to write *An Essay on the Principle of Population as it affects the Future Improvement of Society* (1798), which argued that any reformed society would soon collapse under the weight of overpopulation. Since population growth always outstrips food supply, he argued that the 'natural' checks of war, vice and misery were necessary and inevitable. Godwin, however, was confident that careful husbandry could increase the fertility of the earth and 'moral restraint' could check excessive population. Moreover, like the Taoists, Godwin believed in natural order and that 'there is a principle in the nature of human society by means of which everything seems to tend to its level, and to proceed in the most auspicious way, when least interfered with by the mode of regulation'.[11] If meddling humans can hold back, a harmonious balance will prevail in nature and society in the long run.

Godwin was the philosophical father of Robert Owen (1771–1858), usually acknowledged to be the father of British socialism. Hazlitt recognized that Owen had borrowed his doctrine of universal benevolence and his belief in the omnipotence of truth and the perfectibility of human nature from Godwin, and that Owen's vision of *A New View of Society* (1813/14) was to be found in the old *Enquiry concerning Political Justice*.[12] Like Godwin, Owen built his theory of progress on the premises that characters are formed by their circumstances; that vice is ignorance; and that truth will eventually triumph over error. He stressed the need for moral regeneration first and foremost and advocated economic before political reform. The proper means to eradicating social evils was through education and enlightenment. He looked to the voluntary redistribution of wealth. His ultimate social ideal was a decentralized society of small self-governing communities.

Unlike Godwin, Owen was prepared to accept political leaders, and when he tried to put his theory into practice in a series of model communities – first at New Lanark in Scotland, and then in the Co-operative Community of New Harmony in the United States – he planned it all for the workers, rather than letting them plan it for themselves. Owen further made plans for villages of Unity and Mutual Cooperation, which combined factories with farming. At New Lanark, he set up 'a self-employing, self-supporting, self-educating, and self-governing population'.[13] They undoubtedly enjoyed the best schools, best wages and cleanest surroundings of any workers in Britain at that time.

### Charles Fourier and the phalanx of love

The Frenchman Charles Fourier (1772–1837) has been called the first social ecologist to surface in Western radical thought.[14] He was certainly one of the most profound and original. He conceived of the universe as a vast living organism. In order to complete Newton's world, he proposed his own 'law of passionate attraction' in which all beings and things, including stars, have sexual tendencies. In his sister 'theory of universal analogy', Fourier further presented man as a microcosm of the universe, which is a unified system, a web of hidden correspondences. Man is therefore not separate, but an integral part of it. Moreover, behind the apparent chaos of the world, there is an underlying harmony and natural order governed by universal law.

Fourier rejected entirely existing Western civilization with its repressive moral codes. In his *New Industrial and Social World* (1829), he advocated a society of ideal communities or 'phalanxes', destined to conduct the human race to 'opulence, sensual pleasures and global unity'.[15] If human beings could only attune to the 'Universal Harmony', they would regain their mental health, live without crime, and freely satisfy their passions.

In his utopian writings, Fourier made elaborate plans to maximize sensual pleasure and to transform work into meaningful play. Freedom for Fourier meant not only free choice but freedom from the psychological compulsion to work. In his hedonistic utopia called 'Harmony', there would be agreeable and voluntary labour, nonrepressive sexuality, communal education and living. He divided each phalanx into a number of of self-managing and self-sustaining associations of individuals. Work would be cooperative and property enjoyed in common. Everyone would have the right to work, which would be made as playful and meaningful as possible, and everyone would receive a 'social minimum', a guaranteed annual income. Every effort would be made to promote unity in diversity, and combine personal freedom with communal solidarity. The equality of unequals would prevail as special needs would be met. He called for a guaranteed 'sexual minimum' to be arranged by a 'Court of Love' as well as a social minimum, so that everyone's basic needs could be met.

Unlike Proudhon, Fourier considered woman's emancipation to be central to human improvement: 'social progress and changes of period are brought about by virtue of the progress of women towards liberty,' he insisted. He extended his sympathy to animals, and made it a principle in his ideal society that 'a man who mistreats them is himself more of an animal that the defenceless beasts he persecutes'.[16] Even so, there is an unpleasant element of regimentation in Fourier's *New Industrial and Social World*, with his 'Court of Love' manipulated by a hierarchy of officials, and the arrangements of everyday life so minutely described that they leave little room for innovation.

### Pierre-Joseph Proudhon and the love of the soil

In nineteenth-century France, social thinkers were also dreaming of a post-industrial society in harmony with nature. Pierre-Joseph Proudhon (1809–65) was the first person to call himself an anarchist and his system of mutualism had enormous influence throughout Europe and North America. He is a direct forerunner of those social ecologists who argue that society should be reorganized on federal and decentralist lines.

Proudhon was proud that he came from peasant stock and considered himself 'moulded from the pure limestone of the Jura'.[17] His childhood in the country left him with a powerful feeling for the earth. It fostered an ecological sensibility which led him to lament the loss of the 'deep feeling of nature' that only country life can give. But although Proudhon felt that man loves nature more deeply than anything else, he saw that people were no longer attached to the land as they used to be and treated it merely as a tool and a source of revenue:

> Men no longer love the soil. Landowners sell it, lease it, divide it into shares, prostitute it, bargain with it and treat it as an object of speculation. Farmers torture it, violate it, exhaust it and sacrifice it with their impatient desire for gain. They never become one with it.

He regretted the loss of the powerful attraction and sense of communion which had previously existed between humanity and nature:

> Our generation loves the fields and woods as the magpie loves the gold it steals. We want them only for their investment value, so that we can indulge our rustic fantasies and build country nursing homes, or so that we can experience pride of possession and be able to say 'this is mine'.[18]

Proudhon was not only the first person to call himself an anarchist, but he launched the slogan 'Property is Theft'. The principle needs clarification. By property, Proudhon meant the unjust appropriation of another person's labour. He did not assail private property as such, and was opposed to the community of goods. He was in favour of 'possession' as long as the privileges of ownership were limited to the benefits accruing from it. Indeed, towards the end of his life, he saw property as a mainstay of personal independence.

Proudhon also declared: 'Anarchy is Order.' Like the Taoists and Godwin he believed in natural order. It was authoritarian government and the unequal distribution of wealth that created conflict and chaos in society. Few have offered such an eloquent tirade against government and bureaucracy:

> To be governed is to be watched over, inspected, spied on, direc-ted, legislated, regimented, closed in, indoctrinated, preached at, controlled, assessed, evaluated, censored, commanded . . . To be governed means that at every move, operation, or transaction one is noted, registered, entered into a census, taxed, stamped, priced, assessed, patented, licensed, authorized, recommended, admonished, prevented, reformed, set right, corrected. Gov-ernment means to be subjected to tribute, trained, ransomed, exploited, monopolized, extorted, pressured, mystified, robbed; all in the name of public utility and the general good. Then, at the first sign of resistance or word of complaint, one is repressed, fined, despised, vexed, pursued, hustled, beaten up, garrotted, imprisoned, shot, machine-gunned, judged, sentenced, deported, sacrificed, sold, betrayed, and to cap it all, ridiculed, mocked, outraged and dishonoured. *That* is government, *that* is its justice and its morality![19]

Proudhon was convinced that, left to themselves, people could manage their own lives productively and peacefully.

Ecologists find in Proudhon two of their most cherished social principles: federalism and decentralization. He proposed that power should be decentralized to districts, and that society be organized into a federation of self-managing communities. He recommended the forming of workers' cooperatives and founded a People's Bank which would give free credit and exchange notes based on labour time.

Proudhon was confident that a society without government would flourish. He rejected the traditional Christian God: 'God is evil,' he declared. In his view, 'Each step in our progress represents one more victory in which we annihilate the Deity.' However, he was convinced that there is an immanent principle of justice in nature. Nature and human nature are intrinsically good. Justice is Proudhon's key idea. It operates in the world as a kind of providence; it is 'the supreme God; it is the living God'.[20]

Unlike Godwin, Proudhon does not see that reason is essential to morality. Justice reveals itself spontaneously to the conscience, which, if uncorrupted by false education and governmental tyranny, can be a sure guide for conduct. He also associated justice with equality and argued that it implies a respect for human dignity. We should respect others as we would wish to be respected ourselves.

Proudhon's system of justice has its limitations. Although he was opposed to authority in wider society, he was a patriarch at home. 'The complete being,' he insisted, 'is the male. The female is diminutive of man.'21 Woman is the mean term between man and the rest of the animal realm; where he is the maker, she is the user; where he has a thinking mind, she has a feeling heart. Proudhon lamentably crystallized the age-old stereotypes of male and female which re-emerge in some contemporary New Age thinking.

He also felt that there was a close link between blood and soil. He insists: 'Land belongs to the race of people born on it, since no other is able to develop it according to its need. The Caucasian has never been able to take root in Egypt.'22 While this might seem to confirm the deep ecologists' concern with breaking nation-states down into 'bioregions' which follow natural and cultural boundaries, it has extreme nationalist overtones. Proudhon was anti-Semitic and a French chauvinist. His talk of blood and soil moreover was to be echoed in National Socialism in Germany, which was closely linked to the burgeoning ecology movement, and in some deep ecologists who think that people should stay in their own patches on the earth and be left to fend for themselves.

Nevertheless, Proudhon stands as an important forerunner of the modern ecological movement for his stress on the close communion between humanity and nature, for his belief in natural justice, for his doctrine of federalism and for his insight that liberty is the mother and not the daughter of order.

## Peter Kropotkin and mutual aid

Kropotkin is often remembered as a geographer but after Godwin he contributed most to the creation of an ecological society. Born into the highest ranks of the Russian aristocracy, Prince Peter Kropotkin (1842–1921) was forced to leave his country as a young man because of his revolutionary social views. He became one of the most attractive and thoughtful of anarchist thinkers; Oscar Wilde described him as 'a man with a soul of the beautiful white Christ which seems coming out of Russia'.[23] Kropotkin's happy childhood on his family estate in the bosom of nature left an indelible impression:

> The never-ceasing life of the universe, which I conceive as *life* and evolution, became for me an inexhaustible source of higher poetical thought, and gradually the sense of Man's oneness with Nature, both animate and inanimate – the poetry of nature – became the philosophy of my life.[24]

After becoming a page to the tsar and experiencing the frivolities of court life, Kropotkin spent five years as an administrator in a Cossack regiment in Siberia. His researches there laid the foundations of his later fame as a geographer (he correctly concluded that the structural lines of Asia run diagonally). His close contact with the peasants and their way of life made him lose any lingering confidence in the discipline of the state. He became an anarchist and went into exile, eventually spending much of his life in England.

Despite his feeling for the oneness of nature, Kropotkin based his social views on 'a mechanical explanation of all phenomena, embracing the whole of nature – that is, including in it the life of human societies and their economic, political and moral problems'. He wanted to investigate society with the methods of the exact sciences and to construct a synthetic philosophy comprehending 'in one generalization all the phenomena of nature'[25] In this, he wanted to show that anarchism is not a faith or creed but based on observable and verifiable tendencies in nature and society. It follows that the movement of both natural and social science points in the direction of the anarchist ideal.

To this end, Kropotkin threw himself into the contemporary debate over Charles Darwin's evolutionary theory which came to be known as Social Darwinism. Darwin in his *Origin of Species* had shown that all species had a common ancestry and that evolution occurred through natural selection in the struggle for existence. His supporter T. H. Huxley presented the life of man as a 'continuous free fight'. Such a view seemed to confirm the dark forebodings of Hobbes that the state of nature is a state of universal war. The English philosopher Herbert Spencer argued that the struggle for existence in society led to the 'survival of the fittest'; it was then left to anyone to define 'fittest' as they saw fit.

Kropotkin's observations of animals and the natural world led him in an opposite direction. In his famous *Mutual Aid* (1902), he argued with a rich array of data that in the struggle for life cooperation rather than competition prevails among members of the most successful species. It is not competition but mutual aid that is the most important factor in evolution:

> We maintain that under *any* circumstances sociability is the greatest advantage in the struggle for life ... The animal species, in which individual struggle has been reduced to its narrowest limits, and the practice of mutual aid has attained the greatest development, are invariably the most numerous, the most prosperous, and the most open to further progress.[26]

The real struggle for existence which takes place is not between individuals but against adverse circumstances.

Like modern ecologists, Kropotkin tried to ground morality in an objective philosophy of nature, to deduce moral principles from the social needs and habits of humanity. Humans, he thought, are naturally social and moral. Nature is *'the first ethical teacher of man*. The social instinct, innate in men as well as in all the social animals, – this is the origin of all ethical conceptions and all the subsequent development of morality.'[27] In his study of natural and human history, Kropotkin discerned a double tendency: on one side, towards a greater sociability; on the other, towards an intensity of life. Both aspects should therefore be encouraged in a society which tries to be in harmony with nature.

Kropotkin applies these scientific observations to society. He maintains that society is a natural phenomenon and that man is adapted to live in society without artificial regulations. He draws on the findings of anthropology to argue that in traditional societies human beings have lived in clans and tribes in which customs and taboos ensured mutual aid and harmony. It was only with the rise of coercive institutions of the modern centralized state from the sixteenth century that the traditional practice of mutual aid began to break down in an era of capitalist competition.

Although Kropotkin emphasized the close link between humanity and other species, he wanted to develop the full potential of human beings. He argued in *The Conquest of Bread* that needs of an artistic nature need to be attended to. After securing bread for all, leisure is the supreme aim. True civilization for Kropotkin does not mean leaving the natural state but enabling individuality to flourish. Luxury would become not an ostentatious display but an artistic pleasure.

The ideal for Kropotkin would be a society without government and the state. As with Godwin, it would consist of a network of voluntary associations ('communes') of free and equal individuals who are consumers and producers. The commune, linked by local sympathies and interests, would be the basic cell of society and the centre of life in town and country. Society would thus become a web, 'an interwoven network, composed of an infinite variety of groups and federations of all sizes and degrees, local, regional, national and international – temporary or more or less permanent – for all possible purposes'.[28]

The local communes would federate at different levels to solve disputes, organize production and distribution, and arrange defence. Delegates, immediately accountable and recallable, would be sent to the various assemblies to express the will of the communes. There would be no laws; people would manage their affairs through voluntary contracts. Since wealth is a social product, there would be a form of voluntary communism which recognizes the greatest degree of liberty of the individual with no compulsion to work. The division of labour would be overcome and people would choose their own work and develop freely their mental and manual skills.

In his *Fields, Factories and Workshops* (1899), Kropotkin argued for a harmonious balance between agriculture and industry. Instead of the concentration of large factories in cities, he called for economic decentralization, believing that diversity is the best way to organize production by mutual cooperation. He favoured the scattering of industry throughout the country and the integration of industry and agriculture at the local level:

> Have the factory and the workshop at the gates of your fields and your gardens, and work in them. Not those large establishments, of course, in which huge masses of metals have to be dealt with and which are better placed at certain spots indicated by Nature, but the countless variety of workshops and factories which arise to satisfy the infinite diversity of tastes among civilized men.[29]

Kropotkin felt there was no serious threat from overpopulation to upset his vision of a free and balanced society. There was still an enormous stock of energy in nature and the means of subsistence could be increased by the appropriate use of technology, careful husbandry of resources, and modern methods of intensive gardening. Kropotkin was still sufficiently a nineteenth-century thinker to believe in 'industrial progress'; the conquest of bread, in his view, involved for the time being man's 'conquest over nature'.[30] Even so, Kropotkin remains a great inspiration to the modern ecological movement for his understanding of the role of mutual aid in evolution, his attempt to ground ethics in a philosophy of nature, and his vision of a decentralized and federal society encouraging diversity and individuality within overall harmony.

## William Morris and News from Nowhere

The English poet and artist William Morris (1834–96), whom Kropotkin knew, hated the physical ugliness and emotional constraint of the industrial civilization he saw about him. He made it his life's task to create beautiful things in a beautiful society. As he grew older, he became increasingly radical. As he became aware of what Victorian society was doing to the town and countryside and to their inhabitants, the 'idle singer of an empty day' in his epic poem The Earthly Paradise (1868–70) was transformed into a socialist revolutionary. What he so disliked about the capitalism of his day was its classes, its crude utilitarianism, its mass production, its compulsory labour and its machine-dominated mind. He therefore left behind the ideal world of his dreams evoked by the Middle Ages and Celtic and Norse mythology to describe a vision of a free society in harmony with nature. Although Morris became a Marxist of sorts (he admired Marx's class analysis although he could not read his Capital), his socialism was libertarian in the extreme.

Morris hoped that the society of the future would give personal freedom and allow the unrestricted cultivation of the individual will. Life in the society he advocated would be simple and natural. It would be a society which does not know

> the meaning of the words rich and poor, or the rights of property, or law or legality, or nationality: a society which has no consciousness of being governed; in which equality of condition is a matter of course, and in which no man is rewarded

for having served the community by having the power given to injure it.

What makes Morris an advanced ecological thinker, however, is his conscious wish 'to keep life simple, to forgo some of the power over nature won by past ages in order to be more human and less mechanical, and willing to sacrifice something to this end'.[31]

Morris gave a detailed sketch of what this society might be like in his utopian romance News from Nowhere; or, an Epoch of Rest (1890). In it he describes an England in the twenty-first century which has passed through a revolution. There is no longer any government, private property, law, crime, marriage, money or exchange. Government is no longer necessary. There is no tyrannical code of public opinion to replace the law courts nor any conventional set of rules to judge people by; 'no bed of Procrustes to stretch or cramp their minds and lives'.[32] The Houses of Parliament are no longer a talking shop of the elite; they have become something far more useful, a dung market. The whole people are now the parliament in their popular assemblies.

Society consists of a federation of communes (based on the old wards and parishes). Affairs are largely managed by general custom reached by general assent. If differences of opinion arise, the assembly of neighbours (or 'mote') discusses the matter until there is general agreement. If it is necessary to decide a question by a show of hands, the majority will never impose its will on the minority, however small. The minority will be invited to enact the decision of the majority but never forced to. And if the way of the majority proves faulty, then they in turn should be willing to try the suggestion of the minority.

In Morris's ideal commonwealth, people live responsible lives in equal conditions, fully aware that harm to one means harm to all. They enjoy an abundance of life; there is space and elbow room for all. Big centralized factories have been replaced by scattered local workshops. People find joy in their freely chosen and voluntary labour. Useful work has replaced useless toil. Nothing is made unless it is genuinely needed. Crafts flourish once again but all work which is found irksome to do by hand is done by improved machines. The only reward for labour is the reward of creation and of life itself. People live simple yet beautiful lives in harmony with nature. The steel bridges over the river Thames have been replaced by stone masonry, and salmon leap in the crystal waters of the river. *News from Nowhere* provides the best ecotopia so far imagined.

## Karl Marx's inorganic body

Karl Marx (1818–83) was profoundly influenced as a young man by Hegel's philosophy ('a giant of a thinker') although under the impact of the atheist Feuerbach he rejected philosophical idealism in favour of dialectical materialism. Marx thought Hegel was standing on his head; rather than going from earth to heaven, he descended from heaven to earth. Man makes religion, religion does not make man. Marx therefore stood 'Hegel on the head' by making matter and not mind the ultimate reality.

At the same time, he adopted Hegel's dialectical way of thinking and agreed that the pursuit of truth involves transforming the world. As the words engraved on Marx's tombstone in Highgate Cemetery put it: 'The philosophers have only interpreted the world in various ways; the point is, however, to change it.' Just as Hegel sought to overcome the estrangement of the mind from its objects, so the early Marx sought to end the alienation of man from his own nature and from external nature.

The early Marx appears ecological in many ways. He lamented how man under capitalism had become estranged from the natural world and its objects appeared as 'an alien and hostile world opposed to him'. In his essay on 'The Jewish Question', Marx also argued that the view of nature which developed under the domination of private property and money is the 'actual despising and degrading of nature'. He expressed agreement with Thomas Münzer's view that it is intolerable that 'all of creation has been made into property: the fish in the water, the bird in the air, the off-spring of the earth – creation, too, must become free'.[33]

The way to resolve man's alienation from himself, his fellows and the natural world was for Marx to create through the labour process a communist society. 'Communism as completed naturalism is humanism and as completed humanism is naturalism. It is the genuine solution of the antagonism between man and nature and between man and man.'[34] This dialectical process in which labour 'humanizes' nature and 'naturalizes' humanity suggests that the early Marx recognized that man 'participates organically, i.e, dialectically, in nature' and human society and nature penetrate each other within 'the natural whole'.[35]

The main claim for Marx having an appreciation of ecology rests on the character of dialectical materialism, which allegedly recognizes the unity of nature and man. The dynamic processes of the dialectic may also be equated with ecological processes. But this interpretation of dialectical materialism hardly offers firm evidence for the idea that Marx is really a green masquerading as a red. Marxism is fundamentally man-centred and values nature in so far as it is a setting for the liberation of humanity.

In his work on the *Dialectics of Nature*, Engels directly confronts the question of man's domination over nature. He stresses man's superiority to animals and suggests that it is inherent in human nature to dominate. But his actions have unintended consequences; his mastery over nature is accompanied by increasing misery. Engels does not criticize this tendency to dominate but rather laments man's past failure to aim straight and achieve his end. His weakness comes from his animal nature, which must be overcome:

> Only the conscious organization of social activity with planned production and distribution can give man his social freedom and liberate him from the remnants of his animality, just as production itself gave him his biological freedom ... From the achievement of this organization will date a new era of history, when man, and with him all branches of his activity (natural science in particular) will take on such a brilliance that all that has gone before will be thrown into deep shadow.[36]

Hardly an ecological message! It is the old Promethean dream combined with Bacon's faith in science to transform the world.

Even the early Marx appears far from green. While recognizing that man is a part of nature and, like other animals, lives off it, Marx describes 'the whole of nature' as man's 'inorganic body' in that it is both his immediate means of sustenance and also the material object and tool of his activity.[37] Where man's own body is organic, nature – the 'sensuous exterior world' – is reduced to a mechanical body with which he is obliged to have a constant interchange if he is to live. Human history might be part of natural history, but nature stands as something separate from *Homo sapiens* and *Homo faber*. Nature is not therefore valued for itself but as a direct means to human life, an instrument of man's self-creation. There is no value except human labour; indeed, Marx stresses that the *whole of what is called world history* is nothing but the creation of man by human labour'.[38]

Human evolution had always been a struggle with nature and it was Marx's hope that in the near future the productive forces of nature would be developed to such an extent that the antagonism between humanity and nature would eventually be resolved. But with Marx the relationship is always one-sided. Humanity passes from the realm of necessity to the realm of freedom when man has mastered nature with his technology to such a degree that it is no longer a threat. Yet, as far as the rest of nature is concerned, humanity must appear in this process an even greater threat than before.

Although Marx was more at home on Hampstead Heath than in a dark forest, he describes his ideal communist society without the division of labour in distinctly bucolic terms:

> Society regulates general production and thus makes it possible for me to do one thing today and another tomorrow, to hunt in the morning, fish in the afternoon, rear cattle in the evening, criticize after dinner, just as I have a mind, without ever becoming hunter, fisherman, shepherd or critic.[39]

But the vision is entirely one of dominating and carnivorous man who pursues cattle, birds and fish entirely for his own use. In the long run Marx's communist society does not transcend the dualism between man and nature but continues the tradition of human domination which it claims to end.

Marx was rigidly urban-centred, giving a special historical role to the proletariat as the most advanced class and leaders of the revolution. He talked of 'rural idiocy', despised peasants as a 'servile rabble' and declared that they were historically doomed.[40] He felt that in Europe the individualism of the peasantry and their attachment to the land made them reactionary. As for Asia, traditional Indian villages, in Marx's view, 'restrained the human mind within the smallest possible compass, making it the unresisting tool of superstition, enslaving it beneath traditional rules, depriving it of all grandeur and historical energies'.[41]

Although in the *Communist Manifesto*, Marx and Engels recommended the combination of agriculture and industry, and the gradual abolition of the distinction between town and country, it was a case of urban civilization invading the country and transforming it in its own image.

Marx saw the ancient worship of nature as a chain of illusion. Earlier people, he argued, were 'overawed like beasts' by nature's 'all-powerful and unassailable force'.[42] In the process of evolution, however, man becomes increasingly independent of nature and in the process of transforming nature, he transforms himself. As a result, he emancipates himself from religion. Capital thus has a great civilizing influence by pushing beyond the deification of nature and the traditional way of life, leading to

> its production of a stage of society compared with which all earlier stages appear to be merely *local progress* and idolatry of nature. Nature becomes for the first time simply an object of mankind, purely a matter of utility; it ceases to be recognised as a power in its own right; and the theoretical knowledge of its independent laws appears only as a stratagem designed to subdue it to human requirements, whether as an object of consumption or as the means of production.[43]

This process of disenchantment and mastery over nature is positively welcomed by Marx, although of course he would like to go beyond the class society of capitalism and release its fetters on further economic development. Man emancipates himself from nature through his work, and Marx looked to man's growing mastery over nature to render superfluous the 'miracles of god' by the 'miracles of industry'.[44]

Marx and Engels saw industrial capitalism as a necessary stage in human history. They saw the factory as a vehicle not of slavery but of liberation, essential even in its hierarchical and authoritarian form to transcend the realm of necessity and to achieve economic abundance. Through Marx and Engels, the ideal of social progress through the technological mastery of nature became a central tenet of the labour movement. They ensured that economics took priority over other aspects of cultural and social life and looked forward to the triumph of human science over natural forces.

For all his early Hegelian talk about the ultimate reconciliation of man and nature and his Romantic vision of communist society as the goal of history, Marx remained a humanist and a rationalist. He combined German idealism with the Enlightenment's faith in the perfectibility of man. His favourite maxim was from Terentius: *Nihil humanum a mihi alienum puto* (I believe nothing human to be alien to me).

Unfortunately, nature as a living organism remained alien. It comes as no surprise that Marx believed that Prometheus was 'the foremost saint and martyr in the philosopher's calendar'.[45] The disastrous ecological results of the Marxist-Leninist attempt to achieve mastery over nature have been graphically recorded in the twentieth century, from the brown, dead waters of Lake Baikal to the Chernobyl nuclear catastrophe.

# 23

## DARWINISM AND THE WEB OF LIFE

> The question of questions for mankind – the problem which underlies all others, and is more deeply interesting than any other – is the ascertainment of the place which Man occupies in nature and his relations to the universe of things. Whence our race has come; what are the limits of our power over nature, and of nature's power over us; to what goal we are tending; are the problems which present themselves anew and with undiminished interest to every man born into the world.
>
> T. H. Huxley

Charles Darwin (1809–82) has been called the single most important figure in the history of ecology in the last three hundred years.[1] He contributed more than anyone else to the growth of ecology into a science. He also brought about a Copernican revolution in science, theology and philosophy which transformed humanity's place in nature.

Darwin of course published his theory of evolution in *The Origin of Species by Means of Natural Selection, or the Preservation of Favoured Races in the Struggle for Life* (1859). It was the result of many years' careful observation of the natural world and puzzled thinking. The theory was as least as ancient as Anaximander, who 600 years before Christ had suggested that we had all evolved from primeval slime. Among Darwin's immediate predecessors, the French naturalists Buffon and Lamarck, and his grandfather Erasmus Darwin, had all put forward evolutionary ideas. Lamarck in particular had argued that evolution takes place through acquired characteristics being passed down from one generation to the next. For example, a giraffe whose neck had lengthened during a lifetime of stretching for leaves would have offspring with longer necks.

There had also been a discovery of time of unimaginable duration:

319

Charles Lyell in his *Principles of Geology* (1830–33) had argued that the earth had evolved gradually over millions of years and was not – as biblical scholars and the *Encyclopaedia Britannica* in 1830 claimed – created some 4,000 years before Christ. He rejected the catastrophe theory put forward by Christian fundamentalists to explain the increasingly puzzling fossil record (with fish at the top of mountains and extinct monsters lying in chalk) which held that God had ordained a series of cataclysms. Instead he advocated 'uniformitarianism' – a steady-state view which asserted that all geological change was due to ordinary natural causes that had operated in much the same way since the beginning of the creation. Lyell also put forward geological evidence for the antiquity of man.

After his desultory career at Cambridge, Charles Darwin embarked on HMS *Beagle* as a naturalist. During the voyage around the world, he read and reread Lyell's work and it served as a model of scientific enquiry. Working on what he considered Baconian principles of collecting facts, Darwin observed many life forms which were incompatible with the doctrine of the 'fixity of the species', that is to say that all forms of organic life were made separate and diverse in a single act of creation at the beginning of time. But he had no adequate theory to replace the doctrine of fixed species until a chance reading – 'for amusement' – in 1838 of Thomas Malthus's *Essay on the Principle of Population* (1798). In his Introduction to *The Origin of Species*, Darwin later wrote that his theory of evolution through natural selection was 'the doctrine of Malthus applied to the whole animal and vegetable kingdoms'.[2]

Although Darwin did not publish his theory for many years, the strain of elaborating it and accumulating data to support it had a terrible effect on his mental life. He complained later in life: 'My mind seems to have become a kind of machine for grinding general laws out of large collections of facts.' His favourite reading during the voyage on the *Beagle* had been Milton's *Paradise Lost*, but as he grew older he lamented: 'I wholly lost, to my great regret, all pleasure from poetry of any kind.'[3] So much for the Baconian method.

### Malthus's melancholy nightmares

What Darwin got from Malthus was a quasi-scientific account of the struggle for existence. Malthus, however, was specifically writing against the rational philosopher and anarchist William Godwin and other eighteenth-century social reformers who believed in the perfectibility of man and illimitable progress. Malthus argued that the earth imposes limits to the growth of population and the wellbeing of humanity.

Malthus asserted that the power of population is mathematically greater than the ability of the earth to produce sustenance. He based this on the 'fixed laws of nature' that food is necessary to the existence of humanity and that the passion between the sexes is constant. It follows that 'population, when unchecked, increases in a geometrical ratio. Substance increases only in an arithmetical ratio.'[4] From these premises, Malthus deduced the proposition that there will always be a struggle for existence. Moreover, it is only the 'natural' checks of vice and disease that keep the existing population down. (Malthus regarded contraception and abortion as forms of vice.) Any attempt to improve society by eliminating vice and misery would therefore result in an increase in population and the consequent destruction of the new benefits.

Faced with these inexorable and fixed 'laws of nature', human institutions are 'mere feathers that float on the surface, in comparison with those deeper seated causes of impurity that corrupt the springs and render turbid the whole stream of human life'. Godwin's belief in benevolence as the moving principle of society is therefore 'little better than a dream, a beautiful phantom of the imagination'.[5]

Godwin counterattacked with his doctrine of moral restraint – abstaining from sex. Malthus acknowledged this check in subsequent editions of his essay on population, but felt it would have little influence compared to the great preventive check of vice and the positive check of misery. It was just too bad for those 'unhappy persons, who in the great lottery of life, have drawn a blank'. Humanity in general was therefore doomed to suffer in a world of competition and pain.

Malthus admitted that his essay had a 'melancholy hue' and he was chiefly responsible for turning the new study of political economy into a 'dismal science'. Marx called it a 'libel on the human race'. With his tragic cycle of expansion, competition and death, Malthus added an ecological dimension to Adam Smith's laissez-faire economics, and a depressing reinterpretation of the economy of nature. Poverty was not a social evil but a result of the laws of nature. Insatiable human sexuality and fecundity would make ancient dreams of abundance for all impossible. Ironically, the Reverend Malthus had his own version of utopia, and saw the struggle as grounds for self-discipline, thrift and work which could lift the elect into a state of economic grace. The way to salvation lay in controlling sexual appetite, not in creating a more equal and just society.

Soundly grounded in Newtonian physics, Malthus's conceptual scheme is very similar to classical mechanics: like the First Law of Motion, population increases until checked.[6] He also presents his ratios in mathematical terms, although in practice both are not constant. Human beings are not breeding machines; animals do not reproduce regardless of their environment. Population does not always grow geometrically, and depends on variables such as age and sex distribution. Food supply can also grow faster than arithmetically, as modern techniques of farming have demonstrated.

Above all, Malthus underestimated the potential check of birth control as well as moral restraint. Population growth has slowed down in those countries where contraception is readily available. It might well cease altogether if contraception were available to all those who now say they wish to use it, thereby enabling more women to take advantage of the benefits of education. In our era, it is precisely in countries with high standards of living that population growth has slowed down or even been reversed: the message that small families enjoy a better life has got across. It is in poor countries that there are high birth rates since parents must rely on their offspring and not the community to provide for their old age.

Some deep ecologists have recently espoused Malthus's nightmare and prophesized that the world will be for ever reduced to misery because of the inexorable increase in the human population. They add a further burden of misery in the form of a defiled environment as a result of the excess of numbers. The biologist Paul Ehrlich, for one, has been warning that the end of the world is nigh: we will all be killed by overpopulation. His best-selling work *The Population Bomb* (1968) launched an organization in the United States called Zero Population Growth. Recognizing that an American baby will consume during its life roughly fifty times more that the average Indian born at the same time, Ehrlich concludes that there are too many babies of affluent Americans. He relies on shock tactics to get his simplistic message across: 'Overpopulation means greed which means international tension which means war.'[7]

Not all neo-Malthusians are so extreme. The American biologist

Barry Commoner in *The Closing Circle* (1971) maintains that population control is not a biological problem but a social, economic and political one, recognizing that 'the population bomb is a natural consequence of the development of advanced technology, and it is a product of exploitation not only of the natural resources of underdeveloped countries, but also of their people'.[8] While clearly there is a limit to the carrying capacity of an ecosystem, it has not been reached yet in the ecosphere and the misery experienced in two thirds of the world is largely the result of unjust distribution and the profligate luxury of the richest third of the world. There would be more than enough food for all if eating habits were changed and it were evenly distributed. The importance of Malthus, however, lies in making reproduction a moral and social issue, and in showing the link between growth in population and the available food supply. As an 'equilibrium' theorist, he also questions the possibility of illimitable growth in numbers.

## Struggle for existence and natural selection

Darwin's reading of Malthus has been called 'the single most important event in the history of Anglo-American ecological thought'.[9] What impressed Darwin was Malthus's depiction of the struggle for existence which everywhere goes on. It struck him after his long observation of the habits of animals and plants that in such a struggle favourable variations would tend to be preserved and unfavourable ones destroyed. On the whole and in the long term the fittest would survive.

Darwin's theory of evolution through natural selection, the most unifying of all biological theories, is based on three observations and two deductions. The first observation is that organisms tend to increase at a geometrical rate; the second, that the populations of different species are more or less static. From this he deduces that vast numbers of organisms die before they can reproduce. The third observation is that there are inherited variations between the same members of a species. The final deduction is that in the struggle for existence those variations which make the organism best adapted to its environment will give it a better chance to survive and reproduce. The result will be the gradual evolution of different species and the formation of new species.

Darwin never used the phrase 'survival of the fittest' in *The Origin of Species*; and only later adopted the phrase from Herbert Spencer in place of his own 'natural selection'. But he used 'fit' only in the sense of related to a given environment, not to a scale of perfection. He provided no independent criterion of fitness. He also made clear that he used the term 'struggle for existence', which he had picked up from Malthus, in a 'large and metaphorical sense, including dependence of one being on another, and including (which is more important) not only the life of the individual, but success in leaving progeny'.[10] Indeed, as Kropotkin demonstrated in his work on *Mutual Aid*, cooperation as well as competition is an important factor in evolution. Throughout *The Origin of Species*, Darwin steered clear of making any comments about the relevance of his theory to the human species; at the end, he merely observed that 'light will be thrown on the origin of man and his history'. Nevertheless, he could not help being awed by the grandeur of evolution. When he viewed all beings not as special creations but as lineal descendants of a few living beings, they seemed to become ennobled. Having come so far in the past, he was confident (expressing the optimism of the Victorian age) of 'a secure future of equally inappreciable length, and as natural selection works solely by and for the good of each being, all corporeal and mental endowments will tend to progress towards perfection'.[11]

Darwin would seem to be offering here natural selection as a guarantee of progress, as a both descriptive and deductive law, but the guarantee is not warranted by his theory.[12] Palaeontologists understandably use the terms 'higher' and 'lower' to describe strata of fossils. It is also easy in studying a process of development over time to believe that the latest products of development are better than earlier ones. But it does not inevitably follow. Darwin himself was aware of the dangers of this kind of hierarchical and linear thinking, and pinned into his copy of *Vestiges of the Natural History of Creation* (1844) the memorandum slip: 'Never use the words *higher* and *lower*'. Darwin in reality did not believe in a 'law of necessary development'.[13] The best his theory can imply is that there are trends in evolution and not iron laws, and that while the present trend may be towards greater complexity and consciousness, it may not always be the case. And what comes after is not necessarily better than what went before.

## The entangled bank

Darwin had a very holistic view of nature and was moved by its complexity and beauty. This was encouraged by a reading of Alexander von Humboldt's *Personal Narrative*, which influenced the whole course of his life. It was Humboldt's intention during his travels in Latin America from 1799 to 1804 'to find out how nature's forces act upon one another, and in what manner the geographic environment exerts its influence on animals and plants. *In short, I must find out about the harmony of nature.*' Under the influence of Goethe, he conceived the cosmos as 'one great whole animated by the breath of life'.[14] Darwin too observed that for brevity's sake he sometimes spoke of natural selection as an 'intelligent power' and often personified the word Nature – 'for I have found it difficult to avoid this ambiguity'. This Romantic tendency to see Nature in terms of a mother has been called the 'hidden Goddess of Darwinism'.[15]

Although Darwin, following Malthus, laid great stress on the struggle and competition within nature, like modern ecologists, he was no less struck by the interdependence of species which leads to an equilibrium, by just 'how plants and animals, most remote in the scale of nature, are bound together by a web of complex relations'.[16] No individual organism or species can live independently; every creature is a set of relationships. Even the most insignificant are important to the wellbeing of others, and are 'essential members of society, or at some former period may have been so'. The 'web of life' has become one of the key phrases of the ecologists, and Darwin's main contribution is to have shown how humanity is just one thread in nature's web.

Darwin left a wonderful description of the kind of ecosystems which are fast disappearing in our age of agribusiness and prairie farming:

> It is interesting to contemplate an entangled bank, clothed with many plants of many kinds, with birds singing on the bushes, with various insects flitting about, and with worms crawling through the damp earth, and to reflect that these elaborately constructed forms, so different from each other, and dependent on each other in so complex a manner, have all been produced by laws [of evolution] acting around of us . . .
> There is grandeur in this view of life, with its several powers,

having been originally breathed into a few forms or into one; and that, whilst this planet has gone cycling on according to the fixed law of gravity, from so simple a beginning endless forms most beautiful and most wonderful have been, and are being, evolved.[17]

Darwin introduced the 'Tree of Life' image to explain the process of evolution, thereby replacing the linear model of the Chain of Being. It has the advantage of suggesting that while there is a potential shape, the growing pattern does not fit into a preordained space. The image of the Tree of Life recalls the biblical image, but rather than being static, as in the Christian creationists' view, it is alive and still growing:

> The green and budding twigs may represent existing species; and those produced during each former year may represent the long succession of extinct species . . . As buds give rise by growth to fresh buds, and these, if vigorous, branch out and overtop on all sides many a feebler branch, so by generation I believe it has been with the great Tree of Life, which fills with its dead and broken branches the crust of the earth, and covers the surface with its ever branching and beautiful ramifications.[18]

In this way Darwin presented man as related to the apes, not as their direct descendant, but with a common progenitor. The tree metaphor, however, has it limits. Wedded to the idea of competitive replacement, Darwin suggests that new branches somehow must destroy the less vigorous ones, thereby transforming his organic symbol of mutually beneficial growth into a mechanical model of conflict.

Again, Darwin recognized that nature is a system of 'places', or, as later ecologists put it, 'niches'. But like Linnaeus he tended to isolate their occupants from the complex relations. While recognizing how diversity is nature's way of overcoming severe competition for limited resources in a given area, he tended to follow Malthus rather than Humboldt in stressing the struggle within nature rather than its overall harmony. In 1859, he declared: 'All organic beings are striving to seize on each place in the economy of nature'.[19] The mechanical aspect of Darwin's thinking got the better of the organic ultimately. There was no room for tolerance; competitive replacement was his theme. In the long run, he forecast, the orang-utang would be beaten and exterminated by man in the struggle for survival; the two could not simply occupy the same place in nature.

## The descent of man

Although Darwin mentioned human evolution only in passing in *The Origin of Species*, he deliberately set out in *The Descent of Man* (1871) to argue that man is descended from some lowly organism. The view was highly distasteful to many, particularly its implication that we are descended from the apes. Darwin himself was sufficiently a man of his imperial age to be shocked by the thought that 'we' – his European readers – 'are descended from barbarians'. When he first saw a party of Fuegians on a wild and broken South American shore, he was deeply shocked by the reflection that such were his ancestors. He concluded:

> For my part I would as soon be descended from that heroic little monkey, who braved his dreaded enemy in order to save the life of his keeper, or from that old baboon, who descending from the mountains, carried away in triumph his young comrade from a crowd of astonished dogs – as from a savage who delights to torture his enemies, offers up bloody sacrifices, practises infanticide without remorse, treats his wives like slaves, knows no decency, and is haunted by the grossest superstitions.[20]

Darwin thought it was a law of history and progress that the 'endless number of lower races' had to be wiped out by the 'higher civilized races'.[21] War too was inevitable on earth.

Darwin was deeply affected by the implications of his theory of evolution through natural selection. He made a brief abstract of his theory in 1842, wrote it more fully in 1844 but did not publish it until 1859, and then only because his contemporary Alfred Russell Wallace was about to publish his own theory of evolution. It was probably the frightful emotional and moral implications of the theory that made him reluctant to publish it for many years and kept him on his couch in his country retreat in Kent with some mysterious debilitating malady. Yet Darwin never abandoned the idea that however man might have risen 'to the very summit of the organic scale', he still 'bears in his bodily frame the indelible stamp of his lowly origin'.[22] Whatever Christianity might claim, man is not a special act of creation but wholly part of nature. His ethics are not God-given for all time, but originate in the natural world and evolve like all things on earth.

## Darwin's bulldog

It fell to the English biologist Thomas Henry Huxley (1825–95) to take up the cudgels on Darwin's behalf, defending his 'ape theory' against the howling pack of bishops, burghers and philosophers. Huxley declared that he was ready to go to the stake to defend the theory. As a result, he became known as Darwin's 'bulldog'. But Huxley had his own bones to chew. While recognizing the struggle for existence in Darwin's view of nature, he argued that modern science depicted the world as 'harmonious order governing eternally continuous progress – the web and woof of matter and force interweaving by slow degress, without a broken thread, that veil which lies between us and the Infinite'.[23]

Huxley was horrified by the struggle for existence and condemned those who tried to apply the analogy of cosmic nature to society to justify their ruthless individualism. He thought it a misapplication of the stoical injunction to follow nature and insisted that the cosmic process has no sort of relation to moral ends. Yet, in his evolutionary ethics, Huxley fell back on the humanism of the Enlightenment. He accepted Darwin's thesis that man has descended with other species from a common origin and that there is no absolute structural line of demarcation between animals and men. At the same time, he insisted that 'no one is more strongly convinced than I am of the vastness of the gulf between civilized man and the brutes; or is more certain that whether *from* them or not, he is assuredly not *of* them.'[24]

In his Romanes Lecture on 'Evolution and Ethics' in 1893, Huxley argued that the ethical progress of society depends 'not on imitating the cosmic process, still less in running away from it, but in combating it'. Such an audacious proposal meant 'to pit the microcosm against the macrocosm and to set man to subdue nature to his higher moral ends'.[25] In a note, he explained that the general cosmic process begins to be checked by a rudimentary ethical process which is part of the former 'just as the "governor" in a steam-engine is part of the mechanism of the engine'.

Huxley also adopted the mechanical materialism of the *philosophes*.

He rejected Descartes' view that animals are unconscious automata, maintaining that they have 'a consciousness which, more or less distinctly, foreshadows our own'. But while recognizing that molecular changes in the brain can cause changes of consciousness, he saw no evidence for the process operating in the other direction: 'The consciousness of brutes would appear to be related to the mechanism of their body simply as a collateral product of its working as the steam whistle which accompanies the working of a locomotive engine is without influence upon its machinery.'[26]

## The Darwinian legacy

Although Darwin tried to limit his speculations in *The Origin of Species* to scientific matters, his theory had enormous philosophical and religious implications. In the history of thought, Darwinism resulted in a momentous shift of consciousness. It encouraged an organic and evolutionary way of looking at the world; no longer seen as a static machine, it was transformed into an evolving organism in a constant state of flux. It dissolved the old certainties, the absolutes of right and wrong, and implied that all was a question of degree. It transformed man's view of himself and of his place in nature. No longer could he consider himself the apex of being and the lord of creation; his immediate cousins were the apes and he shared the same ancestry as the worm.

Darwin argued that there is only a difference in degree and not in kind between humans and other species. They are not eternally separated on their own railway tracks of life. Darwin made this connection even more explicit in *The Descent of Man*. In his own day, his hypothesis came to be called the 'ape theory' and ever since then, theorists have tried to argue that we are merely 'naked apes'. Such a view broke down the boundary which traditional Christianity and rationalist philosophy had tried to erect between humans and the rest of the creation. It is no wonder that bishops got hot under their collars and God-fearing states began to ban Darwin's books. Botanizing clergymen, who dipped their jars in ponds and caught butterflies in their nets, no longer saw the face of God in their collections, but the irrefutable evidence of evolutionary theory. William Paley's *Natural Theology: or Evidences of the Existence and Attributes of the Deity* (1802) lay unread on the shelf; bug-hunting became 'the Trojan horse of Victorian agnosticism'.[27]

In philosophy, Darwinism offered scientific refutation of Descartes' dualism of mind and body. It also undermined the view that animals are mere automata; indeed, Darwin argued that they have emotions and those with social instincts can develop a moral sense. He also rejected the idea that language is an impassable barrier between animals and man and claimed that animals have a latent ability to speak. The chief distinction between man and apes is his mental powers, and though the difference between the mind of the 'lowest man' and that of the 'highest animal' is immense, the difference is still one of degree and not of kind.[28]

Not surprisingly, Darwin's evolutionary views pitched the Victorians into a sea of doubt and anxiety. If Darwin is right, troubled minds meditated, and change takes place though random mutations, then Lord Chance rules in the universe. And if man is taught that he is a brute, or at least descended from one, then there is nothing to stop him from becoming one. The thin veneer of civilization, carefully built up over centuries, would be torn asunder and humanity fall back into a savage state of nature where all would prey on all.

When one focused on the struggle in nature for survival, and the vast amount of beings lost in the struggle, nature further appeared to be a 'gladiators' show', a continuous free-for-all. For many it struck a devastating blow against the Romantic 'pathetic fallacy' which saw nature reflecting human moods. The consoling mother of the Romantic poets had become 'nature red in tooth and claw'. Tennyson in particular was struck by the unfeeling profligacy of nature:

> So careful of the type she seems,
> So careless of the single life;
> . . . of fifty seeds,
> She often brings but one to bear,
> I falter where I firmly trod, . . .
> 'So careful of the type'? but no,
> From scarped cliff and quarried stone
> She cries, 'A thousand types are gone:
> I care for nothing, all shall go.'[29]

Those who wanted to find justification for competition among individuals in society now felt able to call it a 'law of nature'. Misapplying Darwin's theory of natural selection through the struggle of existence to society, Social Darwinists began to argue that capitalism, racism and imperialism were confirmed by science and vindicated by the laws of nature. The 'fittest' to rule was variably described as an individual, class, nation or race. Absorbing Social Darwinism in the Vienna of his youth, Hitler maintained that 'if we did not respect the law of nature, imposing our will by the right of the stronger, a day would come when the wild animals would devour us – then the insects would eat the wild animals, and finally nothing would exist on earth except the microbes'.[30]

The most important legacy of the Darwinian revolution is that it has undermined once and for all the attempt to defend the notion of human uniqueness on the grounds of intelligence. Humans are social animals who have developed reason, speech and a moral sense more than their fellow animals. Certainly reason would seem to be a function of higher primates and cetaceans. Dolphins and whales show the tentative beginnings of analytical abilities. Indeed, whales may well be as 'humane' as humans, if not more so. They may also be more intelligent, pondering in the deep on the folly of men.

Aristotle in *The Parts of Animals* observed that of all animals, man has the largest brain in proportion to his size (he left whales out of his list). This is no doubt partly man's triumph and his disaster. It seems the peculiar feature of his intelligence that he knows a great deal in a small area, but above all knows that he does not know very much in the big questions of life. He seems forced to search for certainty in a sea of doubt, to enquire after truth in a world of falsehoods. He knows how to make amazing instruments of construction but does not know how to control his urge to use them for destructive purposes. Pessimists put this down to the ineradicable aggression inherited from our hunting ancestors; the more likely explanation is that it is due to the competition for a perceived scarcity of resources.

In the long evolutionary history of our species, it seems that the left hemisphere of our brain has become the seat of reason, and the right, the centre of intuition. Our ancestors probably used the intuitive right hemisphere to perceive the world, and fully verbal rational thinking is probably only some hundred thousands of years old. Yet in the modern world, especially in the West, we have made so much of the left hemisphere and lost contact with the right – to the detriment of our imagination, feelings and knowledge. The 'enlightening' effect of certain meditation techniques and drugs is probably due to the temporary suppression of cerebral activity of the left hemisphere, thereby permitting 'the stars to come out'.[31] It is time now to reunite the left and the right hemispheres of the brain and all that they represent.

Darwin was a man who looked up at the stars on his long voyage in the *Beagle*, and conjured up a marvellous vision of the evolving universe. He used his reason in service of his intuition, and the earth has been a richer place ever since. We could do well to follow in his wake.

# 24

# THE NEW WORLD OF ECOLOGY

All Bodies have some Dependence upon one another.
Richard Bradley

One of the earliest scientific observations about ecology was made in 1721 by Richard Bradley, who wrote: 'All Bodies have some Dependence upon one another and . . . every distinct Part of Nature's work is necessary for the support of the rest; and . . . if any one was wanting all the rest must be consequently out of order'.[1] Nevertheless, ecology as a science did not emerge until the latter part of the ninteteenth century. The term 'ecology' was adopted by the scientific community after the International Botanical Congress in 1893.

From the beginning it was closely linked with ethology, the study of animal behaviour in its environment. By the end of the century, however, the term began to be applied to a wide variety of fields. Holistically minded biologists showed that man and animals were living interdependently in a balanced environment. The physical sciences warned that the dissipation of energy might threaten human existence and the very life of the planet. Then geographers drew attention to the finite and fragile nature of land. By the beginning of the twentieth century, the scientific scope of the term 'ecology' had largely been set.

### Haeckel's Earth House Hold

Although Ernst Heinrich Haeckel (1834–1919) was the first to use the word *oecologie*, in his *Generelle Morphologie der Organismen* (1866), he did not show much insight into the dynamic principles of ecology. He is to be remembered however for having helped to develop a contextual and holistic approach to biology.

Haeckel had considerable influence as a moralist as well as a biologist, popularizing his love of nature and pantheist creed in books with titles like *The Riddle of the Universe* (1900) and *The*

*Wonders of Life* (1904). As a philosophical monist, he argued that
matter and spirit are attributes of a single substance. Referring to
Bruno, Spinoza and Goethe as his intellectual ancestors, he argued
that they all show 'the oneness of the cosmos, the indissoluble
connection between energy and matter . . . mind and embodiment
. . . God and the world'.[2] Towards the end of his life, Haeckel's
monism took an increasingly spiritual turn. He finally moved to a
vitalist position in his last work *God-Nature* (1914), in which all is
one spirit.

One of his students, the embryologist Hans Driesch, further
postulated in *The Philosophy of the Organic* (1909) a 'dynamic
teleology', a kind of life force behind everything in the universe.
The more complex the life form, the more developed will be its will
and purpose. Like Aristotle, he called this purposeful, vital element
'entelechy': the entelechy of an organism somehow contains in it the
pattern of the adult organism. The theory introduced a vitalist and
indeterminate factor into the determinist physics of the day – a factor
which only became acceptable in the wider scientific community with
the development of quantum theory.

Haeckel insisted like Darwin that there is no gulf between man and
animals: the first beginnings of reason, social virtues and religious
and ethical conduct can be discerned in the most highly developed
vertebrates. On these grounds, he criticized traditional Christianity
for placing man above animals and nature: 'It has contributed not
only to an extremely injurious isolation from our glorious mother
"nature", but also to a regrettable contempt of all other organisms.'
He considered humans to be 'children of the earth' who have the good
fortune 'to drink the inexhaustible fountain of its beauty, and to trace
out the marvellous play of its forces'.[3]

Haeckel anticipated modern ecologists by seeing the universe as a
unified and balanced organism and asserting that man and animals
had the same natural status. Above all, he maintained that nature was
the source of truth and was a wise and secure guide to human life.
Like the Social Darwinists, he believed that scientific observations of
the natural world can form a sound base for organizing society. In this
way, the science of ecology provided the matrix for the development
of the ethics and politics of the green movement.

Haeckel's sketch of an ideal society shows, however, the shortcomings and dangers of the 'naturalistic fallacy', of inferring how
society should be from how nature is. On the analogy of the

brain and the nervous system, he proposed a centralized and hier-archical model with a strong emphasis on duty for survival. It was a short step to National Socialism, which took up many of Haeckel's ecological ideas. Contemporary deep ecologists find the science of ecology supporting the principle of 'biocentric equality' and find no ground for social hierarchy in nature. The case of Haeckel shows that it is only too easy to read human values into nature to justify moral and social views in the opposite direction. Ecology can be as anthropocentric as any other science when it tries to extrapolate from animal to human behaviour, from nature to society.

## Ethology and the wolf at the fireside

At first ecology was closely linked with ethology, the science of animal behaviour. By the First World War, ethologists had developed into two camps: the vitalists, who believed in instinctive drives, and the behavourists, who did not go beyond describing what they saw in laboratories. But an increasing number were determined to observe animal behaviour in their natural surroundings in the wild. The idea revolutionized zoology. The pioneers had to struggle to get out of the laboratory and to go beyond the bars of zoos in order to study animals in their natural habitats. Unlike their fellow zoologists, the ethologists recognized the interaction between the observer and the observed and tried to work with their imagination as well as their reason.

The Austrian Konrad Lorenz (1903–89), one of the great popularizers of ethology, started off as a behaviourist but his close observation of aggression in geese led him to conclude that animal behaviour is governed by inbuilt instincts. His method was one of empathy: he talked with the animals and described their behaviour in human terms. In *On Aggression*, he claimed that animals will defend their territory and their kin-group and show signs of aggression in order to protect themselves. But whereas predatory animals like wolves have developed innate mechanisms to control their aggressive behaviour (when one wolf submits, the dominant one will back off), humans are fundamentally peaceful but when aroused do not know when and how to stop.

Although Lorenz's book was a plea to avoid war, it was taken to justify violence and to support the view that man is innately violent. Lorenz's work triggered off a whole series of popular books in which naked apes are driven by territorial instincts. Man is presented as the 'Imperial Animal' – fundamentally undemocratic, adulterous, acquisitive and status-seeking. Such books tried to use the observation of animals in the wild to explain and justify human behaviour in society.

After the Second World War, a new breed of sociobiologists took up where the Social Darwinists of the previous century had left off. They claimed that practices of existing Western society were based in biological roots. After studying the social insects, Edward O. Wilson in his *Sociobiology: The New Synthesis* (1975) argued that ethics should be explained in evolutionary terms as an aid to survival. From this perspective, he called for a deep conservation ethic based on 'biophilia', but his ethics are narrowly utilitarian and instrumental. Since humanity was now jeopardizing its own existence by reducing biological diversity, he argued that the only way to make conservation work is 'to ground it in ultimately selfish reasoning . . . People will conserve land and species fiercely if they foresee a material gain for themselves, their kin and their tribe.'[4]

This way of thinking has found an echo in Richard Dawkins's celebration of the 'selfish gene'. In the shuffling of genes that determines the mutations from one generation to the next, genes are engaged in 'evolutionary arms races' in their drive to survive. Human beings and other organisms are to the genes mere 'throw-away survival machines'.[5] Dawkin thus gives a scientific gloss to old-fashioned misanthropy and Hobbes's vision of war of all against all in the natural state. He assumes that human nature is fundamentally aggressive and territorial, although he appeals to the principle of self-interest in order to recognize the interests of others.

The positive aspect of popular ethology has been to make people interested in the behaviour of animals in the wild and concerned about conserving their habitats. It has reminded humans that the dog at their fireside has a common ancestry with the wolves in the dark. Ethology as a science has also overlapped with ecology by extending the web of relationships from the physical sphere (energy circling between earth and heaven, between animals and plants) to encompass instinctive drives and learned adaptations. Without the central concept of ecology that the natural world forms an interrelated whole, the relations between organisms and their environments could not have been fully understood.

## The widening embrace of ecology

The most important cultural revolution in the twentieth century has been the transference of the insights of ecology from the scientific to the moral and political field, and the recognition that they cannot be kept separate. Ecology in a broad sense assumes that humans and nonhumans are comparable, and then applies observations about nature to human societies. It is therefore used both in a descriptive and a normative way to suggest how we ought to act.

Earlier in the century, professional ecologists like Charles Elton defined ecology as no more than scientific natural history. A new breed of ecologists described their phenomena in quantitative terms, giving the subject a highly rigorous mathematical treatment. But others were quite at home making much bigger generalizations about the natural world. The American F. E. Clements, who introduced the notion of a succession of colonizing plants into an area until it reached climax growth, talked of plant associations in terms of superorganism: 'the plant formation . . . a complex organism, which possesses functions and structures, and passes through a cycle of development similar to that of a plant.'[6] It was not long before the key concepts of ecology, such as niche, food web, community, ecosystem, diversity and stability, became established, although they remained somewhat vague. Scientists, both in social and in physical sciences, increasingly took note of ecology's holistic way of thinking. Social as well as natural communities were seen to be interrelated and interdependent organisms.

As a social and cultural movement, however, ecology began to develop only after the Second World War, and did not really catch on until the 1960s. It initially combined the anti-mechanistic and holistic approach to biology pioneered by Haeckel with the new approach to economics called 'energy economics' which focused on the problem of scarce and nonrenewable resources. It quickly burst out of these confines and began to appreciate the rich philosophical and literary soil from which its organic ideas and values had grown. Today it draws on a wide variety of philosophical and religious traditions, as we have seen. In the popular mind, it has virtually become synonymous with conservation or the environment; it is even considered by some as a kind of left-wing conspiracy against economic growth.

Ecology has become a scientific enquiry into the interrelationships of all life and the environment, as well as a broader study of man's place within nature. It is has grown from being a minor branch of biology to an interdisciplinary study which, as the subtitle of E. P. Odum's work *Ecology* (1963) suggests, provides *The Link Between the Natural and the Social Sciences*.

Ecology has supported the fundamental insights that humans are not unique in nature, that all life is interdependent, and that the earth itself forms an interwoven whole. It implies that humans can only change their way of life if they take into account their natural capacities and their complex relationship with their environment. It emphasizes our intimate links with the four elements of ancient science – earth, fire, air and water. It has erased the old, fixed boundaries between humanity and other species, between mind and body, matter and spirit. It has going some way in healing the nineteenth-century rift between science and religion so that children can see the face of God in the amoeba at the end of a telescope.

In the future, it may seem no less odd to consider man a unique and separate being from the rest of the creation than it is today to believe that the earth is flat. Ecology has undermined the traditional anthropomorphism and anthropocentrism of the West to such a degree that some ecologists now argue that it is wrong to distinguish between the moral standing of different species. All creatures should be considered of equal worth in the evolution of this strange and wondrous world. All are threads in nature's web, and if one thread is torn all the others are affected.

### The ecological impact of the human species

The universe was probably created in a big bang about 15 billion years ago. For hundreds of thousands of years, life had only a tiny foothold on earth, limited by its habitat and energy source in a violent physical world. The first photosynthetic algae, which were able to make food from simple inorganic substances and released gaseous oxygen as a by-product, brought about great changes. As organisms adapted to the oxygen diffused into the atmosphere, new forms of life began to spread to all parts of the globe. There followed an explosive period of evolution of increasingly complex organisms.

Man did not appear on earth until very late in the process – probably about 3.5 million years ago in East Africa. Early man survived with little impact on natural ecosystems. The discovery of fire was the first technological breakthrough, and made him able to cook food and to destroy vegetation on a large scale. About the same time, the making and use of tools and weapons increased his power as a predator. But it was the invention of agriculture and the domestication of animals that enabled him to grow more food and increase his numbers. Henceforth he began to make deep inroads in natural ecosystems.

It took hundreds of thousands of years for the human population to reach its first 1,000 million by about 1830. As a result of improved agriculture and industry and better living conditions, it rose to 2,000 million by 1930; 3,000 million by 1960. In 1976 it passed 4,000 million; in 1986 it passed 5,000 million. Humankind has only in the last 10,000 years made a significant impact on the planet, and it is only in the last two centuries that is has become critical.

Man is the only creature on earth to consume fuels in large quantities as a source of energy and substantially redistribute metals and other materials. The process has had a devastating effect on natural ecosystems and other species of plants and animals. The cultivation of plants and the domestication of animals have had an even greater impact on upsetting the equilibrium of nature. In recent times, this has been exacerbated by the abandonment of traditional methods of agriculture – growing for oneself – for large-scale production of cash crops to the detriment of local consumption and the quality of the soil. When a rainforest is cut down for short-lived pastureland, an enormously complex ecosystem is destroyed for an artificial environment which can only be maintained by human interference. One of the worst examples of this is the so-called Green Revolution, which increased production by introducing new strains of wheat, rice and other cereals but is dependent on the massive input of fertilizers, pesticides and weedkillers – all of dubious value for peasant cultivators and their land.

Natural communities are relatively stable, and the more varied the species present, the greater the likelihood of long-term stability.[7] There is a definite benefit in organic diversity. A complex natural environment like a tropical forest regulates itself and reaches a natural equilibrium which is remarkably resistant to colonization by new species unless the equilibrium is disturbed. But ever since man invented agriculture some 10,000 years ago in Asia, he has been transforming complex ecosystems into virtual lawns. A lawn does not contain plants other than grass, but provides an environment which favours colonization by other plants; it requires constant human interference to suppress the unwanted plants.

In ecological terms, the creation of such monocultures means that the natural diversity of ecosystems is reduced by eliminating all but the desired species. When an environment is simplified by the development of a monoculture, most species disappear as their resources diminish, but a few are able to exploit the new circumstances. These become known as pests and weeds. The most efficient and cheapest way to get rid of them in the short term is to apply pesticides, weedkillers and fertilizers, a process which eventually ends up poisoning the consumers of the desired crop. Given the intricacies of the food web – the transfer of food energy from its source in plants through a series of organisms – there are bound to be widespread adverse consequences elsewhere.

Since the advent of agriculture and the domestication of animals, man has altered an enormous number of organisms through artificial selection; virtually all the plants in our gardens and the animals in our fields are a result of this process. At the same time, there has been widespread destruction of natural ecosystems and a massive increase in industrial pollution. Wild species of plants and animals are disappearing at an ever-increasing rate. The species composition of virtually all communities has now been altered. There are no areas in the world – however remote, cold, hot, barren, deep or high – which are not free from human influence. There is no place on earth, not even on the highest peaks or in the deepest oceans, which has escaped the polluting and interfering hand of humankind. We have not only transformed the earth's surface but we have begun to change the atmosphere and the weather. It makes bitter sense to talk of the end of nature as a world apart from man: 'We have built a greenhouse, *a human creation*, where once there bloomed a sweet and wild garden.'[8]

## Ecological inequality

Like other animals, humans are essentially dependent on plants as a source of food, and ultimately numbers will be limited by the carrying capacity of the world defined in terms of the availability of food. But there are enormous individual and regional differences. Two thirds of the world's human population live in poverty while the remaining third enjoy comparative luxury. The poor consume a small amount of the world's nonrenewable resources but their growth in population is double that of those living in developed countries. The average European consumes 600 times more steel than the average African; if everyone used oil like the average American, there would be no oil left on the planet in a few years.

The poor two thirds of the world are caught in a bind: one of the main ways of improving living conditions in the long term is to limit the numbers of their offspring, yet in the short term, without any welfare net to support them, having many children increases their own chances of survival in old age. Again, while industrially underdeveloped countries provide raw materials for industries in the developed countries, they are unable to enjoy the full benefits of industrialization; they are condemned to produce materials for others to consume.

As Europeans colonized the world, they brought with them their culture as well as their technology, a culture which saw 'development' and 'progress' in terms of technological mastery over nature. The message was simple and stark: the world is there to be exploited and despoiled. But the Western way of life can never be adopted universally because there are simply not enough resources to go round. The poor countries of the world have developed a taste for consumer goods which they will never be able to satisfy – except for their elites. So the cycle of famine and misery will continue unless there is a fair distribution of resources, less consumption in the richer countries, and a move towards a sustainable global economy which recycles materials and uses renewable energy supplies. If not, then those in the West will probably continue to sit in front of colour television sets, eating processed meals in centrally heated houses, and watch images of others starving to death transmitted 'live' via satellites orbiting the earth.

## Thinking ecologically

The most important lesson of ecology is that human beings are part of nature and that the rest of nature is not there merely for them to exploit. They are a product of evolution, and whatever special attributes they may possess, whether it be reason, speech or spirit, they remain an integral strand in the living web of nature. Once we acknowledge our common origin with other organisms, we may begin to see ourselves in an ecological perspective.

It is an axiom of ecological theory that all organisms modify to some extent the ecosystems in which they live. It is also evident that 'complexity (in terms of species diversity) is correlated with stability'.[9] In terms of population, the message is simple: food supply can be increased, but in the long run human numbers must remain stable in order to avoid a sudden crash. Thinking ecologically in this way, we can anticipate the possible consequences for our present actions. And what is true of population is also true of our present drive for economic growth and scramble for the remaining world resources.

The human species is a recent and temporary occupant on earth, yet its impact is far greater than that of other species. Humans have converted much of the world to suit their own purposes, despite the resistance and vitality of other organisms such as the AIDS virus, the mosquito, the rat or the grey squirrel.

As the third millennium approaches, humans are at a fork: they can go down one path to ecological disaster, or try the other path to a sustainable and harmonious future. If we choose the latter, then we must think about the consequences of population growth, which is near the maximum carrying capacity of many regions on earth. Above all, we should question the consumer ethic, which uses up nonrenewable resources, creates inequality and injustice, generates pollution, destroys other species and upsets the balance of nature. The word 'pollution' is derived from the Greek root for 'defilement'. The consumer ethic not only defiles the environment by creating undesirable change in the biosphere but also corrupts the mind and body by defining pleasure in terms of ownership and absorption.

Waste itself is a human concept; everything in nature is eventually used. If human beings carry on in their present ways, they will one day be recycled along with the dinosaurs.

## Ecology and systems theory

Since the Second World War, ecology, with its key concept of an ecosystem, has been drawn to systems theory as a tool of analysis, with its notions of information, communication and control, loops and feedback, to support the idea of the earth as a self-regulating organism. Systems theory looks at the world in terms of integrated wholes which cannot be reduced to their smaller parts. Rather than looking at basic building blocks, it focuses on fundamental principles of organization. It is also a form of process thinking, and looks for interactions.[10]

An ecosystem is the totality of a community and its environment. It is independent of external sources of matter and energy, except for light from the sun, and it circulates material to maintain life. It includes everything that contributes to the maintenance of life within a specific space and time. An ecosystem can be centred on a single plant, a wood or even the whole of the living world. Even evolution can be described in terms of a dynamic system within a self-organizing universe.[11] Humanity has a peculiar role in modifying natural ecosystems (such as rainforests) and creating new ones (such as farms artificially sustained by pesticides, fertilizers and machinery).

Living organisms are largely self-organizing and self-regulating systems, but they are open systems, constantly interacting with their environment and embedded in an ecosystem. Perhaps the most striking example of an ecosystem is a coral reef, in which the plants, fish and coral interact to form a living whole which seems to operate in a highly coordinated way. It forms an intricate web of relations involving the exchange of energy in continual cycles.

According to systems theory the starting point in any system is homeostasis. When a system is disturbed, it tries to maintain its stability by means of negative feedback systems. But fluctuations can occur which eventually transform the system into a new structure.[12] From this perspective evolution occurs through an interplay of adaptation and creation. It does not proceed, as the French biologist Jacques Monod has recently argued, through a sequence of chance and necessity, of chance mutations and necessity of survival.[13] It is neither governed by randomness nor does it betray a purpose but represents 'an unfolding of order and complexity that can be seen as a kind of learning process, involving freedom and choice'.[14]

The British anthropologist and psychologist Gregory Bateson in his *Steps to an Ecology of Mind* (1972) has suggestively used systems theory to interpret human consciousness in ecological terms, arguing that people are 'self-corrective systems' and 'man is only part of larger systems and that part can never control the whole'. In his new approach of 'cybernetic epistemology', there is a 'larger Mind of which the individual mind is only a sub-system'. The larger mind is comparable to God but it is immanent in the 'total interconnected social system and planetary ecology'.[15] Fritjof Capra has further claimed that the systems view of life is 'spiritual in its deepest essence and thus consistent with many ideas held in mystical traditions'.[16]

Systems theory has undoubtedly transformed ecology as a science. It deals with organic wholes, stresses the interdependence of all things, and depicts nature as self-organizing and self-maintaining. But it does have its limitations. It is common for systems theorists to talk in terms of 'stratified order' in nature. Ecologists using systems theory often present nature in terms of a hierarchical pyramid with the predator with the fewest numbers at the top of the food chain. Like the Great Chain of Being, the hierarchy is a continuous one. E.P. Odum, for instance, claims that the central 'principle of integrative levels' within ecology is the 'principle of hierarchical control' which states: 'As components combine to produce larger functional wholes in a hierarchical series, new properties emerge.'[17] But while there are undoubtedly degrees of complexity in ecosystems, they do not necessarily form a hierarchy.

The word hierarchy (from the Greek *hieros* 'sacred' and *arkhia* 'rule') originally referred to the government of the Church and implies a pyramid of power with subordinate ranks at different levels. The notion of hierarchy is part of the old Cartesian grid which Western thinkers have imposed on nature. Any 'level' looked at in a system is really the level of the observer's attention.[18]

An ecological way of thinking does not necessarily imply hierarchy. A more complex being or system is not necessarily superior to a simple one, any more than a higher layer of fossils in strata is superior to a lower one. Indeed, to maintain the diversity of the healthy ecosystem of the earth, both complex and simple systems are equally necessary. As in any spectrum, the divisions are arbitrary and made for convenience; they need not be seen in hierarchical terms.

To avoid the concept of hierarchy, Capra has suggested the notion of a tree as a more appropriate symbol for the ecological nature of stratification in living systems, with power in the tree flowing in both directions.[19] An even better metaphor might be a 'web' (as in Darwin's 'web of life'), an organic network which stresses the interrelation between all parts and implies that no one part is superior to another. All support each other in overall harmony. Humans are not the apex of the creation, the top of the hierarchy, but strands along with other species forming the warp and weft of nature's intricate and seamless web. They may be capable of unravelling more strands than their neighbours, but in the end all strands are equally interdependent in the exquisite gossamer of the planet.

Again, while systems theory may be suggestive for closed systems – as in the American ecologist Kenneth Boulding's popularization of the concept of spaceship Earth – it is more problematical for open systems and for describing the relationships between different systems. Its fundamental assumption is based on a notion of rest – all remains in a state of homeostasis unless disturbed by fluctuations. Its concept of change cannot represent gradual development well, for it suggests that a system will undergo quantitative changes and then suddenly flip over into a qualitatively new system. And even Boulding's metaphor is misleading because it implies that humans are pilots and engineers in charge of spaceship Earth rather than one species among others travelling together in the odyssey of evolution.

Systems theory, and its sub-branch of cybernetics, can provide imaginative models of the earth and its organisms, making comparisons between man-made and biological systems. But ultimately, with its talk of homeostasis, feedback and functions, it remains a formal, nonsensuous method. It fosters a neutral and abstract view of the living world. It betrays the very mechanical way of thinking which ecology challenges. Above all, it can easily mistake a formal map for the living territory.

## Evolutionary ethics

Ecology is a value-laden science as any other, based on interpretation, arbitrary distinctions and convenient models. Like any other science, it reflects the intellectual framework of its time and place. Many orthodox scientists moreover have found scientific ecology wanting because it is not principally concerned with testing hypotheses. Its findings are more analytical than empirical – they are true by definition rather than by experiment. Ecologists tend to see in nature what they are looking for; they see organic wholes because they have been trained to see them. In general, then, ecology may be said to offer a perspective on nature, rather than a firm body of scientific findings.

The greatest contribution ecology has made to the twentieth century is to ethics. The assumptions and findings of ecology have transformed and revitalized traditional humanist morality. The evolutionary ethics

of the Social Darwinists has given way to environmental ethics which
is principally concerned with man's rightful place in nature and
how he should relate to his surroundings. The issues are highly
controversial and hotly debated. They are also essential to future
wellbeing on earth.

In 1893 T. H. Huxley argued that the ethical progress of society
depended on combating the cosmic process. Fifty years later his
grandson Sir Julian Huxley asserted that 'man can impose moral
principles upon ever-widening areas of the cosmic process, in whose
further slow unfolding he is now the protagonist. He can inject his
ethics into the heart of evolution.'[20] Seeing man as the most evolved
species, Huxley claimed a unique role for humanity in furthering
evolutionary 'progress'. Man need not feel himself insignificant in
relation to the cosmos, for he can control matter by means of mind:

> In the light of evolutionary biology man can now see himself as
> the sole agent for further evolutionary advance on this planet,
> and one of the few possible instruments of progress in the
> universe at large. He finds himself in the unexpected position
> of business manager for the cosmic process of evolution.[21]

If this is the case, he is running a business approaching bankruptcy.
The human being might be the most powerful animal on earth, but he
is hardly an agent for evolutionary progress. The findings of science
are descriptive and not imperative; it is up to us to decide whether we
want to change or encourage existing trends. The evolutionary process
can point the way but it cannot in itself supply us with a criterion
of the good. As Bertrand Russell has warned, 'if evolutionary ethics
were sound, we ought to be entirely indifferent as to what the course
of evolution may be, since whatever it is it is thereby proved to be the
best'.[22]

A more benign view of the management of the universe has
been put forward by Charles Elton, who wrote the famous text
*Animal Ecology* (1927) and helped form the Nature Conservancy
Council in Britain. 'The world's future has to be managed, but
the management would not be just a game of chess – more like
steering a boat.'[23] Ecology can undoubtedly help us appreciate the
direction of the winds and currents as we sail our boat on the
unknown seas of the universe, but it remains to be seen whether
our steering will be effective. All the same, as we ride the waves of

evolution, we can avoid killing the whale below and the albatross above on our exhilarating voyage of discovery. And knowing our place in the scheme of things does not mean that we cannot on occasion make quite a splash and enjoy its myriad diamonds in the sun.

# 25

# PHILOSOPHERS OF THE EARTH

> Would not the world suffer by the banishment of a single weed?
>
> John Muir

One of the great legacies of the twentieth century has been the development of environmental ethics. It goes beyond the humanism of the Renaissance and the Enlightenment to place humanity within and not outside nature, and to call for a more caring attitude to the natural world and its creatures. With increasing concern for the environment and the growth of the green movement in the last couple of decades, the work of a number of earlier thinkers who spoke up on behalf of the silent and suffering creation is being reassessed. Notable among these are the Americans John Muir and Aldo Leopold and the German Albert Schweitzer, who have all made a special contribution to ecosophy, or earth wisdom.

## John Muir's orchids and alligators

In the United States, John Muir in the late nineteenth century followed Thoreau in his concern for the wilderness and was the first to develop a conscious environmental ethic. His insight that everything in nature has intrinsic value occurred as a revelation in the Canadian wilderness near Lake Huron. Escaping from the military draft, he wandered into a dark swamp where he came upon a cluster of rare white orchids. They were so beautiful that he 'sat down beside them and wept for joy'. He later interpreted this as a sudden awareness that the orchids had no relevance for human beings; they would have lived and died, whether a human had seen them or not.

But Muir was not only concerned with the beautiful. 'Would not the world suffer,' he asked, 'by the banishment of a single weed?' Even alligators are beautiful in the eyes of God, and rattlesnakes are good for themselves; we should not begrudge them their share of life. All animals and plants have a right to happiness and were not made for the happiness of one. 'Why should man value himself as more than a small part of the one great unit of creation?'[1]

Muir's ecological sensibility was inspired by a belief in God in all things. Animals, plants, rocks and water are all 'sparks of the Divine Soul'. He was ready to entertain the idea that even rocks have sensations and are capable of happiness. But this concern for the natural world was coupled with a certain misanthropy. He was indifferent, for instance, to the freeing of human slaves, and if a war broke out between man and the animals, he said he would be tempted to take the side of the animals.

As he grew older, however, Muir's public voice changed and he became increasingly utilitarian and pragmatic. After helping set up the Yosemite National Park and the Sierra Club, Muir argued that the primary value of nature was not for the benefit of nature itself but for the benefit of people: for *their* recreation and *their* nourishment. It is a contradiction often seen among conservationists who appeal to man's worst impulses of self-interest in order to further their cause, believing that the end justifies the means.

## Albert Schweitzer's organs and hippopotamuses

The Franco-German Albert Schweitzer (1875–1965) perhaps better than any other moralist makes the case for environmental ethics based on love for all creation. As a devout Christian, he claimed that Christ was not merely a moral teacher but the herald of God's kingdom to come on earth. At the age of twenty-one, Schweitzer decided that he would live for science and art until he was thirty and then devote the rest of his life to serving humanity. In 1905, he gave up his career as an organist, which was earning him an international reputation, and his academic posts as a philosopher and theologian, in order to study medicine. Eight years later he set off with his new wife to establish a hospital to fight leprosy and sleeping sickness at a remote mission station in the heart of French Equatorial Africa (now Gabon). He spent most of his remaining life helping Africans, in a spirit 'not of benevolence but of atonement'.

Steaming along the Ogooué River to a mission at Lambaréné in September 1915, he had a revelation after passing through a herd of hippos. He was meditating on an old problem: what is the soundest basis for ethics? Suddenly there flashed on his mind, 'unforseen and unsought', the phrase 'Reverence for Life'.[2]

The phrase suggests the Buddhist concept of compassion for all beings and the Hindu principle of *ahimsa*, or non injury. But the German word used by Schweitzer, *Ehrfurcht*, has the Western connotation of the sublime, of a sense of awe in the presence of a vast and mysterious power. Recognizing a 'will-to-live' in all creatures, he adapted the Christian golden rule to define virtue as giving 'to every will-to-live the same reverence for life he gives his own'.[3] He developed this insight in relation to European civilization in *The Decay and Restoration of Civilization* (1923) and in his more philosophical *Culture and Ethics* (1924).

Schweitzer's ethics are not without difficulties. In a marvellous sentence, he wrote in 1923 that the moral person 'shatters no ice crystal that sparkles in the sun, tears no leaf from its tree, breaks off no flower, and is careful not to crush any insect as he walks'.[4] But how could Schweitzer justify killing animals to eat or killing germs to avoid disease? His constraint is the utilitarian one – we can kill only when it is necessary to enhance another life. But who is to define necessity and enhancement? The cannibal could make a case for eating his enemy, as the British Meat Board does for the production of veal.

Of course Schweitzer would reject such reasoning, and he insists that the taking of any life should be accompanied by the minimum of pain and a compassionate sense of 'responsibility for the life which is sacrificed'.[5] In addition, the necessary sacrifice of animal and plant life for humanity creates an obligation for everyone 'to do as much good as we possibly can to all creatures in all sorts of circumstances'.[6] Such conduct would also be a form of atonement, removing some of the collective guilt of humanity for their crimes against the nonhuman world. For Schweitzer, this meant removing an insect struggling in a pool of water, or an earthworm stranded on a pavement after a rainstorm; for others, it might mean not washing spiders down the plughole in the bath or releasing flies buzzing against the window.

Clearly, everyone applying Schweitzer's principle of 'reverence for life' has to draw their own boundaries of ethical behaviour. He thought it acceptable for the farmer to mow down thousands of flowers in his meadow in order to feed his cows, but wrong for the same farmer to strike off the head of a single flower by the side of the road on his way home. Vegans would say that you do not need cows; fruitarians, that you do not need fields. Schweitzer approved the killing of animals for medical research where 'truly necessary'; anti-vivisectionists claim that such necessity never arises. The problem is not so much with the principle of reverence but how one decides what is justifiable killing in order to prolong human life.

Schweitzer's main contribution to environmental ethics was his insistence that ethics should not only deal with relations of man to man but the relations of man to all life: 'A man is ethical only when life, as such, is sacred to him, that of plants and animals as that of his fellow men.' He wished to make kindness to animals a moral claim as much as kindness to human beings. The privileged position of power they have in the world confers on them the responsibility to protect others, not the right to exploit them for their own ends. Indeed, like Godwin, Schweitzer thought the moral person should widen his circle of concern from the family, clan, tribe, nation to embrace all humanity, but went further to argue that by reason of our common nature, one should declare 'the unity of mankind with all created beings'.[7]

Like Darwin, Schweitzer saw the possibility of moral as well as biological evolution. As early as 1923 he looked forward to a time when people would be amazed that it took humanity so long 'to recognize that thoughtless injury to life was incompatible with ethics'.[8] Such a view of course overlooks thousands of years of Oriental ethics. Nevertheless, Schweitzer's international reputation helped popularize in the West the ecological and moral principle that every life is intrinsically valuable in nature and we should treat all life with reverence.

## Rachel Carson's silent spring

The American marine biologist Rachel Carson's enormously influential *Silent Spring* (1962) about the consequences of pesticides was dedicated to Schweitzer and she followed him in her conviction that 'life is a miracle beyond our comprehension, and we should reverence it even when we have to struggle against it'.[9] All life forms, even insects, are worthy of consideration. Yet in the drive to conquer and dominate nature humanity had created a sick society and a poisoned planet.

Carson (1907–64) became something of a heroine in the environmental movement. A profound sense of wonder pervades her writings, especially about the teeming life of the sea. It was not hippos but the sight of a small crab at night perfectly at home on the edge of the roaring surf which proved a moral revelation. Yet, like Schweitzer, she too had her limitations and contradictions. Although she rejected the idea of the 'control of nature' as a form of human arrogance, she nevertheless divided the insect world into 'friends' and 'enemies', and advocated 'biological control' of the latter by the former. In the long run, she was in favour of the all-too-familiar anthropocentric and utilitarian principle of 'keeping the balance of nature tilted in our favour'.[10]

## Leopold and the wolf

Although comparatively unknown in Europe, one of the towering figures of the American environmental movement is Aldo Leopold. His slim volume *A Sand County Almanac* (1949), a collection of natural-history sketches, gained few readers when it first appeared but was rediscovered in the sixties. It has been described by René Dubos as the 'the Holy Writ of American Conservation'; Dave Foreman, founding member of the direct-action group Earth First!, has called it the most important book ever written. Leopold has recently been described as 'the most important source of modern biocentric or holistic ethics'.[11]

Leopold was originally a forester, with a penchant for hunting, and he started out in 1909 as a manager of national forests in Arizona and New Mexico. One of his tasks was to exterminate 'bad' predators in the alleged interest of the 'good' animals, such as deer and cattle, and he promised to perservere until the last wolf or lion was dead in New Mexico. In his book *Game Management* (1933), which became for a while the bible of the wildlife profession in America, he favoured treating game like deer and quail as 'crops' that should be cultivated and harvested in the wild in the name of 'greater productivity'.[12] He also wanted to provide opportunities for the average American citizen to play the hunter in the carefully nurtured 'wild'. Although in an essay called 'The Conservation Ethic' (1933), Leopold questioned whether a landowner should be able to use his land as he saw fit without any wider obligations, his economic approach to wildlife management undoubtedly appealed to landowners at the time.

Leopold later recalled how after shooting a wolf he watched 'a fierce green fire dying in her eyes'.[13] It haunted him for thirty years, and he came to adopt the wider view that wolves are as necessary as deer to a healthy ecosystem. Although he often used the mechanical metaphor of nature as an engine where all the parts are essential to its functioning, he nevertheless adopted a holistic conception of nature and denied the distinction between the organic and inorganic. Indeed, he suggested that the 'complexity of the land organism' was the outstanding scientific discovery of the twentieth century.[14] Inspired by the Russian philosopher Peter Ouspensky, he concluded that the earth was alive, a living being, which deserved respect. To transcend his earlier anthropocentric position was for him, as the title of a 1944 essay put it, 'Thinking like a Mountain'.

Leopold's great contribution was to help provide a scientific basis for an environmental ethic. The final chapter of *A Sand County Almanac*, entitled 'A Land Ethic', is his principal claim to fame. Ethics, he argues, are a body of self-imposed limitations on freedom of action that is derived from the recognition that the individual is a member of a wider community. A genuine land ethic therefore 'changes the role of *Homo sapiens* from the conqueror of the land-community to plain member and citizen of it. It implies respect for his fellow-members, and also respect for the community as such.' Although members of a 'biotic team', human beings are clearly the most powerful species and for this reason they need the restraints of a land ethic in their dealings with nature. In the long run, this means no longer abusing land as a commodity. 'When we see land as a community to which we belong, we may begin to use it with love and respect.' Leopold's most interesting claim, however, was for 'the biotic right' to continued existence of animals, plants, waters and soils, whatever their use to us.[15]

Leopold thus applied the liberal notion of the right to life to the 'biotic community', the environment as a whole. At the end of his life, he had come to realize that predators were as important as their prey to a healthy ecosystem;

> Harmony with land is like harmony with a friend; you cannot cherish his right hand and chop off his left. That is to say, you cannot love game and hate predators; you cannot conserve the waters and waste the ranges; you cannot build the forest and mine the farm. The land is one organism.[16]

This did not mean that human beings should have no impact on the environment, even in wilderness areas. The reservations of Schweitzer about taking life cut little ice with Leopold. The gamekeeper happily endorsed hunting and eating dead flesh. The alteration, management and use of an ecosystem were in his view acceptable interferences in the course of nature. As a rule of thumb, he proposed the formula that any decision about the land is 'right when it tends to preserve the integrity, stability and beauty of the biotic community. It is wrong when it tends otherwise'.[17]

The criterion is full of difficulties. Integrity and stability have a specific scientific sense in terms of an ecosystem, but they have a wider moral connotation which is deeply conservative. They do not allow room for dynamic evolution. The principle of beauty opens a beehive of aesthetics: beauty is notoriously in the eye of the beholder, and what is considered beautiful in nature has changed dramatically since the Renaissance. But Leopold breaks through such considerations like a bull out of a corral. As a professional game manager, he did not bat an eyelid at killing thousands of animals if he thought their population exceeded the carrying capacity of their environment. Culling is quite acceptable if it enhances the beauty of an ecosystem – does that include Muir's alligators? Leopold leaves the issue to the 'expert' in wildlife management who takes as his criterion the 'healthy functioning' of the 'bionic mechanism'.[18]

There is a further contradiction here. On the one hand, Leopold's talk of biotic rights of individual organisms would seem to clash with his holistic land ethic where he thinks in terms of the whole rather than the parts. Despite the look of the dying wolf, he cared about the threat to wolves as a species, not as individuals. In the latter case, the loss of individual lives in the economy of nature meant little if nature prospered as a whole. God might worry about the death of a sparrow as it falls from a branch, but not a mountain. The writhing of a worm on a pavement did not hold back Leopold's firm step.

The seeds of more authoritarian strands in the environmental movement, which have germinated organizations like Earth First!, lie in this attitude. If humans are ecological equals in a biotic community, why not cull excessive humans if they threaten the ecosystem in a part of the world? It is a logical extension of Leopold's position, and a view hinted at by Foreman when he suggests that the famine-stricken in Africa should be left to starve in order to re-establish the right carrying capacity of the land in that region.

Calling for an 'Ecological Conscience' in 1947, Leopold suggested that it might take 2,000 years to evolve a code of decency for 'man-to-land contact'. As a start, one should not let economics dictate ethics; a wrong action should not be condoned simply because it pays. But like Muir, Leopold often appealed to human self-interest in his campaign to conserve nature; we should not become like the potato bug which kills itself by killing its host. His land ethic was rather like the enlightened interest or cool self-love of eighteenth-century philosophers.

Leopold's originality has been greatly overrated; there is little new in his essays, for instance, which cannot be found in Darwin, Salt and Schweitzer. He focuses narrowly on the land and has little to say about the sea. His mechanical metaphors sit uneasily with his organic cosmology. He does not question property relations which make it possible for humans to consider that they can do what they like with their land; he just calls for a new attitude to property. He does not realize that in the American tradition, the right to life, especially when extended to embrace nonhuman beings, clashes with the right to property. He looks to coercive legislation by the state to impose its will on people.

But Leopold's enormous influence is probably due to the fact that he was a woodsman who spoke poetically to the general public, evoking a deep love of nature. He was prepared to query the ethical roots of existing conservation practices. He extended the so-called natural rights enjoyed by all Americans to the rights of nature itself. He challenged the great frontier tradition of America, calling for restraint and care in dealings with the environment. Above all, he rejected the conqueror role of man in the Judaeo-Christian tradition, and argued that 'men are fellow-voyagers with other creatures in the odyssey of evolution'.[19]

### Smallpox and wild flowers

The American bacteriologist René Dubos applied Leopold's land ethic to microscopic life and concluded that even germs should not be eradicated since 'disease is part of the total harmony'. In his view, a healthy human organism should rely on its own resistance to infection; malaria had a place in the world with wolves and tarantulas. In *God Within* (1972), he called for an 'enlightened anthropocentrism' which recognized that the world's good in the long run always coincides with human good; we should love nature for its own sake as well as ours. But he still thought that man is the most crucial part of the environment: in order to improve our wellbeing, we must first understand and then control our effect on the environment. Since virtually all the world is now a man-made environment, he sees the problem as one not of conservation but of 'intelligent management'.[20]

The American ecologist David Ehrenfeld, like Leopold, sees in nature the 'unimpeachable right to continued existence'. He considers it the 'arrogance of humanism' to have bias in favour of the human species and against other species; such bias is comparable to sexism and racism.[21] He also wishes to defend the rights of so-called 'non-resources'. This means including in the land ethic members of the biotic community whose disappearance would be unlikely to affect adversely its healthy functioning. Ehrenfeld has gone so far as to argue that even an organism – such as smallpox – whose only function is to prey on people has a right to existence, and vaccination programmes should not eliminate the germ in its only natural habitat within the human body.

It is perhaps a fine ideal to be ready to relinquish human wellbeing to the rights of germs, but the obvious question remains: if Ehrenfeld's community were invaded by smallpox, would he have his own children – if he has any – vaccinated? Should all work on eliminating the AIDS virus stop? These questions raise the broader issue of whether the ecological principle of diversity is sacrosanct at all costs. It would seem to be reasonable (for the enlightened Romanticist at least) to contain some germs, as we would contain bracken and stinging nettles from taking over a field, if they threaten our wellbeing. But this does not mean they should be eradicated entirely from the face of the earth, however obnoxious they may appear. A healthy person, as much as a healthy society and ecosystem, should be able to support some parasites at least; indeed, the degree of health might be measured by the number of parasites which could be tolerated.

The American philosopher J. Baird Callicott is another admirer of Leopold, although he criticizes his stress on the natural rights of organisms. The land ethic for Callicott is important because it is holistic and has as its objective 'the good of the community of the whole'. Such ethical holism calculates right and wrong in relation not to individuals but to the biotic community. The argument reflects the controversy at the time of the French Revolution between those like Thomas Paine who called for the rights of man and those like Bentham who considered such a doctrine 'nonsense on stilts' and advocated the utilitarian principle of the good of the whole. From the point of view of the whole, Callicott argues that oceans and lakes, mountains, forests and wetlands have greater value than individual animals, including humans. In his biotic calculus, soil bacteria and plankton carry more weight than human beings in the food web. He shares the view of the American writer Edward Abbey, who advocated the use of monkey wrenches in defence of the wild, and who has claimed that in certain circumstances he would rather kill a man than a snake.

This biocentric ethic can lead to a hatred of humanity; indeed, Callicott has declared: 'The extent of misanthropy in modern environmentalism may be taken as a measure of the degree to which it has become biocentric.'[22] Such a view has violent overtones, and considers human life cheap. The American philosopher Paul Taylor has taken this biocentric morality, which sees all organisms as having equal intrinsic value, so far as to entertain the idea that unless there are extenuating circumstances providing an adequate moral reason, the wanton killing of a wild flower is just as wrong as killing a human in self-defence. Respect for nature means according to all beings a similar opportunity to fulfil their different potentials, whatever their place in the biotic community.[23]

This kind of biocentric holism, in which the interests and even lives of individual organisms are sacrificed in the alleged interest of the ecosystem, can easily degenerate into a form of ecological fascism. At the same time, the atomistic approach of the rights theorists dwells too narrowly on the calculations of individuals, even when they extend rights to items like trees and rivers. What is urgently required is an environmental ethic which is holistic in orientation but which is not ready to sacrifice individuals to the well-being of the whole; an ethic which gives equal consideration to the interests of humans and nonhumans without losing sight of the collective interests of the wider community in which they live. Such an ethic should be based on the principle of reverence for all life. While trying to minimize suffering, it would attempt to maximize the well-being of the ecosphere and help realize the evolutionary potential of nature as a whole.

# 26

## TIME AND BEING:

### Modern Organic Philosophy

We are too late for the gods and too early for Being.
Martin Heidegger

Three of the most important philosophers who have contributed to
the creation of an organic cosmology this century are the Frenchman
Henri Bergson, the Englishman Alfred North Whitehead and the
German Martin Heidegger. They form a holistic trio, protesting
against the dominant mechanical and materialistic philosophy of
the Western tradition.

### Process and reality: Alfred North Whitehead

Whitehead (1861–1947) was a physicist and mathematician who
worked with Bertrand Russell on *Principia Mathematica*, a vast treatise on the logic of mathematics. But he left Newton's mechanical and
mathematical view of the world behind to develop a thoroughgoing
holistic philosophy.

Whitehead was particularly critical of the mechanistic materialism
of Galileo, Descartes and Newton who attempted to reduce all
human experience to 'clear-cut definite things, with clear-cut definite
relations'. In their heads, nature appeared 'senseless, valueless,
purposeless'; all was reduced to abstract physical and chemical
laws.[1] Such a simplified view of nature had transformed human
life, thoughts, technologies, social behaviour and ambitions, and
had left humanity considerably the poorer. It had been bedevilled
by the 'Dogmatic Fallacy' which consists in the persuasion that we
can produce notions adequately defined to illustrate the 'complexity
of relationship' in the real world.[2]

Whitehead was inspired by the new theory of relativity, the study
of quantum mechanics, and the principle of the indeterminacy in
matter; one of his works was entitled *The Principle of Relativity*

*with Applications to Physical Science*. Newtonian physics is based upon the individuality of each bit of matter: each stone is conceived as fully describable without any reference to any other portion of matter. This doctrine of 'simple location' and of 'external relations' has been dissolved by modern physics with its wave theory of matter. The physical things which we term stones, stars, planets, molecules, electrons, protons, quanta or energy are each to be conceived as 'modifications of conditions within space-time, extending throughout its whole range'. The notion of physical energy, which is at the base of modern physics, is itself an abstraction from 'the complex energy, emotional and purposeful, inherent in the subjective form of the final synthesis in which each occasion completes itself'. In the new science, Whitehead claimed, 'biology is the study of the larger organisms, whereas physics is the study of the smaller organisms'.[3]

Whitehead in *Science and the Modern World* (1925) therefore rebelled against the abstract and mechanical world-view which had dominated Western thinking for three centuries. Like Wordsworth and the Romantic poets, he felt a moral repulsion against the mechanistic philosophy which left so much out; it reduced morality and beauty to mere 'secondary' properties in the mind of the observer. Above all, it claimed that bodies and minds are 'independent, individual substances, each existing in its own right apart from any necessary reference to each other'.[4] Such an atomistic cosmology merely reflected the prevailing economic and social ethic of *laissez faire* and individualism.

Instead, Whitehead called for an 'age of reconstruction' which would overthrow the sovereignty of the physical sciences, appreciate the findings of biology, and emphasize process, indefiniteness and creativity. It would see nature again as the 'organic unity of the whole' with 'the realization of events disposed in an interlocked community'.[5] There was an urgent need to revive a vision of vital relatedness, to recognize that all is interlinked in the universe. The various parts of nature are so interdependent that they cannot be abstracted without altering their identity and that of the whole.

To illustrate his theme, Whitehead likened nature to a Brazilian rainforest where the wide diversity of trees work together to form overall harmony and vitality:

You may obtain individual specimens of fine trees either in exceptional circumstances, or where human cultivation has

intervened. But in nature the normal way in which trees flourish
is by their association in a forest. Each tree may lose something
of its individual perfection of growth, but they mutually assist
each other in preserving the conditions for survival. The soil is
preserved and shaded; and the microbes necessary for its fertility
are neither scorched, nor frozen, nor washed away. A forest is the
triumph of the organisation of mutually dependent species.[6]

By stressing the relatedness within the natural world, science would
encourage humanity to cooperate more fully. In addition, the scientist
should be aware of the aesthetic and ethical values inherent in
his work.

While as individuals we might experience ourselves as separate
unities, we are in Whitehead's opinion all parts of the whole.
Adopting the doctrine of immanence – that is, the doctrine of the
unity of nature and of the unity of each human life – he concluded
that 'our consciousness of self-identity pervading our life-thread of
occasions is nothing other than knowledge of a special strand of unity
within the general unity of nature'.[7]

In *The Concept of Nature* (1920) Whitehead offered a philosophical account of physics, but in his *Process and Reality: An Essay in
Cosmology* (1929) he presented a grand metaphysical system. He
called his own philosophy the 'philosophy of organism'. Indeed, as
the philosopher R. G. Collingwood has written:

> No one has more vividly realized and described the resemblances,
> the fundamental continuity, running all through the world of
> nature, from its most rudimentary forms in the electron and
> proton and the rest of them to its highest development known
> to us in the mental life of man.[8]

First and foremost, Whitehead is a holistic thinker. Nature for him
consists of moving patterns, the movement of which is essential to
their being. He analyses these patterns into what he calls 'events'.
There are no static substances or concepts in the world, only a
continuous network of events. At the same time, Whitehead does
not think it is possible to discover the real essence of a complex
thing by analysing it into its events or parts (as the logical positivists
asserted). As a holistic thinker, he believes every whole is more than
the sum of its parts.

Everything that exists therefore has its place in the order of nature, which consists of 'actual entities' organized into 'societies'. A society in this sense is 'more than a set of entities to which a class-name applies; that is to say it involves more than a merely mathematical conception of order'.[9] Indeed, in Whitehead's view of the world, all things and events are sensitive to the existence of all others and the relations between them consist of a kind of feeling or desire.

Nature is therefore an organism; that is to say, every existing thing resembles a living organism since its essence depends on the pattern or structure which its components make up. There is no point asking whether a tree *is* green or *appears* green. Human beings who perceive the tree and the tree itself are equally real, elements in the 'society' of living beings. The colour (and beauty) of the tree are real features of the society, but if nobody was looking at the tree it would be completely different because the situation would be different. In this sense, Whitehead can be seen in the British empirical tradition, in believing that nature is nothing more than that which is observed in perception by the senses. Natural science should therefore simply offer an account of the content of perception, not speculate about the cause.

Whitehead rejects the distinction between inorganic nature and organic nature made by physical science. He equally denies the 'bifurcation of nature' into two unequal systems of reality based on Descartes' model of mind and matter. Instead, he argues there is only one reality; whatever appears, is real. Dualism exists only in the sense of the transient and the eternal, the physical and the mental, but ultimately the 'Universe is *one*, because of the universal immanence. There is thus a dualism in this contrast between the unity and multiplicity. Throughout the Universe there reigns the union of opposites which is the ground of dualism.'[10]

Whitehead defines life as having three ingredients – self-enjoyment, creative activity and aim – and argues that all three are present in all things and beings. It is quite wrong, in his view, to consider the 'inorganic' nature (of mountains, seas and skies, for instance) as an abstraction, as a kind of setting or environment for life. Life is all-pervasive; it is everywhere, equally in a child's cry and in a falling stone.

The human mind too is not separate from the rest of nature. Everything enjoys what he calls 'prehensions'; that is, it absorbs what is outside itself into its own being. A compass needle 'prehends' magnetic north by reacting to its magnetic field. A tree prehends the sunlight, and turns its energy into leaves. Human minds are special in being able to prehend propositions, but that does not cut them off from the rest of the creation. They have merely developed functions belonging to life in general, including 'living' stones. Thus subject and object are relative terms.[11] It follows that there is a fundamental continuity in nature which balances the individuality of each occasion of experience.

Nature is a process as well as an organism. The activities of the organism are united into a single activity which is the organism itself. Substance and activity are one and the same. The process of nature is not therefore merely cyclic but a kind of 'creative advance'. Like Bergson, Whitehead thought that the organism undergoes a process of evolution in which it constantly takes on new forms and produces new forms in every part of itself. The cosmic process, according to Whitehead, has two main characteristics: 'extensiveness', in that it develops in a setting of time and space; and 'aim', that is, it develops towards a goal.

Our world is only one among many possible worlds which no doubt exist in other 'cosmic epochs'. Since the laws which define it are arbitrary, and not always perfectly obeyed, disorder enters the natural order. But this gives rise to change; there is accordingly a gradual transition to a new type of order.

No doubt partly owing to his mathematical training, Whitehead assumes that a world of necessary and eternal truths is behind the cosmic process. He rejects Bergson's relativistic anti-rationality. His cosmic process therefore rests on space-time and eternal objects. As in the work of Plato, the 'eternal object' attracts and encourages the process of a living thing towards its realization. In Whitehead's expression, it acts as a 'lure'. Even the brownness of compost and the greenness of a tree partake of eternal objects. The world of eternal objects is the source or ground of natural processes in the everyday world. And in Platonic fashion, he asserts that 'the real world is good when it is beautiful'.[12]

For Whitehead, God too is an eternal object and his primordial nature encompasses the possibilities of eternal objects themselves. God is also infinite, the infinite lure towards which all process aims: 'He is the lure of feeling, the eternal urge of desire.' All things are therefore involved in creative and end-directed activity for which God supplies the initial desire. As such, he is like Aristotle's unmoved mover, a first cause which is causeless. He is the source of all creativity.

Whitehead's organic philosophy is not without its flaws. While reacting against the positivism of the nineteenth century, he retained many of the aspirations of the Enlightenment. In his *Adventures in Ideas* (1933), he tried to depict the effect of certain ideas in promoting 'the slow drift of mankind to civilization'. He was firmly wedded to the idea of progress, and betrayed a Whig conception of history as the expansion of freedom and the move from force to persuasion (he was writing before the rise of Hitler). He saw in particular that the 'Western races' had advanced far from the 'savage' state to 'civilization', which he defined as a society exhibiting the five qualities of 'Truth, Beauty, Adventure, Art, Peace'.[13] His discussions of 'lower' and 'higher' civilizations and of the vigour of different races recall the worst vapourings of the Social Darwinists.

In the long run, however, Whitehead promotes an idea of civilization as a condition of peace which combines a 'Harmony of Harmonies' from which restless egotism is excluded. It also has a 'Unity of Adventure' which includes Eros, the 'living urge towards all possibilities, claiming the goodness of their realization'.[14]

It remains unclear in Whitehead's philosophy how the world of eternal objects or forms is organized and how it is connected to this world. Such a Platonic idea would also seem to go against his organic philosophy of process and desire. Nevertheless, with all the complex and subtle understanding of modern physics, logic and mathematics, he elaborated a philosophy which is profoundly in tune with ancient 'earth wisdom' and can inspire the best in modern green thinking.

## *Creative Evolution: Henri Bergson*

Bergson (1859–1941) was the most influential of modern anti-mechanistic and process metaphysicians and his dynamic philosophy offers important insights for the creation of a new ecological sensibility. Outwardly his life was uneventful; with an English mother and a Polish father, he lived and died in France. Straddling two centuries, he was elected in 1900 to the chair of modern philosophy at the Collège de France. But behind the scholarly appearance lay a revolutionary mind in flux. He criticized dogmatic naturalism (which insisted that only natural science could lead to truth) as well as the static materialism of the nineteenth century.

Bergson was not against the proper use of reason, but tried to show the inadequacy of reason to grasp experience and comprehend life fully. Intelligence helps man go beyond instinct and orders the world about him but intuition surpasses it and achieves true knowledge. Beyond the two habitual modes of mental activity, instinct and intelligence, intuition is a kind of empathy: 'By the sympathetic communication which it establishes between us and the rest of beings ... it introduces us into the real domain of life, which is reciprocal interpenetration [compénétration réciproque], indefinitely continued creation.'[15]

Intuition is a combination of scientific objectivity and artistic subjectivity. Unlike the intellect, it does not treat facts and things as outside, external, discrete existences which we analyse and judge. Like the imagination, it can penetrate the veil of appearance to comprehend the true nature of things. It is a completion rather than a denial of reason. Above all, it shows the world to be in constant flux; Bergson's is a philosophy of change.[16]

Central to Bergson's world-view is the notion of duration (durée) which is revealed to the individual in immediate experience. We may conceive of time in two principal ways. There is calendar or clock time, which presents time as discrete moments linked in a linear sequence, stretching behind us and ahead of us. It depicts time in spatial terms, as a succession of events. But there is also time as flux, a time flow not measurable in relation to some standard; it is absolute, always present and yet never ceasing. This flux is known to us by a direct inner perceiving, by intuition and not by an intellectual act. It coincides with our subjective experience of life as an indivisible continuum and not as a series of separate states.

In his first work, Time and Free Will (1889), Bergson introduced the idea of 'pure time' as 'real duration' (durée réelle). In everyday life, we easily fall victim to the artificial notion of time as a succession of separate events and thereby lose contact with our true selves and reality:

> Consciousness, goaded by an insatiable desire to separate, substitutes the symbol for the reality, or perceives the reality only through a symbol. As the self thus refracted, and thereby broken to pieces, is much better adapted to the requirements of

social life in general and language in particular, consciousness prefers it and gradually loses sight of the fundamental self.[17]

With this view of time, Bergson rejected any mechanistic approach to understanding reality. In his view, a vital principle, an original life force (*élan vital*) is at work in mind and matter throughout the universe. In his most famous work, *Creative Evolution* (1907), Bergson argued that it is this creative urge, and not Darwin's principle of natural selection, that is at the heart of evolution. The life force is passed down from one generation of living beings to another by way of individual organisms. But creative evolution is also 'pluri-dimensional', for the life force is responsible for creating all the numerous varieties of living forms. It is the 'profound cause' of variations which are transmitted regularly and form new species.[18] Bergson conceived of the life force as if it were a river flowing among the rocks and mountains of the world. It is like a visible current, rising at a certain moment, diverging but always intensifying as it advances.

Just as the smallest grain of dust is an integral part of the entire solar system, all organized beings give way to the same drive:

> The animal takes off from the plant, man rides on animality, and the whole of humanity, in space and time, is an immense army which gallops alongside each of us, in front and behind us, in a sweeping charge capable of toppling all resistances and leaping over many obstacles, perhaps even death.[19]

Bergson is still sufficiently Promethean to see evolution in such aggressive terms as a cavalry charge destroying all before it. He presents life as a cosmic battle between matter and spirit. He also speaks of man as the purpose and end of evolution. Although we are only the result of one divergent tendency, and might well have developed in a different direction, it is our species alone that has broken free from the weight of dead matter. Man is pre-eminently intellectual, but he can further evolve in a spiritual direction and develop his intuition. We are at a crucial stage in our development:

> Life as a whole, from the initial impulsion that thrusts it into the world, appears as a wave which rises, and which is opposed by the descending movement of matter. On the greater part of its

surface, at different heights, the current is converted by matter
into a vortex. At one point it passes freely, dragging with it the
obstacle which will weigh on its progress but it will not stop it.
At that point is humanity: it is our privileged situation.[20]

In ancient metaphysics and nineteenth-century physics, as Bergson
put it, 'all is given' (*tout est donné*); the future is predetermined by the
past. In Bergson's world, however, the doors of the future are open to
creative and spontaneous change. The world of physics results from
the self-creative activity of life itself. There are no final causes; the
laws of nature are merely the shapes which for a time nature takes.
Ultimately, there is only the play of energy and life in the organic
whole of the universe.

Bergson sometimes wrote as if spirit and matter were separate.
At first sight in *Matter and Memory* (1910), he appears profoundly
dualistic. But while recognizing the reality of spirit and the reality
of matter, he hoped to overcome the theoretical difficulties which
have traditionally beset dualism. He defines matter as 'an aggregate
of "images"'. Matter is a devitalized form of life which moves
in an opposite direction to consciousness: 'Matter is necessity,
consciousness is freedom. This is what life is: freedom inserting
itself within necessity, turning it to its own use.'[21]

The brain is a kind of active filter, selecting and sorting messages:
it is the 'organ of attention to life'.[22] The body is a centre of action;
the moving point pressing forward, in which consciousness manifests
itself in universal becoming. The spirit is 'pure-time' existence, it is the
prolonging of the past into the present; it unites with matter in the act
of perception, but the union can only be expressed in terms of time
and not of space. This act involves overcoming the distinction between
matter and spirit; at a deeper intuitive level all is one. No wonder that
Bergson was elected president of the Society for Psychical Research
in 1913.

Ultimately, Bergson, like Plotinus, identified the individual spirit
in man with the universal world-spirit. While calling for a union
between science and metaphysics, Bergson went beyond both to enter
the realm of pure mysticism. Mystical insight is achieved not through
concentration but through relaxation: it involves letting go, floating
with the living stream of life: 'True mystics simply open their souls
to the oncoming wave.'[23] They are nothing less than surf-riders of
the infinite.

Bergson's great contribution to eco-philosophy was his revolt against mechanistic materialism. He reintroduced the notion of process and energy into Western metaphysics, breaking down the old rigid distinction between the mind and the body, the observer and the observed, the whole and its parts. His depiction of time as a continuous flow has been widely influential; it can be be traced in the 'stream of consciousness' novels of James Joyce and Virginia Woolf as well as in surrealism. He placed great emphasis on direct experience and intuition in understanding the living world. In doing so, he provides a living philosophy relevant to our era. His great insight is that to understand the movement of life one must move with the current; it is not enough to remain on the bank as a detached and lonely onlooker.[24] Bergson should find a central place in the green pantheon for his vision of the dynamic nature of the world with its vital, evolving, never-ending processes.

### Shepherd of being: Martin Heidegger

Bergson and Whitehead are difficult thinkers; the German metaphysician Heidegger (1889-1976) is notoriously so. Many have found his metaphysics incomprehensible. Nevertheless, he is one of the most creative philosophers of the twentieth century and he amply repays the effort to understand his work. The American scholar George Steiner has called him 'the metaphysician of ecologism'; certainly his philosophy has a great deal to say about our place on earth.[25]

Heidegger's primarily interest is in ontology; that is, the study of being. Inspired by the pre-Socratic thinkers, he criticized and dismissed the whole of Western philosophy from Plato onwards for having lost touch with being. Recognizing that 'language is the house of Being', Heidegger paid particular attention to the etymology of words, and tried to revive their original meaning by going back to their root.[26] He therefore reminds his readers that the Greeks understood truth to be *a-lethia*, 'un-hiddenness'. Truth for Heidegger involves 'letting-be', letting something be what it is, something which 'exposes itself to what is, as such'.[27]

In Heidegger's view, there is an inextricable link between the classificatory manner of Western metaphysics and the will to the rational and technological mastery over nature. He calls this nihilism. He was deeply critical of the technocratic mentality and of the rampant consumerism in industrial societies. In their place, he

recommended a kind of 'essential thinking' which listens to the
voice of being, as opposed to analytical thinking which destroys
what it dissects. Towards the end of his life, he recommended that
humans should cease being lords of creation and become 'shepherds
of Being'. Heidegger started out life as a professional philosopher
only to end up as a mystical poet.

Heidegger was a key existentialist thinker in his analysis of the
human condition and his major work *Time and Being* (1927) had
a profound influence on Jean-Paul Sartre's *Being and Nothingness*.
But, like several German ecologists at the time, Heidegger was drawn
to National Socialism; as rector of a German university, he unwisely
told his students that the state of the Third Reich represented reality
and the *Führer* was a vehicle for truth.[28] He was no doubt attracted
by the Nazi attachment to the soil and peasant life.[29] He never
repudiated his support for National Socialism and remained silent
about the holocaust, but it would be wrong to dismiss Heidegger's
philosophy as intrinsically 'fascist'; in the search for being, he leaves
politics far behind him.

In his philosophizing, Heidegger adopts a phenomenological
approach; that is to say, his method is not one of proof but of
description, inviting others to see things his way. In his desire to
examine the data of experience, he makes no distinction between
consciousness and the external world. There is no such thing as a
perceiving subject who is a spectator of an objective world; there is no
gap between the observer and the observed. Heidegger's philosophy
thus does not begin from the observation of external phenomena,
nor from the introspective investigation of the mind, but from a
living participation in the world. No abstract rationalist, Heidegger
recognizes the importance of feeling and intuition in philosophical
understanding: moods, such as *angst* (dread or anxiety), can light up
'the way we find ourselves'.

Heidegger's overriding concern is with ontology, the study of being.
But he starts his study of the totality of being through a particular
being, man. In his analysis of human existence, Heidegger shows
how man's 'being-in-the-world' is characterized by his relationship
to members of his community and surrounding objects.[30] His being
is inextricably linked to nothingness; man stands out from the world
as being incomplete and uniquely conscious of his own death: 'In
anguish, the human being discovers himself confronted by Nothing,
which is the possible impossibility of his existence.' It is his awareness

of the 'nothingness', which is an integral part of his 'being', that sets him from other beings and objects. In this sense, 'man alone exists. Rocks are.'

Man consists of 'facticity' (the set of facts about him, all those elements in life which are simply given) as well as 'possibility' (his open and unmade future). He cannot change or deny his facticity but he is responsible for how he views it and how he creates his own future through his actions. What Heidegger calls *Dasein* ('being there') involves an individual's awareness of having a purpose and potential. Man is 'thrown' into the world and finds himself there, not knowing where he has come from or where he is going.

In Western civilization, it is very easy for human beings to remain 'fallen' (*verfallen*) to be absorbed in everyday affairs and preoccupations, thereby abandoning their possibilities. Such a condition is 'inauthentic'.[31] It involves being lost in the 'mass' of society and living only in the present. It means 'being in the midst of the world', living in an artificial man-made world with a mechanical culture. It fails to take into account the inevitability of one's own death. Overwhelmed by anxiety and fear, the inauthentic individual defines himself as merely a passive object among objects.

Heidegger sees our environment as consisting of objects (things and beings) that can be used; our relation to them as such is characterized by concern. They have the fundamental property of being 'ready-at-hand' but when investigated scientifically or exploited commercially they appear as being 'present-on-hand'. A mountain is 'ready-at-hand', a quarry is 'present-on-hand'. The inauthentic or alienated person reduces the self and others to 'on-hand' beings.

Heidegger makes a similar distinction in his account of time. Objective time can be seen as a succession of discrete moments. Experienced subjectively, as Bergson observed, it reveals itself as inseparable phases of existence, in which the past and the future are as real as the present. In a sense, the future comes before the present, for present action is a realization of future projects. Heidegger rejects the notion of eternity, and insists that life is one of passing time.

Our Western industrial-technocratic society has created an inauthentic world in which things and beings are seen merely as objects to be used and exploited, means to our ends, 'things-on-hand'. The authentic person, however, can break out of the circle. He takes up his own past ('facticity') and launches himself into the future, aware that he can realize his potential and shape himself through his choices. He recognizes that he stands out as the only being that is open and responsible for what he is. He sees himself as a unique being among a community of other beings that are 'at-hand' and not 'on-hand'. He can overcome feelings of guilt (for what he has not done) and anxiety (provoked by a sense of the 'nothingness' at the centre of being) and acknowledge boldly his finitude on earth. He can make himself authentic through his deliberate choice.

Towards the end of his life, Heidegger became interested not so much in human beings as in being in general. He felt that 'the Being of beings' is the only proper object of ontological thought; it meant going beyond a description of the world to reveal it as it is. Where geology, for instance, studies the material composition and history of rocks, ontology tries to 'think the being of the rock', to experience how being manifests itself in the rock.[32]

Heidegger looked forward to a time when we would overcome the 'technological-scientific-industrial character' as the sole criterion of our sojourn on earth.[33] He felt that the anthropocentric attitude in Western civilization had led to the technocratic mentality and the desire to dominate and conquer nature for our own ends. Technology turns all beings into objective, quantifiable and disposable material. In the modern era,

> the object-character of technological domination spreads itself over the earth ever more quickly, ruthlessly and completely . . . the humanness of man and the thingness of things dissolve into the calculated market value of a market which not only spans the whole earth . . . but also . . . trades in the nature of Being and thus subjects all beings to the trade of a calculation that dominates most tenaciously in those areas where there is no need of numbers.[34]

Technology, according to Heidegger, is a 'setting-upon' and 'ordering' of nature. The misuse of technology in the past has led to the violation of nature. Anticipating all the central concerns of modern ecologists, Heidegger wrote in 1949:

> The revealing that rules in modern technology is a challenging, which puts to nature the unreasonable demand that it supply energy which can be extracted and stored as such. But does this not hold true for the old windmill as well? No. Its sails do indeed turn in the wind; they are left entirely to the wind's

blowing. But the windmill does not unlock energy from the air currents in order to store it.

In contrast, a tract of land is challenged in the hauling out of coal and ore. The earth now reveals itself as a coal mining district, the soil as a mineral deposit. The field that the peasant formerly cultivated and set in order appears different from how it did when to set in order still meant to take care and maintain. The work of the peasant does not challenge the soil of the field. In sowing grain it places seed in the keeping of the forces of growth and watches over its increase. But meanwhile even the cultivation of the field has come under the grip of another kind of setting-in-order, which *sets upon* nature. It sets upon it in the sense of challenging it. Agriculture is now the mechanized food industry. Air is now set upon to yield nitrogen, the earth to yield ore, ore to yield uranium, for example; uranium is set upon to yield atomic energy, which can be released for destruction or for peaceful use.[35]

Heidegger argued like ecologists that man should not be the master of nature but let beings display themselves and reach their fruition. He goes beyond Sartre's humanistic existentialism, which places man at the centre of the world. He also went beyond the kind of stewardship which still husbands nature for human ends. What Heidegger sought was true being, which is 'ecstatic dwelling in the nearness of Being. It is the guardianship, that is, the care for Being.'[36]

The earth is not to be associated with the idea of the mass of matter deposited somewhere, or with the merely astronomical idea of the planet: 'In the things that arise, earth occurs essentially as the sheltering agent.'[37] Authentic individuals save the earth. 'Saving the earth does not master the earth and does not subjugate it, which is merely one step from boundless spoilation.'[38] Dwelling on the earth, man should become and make himself open to what Heidegger calls the 'fourfold of Being': 'By a *primal oneness* the four – earth and sky, divinities and mortals – become together in one.'[39]

Descartes once described philosophy as a tree, of which the branches are the several sciences and the root is metaphysics. Heidegger believed that we must go beyond the root of the tree to the ground which supports it. And the ground is the light or truth of being. He wished to go beyond analytical thinking to what he called 'essential thinking', a thinking which does not calculate and dissect but which listens to the soundless voice of being. It asks no questions. It is reverential and primordial. As he says in 'The End of Philosophy and the Task of Thinking' (1966), 'the meditative man is to experience the untrembling heart of unconcealment' in 'the place of stillness'.[40] It seems very close to the Taoist idea of contemplation as a passive and receptive opening of oneself to the world.

Language is the 'house of Being', but in the end Heidegger felt that it was impossible to convey the meaning of being. In his later works, he referred to *Dasein* (being) with two crossed strokes through the word to show that he could not really discuss it.[41] He was trying to say something about the unsayable, about something which is about to be revealed but never is. In the end he was reduced to poetry, 'the establishment of Being by means of the word':

> When the early morning light quietly
> grows above the mountains . . .

> The world's darkening never reaches
> to the light of Being.

> We are too late for the gods and too
> early for Being. Being's poem,
> just begun, is man.

British philosophers brought up in an empirical and analytical tradition are naturally unsympathetic to Heidegger. Gilbert Ryle talked of his 'self-ruinous subjectivism or windy mysticism'; A. J. Ayer dismissed contemptuously his philosophy as a systematic act of misunderstanding of the word 'to be'. In Heidegger's eyes they had simply given up their birthright to dwell in the house of language. He finds company with the great mystics; but while he replaced God with Being, he renounced eternity and remained faithful to the earth with its passing seasons and cycle of life and death. His understanding of Western man's fallen being in the midst of the world, his criticism of his dominant technology and rational metaphysics, his call for authentic dwelling on earth, his search for reverential thinking and, finally, his openness to the Being of all beings provide fertile soil for the growth of a vigorous eco-philosophy for our dismal times. Ecology after all is the study of where we dwell.

# 27

# THE COSMIC JOY OF
# THE NEW SCIENCE

> The world thus appears as a complicated tissue of
> events, in which connections of different kinds alternate
> or overlap or combine and thereby determine the texture
> of the whole.
>
> Werner Heisenberg

The old view of the universe as a machine made up of hard, separate atoms is now obsolete. Modern physics presents the universe as a constant flow of transforming energy. The traditional distinction between substance and form, energy and matter, no longer applies. The new model of reality is remarkably similar to that of the ancient Chinese and early Greek philosophers who saw everything interconnected, living and changing. The distinction embedded in the structure of European languages between the subject and object can no longer hold in philosophy and science: both being part of a larger whole, the observer affects the observed, and the scientist cannot separate himself from his experiment. As a result, the universe has become a much more indeterminate, dynamic and mysterious place.

Nature is once again considered to be self-organizing and self-regulating. Creativity, spontaneity and freedom are central features of this new picture of the natural world. Immanent ends are revealed. The new vision of the universe is evolutionary. It links up with the holistic thinking of ecology, and it revives an animistic view of nature which existed in Europe before the scientific revolution, and which still holds sway in many parts of the world. In short, it is now possible to talk of the rebirth of nature.[1]

## The origin and fate of the universe

Since humans first began to ponder the origin and destiny of the universe, there have been three major competing views or models.

The Judaeo-Christian and Muslim traditions claim that there was a creator not long ago who set everything rolling. The Greeks believed that the world had always existed and would always exist, moving on in cycles forever. A third view holds that the world was created at a stroke a long time ago and will end in a moment of destruction in a finite time.

The last view has recently been given scientific backing. Cosmologists have been talking of the initial act of creation as a Big Bang occurring some 15 billion years ago (the English astronomer Fred Hoyle coined the phrase although he did not like the idea). In this scenario, the universe of matter and energy, space and time, appeared in an infinitely small and dense state and has been expanding and 'thinning out' ever since.[2] In 1929 the American astronomer Edwin Hubble observed that wherever you look, distant galaxies are moving quickly away from us, and concluded that the universe must be expanding.

The Big Bang is the 'primal orgasm'. The cosmos is like a growing organism, within which everything is related: microbes, plants and animals all evolving from the same common ground. Like the ancient Greek creation myth of the Orphic egg, it suggests that all things came from a common living source. But where is evolution heading?

According to the calculations of many modern cosmologists, two possible alternatives exist for the future, depending on how much mass there is in the observable universe: either it will continue to expand for ever, becoming darker as stars grow old and die, or the expansion will one day come to a halt and be reversed. The universe would then contract and implode on itself.

The universe remains a mysterious and awesome presence. One recent speculation is that a kind of matter exists the nature of which is entirely unknown. This matter has generally been called 'dark matter', although some astronomers have called it 'missing mass'.[3] Its existence has been inferred from a study of the conduct of galaxies and of the haloes of gas which surround them. It is impossible to explain the behaviour of galaxies, especially the way they form, simply by the gravitational attraction of the observable stars and gas within them, without supposing there is a great deal of hidden matter. Recent estimates suggest that this 'dark matter' makes up anything from 90 per cent to 99 per cent of the universe.

Some of this strange matter may well be the remnants of stars. It also includes black holes, made when stars die and collapse in upon themselves under their own gravity, or when matter funnels on to a supermassive core at the heart of a galaxy or quasar. Most of it is likely to consist of utterly unknown and strange particles. By their very nature, they are extremely difficult to detect and measure; they are only inferred by their gravitational effects. Black holes are not really black, but glow like a hot body, and the smaller ones are easier to detect since they glow more than the bigger ones.

If there is more than a critical amount of dark matter, the cosmic expansion will gradually come to an end and the universe will begin to contract again, pulled together in a final collapse. Time, space and matter will be crushed out of existence. The ultimate fate of the universe will be a catastrophic implosion: having begun with a Big Bang, the world might well end with a Big Crunch.[4]

## All is relative, to a degree

None of these speculations could have got off the ground without the tremendous revolution in physics earlier in the twentieth century, which arguably was more important for our view of the world than the Copernican and Darwinian revolutions. The development of relativity theory and quantum mechanics resulted in a complete change of the paradigm within which scientists perceive the physical world and our place within it.[5] It not only transformed our notions of time and space, but transformed the old static view of the universe into a dance of cosmic energy.

One of the most important notions underlying the theory of relativity is the notion of fields of energy. The nineteenth-century English physicist Michael Faraday, who believed in the unity of nature, first introduced the idea of an electromagnetic field. He thought of fields in terms of patterns of forces, like the lines of force around a magnet, which existed either in empty space or in what he called 'aether'. Although Faraday established the existence of electrical and magnetic fields, it was left to the Scottish physicist James Clerk Maxwell to give a quantitative description of them in mathematical equations which struck Einstein like a revelation. For Maxwell the invisible field animated space: it not only governs the compass needle but, as he put it, could 'weave a web across the sky'.[6]

Albert Einstein (1879–1955) took up the notion of an electromagnetic field but dispensed with the idea of ether, arguing in his special theory of relativity in 1905 that the electromagnetic field permeates all space. Although it can interact with matter, it is independent of it and has energy and momentum. Einstein made the final synthesis in his famous equation $E=mc^2$ (where E is energy, m mass and c the speed of light), maintaining the equivalence of mass and energy and that they can be converted into each other.

In his first theory of special relativity, Einstein showed that the only reference point in the universe is the speed of light: it remains a constant absolute unrelated to anything else. All observers thus measure the same speed of light, however fast they may be moving. This simple idea established the equation of the relationship between mass and energy. One of the practical applications of this theory of relativity was the conversion of mass into energy in the atom bomb.[7] The world has not been the same since.

The theory of special relativity has fundamentally changed our understanding of the nature of time. In Newtonian physics, time, like space, was considered absolute and independent. With Einstein, notions of 'before', 'now' and 'after' in an arrow of time going in one direction become relative terms. Since information cannot travel faster than the speed of light and the speed of light is constant, for observers in different frames of reference 'now' has different meanings. For instance, to an astronomer on earth, an event in his observatory may appear to be simultaneous with an event observed through his telescope on Mars. Given the speed of light, the event in the earthbound observatory would have occurred *after* the event on Mars. And to an observer on Mars, the event on Mars would have occurred *before* the event on earth. The mind-boggling implication is that the future is somehow enfolded in the past and that time travel may be theoretically possible.

The second part of Einstein's theory, elaborated in 1915, known as the general theory of relativity, covers the relative motion between accelerated systems. By extending the concept of field to gravitation, it describes the gravitational field as a space-time continuum 'curved' or 'warped' in the presence of matter. Gravity may not therefore be a force like other forces.

General relativity further predicts that time will run more slowly near a massive body like the earth. The notion puts an end to absolute time, and implies that each observer must have his own measure of time as recorded by a clock carried with him. The clocks of different observers would not agree: a clock in a ski hut does not tick at the same speed as one in a mine.

Before Einstein's discovery in 1905, space and time were considered a fixed and static arena in which events took place, but which was not influenced by what went on in it. Bodies moved about, forces attracted and repelled, yet time and space continued on for ever. With the general theory of relativity, space and time are now thought of as dynamic qualities in an interrelated and interdependent universe. The English physicist Stephen Hawking sums up its implications: 'When a body moves, or a force acts, it affects the curvature of space and time – and in turn the structure of space-time affects the way in which bodies move and forces act. Space and time not only affect but also are affected by everything that happens in the universe.'[8]

The old notion of a static and eternal universe has therefore given way to the idea of a dynamic, expanding universe which probably had a finite beginning (possibly 15 billion years ago) and will probably have a finite end. The result is that modern physics explores processes ranging from quarks to quasars, and portrays the entire material world 'as but a grand illusion, spun on the loom of the force fields'.[9]

## The uncertainty of quantum mechanics

The second great revolution in science which has helped transform our concept of the universe has been quantum mechanics, a system to explain the behaviour of small phenomena: atoms, molecules and elementary particles. In quantum theory, elementary particles such as protons and electrons are considered to be wave packets, or vibrating quanta. They take a wave or a particle form in fields which are part of a vacuum. Yet it would be wrong to infer that it is empty and lifeless. 'A vacuum is not inert and featureless, but alive with throbbing energy and vitality.'[10]

The German physicist Werner Heisenberg (1901–76), who helped develop quantum mechanics, further helped change with his 'uncertainty principle' our notion of causation and overthrow the doctrine of scientific determinism. It punctured once and for all the hope of developing a science which would enable us to predict everything if we could only know the complete state of the universe at any given moment.

Heisenberg's uncertainty principle asserts that the position and momentum of a particle cannot both be known with certainty because the process of establishing the former must affect the latter: a quantum of light used to measure the position of a particle will disturb the particle and change its velocity in a way which cannot be predicted. The more certain we are concerning the location of a particle, the less certain we are concerning its momentum, and vice versa. The position of an electron travelling at a known velocity, for instance, can only be expressed in terms of a probability. This implies an uncertainty of both its identity and destiny, and if identity and destiny are in doubt one cannot be certain what effects will follow from a given cause. Jerky transitions take place from one form of energy to another through discrete quantum leaps; the forms are related but cannot said to be causally connected. Quantum mechanics thus introduces an element of unpredictability and randomness into physics; all that the scientist is left with is statistical probabilities.

## The grand unified theory

The general theory of relativity describes the large-scale structure of the universe, while quantum mechanics covers the extremely small-scale phenomena. But there may well be a new synthesis afoot: particle physics, the study of the smallest structures in nature, may be about to combine with cosmology, the study of the universe as a whole: the microcosm with the macrocosm, the centre with the circumference.[11]

Many theoretical physicists have tried to do away with the idea implicit in the Big Bang theory of an arrow of time going in a particular direction. Stephen Hawking, for instance, who contributed to the Big Bang theory in his early work, has recently tried to do away with the moment of creation – the edge of time called a 'singularity' by mathematicians – in his search for a new theory that will incorporate general relativity and quantum mechanics into a single, unified quantum theory for large and small parts of the universe. In his view, 'there is a possibility that the singularity may be smeared out and that space and time together may form a closed four-dimensional surface without a boundary or edge, like the surface of the Earth but with two extra dimensions. This would mean that the universe was completely self-contained.'[12]

This description of the universe in terms of a closed space-time, completely self-contained with no edges and no beginning or end, leaves nothing for a creator to do.[13] The notion derives from the 'many worlds' interpretation, which claims that in theory there are many different worlds, with many different sizes. In its extreme form, it suggests that the whole universe splits into two or more replicas of itself every time any quantum system is obliged to choose between two possible states.[14]

This kind of speculation about the universe does, of course, have its limitations. It may be by chance that we are living in a region of the universe which appears smooth and uniform, but elsewhere it may be very different and more chaotic. Indeed, the very appearance of smoothness in the universe may be simply a result of the way we see it. In other words, the universe appears the way it is simply because we exist. This has been called the 'anthropic principle', and in a strong form it suggests that there may be many different regions of a single universe, each with its own structure and laws, only a few of which would perhaps have conditions like the earth for sentient and intelligent life. The answer to the question why the universe is the way we see it, would then be that it could not have been otherwise: if it had been different we would not be there to ask the questions.

Whereas traditional physics was the greatest threat to the growth of an ecological consciousness, the new physics can inspire it. It has destroyed the myth of the scientist as a passive observer conducting experiments with complete objectivity. Every act at the particle level is disruptive, and the manner in which we choose to make an observation influences the results of the interaction. It reaffirms the Kantian belief that we do not see things in themselves but only aspects of things. It depicts the world as an assembly of animated fields and nature as an invisible web of forces. On a broader front, it has helped break down the traditional dichotomy in Western philosophy between the perceiving subject (man) and the perceived object (nature). It overthrows the illusion of apartness – that man is separate from nature.

Taken together, the findings of relativity theory and quantum physics transcend old-style materialism and reanimate the physical world. By describing the fundamental particles of nature as being like waves, they challenge the dominant scientific view since Democritus of the world as an arrangement of changeless and separate atoms in a flat and absolute grid of time and space. They displace the deterministic picture of the universe of traditional physics and introduce the principle of indeterminacy.

Nature now appears as a constant flow of energy fluctuations and transformations. The modern concept of the universe as a sea of energy thus is not only closer to Aristotle's vision than to Newton's, but presents a picture of reality which is very close to that of the founders of science, the Chinese Taoists. The essential feature of the universe, Chuang Tzu observed, some 2,300 years ago, is 'the constant flow of transformation and change'.[15]

## Chaos: the centre cannot hold

Quantum theory suggests that at a particle level, physical processes are essentially indeterminate, predictable only in terms of probabilities. In recent years, there has been a growing awareness among mathematicians, physicists, biologists, chemists, meteorologists and ecologists that indeterminacy may well be inherent in systems at different levels of complexity. To deal with this indeterminism and uncertainty at the heart of nature, a new theory has developed, known as chaos theory. A sign that it has come of age is that a Centre for Nonlinear Studies has been set up at the famous scientific establishment at Los Alamos in the United States to coordinate the work on chaos.

'Where chaos begins, classical science stops.'[16] In the surreal world of chaos theory, familiar geometrical shapes such as circles and ellipses can suddenly give way to complex mathematical structures known as fractals. First developed by mathematicians and meteorologists, the theory cuts across traditional boundaries of science, and considers all kinds of wildness and irregularity observed in nature: the turbulence of weather, the formation of clouds, the eddying of water in a stream, the swirling of sand in a desert storm, the clustering of stars, the crashing of a sea wave, the fluctuations of wildlife populations, the oscillations of the heart and the brain, the dripping of a tap, the motion of a boat moored to a buoy, the collisions of atoms in a gas. Systems which seem to have obeyed precise laws can act in a chaotic manner. A whole new world of possibilities is opening up.

Pierre-Simon de Laplace, an eighteenth-century French mathematican, believed that the universe followed a predetermined path.

It could not be otherwise and all was theoretically predictable. In his *Philosophical Essays on Probabilities*, he surmised:

> An intelligence knowing, at a given instance of time, all forces acting in nature, as well as the momentary position of all things of which the universe consists, would be able to comprehend the motions of the largest bodies of the world and those of the lightest atoms in one single formula, provided his intellect were sufficiently powerful to subject all data to analysis; to him nothing would be uncertain, both past and future would be present in his eyes.[17]

The possibility of total prediction, long taken to be the basis of scientific method, is now in extreme doubt. In the history of the physical sciences, the twentieth century may well be remembered for three great revolutions: relativity theory, quantum mechanics and chaos theory.

Chaos theory was a product of the mathematical imagination inspired by physics. It has helped refine our concept of randomness; it has shown the complexity of nature; it has punctured the illusion of discovering a theory which is capable of predicting all phenomena. It has checked the reductionist trend in science which seeks to break down natural systems into their constituent parts – quarks, chromosomes or neurons – and has gone looking once again for the whole picture. Chaos is a science of process rather than of stability, of becoming rather than being.

Some chaos theorists, no doubt reflecting the chaotic nature of late-twentieth-century life, have even suggested that it rings the death knell of their subjects. The American ecologist William M. Schaffer, for instance, believes that the theory undermines the basic assumptions of ecology that there is a natural balance in nature, that states of equilibrium are reached in an ecosystem through the most efficient use of food resources and the least waste, and that nature left alone will follow a beneficial path. 'What passes for fundamental concepts in ecology is a mist before the fury of the storm – in this case, a full, nonlinear storm.'[18]

It may be difficult to make mathematical models with enough variables to make them capable of predicting the fluctuation of bee populations, for example, but it does not follow that the existing findings of ecology are going to be overthrown by chaos theory.

On the contrary, in many areas it confirms the traditional insights
of ecology. Chaos theory does not deny natural order; it denies static
equilibrium, and reaffirms Heraclitus' notion of flux. The universe
may not be ruled by eternal, unchanging laws but this does not mean
that the observed regularities in nature are nonexistent.

Chaos theory reintroduces into science the ancient notion of
'self-similarity', of the correspondence between the microcosm and
the macrocosm. As soon as man began thinking about these things, it
seemed natural to imagine the very big and the very small as extensions
of the known. Not only did the poet Blake see the world in a grain of
sand, but the philosopher and mathematician Leibniz also imagined
a drop of water containing a whole universe. While modern physicists
have been breaking things apart – with massive machines – in order
to examine each part one at a time, chaos theory has suggested that
if one looks at the whole, the power of self-similarity exists at much
greater levels of complexity.[19]

It also reintroduces an organic way of perceiving the world. Just as,
in biology, life creates order from a sea of disorder, so in physics it
would seem to create patterns out of formlessness. Erwin Schrödinger,
quantum pioneer, observed: 'A living organism has the astonishing
gift of concentrating a "stream of disorder" on itself and thus escaping
the decay into atomic chaos.'[20]

In mathematical models of chaotic processes, objects do not
establish a simple equilibrium, but develop in complex, nonrepetitive
patterns. Comparatively simple systems like a couple of pendulums
have been found to behave chaotically, and so have highly complex
ones like the solar system. An inherent spontaneity in the life of
nature, denied by Newtonian physics but recognized by Bergson
and biological vitalists, would therefore appear to exist. The chaos
of nature thus provides 'the matrix for evolutionary creativity.'[21]

The mechanism of evolutionary change according to neo-Darwinian
theory is random mutation caused by genetic shuffling. From this
perspective, chance rules in the universe. But is this point of view
confirmed by chaos theory?

There may be principles or laws yet to be discovered, influencing
the organization of complex systems. Despite the prevailing fashion
for chaos theory, at a deeper level the apparent randomness may
follow underlying patterns: there may be general laws of disorder, a
kind of 'deterministic chaos'. The American mathematician Mitchell
Feigenbaum, for instance, who was one of the founders of chaos

theory at Los Alamos, has discovered that the onset of chaos occurs in a defined sequence of steps, with apparent mathematical regularities characterized by two universal numbers. Such universality suggests that complex systems may remain subject to general laws or principles which do not necessarily conflict with the underlying laws of physics.

Einstein, for one, was very unhappy about the implications of relativity and quantum physics in placing chance and randomness at the heart of the universe. It was not only against his 'scientific instincts' but he felt that such a view reflected the 'rules of the gaming house'. He wrote to his colleague Max Born:

> You believe in a God who plays dice, and I in complete law and order in a world which objectively exists, and which I, in a wildly speculative way, am trying to capture. I firmly *believe*, but I hope that someone will discover a more realistic way, or rather a more tangible basis than it has been my lot to do. Even the great initial success of the quantum theory does not make me believe in the fundamental dice game, although I am well aware that your younger colleagues interpret this as a consequence of senility.[22]

Developing Einstein's famous statement that God does not play dice, Joseph Ford, a physicist at the Georgia Institute of Technology, has declared: 'God plays dice with the universe. But they're loaded dice. And the main objective of physics now is to find out by what rules were they loaded and how can we use them for our own ends.'[23] In his view, evolution is 'chaos with feedback': the universe is randomness and dissipation but it can produce surprising complexity.

It may well be that the rhythms of nature are harmonious with chaotic and random elements. It is the latter that provide room for spontaneity, improvisation and creativity and enable nature to evolve. As the Chinese physicist Hao Bai-Lin defines chaos, it stands for 'a kind of order without periodicity'.[24] Chaos may lurk beneath the veneer of order, ready to pull down any apparent equilibrium, but within what appears to be chaos lies a deeper and more mysterious order.

Despite the clamourings of the more radical chaos theorists, who apply the idea to insurance, international politics and military financing as well as to science, nature may well be playing a deeper game than dice, a game that we have not yet begun fully to understand. Beneath every phenomenon that manifests irregularity, there may still be an underlying pattern which scientists have not yet discerned. Chaos and order are not mutually exclusive within a larger whole.

Both relativity and quantum theory imply that the universe is an unbroken whole, and chaos theory does not undermine such a view. Relativity theory and quantum mechanics have different notions of order: in the former, movement is continuous, causally determinate and well-defined; in the latter, it is discontinuous and indeterminate. However, it is possible, as the English physicist David Bohm has argued, to discern a form of *'implicate* or *enfolded* order' which affirms 'the unbroken wholeness of the totality of existence as an undivided flowing movement without borders'.[25]

From this perspective, all of reality is enfolded in each of its parts. It implies that what we call empty space contains an immense background of energy, and that matter as we know it is 'a small, "quantized" wavelike excitation on top of this background, rather like a tiny ripple on a vast sea'.[26] It is a view remarkably close to that of the school of Parmenides and Zeno in ancient Greece, who held that space is a plenum, the ground for the existence of all being, including ourselves. The Big Bang could be said to have created a vast ocean of cosmic energy, an immense, multidimensional common ground for the eventual evolution of matter and mind.

The new theory of the universe described by modern physics has an uncanny similarity with early myths. In the Western tradition, it is written in Genesis: 'In the beginning God created the heaven and the earth. And the earth was without form and void; and darkness *was* upon the face of the deep' (Genesis 1:1–2). Order came later. The Greeks had among their gods Dionysus and Apollo, symbols of energy and disorder, harmony and form, respectively. Both are central to creation: the artist creates beauty out of the chaos of experience. In the Hindu tradition, Brahma (the god of creation), Shiva (the god of disorder) and Vishnu (the god of maintenance) mirror the threefold processes of birth, life and death in the earthly cycle. Order and chaos are not separate like God and the devil, but two distinct aspects of the common ground of being, just as the mind and the body are two aspects of a human being. Instead of two binary and separate opposites, order and chaos are ends of a continuous spectrum, or, in more dialectical terms, they are the thesis and antithesis which come together in a higher synthesis. 'As harmony and discord combine in musical beauty, so order and chaos combine in mathematical beauty.'[27]

## Heat death or creative life?

For all the natural and mathematical beauty of the world, there remains one deeply worrying prospect. The earth is dying, not through human interference, but through its own momentum. According to one interpretation of the second law of thermodynamics, known as entropy, nature is inexorably running down as loss of energy leads to increasing disorder.

Rudolf Clausius, a German physicist who was one of the pioneers of thermodynamics, summed up the first and second laws in 1865: the energy of the world is constant; the entropy of the world is increasing. Entropy measures the extent to which the energy of a closed system is available to do work. It also has come to be the measure of disorder in a system: decreasing order in a system corresponds to increasing entropy. It has been argued that all real energy changes in a closed system are to some extent irreversible and that in such changes there is a loss in the amount of energy to do work. It follows that the entropy of the universe must be continuously increasing. Eventually, when entropy reaches its maximum, the universe will experience a 'heat death' – no more energy will be available to do work. All will be reduced to a condition of lifelessness in perpetual night, the temperature will be uniform, and there can be no change as there will be no flow of heat from one place to another.

Arthur Eddington, an English astronomer and physicist, claimed that the law that entropy increases – the second law of thermodynamics – holds the supreme position among the laws of nature.[28] Many of those who have thought through the implications of this claim for the destiny of the universe have been devastated. Having been spun in space by the notion of relativity, they have been thrown forwards into darkening night. The cosmic optimism of the eighteenth century – which declared that this is the best of all possible worlds – has given way to cosmic pessimism.

The possibility of the dissipation of energy on earth is undoubtedly alarming. Even if the argument for entropy proves wrong and the universe does not face a heat death in the future, it may well be that it could happen in some parts of the universe, including our own.

The implication of all this for ecologists is that we should not interfere with the mechanism on earth which enables it to sustain its equilibrium by interacting with its source of energy (the sun) and by responding to energy loss. Neither should humans waste energy or use up nonrenewable energy resources. The American writer Garrett Hardin has interpreted the three laws of thermodynamics to mean: 'We can't win. We are sure to lose. We can't get out of the game.'[29]

The second law of thermodynamics, which states that the entropy of a closed system must increase, means that all life must end. Yet the inevitable death of some organisms enables others to live; it is part of the endless renewal of life on earth which swims against the current of entropy. The amount of energy on earth is relatively constant: the energy used by a herd of wild horses or a flower, for instance, is constantly being replaced by the high-quality energy from the sun.

The second law of thermodynamics can also be interpreted to mean that energy is conserved, and therefore there cannot be an energy crisis, as popular ecologists make out. However, by burning oil or coal we convert one form of energy to another with a loss of energy.

The prospect of the universe experiencing heat death is now being challenged by a growing number of scientists in physics, chemistry, biology, mathematics and computing science. A state of thermal equilibrium may well be the state of the universe (despite deviations from the statistical mean in some regions of the universe). More important, scientists are increasingly recognizing the ability of matter and energy to organize itself. There may well be a creative potency – not God or an occult force – that carries the universe forward to higher organizational states. This could mean that the universe will escape the heat death apparently decreed by the second law of thermodynamics.[30] There could be a latent purpose within the spontaneity of evolution.

## Creative evolution

Traditionally, scientists and philosophers have considered the laws of nature to be eternal and universally applicable. But with the emergence of evolutionary cosmology, this view has been been toned down to the claim that new laws come into being as nature evolves and only when they appear can they be applied universally. Some modern physicists have gone so far as to suggest that the laws of nature exist only in the disembodied mind.

One of the main architects of quantum theory, John von Neumann, has argued that the sciences do not explain and they hardly even try to interpret. In his view, they mainly make models. 'By a model is meant a mathematical construct which, with the addition of certain verbal interpretations, describes observed phenomena. The justification of such a mathematical construct is solely and precisely that it is expected to work.'[31] Stephen Hawking goes even further to assert that 'a theory is just a model of the universe, or a restricted part of it, and a set of rules which relate quantities in the model to observations that we make. It exists only in our minds and does not have any other reality (whatever that might mean).'[32]

It is very easy for mathematicians to lose touch with the sensuous world. The so-called laws of nature are not eternal and unchanging, as Newton held, but nor are they merely mental or mathematical constructs, as von Neumann and Hawking would have us believe. They describe a world which exists independently of the human mind; they are based on observations and can be tested. The laws of nature would appear to be observed regularities based on probability; they are interpretations which change as our understanding increases and as nature develops. They describe habitual trends, not fixed patterns and may well be evolving. And the habits themselves are only temporary and change within evolving nature.[33]

The synthesis of evolutionary theory developed in the 1920s and 1930s still claimed, with Darwin, that change occurred through random genetic mutations in a purposeless universe. The mutations may now be defined as the inheritable changes in the particular sequences that make up the instructions in the DNA molecule.[34] This biological approach is, however, still mechanistic, depicting living organisms as chemical machines. The genetic code of the DNA molecules determines the sequence of amino-acid building blocks in protein molecules, but it does not determine the way the proteins are arranged in cells, and the cells into complex organisms.

The machine analogy of traditional biology may throw some light on the functioning of adult organisms, but it cannot deal adequately with their growth and development, that is to say, their morphogenesis. In order to overcome this problem, a number of biologists in the 1920s, known as vitalists, proposed a new way of thinking about biological morphogenesis in terms of fields. It has been argued that 'morphogenetic fields' exist within and around organisms. Within each organism, there are further, different fields around organs, cells, tissues and so on. It is the morphogenetic field of a piece of flatworm – which contains the complete flatworm field – that enables it to regenerate itself into a complete flatworm. The exact nature of the fields remain obscure, however.

According to his intriguing hypothesis of 'formative causation', the British biologist Rupert Sheldrake believes such fields contain a kind of collective memory on which a member of the species draws, and to which it in turn contributes. In a series of well-argued books, he has claimed that the fields are the means by which the habits of the species are built up, maintained and inherited.[35]

If this is the case, then the evolutionary process involves both creativity and habit. Without creativity, no new habit would come into being; without the controlling influence of habit-formation, creativity would lead to a chaotic process of change. Through evolutionary creativity, new patterns of organization emerge, and through repetition, these new patterns become increasingly habitual if favoured by natural selection. As observed regularities in nature, these habits appear what may be termed 'laws of nature'.

Organicists like Sheldrake have tried to go beyond the vitalist–mechanist divide by stressing the holistic properties of living organisms. They would agree with Whitehead, who claimed that biology is the study of larger organisms, whereas 'physics is the study of smaller organisms'.[36] The writer Arthur Koestler, too, argued that biological organisms are examples of holistic systems found at all levels of complexity, from atoms to galaxies. He called biological and social individuals 'holons' – self-regulating systems which display both 'the autonomous properties of wholes and the dependent properties of parts'. Such a holon can preserve its individuality while functioning as 'an integrated part of an (existing or evolving) larger whole'.[37]

Sheldrake has gone further to claim that self-organizing systems, including molecules, crystals, cells, tissues, organisms and even societies of organisms, are organized by what he calls 'morphic fields'. They have observable effects and may be responsible for 'the character and form and organization of systems at all levels of complexity'. Living organisms therefore may inherit not only genes but also morphic fields. As a pattern of behaviour in an organism becomes increasingly habitual, a cumulative memory will emerge which will be passed on to its offspring: 'The developing organism tunes in to the morphic fields of its species, and thus draws upon a pooled or collective memory.'[38]

The controversial hypothesis suggests that memory depends on 'morphic resonance', rather than on material stores. It could explain the collective behaviour of shoals of fish and flocks of birds which appear to move as a single organism. Sheldrake even goes so far as to argue that social morphic fields coordinating behaviour exist in human societies, giving a tribe its habitual patterns of organization. The tribe maintains itself through a process of 'self-resonance', and the field of the tribe includes living and past members.[39]

This, however, would seem to be going too far. Even if tribal societies maintained themselves in such a manner in the past, the field of morphic resonance has been broken in modern industrial societies. It denies, moreover, human freedom by suggesting that we are in the grip of mysterious forces which shape our collective behaviour, rather like a social collective unconscious.

Sheldrake has made grand metaphysical claims for the hypothesis of causal formation, affirming that it is 'the causal efficacy of the conscious self, *and* the existence of a hierarchy of creative agencies immanent in nature, *and* the reality of a transcendental source of the universe'.[40] He claims that there is enough circumstantial evidence to suggest that the morphic fields exist in nature. Although their existence may not be verified through experimental investigation, their effects are observable and testable. If true, the hypothesis certainly adds a missing dimension to Darwin's theory of evolution.

The kind of creative evolution implied in this hypothesis runs counter to the widespread pessimism evoked by the vision of a world-machine slowly running out of steam, heading towards heat death when entropy reaches a maximum. It does not resurrect the naive optimism of the eighteenth century that this is the best of all possible worlds, but it does imply that the cosmos will not necessarily dissolve into chaos and that it may well continue on a creative path to greater complexity, subjectivity and consciousness.

## Reanimating nature

In general, the new science of the twentieth century has not only inspired a new metaphysics but also encouraged the growth of an ecological consciousness. It has helped break down the dominant view of nature as a purposeless collection of dead atoms. Matter re-emerges as a continuous dancing movement. It has confirmed the view of the philosophers Bergson, Whitehead and Heidegger that the earth is like an organism, and a self-regulating one at that. The whole universe appears as an interconnected and intrinsicially dynamic network af relationships. Nature is no longer a machine, but a web, vibrating with life.

The death of nature predicted by the scientists and philosophers of the Renaissance and the scientific revolution has given way to an unexpected resurrection. The universe described by late twentieth-century science is not perfectly symmetrical, like a Platonic idea, nor is it governed by eternal Newtonian laws. But it does have a flowing elegance; in its evolving field of energy, there is room for spontaneity and creativity. It now makes sense to talk about the cosmic joy of the new science.

# 28

# THE RESURRECTION OF GAIA

> At the beginning of all things Mother Earth emerged
> from Chaos and bore her son Uranus as she slept. Gazing
> down fondly at her from the mountains, he showered
> fertile rain upon her secret clefts, and she bore grass,
> flowers, and trees, with the beasts and birds proper to
> each. This same rain made the rivers flow and filled the
> hollow places with water, so that lakes and seas came
> into being.
>
> Olympian creation myth

In the 1980s there was a revolution in our perception of the earth. No longer an inanimate habitat for life, it is now seen as a living whole. This has partly been a result of the space explorations which have brought back pictures of the earth as a marvellous green and blue globe with drifts of white cloud swirling around it, and partly due to the communications revolution which has turned the world into a global village.

The idea of the earth as a living organism is, as we have seen, not new. The first modern Western scientist to propose the idea seriously was James Hutton, who said at a meeting of the Royal Society in Edinburgh in 1785 that the earth was a 'superorganism' and that its proper study should be physiology. Towards the end of the nineteenth century, the Ukrainian Yevgraf Maximovich Korolenko impressed the young Russian scientist Vladimir Vernadsky with his observation that the 'Earth is an organism'. The latter went on to give the term 'biosphere' its modern meaning in 1911 as 'the envelope of life, i.e. the area of living matter . . . of the Earth's crust occupied by transformers which convert cosmic radiations into effective terrestrial energy'.[1] The ecologist F. E. Clements at the beginning of the twentieth century also described groups of plants as forming 'superorganisms', living entities with their own characteristics.

In recent times, the idea of the whole planet being an organism has been resurrected and popularized by the Canadian atmospheric chemist and inventor James Lovelock in his influential book *Gaia: A New Look at Life on Earth* (1979). The idea began to crystallize in his mind while he was working with the American space programme at the National Aeronautics and Space Administration (NASA) in the United States when plans were being made to look for life on Mars. But the name Gaia – the Greek goddess of the earth – was suggested to Lovelock by the novelist William Golding in a casual conversation between neighbours. According to Lovelock,

> the entire range of living matter on Earth, from whales to viruses, and from oaks to algae, could be regarded as constituting a single living entity, capable of manipulating the Earth's atmosphere to suit its overall needs and endowed with faculties and powers far beyond those of its constituent parts.[2]

Unlike the Darwinian view, which holds that life has adapted to evolving planetary conditions (with both evolving their separate ways), the Gaia hypothesis postulates that 'the physical and chemical condition of the surface of the Earth, of the atmosphere, and of the oceans has been and is actively made fit and comfortable by the presence of life itself'.[3] The right balance of gases in the atmosphere necessary for life is maintained not by chance but by the very process of life. It has used the resources of the earth to make it capable of supporting life forms. From this perspective, evolution is the response of the earth to change, and its attempt to achieve a new equilibrium.

The hypothesis is an extension of the notion of an ecosystem to include the whole of life and a good part of the inanimate world. Supporters of the hypothesis point to the relative constancy of the climate, the constant high level of oxygen (21 per cent) and nitrogen (78 per cent) in the atmosphere and the low level of salt in the sea. It seems more than a coincidence that these conditions are ideal for the evolution of complex life forms. There was virtually no oxygen or nitrogen in the earth's atmosphere to begin with and it is only thanks to the activities of bacteria and the process of photosynthesis that nitrogen and oxygen now predominate. A feedback system compensates for alterations in the global climate by adjusting the rates at which such gases as oxygen, methane and carbon dioxide are produced and removed from the atmosphere, maintaining the climate within limits which foster terrestrial life.

The atmosphere, the chemistry of the oceans and the geology of the earth have been so radically altered by biological activities that they cannot be considered apart. Gaia keeps the planet fit for life by regulating the chemical and physical environment. Life would thus seem to swim against the general current of entropy.[4]

Lovelock suggests that some parts of the earth are 'vital organs' which if disturbed would cause the whole organism of the earth to malfunction. He is particularly concerned about the tropical areas and the seas close to the continental shores: 'Here man may sap the vitality of Gaia by reducing and by deleting key species in her life-support system; and he may then exacerbate the situation by releasing into the air or the sea abnormal quantities of compounds which are potentially dangerous on a global scale.'[5] He therefore recommends 'wise husbandry' to allow Gaia to function well. Large regions should be left as international conservation areas to enable the earth to maintain its equilibrium.

By applying the ecological idea of an ecosytem to the earth as a whole, Lovelock has made a lasting contribution to ecology. He uncritically accepts the ecological model of a structured hierarchy of species represented by the food chain. Yet he rejects the recent claim made by the chaos enthusiast Robert May in his *Theoretical Ecology* that 'as a mathematical generality, increasing complexity makes for dynamical fragility rather than robustness'. On the contrary, Gaia theory enlarges theoretical ecology by taking the species and their physical environment together as a single system, and providing mathematical models which demonstrate that 'increased diversity among the species leads to better regulation' and consequently robustness.[6] This confirms the older view that greater complexity leads to greater stability in an ecosystem.

Lovelock's holistic approach undermines the reductionist attempt of neo-Malthusians like Dawkins who interpret evolution in terms of selfish genes battling for survival. To isolate one element like this in the evolutionary biosphere is to miss the splendour of the wood for a tree. He has further answered the criticisms that biological regulation is only partial on earth, and that it is really a 'coevolution' of life and the inorganic, by stressing once again the lasting interdependence of the parts which join together to form Gaia.[7]

The evolution of the human species now poses a great threat to that equilibrium. With their domesticated animals, they have become a major part of the total biomass and are beginning to disrupt the delicate homeostasis of the earth. Lovelock considers the three greatest threats to be cars (emitting carbon dioxide), chainsaws (cutting down forests for short-lived pasture land) and cattle (requiring the pasture cleared from forests and producing methane).

But Lovelock is by no means a radical environmentalist. Indeed, he has argued that the damage done to the ozone layer and the recent increase in acid rain are minor problems. He has also stoutly defended nuclear power as a 'clean' source of energy: 'I have never regarded nuclear radiation or nuclear power as anything other than a normal and inevitable part of the environment.'[8] He goes on to suggest that 'breathing is fifty times more dangerous than the sum total of radiation we normally receive from all sources'. His friend and popularizer Michael Allaby also states that the opposition to nuclear power is based 'on a quite irrational fear'.[9]

Lovelock, whose notion of Gaia has indirectly encouraged earth worship, castigates environmental radicals and their 'reactionary "back to nature" campaign' and those small fringe groups, 'mostly anarchist in flavour, who would hasten our doom by dismantling and destroying all technology'.[10] Pollution, he points out, is an inevitable consequence of life at work; its very concept is anthropocentric and 'may be irrelevant in the Gaian context'. He concludes that there is 'no urgent cause for concern about man's activities'.[11] This Olympian perspective ignores the real harm humans are doing to themselves and other species. It also overlooks the possibility of pollution being a kind of self-poisoning.

Lovelock is not only a stout defender of industrialization, but also highly Eurocentric. While he urges 'us' as a species to change our ways, he suggests that the countries in the tropics pose the greatest threat to Gaia's wellbeing. He seems dangerously overconfident about the ability of industrial societies to solve their environmental problems: 'When urban industrial man does something ecologically bad he notices it and tends to put things to right again.'[12]

## A new relationship with Gaia

The success of the Gaia hypothesis in environmental circles was no doubt partly due to the way it undermined the prevailing view of nature as a primitive force to master and of the planet as a spaceship for ever travelling around the sun. Gaia offers almost a new pagan religion in a secular age; Gaia has in some circles become a kind of earth worship.

Lovelock outlines three principal characteristics of Gaia which should change our relationship with the earth. Gaia has a 'tendency to optimize conditions for all terrestrial life' (thereby fitting in with Darwinian natural selection); its 'vital organs [are] at the core, as well as expendable or redundant ones mainly on the periphery'; and its responses to changes for the worse 'must obey rules of cybernetics'.[13] These are of course hypotheses, yet to be fully tested, but they should have profound implications for the way humans behave in the biosphere.

According to Lovelock, we are inevitably part of the Gaian process of self-regulation, and 'as the transfer of power to our species proceeds, our responsibility for maintaining planetary homeostasis grows with it, whether we are conscious of the fact or not'. The Gaian hypothesis implies that man is 'a part of, or partner in, a very democratic entity'.[14] Lovelock believes that 'we' have a special place in creation through our technology, which makes it necessary for us to become responsible for the planet. He warns that Gaia can eventually get rid of our species if we threaten the rest of life on earth: 'Gaia is not purposefully antihuman but so long as we continue to change the global environment against her preferences, we encourage our replacement with a more environmentally seemly species.'[15]

For Lovelock, man is not the owner or the tenant of the planet, far less a manager or steward in the Christian sense. When it comes to environmental ethics, Lovelock suggests that we should act like shop stewards, representatives of other species, in the vast enterprise of Gaia.[16] The metaphor has a connotation of humanity struggling against a more powerful and exploitative boss, and implies that we are somehow separate from Gaia. In his more pessimistic moments, Lovelock believes that, given their past record, humans should not be given responsibility for anything, let alone regulating the earth.

Lovelock specifically rejects the notion that human beings are like a cancer on the planet; we are, after all, an integral part of Gaia. It is our practices that are to blame and it is bad farming that constitutes probably the greatest threat to Gaia's health, especially the rearing of animals for food. (He wonders whether his great-grandchildren will be vegetarian with cattle living only in zoos and tame-life parks.) More recently, he has called for a geophysiology of the earth, which would bring many sciences together in a planetary perspective in order to understand the evolution of Gaia. It would study in particular the ways in which the biosphere has been able to survive the progressive heating-up of the sun, and to recover from such catastrophic events as the impact of asteroids. He also proposes that human beings become planetary healers, practising 'planetary medicine', experts on the self-regulatory mechanisms that maintain the necessary conditions for life on Earth.[17] This raises the question: Can the planet be our patient?

Lovelock's ideal vision of a future England would, he claims, be like Blake's: to build Jerusalem in a green and pleasant land. It would involve the return to small, densely populated cities with easy access to the countryside; one third of the land reverting to 'natural' woodland and heath and one sixth reserved for wildlife only; and agriculture a mixture of intensive production and small unsubsidized farms. It is a picture of the patchwork of hedgerows and fields familiar before the Second World War, one of the most transformed and 'humanized' landscapes on earth. This son of a Baffinlander has thus opted for the arcadian myth of old England, widely trod and carefully tended, 'a great work of art'.[18]

## Mechanical science and organic nature

In general, the Gaia hypothesis undermines both humanism and mechanical science. Yet, despite his claims to the contrary, Lovelock remains something of a humanist and a mechanist. In his computer models of Gaia, he extends his views of society to nature: the environment and species exert controls on each other: 'a metaphor for our own experience that the family and society do better when firm, but justly applied rules exist than they do with unrestricted freedom'. Like a nineteenth-century liberal, he appeals to 'enlightened self-interest' for us to change our ways.[19]

He warns his readers that Gaia is 'no doting mother tolerant of misdemeanours, nor is she some fragile and delicate damsel in danger from brutal mankind. She is stern and tough, always keeping the world warm and comfortable for those who obey her rules, but ruthless in her destruction of those who trangress.'[20] It recalls the old Kali image of nature as a devouress.

Lovelock worked for much of his life at Shell, who produce oil for the cars he objects to. He considers transnational companies to be more likely to come up with environmental solutions than governments, and he has an active desire to colonize other planets. He not only wrote with Michael Allaby, a former editor of the

*Ecologist*, a science-fiction work called *The Greening of Mars*, but is still sufficiently Promethean to believe that the 'real job of science is trying to make science fiction come true'.[21]

Lovelock is keen on the mechanical science of cybernetics, which is concerned with self-regulation systems of communication and control in living organisms and machines. In *The Ages of Gaia: A Biography of Our Living Earth* (1989), he plays with a cybernetic model of a planet – called Daisyworld – to test the importance of different environmental variables, with a world imagined to contain only daisies. He also employs ecological models of foxes and rabbits to predict population fluctuations. Despite the circular as opposed to linear logic of cybernetic systems, the approach is mechanical and abstract. Using the model of cybernetics, he adopts the old catastrophe notion of evolution (recently revised by the American scientist Stephen Jay Gould), and predicts that the climate and chemical composition of the earth are kept in homeostasis for long periods until some internal contradiction or external force 'causes a jump to a new stable state'.[22]

The computer models Lovelock has elaborated show that Gaia's regulatory processes occur only through mechanistic means, following the laws of chemistry and physics. They have given rise to a commercial computer game based on the Daisyworld program which puts the player 'in control of Gaia' and enables him to move mountains, destroy whole continents and hostile worlds, create intelligent new life forms and colonize other planets. In short, the programme is little more than a tool-kit for megalomaniacs to indulge in the age-old fantasy of human omnipotence.[23]

### Gaia, immanent purpose and God

Lovelock's closest colleagues have been careful to distance themselves from the more extravagant claims made for Gaia. The microbiologist Lynn Margulis, who worked closely with him in the early genesis of the idea, is concerned not to alienate her fellow scientists. She rejects the notion that the earth is alive or that Gaia is an organism: 'Rather Gaia is an extremely complex system with identifiable regulatory properties which are very specific to the lower atmosphere.'[24]

Lovelock's co-author Michael Allaby also sternly warns his readers against worshipping Gaia. Gaia is not a person, far less a goddess. He defines Gaia as a morally neutral concept, 'no more than an

aspect of the planet Earth, a way of describing the way things
are'.[25] Gaia is a metaphor; it is not teleological, saying nothing
about final ends or goals. Moreover, its processes are entirely
mechanical and he compares the self-regulation of the earth –
mainly conducted by microorganisms – with the governor on a
steam engine.[26]

Rupert Sheldrake, on the other hand, is positively inspired by
the idea that Gaia may be alive *and* purposeful, with its purposes
reflected in the evolutionary process. He suggests that the earth
may be the unified field of Gaia, like the primal unified field in
physics, with gravitational and electromagnetic fields as aspects of
this field. Magnetic fields of the earth vary remarkably, for instance,
with the north and south magnetic poles continually wandering, and
reversing themselves quite frequently over millions of years. Is this
a matter of chance, or the result of some deeper organization
principle at work? The earth is undoubtedly influenced by external
forces in the solar system and beyond, but also subject to internal
purposes.

Sheldrake suggests that the field of Gaia can be thought of as
its morphic field, coordinating its various processes. It might be
interacting by 'morphic resonance' with other Gaia-like planets,
and through 'self-resonance' contain an inherent memory.[27] This
interpretation of the field of Gaia would seem to reintroduce the
idea of an invisible soul in scientific guise; to talk of Gaia's purpose
and memory certainly invokes the older notions of Providence. But
while the hypothesis at present remains a speculation, it is highly
suggestive. It helps explain the uncanny accuracy with which the
earth manages to regulate itself without resorting to some transcendental God.

Lovelock has been careful to distance himself from any teleological
interpretation of Gaia and denies that it assumes the earth's ability to
plan and have foresight. Like Allaby, he stresses that the idea of Gaia
is only a hypothesis; it is not proved beyond doubt. There is moreover
no immanent purpose to be discerned in nature. Nevertheless, he
is ready to admit that the whole planet at certain times appears
as if it were celebrating a 'sacred ceremony'. For him Gaia is a
religious as well as a scientific concept: 'She is of this Universe
and, conceivably, a part of God. On Earth she is the source of life
everlasting and is alive now; she gave birth to humankind and we
are part of her.'[28]

The Gaia hypothesis is not ultimately capable of being tested, although its effects are. Strictly speaking, it is nothing more than an intriguing supposition. Nevertheless, it has great value. By reanimating nature, it supports the view of modern physicists that the universe is more like an organism than a machine. By personifying the earth, it implies that it has intrinsic value and that its interests as a whole are worthy of human consideration. If it encourages a sense of reverence for life, it is to be welcomed.

In a Gaian context, humans are quite expendable. Even if we were to blow ourselves to smithereens with our nuclear weapons, life on earth would continue in some form or other. Indeed, it might be advantageous to other forms of life if we did disappear. Our future is in our hands, but the future of the earth is beyond us. As a living organism, it will continue to regulate and sustain itself. Whether we will be there to see it or not, the illuminated globe of Gaia, with its wondrous lands and oceans, will continue to float in space for a long time to come.

*Part IV*

# THE JOINING
# OF THE WAYS

# 29

# ENVIRONMENTAL ETHICS

In wildness is the preservation of the world.
                              Henry David Thoreau

A new ecological consciousness and sensibility is now emerging in what amounts to a new enlightenment. There has also been a remarkable renewal in philosophy, especially in the area of environmental ethics dealing with the place of humanity within nature. The issue of animal liberation is perhaps the most obvious, but a whole array of prevailing moral attitudes are now coming under scrutiny. The moral community is being extended to include not only humans and animals, but also lakes and woods, plants and stones. Trees as well as valleys, it has been argued, have moral standing.

The change was partly prompted in the sixties and seventies by popular works like Rachel Carson's *Silent Spring* (1962), which suggested that if the present use of pesticides continued there would be no dawn chorus, and by documents such as *Limits to Growth* (1972) published by a team of researchers at the Massachusetts Institute of Technology, which called for a complete rethinking of our approach to nature. The Australian philosopher John Passmore reminded people of *Man's Responsibility for Nature* (1974) and Norwegian philosopher Arne Naess went even further to call for a 'deep ecology' which would replace the prevailing Western technocratic model of the universe with an 'organic person-planetary paradigm'.

The new eco-philosophy has been closely linked with the green movement, which tries to put ecological principles into practice. As in any social movement, there is a spectrum of beliefs and values as well as different political wings, reflected in the fundamentalists and realists in Germany, and the light and dark greens in Britain. In the United States, two main philosophical tendencies have emerged, known as the deep ecologists and the social ecologists. Feminists, too, have made their own special contribution to the debate.

Although deep ecology and social ecology overlap, their different emphases have led to disagreements. The social ecologists are

primarily concerned with changing society in order to change our
relationship to nature, while the deep ecologists concentrate on the
direct relationship between the individual and nature unmediated by
society. One stresses the role of society in creating the ecological crisis,
the other the responsibility of each citizen for planet Earth.

Whereas the social ecologists tend to be more humanist, the deep
ecologists are more spiritually oriented. Social ecology draws on the
European libertarian and utopian tradition and seeks some form of
participatory democracy; deep ecology takes inspiration from Eastern
religions and Western process metaphysics. For social ecologists,
humans are agents with special responsibilities; for deep ecologists,
they tend to be seen as nature's pests. The former have sympathy for
the poor and the oppressed in human communities; the latter like to
retreat to the wilderness and identify with bears, trees and rocks.

### Shallow environmentalism

Both deep and social ecologists are radicals; they go beyond shallow
environmentalists who are merely concerned with preservation and
conservation. The measure for shallow environmentalists is man:
humans are the creators of values, and the value of anything is its
usefulness for humanity. According to them, humans are superior to
all other beings and their welfare is paramount.

What most separates shallow environmentalists from radical
ecologists is the question of intrinsic and instrumental value, of
anthropocentric or biocentric ethics. Radical ecologists argue that
natural things exist for their own sake and are to be valued as such.
Shallow environmentalists believe that nature is primarily to be valued
as an instrument for themselves; it is a means to their ends. We thus
have obligations towards nature and its creatures because they are
directly useful to us. Wetlands, for instance, are valued not because
they provide a habitat for migrating birds, but because people like to
come and see the birds nesting. From this perspective, any interference
with nature is justified if it contributes to human wellbeing. This
view finds its source ultimately in the Judaeo-Christian tradition
and is echoed in Kant's claim that only humans can be considered
ends-in-themselves.

This shallow view is still the most widely held in Western democracies. It accepts that humans are apart from nature, and sees nature
as a backdrop or theatre in which they operate. Land is no common

treasury; it is to be owned and exploited. People can do what they like with their property as long as it does not upset other property-holders. Certain domestic animals may have limited legal standing, but not trees or lakes.

Few environmentalists, however shallow, would support the frontier cowboy ethic of unrestrained exploitation and expansion. The myth of superabundance – 'there is always more where that came from' – has been exploded by the oil crisis. Nevertheless, many are still committed to a form of technological optimism: arguing that any environmental problem can be solved by more technology, better planning, greater economic growth. They reflect the optimism of the eighteenth century, the belief that there is nothing that the mind of man cannot imagine, that his hands cannot realize.

There are of course different strands of thinking among shallow environmentalists. The conservationists, for instance, are primarily concerned about the use value of nature, defending green belts around towns and opposing railways through their patch. They recognize in theory that there are limits to material growth. They are keen to use resources efficiently and get the maximum possible yield in a 'sustainable' version of development. The more far-sighted also want to conserve some benefits for future generations.

Preservationists, on the other hand, want to maintain certain landscapes, species and natural systems (like moors, whales and Antarctica) free from human interference, regardless of their immediate usefulness. They value nature because it offers a pool of genetic diversity, provides resources for human science (as in tropical rainforests), a place for recreation, and a source of aesthetic pleasure and spiritual inspiration (as in national parks).

The conservationist is more human-centred, while the preservationist is more nature-oriented. The former tend to be conservative and continue the pattern of domination and ownership which has bedevilled our relationship with nature for centuries. While a conservationist might defend London Zoo, it would not be paradoxical for a preservationist to call for its closure. Both, however, recognize the importance of nature for providing free goods and services for our well-being and for our life-support systems.

The views of conservationists and preservationists, however limited, provide an important starting point. Many humans who enjoy the latest technological aids want to live in a world with some wild places and animals, even if the closest they get to them is watching nature programmes on television. The appreciation of these is often more aesthetic than scientific, but it marks a growing awareness of a nonhumanist, biocentric ethic. An aesthetic appreciation of nature may well be anthropocentric – the landscape is valued because it has human associations – but many appreciate nature for nature's sake.

The value of comparative wilderness, even if reduced to carefully managed national parks, is increasingly appreciated by dwellers in overcrowded cities. There is considerable therapeutic value to be gained from contact with wild places and animals, revitalizing the bonds with nature cut by our artificial environments. For some this can take the form of hunting, although that just continues the age-old pattern of domination. For others, it means climbing mountain ranges, swimming in remote lakes or sailing out to sea. Above all, the wilderness in our authoritarian culture provides a resounding symbol for human freedom and autonomy. The desire to roam freely, denied to most human and animals shut up in their physical and mental corrals, is the most basic of instincts.

## Radical ecology: the larger whole

Radical ecologists call for a fundamental reorientation in the way we think and act in the world. They search for a new creative harmony between individuals, communities and the natural world. They go to the root of things.

Radical ecologists, both deep and social tendencies, tend to be holistic thinkers. Reacting against the mechanical and atomistic legacy of the scientific revolution, they argue that wholes are more than collections of individuals, greater than the sum of their parts. It is simply not possible to explain properties of complex wholes by analysing simple properties of their parts. In this sense, holism is a central feature of green thinking.

An important ecological implication of holism is that natural systems, like the land and the sea, have value because they are greater than their individual parts. Beings and things are not isolated atoms, but form sets of relationships. Their identity cannot be understood without reference to their relationships: a sister stands in a certain relationship to her brother and parents, but they are all part of the same family.

Modern physics comes to the aid of radical ecologists in this respect. Fritjof Capra, for instance, has drawn on the findings of quantum physics to support the claim that the observer cannot be separated from the observed, and that nature forms a seamless web: 'in atomistic physics we can never speak about nature without speaking about ourselves'.[1] Naess too adopts the 'total-field' concept which dissolves the notion of the world as composed of discrete, separate entities; for him, organisms are 'knots in the biospherical net or field of intrinsic relations'.[2] Even the metaphor of a net is misleading if it implies a physical boundary fixed in time and space.

Inspired by scientific ecology, radical ecologists argue that organisms are sets of relations which by definition are interwoven with their environments; all in the biosphere interacts and is interrelated. Animals and plants are part of larger ecosystems, which have an identity in their own right: individual organisms come and go and while the ecosystem continues to exist. The earth itself is the ultimate ecosystem.

The deep ecologists follow nature mystics in believing that it is possible to identify with nature; it is not absurd to think like a glacier or be like a mountain. Their holistic thinking leads them beyond an anthropocentric concern with the personal self or individual ego, to believe that self-realization is only possible through identification with the larger self of the world. Such a process involves intuition and imagination in order to escape the narrow confines of the human mind and its habitual concerns and achieve trans-species experience and an empathetic understanding of nature. To imagine what it is like to be a tree goes some way towards considering its interests interdependent from our own.

In social terms, holism maintains that the individual is a social being, a set of relationships that cannot be isolated from the rest of society. There has been a long tradition since Rousseau and Hegel which maintains that society is greater than the sum of its members. Rousseau regarded society as forming a moral person and argued that the general will is not the same as the sum of the individual wills. Marx thought that membership of a class was the greatest defining characteristic of an individual. Sociology as a discipline, too, claims that society exists as an entity. But to claim that we are merely 'social constructs' is reductionist.

Extreme holism dissolves the notion of the individual as a separate person and denies his autonomy. Human beings, as much as other animals and plants, may be products of their environment, but they also influence their environment in turn.

When applied to society, holism can lead to authoritarian calls for the individual to submerge himself in the community or to sacrifice himself in its interests. In a notorious phrase, Rousseau thought that a recalcitrant individual, blind to his true interests, could be 'forced to be free' by the state in order to realize his 'higher self'. Rulers have long used patriotism and appeals to the 'good of the whole' as a way of uniting their subjects and preparing them to sacrifice themselves for their rule. The kind of personal identification inspired by tribalism, nationalism and racism has resulted in a bloody history of war and plunder. The call of some radical ecologists to put the earth first in all situations and their readiness to sacrifice individual humans for its general wellbeing tread perilously close to eco-fascism.

What is needed is a moderately holistic view which accepts that we are part of the whole, in metaphysical, moral and social terms, but at the same time recognizes our irreducible individuality. If wholes such as ecosystems are considered worthy of moral consideration, so should the individual organisms which go up to make them. Wholes or collections may often be greater than the sum of their parts, but it does not follow that parts are insignificant or expendable. Nature may be profligate with its offspring in the struggle for survival (an octopus produces ten thousands of eggs only to die in the process), but only in the crudest Social Darwinism can this be used to justify the sacrifice of the weaker members of society.

On the contrary, a true understanding of ecology shows that while organisms are systems of relationships, enmeshed in nature's web, to tear part of the web weakens the whole. Neither the community nor the individual has paramount importance; they cannot be separated from each other, and are mutually beneficial. Ecology points in the direction of symbiosis and mutual aid. The goal should therefore be a kind of ecological and communal individuality, in which the freedom of all guarantees the freedom of one. Such an approach – which might be called 'libertarian ecology' – would recognize the claims of the individual as well as those of the social and biotic community.

## Eco-feminism

Feminists have made a profound and provocative contribution to radical ecology and have helped redefine a just relationship with nature. They tend to be critical of the individualistic rights-based approach in ethics and politics, preferring a more organic and holistic philosophy which does not discriminate between sexes or species. By seeing humans as part of a wider network of relationships they stress reciprocity and symbiosis. This type of eco-feminism in some ways goes deeper than deep ecology and is more social than social ecology.

From their position of oppression in patriarchal society, women have been particularly sensitive to the devastating effects of hierarchy and domination. They are traditionally less assertive and more appreciative of the relationships, nets and webs in society and nature. They point out that man's domination of woman was just part of his wider domination of nature. They observe that partriarchal society has been based on four interlocking pillars: sexism, racism, class exploitation and ecological destruction.

Some feminists have stressed the close link between exploited femininity and exploited nature and argue that the hatred of women and the hatred of nature are mutually reinforcing. Many males, they observe, like to conquer, master and dominate women as they do nature; at the same time, they fear women as they fear the encroachment of nature.

The American feminist Ynestra King has argued that eco-feminist principles are based on the following beliefs:

> 1. The building of Western industrial civilization in opposition to nature interacts dialectically with and reinforces the subjugation of women, because women are believed to be closer to nature. Therefore ecofeminists take on the life-struggles of all of nature as our own.
> 2. Life on earth is an interconnected web, not a hierarchy ... Therefore, ecofeminist theory seeks to show the connections between all forms of domination, including the domination of nonhuman nature, and ecofeminist practice is necessarily antihierarchical.[3]

The American historian Carolyn Merchant has pointed out that the mothering image of the natural world in the Middle Ages restrained destructive appetites to a degree. Earlier scientists tried to catch nature and to lift her veil, not to seize her and bind her. But after the scientific revolution, scientists wanted to put nature on the rack, and force her to reveal her secrets.[4] The similarity between the 'rape' of 'virgin' land and the violation of women is clear.

For long in the Western tradition (but not in Egypt), the earth has been considered female, sometimes as a consoling mother (as by the Romantic poets), sometimes as a stern matron (as by James Lovelock). Whereas for the Egyptians, the fecund earth was male and the sheltering sky female, the Greeks and the Romans turned the Egyptian goddess Isis (queen of the gods) into an earth goddess and universal Mother Nature.

The recent resurrection of the Greek earth goddess Gaia has given rise to an earth-based spirituality, with birth as the underlying metaphor and the cosmos as a living body in which we all participate, and even a new version of feminist witchcraft.[5] This has influenced eco-feminism deeply. It does not, however, involve worshipping 'Yahweh with a skirt' but celebrating the rhythms of life and death and recognizing that the 'Goddess Is All'.[6]

Drawing on the ancient Chinese concept of *ying* and *yang*, some feminists have described how the female *ying* of nature is being oppressed and exploited by the *yang* of men, forgetting that both principles are two aspects of a common nature to differing degrees. In this context, Mary Daly in *Gyn/Ecology* has argued that if women align themselves with 'female nature' they will be able to create a 'free space' in which the values of patricentric culture will simply dissolve.[7] As for gender differences, her remedy is 'Mister-Ectomy'.

Mary Wollstonecraft two centuries ago argued that the 'mind has no sex', but some modern feminists are exploiting the age-old stereotype that they are naturally (by nature) more caring than men and somehow 'closer' to nature. Women are said to be more in touch with natural cycles: the process of menstruating follows the movement of the moon; like the earth, they give birth to new life.

The analogy of woman and nature, the idea that women somehow have a 'special' relationship with nature, originates in the old dualisms of men and women and nature and culture. It continues the myth of transcendence, the myth that humanity transcends the realm of nature by entering the realm of culture. Such a view clearly shows a lack of ecological sensibility which recognizes that all subjects, men and women, are interconnected with each other and other life forms within the web of nature.[8]

With its celebration of unity in diversity, ecology goes beyond such reductionist dualism, accepting the real difference between men and women (and their mutual attraction) while at the same time asserting that they all share an evolving *human* personality inextricably linked with wider nature. It claims that gender distinctions do not have relevance everywhere and at all times. It sees women and men as equally capable of subjectivity, autonomy, reason, intuition and imagination. It does not deny the contribution of traditionally 'female' values such as reciprocity and cooperation, but sees the process of 'nurturing' to be a possibility for all human beings.

Most eco-feminists, having experienced the consequences of patriarchal power, do not want to resurrect it in another form. One of the great contributions to ecology is their critique of hierarchy and power relations. They wish to heal the wounds of centuries of destructive male power. Some, like the German Green Party activist Petra Kelly, are concerned with seizing political power, albeit in a more refined form:

> Our aim is radical, nonviolent change *outside* – and *inside* of us! The macrocosm and the microcosm! This has to do with transforming power! Not power over, or power to dominate, or power to terrorize – but shared power as we know it, replacing it with the power of nonviolence or something common to all, to be used *by all* and *for all*![9]

This liberal and democratic interpretation of power is common in many feminist and ecological circles who talk of 'empowering' the oppressed. Such empowering is fine if it simply means developing 'power-from-within', the ability to realize one's potential, as opposed to 'power-over', the ability to manipulate, control and punish. Any attempt to seize power over other beings (whether human or non human) is inevitably coercive. A genuinely ecological approach seeks the dissolution of hierarchy, domination, authority and power.

Of all eco-feminists, perhaps the American novelist Ursula Le Guin (born 1929) is the most persuasive. She has depicted worlds without hierarchy and domination both in her anarchist utopia *The Dispossessed* (1974) and in her more primitivist utopia *Always Coming Home* (1985). Le Guin has pointed out that wilderness for men is usually a place they can go hunting and exploring and have all-male adventures. She then adds the resounding statement: 'Where I live as a woman is to men a wilderness. But to me it is home.'[10]

In her *Dancing at the Edge of the World*, she further tries to develop a holistic perspective which breaks down barriers and categorizations to depict the processes of change. Her aim is to 'subvert as much as possible without hurting anybody's feelings'. She is particularly critical of the kind of science fiction in which 'space and the future are synonymous: they are a place we are going to get to, invade, colonize, exploit and suburbanize'.[11] The rationalist utopia is a future-oriented 'power trip' based on progress and not process; it is Euclidean, obsessed with the idea of regulating all life by reason; it is fundamentally *yang*, hot, steely and domineering.

In its place she advocates a 'utopian imagination' which recognizes that the Golden Age or Dream Time is right here and now on earth. 'In order to speculate safely on an inhabitable future, perhaps we would do well to find a rock crevice and go backward. In order to find our roots we should look for them where roots are usually found.' Based on the Spirit of Place, it would be 'non-European, non-euclidean, non-masculinist', a utopia which goes beyond the binary computer mentality and contains both *yin* and *yang* aspects.[12] It would involve a dance of renewal – a dance at the edge of the world.

To give gender or status to gods and goddesses is a form of idolatry; it separates spirits from nature as free-floating particles, and places them in a transcendental pantheon of human values. An earth goddess who demands obedience, sacrifice and propitiation from its human worshippers is a supreme example of this kind of alienation. Ultimately, nature is neither male nor female; it is both, a complex, mysterious, multifaceted unity.

True spirituality, which enhances and enlivens all aspects of our lives, is a sensitive awareness of the interconnectedness of things. It does not dwell on particulars but flows with the stream of universal energy.

# 30

# DEEP ECOLOGY VERSUS
SOCIAL ECOLOGY

That the myriad things advance and confirm the self is
enlightenment.

Dogen Zenji

The Norwegian philosopher Arne Naess coined the term 'deep ecology' in 1973. He wanted to distinguish between environmentalism, which is chiefly preoccupied with clearing up the planet, and philosophical ecology (what he calls 'ecosophy'), which seeks to change our understanding of ourselves and our place in nature. 'Ecosophy' derives from the Greek *sophia*, 'wisdom', and *eco*, 'house'. It studies our place in the Earth House Hold and concerns itself with 'earth wisdom'. Although partly inspired by the science of ecology and systems theory, it draws on much wider philosophical and religious traditions, including 'native' American philosophy, Zen Buddhism, Taoism and some pre-Socratic Greek thinkers, as well as Spinoza, Thoreau and Leopold closer to home.

Those deep ecologists, like the Americans Bill Devall and George Sessions, who follow in Naess's philosophical steps call for a new ecological consciousness. They reject the dominant world-view and social paradigm based on mechanical thinking, instrumental rationality and economic growth, which render humans isolated from each other and from nature. They call themselves ecologists because they embrace the central insight of ecology that there is an intermingling of all parts of the universe. They are deep because they look to the fundamental principles which are at the root of our environmental crisis. The archstone of their philosophy is that all life forms have the equal right to live and fulfil their potential.

Naess, strongly influenced by Spinoza and Gandhi, insists that his kind of ecology is deep because it seeks answers to the deeper questions of 'why?' and 'how?' The difference between the shallow and the deep ecology movements is one of depth of argumentation

413

and questioning. The latter looks at fundamental presuppositions of valuation as well as fact and hypotheses.[1] For Devall, deep ecology is 'settling into the stream of things as they are. It means moving down into cooler, more profound water.'[2]

Naess has called his philosophy 'Ecophilosophy T', implying by the use of the letter 'T' that it is only one possible formulation. He is not dogmatic and does not offer his philosophy as a system; it is axiomatic, based primarily on intuition. Fritjof Capra, too, has argued that deep ecology is in keeping with the findings of modern science, but that 'it is rooted in a perception of reality that goes beyond the scientific framework to an intuitive awareness of the oneness of all life, the interdependence of its multiple manifestations and its cycles of change and transformation'.[3]

The subtitle of *Deep Ecology* (1989) by Devall and Sessions is 'Living as if Nature Mattered'. In their widely influential book, they state: 'Deep ecology goes beyond the so-called factual scientific level to the level of self and Earth wisdom.'[4] It tries to provide a philosophical foundation for environmental activism. It is not only concerned with cultivating an ecological consciousness but also elaborating sound environmental ethics.

### Self-realization and biocentric equality

The two ultimate intuitions or norms of deep ecology are 'self-realization' and 'biocentric equality'. By self-realization, deep ecologists mean a form of spiritual unfolding which goes beyond the human to embrace the nonhuman world. It involves like Eastern religions the 'realization of the "self-in-the Self" where the "Self" stands for organic wholeness'. It assumes that 'no one is saved until we are all saved', from entire rainforest systems to the tiniest microbes in the soil.[5]

Naess argued that 'the higher the Self-realization' attained by anyone, 'the broader and deeper the identification with others'.[6] The term 'self-realization' refers to the realization of the personal self, which can involve the negative aspects of self-assertion and aggrandizement, while 'Self-realization' with a capital S refers to the realization of as expansive a sense of self as possible. The former should lead to the latter. The ecosophical outlook is therefore developed through 'an identification so deep that one's *own self* is no longer adequately delimited by the personal ego or the organism.

One experiences oneself to be a genuine part of all life.' Cosmological identification follows from the realization that 'life is fundamentally one'. It means going from an alienated, atomized, homeless existence to become part of the ecological and cosmic whole, to be at one with all things: 'Now is the time to share with all life forms . . . and Gaia the fabulous old planet of ours.'[7]

Although the Australian philosopher Warwick Fox claims to leave deep ecology behind in his sketch of a 'transpersonal ecology', he is no less concerned with identification. It means going beyond the attachment and ownership involved in personal identification with one's family, tribe, nation or race to an ontological identification. This leads to the realization that 'things are', and finally to cosmological identification which realizes that 'we and all other entities are aspects of a single unfolding reality'.[8] In this respect it shares the goal of enlightenment of Mahayana Buddhism; in the words of Dogen Zenji: 'That the self advances and confirms the myriad things is called delusion. That the myriad things advance and confirm the self is enlightenment.'[9]

The second intuition of deep ecology – 'biocentric equality' – is a moral principle. Rejecting humanist ethics, which gives a special place to man in nature, deep ecologists argue that since all organisms and entities in the ecosphere are parts of an interrelated whole, they should be considered equal in intrinsic worth. Every form of life should have 'the equal right to live and blossom'. Naess rejects the hierarchical notions of the Great Chain of Being and the scientific ecologists' notion of food chains with predators at the top of the pyramid in favour of a more egalitarian vision in which 'organisms are knots in the biospherical net'.[10]

As Aldo Leopold puts it, human beings should consider themselves nothing more than 'plain citizens' in the biotic community; they have no more rights than amoebae. The practical implication of the principle of 'biocentric equality' is that we should live with minimum impact on other species and on earth. We should follow the Hindu path of *ahimsa* (nonviolence) and do as little harm as possible.

In order to give a popular expression of their philosophy, Naess and Sessions have drawn up a list of basic principles of deep ecology. The first three are the most philosophically important:

1. The well-being and flourishing of human and nonhuman life on Earth have value in themselves (synonyms: inherent worth

    intrinsic value, inherent value). These values are independent
    of the usefulness of the nonhuman world for human purposes.
2. Richness and diversity of life forms contribute to the
    realization of these values and are also values in themselves.
3. Humans have no right to reduce this richness and diversity
    except to satisfy *vital* needs.[11]

In general, deep ecologists would like to allow all entities the freedom
to unfold and evolve in their own way unhindered by human
domination. Let the river live! Let the whales dive and blow!

From this perspective, deep ecologists like David Ehrenfeld have
attacked The *Arrogance of Humanism* (1978). In their 'religion of
humanity', he claims, humanists believe they have the ability to
rearrange the world of nature for their own ends. The result has
been the destruction of the natural world and its creatures.

It would seem that the very existence of human civilization is an
inevitable violation of biocentric equality. For humans to enjoy the
'equal right to live and blossom', to achieve self-realization, they
must destroy plant and animal life. However, this does not mean
they should not keep their impact to a minimum and interfere as
little as possible in natural ecosystems. Nor does it mean trying to
'civilize' the wild by eradicating predators, thereby upsetting the
natural balance. The value of wilderness areas is independent of
human purposes, whether they be full of life, as in the Amazon
rainforest, or comparatively inert, as in Antarctica. They have
intrinsic or existential value. Above all they allow the larger biospheric whole to continue to realize its evolutionary potential.

## Simple in means, rich in ends

In their lifestyle, deep ecologists advocate voluntary simplicity, a
way of life which is 'inwardly rich but outwardly poor'. Modesty
and humility are considered central virtues. Their guiding principle
is to be 'simple in means, rich in ends'. It means living at one with the
Earth; as Devall puts it, 'nothing forced, nothing violent, just settling
into our place'.[12] They go in search of the primitive and ancient ways.
They value ritual and ceremony. Cultivating ecological consciousness
means for them cultivating what the American academic Theodore
Roszak has called the 'rhapsodic intellect'.

On a practical level, deep ecologists act in defence of the Earth. This involves principally protecting wilderness areas, living in bioregions based on natural and not political boundaries, and decreasing the human population.

Wilderness areas, deep ecologists insist, are essential for the well-being of the human spirit as well as the vitality of the ecosphere. To escape from cities and parks and to experience the wild, they argue, is to develop a sense of place and to realize how nature follows its own processes. Like Thoreau, they believe that 'in wilderness is the preservation of the world'.

Not all humans, however, share their love for wild places; most have adapted to concrete and glass, and feel more at home in a flat than on a prairie. Civilization arose with the foundations of the cities, and many urban dwellers like to keep the wildlife at bay in their neat gardens, let alone in their sanitized rooms.

Even the very notion of 'wilderness' is suspect. It suggests that there is a place to tame. The original inhabitants of North America did not consider their region of the earth a 'pristine wilderness', as the colonialists did; they considered it 'home'. At the same time, as managers of national parks are only too well aware, if many more urban dwellers developed a taste for wilderness areas there would quickly be few left on earth. What remains is generally carefully protected.

To limit the human impact on the environment, deep ecologists recommend living in mixed communities in bioregions. This means living well in one's 'life-territory' and being mindful of one's local environment and culture. Bioregionalism begins by acting responsibly at home. It means developing profound roots in one corner of the Earth House Hold. A bioregion can be defined by its ecosystem, watershed, spirit of place or cultural identity.

Having 'watershed consciousness' is the opposite of being a rolling stone. It need not be narrow or nationalist. Nor does it mean staying where one was born; one can adopt a bioregion anywhere in the world. But wherever one settles one should live in a mixed community which has widened its boundaries to include land, water, plants and animals. One should also recognize that humans are nothing more than plain citizens with other organisms in a biospheric democracy.

In their economics, the deep ecologists recognize that the resources of the earth are limited. They therefore advocate recycling, appropriate technology and the use of renewable sources of energy. They wish to reduce needs to only those which are 'vital' (necessary for survival) and serve the larger goal of self-realization. They want to improve the quality of life rather than increase the standard of living.

A central principle of deep ecology, as espoused by Naess, Devall and Sessions, is that the flourishing of nonhuman life requires a substantial decrease in the human population. In a later work, Devall is more specific when he argues that there should be a commitment to reducing the birthrate, 'especially in third world nations'.[13] Even Edward Abbey, who wanted to take democracy 'all the way' and to transform society into 'a voluntary association of self-reliant, self-supporting, autonomous communities', came out in favour of stopping all immigration into the United States by strengthening the state's border forces.[14] The country in his view was already over-crowded with humans who were destroying the environment and other creatures.

The neo-Malthusian concern for population control has led some deep ecologists to reject aid to the Third World, arguing that the 'natural' checks of famine and disease should be allowed to take their toll. This view led the deep ecologist David Foreman to argue that no food aid should be sent to the Ethiopians; nature should take its course; they should be left to starve. It is the 'natural' corollary of his principle: 'Put the Earth first in *all* decisions, even ahead of human welfare if necessary.'

### Changing direction

Deep ecologists call for changes in 'basic economic, technological and ideological structures'.[15] Naess believes that there is a 'core democracy' in the biosphere and in the human sphere which implies no exploitation, no subjection, no class societies and no centralization; in their place, he would like to see local autonomy, self-sufficiency and cooperation.

But these fine ideals often remain vague slogans without substance in the writings of deep ecology. In practice, political change seems to be reduced to vague and pious calls to develop 'maturity', 'character' and 'leadership' and to go beyond the narrow ego to develop an 'ecological self' which affirms 'the integrity of nature in the widest sense'.[16]

Although deep ecologists are philosophically radical, they do not always wish to challenge existing states. Devall, for one, finds that compromise is desirable in the political arena.[17] A growing number of deep ecologists, however, prefer setting up affinity groups and networks rather than political parties and are prepared to engage in direct action and civil disobedience.

As in all social movements, there is an extreme wing which is prepared to take the law into its own hands. In the United States, the group called Earth First! (named in response to a group which wished to see an end to human starvation, called Food First!) insist that there can be 'no compromise in defence of Mother Earth!' In their *Ecodefence: A Field Guide to Monkeywrenching*, Dave Foreman and Bill Haywood have given careful instruction in 'non-violent resistance to the destruction of natural diversity and wilderness'. This involves taking direct action, which can vary from 'monkey-wrenching' (the purposeful disabling of implements used in an environmentally destructive way) and 'ecotage' (disabling a technological or bureaucratic operation in defence of one's place). One of the most radical voices of this approach is Edward Abbey, who wrote the adventure story *The Monkey Wrench Gang* ( 1975) and said in certain circumstances he would rather kill a man than a rattlesnake.

Yet despite these developments, the mainstream politics of the deep ecologists appears conservative in that it makes little attempt to change the status quo. The first principle of Devall and Sessions in the 'management' of natural resources is 'to encourage agencies, legislators, property owners and managers to consider flowing with rather than forcing natural processes'.[18] In this they do not radically question the existing distribution of power and wealth in society. Despite their principle of 'biocentric equality', they do not question the legalized social hierarchy. Even Dave Foreman and Bill Haywood insist that their form of direct action in defence of the earth is not revolutionary and does not aim to overthrow any social, political or economic system.

At the same time, the principle of 'biocentric equality' flattens out distinctions not only between the human species and other species, but between individuals and groups within the human species. Deep ecologists constantly use the pronoun 'we' to refer to the human species as a whole, and in a new version of original sin imply that all humans share a collective guilt for the despoilation of the planet. But this analysis overlooks the far greater responsibility of the developed industrialized countries in the North and of particular classes and groups within those societies for this state of planetary affairs.

Devall recommends that people become 'rainbow warriors' on behalf of nature, recognizing that social and political transformation are part of 'Self-realization'. But his warriors are not overtly political; the weapons they use are the insight that they are part of the web of life and a sense of compassion for the suffering of the world. They follow a 'profoundly objective spiritual *way*'.[19] They stay in their homelands and bioregions and commune with nature.

When it comes to conventional politics, Devall's 'warriors' do not take sides between capitalism and Marxism but are politically neutral: 'They are neither left nor right. They are affirming the inherent worth of rain forests and grizzly bears. They are encouraging broader identification and solidarity.' Charlene Spretnack and Fritjof Capra define green politics in similar terms, insisting that they go beyond the 'Left/Right split of the declining paradigm'.[20] Warwick Fox, defending deep ecologists from the accusation of environmental fascism, argues that ecology teaches old-fashioned American liberalism: just as democracy claims 'no-one is *above* the law', so on the basis of 'ecosphere ethics' 'no entity is *above* the ecology'.[21] In so saying, he defends the very legal system which wiped out the ecologically harmonious way of life of the Indians and continues to plunder 'legally' the world's resources. In general, deep ecology takes an idealistic view of society which fails to show how structures and values interrelate and sees change in terms of cyclical fluctuations rather than any dialectical development.[22]

As a strategy for change, deep ecology mainly recommends performing acts of 'ecotage', reforming the legal system, changing personal lifestyle and increasing awareness through persuasion and example. While all this can be positive, it largely leaves the main sources of human domination and hierarchy – private property and the state – intact.

Another problem with deep ecology is its axiom of biocentric equality and its assertion that everything alive has the 'equal right to live and blossom'. This rights-based approach would seem to be inconsistent with the general holistic orientation of deep ecology.[23] When applying the principle, difficulties also immediately arise. In the first place, it leaves out inanimate objects like mountains and lakes which do not strictly speaking live or blossom, yet have an intrinsic worth as part of an ecosystem. Secondly, it does not distinguish between different creatures. Do simple organisms like smallpox virus have the same right to flourish as a complex one like an elephant? Thirdly, the principle of biocentric equality offers no guidance when a conflict of rights should arise. Is a varied ecosystem more valuable than a simple and common one? Are sacred sites more important than secular ones? Do rare species have more right to survive than common ones? In order to get out of these dilemmas, it would seem necessary to introduce the notion of fairness, which is not the same as equal treatment. Coupled with the principle of impartiality, it will help solve conflicting rights by discriminating in favour of the most worthy.

There are other shortcomings in deep ecology. Most deep ecologists limit their discussion to a 'land ethic', forgetting that about seven tenths of the earth's surface is covered by sea. It would be even more consistent not to end with the earth itself but to extend the principle of wellbeing to the universe as a whole.

Deep ecologists accept that humans have a right to reduce the richness and diversity of life forms in order to satisfy their *vital* needs', but they offer no clear definition of such needs. Devall clouds the issue when he says that deep ecologists seek to satisfy vital needs 'with the most simple, elegant, and least environmentally destructive means'.[24] This leaves open the question of how much life we can take to enable us to live.

Although the principle of biocentric equality denies special human rights, the deep ecologists insist that we have duties. We do not have more worth than other species, yet we have responsibility for them. But to what degree should we interfere?

Again, deep ecology offers only a broad orientation. Indeed, Naess has left the issue of drawing the boundary between justifiable and unjustifiable interference with nature to 'local, regional, and national circumstances and cultural differences'.[25] If that is the case, the very notion of 'biocentric equality' has little content except as a slogan.

On the face of it, the principle of 'biocentric equality' combined with the norm of minimal harm would logically lead to vegetarianism. Devall and Sessions maintain that an intuition of deep ecology is that 'we have no right to destroy other living beings without sufficient reason'. Naess, on the other hand, asserts that the human participation in an ecosystem 'necessitates some killing, exploitation and oppression'.[26] Both qualifications of 'biocentric equality' are so ambiguous and vague that they are virtually meaningless. What constitutes 'sufficient reason' – survival or the vagaries of the palate?

For psychological reasons rather than 'vital needs', many deep ecologists advocate hunting as a means of being more 'in touch' with nature. The American ecologist Paul Shepard, for instance, argues that hunters were 'more fully human' than their descendants, whereas agriculture is an ecological disease which has led to 'humanizing the earth's surface'. In the crudest sociobiology, he argues that we are 'genetically' hunters and gatherers. Devall and Sessions justify their practice of eating meat by the claim that 'mutual predation is a biological fact of life'.[27] A similar argument was employed by the Social Darwinists to justify capitalist and imperialist competition.

Another 'intuition' of deep ecologists which has been made into a 'law of ecology' is that 'Nature knows best'.[28] To assume this, however, is to assume that there is some benevolent force in nature which operates like Providence. Nature may offer the ground for ethics, and ethics has a natural history, but it does not follow that everything which exists in the natural world, including viruses, earthquakes and droughts, is necessarily 'good'.

Clearly the Western attempt to 'improve nature' has had disastrous results when it has not understood the processes of nature or failed to appreciate the long-term consequences of deep intervention. But to assert that any major man-made change in a natural system is likely to be *detrimental* to that system, as Barry Commoner does, is absurd. It implies, for instance, that the whole history of Western medicine has been counterproductive. We should not have tried to eradicate the smallpox virus and we should stop research into AIDS. To believe that 'Nature knows best' would appear to be a modern version of Pope's cosmic Toryism in which 'Whatever is, is right', or Leibniz's unquestioning optimism that we live 'in the best of all possible worlds'.

Deep ecologists often seem to consider themselves to be an elite of enlightened visionaries. They are extremely contemptuous of the vast majority of humans who have been won over to the values and goals of industrial-technocratic civilization. Despite their celebration of the virtues of modesty and humility, many are deeply intolerant of other lifestyles. Their concern for the earth makes some of them appear to be the enemies of the human race.

There is much which is valuable in deep ecology, especially its desire to extend the moral community to include nonhuman life and its call for a wider identification with nature. It rightly insists that the condition of the freedom of humans should be the freedom of the rest of nature. It affirms boldly that all nature has intrinsic value. But is it deep? Although it vociferously opposes 'humanist arrogance', there is a sense in which the very phrase 'deep ecology' is arrogant.

In another sense, deep ecology is little more than a tautology, like cold snow.

## Social ecology

Social ecology developed earlier than deep ecology and has been one of its principal critics. The term, first used by the American ecologist E. A. Gutkind in 1954, has come to describe that tendency within the green movement which sees the present ecological crisis as a result of the breakdown of the organic fabric of both society and nature.[29] It is associated with those radicals who seek fundamental social change as the only way to avoid the 'ecocide' that humanity seems to be heading for. It takes the concerns of the green movement with democracy, community and cooperation to the borders of anarchism and beyond, realizing that it is our institutions of domination and hierarchy, especially embodied in the state and government, that block the possible liberation of nature and humanity.

Inspired by the ecological principles of unity in diversity, spontaneity and complementarity, social ecology sees the balance and integrity of the ecosphere as an end in itself. It aims to create a social movement to transform the way we see our place within nature and to change our relations with each other and the nonhuman world. The most fundamental goal is therefore one of regeneration and rebirth, of nothing less than renewing the earth.[30] In this, social ecology challenges the fundamental premisses of Western civilization.

The science of ecology, according to social ecologists, not only supports libertarian moral principles but provides some essential guidelines of how a free society might be organized. Ecology stresses that the overall harmony of an ecosystem can best be achieved through the increasing differentiation and enrichment of its parts, free of all hierarchy and domination. By stressing the interdependence of all living things and beings and the dynamic balance of nature, it describes an evolving and symbiotic universe.

Social ecologists do not accept the distinction between 'is' and 'ought', the division of experience into descriptive and normative spheres. Instead, they argue that whatever exists has a potential: what should be is contained in what is. Our experience of valuing and seeking the good is merely part of the vast process of the emergence of value in nature in which all beings seek to attain their good.[31] Nature itself is not an arena for ethical

behaviour – that is peculiar to humans – but it can provide a ground
or matrix for ethics and be a rich source of values and ideals.

Social ecology differs from both shallow environmentalism and
deep ecology in its emphasis and direction. Environmentalism merely
reflects an instrumental rationality: it views nature as a passive
habitat composed of potentially useful objects. It is mainly concerned
with the short-term fixes of conservation and pollution control. It
lays the blame for the ecological crisis on inappropriate technology,
overpopulation or industrial growth while ignoring the real cause,
which lies in the institutionalization of domination and hierarchy
and the authoritarian mentality which sustains it.

At the same time, social ecologists criticize deep ecologists for
failing to appreciate that ecological problems have their ultimate
roots in human society. They do not fully appreciate that man's
domination of nature is a social development and the result of a
particular course of human history. They underestimate the special
ability of evolving human beings to create consciously and purposefully their own societies and cultures. They overlook the importance
of social evolution as an extension of biological evolution.

The most outspoken of social ecologists, the American Murray
Bookchin, has accused the deep ecologists of trying 'to regale
metaphorical forms of spiritual mechanism and crude biologism
with Taoist, Buddhist, Christian or shamanistic "Eco-la-la"'. He
calls the deep ecology expounded by Naess, Foreman and Sessions
a 'black hole' of half-digested, ill-formed and half-baked ideas.[32]

Others, like the American philosopher John Clark, recognize
the importance of Taoism to social ecology, and appreciate the
contribution of deep ecology to a holistic respect for the richness
and diversity of life, but feel that it does not offer a coherent
philosophy or praxis. By contrast, he believes that social ecology
presents a comprehensive conception of the self, society and nature.
Starting from the ecological principle of organic unity in diversity,
he asserts that the good of the whole can only be achieved through
the 'rich individuality and complex interrelationship of the parts'.[33]
Social ecology recognizes that evolution progressively unfolds in the
direction of increasing diversification and consciousness.

Social ecologists argue that the environmental crisis is a social
problem and can only be solved by social and political means. They
point out that it is misleading to talk about the 'collective guilt'
of the human species, without recognizing the impact of different

nations, classes and sexes on the planet. They are critical of the deep ecologist 'mountain-men' who contemplate nature in marginal wilderness areas and turn their back on the cities where most humans live. They reject the idea that all creatures are of identical worth and that the only sound ethics is one of strict biocentric equality. They are not ready to sacrifice human beings in the drive to control population.

On a positive level, social ecologists see that the precondition for human survival and planetary health is the creation of a decentralized society of face-to-face communities which adopt an emancipatory technology and a careful balance between agriculture and industry. In such organic communities, the traditional antagonism between humanity and nature would come to an end and the individual self would become part of a larger social and ecological self.

Murray Bookchin, born in 1921 and author of *The Ecology of Freedom* (1982), has been the most influential exponent of social ecology. Despite his bitter attack on deep ecologists, he is a holistic thinker like them and stands firmly within the Western tradition of organic and process metaphysics. As early as 1952, he was complaining about the use of pesticides in food and under the pseudonym of Lewis Herber railed against *Our Synthetic Environment* (1962). It was his essay 'Ecology and Revolutionary Thought', written in 1965 and published in a collection called *Post-Scarcity Anarchism* (1971), which first applied the insights of ecology to the possibility of creating a free society without hierarchy and domination.

Impressed by Marx's dialectic, but not by his political prescriptions, Bookchin describes his own philosophy as a form of 'dialectical naturalism'. Nature for him is not just a 'lump of minerals' but a 'complex web of life' which is charged with ethical meaning.[34] He rejects equally the kind of mechanical materialism which sees nature as a dead collection of resources, and the 'spiritual mechanism' in which all is dissolved in cosmic oneness. Instead, he develops the Greek concept of *nous* which finds meaning and purpose in nature.

Like Lovelock's Gaia, nature for Bookchin has an ability to organize and maintain itself. It also has an inherent striving towards increasing consciousness, complexity and subjectivity. This latent intentionality manifests itself as 'a graded development of self-organization that yields subjectivity and, finally, self-reflexivity in its highly developed human form'.[35] Human nature is thus a kind of 'second nature' made out of primeval 'first nature'. Whereas 'first nature' is the product of biological evolution, 'second nature' comes from social evolution; it is the cultural product of the human mind, which can act creatively and purposefully in a unique way.[36] Human consciousness is not unique to humans but merely nature rendered self-conscious. While Bookchin discerns an inherent purpose in nature in this way, he does not offer a deterministic picture. Like a plant or a child, nature as a whole has a potential which tries to unfold with a dim sense of will and choice.

Drawing on the radical libertarian tradition of Fourier, Kropotkin and William Morris, Bookchin locates the cause of the present ecological crisis firmly in society and history. It is not merely the result of unchecked technology, industrial growth or overpopulation; more harmful has been the emergence of domination and hierarchy in human society: 'The domination of nature by man stems from the very real domination of human by human.'[37] In the past, it was thought necessary to dominate and conquer nature in order to transcend scarcity. But the very concept of dominating nature first emerged from man's domination of woman in patriarchal society and of man's domination of man in hierarchical society. Human beings and the rest of nature have thus become the common victims of oppression and exploitation. To overcome the present ecological crisis it is therefore necessary to end this state of affairs. This can be done only by fundamentally changing society. If we begin to change human relationships, then we simultaneously change the relations of humans with the rest of nature.

Despite his vociferous and often vituperative disagreements with the deep ecologists for leaving social transformation off their platform, Bookchin tries like them to ground his ethics in scientific observations about nature. Nature can provide the ground for ethics and we can evaluate 'what is' in terms of its potential to be realized. He also calls for an 'ecological sensibility' which will develop a holistic outlook, celebrate play and imagination, and 're-enchant' humanity and nature through a new animism. It would involve a form of spiritual escapism but a 'return to earthy naturalism'.[38]

Bookchin's ideal society would consist of a decentralized society of 'ecocommunities' using 'ecotechnologies' situated in local ecosystems. It would consist of a federation of communes in which all members decided on their own affairs through popular assemblies based on majority vote. Production would be agreeable, voluntary and environmentally friendly. Distribution would be based on usufruct rather than need. All individuals would be guaranteed a basic minimum – the irreducible minimum – to enjoy life, whether they worked or not. Rather than equal shares, the principle of the equality of unequals would apply, which compensates for disabilities and special needs. Freedom rather than justice, pleasure rather than happiness, is the ultimate goal. People would be able to satisfy freely their needs.

There are some features in Bookchin's early vision of 'ecotopia' which are questionable. He offends the animal-welfare movement by advocating hunting and stock-raising and the 'rational' and 'humanistic' use of animals; he waxes lyrical about air-conditioned tractors and the 'augermatic feeding of livestock' in feed pens without realizing that such pens are like prisons. He even contemplates the advantages of 'controlled thermonuclear reactions'.[39] His depiction of agrarian communes in *The Ecology of Freedom*, with 'wherever possible the wildlife they may support at the fringes' is a landscape largely transformed by humans.[40] The balance is tipped in favour of humans rather than the surrounding communities.

Bookchin rails against the deep ecologists' idea of 'biocentric equality' as being anti-humanist. But his own proposal to intervene in the evolutionary process, 'consciously abetting the thrust of natural evolution towards a more diversified, varied and fecund biosphere' is too humanist in the other direction.[41] It involves encouraging the human attributes of consciousness and subjectivity in latent life forms. It resurrects the idea of stewardship in which humans are managers rather than fellow travellers in the cosmic process of evolution.

Despite his libertarian position, there is still an apparent echo of Marxism in Bookchin when he asserts: 'Our reentry into natural evolution is no less a *humanization* of nature than a naturalization of humanity'. Bookchin shares the interventionist desire of the early ecologist Charles Elton that humanity should grasp the tiller of evolution: 'The world's future has to be managed, but the management would not be just a game of chess – more like steering a boat.'[42]

In fairness to Bookchin, he has recently qualified his endorsement of Elton's view and re-emphasized that we do not have a 'free rein' in manipulating the biosphere. Yet he continues to stress the unique place of the human species in natural evolution. He also remains faithful to the notion of positive intervention in the natural process in order to protect the biosphere from possible destructive events, to engage in ecological restoration work, and to 'open up new evolutionary pathways that can benefit existing biota'.[43]

Bookchin may be the most notorious theorist of social ecology, but the school is developing a momentum of its own. John Clark is less strident in style, appreciates the ecological insights of Eastern philosophy, and is not so dismissive of deep ecology. For him, social ecology defines freedom as essentially 'self-determination', found at all levels of being, as nature strives towards greater consciousness and diversity. In both nature and human society the progressive unfolding and realization of freedom relies on cooperation and mutual aid.

The implication for ethics is that value is created as each being realizes its potential. As the most richly developed species, this understanding gives an essential place to humanity in attaining the good of the whole, either by 'helping' evolution through 'judicious and restrained co-operation' to realize its potential or by checking it through ecological degradation. Like Bookchin, Clark considers that a degree of intervention in nature is now necessary but his is not so deep: 'We must undertake the regeneration of nature, by reversing the process of destruction of species and ecosystems, and by seeking to co-operate with nature in fostering richness, diversity and complexity.'[44]

Social ecologists are right to call for the development of a new ecological sensibility that recognizes the integrity of the ecosphere as an end in itself. In order to achieve harmony with nature, harmony must also be created within society. This can only be achieved through the development of an environmental ethics which sees human beings as an inextricable part of nature, and which asserts the intrinsic worth of the whole of nature. Such ethics will remain empty talk without the attempt to create a society which seeks to realize the ecological ideal of unity in diversity by combining the greatest degree of individuality consistent with the greatest degree of solidarity.

The passionate divide between the adherents of deep ecology and social ecology is both destructive and unnecessary. Their emphasis may be different but they both recognize that the crucial cause of the present ecological crisis is the deranged relationship between humanity and nature. They share a common appreciation of nature as a living web which has its own purpose and meaning. They both call for a new ecological consciousness which recognizes humanity to be one species among others on an evolving planet.

My own view is that a new synthesis of deep ecology and

social ecology is needed in what might be called libertarian ecology. It will be deep in the sense of going to the roots of the ecological crisis and engaging in profound questioning. It will be social in recognizing that the human domination of nature begins in society and that its freedom will necessarily involve the freedom of humanity as a whole. Finally, it will be libertarian in wanting to liberate both humans and nonhumans, society and nature, allowing all to find their place in the odyssey of evolution.

# 31

# TOWARDS A LIBERTARIAN
# ECOLOGY

When the great Tao is forgotten,
Kindness and morality arise.

Lao Tzu

Is it right to eat animals? Is the life of a mouse more valuable than
that of a mature oak? Whom do we include in our moral community?
Does the earth have interests? What theory can help us decide whether
a dam should be built in a wilderness or whether cattle should displace
trees? What is our place and role in nature? Does a flower have
a right? Is an ecosystem intrinsically valuable or only of value in
relationship to us? These are just a few of the questions that vex
environmental moralists.

It is difficult, if not impossible, to find one single overarching
moral theory – a single set of guidelines and priorities – to cover all
aspects of our relationships with nature. Such a comprehensive theory
remains as elusive as the grand unified theory in physics. It makes
more sense, therefore, to adopt a form of ethical pluralism which
accepts that different moral theories have their merits in different
circumstances and areas. Theories of rights, for instance, are often
at odds with utilitarian ethics, since numbers and consequences have
no sway over the inalienable right to life. Both rights-based and
utilitarian ethics, on the other hand, engender respect for individual
organisms, but are vague about larger systems and collections, like
valleys, rivers and trees, which would require a more holistic
approach.

This is not to say that there should be different sets of principles
directing our relationships with humans and with nonhumans. Such a
view can easily lead to hypocrisy and expediency; for example, that it
is wrong to torture humans but right to continue animal experiments.
It could imply that it is right to put an animal 'out of its misery',
but wrong to kill humans 'painlessly' because they are living a life

430

of suffering through poverty and tyranny. Surely the answer is to stop the misery, not to apply one set of principles to humans and another to animals.

Ethical pluralism does imply, however, that some theories are more appropriate than others when dealing with certain dilemmas and situations. It is not only a form of ethical colonialism but unecological to assert that there are universal moral principles which are not modified by circumstances. Indeed, a libertarian ecology suggests that every case should be considered a rule unto itself.

Ultimately, fully developed people living in harmony with nature have no need for moral guidelines or maps to help them through the maze of life's choices. Their actions are spontaneously right, in keeping with the flow of things. They live good lives without being aware of them; they have dispensed with man-made laws and moral rules to govern their behaviour. Like animals, they simply are. Only when discord is felt does morality arise.

### Animal rights, human and nonhuman

Strolling in Kilburn in London recently, I came across a dispensary of the Royal Society for the Prevention of Cruelty to Animals in a Victorian building which has this war memorial on its façade:

> This tablet records the death by enemy action, disease or accident of 484,143 horses, mules, camels and bullocks, many hundreds of dogs, carrier-pigeons and other creatures on the various fronts during the Great War 1914–1918. Knowing nothing of the cause, looking forward to no final victory, filled only with love, faith and loyalty, they endured much and died for us. May we all remember them with gratitude in the future and commemorate their suffering and death by showing kindness and consideration to living animals.[1]

At first sight, the sentiments expressed would seem honourable and compassionate, yet they are shot through with anthropomorphism. How does the writer know that the horses were 'filled only with love, faith and loyalty' as they were beaten in the mud and urged into the barbed wire? By putting their deaths down to 'enemy action', disease or accident, it also entirely exonerates their military masters from any responsibility. The whole approach assumes that animals have no rights which might prevent them from being sent to war on our behalf.

The theory of rights has a long-established tradition in the political culture of the West, and has been slowly extended to encompass a widening circle of individuals. Locke in the seventeenth century was the first to claim that the notion of 'natural' rights to life, liberty and property was self-evident to all rational beings, but these were limited at first to rational, property-owning European males. In the subsequent struggle for human emancipation, rights took the form of life, liberty and the pursuit of happiness in the American Declaration of Independence, and equality, liberty and fraternity in the French Revolution. But it still did not include women and non-Europeans. Only in the twentieth century have human rights been extended to embrace all humanity, although those enshrined in the United Nations Declaration of Rights are far from being respected in all countries.

Since the 1970s there has been a growing groundswell to widen further our moral horizon and to extend rights to animals as well as humans. The criterion for whether a being is entitled to moral consideration has shifted from rationality (consciousness) to sentience (feeling). But where to draw the line between sentience and nonsentience will always be debatable; the utilitarian philosopher Peter Singer, who has done much to promote animal liberation, draws it near the mollusc – 'somewhere between a shrimp and an oyster'.[2] An octopus, however, is a mollusc, with a powerful memory, apparent feelings (changing colour according to its responses) and problem-solving intelligence. I, for one, would include molluscs in the moral community. I would extend Bentham's principle even further to say that the criterion for moral considerability is not whether an organism *feels*, but whether it *lives*. This would include flora as well as fauna in the category of living things worthy of moral consideration.

Singer's case for animal liberation is based on the utilitarian ethic to maximize pleasure and minimize pain, coupled with the principle of equality. He rightly points out that the basic principle of equality – a moral idea rather than an assertion of fact – does not require equal or identical *treatment* but equal *consideration*.[3] This does not mean that the interests of some organisms are more important than others, but that all should be considered equally. It requires that whatever the nature of a being, if it is capable of feeling, its suffering should be counted equally with like suffering. It asserts that equality must be based on the moral principle of the equal consideration of interests rather than on the possession of some characteristic such as language or reason.

What Singer has successfully popularized is the notion that to deny animals moral consideration – speciesism – is on a par with sexism and racism. He has brought nonhumans into our circle of moral concern, called attention to their suffering at human hands, and made a good case for vegetarianism in the process. From the liberal principle of not causing unnecessary pain, the British philosopher, Stephen Clark, too, has argued persuasively that humans should become vegetarians. Admittedly in pursuit of a fantasy, the British novelist Brigid Brophy has called for a 'Declaration of Independence on Behalf of the Other Animals'.[4]

From a different perspective, the American philosopher Tom Regan has no less cogently argued *The Case for Animal Rights* (1988). His starting point is that animals as 'subjects-of-a-life' have intrinsic worth and an equal natural right to life.[5] His 'subjects' include all 'normal adult mammals', whom he defines as manifesting the characteristics of perception, memory, desire, belief, self-consciousness, intention, a sense of the future, and sentience. These should be treated as Kantian ends-in-themselves and not merely in a utilitarian way as means to the best consequences. All beings with inherent value have an equal right to respectful treatment. It is therefore difficult to justify animal experimentation or hunting, for instance, on utilitarian grounds.

While I agree with Regan's conclusions, the language of rights is unfortunately vague and confusing. All too easily it can degenerate into complacent rhetoric. The lists of rights put forward for approval are often arbitrary and conflicting. A human's right to property, which usually includes domesticated animals, conflicts with the animals' rights to life and liberty. The right to life is appealed to by those who would like to abort a foetus and those who would like to see it born.

Although Locke and others tried to argue that reason demonstrated that the right to life, liberty and property (which could be reduced to the right to 'estate' since they are something which we possess) were 'natural rights' based on the laws of nature, in fact it is clear that they are artifical conventions created by humans for their own interests. Even the editor of the American journal *Environmental*

*Ethics*, criticizing the methods of the Earth First! movement, has reminded its readers approvingly that the sanctity of property was one of Locke's natural rights.[6] In short, rights are usually little more than particular claims made by different people in the pursuit of their interests.

Rights are also framed in legalistic terms, and require the state to enforce them through the threat or actual use of violence. They involve a power struggle, the power of someone or some group over someone else, whether it be the divine right of kings, the rights of man or the rights of animals. They mean asserting a personal boundary which should not be violated, whether of the body, mind or property, and the assertion leads to escalating war. In the final analysis, the state, which claims to defend in liberal democracies the right to life and liberty, claims the right to imprison people and through its agents (soldiers and executioners) the right to kill them.[7]

The doctrine of rights is not only property-based, individualistic and inherently coercive, but it is also often patronizing. It is usually a question of those holding power extending their privileges to others. It implies that animals are inferior to humans and require our legal guardianship. To want to extend the moral community to animals according to consciousness or sentience assumes a hierarchy of moral worth.[8]

The main reason for using the language of rights today is that in our culture it is readily understood by those seeking to expand freedom. They are enmeshed in the historical experience of oppressed groups seeking a fairer deal. But their partial nature should not be overlooked. In the long run, human and animal liberation do not require a new charter of rights but a thorough transformation of our unjust and unequal relationships and the development of an ecological sensibility which recognizes the intrinsic worth and autonomy of all creatures.

While rights theorists and utilitarians go in different directions, they have both helped to close the gap between humans and nonhumans inherited from Western philosophy and the Christian religion. It has become increasingly difficult to maintain that humans are somehow metaphysically unique. We should therefore acknowledge our kinship with animals. Although they may be less conscious than we are and find it difficult to imagine the future, they are still capable of pain and pleasure, fear and contentment; as such they have inherent value and should not be treated for our purposes except in ways that recognize this.

Whatever Descartes and his followers might say, I am convinced that animals have consciousness and sentience as I watch the stray dog that has chosen to live with me curled up asleep by a log fire, whining and trembling in its dreams. It is an intuition confirmed by close observation over ten years. The dog has taught me a lot about human arrogance and chauvinism, about spontaneous affection and play, and about trans-species communication.

It may be anthropomorphic to attribute human characteristics to this dog and other animals, but, where the evidence is overwhelming, not to do so is a form of human chauvinism. I consider the dog and me to be part of the same moral community, held together by mutual obligations and common interests. To 'put him out of his misery' would raise similar problems as euthanasia might in the case of my brother. At the same time, I do not treat the dog like an honorary human. I try to recognize its autonomy as an individual and to consider its canine interests. I leave it lying on the earth, not curled on my lap.

Not only have eco-philosophers been concerned with widening the moral community to include animals, but there has also been an attempt to extend legal standing to natural objects. The case arose when the Sierra Club tried to prevent Walt Disney Enterprises from developing the Mineral King Valley, a remote wilderness area in the United States. It was argued that the wilderness itself should be considered a plaintiff, with the Sierra Club representing the valley as a guardian or attorney. The argument was that valleys and trees should be considered 'legal persons' along with corporations, nations, societies and clubs.[9] The case was thrown out, but it raises the question of whether trees, stones and ecosystems can have moral standing. Although embedded in a legalistic and rights-based culture, this points to a widening of moral community from humans and animals to include plants and trees.

It has been argued that only entities which have 'interests' can have moral and legal standing. This is usually taken to mean only persons who have consciousness. But, as some utilitarian and rights theorists have recently argued, not only consciousness but sentience – the ability to feel – should be taken as a criterion of moral considerability. Since dogs as well as humans are conscious and feel pleasure and pain, they can be judged to have 'interests'. But what about roses in my garden or polyps in an ecosystem? I would say the fact that they exist, and can fare well or ill, gives them interests and we should take them into account in our moral considerations.

## Utility and the general good

Utilitarians claim that each person has a duty to the best of his or her ability to contribute to the general good. Utilitarians have until recently restricted their considerations to the general good of human society which has involved the massive exploitation of nature. Some, as we have seen, extended the moral community to include sentient animals. Others extended the principle of utility to the ecosphere, to promote the general good of nature as a whole. This would go beyond Leopold's 'land ethic' and embrace the sea, and finally the earth and sky and space.

The utilitarian ethic, just like the notion of rights, is fraught with difficulties, in theory and in practice. The immediate problem is in defining 'good'. For Bentham, good meant pleasure and pleasure brought about happiness. He therefore believed that it was right to try to maximize pleasure and minimize pain. Another problem is how to classify different types and degrees of pleasure. For Bentham skittles was as good as poetry but for John Stuart Mill intellectual pleasures were superior to physical pleasures. Is it better to be Socrates dissatisfied or a pig contented? he asked. Then the numbers game began. Bentham defined the general good as the maximum amount of pleasure of the greatest number. For Mill general happiness was considered a good to the sum of all persons, just as each individual's happiness is a good to that individual. The discussion became increasingly abstract and unreal.

When the hedonistic principle of utility is applied in practice, it is difficult to decide not only between competing claims of human communities, but also between different species. Does the happiness of foxes trump the happiness of sheep farmers? It may be possible to take into account the pains and pleasures of more complex mammals like bears, wolves and deer, but what about calculating the pains and pleasures of insects, jellyfish and barnacles? What about the pleasures and pains of collections, such as woods, rivers, beehives and ecosystems? And there is the wider question of deciding when human interference is justified for the 'good' of an ecosystem.

It is virtually impossible to calculate the total distribution of happiness across a mixed group. The utilitarian appeal to maximize personal good is difficult enough when calculating within the confines of a nation-state, particularly since there is, as Sartre observed, 'naturally an infinity of possible projects as there is an infinite possibility of possible human beings'.[10] Imagine the difficulties of calculating the happiness of the greatest number of the global village of humanity, let alone of Gaia itself.

In his 'felicific calculus', Bentham insisted on the egalitarian principle of 'Each to count for one and none for more than one'. Godwin also introduced the principle of impartiality as a beacon in dealing with competing interests in his utilitarian ethics. But it led to conclusions which shocked his contemporaries: if a house caught fire and I could only save one of two people, a philosopher and his maid, whom should I choose? On the principles of utility and impartiality, I should save the philosopher, because of his likelihood to contribute to the general good, rather than his maid – even if the maid be my mother. Such a view of rational impartiality flies in the face of those private affections which are often considered to be the basis of moral feeling. Even Godwin worried over it.

Many would agree with Albert Camus when he said during a speech accepting his Nobel prize for literature that if he had to choose between justice and his mother, he would choose his mother. It was said in the context of the Algerian War of Independence; having been brought up in French Algeria, like so many *pied noirs* he opposed independence and argued merely for equal rights for Algerians and French. But by choosing his mother, he abandoned impartial justice and discriminated in favour of his family, clan, tribe, race and nation. It is this partial morality that environmental ethics tries to go beyond.

But what of the true case of the shipwrecked yacht-owner who found himself in the sea with his dog and cook? He scrambled into the only two-man life raft available, and hauled his dog in with him. Despite the protests of the cook, he refused to let him in as well. When they were rescued, the cook was found dead tied to the raft in the water and the yachtsman and his dog alive inside. A triumph of ecocentric impartiality, or inhuman selfishness of the owner who preferred his dog to a hired hand? Instinctively, most humans would condemn the yacht-owner.

Regan offers another version of the overcrowded-lifeboat case, involving four humans and a dog. But he goes against his own view

that living subjects have equal inherent value, by arguing that if one
of the five has to be thrown over to prevent the lifeboat from sinking,
it should be the dog. The dog would simply have fewer 'opportunities
for satisfaction' than a human and his loss would therefore be the
lesser harm.[11] Numbers do not count: the case would still hold if it
were one human life against the lives of a million dogs. Regan would
seem to be falling back on a speciesist intuition that human life has
supreme value.

To apply the principles of utility or rights from human society to
nature as a whole, we need to overcome our species-partiality, just as
Godwin suggested that we should overcome our family ties, and
think in terms of the good of the whole. In a sense, this would mean
going 'against nature' since it would seem, through the evolutionary
drive for survival, that we have a 'natural' preference for our own
children and our own species. But these urges are not irresistible and
friendship – which is natural – can cross the species barrier.[12] It can
even mean, as the case of the yacht-owner shows, that some prefer a
known dog to a human stranger. Certainly there are very controversial cases where the life of an animal is considered more
important than the interests of a man. Wardens in national parks
in Zimbabwe are prepared to shoot poachers in order to protect
the endangered animals. And what of the easily imagined case of
the last pair of breeding pandas versus two humans intent on
killing them for their fur?

The principle of ecocentric impartiality, while a useful beacon,
is clearly not perfect. If each species is considered to be equally
important in the attempt to maximize the wellbeing of the whole,
how do we discriminate? In favour of the one most likely to contribute
to the overall welfare, a utilitarian would be obliged to answer. On
these grounds, the destructive record of humans would not place them
in a good position; bees, performing the essential task of fertilization
as they flit from flower to flower, might well be considered more
worthy. In the long term, of course, it is in the interest of humanity
that the interests of other species are considered, since we are all
interconnected and mutually dependent. We should realize that
animals, plants, stones, fire, earth, air and water have their vital
place within nature's web.

The principle of ecocentric impartiality would therefore seem an
advance on the principle of biocentric equality for all beings and
things advocated by deep ecologists. The former does not deny that all

beings and things (individuals as well as groups) have inherent value, but it suggests that there is at least a partial ordering of value. The more valuable something is deemed, the more worthy it is of being preserved. In normal circumstances, a human might be considered more valuable than a nonhuman, but where a group or a threatened species is concerned, the latter may have precedence over the former. The criterion for value is the contribution to the wellbeing of the whole, taking into account such ecological principles as diversity, richness, stability and scarcity.

To adopt the principle of ecocentric impartiality might mean on occasion that human interests of a nonvital kind do not trump the vital interests of other organisms. It might well be right to sacrifice our interests as humans to the interests of animals, plants and even ecosystems. We might forgo our pleasure in climbing a mountain or visiting a marsh in order to let it be free to live and develop in its own way.

A sound environmental ethics would seem to require rationality which can think in terms of the long-term interests of the earth and the long-term consequences of our actions; intuition, to see the value of letting nature flourish; and imagination, to appreciate the needs of other beings and things. The latter is the supreme faculty of morality which enables us to go out of ourselves and to imagine what it is like to be a mountain, an orchard or a buzzard. Above all, it enables us to go beyond the boundaries of our own species and identify with the whole of nature.

### Minimum harm

However much we try, it is notoriously difficult to define and bring about the general good. Even when dealing with our neighbour, it it is not always clear how one can maximize his or her good. In some cases it may be best to do nothing; in other cases, we may intervene to prevent damage to others. But however benevolent our intentions, the consequences of our interference can be disastrous through lack of foresight and knowledge. Since this is true for a neighbour, what if the object of our care is society or nature?

Given the obvious difficulties of contributing to the general good, a less ambitious and more reliable way might be to try to minimize harm and cause as little suffering as possible consistent with living.

If all of nature has intrinsic worth, on what grounds can we justifiably kill organisms? In order to live. We cannot live without some killing but, on the principle of minimum harm, we should limit killing to the least sentient organisms and the smallest number of them possible. This means minimizing eating sentient and conscious life such as mammals, birds and fish. A vegan diet is the ideal; vegetarianism is second best, a meatless diet third, and so on. Subsistence hunting might be morally acceptable if there is no alternative source of food but not hunting for sport.

Are there any other grounds on which we can put organisms to death? Only in strict self-defence. If our basic health or survival is at stake, then we can justify killing the threatening organism if there are no alternative means.[13] This would qualify the principle of ecocentric impartiality by making it justifiable to eliminate organisms which make up the smallpox virus or HIV. It would not, however, justify the attempt to wipe out the entire mosquito or tetse-fly population in order to prevent malaria and sleeping sickness from being passed on between humans.

But when do we know that there are no alternative means available? I can remember when I was seventeen listening to the pacifist Christian Lord Soper on a box in Hyde Park Corner in London arguing that we can never justify taking the life of another person in self-defence because we can never be sure that they really mean to harm us. Tolstoy made a similar point when asked whether he would shoot a man who was about to rape his daughter. How can one be certain about actions in the future? Intentions are extremely difficult to discern from outward actions, and threatening behaviour can suddenly change into submission or flight. If one shot the threatening person when he did not in fact intend to kill or rape, one would have the blood of an innocent person on one's hands. The same might be said of a threatening elephant. Nevertheless, despite these caveats, the principle of self-defence, coupled perhaps with the side constraint of minimum harm, is the only morally justifiable reason for killing a conscious being.

The notion of self-defence can be widened to include survival. An ecological awareness makes it difficult to assert 'Thou shalt not kill' as a universal imperative. Cultures and ways of life are inextricably linked to their environments; it would be absurd to expect Inuit to become vegetarian without their ceasing to be Inuit. Masai in East

Africa would no longer be culturally Masai if they gave up their cattle, put on Western clothes and ate maize meal. If it were a question of survival in extreme and unavoidable circumstances, I would eat meat.

## Reverence for being

Ultimately, to consider rights and utility as a basis for moral considerability is too narrow. Ethical systems with this basis are too atomistic: they rely on weighing and measuring interests and consequences; they take isolated entities separated from their relationships as the owners of rights or the beneficiaries of utility. Both ethical approaches are partial; all right up to a certain point, especially when dealing with individuals, but not comprehensive enough to cover all moral decisions, especially those concerned with nature as a whole.

A genuine eco-philosophy needs a broader framework for a life-based ethic, accepting of course that life itself needs to be defined. The deep ecologist's principle of 'equal right to life' can be extended into a broad Buddhist compassion for all life, a Taoist readiness to let things be, and a Jain attempt to cause minimum injury. It takes up Schweitzer's principle of 'reverence for life' and applies it to the whole of nature. It advocates reverence for the Being of all beings.

Reverence for life, and for nature itself, does not mean placing the natural over the human.[14] On the contrary, it means revering oneself and other forms of being as part of an organic whole, and involves a respect for the diversity of life. There are problems concerning the scope and precision of such a principle, as there are with all other moral theories, but this does not lessen its validity.

What characterizes life is striving – against the pressures of entropy – for certain ends. Living systems are not merely self-organizing but also self-renewing. A hedgerow is greater than a blackthorn. Coral reefs try to heal themselves. Indeed, not only biological organisms but all process structures that try to regenerate and organize themselves can be included into the class of living systems. This would include ecosystems, the land, the oceans and the ecosphere – the living organism of Gaia itself – which may be said to have a good of their own and therefore to be worthy of consideration. And to say an entity which has a good of itself is worthy of consideration is simply axiomatic. Without such an assumption, ethics cannot get underway.[15]

## The individual and the whole

Tom Regan, whose rights-based case for animals means that he would sacrifice millions of dogs for one human simply because the latter has more 'opportunities for satisfaction', has accused the advocates of a more holistic view of nature of being guilty of 'environmental fascism'.[16] But this betrays a misunderstanding of the nature of fascism and holistic environmental ethics. When Leopold, whom he singles out, says that 'a thing is right when it tends to preserve the integrity, stability, and beauty of the biotic community' and that 'man is only a member of the biotic team', he is not calling for the sacrifice of individual organisms since they are all an integral and interrelated part of the whole.[17] By breaking individual threads, you destroy the web. Even Regan has latterly accepted that groups of individuals (e.g. ecosystems) are of 'direct moral significance'.[18]

Nevertheless, it is true that a holistic environmental ethic which calculates right and wrong with regard to the biotic community rather than individuals can reach unacceptable conclusions. J. Baird Callicott believes that bacteria and plankton carry more ethical weight than human beings because of their importance to the well being of the ecosphere. He is prepared to assert: 'The extent of misanthropy in modern environmentalism may be taken as a measure of the degree to which it is biocentric.'[19] The philosopher Holmes Rolston also believes, drawing on rights theory, that the species and ecosystem are more important than the individual and the prime object of duty: 'The appropriate survival unit is the appropriate level of concern.'[20] Edward Abbey, of The Monkey Wrench Gang fame, also attacked 'Man the Pest' and declared: 'I could no more sink the blade of an axe into the tissues of a living tree than I could drive it into the flesh of a fellow human.'[21]

Such a mechanistic view fails to take into account that human beings are part of the ecosphere as much as any other species, and to discriminate against them as a species is 'speciesism' in reverse. The biocentric ethic taken to extremes can be a form of neurotic misanthropy masquerading as earth chauvinism; it approximates Swift's view expressed by the King of Brobdingnag in Gulliver's

*Travels* that the human species is 'the most pernicious Race of little odious Vermin that Nature ever suffered to crawl upon the Surface of the Earth'.[22] A real respect for a community means a respect for the individuals which make it up: every individual, whether human or non human, has intrinsic worth.

There are of course difficulties in grounding ethics in a philosophy of nature. It could be argued that human beings as uniquely valuing agents project values on to nature (inevitably human ones) rather than finding them there. This would mean that there are no intrinsic values to be found in nature.

Again, the fact that natural processes operate in a certain way does not mean that human beings who are uniquely capable of moral choice have to follow them. The truly moral life recognizes the autonomy and rationality of moral agents. The science of ecology might demonstrate that overall harmony is increased by diversity, and that symbiosis helps maintain the vitality of communities, but many human beings prefer to go 'against nature' in this respect by following their selfish interests and by creating a uniform society.

Science can also be ideological, like the kind of Social Darwinism and sociobiology which claims that humans are fundamentally aggressive, territorial and selfish animals, thereby offering a so-called 'scientific' defence of capitalism. This kind of morality dressed as science subverts human autonomy and dignity. Garrett Hardin in his essay 'The Tragedy of the Commons'(1968) tried to give 'ecological' backing to his view that 'Freedom in a community brings ruin to all' and that coercive policies are necessary to restrict human population at an optimum level. To illustrate his thesis he uses the example of a group of self-interested herdsmen on an unrestricted commons whose actions 'naturally' end in disaster because 'each man is locked into a system that compels him to increase his herd without limit – in a world that is limited'.[23] This might be true of the Masai in East Africa, whose status is based on the number of cattle owned, a cultural attitude that developed when there was sufficient space for pastoralists to roam at will. But most rational farmers – in Africa as elsewhere – would see the advantage of making voluntary agreements to keeping a healthy balance.

With these reservations in mind, it is still possible for the science of ecology to provide a framework which can motivate certain moral attitudes. It can offer an 'extension of awareness': the more we know about relevant facts, the more sophisticated our evaluations will be.[24]

Science can offer guidelines, lessons to be learn if we are wise enough
to recognize them. 'What is' consists of 'what has been' and 'what
will be': nature is not static and has a completed past and an
unmade future. By becoming aware of the direction of evolution,
we will be in a better position to work with the flow rather than
against it.

Ecology as a disciplinary subject offers a rich backdrop to environmental ethics since it deals with the whole of nature. It provides
a holistic account of the total field of nature, with organisms as
threads in the web of life. It reminds us that the character of
a thing or being partly depends on where it is. It shows that
we are all sets of relationships. It implies that there are natural
constraints on what we can and cannot do in the pursuit of well
being. Our niche may be broad since we are unspecialized animals,
but it has limits and overlaps with others: an Inuit cannot be
fruit-gatherer, and a vegetarian cannot live for long on a desert
island in the Maldives. An ecological account of human nature
recognizes that all humans live within a natural as well as a social
context, and while there is no unchanging human essence in evolving
nature, there are limits and possibilities.[25]

Indeed, ecology shows how inextricably organisms are linked to
their larger wholes or ecosystems. They are all part of the process of
evolution which is moving towards greater complexity, diversity and
subjectivity. Not only the most conscious products of evolution are
valuable – mammals – but the process of evolution itself has value.
Individual organisms would not have evolved without particular
systems and the evolutionary process.[26] Our value as conscious
beings cannot be separated from the things and beings which
make up our environment. The Earth is our House Hold, the
home in which life takes place, but it is not ours in the sense of
private property. Peter Singer has written that 'A stone does not
have interests because it cannot suffer. Nothing that we can do to
it could possible make any difference to its welfare.' But William
Blake once wrote:

> Each grain of sand,
> every stone on the land,
> each rock and each hill,
> each fountain and rill,
> each herb and each tree,

mountain, hill, earth and sea,
cloud, meteor and star,
are men seen afar.[27]

Blake is saying that from one perspective – an ecological one – stones are not different from men: they are beings in different form but like them they exist and are worthy of consideration. They form part of the living organism of the earth.

All things are alive and have value: foxes and frogs, mountains and lakes, ecosystems and habitats, stones and raindrops, and the vibrating earth itself are all included in the category of the living. And 'everything that lives is holy'; it is worthy of our respect. Since the whole of nature is living, we should respect it as a whole.[28] We should therefore abandon the pretence of aspiring to be owners, tenants, managers, partners, stewards, citizens or even passengers in the ecosphere. We should not even be shepherds but guardians of being, nurturing where necessary, but letting things be and find their own way in benign neglect.

I would not, however, go beyond this sketch of a life-based and holistic ethics to suggest that there is a cosmic purpose. I do not share the Polish philosopher Henryk Skolimowski's anthropomorphic version of 'ecological humanism' – that we are perfectible: 'God-in-the-process-of-becoming . . . fragments of grace and spirituality'.[29] I have no certain views on the ultimate ends of evolution and the nature of divine purposes. From the past record and present process, evolution on earth seems to be moving in the direction of greater complexity, individuality, consciousness and freedom. It is a direction that I would not wish to fight against as some fight against the 'animality' of human nature; my environmental ethics are not 'anti-nature' but 'pro-nature'; better still, 'part of nature'.

I do not believe that God's persuasive power is somehow 'luring' all aspects of the universe towards the realization of instances of ever more greatness of experience or intensity of feeling.[30] It is not an intuition that I share. Indeed, I do not see 'God' as a personal being, either in a transcendental or an immanent way. I might be prepared to use the phrase 'God is Nature', not in a pantheistic way with God and Nature being identical, but merely as a metaphor intended to give ultimate value and significance to nature. It is way of saying nature is 'sacred' and 'holy' and worthy of respect. It is better that the world *is* than that it is not.

The German-American philosopher Herbert Marcuse recognized
that man had treated nature as his slave and called for the 'liberation
of nature'. Following Marx, he thought that capitalism had alienated
humanity from nature, and that the communist revolution would
ultimately bring about a reconciliation between the two. Believing
that everything exists primarily for its own sake, he concluded:
'Nature, too, awaits the revolution!'[31]

More recently the social ecologist Murray Bookchin has argued
that the 'human stewardship of the earth' requires a radical integration of 'second nature' (human consciousness) with 'first nature'
(from which we have evolved) and ultimately a transcendence of both
into the new domain of '*free* nature', thereby raising evolution to a
level of 'self-reflexivity'.[32]

But what does this mean? For Bookchin it means actively participating in evolution to give birth to more conscious and higher
life forms – an ecological version of Marx's nursemaid of history
who helps bring about the communist society. Yet this is far too
interventionist; it smacks of the Hegelian state 'helping' its citizens
to realize their 'higher selves'. No, better to free nature negatively
from human constraints so that it is free to realize its potential,
recognizing of course that humanity itself is part of that potential,
one thread in nature's web.

The tension between intervention in and preservation of nature is
inevitable. It may be necessary to intervene sensitively in an informed
attempt to repair the damage executed by earlier generations. But the
ideal is to adopt the Taoist position of letting alone, of letting be: 'If
nothing is done, then all will be well.'

The harmony of nature has been destroyed by dominating and
meddling humanity in the last tens of thousands of years, a fraction
of evolutionary time. The natural condition of humans and all beings
require no artificial rules or laws. It is laws that have been the cause,
not the remedy, of the prevailing social and ecological crisis:

> that the conditions of life are violated, that the will of God does
> not triumph, that the beasts of the field are disorganized, that
> the birds of the air cry at night, that blight reaches the trees and
> the herbs, that destruction spreads among creeping things, – this,
> alas! is the fault of *government*.[33]

Liberating nature would not, therefore, mean deep intervention in the evolutionary process, even if at present it seems to be going in the favourable direction of greater consciousness, subjectivity and diversity. No, it would mean: Hands off! Let Nature live! Let the Tao be!

> Man follows the earth.
> Earth follows heaven.
> Heaven follows the Tao.
> Tao follows what is natural.[34]

# 32

## ECOTOPIA REVISITED

> A map of the world that does not include utopia is not worth even glancing at, for it leaves out the one country at which Humanity is always landing. And when Humanity lands there, it looks out, and, seeing a better country, sets sail. Progress is the realization of Utopias.
>
> Oscar Wilde

Humanity is facing its greatest challenge in the course of its long and troublesome evolution. Through their tool-making genius, humans have transformed the earth, and no part, however deep in the ocean or high in the sky, does not reveal their imprint. Their numbers have swelled to more than five billion, and they multiply in an ever-increasing scramble. They drag out the entrails of the earth for metals and minerals, they sweep the seas for food, they turn the forests into swathes of short-lived pasture and destroy the sheltering sky. They are on the threshold of disaster, and nothing short of a fundamental change in consciousness and society can prevent them from careering towards ecocide.

To create a free and ecological society is an exercise in the utopian imagination. In Greek 'utopia' might mean 'no place', and Marx dismissed utopian thinking as unscientific, but it is just one way of describing how an ideal might be realized. To imagine an ecotopia is more than fantasy; it is rooted in existing practices and develops existing tendencies. In order to go beyond the impasse at which humanity finds itself requires an exercise in utopian imagination. It is in the fiery forges of the imagination that a new vision can arise, a vision which can transform our relationship with each other and the world.

Ecotopia is not intended as a blueprint. All social blueprints are absurd since they deny spontaneity and creativity. It is up to free people to create their own free society. But it makes sense to sketch some of the directions a free and ecological society might take. It would be free because it would allow individuals, communities and nature itself to realize their potential to the maximum degree, and it would be ecological because it would recognize that human survival rests on a harmonious relationship with the natural world.

In social terms, ecology points in the direction of a self-organizing, organic community like nature itself. It implies a pluralist, cooperative society which is committed to a common life, participatory democracy and ecological values. It recognizes the interdependence of all its members and the benefits of symbiosis and mutual aid. It tries to achieve unity in diversity, combining age-old patterns of cooperation with a modern sense of the individual. Since the primary source of men's domination of nature is their domination of their fellow women and men, an ecological society would seek to dissolve hierarchy and oppression. Rather than forming a hierarchy of power, it would try to create a series of overlapping networks in which no group dominates another. It would direct its energies not to power struggles but to the fulfilment of all its members and other life forms in the wider society of nature. The long-term aim would be to create a decentralized society of self-managing communities. Such a society would come to resemble a web with interwoven strands rather than a pyramid.

The basic cell of such a living society would be the 'affinity group', a voluntary association of free individuals formed by those with common interests and purposes. Like an extended family whose members are chosen, it would be convivial and creative, its members helping each other to realize their best without practising fraternal or sisterly terror. Forming horizontal networks with other groups, it would not become rigid or fixed, but continually evolve according to changing circumstances. Each group would work as far as possible through consensus which involves everyone in decision-making without the tyranny of a majority or a minority.

These groups would make up the commune, the fundamental organizing unit of society. The ecological ideal can best be served through the commune, a face-to-face community. The affairs of the commune would perhaps be run through the public forum of a popular assembly, the public sphere of life. A federation would link up the communes within a given territorial area. The assemblies could then federate at the district and regional level and, as long as nations exist, at the national level. Delegates would not follow their own consciences nor members of parties follow the party line, but merely express the will of the individuals in the neighbourhood who choose them. They would be at all times accountable and recallable. The regional and national assemblies could be called whenever necessary in order to solve disputes, coordinate activities and to organize foreign policy and defence. There would be self-management at the workplace, but workers would not have any more power to decide the course of events than other citizens.

Democracy would be direct and participatory. It would be direct in the sense that everyone would be involved in decision-making if they so wished. All members of the local commune would be able to attend the assemblies which decide the running of affairs, as in the *ecclesia* of the Greek *polis*. It would be participatory in the sense that participants would assume an obligation to enact the decisions made in the assemblies in the same way that they would fulfil a promise. But just as a promise can be justifiably broken in certain circumstances, so an individual may change his or her mind if new information or conditions prevail. If decisions were binding, come what may, that would only enable past folly to govern future wisdom.

Consent would always remain voluntary. Decisions would take more the character of invitations than of legal rules enforced by coercive sanctions. Ideally they would be reached through consensus after sufficient discussion for all who wish to air their views and for the will of the assembly to be felt. But if this proved impossible on some occasions, then the assembly might fall back on the principle of majority voting, although the decision of the majority would not be binding on the minority. They might be invited to go along with the majority but would not be obliged to do so. At the same time, if the majority view proved wrong-headed in the outcome, then it should be willing to give way to the minority view. The principle of private judgement would be respected and no one would be forced to carry out decisions with which they disagreed. Any administrative posts would be rotated, either by voting or casting lots, so as to avoid sclerotic bureaucracy or rule by so-called experts who often reveal just trained incapacity. The principal incentive for people to keep their contracts would be the difficulty in forming future ones if they were deemed likely to be broken.

Such a society would be both equal and free. The equal claims to be free and to participate would be respected. It would not involve a levelling-down of society to a grey uniformity, a kind of social entropy. On the contrary the freedom of one would be the condition of the freedom of all and the maximum amount of individuality consistent with solidarity would be encouraged. Any ecological society should have room for the creativity and spontaneity reflected in nature itself. Humanity and nature would be free to take their course in order to achieve their own good and reach fulfilment.

The kind of freedom envisaged would be essentially a negative form of freedom, a lifting of shackles, in which beings would be allowed to follow their own natures and realize their natural potential. What free people wish to do will be decided by free people. But presumably they would not create a regimented or uniform society; aware that the tyranny of custom or public opinion can be as oppressive as law, members of an ecological society would be tolerant of different lifestyles and views. They could try to persuade their neighbours of the rightness of their views, but not coerce them into accepting them.

Equality in an ecological society would not mean merely equal opportunity, equality before the law, or equal shares. Rather, it would be an equality of unequals, recognizing that those with special needs or disabilities would be compensated for according to their respective requirements and situations. Nevertheless, an irreducible minimum to satisfy basic needs, including leisure, would be guaranteed for all by the community. The healthier and more vital the community, the greater the number of 'parasites' it could support.

An ecological society would allow the realization of the 'ecological self', which is many-sided, creative and spontaneous. Such a self would realize its own individuality as part of a larger organic whole of society and nature. It would develop through voluntary, egalitarian relationships with others. Relationships would no longer be mediated by the laws of state and Church, and women no longer expected to provide sexual and domestic services for fictitious security and protection. Free unions would evolve based on trust, lasting as long the consenting partners wished. Children would be looked after by the community as well as by their families.

Human labour would no longer 'appropriate' nature for itself, or try to 'humanize' it. Humanity and nature would work together in the creative process of evolution. Renewed humanity would not impose their grid on nature, but rather try to reveal its sensuous contours, as Michelangelo sought to release the sculpture within the uncarved block.

With the benevolent functions of the state in health and education decentralized to the local assemblies, the state and government would be redundant and therefore be dissolved. While there might be some bodies to coordinate production, distribution, foreign policy and defence, they would have no authority to decide on behalf of the assemblies. The mystique of government would disappear, and social relations become transparent. There would be no concentration or centralization of political and economic power. Indeed, power in the coercive sense of control or authority over others would disappear. Power-over – the ability to control and punish – would be replaced by power-from-within, the inherent ability to realize one's potential.

Some social ecologists believe that it is possible to have politics without hierarchy and domination. But whoever says conventional politics says domination. In an ecological society, there would no longer be politics as it is commonly understood, as the art of directing states and the juggling of parties for power. Even green parties would eventually dissolve themselves so that the people could manage themselves through their federated assemblies. The government of men would give way to the administration of affairs.

After recognizing the principle of human equality – the equality of unequals – an ecological society would apply the principle of ecocentric impartiality. It would recognize that on occasion vital needs of other creatures and natural communities would be given precedence over nonvital human needs. There would be reverence for life, a recognition of the intrinsic worth of all creatures, and an attempt to cause minimum harm. Mixed communities of humans, animals and plants would develop, with other species respected for their own sake and not used merely as a means to our ends. Any gift which one might receive would be passed on.

But to recognize that all living beings and natural communities have intrinsic worth does not mean that they should be treated or considered equally. As a rough rule of thumb, we should perhaps in our moral arithmetic give more weight to the interests of living organisms with high degrees of sentience, but those with less are still worthy of consideration. Our moral community should embrace humans and nonhumans, plants and stones, the wide world itself. Therefore do not ask for whom the bell tolls – whether it be the funeral of a man or a mouse – for it tolls for *us all*. And if a clod

of soil falls into the sea, if a bird falls out of the sky, you and I are
the less.

## Organizing the Earth House Hold

The economy in an ecological society would turn away from maxi-
mizing profits to minimizing harm; it would be concerned not with
for ever producing more goods to consume, but with satisfying
vital needs.

The economy would be decentralized, with a harmonious balance
of agriculture and industry, fields and workshops. While the country
would be brought to the city, the impact of the city on the country
would be minimized.

The economy would aim at being as self-sufficient and self-reliant
as possible, drawing on local materials and plants. But self-sufficiency
need not be an absolute principle since it can isolate and be unfair.
Surpluses from one region can be shared with others through the
coordinated bodies of the federated assemblies. People would be
guaranteed a social and an economic minimum for a decent life,
fulfilling their basic physical, mental and spiritual needs. Buildings
would be primarily dwellings, shaped on the human scale according
to those who use them.

An ecological economy would not be committed to endless growth,
but link production with sustainable resources and renewable energy.
It would aim at producing simple and durable goods. Happiness
would not be defined in terms of ownership and consumption as
at present; there would be no attempt to stimulate artificial desires
and nonvital needs. Such a steady economy need not necessarily
mean no growth – tastes and knowledge will change – but it will
seek the stability of dynamic equilibrium. It would try to adapt the
population to the resources of the region, providing the minimum
material security and the maximum leisure for the wellbeing of all.

The modern ecological movement evolved out a fusion of
the science of ecology and the science of energy economics. An
ecological economy would therefore consume a minimum of
energy and preserve resources. It would recover something of the
original Greek meaning of economy as the *nomie* (organization)
of the *oikos* (household), not only in the minimal sense of good
housekeeping by avoiding waste and maintaining health, but
in recognizing that the dwelling of our home is the earth itself.

## Science and technology

The ideal of science is the disinterested pursuit of knowledge. But science is not value-free. Science treats nature in a particular way. Research is usually oriented towards a specific goal which leads to the exploitation of nature.

Scientists have a responsibility for the research they undertake and for the consequences of their experiments. While the new theoretical physics confirms the ancient wisdom that nature is a living and organic whole, engineers who build bridges and dams still work on Newtonian principles and often treat nature as a collection of dead atoms to be reshaped like Lego. A deeper scientific awareness coupled with an ecological sensibility will help to re-enchant nature, and then perhaps it will be less violated.

The gap between pure science and technology is closing fast. With the use of appropriate technology, it might be possible to pass from the realm of scarcity, which has bedevilled humans ever since they first evolved, to a realm of relative abundance in which the basic needs of all could be satisfied. The technology used to achieve this desirable state of affairs need not pollute the environment. The use of renewable energy – wind, sun and water – is not only harmless and inexhaustible but also has aesthetic value.

Technology should be appropriate, liberatory and unobtrusive. Appropriate, in that it will be environmentally friendly, geared to the bioregion and equal to its task. It will go beyond its usual concern merely with means and consider specific ends and wider consequences. It will be liberatory, by releasing humanity from drudgery while not dominating it or nature. It will try to solve the apparent contradiction between human planning and control and the spontaneity of nature by being sensitive to the needs of the natural world. It will be unobtrusive in that it will not transform the natural contours of the earth's surface nor loom large in everyday life.

There is no such thing as a 'technological imperative' in the sense that technology expands and develops on its own impetus and momentum. It is human beings who decide what technology to develop and use. The steam engine was discovered in the eleventh century but was not fully developed until the Industrial Revolution.

The technologist is not an ecological hero any more than the expert in cybernetics and systems theory. The New Age vision of the technologist guiding 'spaceship Earth' is a dangerous self-delusion. The eco-technologist should listen to the voice of his society and consider the interests of the wider community of the natural world.

## Producing for life

Food is essential to life, and cities and civilizations have developed only where farming has produced a surplus beyond the farmers' needs. In the past, agriculture has proved ecologically disastrous, so much so that some ecologists have argued that human society began to take the wrong path when it developed settled agriculture. But agriculture in an ecological society would be organic and adapted to the locality, living within the constraints of natural systems. It would move away from the 'hard path' of high technology which employs pesticides, herbicides and artificial fertilizer. Biotechnology, genetic engineering and attempts to govern evolution would be dispensed with. Soil fertility can be maintained through careful composting, companion-growing and rotation of crops. Soft pathways would be trod: all-round gardening, exploring the native plant culture and meeting the natural expectations of the land.

In the long run commercial farming can only fail. Like the ancient Chinese, eco-farmers learn from the local rhythms and relationships of the land and work with them; they do not impose technological fixes which increase yields temporarily but rely on huge energy imputs from elsewhere and degrade the wider environment. They grow crops, vegetables and orchards the same way wild plants grow.

When we change the way we grow our food, we change our values and eventually our society. The 'do-nothing' natural farming of the Japanese ecologist Masanobu Fukuoka may not be appropriate for all regions of the world. But his philosophy of *The One-Straw Revolution* (1978) of working with the forces of nature with the minimum of effort and disturbance is universally applicable: 'Simply serve nature and all is well.' Animals fight but do not make war, he reminds us; 'the key to peace lies close to the earth'. It is the polar opposite of the existing approach of Western commercial farming.

At present farmers throughout the world are committed to continual expansion, their merchant mentality transforming crops and animals into substitute money. Finding ways around government decrees, dodging taxes and understanding the latest technology take up all their time. But there should be time for a farmer to write a poem or compose a song; all would benefit. There is wisdom in the old perception of farming as a sacred activity. What is needed is a new relationship with the land – a land ethic of partnership and cooperation – which involves not merely *pursuing* the way of nature but *being* part of it, unconsciously at one with it. This involves a non-opposing, non-discriminating state of mind, an effortless approach which relies on intuition more than on figures and thinks in terms of fulfilment rather than results.

The building of fences was the beginning of the downfall of humanity, and the evolution of razor-sharp, barbed-wire fences is yet another stage in its crazy downward spiral. The so-called primitive and the wise recognize that the land, like air and water, is a common treasury. It should therefore be held as a trust by those who cultivate it or live on it. While people may enjoy the good things of the earth as temporary 'possessions' rather than as absolute 'property', they should recognize that they have a responsibility to tend and nurture the earth for the benefit of all life and future generations.

In certain damaged lands, a degree of restoration work will be required; guardians will have to look after inherited toxic and nuclear wastes. A process of healing the earth's wounds will be necessary so that vital organs can recover health. Dwellers in an ecological society will reverse the anti-evolutionary process of industry and allow evolution to take its course in the direction of greater diversity, complexity and consciousness. But in general humans will aim to tread lightly on the earth, making the minimum disturbance and leaving the slightest traces. Adopting a form of voluntary simplicity, they will combine global thinking with local living. Poor in means, they will be rich in ends.

Applying the principles of ecocentric impartiality and minimum harm, there would be a considerable reduction in meat-eating, which involves the suffering of animals and a wasteful use of resources. A vegetarian diet is not only healthier but requires seven times less land than meat production. Eating no meat or less meat would therefore release pasturelands to be reforested or allow them to return to their original state, thereby enhancing the vitality of Gaia. The domestication of animals would phase itself out, with the prisoners of zoos and laboratories returned to the wild if they could fend for themselves. Vegetarianism would make sense but would not be imposed; in certain extreme habitats, humans would still need to live by fishing or hunting (as the Inuit of Alaska or the hunter-gatherers of the Kalahari). But such activities would be for survival and not for sport, since finding pleasure in the suffering of others is ignoble and unnatural.

Industry would also be transformed, no longer degrading the local environment with filthy rivers and acid rain, or the global environment with the destruction of the ozone layer. It will no longer produce vast quantities of waste matter and waste heat. It will work with renewable energy in the form of water and wind, tide and tempest. Even if a clean version of nuclear fusion could be discovered, offering dreams of unlimited energy, it would not be welcome since it would provide a great temptation to exploit the remaining oils, metals and minerals in the earth.

In an ecological society, factories would be decentralized, drawing on local materials and energy supplies as much as possible. Production would be mainly for local consumption, although surpluses could be distributed to those in need elsewhere. Not only producers but also consumers would be involved in defining agreed needs in their federated assemblies.

Workplaces would be organized on the principle of self-management. The worker would no longer be alienated from his work, his fellows and nature, but fulfil himself in his labour. Useless toil would give way to meaningful play. With a new balance between agriculture and industry, the workshop would come to the field and the field to the workshop. The division of labour would be eroded and everyone would be free to choose the work which most suits their talents and interests. Since a lazy person is usually a round peg in a square hole, there would be no danger of collective idleness, although idleness itself would be considered no sin.

In an ecological community it will be for the people in their assemblies to define their needs, but there are important differences between vital needs and artificial wants. Vital needs are those for material and spiritual wellbeing, those necessary for dwelling and creating on earth. Artificial wants are those which multiply desires without bringing satisfaction and which deplete energy and pollute the consumer and the earth. Life in ecotopia might be simpler in consuming less but it would be more complex in feeling; poorer in material goods, but richer in purpose and meaning.

With fewer needs to satisfy, there would be less necessary work to do and more leisure to develop the full harmony of being. The bread of poetry can be developed simultaneously with the poetry of bread.

We consume in order to live; but increasingly consumption itself is becoming a real killer. Consumption in certain parts of the world would have to be checked, notably in the West, and increased in other parts. It is not possible to carry on consuming goods, however 'environmentally friendly', at the present rate. The United States, containing only 6 per cent of the world's population, consumes 80 per cent of its resources.

Excessive consumption is both unduly selfish and ecologically unsound. Some consumption beyond the satisfaction of vital needs might be acceptable. An ecological society should be a free and celebratory society; it need not be stern, Spartan nor dour. There is no virtue in stoical simplicity and austerity for their own sake. If people so wish, a degree of luxury and ostentation would be possible within the limits of a sustainable economy. In touch with their primitive roots, human beings would be able to enjoy the most creative aspects of civilization.

But would overpopulation threaten ecotopia? Many modern ecologists concur with the Reverend Thomas Malthus that any increase in human numbers would only make living conditions worse. The growth of the population is not only the greatest threat to human society but also to the earth.

With the human population swollen to some 5.3 billion, and with no signs of slowing down except in small pockets, other organisms are under growing threat. As humans increase and spread and bespoil, other creatures are being pushed out of their traditional habitats. Domesticated animals, especially cattle, cause the rainforests to be cut down and produce methane which increases global warming. Even wilderness oases in ecological disaster zones, like the Kruger National Park in South Africa, are under threat from neighbouring humans who see no reason why they should not eat the animals and till the land. In many areas of the globe, owing partly to changing climatic conditions, partly to bad farming methods, human populations are outstripping the food supply.

The increasing economic impoverishment of two thirds of the world in the South is directly related to the growing prosperity in the industrialized North. Industrialized countries should not call for population control elsewhere but should first set their own house in order and consume less. In particular, they should not suck up the world's nonrenewable resources in the form of primary materials and then through advertising create a market for their manufactured goods. Industrialized countries should be aware that they are 'in-dust-realized'.

Man does not have a God-given right to 'multiply, and replenish the earth', whatever the Bible says. There are clearly ecological limits to the number of humans some regions can support, and the claims of other species to wellbeing must be considered. But it is not enough merely to let the so-called 'natural checks' of 'vice and misery' prevail on the other side of the fence. No one should turn their back on a starving baby. Since humans are conscious animals and capable of foresight, the 'artificial' checks of contraception or moral restraint can curb 'natural' passions if need be. In the long run, the most important means to check excessive population is the prospect of a decent life. If life is secure and pleasant, families become smaller. In ecotopia, it would be for the people in their own regions to decide the desirable population in relation to their environment. But neighbours can always offer help and advice.

### Ecological sensibility

If humans walked on all fours they might not perhaps be such a troublesome species. As the most highly developed tool-using animals, they have developed enormous power over nature – so much power that they can now modify the course of natural evolution. Bacon's principle 'knowledge is power' has been amply demonstrated, but what humans have not yet developed is sufficient wisdom to be able to control their greedy and destructive natures. They must curb their power over nature by first controlling themselves. With this tremendous power, most visible in an atomic explosion, must go responsibility. And it is up to the majority – the powerless – to persuade those in authority to relinquish their power and apply their knowledge to enhancing and not to destroying the earth.

We humans have no right or skill to become managers of the cosmic process and govern evolution. Conquest should give way to wise stewardship, but stewardship should eventually be replaced by cooperation. We should not intervene deeply in natural processes through genetic engineering or artificial selection. We may foster diversity and latent life forms (thereby reversing the present anti-evolutionary trend) but we should not try to 'humanize' nature by taking our own species as the ideal model. We should be content to be fellow travellers with other creatures on the voyage of evolution.

Small is not necessarily beautiful (consider the starry heaven or the wide ocean) but eco-communities should be shaped on a human scale in which people can enjoy face-to-face relationships. They would develop ecological as well as historical and cultural identities, linking up in bioregions which follow natural rather than arbitrary political boundaries.

Living locally need not be parochial in the narrow sense. In an ecological society, one would be rooted in a locality, belong to a community, and have a strong sense of place. But one would be able to travel in mind and body. Involvement with others would form a widening circle, rippling out across the earth's surface from home, district and region to identify with the whole of humanity, other species and eventually the entire world. A genuinely ecological society would be internationalist and interplanetary. It would recognize that humanity is only one strand in nature's web.

Ecologically conscious people will not follow private interest but experience ever-widening identification. They will have strong and deep roots, and a keen empathy with the inhabitants, human and nonhuman, of their homeland. They will know its standing stones and its rushing waters, its quiet nooks and busy centres. They will celebrate local connections and be mindful of their environment.

At the same time, they will not identify exclusively with their own ego, family, race, nation or species but go beyond such ties to reach out to embrace the planet and the stars. Like a tree on a mountainside, the deeper they stretch their roots into the earth, the higher their branches will reach into the heaven. They might take as their symbols the eagle and the snake, strength and wisdom, creatures which crawl closest to the earth and soar highest in the sky. They will throw off the spirit of gravity, unify mind and body, reason and imagination, and dance to the music of the spheres.

Above all, a truly ecological society will foster the growth of individuals with an ecological sensibility. The two will go hand in hand. Ecological sensibility will be holistic. It will see the individual as part of the community, the community as part of society, and society as part of the species. The human species in turn is part of the society of species in a wider community of beings.

Ecological sensibility will see the human cell as a microcosm of man and man as a microcosm of the cosmos. Humans cannot get outside the egg of nature. The world is their body.

Ecological sensibility will begin to heal the rift between reason and imagination, mind and body, the creator and the creation, the individual and society, humanity and nature.

Ecological sensibility will not follow man-made clock time. It will experience time as flux and flow with its stream. It will recognize that every beginning has an end, that death is part of life, that nothingness is the ground of being. It will attune itself once again to the rhythm of seasons and to the movement of the stars.

Ecological sensibility will be able to swim with dolphins, think like a horse and sway like a reed.

Ecological sensibility will have a sense of wonder and a reverence for all life. It will develop an intimate relationship with other animals and plants. It will see all beings as brothers and sisters, including the living rock and the dancing atom.

Ecological sensibility will challenge the authority of established institutions and then challenge the principle of human authority itself.

Ecological sensibility will become aware of what one already is and open up to what one already has.

Such sensibility will be rhapsodic, reverential and essential. It will go to the root of things and not be distracted by flashy exteriors and troublesome noise. It will be meditative and contemplative; it will be joyful and spontaneous; it will leap the dance of belonging. Above all, it will listen in silence to the soundless voice of Being.

### Creating ecotopia

Ectopia cannot be created by coercive means. The ends do not justify the means. Means should be considered ends-in-the-making and libertarian means must be used to realize libertarian ends. A free and ecological society, which aims to end hierarchy and domination, cannot be brought about by authoritarian or violent means.

The only sensible way forward is to start from the individual, then work through affinity groups and finally to a wide movement which seeks to decentralize power and create in place of the Nation State a loose federation of organic communities. This emerging movement should try to reverse the present transfer of power to the centre in Europe and deflect it to the regions as the first step in the ultimate dissolution of coercive power and authority. It should commit itself to the principles of nonviolence and truth. It would not resort to weapons except those of persuasion, argument and example. It might however be prepared to organize campaigns of civil disobedience, as Gandhi did, to educate the wider public, to resist injustices, and to defend the earth. But it should adopt a way of acting that refrains from hurting others and a lifestyle based on compassion for all. The aim in any group struggle should be to reduce in the long term the overall amount of violence in the world.

Since consciousness and society are interwoven, they should be changed at the same time. For some this means local campaigns aimed at specific abuses, forming action groups, or building cooperatives and self-managed farms and workshops. For others, it means helping to create alternative communities close to the land or writing books, as I have done, in the hope that people might change their thinking and ways. Every person has her own area of skill and place in society where she is most effective. Whatever encourages diversity, freedom and solidarity is going in the right direction. Individuals may seem drops in the ocean, but combined together they can make up a tidal wave.

Only if a genuinely free and ecological society is created will humanity be able to live in harmony with itself, other species and their environment. In the meantime, if we can ride the rough waters of the present crisis, anything that contributes to the current of libertarian ecology, however small, is to be welcomed. The personal is not only political but the body is the world, and the self is a microcosm of the universe.

Will such a society ever be realized? The seeds of it are already there, beneath the snow, and there are clear signs that a thaw is beginning to set in. It is not too late for the man-made desert to bloom once again. It may well coincide with the dawn of the third millennium.

The Chinese word for crisis is *ji*, which means both 'danger' and 'opportunity'. We have the power to destroy as well as to create. Humanity is on a rope over an abyss stretched between the past and the future, between its animal ancestry and its unknown potential. If we do not reverse our present trend, we may well fall and be lost into swirling space. To the universe it will be a slight disturbance in the cosmic flow. But to our form of life on earth, on this beautiful earth with all its wondrous colours and smells and sensations, it will mean the void, the black emptiness of nothing. We came from nothing; it is too early for us to return to nothing.

# NOTES

Place of publication is London, unless otherwise stated.

## Chapter 1. Taoism

1 See *A Source Book in Chinese Philosophy*, trans. Wing-Tsit Chan (Princeton, NJ.: Princeton University Press, 1963), pp.137–8
2 Joseph Needham, *Science and Civilization in China*, (Cambridge: Cambridge University Press, 1956), II, 35
3 Lao Tsu, *Tao Te Ching*, trans. Gia-Fu Feng & Jane English (New York: Vintage, 1972), ch.28
4 Ibid., 34
5 See Alan Watts, *Nature, Man & Woman* (Abacus, 1976), p.97
6 *Tao Te Ching*, op.cit., ch.40
7 See John Clark, 'Master Lao and the Anarchist Prince', *The Anarchist Moment: Reflections on Culture, Nature and Power* (Montreal: Black Rose Books, 1986), p.170
8 *Chuang Tzu: Taoist Philosopher and Chinese Mystic*, trans. Herbert A. Giles (Unwin Paperbacks, 1980) p.256
9 Ibid., p.267
10 See Watts, *Nature, Man & Woman*, op.cit., p.19
11 Huai Nan Tzu, 9, in Needham, *Science and Civilization in China*, op.cit., II, 561
12 *I Ching*, ed. Raymond van Over, trans. James Legge (New York: New American Library, 1971), p.127
13 See R. G. H. Siu, *Tao of Science* (New York: John Wiley, 1957); Fritjof Capra, *The Tao of Physics* (Wildwood House, 1975)
14 *Tao Te Ching*, ch.8, 28
15 Ibid., 6
16 *Chuang Tzu*, p.98
17 *Tao Te Ching*, ch.38
18 Ibid., 38, 10
19 *Chuang Tzu*, p.90
20 Ibid., p.166
21 *Tao Te Ching*, op.cit., ch.67
22 Ibid., 5
23 *Chuang Tzu*, p.73
24 See Holmes Welch, *Taoism: The Parting of the Way* (Boston: Beacon, 1957), pp.44–5
25 *Chuang Tzu*, p.98
26 Ibid., p.125
27 *Tao Te Ching*, ch.80
28 Ibid., 46
29 Ibid., 30, 42
30 Ibid., 78

31  Ibid., 55
32  *Chuang Tzu*, p.113
33  Ibid., p.87
34  *Tao Te Ching*, ch.53, 18
35  Ibid., 57
36  Ibid., 80
37  *Chuang Tzu*, p.104
38  Ibid., p.106
39  Ibid., pp.255–6

## Chapter 2. Hinduism

1  See D. D. Kosambi, *The Culture and Civilization of Ancient India in Historical Outline* (New Delhi: Vikas, 1981), pp.26–7
2  See K. M. Sen, *Hinduism* (Harmondsworth: Penguin, 1975), p.44
3  *A Source Book in Indian Philosophy*, eds. S. Radhakrishnan & C. A. Moore (Princeton, NJ: Princeton University Press, 1971), p.23
4  'To Prthivi', ibid., p.11
5  'Hymn to Goddess Earth', Book XII, *Atharvaveda*, in Sen, *Hinduism*, op.cit., pp.122–4. In the original translation, from *The Sacred Books of the East*, ed. Max Muller, vol.XLII, 'obeisance' is used for 'reverence', but the latter word evokes better the spirit of the hymn.
6  See 'To Purusa', *Indian Philosophy*, op.cit., pp.19–20
7  *Rigveda*, 21, 164, 46
8  Isa Upanishad, V, 1, *Indian Philosophy*, op.cit., pp.39, 40
9  Brhadaranyaka Upanishad, ibid., p.77
10  Svetasvatara Upanishad, VI, 11–12
11  See Sen, *Hinduism*, op.cit., p.83
12  See Michael N. Nagler, 'Reading the Upanishads', *The Upanishads*, trans. Eknath Easwaran (Arkana, 1988), p.280
13  Prashna, VI. 3–4, ibid., p.167
14  Shveta, IV, 3–4, ibid., p.225
15  Chandogya, III, 19, 1–2, ibid., p.65
16  Mandukya, 1, ibid., p.55
17  Isha, 6–7, Ibid., p.209
18  Chandogya, IV, 17,4
19  Ibid., VIII, 1, 5–6
20  In David Maclagan, *Creation Myths* (Thames & Hudson, 1979), p.10
21  *The Bhagavad-Gita*, trans. Juan Mascaró (Harmondsworth: Penguin, 1975), XVIII, 61, p.120
22  Ibid., III, 25, p.58
23  Ibid., XII, 13, p.97
24  In Sen, *Hinduism*, op.cit., p.103
25  Ibid., pp.104–5
26  Ibid., p.104
27  John Levy, *The Nature of Man according to the Vedanta* (Routledge & Kegan Paul, 1956), p.43
28  *Thus Spake Ramana*, ed. Swami Rajeswarananda (Tiruvannamalai, 1971), pp.19, 29
29  *The Teachings of Bhagawan Sri Ramana Maharshi in his own Words*, ed. Arthur Osborne (Rider, 1962), p.163–4 Ibid., pp.112, 195

## Chapter 3. Buddhism

1 Christmas Humphreys, *Buddhism* (Harmondsworth: Penguin, 1971), p.75
2 *The Teachings of the Compassionate Buddha*, ed. E. A. Burtt (New York: Mentor, 1955), pp.133, 52
3 Chan, *A Source Book of Chinese Philosophy*, op.cit., p.396
4 Ibid., p.412
5 Humphreys, *Buddhism* p. 179
6 D. T. Suzuki, *Essays in Zen Buddhism*, First Series (Rider, 1949), p.111
7 *Zen Buddhism: Selected Writings of D. T. Suzuki*, ed. William Barret, (New York: Anchor, 1956)
8 *Lankavatara Sutra*, in Aldous Huxley, *The Perennial Philosophy* (Triad, 1989), p.24
9 Yung-chia Ta-shih, ibid., p.24
10 Third Patriarch of Zen, ibid., pp.102–3
11 Chan, *A Source Book in Chinese Philosophy*, op.cit., p.446
12 Ibid., p.445
13 *Buddhist Scriptures*, trans. Edward Conze (Penguin, 1975), p.134
14 Chan, *A Source Book in Chinese Philosophy*, op.cit., p.439
15 Ibid., p. 433, 437
16 *Zen Flesh, Zen Bones*, compiled by Paul Reps (Harmondsworth: Penguin, 1986), pp.39–40
17 In Humphreys, *Buddhism*, op.cit., p.183
18 'Record of the Life of the Ch'an Master Po-Chang Huai-Hai', trans. Gary Snyder, *Earth Household* (Toronto: George J. McLeod, 1969) p.76
19 Suzuki, *Selected Writings*, op.cit., p.18
20 Snyder, Real Work: *Interviews and Talks, 1964–79* (New York: New Directions, 1980), p.99
21 In Humphreys, *Buddhism*, op.cit., p.186
22 Suzuki, *Selected Writings*, op.cit., p.240
23 In Alan W. Watts, *The Way of Zen* (Harmondsworth: Penguin, 1957), p.154
24 *Zen Flesh, Zen Bones*, op.cit., pp.75, 54
25 See E. F. Schumacher *Small is Beautiful: Economics as if People Realy Mattered* (Abacus, 1973).
26 *Zen Flesh, Zen Bones*, op.cit., p.73
27 Ibid, p.49
28 Ibid, p.101
29 Watts, *The Way of Zen*, op.cit., p.208
30 *Zen Flesh, Zen Bones*, op.cit., pp.72–3

## Chapter 4. Ancient Egypt

1 W. B. Emery, *Archaic Egypt* (Harmondsworth: Penguin), p.177
2 See John. A. West, *The Travellers' Key to Ancient Egypt* (Harrap Columbus, 1989), p.31
3 See Lucy Lamy, *Egyptian Mysteries: New Light on Ancient Knowledge* (Thames & Hudson, 1989), p.18
4 R. A. Schwaller de Lubicz, *Le Roi de la théocratie pharaonique* (Paris, 1958) in Lamy *Egyptian Mysteries*, op.cit., p.17
5 Ibid., p.10
6 Ibid., p.11

7 E. A. Wallis Budge, *Egyptian Religion* (Arkana, 1987), p.137
8 For Plutarch's account, see Lamy, *Egyptian Mysteries*, op.cit., p.5
9 Serge Sauneron, *Les Fêtes religieuses d'Easna aux dernieres siecles du paganisme*, (Cairo, 1962) V, 100; Lamy, *Egyptian Mysteries* 82.
10 See Wallis Budge, *Egyptian Religion*, op.cit., p.136
11 Budge, *Egyptian Religion*, p.230
12 Ibid., p.231

## Chapter 5. Early Greece

1 In John Passmore, *Man's Responsibility for Nature*, 2nd edn (Duckworth, 1980) p.7
2 Hesiod, *Works and Days*, 109–201 in Robert Graves, *The Greek Myths*, op.cit., I, 36
3 See Robert Graves, *The Greek Myths* (Harmondsworth: Penguin), I, 27
4 See Graves, *The White Goddess: A Historical Grammer of Poetic Myth* (Faber & Faber, 1988), ch.iv
5 See Graves, *The Greek Myths*, op.cit., I, 11–20
6 Ibid., I, 31
7 Carl Kerényi, *The Gods of the Greeks* (Harmondsworth: Pelican, 1958), p.16
8 In Lucy Rees, *The Horse's Mind*, (Stanley Paul, 1984), p.147
9 See Jocelyn Godwin, *Mystery Religions in the Ancient World* (Thames & Hudson, 1981), pp.332–4
10 In Bertrand Russell, *History of Western Philosophy* (Allen & Unwin, 1962), p.46
11 *Heraclitus: The Cosmic Fragments*, ed, G. S. Kirk (Cambridge: Cambridge University Press, 1970), p.307
12 In Russell, *History of Western Philosophy*, op.cit., pp.59–63
13 Ibid., p.52
14 In *The Gaia Atlas of Planetary Management* (Pan, 1985), p.158
15 Plato, *Timaeus*, trans. H. D. P. Lee (Harmondsworth: Penguin, 1965), pp., 54, 42–3
16 Ibid., pp.44–5
17 Plato, *Critias*, trans. B. Jowett (Oxford, 1892), 111b, c.
18 Plato, *Timaeus*, op.cit., pp.34–5
19 Aristotle, *Ethics*, trans. J. A. K. Thomson (Harmondsworth: Penguin, 1963), p.279
20 Ibid., p.83
21 Aristotle, *De Partibus Animalium*, I, 645a, 15f
22 Aristotle, *Ethics*, op.cit., p.299
23 Aristotle, *De Anima*, 414a 29 – 415a 13
24 Aristotle, *Politics*, (Everyman edn.), p.10
25 See Arthur F. Lovejoy, *The Great Chain of Being*, (Cambridge, Mass.: Harvard University Press, 1971), pp.59–60
26 Diogenes Laertius, *Lives of Eminent Philosophers*, trans. R. D. Hicks (Loeb Classical Library, 1925), II, 195
27 In Jon Wynne-Tyson, *Food for a Future* (Centaur Press, 1979) p.138
28 Plutarch, 'Whether land or sea animals are cleverer', *Moralia*, 12, 964–5, trans. W. Helmbold (Loeb Classical Library edn.), p.353
29 In Wynne-Tyson, *Food for a Future*, op.cit., p.131

## Chapter 6. The Romans

1 Joscelyn Godwin, *Mystery Religions in the Ancient World* (Thames & Hudson, 1981), p.98.
2 Ibid., p.13
3 See Carl Kerényi, *Dionysus: Archetypal Image of Indestructible Life* (Princeton, NJ: Princeton University Press, 1976)
4 Cicero, *De Natura Deorum*, Bk 2, in Passmore, *Man's Responsibility for Nature*, op.cit., p.14
5 Ibid., II, 153, Passmore, p.18
6 In Wynne-Tyson, *Food for a Future*, op.cit., p.140
7 In Huxley, *The Perennial Philosophy*, op.cit., p.20
8 Plotinus, *Enneads*, V, 2, 1, ed. Volkmann (1884), II, 176; in Lovejoy, *The Great Chain of Being*, op.cit., p.62
9 Ibid., V, 2, 1–2; Volkmann, II, 176–8; Lovejoy, p.63
10 Ibid., III, 3, 7; Volkmann, I, 259; Ibid., III, 2, 11; Volkmann, I, 239; Lovejoy, pp.64–5
11 In Huxley, *The Perennial Philosophy*, op.cit., p 130
12 Ibid., p.97

## Chapter 7. Celtic Mysteries

1 In T. G. E. Powell, *The Celts* (Thames & Hudson, 1963), pp.73–4
2 See John Sharkey, *Celtic Mysteries: The Ancient Religion* (Thames & Hudson, 1989)
3 In Alwyn Rees & Brinley Rees, *Celtic Heritage: Ancient Tradition in Ireland and Wales* (Thames & Hudson, 1961), p.287
4 Ibid., p.98
5 See Janet and Colin Bord, *Ancient Mysteries of Britain* (Grafton, 1986), p.145
6 *Sir Gawain and the Green Knight*, ed. Israel Gollancz (Oxford: Oxford University Press, 1966), pp.6–7
7 See William Anderson, *The Rise of the Gothic* (Hutchinson, 1985), p.118
8 In Sharkey, *Celtic Mysteries*, op.cit., pp.20–21
9 Julius Caesar, *Gallic Wars*, VI, 4

## Chapter 8. The Judaeo-Christian Tradition

1 John Calvin, *Commentaries on the First Book of Moses, called Genesis* trans. J. King (London, 1847), I, 96
2 See Roderick Frazier Nash, *The Rights of Nature: A History of Environmental Ethics* (London & Madison: University of Wisconsin Press, 1989), p.90
3 See Andre G. Haudricourt, 'Domestications des animaux, culture des plantes et traitement d'autrui', *L'Homme*, 2 (1962)
4 Cf. Carl Sagan, *The Dragons of Eden: Speculations on the Evolution of Human Intelligence* (New York: Ballantine, 1986), pp.98–99
5 See Ian Bradley, *God is Green: Christianity and the Environment* (Darton, Longman, & Todd, 1990), p.57
6 See Basil Willey, *The Seventeenth-Century Background* (Harmondsworth: Penguin, 1964) p.35

7 See George S. Hendry, *Theology of Nature* (Philadelphia: Westminster Press, 1980), p.55

8 John Calvin, *Institutes of the Christian Religion*, ed. J. T. McNeill (SCM, 1961), p.246

9 Blaise Pascal, *Pensées*, trans, A. J. Krailsheimer (Harmondsworth: Penguin, 1975), p.158

10 Ibid., pp.57, 235

11 Ibid., pp.94, 235

12 Ibid., p.95

13 See Louis Ginzeber, *The Legends of the Jews*, trans, Henrietta Szold (1909) (Philadelphia: Jewish Publication Society of America, 1988), I, 352

14 Ibid., V, 269

15 Ibid., I, 49–50

16 Ibid., V, 65

17 See Claus Westermann, *Genesis I–III A Commentary* (SPCK, 1984), p.159

18 Ginzeber, *Legends of the Jews*. op.cit., V, 61

19 Z'ev ben Shimon Halevi, *Kabbalah: Tradition of Hidden knowledge* (Thames & Hudson, 1979), p.5

20 Perle Epstein, *Kabbalah: The Way of the Jewish Mystic* (Boston & London; Shambala, 1988) p.74

21 Ibid., p.6

22 Halevi, *Kabbalah*, op.cit., p.17

23 See ibid., p.13

24 Ibid., p.8

25 See Epstein, *Kabbalah*, op.cit., pp.69–71

26 Ibid., p.109

27 Ibid., p.114

28 Ibid., 117

29 In Halevi, *Kabbalah*, op.cit., p.28

## Chapter 9. Christianity

1 Lynn White, 'The Historical Roots of our Ecological Crisis', *Science*, 155: 3767 (10 March 1967), 1204–7

2 Passmore, *Man's Responsibility for Nature*, op.cit., p.20

3 In Bradley, *God is Green*, op.cit., p.13

4 St Augustine, *The Catholic and Manichaean Ways of Life*, trans. D. A. Gallagher & I. J. Gallagher (Boston, 1966), ch.xvii, p.102

5 St Thomas Aquinas, *Summa Theologica* II, II, Q. 64, art. 1

6 Ibid II, II Q. 24, art. 3. Cf. Singer, *Animal Liberation*, op.cit., pp.198–97

7 Ibid., II, I, Q. 102, art. 6

8 Nash, *The Rights of Nature*, op.cit., p.91. See also his *Wilderness and the American Mind* (New Haven: Yale University Press, 1973) and George H. Williams, *Wilderness and Paradise in Christian Thought* (New York, 1962); Max Oelschlager, *The Idea of Wilderness from Prehistory to the Present* (New Haven: Yale University Press, 1991)

9 Robert Dwyer, 'Worship of the Environment is the New Religion', *Los Angeles Times* (10 August 1973), p.27

10 Benjamin Walker, *Gnosticism: Its History and Influence* (Wellingborough: Crucible, 1989), p.49

11 René Dubos, *A God Within* (New York, 1968), 45, 153–74

12 In Huxley, *The Perennial Philosophy*, op.cit., pp.96, 84

13 St Bonaventura, *Life of St Francis* (SPCK, 1978), p.251
14 See *St Francis of Assisi: His Life and Writings as recorded by his Contemporarie*, trans. L. Sherley-Price (Mowbray, 1959), p.145
15 See Passmore, *Man's Responsibility for Nature*, op.cit., p.112
16 Teilhard de Chardin, 'Catholicism and Science' (1946), *Christ and Science*, trans. René Hague, (Collins, 1965), pp.189–90
17 'My Universe', (1924), ibid., p.45
18 Chardin, 'My Universe', *Science and Christ*, op.cit., p.59
19 *Le milieu divin, An Essay on the Interior Life* (Fontana, 1978), pp.46, 116, 119
20 'My Universe', op.cit., p.67
21 Bradley, *God is Green*, op.cit., p.7
22 Ibid., pp.20, 93
23 Matthew Hale, *The Primitive Origination of Mankind* (1677), p.370
24 Bradley, *God is Green*, op.cit., 103
25 H. Paul Santmire, *Brother Earth: Nature, God and Ecology in Time of Crisis* (New York, 1970), p.101. See also his *The Travail of Nature* (1985)
26 See Charles Birch & John B. Cobb, trans. *The Liberation of Life: From the Cell to the Community* (Cambridge, 1981)
27 John B. Cobb, *Is It Too Late? A Theology of Ecology* (Beverley Hills, Cal.., 1972), p.125
28 Don Cupitt, in Hugh Montefiore, (ed.) *Man and Nature* (1975), p.119
29 William Temple, *Nature, Man and God* in Jonathan Porritt, *Seeing Green The Politics of Ecology Explained* (Oxford: Basil Blackwell, 1984)
30 Montefiore, 'Man and Nature: A Theological Assessment', *Zygon*, 12 (1977), 206

## Chapter 10. Islam

1 See Alfred Guillaume, *Islam* (Harmondsworth: Penguin, 1977), pp.7–9
2 *The Meaning of the Glorious Koran*, trans. Mohammed Marmaduke Pickthall (New York: New American Library, n. d.). Reference to the Surahs in this work are henceforth given in brackets in the text.
3 In Reynold A. Nicholson, *The Mystics of Islam* (1914) (New York: Shocken, 1975), p.118
4 In Timothy Ferris, *Coming of Age in the Milky Way* (Bodley Head, 1988), p.43
5 In Huxley, *The Perennial Philosophy*, op.cit., p.10
6 Ibid., p.268
7 See Annemarie Schimmel, *Mystical Dimensions of Islam* (Capel Hill: Univ. of North Carolina Press, 1975), p.189
8 In *The World's Religions*, (Lion, n.d.), p.318
9 Ibid., p.320
10 In Schimmel, *Mystical Dimensions of Islam* op.cit., p.18
11 Ibid., p.189
12 Ibid., p.428
13 Guillaume, *Islam*, op.cit., p.143
14 Schimmel, *Mystical Dimensions of Islam*, op.cit., p.46
15 Ibid., p.293
16 Huxley, *The Perennial Philosophy*, op.cit., 138
17 Ibid., p.265

## Chapter 11. North American Indians

1 Dee Brown, *Bury My Heart at Wounded Knee: An American History of the American West* (Picador, 1975), pp.261, 250
2 Stan Steiner, *The Vanishing White Man* (1976)
3 See Paul Radin, *The World of Primitive Man* (New York: Grove Press, 1960), p.11
4 Brown, *Bury My Heart at Wounded Knee*, op.cit., p.195
5 In F. Turner, *Beyond Geography: The Western Spirit against the Wilderness* (New Brunswick: Rutgers University Press, 1983), pp.282–3
6 Brown, *Bury My Heart at Wounded Knee*, op.cit., p.137
7 Ella C. Deloria, *Speaking of Indians* (Vermillion: University of South Dakota, 1978), p.52
8 John (Fire) Lame Deer & Richard Erdoes, *Lame Deer: Seeker of Visions* (New York: Pocket Books, 1972), pp.112–113
9 In Maclagan, *Creations Myths*, op.cit., p.26
10 Chief Seattle to President Franklin Pierce, 1854
11 John C. Mohawk, 'Distinguished Traditions', *Renewing the Earth: The Promise of Social Ecology*, ed. John Clark (Green Print, 1990), p.93
12 Segwalise in *Basic Call to Consciousness* (New York: Akwesasne Notes, 1978). See also T. C. McLuhan, ed., *Touch the Earth: A Self Portrait of Indian Existence* (Abacus, 1989)
13 Mohawk, 'Distinguished Traditions', op.cit., p.95
14 *Lame Deer*, op.cit., pp.102–3
15 Deloria, *Speaking of Indians*, op.cit., p.35 Deloria refers to the Sioux as the Dakota, a classification of Indian languages used by the Sioux.
16 *Lame Deer*, op.cit., p.183
17 Hyemeyohsts Storm, *Seven Arrows* (New York: Ballantine Books, 1972) p.5
18 Sun Bear & Waburn, *The Medicine Wheel* (New York: Prentice Hall, 1980), p.xii
19 *Lame Deer*, op.cit., p.6
20 See Deloria, *Speaking of Indians*, op.cit., p.40
21 Frank Waters, *Book of the Hopi* (Harmondsworth: Penguin, 1977), p.293
22 Ibid., p.23
23 Maclagan, *Creation Myths*, op.cit., p.23
24 Waters, *Book of the Hopi*, op.cit., p.7
25 Dorothy Lee, *Freedom and Culture* (Englewood, NJ: Prentice-Hall, 1959), p.47
26 See Waters, *Book of the Hopi*, op.cit., p.334
27 See Weston La Barre, *The Ghost Dance* (New York: Doubleday, 1970), p.301
28 Claude Lévi-Strauss, 'Tristes Atropiques', *Encounter*, XC (April 1961), 40. The quote comes from Jean-Jacques Rousseau, *Discourse on the Origin of Inequality of Mankind* (1754).

## Chapter 12. Alchemy

1 'The Sophic Hydrolith', *The Hermetic Museum*, first translated into English 1678, ed. A. E. White (1893)
2 *Mirror of Alchimy*, (1557) attributed to Roger Bacon, p.19
3 See C. G. Jung, *Psychology and Alchemy* (1944) (Routledge & Kegan Paul, 1953)
4 See Titus Burckhardt, *Alchemy: Science of the Cosmos, Science of the Soul*, trans. William Stoddart (Longmead: Element Books, 1986), p.9

5  See Cherry Gilchrist, *Alchemy: The Great Work* (Wellingborough: Aquarian Press, 1984), pp.11–12
6  See Jack Lindsay, *The Origins of Alchemy in Graeco-Roman Egypt* (Frederick Muller, 1970), ch.vi
7  In Burckhardt, *Alchemy*, op.cit., p.23
8  See Johannes Fabricius, *Alchemy: The Medieval Alchemists and their Royal Art* (Wellingborough: Aquarian Press, 1976), pp.6–7
9  See Mircea Eliade, *Forgerons et alchimistes* (Paris: Collection 'Homo sapiens', 1956)
10  See Camara Laye, *L'Enfant noir* (Paris, 1953)
11  *Corpus Hermeticum*, in Burckhardt, *Alchemy*, op.cit., p.40
12  Plotinus, *Enneads*, III, 8
13  Burckhardt, *Alchemy*, op.cit., p.116
14  *Purissima Revelation*, trans. from Robert Buchère *Le Voile d'Isis* (Paris, 1921), p.183
15  In John Fauvel, Raymond Flood, Michael Shortland, & Robin Wilson, *Let Newton Be! A New Perspective on his Life and Work* (Oxford: Oxford University Press, 1988), p.140
16  In Burckhardt, *Alchemy*, op.cit., pp.196–7
17  *Corpus Hermeticum*, trans. Walter Scott (Dawsons, 1969), Libellus, XI
18  Gilchrist, *Alchemy*, op.cit., p.116; see also Frances Yates, *The Rosicrucian Englightenment* (Routledge & Kegan Paul, 1972)
19  Gilchrist, *Alchemy*, op.cit., p.119. See also Joscelyn Godwin, *Robert Fludd* (Thames & Hudson, 1979)
20  In Burckhardt, *Alchemy*, op.cit., p.31
21  Ibid., p.25
22  Jacob Boehme, *Signatura Rarum* (James Clark, n.d.), pp.13, 89
23  In Betty Dobbs, *The Foundation of Newton's Alchemy* (Cambridge: Cambridge University Press, 1975)
24  Fritjof Capra, *The Tao of Physics*, op.cit., p.71.
25  In Burckhardt, *Alchemy*, op.cit. p.13
26  Plato, *The Republic*, trans. Desmond Lee, (Harmondsworth: Penguin, 1981), p.182
27  In Burckhardt, *Alchemy*, op.cit., p.30
28  In Alan Ereira, *The Heart of the World* (Jonathan Cape, 1990), p.163

## Chapter 13. *The Scientific Revolution*

1  Andreas Vesalius, 'Anatomy and the Art of Medicine' from Preface to *De Humani Corporis Fabrica* (1543), in *The Portable Renaissance Reader*, eds. James Ross & Mary Martin McLaughlin (Harmondsworth: Penguin, 1977), pp.570–2
2  Johannes Kepler to Herwart von Hohenburg, 1605, in David Pepper, *The Roots of Environmentalism* (Routledge, 1990), p.47; Kepler, *Harmonice Mundi* (1691)
3  In R. Collingwood, *The Idea of Nature* (Oxford: Oxford University Press, 1965), p.102
4  Galileo Galilei, *The Assayer* (1623)
5  See Richard Westfall, *Never at Rest: A Biography of Isaac Newton* (Cambridge: Cambridge University Press, 1980), p.292; Fauvel et al, *Let Newton Be!*, op.cit., p.142
6  Ibid., p.133
7  Isaac Newton, *Philosophiae Naturalis Principia Mathematica* (1687), Preface, in J. F. Lively, ed. *The Enlightenment* (Longmans, 1967), pp.15–16

8 Newton, *Optics* (1704) in Fauvel et al, *Let Newton Be!*, op.cit., p.91

9 Newton to Richard Bentley (25 Feb. 1693), Westfall, *Never at Rest*, op.cit., p.505

10 Newton, *Queries* (1706) to *Optics* in Fauvel et al, *Let Newton Be!*, op.cit., pp.94–5

11 In *Let Newton Be!*, op.cit., pp.133, 135

12 See Rupert Sheldrake, *The Rebirth of Nature: The Greening of Science* (Century, 1990), p.63

13 Draft corollary to Proposition VI of the *Principia*, in *Let Newton Be!*, op.cit., p.172

14 Newton, *Optics*, in Lively, *The Enlightenment*, op.cit., p.43

15 General Scholium to the 1713, 3rd. edn. of the *Principia*, in Westfall, *Never at Rest*, op.cit., p.748

16 See Piyo Rattanssi, 'Newton and the Wisdom of the Ancients', *Let Newton Be!*, op.cit., p.198

17 Voltaire, 'A Madame La Marquise du Chatelet', *Oeuvres philosophiques* (Paris: Larousse, 1934), p.35

18 Alexander Pope, *Epitaph* (1730), *The Poems of Alexander Pope*, ed. John Butt, (Methuen, 1968), p.808

19 See Stephen W. Hawking, *A Brief History of Time: From the Big Bang to Black Holes* (Bantam, 1990), pp.181–2

20 In Timothy Ferris, *The Coming of Age in the Milky Way* (Bodley Head, 1988), p.119

21 A. N. Whitehead, *Science and the Modern World*, (Cambridge: Cambridge University Press, 1925), ch.iii

## Chapter 14. Philosophers of the Brave New World

1 See Keith Thomas, *Man and the Natural World: Changing Attitudes in England 1500–1800* (Allen Lane, 1983), pp.92,21

2 Sir Matthew Hale, *The Primitive Origination of Man* (1677), p.68; *Works of Robert Boyle*, IV, 363, V, 469

3 Giovanni Pico della Mirandola, 'The Dignity of Man', *The Portable Renaissance Reader*, eds. James Ross & Mary Martin McLaughlin (Harmondswoth: Penguin, 1977), pp.476, 479

4 Marsilio Ficino, 'The Soul of Man', ibid., pp.387–83

5 See Willey, *The Seventeenth-Century Background*, op.cit., p.37

6 Francis Bacon, *De Augmentis Scientiarum* (1623) (Bohn edn.), pp.6–8, 16

7 Bacon, *Novum Organum* (1620) I, 1xv.

8 Bacon, *Works of Francis Bacon*, eds. J. Spedding, E. L. Ellis & D. D. Heath (1857–9), VII, 253

9 Bacon, 'Of Studies', 'Of Nature in Men', *Essays, The Wisdom of Ancients, The New Atlantis* (Oldham Press, n.d.), pp.134, 166

10 Bacon, *Works*, op.cit., IV, 517

11 Bacon, 'Pan, or Nature', *Essays*, op.cit., p.222

12 'Of Gardens', ibid., p.156

13 *New Atlantis*, op.cit., p.329

14 Ibid., pp.331–2

15 William Blake, *Complete Writings*, op.cit., p.397 ed. Geoffrey Keynes (Oxford: Oxford University Press, 1972)

16 René Descartes, *Discourse on Method and the Meditations*, trans. F. E. Sutcliffe (Harmondsworth: Penguin, 1976), p.78

17 See Alexader Koyré, 'Introduction' to *Descartes: Philosophical Writings*, ed. E. Anscombe & P. T. Geach (Nelson, 1972), p.xxiii
18 Descartes, *Discourse on Method*, op.cit., pp.54–5
19 Ibid., p.55
20 Ibid., pp.65, 129, 139
21 Ibid., pp.75–6.
22 Descartes to Henry More (5 February 1649), quoted in Tom Regan, *The Case for Animal Rights* (Routledge, 1988), p.3.
23 Descartes, *Meditations*, op.cit., p.112
24 See Thomas, *Man and the Natural World*, op.cit., pp.41–50
25 Edward Gibbon, *The History of the Decline and Fall of the Roman Empire*, ed. J. B. Bury (1906 edn.), V, 315, 314
26 Thomas Hobbes, *Leviathan*, ed. C. B. Macpherson, (Harmondsworth: Penguin, 1976), p.160
27 Ibid., p.161
28 Ibid., p.186
29 Ibid., pp.189, 224
30 Ibid., p.151
31 In Macpherson, Introd., ibid., p.61

## Chapter 15. The Philosophical Counter-Revolution

1 See Frances Yates, *Giordano Bruno and the Hermetic Tradition* (Routledge & Kegan Paul, 1964)
2 Lovejoy, *The Great Chain of Being*, op.cit., p.116.
3 Giordano Bruno, *De immenso*(1586), II, ch.13
4 Bruno, *De l'infinito universo e mondi*, in Lovejoy *The Great Chain of Being*, op.cit., p.119
5 Michel de Montaigne, 'Of the Education of Children', 'Of Solitude', *Essays*(1588)
6 *Montaigne's Essays*, trans. John Florio (1603) (1892 edn.), I, 219
7 'Of Cannibals'
8 Ibid.
9 'Apology for Raimond de Sebonde', *Essays*, in Singer, *Animal Liberation*, op.cit., 202.
10 Montaigne, 'On Cruelty', *Essays*, op.cit, II, 126
11 Ibid., II, 119
12 Bernard Pallisy, 'On Nature and Experience', *The Portable Renaissance Reader*, op.cit., pp.575–5, 574
13 Arne Naess, 'Through Spinoza to Mahayana Buddhism, or Through Mahayana Buddhism to Spinoza?', in *Spinoza's Philosophy of Man*, ed. John Wetlesen (Oslo: University Press of Oslo, 1978). See also Bill Devall & George Sessions, *Deep Ecology: Living as if Nature mattered* (Salt Lake City: Peregrine Smith, 1985), pp.237–84
14 Spinoza, *Ethics* (1677), Pt. III, prop.25
15 See Stuart Hampshire, *Spinoza*, (Harmondsworth: Penguin, 1951), p.71
16 Spinoza, *Ethics*, op.cit., Pt. III, prop.7
17 Ibid., Pt. III, note to prop.2
18 Ibid., Pt. I, prop.29
19 Ibid., Pt. III, prop.59, note
20 Ibid., Pt. IV, prop.42
21 Ibid., Pt. IV, prop.47
22 Ibid., Pt. V, prop.24

23 Spinoza, *The Treatise on the Correction of the Understanding*, Pt, II; in Hampshire, *Spinoza*, op.cit., p.110

24 Spinoza, *Ethics*, op.cit., Pt. III, prop.2 note

25 Ibid., Pt. II, prop.11, corollary

26 Hampshire, *Spinoza*, op.cit., p.76

27 Spinoza, *Ethics*, Pt. IV, appendix, para 26, *The Chief Works of Benedictus de Spinoza*, trans. R. H. M. Elves (New York: Dover, 1955), II, 241

28 Hampshire, *Spinoza*, op.cit., p.189

29 Spinoza, *Theological-Political Treatise*, (1670), ch.xx

30 Ibid, ch.i, set.3

31 Ralph Cudworth, *True Intellectual System of the Universe*, ed. Tegg (1845), I, 321

32 Willey, *The Seventeenth-Century Background*, op.cit., p.149

33 John Ray, *The Wisdom of God manifested in the Works of the Creation* (1691) (1701 edn.), p.48

34 Ibid., p.185

35 Ibid. 407

36 See Maurice Cranston, Introduction, John Locke, *An Essay Concerning the Human Understanding* (1689) (Collier-Macmillan, 1965), p.15.

37 Ibid., p.16

38 Locke, *The Educational Writings of John Locke*, ed. James L. Axtell (Cambridge University Press, 1968), pp.225–6

39 Locke, *Two Treatises of Civil Government*(1689) (Dent, 1936), pp.118, 119, 126

40 Ibid., p.129

41 Ibid., p.131

## Chapter 16. The Enlightenment

1 See Peter Gay, *The Enlightenment: An Interpretation* (Wildwood House, 1973), I, xiii

2 d'Alembert *Essai sur les éléments de philosophie*, in J. F. Lively, *The Enlightenment* (Longmans, 1967), pp.4–5

3 Georg Wilhelm Friedrich Hegel, *Philosophy of History* (1821), ibid., pp.98, 100

4 Jean le Rond d'Alembert, *Discours préliminaire* to the *Encyclopédie*, ibid., p.13

5 Ernst Cassirer, *The Philosophy of the Enlightenment* (Princeton, NJ: Princeton University Press, 1951), p.13

6 John Locke, *Essay Concerning Human Understanding* (1689)

7 David Hume, *Treatise of Human Nature* (1739), in Lively, *The Enlightenment*, op.cit., p.23

8 Anne Robert Jacques Turgot, *Discours aux Sorboniques* (11 December 1750)

9 Marquis de Marie Jean Antoine Nicolas Caritat Condorcet, 'Première Mémoire', *Sur l'instruction publique* (1791–2), p.18

10 Pope, 'Essay on Man', *Poems*, op.cit., p.513

11 Ibid., p.537

12 Ibid., p.515. See also Willey, *The Eighteenth-Century Background* (Harmondsworth: Penguin, 1972) p.47

13 Soame Jenyns, *Free Enquiry into the Nature and Origin of Evil* (1757) (1790 edn.), p.37

14 Ibid., pp.71–2

15 Ibid., pp.9–50, 67–8

16 In Lovejoy, *The Great Chain of Being*, op.cit., pp.253–4

## Chapter 17. To Follow Nature

1 See Raymond Williams, 'Nature' in *Keywords: A Vocabulary of Culture and Society* (Fontana, 1976)

2 See Willey, *The Eighteenth-Century Background*, op.cit., p.12.

3 Anthony, Earl of Shaftesbury, 'The Moralists: A Philosophical Rhapsody', *Characteristics of Men, Manners, Opinions, Times* (1711), ed. John M. Robertson, (Indianapolis & New York: Bobbs-Merrill, 1964) II, 65, 102

4 'Miscellaneous Reflections', *Characteristics*, op.cit., II, 268–9

5 'The Moralist', ibid., II, 98

6 Ibid., II, 127, 122

7 Ibid., II, 73

8 Paul Heinrich Dietrich, Baron d'Holbach, *Système de la nature*, (1780 edn.), I, 23

9 Holbach, *Système de la nature* (1770), I, 292–3

10 Holbach, *Christianisme dévoilé*, in Willey, *The Eighteenth-Century Background*, op.cit., p.155

11 Holbach, *Le bon sens*, in Lively., *The Enlightenment*, op.cit., p.61

12 Holbach, *Système de la nature* (1780 edn.) II, 277

13 Ibid., II, 415

14 Ibid., (1770 edn.), II, 257–8

15 La Mettrie, *Histoire naturelle de l'âme* (1745)

16 La Mettrie, 'L'Homme machine', *Oeuvres philosophiques* (Berlin, 1751), p.55

17 Edmund Burke, *A Vindication of Natural Society* (1756), pp.3–5

18 Ibid., p.104

19 Jeremy Bentham, *An Introduction to the Principles of Morals and Legislation* (1789)

20 Ibid., ch.xvii

21 See Singer, *Animal Liberation*, op.cit., p.27

22 Ibid., p.213

23 Immanuel Kant, 'Beantwortung der Frage; Was ist Aufklärung?', Cassirer, *Philosophy of the Enlightenment*, op.cit., p.163

24 Kant, Preface to 2nd edn. (1787) 'Introduction, *Critique of Pure Reason*', trans, J. M. D. Meiklejohn, introd. A. D. Lindsay (Dent, 1978), pp.10–11

25 *The Moral Law: Kant's Groundwork of the Metaphysic of Morals*, trans. H. J. Paton (Hutchinson, 1972) p.97

26 Ibid., p.84

27 Kant, *Lectures on Ethics*, trans. L. Infield (New York: Harper Torchbooks, 1963), pp.239–40

28 *The Moral Law*, op.cit., pp.90–91

29 In S. Körner *Kant*, (Penguin, 1970), p.170

30 Ibid., pp.61, 62

## Chapter 18. Primitivism

1 Gabriel de Foigny, *Les Aventures de Jacques Sadeur dans la découverte de la Terre Australe* (1676) in Marie Louise Berneri, *Journey through Utopia* (Freedom Press, 1982), p.198

2 Jonathan Swift, *Gulliver's Travels and Other Writings*, ed. Ricardo Quintana (New York: Modern Library, 1958), 101

3 Ibid., p.202

4 Denis Diderot, *Le Neveu de Rameau* (1823) in Charles Vereker, *Eighteenth-Century Optimism* (Liverpool: Liverpool University Press, 1967), p.167
5 Diderot, 'Passions', *Encyclopédie*, ibid., p.168
6 Jean-Jacques Rousseau, 'The Origin of Inequality', *The Social Contract and Discourses*, trans. G. D. H. Cole, rev. edn. J. H. Brumfitt & J. C. Hall (Dent, 1973), p.51
7 Ibid., p.39
8 Ibid., pp.55, 66
9 Ibid., p.76
10 Ibid., p.83
11 Ibid., p.89
12 Ibid., p.93
13 Ibid., p.104
14 Ibid., p.82
15 Rousseau, *The Social Contract*, ibid., p.165

## Chapter 19. Changing Sensibilities

1 See Claude Lévi-Strauss, *The Savage Mind* (1966), pp.2, 8
2 In Thomas, *Man and the Natural World*, op.cit., p.62
3 Coleridge, 'The Ancient Mariner', ll. 612–17, *The Portable Coleridge*, ed. I. A. Richards (Harmondsworth: Penguin, 1977), p.104
4 Hume, *Essays Moral, Political and Literary*, ed. T. H. Green & T. H. Grose (1898), II, 85–8; Hale, *The Primitive Origination of Man*, op.cit., p.16
5 Charles White, *Account of the Regular Gradation* (n.d.), p.80
6 See Donald Worster, *Nature's Economy: A History of Ecological Ideas* (Cambridge: Cambridge University Press, 1977), pp.2, 36
7 Gilbert White, *The Natural History of Selborne* (1789) in Worster, *Nature's Economy*, op.cit., pp.7–8
8 In Thomas, *Man and Nature*, op.cit., p.22; Thomas Aquinas, *Summa contra Gentiles*, III, 113
9 Henry More, *An Antidote against Atheism* (2nd edn., 1655), pp.124–5; *The Works, Moral and Religious, of Sir Matthew Hale*, ed. T. Thirlwell (1805), II, 274; *The Diary of Samuel Pepys*, ed. R. Latham & W. Matthews (1970) VII, 246
10 Hume, *Dialogues concerning Natural Religion* (1779); Kant, *Critique of Teleological Judgment* (1790). See C. J. Glacken, *Traces on the Rhodian Shore: Nature and Culture in Western Thought from Ancient Times to the End of the Eighteenth Century* (Berkeley: University of California Press, 1967), ch, xi
11 Edward Bancroft, *An Essay on the Natural History of Guiana* (1769), pp.223–4
12 Blake, 'The Fly', *Complete Writings*, op.cit., p.213
13 Byron, *Don Juan*, canto xiii, stanza 106
14 Wordsworth, 'Lines written in early Spring'
15 Pope, 'Essay on Man', *Works*, op.cit., p.530
16 Spinoza, *Ethic*, IV, prop.37
17 Jacob Bauthumley in Norman Cohn, *The Pursuit of the Millennium* (1962), p.342
18 In Thomas, *Man and the Natural World*, op.cit., p.293
19 Philotheos Physiologus (Thomas Tryon), *The Country-man's Companion* [1683], sig. A2
20 Ibid., p.171
21 Ovid, *Metamorphoses*, trans. Dryden in *The Poems of John Dryden*, ed. James Kinsley, (Oxford, 1958), IV, 1736

22 In Nash, *The Rights of Nature*, op.cit., p.24
23 John Oswald, *The Cry of Nature* (1791), p.ii
24 John Stuart Mill, *Principles of Political Economy* (1848), ed. M. M. Robertson (Toronto, 1965), II, 952
25 Arthur Helps, *Some Talk about Animals and their Masters* (1873)
26 Henry S. Salt, *Animals' Rights considered in relation to Social Progress* (1891) (New York, 1894), p.16
27 Salt, *Cruelties of Civilization* (n.d.), vii
28 Locke, *Two Treatises on Government*, ed. Peter Laslett (Cambridge, 1960), p.201; Thomas, *Man and the Natural World*, op.cit., p.194
29 Joseph Addison, *Spectator*, 393 (31 May 1712); John Clare, 'Poems of the Imagination: Yew Trees', *The Poems of John Clare*, ed. J. W. Tibble (1935), pp.4–5; Wordsworth, 'The Excursion', vii, ll. 590–631
30 Bacon, 'Of Gardens', *Essays*, op.cit., p.156; William Cobbett, in Thomas, *Man and the Natural World*, op.cit., p.240
31 John Lawrence, *The Gentleman's Recreation* (1716); in F. E. Manuel, *A Portrait of Isaac Newton* (Cambridge, Mass., 1968), p.105
32 In David Crouch & Colin Ward, *The Allotment: Its Landscape and Culture* (Faber & Faber, 1990), p.52
33 Thomas, *Man and the Natural World*, op.cit., p.254
34 Henry More, *An Antidote against Atheism* (2nd edn. 1655), p.93
35 William Gilpin, *Remarks on Forest Scenery* (1791), II, 166; *John Constable's Correspondence*, ed. R. B. Beckett (Suffolk Records Society, 1962–8), VI, 98
36 Wordsworth, 'Liberty', l. 32
37 Coleridge to Thomas Wedgwood (14 January 1803) in Basil Willey, *Samuel Taylor Coleridge* (Chatto & Windus, 1972), p.95.
38 Wordsworth, *The Excursion*, viii, ll. 151–5
39 John Bruckner, *A Philosophical Survey of the Animal Creation* (1768) in Worster, *Nature's Economy*, op.cit., p.48
40 Mill, *Principles of Political Economy*, op.cit., IV, 6.2
41 Thoreau, 'Walking' (1862), *The Portable Thoreau*, ed. Carl Bode (Harmondsworth: Penguin, 1979), pp.613, 618. Cf. Nash, *Wilderness and the American Mind* (1982), p.84
42 In Peter J. Schmitt, *Back to Nature* (New York, 1969), p.67
43 Freud, 'Introductory Lectures on Psycho-Analysis' (part iii), *Complete Psychological Works of Sigmund Freud*, trans. James Strachey et al, (1963), XVI, 372

## Chapter 20. The Romantic Mind and Imagination

1 In A. K. Thorlby, *The Romantic Movement* (Longmans, 1966), pp.151, 2
2 Pope, *Essay on Criticism*; Edward Young, *Conjectures on Original Composition* (1759) (New York, 1917), p.45
3 See M. H. Abrams, *The Mirror and the Lamp: Romantic Theory and the Critical Tradition* (1953)
4 Hume, *Treatise of Human Nature*, Bk. II, part iii, sec. 3; Rousseau, *Emile* (1762); Marquis de Luc de Clapier Vauvenargues, in Gay, *The Enlightenment*, op.cit., II, 191
5 Novalis in J. L. Talmon, *Romanticism and Revolt* (Thames & Hudson, 1967), p.156
6 Heine in Lilian R. Furst, *Romanticism* (Methuen, 1969), p.2; Keats to G. & T. Keats (21 December 1817)
7 Johnson on fancy; Keats to Benjamin Bailey, (22 November 1817)

8 Coleridge, *Biographic Literaria* (Dent, 1962), pp.174, 167; Blake, *Complete Writings*, op.cit., p.293; Keats to his brother George (18 September 1819); Shelley, *Defence of Poetry* (1821), *Shelley's Prose; or The Trumpet of Prophecy*, ed. D. L. Clark, (Albuquerque, 1954), p.240

9 George Sand in Furst, *Romanticism*, op.cit., p 3; in my *William Blake: Visionary Anarchist* (Freedom Press, 1988), p.28

10 Edmund Burke, *Philosophical Enquiry into the Origin of Our Ideas of the Sublime and the Beautiful* (1757)

11 Mme de Staël, *De la littérature* (1800)

12 Wordsworth, *The Prelude* (1798–1805) VI; *Ode: Intimations of Immortality from Recollections of Early Childhood* (1802–1804)

13 Keats to Fanny Brawne (25 July 1819)

14 Blake, *Complete Writings*, op.cit., pp.818, 533

15 Ibid., p.793

16 Ibid., pp.777, 379, 149, 160

17 Ibid., p.431

18 Ibid., p.793

19 Wordsworth in Huxley, *The Perennial Philosophy*, op.cit., p.96

20 Wordsworth, *The Prelude*, op. cit.

21 *The Recluse*

22 *Ode: Intimations of Immortality*, op. cit.

23 Coleridge, *Biographia Literaria*, op.cit., p.86

24 *Table Talk* (1835), (25 July 1832)

25 *The Statesman's Manual*, in Lively, *The Enlightenment*, op.cit., p.85

26 Wordsworth, *The Prelude*, op. cit., III, 60; Coleridge to Thomas Poole (23 March 1801)

27 Ibid.

28 Coleridge, 'The First Landing Place', Essay V, *The Friend*; *Aids to Reflection* (1825). See also Basil Willey, *Samuel Taylor Coleridge* (Chatto & Windus, 1972), pp.89, 128, 227

29 Coleridge, *The Friend*, (Bohn edn.), p.366

30 Coleridge, *The Statesman's Manual*, in Lively, *The Enlightenment*, op.cit., p. 85

31 Coleridge to John Thelwall (14 October 1797)

32 Coleridge, *Dejection: An Ode*, original draft

## Chapter 21. Romantic Cosmology

1 See S. Toulmin & J. Goodfield, *The Discovery of Time* (Harmondsworth: Penguin, 1967), p.327

2 Ibid., p.159

3 Ibid., p.167

4 In Thorlby, *The Romantic Movement*, op.cit., p.98

5 Toulmin & Goodfield, *The Discovery of Time*, op.cit., p.168

6 In Thorlby, *The Romantic Movement*, op.cit., p. 97

7 Coleridge, *Biographia Literaria*, op.cit.

8 Wordsworth, *A Poet's Epitaph*

9 See C. C. Gillespie, *The Edge of Objectivity* (1960), ch.v

10 Whitehead, *Science and the Modern World* (1925)

11 *Nature* (1869), I, 9

12 Johann Wolfgang von Goethe, *The Sorrows of Werther* (1774)

13 Goethe, *Faust*, Part II (1832)

14 Percy Bysshe Shelley, *Prometheus Unbound* (1820)

15 Mary Shelley, *Frankenstein; or, The Modern Prometheus* (1818)
16 Johann Gottlieb Fichte, *The Science of Knowledge* (1794)
17 Friedrich Schelling, *Nature Philosophy* (1800)
18 In Talmon, *Romanticism and Revolt*, op.cit., p.160
19 Wilhelm Hegel, Introduction, *Philosophy of History* (1821)
20 *Hegel: The Essential Writings*, ed. Frederick G. Weiss (New York: Harper & Row, 1974), p.262
21 Hegel, conclusion to *Phenomenology of Mind* (1807)
22 See Peter Singer, *Hegel* (Oxford: Oxford University Press, 1983), p.82
23 Hegel, *Essential Writings*, op.cit., p.7
24 Ibid., p.190
25 Ibid., p.78
26 See Theodor W. Adorno, *Negative Dialectics* (New York: Seabury Press, 1973), p.8
27 See J. L. Talmon, *The Origins of Totalitarian Democracy* (Secker & Warburg, 1952)
28 Engels, *Socialism: Utopian and Scientific* (1880)
29 See Max Horkheimer and Theodor Adorno, *Dialectic of Enlightenment* (New York: Herder & Herder, 1972)
30 Horkheimer, *The Eclipse of Reason* (New York: Oxford University Press, 1947), p.176

## Chapter 22. Utopian Seers

1 William Hazlitt, *The Spirit of the Age: or Contemporary Portraits* (1825) (Oxford: Oxford University Press, 1954), pp.19–20. For Godwin's influence, see also my *William Godwin* (London & New Haven: Yale University Press, 1984), ch.viii
2 *The Anarchist Writings of William Godwin*, ed. with introd. Peter Marshall (Freedom Press, 1986), p.61
3 Ibid., p.92
4 Ibid., pp.64, 95
5 Ibid., p.69
6 In my *William Godwin*, op.cit., p.268
7 Godwin, *Anarchist Writings*, op.cit., p.171
8 In my *William Godwin*, op.cit., p.158
9 Godwin, *Anarchist Writings*, op.cit., p.173
10 Ibid., p.51
11 Ibid., p.136
12 In my *William Godwin*, op.cit., p.311
13 In Colin Ward, *Utopia* (Harmondsworth: Penguin, 1974). p.29
14 Murray Bookchin, *The Ecology of Freedom: The Emergence and Dissolution of Hierarchy* (Palo Alto, Calif.: Cheshire Books, 1982), p.331
15 *The Utopian Vision of Charles Fourier*, ed. Jonathan Beecher & Richard Bienvenu (Boston: Beacon Press, 1971), p.1
16 Ibid., pp.196, 321
17 *Selected Writings of Pierre-Joseph Proudhon*, ed. Stewart Edwards, trans. Elisabeth Fraser (Macmillan, 1960), p.197
18 Ibid., p.261–2
19 In my *Demanding the Impossible: A History of Anarchism* (Harper Collins, 1992), p.246
20 Ibid., pp.249–50
21 Ibid., p.256

22 Proudhon, *Selected Writings*, op.cit., p.260

23 Oscar Wilde, *De Profundis and Other Essays* (Harmondsworth: Penguin, 1973), p.80

24 Peter Kropotkin, *Memoirs of a Revolutionist*, ed. Allen Rogers (Cresset, 1988), p.91

25 Kropotkin, *Modern Science and Anarchism* (1905)

26 Kropotkin, *Mutual Aid* (Harmondsworth: Penguin, 1939), p.23

27 Kropotkin, *Ethics: Origin and Development*, ed. N. Lebedev (Dorchester: Prism Press, n. d.), p.45

28 Kropotkin, *Anarchism and Anarchist Communism*, ed. Nicolas Walter (Freedom Press, 1987), p.7

29 Kropotkin, *Fields, Factories and Workshops Tomorrow*, ed. Colin Ward (Allen & Unwin, 1974), p.26

30 Kropotkin, *Mutual Aid*, op.cit., p.233

31 William Morris, *Political Writings*, ed. A. L. Morton (Lawrence & Wishart, 1973), p.201

32 Morris, *News from Nowhere; or, An Epoch of Rest* (Longman, Green, 1907), p.64

33 Karl Marx, *Early Texts* ed. David McLellan (Oxford: Basil Blackwell, 1971), pp.138, 112

34 Ibid., p.148

35 Howard L. Parson, ed., *Marx and Engels on Ecology* (Wesport, Conn.: Greenwood Press, 1977), p.10; Alfred Schimdt, *The Concept of Nature in Marx* (New Left Books, 1973), p.80

36 Engels, *Dialectics of Nature*, Marx & Engels, *Collected Works* (Lawrence & Wishart, 1987), XV, 330–1

37 Marx, *Early Texts*, op.cit., 139

38 Erich Fromm, *Marx's Concept of Man* (New York: Frederick Ungar, 1973), p.26

39 Ibid., p.42

40 See my article 'What Hope for the Rural Idiot?', *New Internationalist* (June, 1978)

41 Marx, 'British Rule in India', Marx & Engels, *Basic Writings on Politics and Philosophy*, ed. Lewis S. Feuer (Fontana, 1969), p.517

42 Marx & Engels, *The German Ideology*, (New York: International Publishers, 1947), p.19 See John P. Clark, 'Marx's Inorganic Body', *Environmental Ethics* (Fall, 1989), XI, 243–58

43 *Marx's Grundrisse*, ed. David McLellan (Macmillan, 1971), p.94.

44 Marx, *Early Texts*, op.cit., 141

45 Ibid., p.14

## Chapter 23. Darwinism

1 See Worster, *Nature's Economy*, op.cit., p.114

2 Charles Darwin, *The Origin of Species* (1859), ed. J. W. Burrow, (Harmondsworth: Penguin, 1968), p.68

3 Darwin, *Autobiography* (Oxford: Oxford University Press, 1974), p.23

4 Thomas Malthus, *An Essay on the Principle of Population* (1798), ed. Anthony Flew (Harmondsworth: Penguin, 1970), p.71

5 Ibid., p.133

6 See Flew, Introduction, ibid., pp.31–2

7 Anne Chisholm, *Philosophers of the Earth. Conversations with Ecologists* (Sidgewick & Jackson 1972), p.144

8 Ibid., p.137–8
9 Worster, *Nature's Economy*, op.cit., p.149
10 Darwin, *The Origin of Species*, op.cit., p.116
11 Ibid. pp.458, 459
12 See A. G. N. Flew, *Evolutionary Ethics* (Macmillan, 1967), p.18
13 Darwin, *The Origin of Species*, op.cit., p.348
14 In Worster, *Nature's Economy*, op.cit., pp.133, 135
15 Darwin, *The Variations of Animals and Plants Under Domestication* (Murray, 1875), pp.7–8; Sheldrake, *The Rebirth of Nature*, op.cit., p.54
16 Darwin, *The Origin of Species*, ibid., pp.124–5
17 Ibid., pp.459–60
18 Ibid., pp.171–2
19 In Worster, *Nature's Economy*, op.cit.,. p.158
20 Darwin, *The Descent of Man* (Watts, 1930), pp.243–4
21 In Worster, *Nature's Economy*, op.cit., p.165
22 Darwin, *The Descent of Man*, op.cit., p.244
23 T. H. Huxley, 'The Origin of the Species', *Man's Place in Nature and Other Essays* (Dent, 1921), p.323
24 Huxley, 'Man's Relations to Lower Animals', *Man's Place in Nature and Other Essays*, op.cit., p.102
25 Huxley, Romanes Lecture on 'Evolution and Ethics', J. S. & T. H. Huxley *Evolution and Ethics* (Pilot Press, 1947), p.82
26 Huxley, 'On the Hypothesis that Animals are Automata, and its History', Lecture delivered to British Association, Belfast, 1874
27 Burrow, Introduction, *The Origin of Species*, op.cit., p.19
28 Darwin, *The Descent of Man*, op.cit., p.140
29 Tennyson, *In Memoriam* (1850)
30 H. R. Trevor-Roper, ed. *Hitler's Table Talk* (Weidenfeld & Nicolson, 1953), p.39
31 See Carl Sagan, *The Dragons of Eden: Speculations on the Evolution of Human Intelligence* (New York: Ballantine, 1986), p.177n

## Chapter 24. The New World of Ecology

1 In R. P. McIntosh, *The Background of Ecology* (Cambridge: Cambridge University Press, 1985), p.78
2 In Anna Bramwell, *Ecology in the 20th Century* (New Haven: Yale University Press, 1989), p.44
3 Ibid., p.49
4 Edward O. Wilson, *Biophilia* (Cambridge, Mass.: Harvard University Press, 1984), p.138
5 See Richard Dawkins, *The Selfish Gene* (Oxford: Oxford University Press, 1976)
6 F. E. Clements, *Research Methods in Ecology* (Lincoln, Nebraska: University Publishing Co., 1909), p.199
7 See D. F. Owen, *What is Ecology?*, 2nd edn, (Oxford: Oxford University Press, 1980), p.135
8 Bill McKibben, *The End of Nature* (Harmondworth: Penguin, 1990), p.84
9 Owen, *What is Ecology?*, op.cit., p.195
10 See Ervin Laszlo, *Introduction to Systems Philosophy* (New York: Harper Torchbooks, 1972)
11 See Erich Jantsch, *The Self-Organizing Universe* (Oxford: Pergamon, 1979)

12 See Ilya Prigogine, *From Being to Becoming* (San Francisco: Freeman, 1980)
13 See Jacques Monod, *Chance and Necessity* (Collins, 1972)
14 Fritjof Capra, *The Turning Point: Science, Society and the Rising Culture* (Flamingo, 1983), p.312
15 Gregory Bateson, *Steps to an Ecology of Mind* (Paladin, 1973), pp.405, 436
16 Capra, *The Turning Point*, op.cit., p.330
17 E. P. Odum, *Ecology: The Link Between the Natural and Social Sciences*, 2nd edn. (New York: Holt, Rinehart & Winston, 1979), p.5
18 See Paul A. Weiss, *Within the Gates of Science and Beyond* (New York: Hafner, 1971), p.276
19 Capra, *The Turning Point*, op.cit., p.305
20 Julian Huxley, 'Evolutionary Ethics' (1943), in *Darwin*, ed. Philip Appleman (New York: Norton, 1970), p.411
21 Huxley, *Evolution in Action* (Harmondsworth: Penguin, 1968), p.139
22 In Flew, *Evolutionary Ethics*, op.cit., p.48
23 Charles Elton, *The Ecology of Invasions by Plants and Animals* (New York: Wiley, 1953), p.101

## Chapter 25. Philosophers of the Earth

1 In Stephen Fox, *The American Conservation Movement: John Muir and his Legacy* (Madison, Wis., 1985), p.44; Muir, *A Thousand-Mile Walk to the Gulf*, ed. W. F. Badé, (Boston, 1917), p.356
2 Albert Schweitzer, *Out of My Life and Thought: An Autobiography* (1931) (New York, 1933), p.185
3 Ibid., p.188
4 Schweitzer, *Philosophy of Civilization: Civilization and Ethics*, trans. John Naish (1923), p.254
5 Schweitzer, *Out of My Life and Thought*, op.cit., p.271
6 In Nash, *The Rights of Nature*, op.cit., p.61
7 Schweitzer, *Out of My Life and Thought*, op.cit., p.188; *Indian Thought and its Development*, trans. C. E. B. Russell (New York, 1936), p.261
8 *The Animal World of Albert Schweitzer*, trans. R. Joy (Boston, 1950), p.169
9 Rachel Carson, *Silent Spring* (Boston, 1962), p.275
10 Ibid., p.251
11 Nash, *The Rights of Nature*, op.cit., pp.63, 70
12 Worster, *Nature's Economy*, op.cit., p.271
13 Aldo Leopold, *A Sand County Almanac* (New York: Oxford University Press, 1949), pp.129–30
14 Leopold, 'Wherefore Wildlife Ecology?', in Nash, *The Rights of Nature*, op.cit., p.64
15 Leopold, *A Sand County Almanac*, op.cit., pp.205, vii, 209
16 Ibid., pp.189–90
17 Ibid., pp.224–5
18 Ibid., p.214
19 Ibid., p.204
20 In Anne Chisholm, *Philosophers of the Earth*, op.cit., p.15
21 David Ehrenfeld, *The Arrogance of Humanism* (Oxford: Oxford University Press, 1978), p.210
22 In Nash, *The Rights of Nature*, op.cit., p.154. See also J. Baird Callicott, *In Defense of the Land Ethic: Essays in Environmental Philosophy* (Albany: State University of New York Press, 1989)

23 See Paul W. Taylor, 'In Defence of Biocentrism', *Environmental Ethics*, 5 (1983), 241–3, and his *Respect for Nature: A Theory of Environmental Ethics* (Princeton, N.J.: Princeton University Press, 1986)

## Chapter 26. Time and Being

1 A. N. Whitehead, *Science and the Modern World* (Cambridge: Cambridge University Press, 1925), pp.58–9
2 See Whithead, *Adventures in Ideas* (Cambridge: Cambridge University Press, 1933), p.185
3 Ibid., pp.201–22, 239; *Science and the Modern World*, op.cit., ch.iii
4 Ibid., pp.79–80
5 Ibid., pp.71, 76.
6 Ibid., pp.184–5
7 *Adventures in Ideas*, op.cit., p.241
8 Collingwood, *The Idea of Nature*, op.cit., p.174
9 Whitehead, *Process and Reality* (Cambridge: Cambridge University Press, 1929), II, iii
10 *Adventures in Ideas*, op.cit., p.245
11 Ibid., pp.226–7
12 Ibid., p.345
13 Ibid., pp.vii, 352–3
14 Ibid., pp.367, 381
15 Henri Bergson, *L'Évolution créatrice*, (1907), 5th edn (Paris: Félix Alcan, 1909), p.193. My translation
16 See H. Wildon Carr, *Henri Bergson: The Philosophy of Change* (Jack, n.d.)
17 Bergson, *Time and Free Will* (1899) (Allen & Unwin, 1910), p.128
18 *Evolution Créatrice*, op.cit., p.95
19 Ibid., p.294
20 In Carr, *Henri Bergson*, op.cit., p.89
21 Bergson, 'Mind Energy' (*L'Energie spirituelle*), *Lectures and Essays* (1920), p.13
22 Ibid., p.47
23 Bergson, *Two Sources of Morality and Religion* (New York: Doubleday, 1953), p.53
24 See John-Francis Phipps, *The Politics of Inner Experience: Dynamics of a Green Spirituality* (Green Imprint, 1990), p.94
25 George Steiner, 'The House of Being', *Times Literary Supplement* (9 October 1981)
26 Martin Heidegger, 'Letter on Humanism' (1947), *Basic Writings,* ed. David Farrell Krell (Routledge, & Kegan Paul, 1978), p.193
27 Heidegger, 'On the Essence of Truth', *Existence and Being,* ed. W. Brock (Chicago: Regnery, 1949), p.306
28 See George Steiner, *Heidegger* (Fontana, 1978), pp.112–116
29 See John Macquarrie, *Martin Heidegger* (Lutterworth, 1968), p.1
30 Heidegger, *Being and Time,* (SCM, 1962), p.78f.
31 See Michael Zimmerman, *Eclipse of Self: The Development of Heidegger's Concept of Authenticity* (Athens: Ohio University Press, 1981)
32 In Steiner, *Heidegger*, op.cit., p.67
33 Heidegger, 'The End of Philosophy and the Task of Thinking', *Basic Writings*, op.cit., p.379
34 'What are Poets For?', *Poetry, Language, Thought* (New York, 1975), pp.114–5
35 'The Question concerning Technology' (1954), *Basic Writings*, op.cit., p.296

36 'Letter on Humanism' (1947), ibid., pp.221, 222
37 'The Origin of the Work of Art', ibid., p.169
38 'Building Dwelling Thinking', ibid., p.328
39 Ibid., p.327
40 'The End of Philosophy and the Task of Thinking' (1966), ibid., p.387
41 See *The Question of Being* (Vision, 1968), p.83

## Chapter 27. The Cosmic Joy of the New Science

1 See Sheldrake, *The Rebirth of Nature*, op.cit., p.75. See also J. B. Cobb & D. R. Griffin, *Mind and Nature: Essays on the Interface of Science and Philosophy* (Washington: University Press of America, 1978); D. R. Griffin, ed., *The Reenchantment of Science: Postmodern Proposals* (Albany: State University of New York Press, 1988)
2 See John Gribben, *In Search of the Big Bang* (Corgi, 1986)
3 Gribben, *The Omega Point: The Search for the Missing Mass and the Ultimate Fate of the Universe* (Corgi, 1988), p.13
4 Ibid., p.11
5 See Paul Davies, *Space and Time in the Modern Universe* (Cambridge: Cambridge University Press, 1977)
6 In Timothy Ferris, *The Coming of Age in the Milky Way* (Bodley Head, 1988), p.187
7 See Richard Rhodes, *The Making of the Atomic Bomb* (New York: Simon & Schuster, 1986)
8 Stephen W. Hawking, *A Brief History of Time: From the Big Bang to Black Holes,* (Bantam, 1990), p.33
9 Ferris, *The Coming of Age in the Milky Way*, op.cit., p.186
10 Paul Davies, *Superforce: The Search for the Grand Unified Theory of Nature* (Heinemann, 1984). p.5; see also Sheldrake, *The Rebirth of Nature*, op.cit., p.68
11 See Ferris, *The Coming of Age in the Milky Way*, op.cit., p.335
12 Stephen W. Hawking, 'The Edge of Spacetime', in William Kaufmann, *Universe* (New York: Freeman, 1985)
13 See Hawking, *A Brief History of Time*, op.cit., p.141
14 See Gribben, *The Omega Point*, op.cit., p.200
15 See Capra, *The Tao of Physics*, op.cit., p.114; See also his *The Turning Point*, op.cit., pp.19–20, 330–1
16 James Gleick, *Chaos: Making a New Science* (Heinemann, 1988), p.3
17 In Ferris, *Coming of Age in the Milky Way*, op.cit., p.291
18 William M. Schaffer, 'Chaos in Ecological Systems: The Coals that Newcastle Forgot', *Trends in Ecological Systems* 1 (1986), p.63
19 Gleick, *Chaos*, op.cit., p.115
20 Erwin Schrödinger, *What is Life?* (Cambridge: Cambridge University Press, 1967), p.82
21 Sheldrake, *The Rebirth of Nature*, op.cit., p.71
22 Albert Einstein to Max Born, in Ian Stewart, *Does God Play Dice? The Mathematics of Chaos* (Basil Blackwell, 1989), p.293
23 Joseph Ford, 'What is Chaos, That We Should Be Mindful Of It', in Gleick, *Chaos*, op.cit., p.306
24 Hao Bai-Lin, *Chaos* (Singapore: World Scientific, 1984), p.i
25 See David Bohm, *Wholeness and the Implicate Order* (Ark, 1985), p.172
26 Ibid., p.191
27 Stewart, *Does God Play Dice?* op.cit., p.22

28 Arthur Eddington, *The Nature of the Physical World* (Cambridge: Cambridge University Press, 1928), p.74
29 In James Lovelock, *Gaia: A New Look at Life on Earth* (Oxford: Oxford University Press, 1979), p.124
30 See Paul Davies, *The Cosmic Blueprint* (Heinemann, 1987)
31 John von Neumann, *Mathematical Foundations of the Quantum Theory* (Princeton, NJ: Princeton University Press, 1955)
32 Hawking, *A Brief History of Time*, op.cit., p.9
33 See Sheldrake, *The Rebirth of Nature*, op.cit., p.105
34 See Sagan, *The Dragons of Eden*, op.cit., p.27
35 See Sheldrake, *A New Science of Life: The Hypothesis of Formative Causation* (Blond & Briggs, 1981), and *The Presence of the Past: Morphic Resonance and the Habits of Nature* (Collins, 1988), and *The Rebirth of Nature* op.cit.
36 See Whitehead, *Science and the Modern World*, op.cit.
37 Arthur Koestler, *The Ghost in the Machine* (Chicago: Regnery, 1967), p.341
38 Sheldrake, *A New Science of Life*, op.cit., p.13; *The Rebirth of Nature*, op.cit., p.90
39 *The Rebirth of Nature*, op.cit., p.96
40 *A New Science of Life*, op.cit., p.207

## Chapter 28. The Resurrection of Gaia

1 In James Lovelock, *The Ages of Gaia: A Biography of Our Living Earth* (Oxford: Oxford University Press, 1989), pp.9–10
2 Lovelock, *Gaia*, op.cit., p.9
3 Ibid., p.152
4 Cf. *The Ages of Gaia*, op.cit., p.23
5 *Gaia*, op.cit., p.121
6 *The Ages of Gaia*, op.cit., pp.51, 62
7 Ibid., p.34f
8 Ibid., p.174–5
9 Ibid., 176; Michael Allaby, *Guide to Gaia*, (Optima, 1989), p.165
10 *Gaia*, op.cit., pp.117, 123
11 Ibid., pp.110, 111
12 Ibid., p.121
13 Ibid., p.127
14 Ibid., p.131, 145
15 *The Ages of Gaia*, op.cit., p.236
16 See John Ryle, 'The Secret of Everything', *Independent on Sunday* (22 September 1991)
17 See Lovelock, *Gaia: The Practical Science of Planetary Medicine* (Gaia Books, 1991)
18 *The Ages of Gaia*, op.cit., p.232
19 Ibid., p.52
20 Ibid., p.212
21 Lovelock to John Ryle, 'The Secret of Everything', op.cit.
22 *The Ages of Gaia*, op.cit., p.13
23 See Brian Walker, 'Battle for the Aped', *Guardian* (21 February 1991)
24 In P. Bunyard & E. Goldsmith, eds., *Gaia: The Thesis, the Mechanisms and the Implications* (Camelford: Wadebridge Ecological Centre, 1988)
25 Allaby, *Guide to Gaia*, op.cit., p.112
26 Ibid., p.95

27  Sheldrake, *The Rebirth of Nature*, op.cit., p.135
28  Lovelock, *The Ages of Gaia*, op.cit., pp.205, 206

## Chapter 29. Environmental Ethics

1  Capra, *The Turning Point*, op.cit., ch.iii
2  Arne Naess, 'the Shallow and the Deep, Long-range Ecology Movement. A Summary', *Inquiry*, 16 (1973)
3  Ynestra King, 'The Ecology of Feminism and the Feminism of Ecology', *Healing the Wounds: The Promise of Eco-feminism*, ed. Judith Plant (Green Print, 1989), p.19
4  See Carolyn Merchant, *The Death of Nature: Women, Ecology and the Scientific Revolution* (San Francisco, 1980), ch.i
5  See Starhawk, 'Feminist, Earth-based spirituality and Ecofeminism', *Healing the Wounds*, op.cit., p.175
6  Charlene Spretnak, 'Towards an Ecofeminist Spirituality', ibid., p.128
7  Mary Daly, *Gyn/Ecology* (Boston: Beacon Press, 1978), p.12
8  See Chiah Heller, 'Toward a Radical Eco-feminism', *Renewing the Earth: The Promise of Social Ecology*, ed., John Clark (Green Print, 1990) pp.160–1
9  Petra Kelly, 'Foreword', *Healing the Wounds*, op.cit., p.x
10  Ursula K. Le Guin 'Women/Wilderness', ibid., p.461
11  Le Guin, *Dancing at the Edge of the World: Thoughts on Words, Women, Places* (Gollancz, 1989), pp.vii, 143
12  Ibid., pp.87, 84, 909

## Chapter 30. Deep Ecology versus Social Ecology

1  Arne Naess, 'Deepness of Questions', in Warwick Fox, *Toward a Transpersonal Ecology: Developing New Foundations for Environmentalism* (Boston: Shambhala, 1990), p.93; Naess, 'Identification as a Source of Deep Ecological Attitudes', in Michael Tobias, ed., *Deep Ecology* (San Diego: Avant Books, 1985), p.256
2  Bill Devall, *Simple in Means, Rich in Ends: Practising Deep Ecology* (Green Print, 1990), p.12
3  Capra, *The Turning Point*, op.cit. p.458
4  Bill Devall & George Sessions, *Deep Ecology: Living as if Nature Mattered* (Salt Lake City: Peregrine Smith Books, 1985), p.65
5  Ibid., p.67
6  Naess, *Ecology, Community and Lifestyle*, trans. & ed. David Rothenberg (Cambridge: Cambridge University Press, 1989), p.196
7  Ibid., pp.174, 166; 'Self-realization: An Ecological Approach to Being in the World', *The Trumpeter* 4(3) (1987), 39–40
8  Fox, *Toward a Transpersonal Ecology*, op.cit., pp.250, 252
9  Dogen Zenji, in Devall & Sessions, *Deep Ecology*, op.cit., p.232
10  Naess, 'The Shallow and the Deep, Long-Range Ecology Movement: A Summary', *Inquiry* 16 (1973), 96, 95
11  Devall & Sessions, *Deep Ecology*, op.cit., p.70
12  See Devall, *Simple in Means, Rich in Ends*, op.cit. p.203
13  Devall, *Simple in Means, Rich in End*, op.cit., p.16
14  Edward Abbey, 'Theory of Anarchy'; 'Immigration and Liberal Taboos' in *One Life at a Time, Please* (New York: Henry Holt, 1988)
15  Devall & Sessions, *Deep Ecology*, op.cit., p.70

16 Devall, *Simple in Means, Rich in Ends*, op.cit., p.69
17 Ibid., p.32
18 Devall & Sessions, *Deep Ecology*, op.cit., p.145
19 Sessions, *Simple in Means, Rich in Ends*, op.cit., pp.123, 201
20 Ibid., p.202; Charlene Spretnak & Fritjof Capra, *Green Politics. The Global Promise* (Santa Fe, NM: Bear & Co, 1986), p.xxvi
21 Fox, *Toward a Transpersonal Ecology*, op.cit., p.179
22 See Stephen Elkins, 'The Politics of Mystical Ecology', *Telos*, 82 (1989–90), 57
23 See Richard Sylvan, 'A Critique of Deep Ecology', *Radical Philosophy*, 40 (1985), 7
24 Devall, *Simple in Means, Rich in Ends*, op.cit., p.16
25 Naess, 'Sustainable Development and the Deep Long-Range Ecology Movement', *The Trumpeter* 5 (1988), 139
26 Devall & Sessions. *Deep Ecology*, op.cit., p.67; Naess, 'Shallow and Deep Ecology', op.cit., p.95
27 See Paul Shepard, *The Tender Carnivore and the Sacred Game* (New York: Scribner's 1973)
28 See Barry Commoner, *The Closing Circle* (1971)
29 See E. A. Gutkind, *Community and Environment* (1954)
30 See Clark, *The Renewing the Earth*, op.cit., pp.1–2
31 See Bookchin, *The Philosophy of Social Ecology*, op.cit., p.175; Clark, *Renewing the Earth*, op.cit., p.7
32 Bookchin, 'Social Ecology versus "Deep Ecology"', pp. 4–5; *Green Perspectives* (Summer 1987), 19, 4
33 Clark, 'What is Social Ecology', *Renewing the Earth*, op.cit., p.5. See also his *The Anarchist Moment*, op.cit., ch.vii
34 Bookchin, 'Ecology and Revolutionary Thought', *Post-Scarcity Anarchism* (Wildwood House, 1974), p.64
35 Bookchin, *Ecology of Freedom* op.cit., p.237
36 'Social Ecology versus "Deep Ecology"', op.cit., pp.9–10
37 *The Ecology of Freedom*, op.cit., p.1
38 'Social Ecology versus "Deep Ecology"', op.cit., p.10
39 *Post-Scarcity Anarchism*, op.cit., pp.115, 119
40 Bookchin, *The Ecology of Freedom*, op.cit., p.344
41 Ibid., p.342
42 Ibid., pp.315, 25
43 'Recovering Evolution', *Environmental Ethics* 12 (Fall 1990), 257; 272–4
44 Clark, *Renewing the Earth*, op.cit., pp.7, 3

## Chapter 31. Towards a Libertarian Ecology

1 The Animals War Memorial, RSPCA Dispensary, Cambridge Avenue, Kilburn, London NW6. It is also recorded on the same memorial that 725, 216 various animals were wounded.
2 Singer, *Animal Liberation*, op.cit., p.178
3 Ibid., p.22. See also his 'Ten Years of Animal Liberation', *New York Review* (17 January 1985)
4 Stephen R. L. Clark, *The Moral Status of Animals* (Oxford: Clarendon Press, 1977), pp.34–5; Brigid Brophy, 'In Pursuit of A Fantasy', in Stanley & Roslind Godlovitch & John Harris, eds., *Animals, Men and Morals* (Gollancz, 1972), p.128
5 Tom Regan, *The Case for Animal Rights* (Routledge, 1988), p.243

6 See Eugene Hargrove, 'Ecological Sabotage: Pranks or Terrorism', *Environmental Ethics* 4 (Winter 1982), 292

7 Karl Hess, 'Rights and Reality', *Renewing the Earth*, op.cit., pp.130–1

8 See John Rodman, 'The Liberation of Nature?', *Inquiry* 20 (1977), 94–101

9 See Christopher D. Stone, *Should Trees have Standing? Toward Legal Rights for Natural Objects* (Los Altos, CA: William Kaufmann, 1974)

10 Jean-Paul Sartre, *Being and Nothingness*, trans. H. E. Barnes (Methuen, 1985), p.564.

11 Regan, *The Case for Animal Rights*, op.cit., 324

12 See Mary Midgley, *Animals and Why They Matter: A Journey around the Species Barrier* (Harmondsworth: Penguin, 1983)

13 See Paul Taylor, *Respect for Nature*, op.cit.

14 See Bookchin, *The Philosophy of Social Ecology*, op.cit., p.114

15 See Fox, *Toward a Transpersonal Ecology*, op.cit., pp.166–70, 192–3

16 Regan, *The Case for Animal Rights*, op.cit., p.362

17 Leopold, *A Sand County Almanac*, op.cit., pp.217, 209

18 See Regan, ed., *All That Dwell Therein: Animal Rights and Environmental Ethics* (Berkeley, CA: University of California Press, 1982)

19 In Nash, *The Rights of Nature*, op.cit., 154. See also J. Baird Callicott, *In Defense of the Land Ethic*, op.cit.

20 See Holmes Rolston III, *Environmental Ethics: Duties to and Values in the Natural World* (Philadelphia: Temple University Press, 1988)

21 Edward Abbey, *The Journey Home* (New York, 1977), p.208

22 Swift, *Gulliver's Travels and Other Writings*, op.cit., p.101

23 Garrett Hardin, *Exploring New Ethics for Survival* (New York: Viking, 1972), pp.256, 254.

24 Andrew Brennan, *Thinking about Nature: An Investigation of Nature, Value and Ecology* (Routledge, 1988), p.135

25 See my essay, 'Human Nature and Anarchism', in *For Anarchism: History, Theory, and Practice*, ed. David Goodway (Routledge, 1988), ch.iv

26 See Royston, *Environmental Ethics*, op.cit.

27 Singer, *Animal Liberation*, op.cit., p.164; Blake, *Complete Writings*, op.cit., pp.804–5

28 Taylor, *Respect for Nature*, op.cit.

29 Henryk Skolimowski, *Eco-philosophy: Designing New Tactics for Living* (Marion Boyars, 1981), p.115

30 See Charles Birch & John B. Cobb, Jr., *The Liberation of Life: From the Cell to the Community* (Cambridge: Cambridge University Press, 1981)

31 Herbert Marcuse, *Counterrevolution and Revolt* (Boston, 1972), pp.59, 74

32 Bookchin, *The Philosophy of Social Ecology*, op.cit., pp.177, 182–3

33 *Chuang Tzu*, op.cit., p.113

34 Lao Tse, *Tao Te Ching*, op.cit., ch.25

# SELECT BIBLIOGRAPHY

Articles referred to are given in the notes. Place of publication is London, unless otherwise indicated.

## Bibliographies

Anglemyer, Mary & Eleanor R. Seagraves, *The Natural Environment: An Annotated Bibliography of Attitudes and Values* (Washington: Smithsonian Institution Press, 1984)

Brennan, Andrew & Sean Smith, *Two Decades of Environmental Philosophy* (Department of Philosophy, University of Stirling, 1990)

Davis, D. E., *Ecophilosophy: A Field Guide to the Literature* (San Pedro, CA: R. & E. Miles, 1989)

## Before 1900

Aquinas, St Thomas. *Summa Theologiae*, ed. Timothy Mc Dermont (Eyre & Spottiswoode, 1989)

Bacon, Francis, *The Essays, the Wisdom of the Ancients and the New Atlantis* (Odhams Press, n.d.)

Bentham, Jeremy, *An Introduction to the Principles of Morals and Legislation* (1789)

*The Bhagavad Gita*, trans. Juan Mascaró (Harmondsworth: Penguin, 1975)

Blake, William, *Complete Writings* ed. Geoffrey Keynes (Oxford: Oxford University Press, 1972)

*Buddhist Scriptures*, trans. Edward Conze (Harmondsworth: Penguin, 1975)

*Chuang Tzu*, trans. Hebert A. Giles, (Unwin Paperbacks, 1980)

Coleridge, Samuel Taylor, *The Portable Coleridge* ed. I.A. Richards (Harmondsworth: Penguin, 1977)

——, *Biographia Literaria* (Dent, 1962)

Darwin, Charles, *The Origin of Species*, (1859) ed. J. W. Burrow (Harmondsworth: Penguin, 1968)

——, *The Variation of Animals and Plants under Domestication* (Murray, 1875)

——, *Autobiography* (Oxford: Oxford University Press, 1974)

Descartes, René, *Discourse on Method and the Meditations* trans. F. E. Sutcliffe (Harmondsworth: Penguin, 1976)

——, *Philosophical Writings* ed. E. Anscombe & P. T. Geach (Nelson, 1972)

*St Francis of Assisi: His Life and Writings as recorded by his Contemporaries*, trans. L. Shirley-Price (Mowbray, 1959)

Godwin, William, *The Anarchist Writings of William Godwin*, ed. Peter Marshall (Freedom Press, 1986)

*Heraclitus: The Cosmic Fragments*, ed. G. S. Kirk (Cambridge: Cambridge University Press, 1970)

Hobbes, Thomas, *Leviathan* (1651) ed. C. B. Macpherson (Harmondsworth:

Penguin, 1976)

*I Ching*, trans. James Legge, ed. Raymond van Over (New York: Mentor, 1971)

*The Glorious Koran*, trans. Mohammed Marmaduke Pickthall (New York: Mentor, n.d.)

Lao Tsu, *Tao Te Ching*, trans. Gia-Fu Feng & Jane English (New York: Vintage, 1972)

Locke, John, *Two Treatises of Civil Government* (1689)

Malthus, Thomas, *An Essay on the Principle of Population* (1798) ed. Anthony Fleur (Harmondsworth: Penguin, 1970)

Morris, William, *News from Nowhere* (1890) (Longmans, Green & Co., 1907)

——, *Political Writings*, ed. A. L. Morton (Lawrence & Wishart, 1973)

Salt, H. S., *Animal Rights*

*A Source Book in Chinese Philosophy*, trans. Wing-Tsit Chan (Princeton, NJ: Princeton University Press, 1973)

*A Source Book in Indian Philosophy*, eds. Sarvepalli Radhakrishnan & Charles A. Moore (Princeton, NJ: Princeton University Press, 1971)

*The Teachings of the Compassionate Buddha*, ed. E. A. Burtt (New York: Mentor, 1955)

*The Upanishads*, trans. Eknath Easwaran (Arkana, 1988)

*Zohar: The Book of the Enlightenment*, trans. D. C. Matt (SPCK, 1983)

## General

Abbey, Edward, *The Journey Home: Some Words in Defense of the American West* (New York: Dutton, 1977)

——, *Desert Solitaire* (Salt Lake City, UT: Peregrine Smith, 1981)

Allaby, Michael, *Inventing Tomorrow: How to live in a Changing World* (1977) (Abacus, 1977)

——, *Guide to Gaia* (Optima, 1989)

——, ed., *Thinking Green: An Anthology of Essential Ecological Writing* (Barrie & Jenkins, 1989)

Anderson, Walter Truett, *To Govern Evolution: Further Adventures of the Political Animal* (New York: Harcourt, Brace, Jovanovich, 1987)

Anderson, William, *The Rise of the Gothic* (Hutchinson, 1985)

Anderson, William & Clive Hicks, *Green Man* (HarperCollins, 1990)

Appleman, Philip, ed., *Darwin* (New York: Norton, 1970)

Ashby, Eric, *Reconciling Man with the Environment* (Oxford: Oxford University Press, 1978)

Attfield, Robin, *The Ethics of Environmental Concern* (Oxford: Basil Blackwell, 1983)


Baden, John & Garrett Hardin, *Managing the Commons* (San Francisco: W. H. Freeman, 1977)

Bahro, R., *From Red to Green: Interviews with the New Left Review* (Verso, 1984)

——, *Building the Green Movement* (Heretic, 1986)

——, *The Logic of Deliverance: On the Foundations of an Ecological Politics* (Schumacher Society Lecture, 1986)

Barbour, Ian G., *Earth Might Be Fair: Reflections on Ethics, Religion and Ecology* (Englewood Cliffs, NJ: Prentice Hall, 1972)

——, *Western Man and Environmental Ethics* (Menlo Park: Addison Wesley,

1973)

Barclay, Harold, *People without Government*: *An Anthropology of Anarchism* (Kahn & Averill and Cienfuegos Press, 1982)

Barr James, *Christianity and Ecology* (Manchester, 1983)

Bateson, Gregory, *Steps to an Ecology of Mind* (Paladin, 1973)

Berger, John, *Restoring the Earth*: *How Americans are Working to Renew Our Damaged Earth* (New York: Alfred Knopf, 1985)

Bergson, Henri, *L'Évolution créatricé*, (1907) 5th edn. (Paris: Félix Alcan, 1909)

Berman, Morris, *The Reenchantment of the World* (Ithaca: Cornell University Press, 1981)

——, *Coming to our Senses*: *Body and Spirit in the Hidden History of the West* (New York: Simon & Schuster, 1989)

Berneri, Marie Louise, *Journey through Utopia* (1950) (Freedom Press, 1982)

Berry, Wendell, *The Unsettling of America* (San Francisco: Sierra Club, 1977)

Birch, Charles, *Nature and God* (SCM, 1965)

Birch, C. & J. B. Cobb, Jr., *The Liberation of Life*: *From the Cell to the Community* (Cambridge: Cambridge University Press, 1981)

Black, John, *The Dominion of Man*: *The Search for Ecological Responsibility* (Edinburgh: Edinburgh University Press, 1970)

Blackstone, William T., ed., *Philosophy and the Environmental Crisis* (Athens, GA, 1974)

Bohm, David, *Wholeness and the Implicate Order* (Ark, 1984)

Bookchin, Murray, *Post-Scarcity Anarchism* (Wildwood House, 1974)

——, *The Ecology of Freedom*: *The Emergence and Dissolution of Hierarchy* (Palo Alto: Cheshire, 1982)

——, *Toward an Ecological Society* (Montréal: Black Rose, 1986)

——, *The Modern Crisis*, 2nd edn. (Montréal: Black Rose, 1987)

——, *Remaking Society* (Montréal: Black Rose, 1989)

——, *The Philosophy of Social Ecology*: *Essays on Dialectical Naturalism* (Montréal: Black Rose, 1990)

Bord, Janet & Colin, *Ancient Mysteries of Britain* (Grafton, 1986)

Bradley, Ian, *God is Green*: *Christianity and the Environment* (Darton, Longman & Todd, 1990)

Bramwell, Anna, *Ecology in the 20th Century*: *A History* (New Haven: Yale University Press, 1989)

Brandt Commission, *North-South*: *A Programme for Survival* (Pan, 1980)

Brennan, Andrew, *Thinking about Nature*: *An Investigation of Nature, Value and Ecology* (Routledge, 1988)

Brown, Dee, *Bury my Heart at Wounded Knee*: *An Indian History of the American West* (Picador, 1978)

Brown, Lester R., ed., *Building a Sustainable Society* (New York: Norton, 1981)

Brundtland, G. H. et al, *Our Common Future* (Oxford: Oxford University Press, 1987)

Bulbus, Isaac, *Marxism and Domination* (Princeton, NJ: Princeton University Press, 1982)

Bunyard, Peter & Fern Morgan-Grenville, eds., *The Green Alternative*: *Guide to Good Living* (Methuen, 1987)

Burckhardt, Titus, *Alchemy*: *Science of the Cosmos, Science of the Soul*, trans. William Stoddart (Longmead: Element Books, 1986)

Burke, Tom & John Elkington, *The Green Capitalists* (Gollancz, 1987)

Callenbach, Ernest, *Ecotopia* (Berkeley, CA: Banyan Tree Books, 1975)

Callicott, J. Baird, *In Defence of the Land Ethic: Essays in Environmental Philosophy* (Albany: State University of New York Press, 1989)

Callicoot, J. Baird & Roger T. Ames, eds., *Environmental Philosophy: The Nature of Nature in Asian Traditions of Thought* (Albany, NY: State University of New York Press, 1989)

Caplan, A. L., *The Sociobiology Debate: Readings* (1978)

Capra, Fritjof, *The Tao of Physics* (Wildwood House, 1975)

——, *The Turning Point: Science, Society and the Rising Culture* (Flamingo, 1983)

Carson, Rachel, *The Sea Around Us* (New York: New American Library, 1961)

——, *Silent Spring* (Hamish Hamilton, 1962)

Chardin, Teilhard de, *Science and Christ*, trans. René Hague (Collins, 1968)

——, *Le milieu divin: An Essay on the Interior Life* (Fontana, 1978)

——, *The Future of Man* (Fount, 1982)

Chisholm, Anne, *Philosophers of the Earth: Conversations with Ecologists* (Sidgwick & Jackson, 1972)

Clark, John, *The Anarchist Moment: Reflections on Culture, Nature and Power* (Montréal: Black Rose, 1984)

——, ed. *Renewing the Earth: The Promise of Social Ecology* (Green Print, 1990)

Clark, Stephen R. L., *The Moral Status of Animals* (Oxford: Clarendon Press, 1977)

Clarke, P. & A. Linzey, eds., *Political Theory and Animal Rights* (Pluto, 1991)

Clastres, Pierre, *Society against the State: The Leader as Servant and the Humane Use of Power among the Indians of the Americas* (New York: Urizen, 1977)

Clements, F. E., *Research Methods in Ecology* (Lincoln, Nebraska: University Publishing Co., 1905)

Cobb, J. B. & D. R. Griffin, *Mind in Nature: Essays on the Interface of Science and Philosophy* (Washington: University Press of America, 1978)

Cohen, Boaz, ed., *The Legends of the Jews* (Philadelphia: Jewish Publication Society of America, 1966)

Cohen, M. P., *The Pathless Way: John Muir and American Wilderness* (Madison: University of Wisconsin Press, 1984)

Cohn, Norman, *The Pursuit of the Millennium* (Paladin, 1984)

Collingwood, R. G., *The Idea of Nature* (1945) (Oxford: Clarendon Press, 1965)

Commoner, Barry, *The Closing Circle: Nature, Man and Technology* (Cape, 1972)

——, *Making Peace with the Planet* (Gollancz, 1990)

Crouch, David & Colin Ward, *The Allotment: Its Landscape and Culture* (Faber & Faber, 1980)

Daly, Mary, *Gyn/Ecology: The Meta-Ethics of Radical Feminism* (Boston: Beacon Press, 1978)

Davies, Paul, *Space and Time in the Modern Universe* (Cambridge: Cambridge University Press, 1977)

——, *God and the New Physics* (Harmondsworth: Penguin, 1983)

——, *Superforce: The Search for the Grand Unified Theory of Nature* (Heinemann, 1984)

——, *The Cosmic Blueprint* (Heinemann, 1987)

Dawkins, Richard, *The Selfish Gene* (Oxford: Oxford University Press, 1976)

Deloria, Ella C., *Speaking of Indians* (Vermillion: Dakota University Press, 1979)

Devall, Bill, *Simple in Means Rich in Ends: Practising Deep Ecology* (1988) (Green Imprint, 1990)

Devall, Bill & George Sessions, *Deep Ecology: Living as if Nature Mattered* (Salt Lake City: Peregrine Smith Books, 1985)

Diamond, Stanley, *In Search of the Primitive: A Critique of Civilization* (New Brunswick, NJ: Transaction Books, 1974)

Dobbs, Betty, *The Foundation of Newton's Alchemy* (Cambridge: Cambridge University Press, 1975)

Driesch, H., *Science and Philosophy of the Organism* (Black, 1908)

Dubos, René, *A God Within* (Angus & Robertson, 1972)

Dubos, René & Barbara Ward, *Only One Earth* (New York: Norton, 1972)

Eckholm, Erik, *Down to Earth* (Pluto, 1982)

Ehrenfeld, David, *The Arrogance of Humanism* (Oxford: Oxford University Press, 1978)

Ehrlich, Paul R., *The Machinery of Nature: The Living World Around Us – And How It Works* (New York: Simon & Schuster, 1986)

Ehrlich, Paul R. & Anne H., *Extinction: The Causes and Consequences of the Disappearance of Species* (New York: Ballantine, 1983)

——, *Earth* (New York: Franklin Watts, 1987)

Ekins, Paul, ed., *The Living Economy: A New Economics in the Making* (Routledge & Kegan Paul, 1986)

Elder, John, *Imagining the Earth: Poetry and the Vision of Nature* (Urbana: University of Illinois Press, 1985)

Elgin, Duane, *Voluntary Simplicity: Toward a Way of Life That is Outwardly Simple, Inwardly Rich* (New York: William Morrow, 1981)

Eliade, Mircea, *The Sacred and the Profane: The Nature of Religion* (New York: Harcourt, Brace & World, 1959)

——, *The Forge and the Crucible* (New York: Harper & Row, 1971)

Elkington, John & Julia Hailes, *The Green Consumer Guide* (Gollancz, 1988)

Elliot, R. & A. Gare, eds., *Environmental Philosophy* (Milton Keynes: Open University Press, 1983)

Elton, Charles, *Animal Ecology* (1935)

——, *The Ecology of Invasions by Plants and Animals* (New York: John W. Wiley, 1953)

Emery, W. B., *Archaic Egypt* (Harmondsworth: Penguin, n. d.)

Epstein, Perle, *Kabbalah: The Way of the Jewish Mystic* (Boston: Shambhala, 1988)

Ereira, Alan, *The Heart of the World* (Cape, 1990)

Fabricius, Johannes, *Alchemy: The Medieval Alchemists and their Royal Art* (Wellingborough: Aquarian Press, 1976)

Fauvel, John, Raymond Flood, Michael Shortland, & Robin Wilson, *Let Newton Be! A New Perspective on his Life and Works* (Oxford: Oxford University Press, 1988)

Ferris, Timothy, *Coming of Age in the Milky Way* (Bodley Head, 1988)

Flew, A. G. N., *Evolutionary Ethics* (Macmillan, 1967)

Foreman, David, ed., *Ecodefense: A Field Guide to Monkeywrenching* (Tucson, AZ: Ned Ludd Books, 1985)

Forster, L. & J. Todd, *Readings on the Ecological Revolution* (Lexington, MA.: Heath & Co., 1971)

Fox, Stephen, *John Muir and his Legacy* (Boston: Little Brown, 1981)

Fox, Warwick, *Toward a Transpersonal Ecology: Developing New Foundations for Environmentalism* (Boston: Shambhala, 1990)

Frankel, B. *The Post Industrial Utopians* (Cambridge: Polity Press, 1987)
Frazer, James George, *The Golden Bough: A Study in Magic and Religion* (Macmillan, 1924)
Fromm, Erich, *To Have or To Be* (Abacus, 1979)
——, *Marx's Concept of Man* (New York: Frederick Unger, 1973)
Fukuoka, Masanobu, *The One-Straw Revolution: An Introduction to Natural Farming* (Emmaus: Rodale Press, 1978)

Gay, Peter, *The Enlightenment: An Interpretation* (Wildwood House, 1973)
Gilchrist, Cherry, *Alchemy: The Great Work* (Wellingborough: Aquarian Press, 1984)
Ginzeber, Louis, *The Legends of the Jews* trans. Henrietta Szold (1909) (Philadelphia: Jewish Publication Society of America, 1988)
Glacken, C. J., *Traces on the Rhodian Shore: Nature and Culture in Western Thought from Ancient Times to the End of the Eighteenth Century* (Berkeley: University of California Press, 1967)
Gleick, James, *Chaos: Making a New Science* (Heinemann, 1988)
Godlovitch, Stanley & Rosalind & John Harris, eds., *Animals, Men and Morals* (Gollancz, 1972)
Godwin, Joscelyn, *Mystery Religions in the Ancient World* (Thames & Hudson, 1981)
Goldsmith, Edward *et al.*, *A Blueprint for Survival* (Harmondsworth: Penguin, 1964)
Goldsmith, Edward & Nicholas Hildyard, eds., *Battle for the Earth: Today's Key Environmental Issues* (Mitchell Beazley, 1988)
——, *The Earth Report 2: Monitoring the Battle of our Environment* (Mitchell Beazley, 1990)
Gollancz, Israel, *Sir Gawaine and the Green Knight* (Oxford: Oxford University Press, 1966)
Goodway, David, ed., *For Anarchism: History, Theory and Practice* (Routledge, 1989)
Gorz, Andre, *Paths to Paradise or the Liberation from Work* (Pluto, 1985)
Gould, Stephen Jay, *Wonderful Life; The Burgess Shale and the Nature of History* (Hutchinson Radius, 1989)
Graves, Robert, *The White Goddess* (Faber & Faber, 1988)
——, *The Greek Myths*, vol. I, (Harmondsworth: Penguin, 1955)
Gribben, John, *In Search of Schrödinger's Cat* (Corgi, 1984)
——, *In Search of the Big Bang* (Coregi, 1986)
——, *The Omega Point: The Search for the Missing Mass and the Ultimate Fate of the Universe* (Corgi, 1987)
Griffin, D. R., ed., *The Reenchantment of Science: Postmodern Proposals* (Albany: State University of New York Press, 1988)
Griffin, Susan, *Women and Nature* (New York: Harper & Row, 1978)
Guillaume, Alfred, *Islam* (Harmondsworth: Penguin, 1977)
Gutkind, E. A., *Community and Environment* (New York: Philosophical Library, 1954)

Halevi, Z'ev ben Shimon, *Kabbalah: Tradition of Hidden Knowledge* (Thames & Hudson, 1988)
Hall, Rebecca, *Animals are Equal* (Wildwood House, 1980)
Hampshire, Stuart, *Spinoza* (Harmondsworth: Penguin, 1965)
Hardin, Garrett, *Exploring New Ethics for Survival* (New York: Viking, 1972)

——, *The Limits of Altruism* (Bloomington, IN: Indiana University Press, 1977)

Hardin, Garrett & John Baden, eds., *Managing the Commons* (San Francisco, CA: W. H. Freeman, 1977)

Hardy, A., *The Living Stream* (Collins, 1965)

Hargrove, Eugene C., ed., *Religion and Environmental Crisis* (Athens, GA, 1986)

——, *Foundations of Environmental Ethics* (New Jersey: Prentice-Hall, 1989)

Hawking, Stephen W., *A Brief History of Time: From the Big Bang to Black Holes* (Bantam, 1990)

Heidegger, Martin, *Basic Writings*, ed., D. F. Krell (Routledge & Kegan Paul, 1978)

——, *The Question of Being*, trans. W. Kluback & J. T. Wilde (Vision, 1968)

——, *Poetry, Language, Thought* (New York, 1975)

Henderson, Hazel, *The Politics of the Solar Age: Alternatives to Economics* (Anchor, 1981)

Hendry, George S., *Theology of Nature* (Philadelphia: Westminster Press, 1980)

Horkeimer, Max & Theodor Adorno, *Dialectic of Enlightenment* (New York: Herder & Herder, 1972)

Horkeimer, Max, *The Eclipse of Reason* (New York: Oxford University Press, 1947)

Hughes, J. Donald, *Ecology and Ancient Civilization* (Albuerquerque, NM: University of New Mexico Press, 1975)

——, *American Indian Ecology* (El Paso, TX: Texas Western Press, 1983)

Hughes, J. D. & R. C. Schultz eds., *Ecological Consciousness* (Washington, DC: University Press of America, 1981)

Humphreys, Christmas, *Buddhism* (Harmondsworth: Penguin, 1971)

Huxley, Aldous, *The Perennial Philosophy* (1945) (Triad Grafton, 1989)

Irvine, Sandy & Alec Ponton, *A Green Manifesto: Policies for a Green Future* (Optima, 1988)

Jantsch, Erich, *The Self-Organizing Universe* (Oxford: Pergamon, 1979)

Johnson, Colin, *Green Dictionary* (Optima, 1991)

Jonas, Hans, *The Phenomenon of Life* (New York: Dell, 1966)

Jung, C. G., *Pyschology and Alchemy* (Routledge & Kegan Paul, 1953)

Kerényi, Carl, *The Gods of the Greeks* (Harmondsworth: Penguin, 1958)

Koestler, Arthur, *The Ghost in the Machine* (Chicago: Regnery, 1967)

Kosambi, D. D., *The Culture and Civilisation of Ancient India in Historical Outline* (New Delhi: Vikas, 1981)

Kropotkin, Peter, *Fields, Factories and Workshops Tomorrow*, ed. Colin Ward (George Allen & Unwin, 1974)

La Barre, Weston, *The Ghost Dance* (New York: Doubleday, 1970)

LaChapelle, Dolores, *Earth Wisdom* (1978)

Lame Deer, John (Fire) & Richard Erdoes, *Lame Deer: Seeker of Visions* (New York: Pocket Books, 1976)

Lamy Lucy, *Egyptian Mysteries: New Light on Ancient Knowledge* (Thames & Hudson, 1989)

Laye, Camara, *L'Enfant noir* (Paris, 1953)

Lee, Dorothy, *Freedom and Culture* (Englewood, NJ: Prentice Hall, 1959)

Leiss, William, *The Domination of Nature* (New York: Braziller, 1972)

Le Guin, Ursula K., *Always Coming Home* (New York: Harper & Row, 1985)

——, *Dancing at the Edge of the World: Thoughts on Words, Women, Places* (Gollancz, 1989)

Leland, Stephanie & Leonie Caldecott eds., *Reclaim the Earth* (Women's Press, 1983)

Leopold, Aldo, *Sand County Almanac* (1949) (Oxford: Oxford University Press, 1968)

Levy, John, *The Nature of Man according to the Vedanta* (Routledge & Kegan Paul, 1956)

Lindsay, Jack, *The Origins of Alchemy in Graeco-Roman Egypt* (Frederick Muller, 1970)

Lorenz, K., *On Aggression* (1966)

Lovejoy, A. F., ed. *A Documentary History of Primitivism and Related Ideas* (Baltimore: John Hopkins University Press, 1935)

——, *The Great Chain of Being* (Cambridge, Mass.: Harvard University Press, 1971)

Lovelock, James, *Gaia: A New Look at Life on Earth* (Oxford: Oxford University Press, 1979)

——, *The Ages of Gaia: A Biography of our Living Earth* (Oxford: Oxford University Press, 1989)

——, *Gaia: The Practical Science of Planetary Medicine* (Gaia Books, 1991)

Lowe, Philip &Jane Goyder, *Environmental Groups in Politics* (George Allen,1983)


Maharshi, Ramana, *The Teachings of Bhagavan Sri Ramana Maharshi in his Own Words*, ed. Arthur Osborne (Rider, 1975)

Marcuse, Herbert, *Eros and Civilization* (Boston: Beacon Press, 1955)

Marshall, Peter, *William Godwin* (New Haven: Yale University Press, 1984)

——, ed., *The Anarchist Writings of William Godwin* (Freedom Press, 1986)

——, *Cuba Libre: Breaking the Chains?* (Gollancz,1987; Unwin Paperbacks,1988; Boston: Faber & Faber, 1988)

——, *William Blake: Visionary Anarchist* (Freedom Press, 1988)

——, *Demanding the Impossible: A History of Anarchism* (HarperCollins, 1992)

Marx, Leo, *The Machine in the Garden: Technology and the Pastoral Idea in America* (Oxford: Oxford University Press, 1964)

Matthews, Freya, *The Ecological Self* (Routledge, 1990)

MacLagan, David, *Creation Myths: Man's Introduction to the World* (Thames & Hudson, 1979)

McCormick, John, *The Global Environment Movement: Reclaiming Paradise* (Belhaven Press, 1989)

McDonagh, Sean, *To Care for the Earth* (Geoffrey Chapman, 1986)

McIntosh, R. P., *The Background of Ecology* (Cambridge: Cambridge University Press, 1985)

McKibben, Bill, *The End of Nature* (Harmondsworth: Penguin, 1990)

McLuhan, T. C., ed., *Touch the Earth: A Self Portrait of Indian Existence* (Abacus, 1989)

McMillan, Carol, *Women, Reason and Nature* (Princeton, NJ: Princeton University Press, 1982)

Meadows, Dennis *et al.*, *The Limits to Growth: A Report for the Club of Rome's Project on the Predicament of Mankind* (Earth Island, 1972)

Merchant, Carolyn, *The Death of Nature: Women, Ecology, and the Scientific Revolution* (San Francisco: Harper & Row, 1983)

——, *Radical Ecology: The Search for a Livable World* (New York: Routledge, 1992)

Michell, John, *The Earth Spirit: Its Ways, Shrines and Mysteries* (Thames & Hudson, 1989)

Midgley, Mary, *Beast & Man: The Roots of Human Nature* (Methuen, 1980)
——, *Heart and Mind* (New York: St Martin's Press, 198t)
——, *Animals and Why They Matter* (Harmondsworth: Penguin, 1983)
Monod, Jacques, *Chance and Necessity* (Collins, 1972)
Montefiore, Hugh, ed., *Man and Nature* (Collins, 1975)
Morris, Richard Knowles & Michael W. Fox, eds., *On the Fifth Day: Animal Rights and Human Ethics* (Washington, DC, 1978)
Mumford, Lewis., *Technics and Civilization* (New York, 1934)
——, *The Culture of the Cities* (1940)
Myers, Norman, *The Sinking Ark* (Oxford: Pergamon, 1979)
——, ed., *The Gaia Atlas of Planetary Management* (Pan, 1985)

Naess, Arne, *Freedom, Emotion and Self-Subsistence* (Oslo: Universite-forlaget, 1975)
——, *Ecology, Community and Lifestyle: Outline of an Ecosophy*, trans. D. Rothenberg (Cambridge: Cambridge University Press, 1989)
Nash, Roderick Frazier, *Wilderness and the American Mind* (New Haven: Yale University Press, 1973)
——, *The Rights of Nature: A History of Environmental Ethics* (Madison: University of Wisconsin Press, 1989)
Needham, Joseph, *Science and Civilization in China* Vol. 11, (Cambridge: Cambridge University Press, 1956)
Needleman, Jacob, *A Sense of the Cosmos: The Encounter of Ancient Wisdom and Modern Science* (Garden City, NY: Doubleday, 1975)
Nicholson, R. A., *The Mystics of Islam* (New York: Shocken, 1975)
Nollman, Jim, *Animal Dreaming: The Art and Science of Interspecies Communication* (New York: Bantam Books, 1987)
Norton, Bryan, *Why Preserve Natural Variety?* (Princeton, NJ: Princeton University Press, 1988)
Noss, John B., *Man's Religions*, 6th edn., (New York: Macmillan, 1980)

Odum, Eugene P., *Ecology: The Link between the Natural and the Social Sciences*, 2nd edn., (Holt Rinehart & Winston, 1975)
Ophuls. W., *Ecology and the Politics of Scarcity: Prologue to a Political Theory of the Steady State* (San Francisco: W. H. Freeman, 1977)
O'Riordan, T., *Environmentalism* (Pion, 1976)
Owen, D. F., *What is Ecology?* (Oxford: Oxford University Press, 1980)

Paehlke, Robert, *Environmentalism and the Future of Progressive Politics* (New Haven: Yale University Press, 1989)
Partridge, Ernest, ed., *Responsibilities to Future Generations: Environmental Ethics* (Buffalo, NY, 1981)
Passmore, John, *The Perfectibility of Man* (Duckworth, 1972)
——, *Man's Responsibility for Nature. Ecological Problems and Western Traditions*, 2nd edn. (Duckworth, 1980)
Phipps, John-Francis, *The Politics of Inner Experience: Dynamics of Green Spirituality* (Green Print, 1990)
Pepper, David, *The Roots of Modern Environmentalism* (1984) (Routledge, 1989)
Peters, R. S., ed., *Nature and Conduct* (Macmillan, 1975)
Pietroni, Patrick, *Holistic Living* (Dent, 1986)

Plant, Judith, ed., *Healing the Wounds: The Promise of Ecofeminism* (Green Print, 1989)

Pollard, Sidney, *The Idea of Progress* (Harmondsworth: Penguin, 1971)

Ponting, Clive, *A Green History of the World* (Sinclair-Stevenson, 1991)

Porritt, Jonathon, *Seeing Green: The Politics of Ecology Explained* (Oxford: Basil Blackwell, 1984)

Porritt, Jonathon & David Winner, *The Coming of the Greens* (Fontana, 1988)

Powell, T. G. E., *The Celts* (Thames & Hudson, 1963)

Prigogine, Ilya & Isabelle Steigers, *Order out of Chaos: Man's New Dialogue with Nature* (Heinemann, 1984)

Prigogine, I., *From Being to Becoming* (San Francisco, 1980)

Radin, Paul, *The World of Primitive Man* (New York: Grove Press, 1960)

Reader, John, *The Rise of Life: The First 3.5 Billion Years* (New York: Knopf, 1986)

Rees, Alwyn & Brinley Rees, *Celtic Heritage: Ancient Tradition in Ireland and Wales* (Thames & Hudson, 1973)

Rees, Lucy, *The Horse's Mind* (Stanley Paul, 1984)

Regan, Tom, ed., *Earthbound: New Introductory Essays in Environmental Ethics* (New York: Random House, 1984)

——, *All That Dwell Therein: Animal Rights and Environmental Ethics* (Berkeley, CA: University of California Press, 1982)

——, *The Case for Animal Rights* (Routledge, 1988)

Regan, Tom & Peter Singer, eds., *Animal Rights and Human Obligations* (Englewood Cliffs, NJ: Prentice Hall, 1976)

Reps, Paul, ed., *Zen Flesh, Zen Bones* (Harmondsworth: Penguin, 1975)

Rhodes, Richard, *The Making of the Atomic Bomb* (Harmondsworth: Penguin, 1988)

Rifkind, J. & T. Howard, *Entropy: A New World View* (1985)

Rolston 111, Holmes, *Philosophy Gone Wild* (Buffalo, NY: Prometheus, 1986)

——, *Environmental Ethics* (Philadelphia: Temple University Press, 1988)

Ross, J. B. & M. M. Mclaughlin, eds., *The Portable Renaissance Reader* (Harmondsworth: Penguin, 1985)

Roszak, Theodore, *Where the Wasteland Ends* (Faber, 1974)

——, *Person/Planet* (Gollancz, 1979)

Russell, Bertrand, *History of Western Philosophy* (Allen & Unwin, 1962)

Ryder, Richard D., *Animal Revolution: Changing Attitudes towards Specieism* (Oxford: Blackwell, 1989)

Ryle, M., *Ecology and Socialism* (Radius, 1988)

Sagan, Carl, *The Dragons of Eden: Speculations on the Evolution of Human Intelligence* (New York: Ballantine, 1977)

Sagoff, Mark, *The Economy of the Earth: Philosophy, Law, and the Environment* (Cambridge: Cambridge University Press, 1988)

Sale, Kirkpatrick, *Human Scale* (Secker & Warburg, 1980)

——, *Dwellers in the Land: The Bioregional Vision* (San Francisco: Sierra Club, 1985)

Santmire, H. Paul, *The Travail of Nature: The Ambiguous Ecological Promise of Christian Theology* (Philadelphia, 1985)

Sartre, Jean-Paul, *Being and Nothingness*, trans. H. E. Barnes (Methuen, 1985)

Scherer, Donald & Thomas Attig, eds., *Ethics and the Environment* (Englewood Cliffs, NJ: Prentice Hall, 1983)

Schell, J., *The Fate of the Earth* (Picador, 1982)

Schimmel, Annemarie, *Mystical Dimensions of Islam* (Capel Hill: University of North Carolina Press, 1975)

Schmidt, Alfred, *The Concept of Nature in Marx* (New York: Humanities Press, 1972)

Schmidt, Paul F., *Perception and Cosmology in Whitehead's Philosophy* (Rutgers University Press, 1967)

——, *Rebelling, Loving and Liberation: A Metaphysics of the Concrete* (Albuquerque: Hummingbird Press, 1971)

Schumacher, E. F., *Small is Beautiful: A Study of Economics as if People Mattered* (Abacus, 1974)

——, *A Guide for the Perplexed* (Abacus, 1978)

——, *Good Work* (New York: Harper Colophon, 1979)

Schwarz, Walter & Dorothy, *Breaking Through: Theory and Practice of Wholistic Living* (Bideford: Green Books, 1987)

Schweitzer, Albert, *The Teaching of Reverence for Life*, trans. R. Winston & C. Holt (New York: Rinehart & Winston, 1965)

Sen, K. M., *Hinduism* (Harmondsworth: Penguin, 1975)

Seymour, J. & Girardet, H., *Blueprint for a Green Planet* (Dorling Kindersley, 1987)

Sharkey, John, *Celtic Mysteries: The Ancient Religion* (Thames & Hudson, 1989)

Sheldrake, Rupert, *A New Science of Life: The Hypothesis of Formative Causation* (Blond & Briggs, 1981)

——, *The Presence of the Past: Morphic Resonance and the Habits of Nature* (Collins, 1988)

——, *The Rebirth of Nature: The Greening of Science and God* (Century, 1990)

Shepard, Paul & Daniel McKinley, eds., *The Subversive Science: Essays toward an Ecology of Man* (Boston: Houghton Mifflin, 1969)

Shepard Paul, *The Tender Carnivore and the Sacred Game* (New York: Scribner's, 1973)

——, *Thinking Animals: Animals and the Development of Human Intelligence* (New York: Viking Press, 1978)

——, *Nature and Madness* (San Francisco: Sierra Club, 1982)

Sikora, Richard & Brian Barry, eds., *Obligations to Future Generations* (Philadelphia, 1978)

Singer, Peter, *Animal Liberation: Towards an End to Man's Inhumanity to Animals* (Paladin, 1977)

——, *The Expanding Circle* (Oxford: Oxford University Press, 1981)

——, ed., *In Defence of Animals* (Oxford: Basil Blackwell, 1985)

——, ed., *Applied Ethics* (Oxford: Oxford University Press, 1986)

——, *Hegel* (Oxford: Oxford University Press, 1988)

Skolimowski, Henryk, *Eco-Philosophy: Designing New Tactics for Living* (Marion Boyars, 1981)

Snyder, Gary, *Earth Household* (Toronto: George J. McLeod, 1969)

——, *Turtle Island* (New York: New Directions, 1974)

——, *The Old Ways* (San Francisco: City Lights Books, 1977)

——, *Real Work: Interviews and Talks, 1964–1979* (New York: New Directions, 1980)

*Society and Environment*, ed. anon., (Moscow: Progress Publishers, 1977)

Spretnak, Charlene, *The Spiritual Dimension of Green Politics* (Santa Fe, NM: Bear & Co., 1984)

Spretnak, Charlene & Fritjof Capra, *Green Politics* (Paladin, 1985)

Spring, D. & E., *Ecology and Religion in History* (New York, 1974)

Starhawk, *Dreaming the Dark: Magic, Sex and Politics* (Boston: Beacon Press, 1982)

Stewart, Ian, *Does God Play Dice? The Mathematics of Chaos* (Oxford: Basil Blackwell, 1989)

Stone, Christopher D., *Should Trees Have Standing? Toward Legal Rights for Natural Objects* (Los Altos, CA: William Kaufmann, 1974)

——, *Earth and Other Ethics* (New York: Harper & Row, 1988)

Storm, Hyemeyohsts, *Seven Arrows* (New York: Ballantine, 1972)

Suzuki, D. T., *Zen Buddhism: Selected Writings*, ed. William Barrett (New York: Doubleday Anchor, 1956)


Taylor, Paul W., *Respect for Nature: A Theory of Environmental Ethics* (Princeton, NJ: Princeton University Press, 1986)

Thomas, Keith, *Religion and the Decline of Magic* (Harmondsworth: Penguin, 1973)

——, *Man and the Natural World: Changing Attitudes in England 1500–1800* (Allen Lane, 1983)

Tobias, Michael ed., *Deep Ecoology* (San Diego, CA: Avant Books, 1985)

Tokar, Brian, *The Green Alternative* (San Pedro: R. & E. Miles, 1987)

Toulmin, Stephen & June Goodfield, *The Discovery of Time* (Harmondsworth: Penguin, 1967)

Turner, F., *Beyond Geography: The Western Spirit against the Wilderness* (New Brunswick: Rutgers University Press, 1983)


Van De Veer, Donald & Christine Pierce, eds., *People, Penguins and Plastic Trees: Basic Issues in Environmental Ethics* (Belmont, CA: Wadsworth, 1986)


Walker, Benjamin, *Gnosticism: Its History and Influence* (Wellingborough: Crucible, 1989)

Wallis Budge, E. A., *Egyptian Religion* (Arkana, 1987)

Waters, Frank, *Book of the Hopi* (Harmondsworth: Penguin, 1977)

Watts, Alan, *Nature, Man and Woman* (New York: Vintage, 1970)

——, *Psychotherapy East and West* (New York: Vintage, 1961)

——, *The Way of Zen* (Harmondsworth: Penguin, 1962)

Welch, Holmes, *Taoism: The Parting of the Way* (Boston: Beacon, 1957)

West, John, *The Traveller's Key to Ancient Egypt* (Harrap Columbus, 1989)

Whitehead, A. N., *Science and the Modern World* (Cambridge: Cambridge University Press, 1925)

Wilde, Oscar, *De Profundis and Other Essays* (Harmondsworth: Penguin 1973)

Willey, Basil, *The Seventeenth-Century Background* (Harmondsworth: Penguin, 1964)

Williams, Raymond, *Keywords: A Vocabulary of Culture and Society* (Fontana, 1976)

Worster, Donald, *Nature's Economy. The Roots of Ecology* (San Francisco: Sierra Club, 1977)

Wynne-Tyson, Jon, *Food for a Future* (Centaur Press, 1979)


Yates, Frances, *Giordano Bruno and the Hermetic Tradition* (Routledge & Kegan Paul, 1964)

# INDEX